The Constitution before the Judgment Seat

THE CONSTITUTION
BEFORE THE JUDGMENT SEAT

The Prehistory and Ratification of the American Constitution, 1787–1791

Jürgen Heideking

EDITED BY
JOHN P. KAMINSKI AND
RICHARD LEFFLER

University of Virginia Press Charlottesville and London

University of Virginia Press

Printed in the United States of America on acid-free paper

First published 2012

1 3 5 7 9 8 6 4 2

LIBRARY OF CONGRESS CATALOGING-IN-PUBLICATION DATA

Heideking, Jürgen, 1947–2000

[Verfassung vor dem Richterstuhl. English]

The Constitution before the judgment seat : the prehistory and ratification of the American Constitution, 1787–1791 / Jürgen Heideking ; edited by John P. Kaminski and Richard Leffler.

p. cm.

Originally published in German as Die Verfassung vor dem Richterstuhl in 1988.

Includes bibliographical references and index.

ISBN 978-0-8139-3174-6 (cloth : alk. paper)

1. Constitutional history—United States. 2. United States—Politics and government—1783–1809. 3. United States—Intellectual life—18th century. 4. United States. Constitutional Convention (1787) I. Kaminski, John P. II. Leffler, Richard. III. Title.

KF4520.H4513 2011

342.7302′9—dc22

2011012444

The present state of American politics will form the most important area that ever engaged the pen of the historian.

BALTIMORE *MARYLAND GAZETTE,* JULY 13, 1787

I have either read or heard this truth, which Americans should never forget, —That the silence of historians is the surest record of the happiness of a people.

"A FARMER," BALTIMORE *MARYLAND GAZETTE,* MARCH 7, 1788

CONTENTS

PREFACE

The story of how this English translation of Jürgen Heideking's award-winning work came to fruition is a bit complicated. Madison House Publishers obtained a grant for Jerry Neeb-Crippen to translate the original text from German into English. Jürgen, who had made substantial deletions to the manuscript before the translation, then worked with Richard Leffler in revising the translation of the first three chapters. Shortly thereafter, in the year 2000, Jürgen was tragically killed in an automobile accident. The manuscript lay dormant for several years. In the interim, Rowman & Littlefield Publishers bought Madison House.

Several years later, the present volume's editors reinitiated the editing process. Rowman & Littlefield graciously stepped aside, making it possible for the University of Virginia Press to publish an English-language edition, including an editors' introduction placing Jürgen's work within the historiography of the twenty years that had elapsed since Jürgen first wrote his book.

The German Historical Institute, through the good auspices of its former director Christof Mauch, now a professor of American cultural history at the Ludwig Maximilians University Munich, provided a generous subvention, making it possible to publish this long book at a reasonable price.

John P. Kaminski and Richard Leffler

EDITORS' INTRODUCTION

Some years ago, William Pencak, in his review of Richard R. Beeman's *Variety of Political Experiences in Eighteenth Century America* (Philadelphia, 2004), commented that most of Beeman's citations were to pre-1980 scholarship, "which is not so much a judgment of his research but an indication that political history is no longer at the top of the agenda for early Americanists."[1] Similarly, Pauline Maier recalled that an audience member at a session at the annual meeting of the Organization of American Historians said that "when he teaches the American Revolution he finds himself assigning books that were published thirty years ago."[2] But political history has seen a revival using new sources and methodologies,[3] and to these have been added schools of "Atlantic history," "postcolonial theory," and "public-sphere history." Contemporaneous with the earliest expressions of these developing ideas, and preceding most of them, Jürgen Heideking, a professor of British and North American history at the University of Tübingen and then at the University of Cologne, published *Die Verfassung vor dem Richterstuhl: Vorgeschichte und Ratifizierung der Amerikanischen Verfassung, 1787–1791* (Berlin, 1988), which looked at important political, economic, social, and cultural elements of the post-Revolutionary settlement in America, culminating in the ratification of the Constitution. Jürgen's work looked back to earlier historians as well as to contemporaries; it was often innovative, but it was always based on remarkably thorough research into the original sources on the ratification of the Constitution.

Jürgen brought a unique perspective to his work. He wrote as a European with a viewpoint born of the ongoing evolution of "Europe," a work still in progress. Although his writing is not tendentious or didactic, Jürgen believed that the period of American history during the Confederation, from 1781 to 1789, resembles the modern condition of "Europe" as it transcends the polities of the individual nation-states. Therefore, Jürgen began his study with a "Historical Background," a brief analysis of the "United States during the 'Critical Period,'" which is remarkably concise but which captures the constitutional, legal, political, and economic issues that led eventually to the Constitutional Convention in the summer of 1787. As he says in his acknowledgments, his hope was that the American experience during the Confederation would be instructive, and "that the process of European integration might benefit from the example of the thirteen American states which, in free and open debate, crafted a constitutional framework for a common future."[4]

Perhaps Jürgen's background as a German Social-Democrat had an influence on him, because at a time when both "an economic interpretation" and the view that there was a general reaction against the radical democracies created by the state constitutions after the Revolution were very much out of favor, Jürgen was interested in both ideas. He notes that there were cries of "too much democracy" and "tyranny of the majority" during the Confederation. In Jürgen's view, economic conditions and the actions taken in the states in the years before 1787 persuaded nationalists that there was a "deep-seated moral crisis, symptomatic of the loss of virtue regarded as the lifeblood of republics. For this reason, the planned revision of the Articles of Confederation would have to go beyond merely redistributing power between the states and the central government, and root out the mechanism of self-destruction which had apparently been embedded in the state constitutions" (see p. 13).

On the other hand, many people were deeply suspicious of any new, stronger government, such as that created by the Constitution. They feared that Federalists in power in a new national government "would use it as against the interests of the 'common man'" (133). Large electoral districts, possible under the Constitution and required in the Senate, "favored widely known or wealthy candidates, resulting in the exclusion of the 'middling classes' supported by the Antifederalists" (133). The new government under the Constitution, if controlled by the Federalists, would create "an aristocratic regiment consisting of the president, Congress, and the Supreme Court [who] could join forces to isolate itself from the states and people, thus permitting 'energetic' government action in the broadest sense of the word" (133). And what was this broadest sense? If the "better sort," represented by the Federalists, controlled the new government, they would seek fame and power, "to the detriment of the common man." Heideking continued: "The cost of their aspirations for national glory would be devastating wars and a massive national debt; to raise the money needed for arms and interest payments, taxes would soar and be collected by force if necessary; the concern for the common weal would give way to private profit-seeking and unbridled egoism, leading to the complete subjugation of the middling and lower classes to a phalanx of merchants, lawyers, and creditors. . . . America was on the verge of imitating all the mistakes already endured by Europeans" (133).

Even if these aspects of the debate over the Constitution were of little interest to the academic consensus at the time Jürgen was writing, he looked at these issues freshly and persuasively. Both sides, Federalist and Antifederalist, remarked on the transformation of post-Revolutionary attitudes about "democracy" and "liberty" that was taking place only a few short years since 1776. In fact, Jürgen argues, there was a "popular repudiation of the radical republican tradition" in the last years of the Confederation, and many Antifederalists—John Quincy Adams for one—were extremely distressed by this transformation of the Revolutionary ethos they had "grown up with and internalized" (66). To Jürgen, the Federalists "were indeed the revolutionaries of 1787–88." These revolutionaries, however, "intended their revolution to achieve stability, order, security, and predictability." He goes on: "To accomplish this, though they had little faith in the political wisdom of the common man, they were forced by the social and political realities of Revolutionary America to respect the sovereignty of the people and to win the majority to their side." They rallied round the Constitution, but they believed it did not go nearly far enough in concentrating power or restraining "the destructive forces inherent in republics." Jürgen quotes many Federalists, such as the Constitutional Convention delegate Oliver Ellsworth of Connecticut, who wrote, "The danger of the constitution is not aristocracy or monarchy, but anarchy" (134).

In addition to this debate over the distribution of power and the need for political and social restraints, there was also the related question of control over money and taxes. Americans everywhere—and of all classes and trades but especially the dominant group, farmers—were affected by debt and vastly increased tax obligations after the war, and by the shortage of specie or any other circulating medium. This "prompted New England farmers as well as Southern planters to oppose the Constitution that prohibited paper money" and had vast new taxing power, which had already been used in the states to finance the repayment of debt (250). The possibility that the liquidity provided by paper money might be eliminated and that additional taxes would be imposed was alarming. In the years since Jürgen died in 2000, there has been a resurgent interest in these economic and social issues related to the Constitution, and recent analyses have generally supported Jürgen's interpretation. In this, as in other aspects of his work, Jürgen anticipated what has become important in current historical writing.[5]

Closely related to these issues prevalent during the Confederation (and of interest to anyone concerned with developments in Europe today) was the effort in post-Revolutionary America to create a modern nation-state with power to act in the national interest and to defend the nation without the mediation of the states. Radical nationalists supported the Constitution as "the only realistic alternative to the weak Congress" under the Confederation. They had an exaggerated sense of conditions under the Articles, and they were cognizant of the predictions, in Britain and on the Continent, that the post-Revolutionary American condition would be marked by catastrophe. A weak and unstable Confederation would tempt the European powers to engage in war with America. "Only a sound federation could act with enough self-confidence in the international arena to be treated with respect by potential adversaries" (138). The alternative was weak regional confederacies backed by the various European powers—a series of small nation-states dominated by the European state system. Federalists like Alexander Hamilton believed that the federal government needed unrestricted power to raise an army, and this required the power to borrow money on short notice and to raise the revenues needed to finance the debt. "Money," Hamilton wrote, "is with propriety, considered as the vital principle of the body politic; as that which sustains its life and motion and enables it to perform its most essential functions. A complete power, therefore, to procure a regular and adequate supply of revenue, as far as the resources of the community will permit, may be regarded as an indispensable ingredient in every constitution." Similarly, the power to raise armies and navies, to direct their operations, and to "provide for their support" . . . "ought to exist without limitation: Because it is impossible to foresee or define the extent and variety of national exigencies, and the correspondent extent & variety of the means which may be necessary to satisfy them" (147).[6] It was, therefore, "difficult to obtain new foreign loans as long as the repayment of the existing debts in France and the Netherlands remained doubtful" (11). "Only if Congress could be ensured an 'independent income' would it have the necessary authority to deal with states and foreign powers" (10). Here Jürgen is suggesting a line of thought that has burgeoned in the last decade, one that extends his ideas and makes explicit the intimate connection between the powers to tax, to borrow, and to make war as one condition of the modern nation-state.[7]

There was also a profound disagreement between Federalists and Antifederalists over the place of the United States in the world. Both sides hoped and expected that America would be part of the Atlantic commercial world, and that a reformed American government would encourage vast numbers of Europeans to emigrate to America. Before the war the American colonies were part of the British colonial system, and Americans hoped to become part of the British trading system again. Antifederalists wanted the United States to remain separate and different from the European state system. American nationalists, like Washington, Hamilton, and Madison, conceived of the United States as necessarily part of the greater Atlantic community, and wanted to be able to defend the nation within that system, to be a major player within it—or, as the American Peace Commissioners said in 1783, to "move like a Primary & not like a Secondary Planet . . . in the Political System of the World."[8] And some Americans had a vision as well of becoming a continental empire in the western hemisphere. Federalists "took the 'westward course of empire' metaphor seriously, which implied that the center of world power, having migrated from Asia to Greece, Rome, and then England, would some day shift to the American continent" (161). Antifederalists were less than enthusiastic about this world ambition and the governmental power needed to achieve it. "They often admonished their compatriots to place 'domestic peace and justice' before 'national glory.'" Antifederalists "agreed that America should assume its appropriate place in the circle of world powers; however, the United States was created as a "fœderal union," not as a "Universal Empire'" (161). As a European, and as a student and professor of American history, Jürgen understood well the importance of Europe to America's commercial prosperity and the desire by some Americans at the time of the ratification debate to depend on European political theory; to look to the forms of European governments as examples for America; to view the great European empires past and present as something for America to emulate or as something to avoid; and to play an appropriate role in the Atlantic world, though Americans might disagree strongly about what was an appropriate role. When Jürgen wrote *Die Verfassing,* "Atlantic history" and "postcolonial theory" were in their beginning stages. By the time he undertook the revision and translation, they had become huge forces in the writing of American history.[9]

Another aspect of Jürgen's work concerns the political process that was used to adopt the Constitution. An important element in the process of ratifying the Constitution was the campaign in each of the states to elect delegates to a state ratifying convention. As with any election, various methods and venues were used to influence public opinion. Newspapers, magazines, broadsides, and pamphlets; public meetings and parades; legislative debates; existing political parties and ethnic groups; and organizations of workmen—all were part of the electoral process. Although Jürgen Heideking wrote *Die Verfassing* well after Jürgen Habermas published his work on the "public sphere" in 1962, Heideking's work was published a year before Habermas's was translated into English, and was, therefore, among the earliest applications of "public-sphere" theory to early American political history, where it has become so important.[10] Jürgen writes about the public mood, public opinion, and about the press. He writes about the "republican festive culture"—including the public celebrations of ratification in various cities throughout America—which, as he said elsewhere, was not just a reflection of social practices but had "the elemental power to create and 'construct' (or 'desconstruct') political concepts and cultural meaning. In this sense, festive culture is part of the historical process that shapes and transforms power relations, social structures, and popular mentalities."[11] He writes of the ratification of the Constitution as "a political process and cultural event of the highest order," which played a "pivotal role . . . in the transition from the struggle for independence to national integration and—within the broader scope of the eighteenth century's 'democratic revolution'—the progression from a traditional to a modern society" (4). This process, he says, "affected public as well as private life, and altered the traditional methods of influencing public opinion" (3). The debate took place in "private circles and letters, in representative institutions, and, above all else, in the 'public sphere' situated between the private and the official levels" (4). The ratification debate was an effort by each side to win the support of public opinion, "a vital element of American politics." As Jürgen continues: "In contrast to Europe, where public opinion was slowly evolving in opposition to the established ruling powers, and where it had at best a corrective influence, public opinion in America constituted a driving force of political development" (53). Jürgen's analysis of the role of the press—the way it functioned to distribute news and opinion nationally, its relationship to public opinion, the circulation size and distribution of the newspapers, the politicization of the printers, and the pressures exerted on the Antifederalist press—is the finest and most comprehensive in print. As he asserts, "The debate over the Constitution led to the emergence of a national party press which was to develop its full potential during the following decade in the dispute between Federalist and opposition Republican newspapers" (85). Jürgen brings a dramatic insight to the story when he notes that "interstate political and publishing activities [during the ratification debate] contributed to the nationalization of political life in post-Revolutionary America," and that printers, by appealing "to a national audience[,] . . . [were] contributing to the construction of a common American identity" (93). For instance, the cooperation among Antifederalists in New York, and with Antifederalists in other states, "marked the transition to a national party organization and political culture" (100). "As an early form of party activity on the national level," Jürgen concludes, "its significance transcends the ratification debate" (104). Jürgen thus anticipated the work that would be done after him, and with unmatched detail.

But it is in his discussion of the celebrations of ratification that took place throughout America (and, in some places, the reaction against these celebrations) that Jürgen best displays his extraordinary mastery of the documentary record and his ability to extract from these events the full meaning of the ratification debate and, really, the agenda of Federalists from 1787 to 1801. He captures here the political, economic, and social agenda of Federalists as no one has before or since.[12] First, he describes in great detail the celebrations in Boston, Philadelphia, New York, Baltimore, and elsewhere. He contrasts these celebrations with other rituals honoring the Revolution that had taken place since 1776 that contained an "anti-authoritarian and rebellious aspect which somehow seemed incompatible with the principles of an upstanding, self-governing citizenry" (344–45). He then analyzes the elements of these ratification rituals with intelligible, believable, and exciting insights. The ratification rituals were, at bottom, portrayals of the Constitution as "the logical conclusion of the prolonged struggle for political and religious freedom and represented the consummation of national unity" (352). The celebrations had a multilayered meaning and revealed much about the way in which the Constitution, and later the federal government, were portrayed by Federalists. The celebrations were a demonstration to Antifederalists that they were "running the risk of political isolation and social quarantine. At once an appeal and a warning, they coaxed the opposition into line with Federalist attitudes" (362). They encouraged opponents to join the new government as a way of achieving their desired goal of adopting amendments to the Constitution.

The celebrations were a reflection of the Federalist theme that the Constitution would end the economic depression of the 1780s under the Articles of Confederation and restore the unity and patriotism of the Revolution. "The parades essentially represented the symbolic banishment of economic hardship and optimism for the future" (362). That "the storm had been weathered and brighter days were in store was manifested in the rising-sun metaphor" that was common in the processions and celebrations (362). A persistent theme was a demand for the protection of the domestic manufacturing industries that had arisen in America since the 1760s. Marching tradesmen in the parades carried signs that called unambiguously for protection, and expressed their preference for domestically produced goods over imports. The Baltimore silversmiths proclaimed, "No importation and we shall live." The New York clothing workers urged, "Americans, encourage your own manufacturers." At the celebratory banquets that accompanied the processions it was always noted that the food and drink were American: "federal food," "federal beverages," home brews, and "ale, proper drink for Americans" (363).

Another theme was that the economic and political crises of the 1780s had to be resolved by "working together and avoiding clashes between classes and special interests." The urban middle classes were staking "their claim to a position of economic and political equality with the elite" (363). Boston merchants jumped at the chance to create a solidarity with workers by raising money to commission three new ships from local shipyards (the shipbuilding industry had been decimated during the depression), and the *Massachusetts Centinel* declared, on March 26, 1788, that "this unequivocal proof of federalism . . . will be a great relief to a number of our industrious mechanicks, whom the decline of commerce . . . has deprived of employment" (363–64). When the new government was launched, tradesmen's groups from various cities demanded that Congress provide protectionist measures for their industries.

The organization, symbolism, and slogans of the celebrations were intended to justify the Constitution as "an inevitable and universally accepted link in an unbroken chain of events from the discovery and settlement of America to the Revolution" and the war. The Constitution "represented the final step toward the foundation of an American nation-state. The struggle for ratification was seen as the continuation and culmination of the struggle for independence" (364). Jürgen quotes from Benjamin Rush's description of the Philadelphia July 4th parade, a revealing insight into Federalist motives: "The connection of the great event of Independence—the French alliance—the Peace—and name of General Washington, with the adoption of the Constitution, was happily calculated to unite the most remarkable transports of the mind which were felt during the war with the great event of the day, and to produce such a tide of joy as has seldom been felt in any age or country." Rush concluded: "'Tis done! We have become a nation" (364).

The word "federal" now came to replace the word "national." Tradesmen were "federal" carpenters, "federal" cordwainers. As one writer in the *Massachusetts Centinel* observed on January 18, 1788, the word "federal" invoked "national honour, dignity, freedom, happiness, and every republican privilege," as opposed to the term "anti-federalism," which stood for "anarchy, confusion, rebellion, treason, sacrilege, and rapine" (365). This was the Federalist platform, not just in 1787–88, but throughout the Federalist era. And Jürgen provides a remarkable analysis of the architectural metaphors of the federal celebrations, in language, in cartoons, and in actual structures. He notes references to the "Grand Federal Edifice," the "Grand Republican Superstructure," the "New Roof," the "Fœderal Temple," and the "Temple of American Liberty." These are allusions to buildings that were "designed to illustrate the innovative principle of federalism itself, the interconnections and interdependencies between the central government and the states" (366). The federal government was the roof supported by pillars representing the states, indicating the intended power relationship in the federal system. The temple-and-dome symbolism was intended "to combine classical form and aestheticism with Christian values" (366).

Ironically, amidst all this symbolism, the Constitution itself became a focal point only gradually. But by July 4, 1788, it had become a central element. Pennsylvania's chief justice Thomas McKean, a leading Federalist in that state's convention, participated in the Philadelphia parade, holding a scroll of the Constitution. Jürgen quotes Benjamin Rush's account of this scene: "The triumphal car was truly sublime—It was raised above every other object. The Constitution was carried by a great Law-officer, to denote the elevation of the government, and of law and justice, above every thing else in the United States" (366). In the July 23rd New York procession, a life-sized image of Washington held a copy of the Constitution. Jürgen observes that these images of the Constitution began the portrayal of the Constitution as sacred.

These processions of 1788 were not haphazard. They were, as Jürgen says, "public works of art," a form of expression intended to convey a message. In this case, "They rendered the Federalist ideology tangible by converting its message into movement, images, and sound" (367). The designers of these events were some of the most important artists of the age, including Charles Willson Peale, Francis Hopkinson, Alexander Reinagle, Noah Webster, Samuel Low, and Pierre L'Enfant. "They built temples and colonnades, modeled figures, designed illuminations, set off fireworks, and painted allegorical pictures and portraits of Washington for public display; they wrote songs, recited poems, and put on plays; they composed marches, odes, and hymns, set Psalms to music, and held concerts" (367). The processions consciously conveyed the idea that the arts, literature, and education—represented by students, teachers, and professors—would be encouraged as never before under the government created by the Constitution. Jürgen quotes James Wilson's oration at the Philadelphia July 4th procession on the value of such republican parades: "They may *instruct* and *improve,* while they *entertain* and *please.* They may point out the elegance or usefulness of the sciences and the arts. They may preserve the memory, and engrave the importance of great *political events.* They may represent, with peculiar felicity and force, the operation and effects of great *political truths*" (369).

The actual events, the behavior of the people who participated, also were intended to convey a message of what the future would be under the Constitution: a "new republican society" marked by "liberty and equality yet still structured, orderly, and disciplined." At the banquets that often concluded the processions, all orders of people "dined together in the most perfect harmony." Social deference and partisan division were transformed into "harmony and friendship," and because these processions involved a very high percentage of the population, they were clearly "sanctioned by the majesty of a Free People," in pointed contrast to European practice, in which processions were celebrations of the political and social elites (373). Again Jürgen quotes from Rush, who contrasts the egalitarian nature of the American events as opposed to the European celebrations of great personages. In America, the lowliest apprentice participated along with farmers and tradesmen: "Such is the difference between the effects of a republican and a monarchical government upon the minds of men!" Jürgen points to the motto of the Philadelphia masons in the procession: "Both buildings and rulers are the works of our hands" (370).

The Constitution was a purely secular document. In the states, traditionally established churches were disestablished completely or converted to one-among-several state-supported churches, at least in theory. Still, there was a wide perception that government needed the support of religion for the maintenance of that civic virtue, without which republicanism could not survive. Organizers of the processions included clergy prominently. As Rush explained: "Pains were taken to connect Ministers of the most dissimilar religious principles together, thereby to shew the influence of a free government in promoting christian charity. The Rabbi of the Jews, locked in the arms of two ministers of the gospel, was a most delightful sight. There could not have been a more happy emblem contrived, of that section of the constitution, which opens all its power and offices alike, not only to every sect of christians, but to worthy men of *every* religion" (373). Federalists were in the process of creating a "civil religion," Jürgen says, in which a secular government would be sanctified by religious beliefs of all kinds.

In Jürgen's view, these celebrations "laid the foundation for a distinct festive culture, whose forms, style, and spirit can still be observed in public life in the United States today" (374). As he describes and analyzes these events, he captures the Federalist paradigm of 1787–88, and really of the following decade. The "public sphere" has never been explicated better.

In 1997, the great historian of early America, Edmund S. Morgan, commented that the modern documentary editions of the Founding Fathers "stand as the single most important achievement of American historical scholarship in this century."[13] More recently, Professor Max Edling wrote that, "thanks to the publication of *The Documentary History of the Ratification of the Constitution,* it is now possible to investigate the Federalist side of the debate [over the Constitution] more inclusively than has previously been the case."[14] The mass of information, the detail, that Jürgen had at his disposal was possible because of the modern documentary editions he had at his disposal—in particular, the works of the Ratification Project at the University of Wisconsin–Madison. Jürgen spent a year in Madison searching the files thoroughly, and he was completely familiar with the volumes that had been published up to the time of his death. The depth of his research is reflected in the present remarkable account of the complex political, intellectual, and cultural process of ratifying the Constitution. It is the most complete description that has ever been written, and he has added to this mastery of fact an insightfulness characteristic of a great historian.[15] As with all fine historical writing, Jürgen's work has been confirmed and amplified by those who came after him. This volume, now available in English for the first time, will have value for years to come.

AUTHOR'S ACKNOWLEDGMENTS

The German edition of this book appeared in 1988 as a contribution to the Bicentennial of the American Constitution. Yet it was my sincerest hope that the book's significance would extend beyond this occasion, and that the process of European integration might benefit from the example of the thirteen American states which, in free and open debate, crafted a constitutional framework for a common future.

The initial impulse for a project on the birth of the American Constitution came from my mentor, Professor Gerhard Schulz. As the director of the Institute for Contemporary History at the University of Tübingen, he has never restricted his area of interest to the twentieth century, having broadened his scope to include the intellectual, political, and social origins of the modern world and, further, the era of the discovery and settlement of America. I am indebted to him for his efforts to deepen my understanding of interrelated aspects of Atlantic history and culture, as well as for his continual support of my academic career, which I began as a research assistant, and then as an assistant professor, in his institute.

It was on his advice that, in late 1979, I contacted Professor Merrill Jensen in Madison, Wisconsin, the director of the monumental *Documentary History of the Ratification of the Constitution.* He encouraged me to take a fresh look at the formation of the American Constitution—a highly controversial issue since the publication of Charles A. Beard's economic interpretation in 1913—from the unbiased perspective of an "outsider," and invited me to Madison to study the relevant source material. I was regrettably never able to meet Merrill Jensen in person, as he died prior to my first trip to the United States in the spring of 1980. I was warmly received, however, by his disciples and successors as the editors of the *Documentary History,* John P. Kaminski, Richard Leffler, and Gaspare J. Saladino. During a subsequent research visit in Madison in 1983–84, made possible by a Feodor-Lynen Fellowship from the Alexander von Humboldt Foundation, my association with these scholars and their families developed into a true friendship. Their help and advice also enabled my wife and our two children to share in the ups and downs of everyday life in America for an entire year. Professor John Boyer, who had been kind enough to invite me to the United States as a former Humboldt Fellow, instructed me on the use of the research facilities at the University of

Chicago and introduced me to other historians working there. Yet my main "base" always remained the University of Wisconsin in Madison, whose History department, then chaired by Theodore S. Hamerow, unbureaucratically took me in as a visiting scholar.

From the standpoint of my academic development, the almost daily interaction with the editors of the *Documentary History of the Ratification of the Constitution* was of inestimable value. The knowledge they had painstakingly accumulated through the years was passed on freely to the guest from Europe. I was assigned my own workspace in their institute, now renowned in the United States and beyond as the "Center for the Study of the American Constitution." Almost in passing I was introduced to modern editing techniques and initiated into the world of the personal computer. What impressed me the most was their meticulous treatment of the historical material and the respect they showed toward original quotes from the sources, particularly the observations of the "common people." Through their mediation I was able to benefit from the research findings of other extensive editing projects: the *Documentary History of the First Federal Elections,* also compiled in Madison; and the *Documentary History of the First Federal Congress,* based at George Washington University in the nation's capital. I would also like to express my gratitude to the directors and staff of these institutions, especially Charlene B. Bickford, Kenneth R. Bowling, and Gordon DenBoer, for their advice and support.

John Kaminski and Richard Leffler encouraged me to publish an English edition of my book and put me in contact with Madison House and its director, Gregory M. Britton. The project was delayed by my assignment to the German Historical Institute, just founded in 1987 in Washington, D.C., and by the taking up of a teaching position in North American History at the University of Tübingen. It received new impetus when my Habilitationsschrift won a distinction in Heidelberg in 1997 as the best book on American history and *Inter Nationes* in Bonn provided a generous grant for the cost of translation. We were able to complete the English version quickly thanks to the excellent cooperation between the publishing houses de Gruyter in Berlin and Madison House, as well as the diligence and competence of translator Jerry Neeb-Crippen. My friends in Madison proofread the manuscript and offered numerous suggestions for improvement. I accept full responsibility nonetheless for any oversights or errors the book may contain.

Jürgen Heideking

RATIFICATION CHRONOLOGY, 1786–1791

1786

21 January	Virginia calls meeting to consider granting Congress power to regulate trade
11–14 September	Annapolis Convention
20 September	Congress receives Annapolis Convention report recommending that states elect delegates to a convention at Philadelphia in May 1787
11 October	Congress appoints committee to consider Annapolis Convention report
23 November	Virginia authorizes election of delegates to Convention at Philadelphia; New Jersey elects delegates
4 December	Virginia elects delegates
30 December	Pennsylvania elects delegates

1787

6 January	North Carolina elects delegates
17 January	New Hampshire elects delegates
3 February	Delaware elects delegates
10 February	Georgia elects delegates
21 February	Congress calls Constitutional Convention
22 February	Massachusetts authorizes election of delegates
28 February	New York authorizes election of delegates
3 March	Massachusetts elects delegates
6 March	New York elects delegates
8 March	South Carolina elects delegates
14 March	Rhode Island refuses to elect delegates
23 April–26 May	Maryland elects delegates
5 May	Rhode Island again refuses to elect delegates
14 May	Convention meets; quorum not present
14–17 May	Connecticut elects delegates
25 May	Convention begins with quorum of seven states
16 June	Rhode Island again refuses to elect delegates
27 June	New Hampshire renews election of delegates

13 July	Congress adopts Northwest Ordinance
6 August	Committee of Detail submits draft constitution to Convention
12 September	Committee of Style submits draft constitution to Convention
17 September	Constitution signed and convention adjourns *sine die*
20 September	Congress reads Constitution
26–28 September	Congress debates Constitution
28 September	Congress transmits Constitution to the states
28–29 September	Pennsylvania calls state convention
17 October	Connecticut calls state convention
25 October	Massachusetts calls state convention
26 October	Georgia calls state convention
31 October	Virginia calls state convention
1 November	New Jersey calls state convention
6 November	Pennsylvania elects delegates to state convention
10 November	Delaware calls state convention
12 November	Connecticut elects delegates to state convention
19 November–7 January 1788	Massachusetts elects delegates to state convention
20 November–15 December	Pennsylvania convention
26 November	Delaware elects delegates to state convention
27 November–1 December	Maryland calls state convention; New Jersey elects delegates to state convention
3–7 December	Delaware convention
4–5 December	Georgia elects delegates to state convention
6 December	North Carolina calls state convention
7 December	Delaware convention ratifies Constitution, 30 to 0
11–20 December	New Jersey convention
12 December	Pennsylvania convention ratifies Constitution, 46 to 23
14 December	New Hampshire calls state convention
18 December	New Jersey convention ratifies Constitution, 38 to 0
25 December–5 January 1788	Georgia convention
31 December	Georgia convention ratifies Constitution, 26 to 0
31 December–12 February 1788	New Hampshire elects delegates to state convention

1788

3–9 January	Connecticut convention
9 January	Connecticut convention ratifies Constitution, 128 to 40
9 January–7 February	Massachusetts convention
19 January	South Carolina calls state convention
1 February	New York calls state convention
6 February	Massachusetts convention ratifies Constitution, 187 to 168, and proposes amendments
13–22 February	New Hampshire convention: first session
1 March	Rhode Island calls statewide referendum on Constitution
3–27 March	Virginia elects delegates to state convention
24 March	Rhode Island referendum: voters reject Constitution, 2,714 to 238
28–29 March	North Carolina elects delegates to state convention
7 April	Maryland elects delegates to state convention
11–12 April	South Carolina elects delegates to state convention
21–29 April	Maryland convention
26 April	Maryland convention ratifies Constitution, 63 to 11
29 April–3 May	New York elects delegates to state convention
12–24 May	South Carolina convention
23 May	South Carolina convention ratifies Constitution, 149 to 73, and proposes amendments
2–27 June	Virginia convention
17 June–26 July	New York convention
18–21 June	New Hampshire convention: second session
21 June	New Hampshire convention ratifies Constitution, 57 to 47, and proposes amendments
25 June	Virginia convention ratifies Constitution, 89 to 79
27 June	Virginia convention proposes amendments
2 July	New Hampshire ratification read in Congress; Congress appoints committee to report an act for putting the Constitution into operation
21 July–4 August	First North Carolina convention
26 July	New York convention circular letter calls for second constitutional convention; New York convention ratifies Constitution, 30 to 27, and proposes amendments
2 August	North Carolina convention proposes amendments and refuses to ratify until amendments are submitted to Congress and to a second constitutional convention

13 September	Congress sets dates for election of president and meeting of new government under the Constitution
20 November	Virginia requests Congress under the Constitution to call a second constitutional convention
30 November	North Carolina calls second state convention

1789

4 March	First Federal Congress convenes
1 April	House of Representatives attains quorum
6 April	Senate attains quorum
30 April	George Washington inaugurated as first president
8 June	James Madison proposes Bill of Rights in Congress
21–22 August	North Carolina elects delegates to second state convention
25 September	Congress adopts twelve amendments to Constitution to be submitted to the states
16–23 November	Second North Carolina convention
21 November	Second North Carolina convention ratifies Constitution, 194 to 77, and proposes amendments

1790

17 January	Rhode Island calls state convention
8 February	Rhode Island elects delegates to state convention
1–6 March	Rhode Island convention: first session
24–29 May	Rhode Island convention: second session
29 May	Rhode Island convention ratifies Constitution, 34 to 32, and proposes amendments

1791

15 December	Bill of Rights adopted

The Constitution before the Judgment Seat

INTRODUCTION

The Historical Significance of the Debate over the American Constitution

The Constitution is now before the judgment seat.—It has, as was expected, its adversaries, and its supporters, which will preponderate is yet to be decided.

GEORGE WASHINGTON TO HENRY KNOX, OCTOBER 15, 1787

It was a time when men in a Confederation, which had been sufficiently strong to hold them together in war, were arguing in disorder about a greater union which—in unity and security—could hold for them a full measuring of their victory. They came in no calm conversation to our Constitution. It was born in invective, pamphleteering, and plain politics.

DRAFT OF A SPEECH BY PRESIDENT FRANKLIN D. ROOSEVELT FOR JEFFERSON DAY, 1945

Every politically minded individual, particularly a native of central Europe, with its painful, cataclysmic history, must regard it as a supreme intellectual challenge to study a constitutional system which for over two hundred years has continually provided the foundation and framework for the political and social life of a great nation.[1] Drafted in Philadelphia between May and September 1787, ratified by voters in the thirteen states after a thorough public debate, expanded by the First Congress to include a Bill of Rights, and later enhanced by a small number of carefully chosen amendments, the American Constitution has proven itself fully capable, both in terms of its principles and its institutional structure, of guiding a loosely knit, diverse, and heterogeneous Union as it rose to become a democratic world power. The serious crises that have hitherto faced the American system of government—civil war, world wars, economic depressions, race conflicts, Vietnam, and Watergate—have only served to highlight its unbroken strength and vitality as a symbol of national unity and collective identity. In the course of these two hundred years, more than fifty million immigrants have been introduced to the spiritual and cultural values of the New World by way of the Declaration of Independence, the Constitution, and the Bill of Rights. This phenomenal success makes the American founding one of the most important and influential events in world history. In light of modern-day experiences with authoritarian and totalitarian regimes, we can perhaps understand better than ever before the significance of British Prime Minister William Gladstone's assessment of the American Constitution as "the most wonderful work ever struck off at a given time by the brain and purpose of man."[2]

For historians, however, whose job it is to trace the origins of historical developments and place them in context, such eulogies can never be the goal of their work or a purpose in themselves. In fact, they are often merely a starting point for all-the-more intensive research. The awe-inspiring age of the Constitution should thus not lead us to forget that the work of the Philadelphia Convention by no means met with unanimous approval, and that enormous effort was required of its proponents to secure its adoption in place of the Articles of Confederation, in force since 1781. This study focuses on the debate over the Constitution and the Bill of Rights in the years 1787 to 1791, which culminated in the United States' first controversy on a national scale, galvanizing large segments of the population and forcing them to take a stance. The opinion-forming and decision-making process that preceded the adoption of the Constitution and the Bill of Rights provides a key to understanding their lasting stability and legitimation. To the extent that the debate dealt with such fundamental issues as the nature of government, sovereignty, the separation of powers, federalism, representation, political participation, and human rights and liberties, it has lost none of its relevance or importance through the ages.

The last quarter of the eighteenth century is undoubtedly one of the most thoroughly researched periods in American history. Yet compared with the immense volume of research on the Revolution and early national period, the attention accorded the ratification debate has to date been relatively modest. Few historians have followed up on Franklin D. Roosevelt's observation that the Constitution "was born in invective, pamphleteering, and plain politics." There are both practical and methodological reasons for this neglect. In those accounts of the Revolution that extend beyond the winning of independence in 1783, the debate is usually treated as a mere appendage to the Philadelphia Convention. Monographs depicting the history of the early Republic, on the other hand, almost always build on assumed knowledge of the origins and adoption of the Constitution, so that the ratification debate often lies nearly concealed from view, in a historical blind spot.[3] A more serious defect derives from the circumstance that, for a long time, nearly every study was guided by a single-minded determination to prove or disprove the theory propounded by Charles A. Beard in 1913 regarding the economic origins of the Constitution.[4] Due to this narrowing of the perspective to the founding fathers' material interests and motives, the ratification debate has rarely been approached as a complex social phenomenon and communicative process. Conversely, the events have often been reduced to a dispute over political theory, in which case it seemed sufficient to concentrate on a few important sources like the *Federalist Papers*. Significant exceptions include the works of Robert A. Rutland, Cecelia M. Kenyon, Steven R. Boyd, and Jackson Turner Main, which capture the dramatic atmosphere of the ratification struggle.[5] When they wrote their books in the 1960s and 1970s, however, the full documentary record was not yet available, and the scholarly interest focused somewhat one-sidedly on the opponents of the Constitution, the Antifederalists.[6] The situation improved in the 1970s with the publication of the first volumes of the three major editorial projects of the founding era. No single scholar could have managed to collect all the source material in the various archives which, from then on, successively appeared (and still appears) in printed form.[7] In the 1980s, the Bicentennial of the Constitution inspired a number of new monographs, articles, collections of essays, and biographies of leading political figures of the founding era.[8] The general scholarly interest now shifted rather sharply from social and economic issues to ideological concepts, especially the relationship between republicanism and liberalism in the Revolutionary and post-Revolutionary discourse.[9] For the most part, these works aimed at reconstructing and evaluating the different "languages" used by the contemporaries, and they significantly broadened our understanding of the intellectual climate of the time.[10] On the other hand, the authors often showed only scant interest in questions of political strategy and tactics, or in fascinating phenomena of popular culture such as the ratification celebrations of 1788. Yet what is needed is precisely an understanding of the correlation between legal concepts, ideologies, and material interests, coupled with an approach that brings the languages of and interactions between individuals and groups into focus against the backdrop of social relationships and economic developments. The passionate debate over the future course of the American Union in 1787–88 would appear to be an ideal and worthwhile candidate for this kind of scholarly synthesis.

The goal of this study therefore is to present the ratification debate as a complex event involving all strata of society and worthy of attention in and of itself. The process of ratification took place on the national, state, and local levels, affected public as well as private life, and altered the traditional methods of influencing public opinion. The fierce clash between advocates and opponents of the Constitution brought to light the tremendous dynamism of the American society, which was simultaneously seeking to establish a lasting political order and striving to find a deeper meaning behind its collective experience since the separation from Great Britain. This becomes evident if the people are allowed to speak for themselves in their incredibly vibrant, forceful language, modeled on the Bible and classical authors in addition to English philosophers and literary figures. Only if the entire mass of available source material is surveyed, from the records of legislative bodies and ratification conventions to private notes and letters to the flood of newspaper articles and pamphlets, can the debate be revealed as a political process and cultural event of the highest order. This awareness in turn is necessary if one is to grasp the pivotal role the ratification of the Constitution played in the transition from the struggle for independence to national integration and—within the broader scope of the eighteenth century's "democratic revolution"—the progression from a traditional to a modern society.[11]

The Constitution pulled from a Philadelphia printing press on September 18–19, 1787—containing just enough text to cover four pages of newspaper—unleashed a lively and exhaustive debate waged in private circles and letters, in representative institutions, and, above all else, in the "public sphere" situated between the private and the official levels. For over a year this constitutional issue transfixed Americans, just as it captured the attention of foreign observers. Two opposing political camps sprang into existence, the pro-Constitution Federalists and the Antifederalists, both of which harbored a wide range of ideological views, and neither of which would ever obtain any semblance of monolithic uniformity. Caught in a relentless tug-of-war between the two parties was the group of undecided, doubtful, and neutral constituents. Both the friends and foes of the Constitution were aware of the occasion's historic import. And they agreed that the Union's long-feared and anticipated crisis had entered its decisive phase. The outcome of the dispute would determine the fate not only of contemporary Americans but of generations to come—perhaps even all of humanity. In the first "Publius" essay of October 27, 1787, Alexander Hamilton expressed what many people were thinking, namely, "that it seems to have been reserved to the people of this country, by their conduct and example, to decide the important question, whether societies of men are really capable or not, of establishing good government from reflection and choice, or whether they are forever destined to depend, for their political constitutions, on accident and force." Whereas Hamilton and his supporters were convinced the adoption of the Constitution would improve life across the board, their opponents warned of a threat to state sovereignty and civil liberty. Accordingly, Revolutionary War hero Patrick Henry implored his fellow Virginians: "You ought to be extremely cautious, watchful, jealous of your liberty; for, instead of securing your rights, you may lose them forever. If a wrong step be now made, the republic may be lost forever." Americans were running the risk of divesting the old order of its binding force without finding a new one to take its place. As a result, the exuberant feeling of being party to an epoch-making decision was tempered by the fear of failure and decline. Every analysis of the ratification debate must take this ambivalent, fluctuating mood into consideration along with the temporal aspect of the proceedings: the rushes, the delays, the juxtaposition of various events, and the dramatic climaxes. Many contemporaries experienced the whole process as a kind of miracle, and the metaphor of the "judgment seat" used by George Washington did not just mean public opinion but clearly had religious connotations.[12] To a certain extent, the events leading to the adoption of the Constitution and the addition of the Bill of Rights were composed of thirteen separate debates. Each state in the Union had to examine the proposal and reach its own conclusion, and every decision largely depended on the political and economic constellations that had formed in the particular state since the Revolution. At the same time, the Constitution triggered an encompassing, national discussion which set the stage for the political, economic, and cultural development of the United States under the new system of government. It is precisely this interplay between local and national aspects, and between the forces of tradition and modernity, that makes the matter so complex and interesting.

1

Historical Background

The evils we experience do not proceed from minute or partial imperfections, but from fundamental errors in the structure of the building, which cannot be amended otherwise than by an alteration in the first principles and main pillars of the fabric.

ALEXANDER HAMILTON, *FEDERALIST* NO. 15

It must, however, be admitted, that our federal system is defective, and that some of the state governments are not well administered; but, then, we impute to the defects in our governments, many evils and embarrassments which are most clearly the result of the late war.

"FEDERAL FARMER," NOVEMBER 8, 1787

The United States during the "Critical Period"

Achievement and Failings of the Confederation

In all of his writings, Merrill Jensen challenged the conventional notion that the history of the United States under the Articles of Confederation consisted of a chain of failures and was typified by political blunders and moral decline. He countered this one-sided interpretation by correctly pointing to the forward-looking accomplishments of these years and showing how the Revolution had actually kindled the enterprising spirit of Americans. There was first of all the Northwest Ordinance of 1787, which blocked the spread of slavery in the North and laid the foundation for the further expansion of the United States.[1] After the "landed" states had relinquished their territorial claims in the West, Congress created a "national domain" that was open to settlers and could serve as a source of revenue for the Confederation government. By acting as a mediator in border disputes between states, Congress fostered a sense of unity and brought about an increased awareness of the necessity of national jurisdiction.[2] The exigencies of war and postwar anxieties prompted Congress to mold the system of committees and commissions into a framework for government administration, creating the presidency and the secretariat of Congress as well as the Post Office and the three most important "executive departments": the Office of Foreign Affairs; the Department of War; and the Finance Department, headed by Superintendent of Finance Robert Morris until his replacement by a three-member Board of Treasury in 1784. All of these offices and departments introduced concepts and instituted reforms that were further developed in the federal government under the new Constitution.

Beyond these administrative improvements, the Confederation period was also a time of political experimentation and of the application of Enlightenment theory. Starting in Virginia, the privileges of the "established" churches gradually fell to the principle of separation of church and state. Evidence of the humanitarian movement can be seen in the first legislative measures against slavery in the northern states, in criminal law reforms, and in improvements in the field of education. Across the country, academies and private associations were founded dedicated to the progress of science and medicine. Although westward emigration increased after 1783, the coastal cities continued to grow, reorganize their administration, and enhance education and culture. All of these developments were rooted in the colonial period, yet to a large measure they were also the product of a widespread feeling that the successful struggle for independence signaled the dawn of a new age.[3]

These promising trends notwithstanding, the postwar period was characterized by a sense of dissatisfaction and self-doubt. Only temporarily suppressed by the joy over the Treaty of Paris in 1783, this discontent grew into a general sense of crisis by the end of 1785. To a certain extent, the feeling that the Articles of Confederation were not equal to the demands of the times was the outgrowth of a spirit of experimentation and reform that was never satisfied with the status quo, constantly propelled by a desire for change and restructuring. However, this feeling was also based on the experience of actual deficiencies, the sources of which were a weak Congress combined with political and social instability in the states. Whereas the authority of the Confederation Congress had been the focal point of political discussion until 1783, the main concern began to shift more and more to the states. The desire for change was thus motivated by two separate, though related, factors: the inability of Congress to act decisively threatened the dissolution of the Union; and the imminent collapse of law and order in the states signaled the ignominious end of the republican experiment.

The Efforts to Reform the Articles of Confederation

The Articles of Confederation created a "firm league of friendship" and a "permanent union" whose members retained their "sovereignty, freedom and independence, and every Power, Jurisdiction and right, which is not by this confederation expressly delegated to the United States, in Congress assembled."[4] The Confederation Congress was to be a coordinating body, and its members, the delegates to Congress, were usually elected by the state legislatures.[5] Each state could send up to seven delegates, but each delegation had only one vote. Resolutions on important issues required the approval of at least nine states, while constitutional amendments could only be adopted by the unanimous consent of the state legislatures. The states forfeited a portion of their rights to the Union and delegated "expressly" defined powers to Congress. According to Article IX, for example, the Confederation had "the sole and exclusive right and power of determining on peace and war . . . of sending and receiving ambassadors [and of] entering into treaties and alliances." It was also responsible for conducting war on land and at sea and was authorized to borrow money, issue bonds, and emit paper money. The states agreed to comply with demands for financial and military support, which were to be presented by Congress in the form of requisitions.

On paper, the provisions seemed to guarantee the central administration's ability jointly and energetically to conduct war and pursue foreign policy. Yet even before Maryland became the last of the thirteen states to ratify the Articles in 1781, doubts had surfaced regarding the practicability of the system and changes and reforms were considered. Open criticism was expressed, among others, by Alexander Hamilton in his *Continentalist* essays, and by Thomas Paine, who evoked the image of a powerful North American nation-state in his pamphlet *Common Sense* and in the *American Crisis* series.[6] These "nationalists" saw their views confirmed by a series of military defeats in addition to the enormous economic problems facing Congress. To remedy the situation, they proposed strengthening the authority of the central government, focusing their reform efforts on three key demands: Congress was to be granted the power to regulate domestic and foreign trade; to secure for itself a regular income through customs duties and taxes; and to use force against dilatory or recalcitrant states. There were differences of opinion, however, regarding the proper extent of the revisions and the best way of instituting them. There were basically three options, all of which were tested. First, an attempt was made to interpret the Articles of Confederation so broadly as to render constitutional amendments unnecessary. For instance, it was argued that since the Articles put the burden of conducting war on Congress, they also implicitly apportioned to it the authority required to meet this obligation. Several delegates wanted to contrive precedents to establish the validity of this "implied powers" theory. They were thwarted, however, by the vigilance of the advocates of state sovereignty, who effectively resisted the "silent" extension of the central government's power. It then appeared that the most promising method was to convince the states of the need for reforms in order to bring about amendments in the prescribed manner. From 1781 to 1786, Congressional committees therefore drafted one proposal after another designed to improve the efficiency of the Confederation government. Although several of these plans met with broad approval, none was able to clear the high hurdle of unanimous ratification. A third, more radical alternative involved calling a convention for the express purpose of revising the Articles of Confederation. This idea had also entered the discussion at an early stage, and had backers in Congress as well as a number of states. Yet, for a time, even such emphatic champions of reforms as Virginians James Madison and Edmund Randolph were hesitant to embark on so uncertain a venture as a constitutional convention. Not until all other possibilities had been exhausted and the sense of crisis had reached a climax did this concept prevail, leading from the Annapolis Convention in 1786 to the Federal Convention in Philadelphia the following year.

The nationalists attempted their first offensive between 1780 and 1783. They were initially prompted to act by the precarious situation during the war, then by the fear that a favorable peace agreement would reduce interest in reforms. The concepts of leading figures like Philadelphia merchant Robert Morris and energetic, ambitious Alexander Hamilton combined political, constitutional, and economic components in a single reform package. The key element was the "power of the purse," the control over the Union's fiscal policies. Only if Congress could be ensured an "independent income" would it have the necessary authority to deal with the states and foreign powers. The revenues were to be used principally to pay the interest owed to public creditors, who had helped to finance the war effort. In this way, the domestic debt could be used to form a "bond of union" around which all the commercial classes would rally in their own interest. Moreover, funding the national debt would create capital for investments.

The nationalists came very close to implementing their concept when Congress named Robert Morris as superintendent of finance in 1781 and proposed a 5 percent duty on imports. This "Impost of 1781" was to remain in force until the national debt had been "fully & finally discharged."[7] To drum up support for the plan, Morris and Hamilton directed their efforts at merchants, Continental Army officers, and public creditors. It was their intention to found the power of the central administration on the loyalty of these influential groups.[8] The impost never went into effect, however, as Rhode Island refused to ratify the proposal and the Virginia legislature rescinded its approval of the plan in late 1782. The mobilization of the targeted special interest groups was also less than successful. Some of the merchants and creditors pinned their hopes on the states, which were preparing to assume their share of the Revolutionary debts and set up policies of their own for redeeming loans and paying interest. It was not possible to exert strong political influence over the officers' corps, either, against the will of Commander in Chief George Washington, who was averse to using the army for political purposes.[9]

The peace treaty, Morris's resignation, and the departure of other prominent "nationalists" from Congress on account of rotation provisions in the Articles of Confederation weakened, but did not stop, the reform crusade. A circular letter sent by George Washington to the state executives in June 1783 helped to keep the continental vision and the national movement alive. In the words of the retiring commander in chief, America's well-being required that Congress be recognized as the "supreme power" and be granted the ability "to regulate and govern the general concerns of the confederated republic." The people of the United States would have to put their "local prejudices and politics" aside and be willing to make "mutual concessions."[10]

The problems in this time of peace opened more and more citizens' eyes to the shortcomings of the Confederation system. When the British government imposed trade restrictions on the United States in 1783, Congress was unable to implement countermeasures because it lacked the power to regulate commerce. The postwar recession, aggravated by a deflationary financial crisis, fueled protectionist tendencies and strained relations between the states. There were increasing complaints from the frontier about inadequate military protection against Indian raids. The popularity of separatist groups threatening to set up their own governments was growing in the western territories. The most pressing problem concerned the Union's financial situation. The revenue from requisitions, which the states had only sporadically complied with even during the war, dropped off to a mere trickle. It was difficult to obtain new foreign loans as long as the repayment of the existing debts in France and the Netherlands remained doubtful. While the states were wrestling with problems of their own, the Confederation government was in danger of becoming completely insolvent. The Confederation Congress, which met at various places after leaving Philadelphia in 1783, was repeatedly unable to obtain a quorum. On top of this, the delegates became embroiled in a heated North-South dispute in the summer of 1786 over relations with Spain and navigation rights on the Mississippi.[11]

At this juncture, all hopes rested on another amendment proposal introduced in Congress in 1783 in place of the failed Impost of 1781. It comprised, in effect, a complex economic reform package which the states had to adopt in its entirety if they wanted to take advantage of the benefits it offered. The central element was again an import duty; this time, however, the impost was only to remain in force for twenty-five years. In addition, Congress approached the states in April 1784 with the request that it be granted the "power to regulate commerce," though again only for a limited time.[12] At the beginning of 1786, the delegates were faced with the situation that not all of the states had yet ratified the amendment. Furthermore, several legislatures had approved the proposal only on certain conditions and with restrictions. At that point, the calls for a general convention to revise the Articles could no longer be ignored. Representatives from five states met in Annapolis in September 1786 at the invitation of Virginia to discuss common trade problems. Other delegates were on their way, but those in attendance quickly wrote a report and adjourned. The report, written by Alexander Hamilton, recommended that a convention of the states be held in May 1787 in Philadelphia, "to take into consideration the situation of the United States, to devise such further provisions as shall appear to them necessary to render the constitution of the Federal Government adequate to the exigencies of the Union; and to report such an Act for that purpose to the United States in Congress Assembled, as when agreed to, by them, and afterwards confirmed by the Legislatures of every State will effectually provide for the same."[13] The New York legislature put an end to the quest for amendments once and for all on February 15, 1787, by not removing conditions on its ratification of the Impost of 1783 that were unacceptable to Congress. A week later, Congress approved an amended proposal by the delegation from Massachusetts to call a convention "for the sole and express purpose of revising the Articles of Confederation."[14] It was agreed that the delegates should be elected by the state legislatures. During the weeks that followed, every state except Rhode Island complied with the request by Congress to appoint delegates.

Concerns about Domestic Tranquility and the Survival of the Republican Order

From 1783 on, an increasing number of Americans beyond the narrow circle of zealous nationalists were beginning to acknowledge the need to expand the powers of the Confederation government, especially in the economic and financial sectors. This growing consensus, which included many future Antifederalists, was only half of the picture.[15] Besides the inability of Congress to act decisively, criticism was also being directed at the independent status and vast powers of the states. This was not merely a question of properly apportioning authority. Many observers among the educated and property-owning class feared developments on the state level could careen out of control and wreck the accomplishments of the Revolution. Their concerns were not only with specific measures and laws, but with the structure of the state constitutions themselves, which placed few restraints on the majorities in the assemblies. These misgivings stood in marked contrast to the satisfaction with which the new state constitutions originally had been received and hailed as the embodiment of republican political theory. To be sure, concerns had been voiced about "too much democracy," the "tyranny of the majority," and a slide into anarchy and despotism. Yet these isolated warnings were offset by the hope that Americans possessed sufficient civic virtue to repel such threats. This optimism was temporarily restored in 1783–84, before quickly giving way to disillusionment and skepticism. Triggering the chain of events were efforts in several states to alleviate the hardships caused by the economic recession through the issuance of paper money and the passing of laws designed to relieve debtors. These measures brought to mind the runaway inflation of the war years and were seen as an indication that private property was no longer secure. The multitude of debt, or loan certificates, in circulation were drawn into the whirlpool of inflation, adding to the chaos already prevailing in the currency system. This was fertile ground for all kinds of speculative projects, especially for buying up cheap Continental certificates in the expectation of rising prices after the establishment of a stronger central government. Another ominous sign was the fierce partisan debate that ensued over this and other issues—from the treatment of the remaining or returning loyalists to the validity of certain clauses of the peace treaty. The economic decline appeared to be the outward manifestation of a deep-seated moral crisis, symptomatic of the loss of virtue regarded as the lifeblood of republics. For this reason, the planned revision of the Articles of Confederation would have to go beyond merely redistributing power between the states and the central government, and root out the mechanism of self-destruction which had apparently been embedded in the state constitutions.

This sense of foreboding was confirmed by two incidents. In Rhode Island, the radical Country Party triumphed in the elections of April 1786, winning the governorship along with a majority in both houses of the legislature. The party immediately implemented a program to use the depreciation of newly issued paper money to ease the private and public burden of debts. The agrarian Country representatives disregarded the protests of merchants, creditors, and artisans, whose hard-currency claims could now be settled with severely depreciated paper money. They were equally undeterred by a ruling of the Rhode Island Supreme Court that obstructed the operation of the law. Another election victory in the spring of 1787 enabled the majority to replace uncooperative judges and to expand their paper-money policy, which was widely regarded as a mockery of the fundamental principles of justice and morality. To many observers, Rhode Island served as an example of unchecked democracy trampling on the rights and interests of the minority.[16]

Just as disquieting were reports that had been coming from Massachusetts since the middle of 1786. At the urging of the eastern business community, the state legislature had resolved to pursue an agenda which kept money in short supply in conjunction with a firm stabilization policy. Taxes were raised so the government could punctually discharge its obligations to public creditors. This provoked protests by farmers who did not have the money to pay their debts or their taxes. These protests culminated in open rebellion in August 1786. Groups of armed farmers hindered the collection of taxes, prevented forced auctions, and obstructed the work of local courts. Finally, they banded together in military formations and marched on a federal weapons arsenal in Springfield. There were rumors at the seat of Congress in New York that the rebels intended to use "agrarian laws" to abolish debts and bring about an equitable distribution of property.[17] The news of these events spread like wildfire across the Union, eliciting excited, at times hysterical reactions. Even an otherwise prudent man like George Washington now concluded "that mankind when left to themselves are unfit for their own Government." The reports from Massachusetts led him to believe the United States was heading down the path of "anarchy and confusion."[18] Others regarded Shays's Rebellion as a salutary shock that would ultimately enhance the chances for substantial reform. The outrage of law-abiding citizens must be exploited, Stephen Higginson wrote to Henry Knox: "The public mind is now in a fit State . . . to come forward with a System competent to the great purpose of all Civil Arrangements, that of promoting and securing the happiness of Society."[19] Although the Massachusetts militia had relatively little trouble quashing the rebellion in early 1787, the psychological repercussions continued to reverberate even after the Constitutional Convention. During the ratification debate, Federalists often termed opponents of the Constitution "Shaysites."

No one expressed the concerns about the states' inner affairs more succinctly than James Madison. As a Virginia delegate to Congress, Madison had already advocated strengthening the central government, but it was his experiences as member of the Virginia legislature from 1784 to 1786 that made him an ardent supporter of the convention idea. Even before the end of his first year in the assembly, he declared that the imperfect systems of the Revolutionary era must not be allowed to become "habits."[20] In March 1786, Madison described the growing economic tensions between the states in a letter to Jefferson: "The States are every day giving proof that separate regulations are more likely to set them by the ears, than to attain the common object. When Masssts. set on foot a retaliation of the policy of G. B. Connecticut declared her ports free. N. Jersey served N. York in the same way. And Delaware I am told has lately followed the same example in opposition to the commercial plans of Penna."[21] Madison returned to the Congress in February 1787 amid alarming reports from Rhode Island and Massachusetts. There he wrote a memorandum entitled "Vices of the Political System of the United States," which contained the key thoughts later propounded and refined in his speeches at the Philadelphia Convention and reiterated in his *Federalist* essays and in the debates of the Virginia ratifying convention. In a few brief sections, he addressed the impotence of Congress and the structural weaknesses of the Articles of Confederation. His main point of emphasis, however, concerned the blunders and irregular behavior of the state legislatures: "If the multiplicity and mutability of laws prove a want of wisdom, their injustice betrays a defect still more alarming: more alarming not merely because it is a greater evil in itself, but because it brings more into question the fundamental principle of republican Government, that the majority who rule in such Governments, are the safest Guardians both of public Good and of private rights."[22] Madison was certainly not alone in his thinking on this issue. Similar doubts regarding the moral and constitutional foundations on which the states had risen from the Revolution were expressed by Alexander Hamilton in New York and Congressman Rufus King of Massachusetts, who wrote in October 1786: "But if . . . the great Body of people are without Virtue, and not governed by any internal Restraints of Conscience, there is but too much room to fear that the Framers of our constitutions and laws have proceeded on principles that do not exist, and that America, which the Friends of Freedom have looked to as an Asylum when persecuted, will not afford that Refuge."[23]

The "firm league of friendship" uniting the thirteen sovereign republics would thus have to be replaced by a system that vested the Union government with sufficient "coercive authority" over the states. In Madison's opinion, the most efficient means of control would be a right of veto, allowing Congress to intervene in the legislative affairs of the states and to nullify inappropriate measures. He attached great importance to this idea and was prepared to fight for it at the convention in Philadelphia.[24] Madison believed that the calling of the convention and the public's willingness to accept reforms were more the result of the social and economic ills caused by the actions of state legislatures than the harm "which accrued to our national character and interest from the inadequacy of the Confederation to its immediate objects."[25] At the time he wrote these words to Jefferson on October 24, 1787, it was by no means clear whether the "public mind" would indeed sanction the Philadelphia plan, which, even without the right to veto state laws, went far beyond a mere reform of the Articles of Confederation.

Contemporary Views of the Economic State of the Confederation

The economic realities of the late 1780s did not justify the nationalists' prophecies of doom any more than the placating rhetoric of their opponents. Hardly a dramatic collapse, the "critical period" was one of several intervals of stagnation woven into the colonial economy's secular process of growth. It was particularly difficult for Americans to come to terms with the situation because they had reached a comparatively high standard of living before the war and entertained such high expectations. The true problem had less to do with treating the ills of a slumping economy than with overcoming the aftermath of war and properly exploiting the Union's potential. This necessitated the reorientation of thirteen separate economies, now forced to function outside of the British mercantile system. The time of the ratification debate was thus also a period of transition in an economic sense, during which the public mood oscillated between hope and fear, doubt and confidence. Nobody possessed all the information necessary to evaluate accurately the overall economic situation. Congress itself lacked a statistical overview of commercial activity, much less an analysis or prognosis of economic developments. As a result, judgments were often based on local or regional circumstances combined with information supplied by friends and acquaintances, travel reports, and newspaper articles. Just how inadequate this method was can be seen in Madison's admission in August 1786 that he knew as much about Georgia as about Kamchatka, namely, nothing at all.[26] Americans disagreed sharply about the economic state of the Confederation. Alexander Hamilton lamented the "melancholy situation" of the United States, asking his countrymen to reflect whether they had not sunk to the farthest depths of national humiliation: "Is public credit an indispensable resource in time of public danger? We seem to have abandoned its cause as desperate and irretrievable. Is commerce of importance to national wealth? Ours is at the lowest point of declension. . . . Is a violent and unnatural decrease in the value of land a symptom of national distress? The price of improved land in most parts of the country is much lower than can be accounted for by the quantity of waste land at market, and can only be fully explained by the want of private and public confidence . . . it may in general be demanded, what indication is there of national disorder, poverty, and insignificance that could befall a community so peculiarly blessed with natural advantages as we are, which does not form a part of the dark catalogue of our public misfortunes?"[27] This gloomy picture predominated in contemporary reports, and it was often accompanied by the assumption that only a speedy adoption of the new Constitution could stop the descent of the whole country into bankruptcy and ruin.

Conversely, anyone who read James Winthrop's "Agrippa" letters or the "Hanno" essay in the *Massachusetts Gazette* was given the impression that Massachusetts, at least, had already overcome the crisis. Shays's Rebellion was a thing of the past, and the people were once again enjoying the fruits of liberty in a prospering republic: "The people have applied with diligence to their several occupations, and the whole country wears one face of improvement. Agriculture has been improved, manufactures multiplied, and trade prodigiously enlarged. These are the advantages of freedom in a growing country. . . . Let any man look round his own neighbourhood, and see if the people are not, with a very few exceptions, peaceable and attached to the government; if the country had ever within their knowledge more appearance of industry, improvement, and tranquillity; if there was ever more of the produce of all kinds together for the market; if their stock does not rapidly increase; if there was ever a more ready vent for their surplus; & if the average of prices is not about as high as was usual in a plentiful year before the war."[28] "Hanno" agreed entirely: "Perhaps the effects of sudden industry were never more apparent than they now are in every part of the commonwealth. By means of it, the trade of this town [Boston], particularly the export trade, is very considerably augmented, beyond what was ever known. Tho' this may, from the increase of business, alone produce an occasional scarcity of cash, the evil will every day diminish by the returns of your voyages." According to "Hanno," this progress could only be threatened by the establishment of a national capital in Philadelphia: "[Boston] is now the seat of sovereign power. . . . When the seat of power is removed, this town, which is now the resort of all nations, and which sends ships to every part of the habitable world, must bow her fair head to a successful rival, and mourn for departed glory."[29] Like "Agrippa" and "Hanno," "Candidus" believed the problems that remained could not be solved by adopting the new Constitution. What was needed was public virtue, hard work, and austerity: "We may contend about forms of government, but no establishment will enrich a people, who wantonly spend beyond their income."[30] Another adversary of the constitutional reforms concluded: "I had rather be a free citizen of the small republic of Massachusetts, than an oppressed subject of the great American empire."[31] "Federal Farmer," published as a pamphlet in New York, was upbeat as well, if more down to earth. "Our governments answer all present exigencies, except the regulation of trade, securing credit, in some cases, and providing for the interest, in some instances, of the public debt. . . . We are hardly recovered from a long and distressing war: The farmers, fishermen, &c. have not yet fully repaired the waste made by it. Industry and frugality are again assuming their proper station. Private debts are lessened, and public debts incurred by the war, have been, by various ways, diminished. I know uneasy men, who wish very much to precipitate, do not admit all these facts; but they are facts well known to all men who are thoroughly informed in the affairs of this country. It must, however, be admitted, that our federal system is defective, and that some of the state governments are not well administered; but, then, we impute to the defects in our governments, many evils and embarrassments which are most clearly the result of the late war."[32]

Hence, there was disagreement among contemporaries regarding the extent of the post-Revolutionary crisis and whether a fundamental constitutional reform was required to rectify the situation. Indeed, the question of the economic and political state of the Union became an integral component of the dispute over ratification that began in the fall of 1787.

The Philadelphia Convention and the Sovereignty of the People

Conventions and Constituent Power

The Philadelphia Convention signified the triumph of the idea that the constitutional framework of the American government was in need of a complete reorganization, and that this change would have to be effected outside the procedures set down in the Articles of Confederation. At the same time, Madison's notions about the necessary relationship between the states and the national government were gaining ground. The only way to prevent state legislatures from infringing on the private rights of citizens was to erect an insurmountable protective barrier in the form of a strong central government. Accordingly, the delegates did not linger long over an attempt to reform the Articles of Confederation, devising instead an entirely new system of government. The most crucial change involved the relationship between the federal government and the people. Previously, Congress could only approach the citizens by way of state legislatures. The new government, by contrast, was to derive its authority from the consent of the people. This would invest it with the power to act directly on the "people of the United States." The delegates' intention to endow their work with the unquestionable legitimacy of the peoples' sovereign will was the result of this desire to have a close tie to the people coupled with the realization that they were deviating from the narrow mandate granted to them by Congress and their state legislatures. This presupposition at the outset of deliberations, however, only served to confirm the fears of those few who had opposed the convention as an instrument of constitutional reform.

Since the Revolution, the term "convention" had been associated with the concept of the sovereignty of the people and their right to resist oppressive government, as well as the belief that legislative and constituent powers were two distinct entities. Conventions, committees, and assemblies had often been viewed since 1774 as supplementary authorities that superseded the organs of colonial rule, the latter having either lost their popular support or been dissolved.[33] The existence of these bodies indicated that the political system was crumbling and a new source of legitimation would have to be sought. Beginning in 1776, the argument was raised in several states that the "normal" organs of representation—even those elected by the people—had no authority to create a constitution. Any constitution enacted by a regular legislative body could just as easily be amended—or even rescinded—by another legislature. A new system of government could only be based on the ultimate political sovereignty of the people themselves. And only a constitutional convention whose members were elected for this specific purpose could claim to represent the authentic voice of the people.[34] The first convention of this type was held in Delaware in 1776, after the Continental Congress in November 1775 had directed the thirteen legislatures to "call a full and free representation of the people, and that the representatives, if they think it necessary, establish such a form of government, as in their judgment will best produce the happiness of the people."[35]

The most thorough discussion of the principle that the sovereign will of the people could best be expressed through conventions took place among the citizens of Massachusetts. As the legislature elected by the towns, the General Court in Boston considered itself legally competent to draft a constitution. Radical revolutionaries from the backcountry, on the other hand, pressed right from the start for a "Convention, or Congress . . . immediately Chosen, to form & establish a Constitution, by the Inhabitants of the Respective Towns in this State."[36] Not until the General Court's proposed constitution had been thwarted by town meetings in 1778 did the legislators give in to the demands for a convention. In June 1779, they resolved "That it be and

Hereby is recommended to the several Inhabitants of the several towns of this State to form a Convention for the sole purpose of forming a new Constitution."[37] The delegates were to be elected by all white males over 21 without linking voting rights to property ownership or the payment of taxes. A constitution was subsequently drafted by the elected delegates and presented to the towns for approval. After an analysis of the towns' written responses revealed that the requisite two-thirds majority had been creatively obtained, the new constitution went into effect in 1780. In Massachusetts, at least, the principle that the constituent power lay in the hands of the people had been formally recognized and put into practice. The central concept of the contract theory, according to which the right to govern is derived from the consent of the people, had finally shed the unreal, theoretical quality attached to it in Europe.[38] As "fundamental law," the written constitution also acquired an almost sacred validity not possessed by the statutes enacted by legislatures.[39] No longer a mere synonym for government, constitutions had now been elevated to a loftier position: they dictated the limits of power and the rules of procedure.

A national constitution founded on the will of the American people was first proposed by Thomas Paine in 1776. With his usual mixture of vision and pathos, he proposed in *Common Sense* the idea of a "continental conference" for the purpose of writing a "Continental Charter" comparable to the venerable Magna Carta. His disappointment over the Articles of Confederation led him to take up this subject again in 1780. In *Public Good,* he predicted: "The several states will, sooner or later, see the convenience if not the necessity of adopting; which is, that of electing a Continental Convention, for the purpose of forming a Continental Constitution, defining and describing the powers and authorities of Congress."[40] In September of the same year, Alexander Hamilton was also contemplating various methods of strengthening the central government, among them a "convention of all the States, with full authority to conclude finally upon a general confederation." An assembly of this nature would also rekindle the citizens' sense of hope and funnel their passions in a new direction.[41] Two months later, representatives from the New England states and New York met in Hartford, Connecticut, to suggest vesting almost dictatorial authority in General Washington and granting Congress the "power of Coertion" against recalcitrant states.[42]

From this point on, there was a sporadic debate on the virtues of a national convention. For many people, conventions still had the dual character of an institution capable of either pursuing extralegal, revolutionary goals or of providing order and legitimacy. Conservatives were concerned about county conventions being held in many communities. Allegedly representing the "voice of the people," these county conventions criticized acts passed by state legislatures and denounced the coastal regions' over-representation in the assemblies. The proponents of state sovereignty also expressed reservations about these conventions, though they were even more distressed by the convention plans of the nationalists, which they viewed as a deliberate attack on the system of government they had fought for in the Revolution. As late as 1785, the Massachusetts congressional delegates refused to follow instructions from their legislature to propose the calling of a general convention. They informed the governor that the Articles of Confederation and the state constitutions represented the "Great Bulwarks of Liberty." If revisions by conventions were allowed for trivial—or even significant—reasons, the value of those works as "effectual and sacred Barriers" would be lost. In the delegates' mind, the campaign for a national convention was part of elaborate and vigorously pursued plans, "which, had they been successful, We think would inevitably have changed our republican Governments, into baneful Aristocracies." Americans would be well advised to make do with the shortcomings of the system in place rather than to risk "general Dissentions and Animosities" with ruinous consequences for the Union.[43] In October 1786, when Congress had already received the report of the Annapolis Convention, Rufus King told the Massachusetts House of Representatives: "The Confederation was the act of the people. No part could be altered but by consent of Congress and confirmation of the several legislatures. Congress therefore ought to make the examination first, because if it was done by a convention, no legislature could have a right to confirm it."[44]

When the report of the Annapolis Convention was finally discussed by Congress in February 1787, Shays's Rebellion had changed the minds of the Massachusetts delegates. They no longer opposed the idea of a convention, but they successfully limited the purpose of the proposed Philadelphia Convention. Instead of authorizing the delegates simply to render the federal government "adequate to the exigencies of the Union," the Massachusetts resolution stipulated that the convention meet "for the sole and express purpose of revising the Articles of Confederation and reporting to Congress and the several legislatures such alterations and provisions therein as shall when agreed to in Congress and confirmed by the states render the federal constitution adequate to the exigencies of government and the preservation of the Union."[45] Connecticut's congressional delegates, who consistently opposed a convention, alone voted against this resolution. Only on May 17 did the Connecticut legislature adopt an "Act Electing and Empowering Delegates" to the Philadelphia Convention. Rhode Island, which was not represented when Congress discussed the convention resolution, flatly refused to go along with its recommendations. The justification given several months later by the Rhode Island General Assembly in a letter to Congress reflected the opinions held by a majority of Americans right up to Shays's Rebellion: any deviation from the amendment procedure contained in the Articles of Confederation would run the risk of annulling the existing compact with the states, plunging all Americans into "a common ruin." Besides, only the freemen had the right to choose convention delegates in town meetings. The state government did not have the jurisdiction to send representatives to a convention "which might be the means of dissolving the Congress of the Union."[46] Thus, on the eve of the gathering in Philadelphia, there was a general awareness that the convention would be hard to control and might take a surprising turn. This uncertainty and volatility was precisely what men like Washington, Hamilton, Madison, Robert Morris, Gouverneur Morris, and James Wilson saw as a unique opportunity. They were convinced they could use the convention to propose profound change in the constitutional arrangement of the Union.[47]

The Philadelphia Convention Writes a New Constitution

The convention met in the Philadelphia State House on May 14, 1787, but a quorum of seven states was not present until May 25. George Washington then was elected convention president, and a committee was appointed to draw up rules. From May 29 on, the delegates—who for six weeks often went into committee of whole with Nathaniel Gorham of Massachusetts presiding—spent every workday deliberating for five to six hours behind closed doors. The only interruption in this routine occurred between July 26 and August 6, when a committee of five—the Committee of Detail—arranged the resolutions agreed upon into a draft constitution. On September 17, the convention adjourned *sine die*. Of the seventy-four delegates originally appointed, fifty-five actually participated in the convention at one time or another. Rhode Island was not represented, the New Hampshire delegation did not arrive until July 23, and New York lost its right to vote when John Lansing and Robert Yates went home on July 10, leaving Hamilton behind as the state's lone representative. In the end, the Constitution was signed by thirty-nine delegates from twelve states. George Mason and Edmund Randolph from Virginia and Elbridge Gerry from Massachusetts were the only delegates in attendance on September 17 who withheld their signatures.[48]

A few exceptions notwithstanding, the delegates can be divided into three groups: the nationalists, including Alexander Hamilton, Robert Morris, Gouverneur Morris, James Wilson, Nathaniel Gorham, James Madison, and George Washington; the proponents of state sovereignty, led by Lansing, Yates, Luther Martin from Maryland, and William Paterson from New Jersey; and a group of delegates dedicated to reconciling the other two camps, among them Roger Sherman and Oliver Ellsworth from Connecticut, John Dickinson from Delaware, John Rutledge from South Carolina, Elbridge Gerry and Rufus King from Massachusetts, and George Mason from Virginia. The nationalists doubtlessly benefited from the fact that a number of prominent popular leaders—such as Virginians Patrick Henry and Richard Henry Lee, Governor John Hancock and Samuel Adams of Massachusetts, Governor of New York George Clinton, Abraham Clark of New Jersey, Samuel Chase from Maryland, and Willie Jones from North Carolina—had either declined to seek an appointment to the Convention or had turned down appointments.

On the second day of debate, the convention decided to abandon the Articles of Confederation and adopt instead the resolutions put forward by the Virginia delegation as the basis of a new constitution. On May 30, six of the eight states in attendance approved the crucial first resolution, introduced by Virginia Governor Edmund Randolph, "that a *national* Government ought to be established consisting of a *supreme* Legislative, Executive & Judiciary." This consensus was threatened in mid-June, however, when William Paterson presented an alternative plan adapted to the interests of the smaller states and limited to amending the Articles of Confederation. Two days later Alexander Hamilton delivered a four-hour speech calling for a plan that some thought smacked of monarchy. Some delegates supported Paterson's plan because they remained attached to the principle of state sovereignty, others—such as Sherman and Ellsworth—because they wanted a better representation for their small states in a national government. After an intense debate, however, Paterson's proposal was rejected and the convention returned its attention to the modified Virginia plan.[49]

In their speeches, the delegates alluded to the leading ancient and modern authorities on constitutional law and history, from Aristotle and Polybius, to Locke, Montesquieu, and Blackstone. Their main sources of inspiration, however, were the British system of government and their own state constitutions. The discussion centered around four main issues: the distribution of power between the states and the new central government; the internal structure of this envisaged central government; the representation of individuals as well as states in the new "national" or "federal" legislature; and the balance of interests between the large and small states on the one hand and between northern and southern states on the other.[50] In the resolutions submitted to the Committee of Detail in late July, the majority assented to the replacement of the troublesome expression "national government" by "the government of the United States."[51] However, the convention left no doubt as to the dominant position of this new "general," or "federal," government. The laws, treaties, and Constitution of the United States formed the "supreme Law of the Land" with binding force on all judges, "any Thing in the Constitution or Laws of any State to the Contrary notwithstanding." While the federal government gained new powers not included in the Articles of Confederation, the states were compelled to accept several important restrictions. Congress was granted the authority to levy "Taxes, Duties, Imposts and Excises"; it had power to regulate interstate and foreign commerce, oversee the military, and enact any laws deemed "necessary and proper for carrying into Execution" the powers specified in the Constitution. Congress could also declare war, raise and support armies, provide and maintain a navy, and call forth the state militias "to execute the Laws of the Union, suppress Insurrections and repel Invasions." The states, by comparison, were prohibited from coining money and issuing paper money, impairing the obligation of private contracts, or levying import duties. This shift of power in the direction of a central government acting immediately on individuals, the restrictions on the power of the states, and the supremacy clause rendered a Congressional right to veto state legislation, so fervently supported by Madison, unnecessary.[52]

The division between the South and the North had been a source of considerable turmoil for the Confederation Congress (the controversy over navigation on the Mississippi, for example). During the course of the convention, three issues had become firmly entwined in a seemingly inextricable knot of contention: the mode of representation; the system of slavery, including the slave trade; and the authority of Congress in matters of commerce and the economy. As early as June it had been agreed that both the apportionment of seats in the House of Representatives and the levying of direct taxes should be based on population. As a concession to the South, three-fifths of the slaves were to be included in the enumerations. Despite this compromise, the southern delegates still feared the northern and middle states might abuse their numerical superiority in Congress to create a shipping and trade monopoly. They therefore demanded a two-thirds majority for laws regulating trade and the prohibition of duties on exports. The northern delegates deeply resented such a de facto veto power in trade matters, and they resisted the two-thirds clause. These seemingly irreconcilable differences brought the convention to the brink of dissolution. Not until the end of August was a compromise reached by a committee expressly created for that purpose. The three-fifths clause and the prohibition of export duties were included in the draft constitution; Congress was allowed to impose a maximum import duty of $10 per slave but could not prohibit their importation before 1808; in exchange, a simple majority would suffice in both houses of Congress for the passage of bills regulating commerce.[53] When the states represented at the convention approved this complicated formula by a vote of 7 to 4, the convention was able to proceed to a successful conclusion.

The Convention and the Problem of Ratification

In order to allow the delegates to speak candidly, the convention agreed at the outset that "nothing spoken in the House [could] be printed, or otherwise published, or communicated without leave."[54] But if the doors of the State House remained closed to the public, the "common man" made his presence indelibly felt at the debates. Time and again, the speakers evoked the "genius of the people," alluded to the "sentiments of the people" and the "popular current," or strove to divine the "public mind."[55] Pierce Butler of South Carolina expressed the feelings of the majority of the delegates when he declared: "We must follow the example of Solon who gave the Athenians not the best Government he could devise; but the best they would receive."[56] The congressional veto of state laws was definitively dropped in August, the delegates largely agreeing with John Rutledge of South Carolina that this provision alone "would damn and ought to damn the Constitution." Hamilton's plan of government, according to which the president and senators would be elected for life, with state governors appointed by the central government, was never seriously considered.[57] The nationalists' rhetoric against the "excesses and follies of democracy" and its "levelling spirit" (joined in even by Elbridge Gerry),[58] was therefore only one side of the coin. The other side was characterized by respect for public opinion and efforts to find balanced solutions. Despite George Mason's assertion on the final day of the Convention that the Constitution had been created "without the knowledge or idea of the people,"[59] the truth was that the delegates were sensitive to the difficulties of the upcoming struggle over ratification.

There were no precedents to guide the ratification process. As indicated above, most state constitutions had taken effect without being submitted to the public for approval. Their validity was thus challenged in several states, because they were not based on the sovereignty of the people.[60] The ratification of the Articles of Confederation seemed even more flawed. First of all, the Articles had been drawn up by Congress itself instead of an independent body. In addition, the act of ratification varied from state to state, ranging from resolutions to formal enactments. Finally, not all state constitutions officially recognized the Articles of Confederation. As a result, it was sometimes a matter of dispute whether ordinances and resolutions of Congress had precedence over state laws.[61] In Madison's view, the Confederation thus contained the seeds of its own destruction: from the "doctrine of compacts" it followed "that a breach of any of the articles of the confederation by any of the parties to it, absolves the other parties from their respective obligations, and gives them a right if they chuse to exert it, of dissolving the Union altogether."[62] The lesson Madison drew here was that the new Constitution needed the explicit endorsement of the people if it was to have a lasting, binding effect on citizens and states alike. He used this argument on June 5 to defend the fifteenth, and final, Virginia resolution stipulating that, subsequent to its approval by Congress, the Constitution was to be submitted to "an assembly or assemblies of Representatives, recommended by the several Legislatures to be expressly chosen by the people, to consider & decide thereon." Madison regarded this as essential, for the document they were framing in Philadelphia "should be ratified in the most unexceptionable form, and by the supreme authority of the people themselves."[63]

This concept was not immediately received with great enthusiasm by the delegates. They consequently returned to this subject again and again to weigh alternatives. Adoption by state legislatures found considerable support, though a Union-wide second convention was also suggested for this purpose. A general referendum seemed contrary to the federal principle, whereas communal referenda were ruled out immediately on the basis of previous experiences in Massachusetts and New Hampshire, where the towns voted. While most nationalists preferred state ratifying conventions, ratification by state legislatures appealed to those delegates like Sherman, Gerry, and Martin who wished to avoid the complete abandonment of the Confederation. The lines between the two camps were not clearly drawn, however. Oliver Ellsworth, for instance, normally a proponent of the nationalist view, complained that "a new sett of ideas seemed to have crept in since the Articles of Confederation were established. Conventions of the people, or with power derived expressly from the people, were not then thought of." In Ellsworth's view, conventions were more likely "to pull down than to build up Constitutions."[64] Madison was supported, on the other hand, by fellow Virginian George Mason, who emphatically denied the authority of state legislatures to ratify the Constitution: "Whither then must we resort? To the people with whom all power remains that has not been given up in the Constitutions derived from them. It was a great moment . . . that this doctrine should be cherished as the basis of free Government."[65]

There were several practical arguments for ratification by conventions instead of state legislatures. It was feared that the Constitution's opponents might resort to tactical ploys to delay or obstruct the ratification process by using the relatively cumbersome bicameral political system in place in eleven of the thirteen states. Only thirteen conventions would consider the Constitution, whereas twenty-four legislative bodies would have to consider it. Advocates of state sovereignty were said to be strongly influential in state governments and legislatures. They would surely not be willing to relinquish some of their power to strengthen the Union. By contrast, a number of "capable men" might volunteer to serve in state conventions who had long ago turned their backs on the small-minded pursuits of state politics, or who were ineligible to sit in legislatures, as was the case for clergymen in five states.[66] Still more weight was attached to reservations of a general nature. Most delegates found ratification by state legislatures too reminiscent of the outdated system of the Articles of Confederation. When this method was formally proposed by Ellsworth and Paterson, Gouverneur Morris retorted that they had apparently not yet grasped the true purpose of the deliberations, and that their suggestion was rooted in the false assumption "that we are proceeding on the basis of the Confederation. This Convention is unknown to the Confederation." Madison, who also drew a sharp dividing line between the Articles of Confederation and the Constitution, considered "the difference between a system founded on the Legislatures only, and one founded on the people, to be the true difference between a *league* or *treaty,* and a *Constitution.*" Popular ratification mobilized the revolutionary power of the people and would give legitimacy to what the convention proposed. Madison argued that "the people were in fact, the fountain of all power, and by resorting to them, all difficulties were got over. They could alter constitutions as they pleased." Rufus King and James Wilson also spoke in favor of a "recurrence to first principles" and a reversion to the "original powers of Society" in accordance with republican theories on the establishment of a new social contract.[67] Seen from this angle, possible compromises like a combination of ratification by state legislatures and conventions seemed not merely impractical, but inadequate and even dangerous.

Once a decision had been reached in favor of state ratifying conventions, it remained to be determined how many state ratifications should be required for the Constitution to take effect. Suggestions ranged from a majority of seven states to unanimous approval in accordance with the amendment provisions of the Articles of Confederation. The latter alternative seemed unrealistic in view of Rhode Island's position and was thus dismissed. Out of consideration for republican principles, Madison and Wilson advocated a majority of both the states and the population. In the end, the delegates settled on nine states, the same number required by the Confederation Congress for decisions on fundamental issues. Article VII of the Constitution read as follows: "The Ratification of the Conventions of nine States, shall be sufficient for the Establishment of this Constitution between the States so ratifying the Same." This formulation ruled out the possibility of one or two states blocking the adoption of the Constitution. By opting for the state-convention model, the delegates indirectly addressed the complicated issue of sovereignty. The Constitution was not being submitted to the American people as a whole for ratification, but rather to the citizens of the United States in their capacity as residents of individual states. Hence, sovereignty remained in the hands of the people as inhabitants of their state.[68] In *Federalist* No. 39, Madison states that the ratification process was both federal (by states) and national (by the people). A final matter of concern was whether the consent of Congress was to be required as stipulated in the Articles of Confederation and in the February congressional resolution that called the Constitutional Convention. It was decided that this should be waived. Delegates feared there might be enough opposition in Congress to delay or even destroy the prospect of ratification.[69] It also seemed unbecoming to require the Confederation Congress to endorse its own death warrant. These three crucial decisions—giving preference to state conventions over state legislatures, reducing the number of required ratifications from thirteen to nine, and forgoing congressional approval—sealed the end of the Confederation and paved the way for the emergence of a new system of federal government in a manner "unknown to the Confederation."

In the minds of most delegates, reservations about "democracy" were paradoxically accompanied by a reliance on the power of the people to invest legitimacy in the new government. Even as the delegates were intent on creating the most favorable conditions possible for the adoption of the Constitution, they never hesitated to leave the last word up to the citizens. In this way, the Philadelphia Convention fulfilled a dual function, at once innovative and conservative, in the tradition of revolutionary conventions. Operating outside the legal framework of the Articles of Confederation, the delegates helped to dispose of the existing constitutional system so as to found a new order. The sovereignty of the people, championed primarily by the radical patriots at the outset of the Revolution, now seemed to be the only credible form of legitimation available even to the more conservative delegates. They perceived the concept of popular sovereignty as an excellent means of reversing the alarming trend toward unrestrained rule by state legislatures. In the process, the idea of an overriding national government acting directly on the people, and directly or indirectly accountable to them, merged with the republican theory of popular consent. Still, no one doubted that a difficult road lay ahead. Edmund Randolph felt that "one idea has pervaded all our proceedings, to wit, that opposition as well from the States as from individuals, will be made to the System proposed." Gouverneur Morris feared the initial enthusiasm for the Constitution might be of short duration: "By degrees the State officers, & those interested in the State Governments will intrigue & turn the popular current against it." Some thought was even given by Rufus King to burning the minutes of the convention: "If suffered to be made public, a bad use would be made of them by those who would wish to prevent the adoption of the Constitution."[70]

A feeling of dark foreboding was particularly prevalent among those delegates who opposed the Constitution in the convention. Elbridge Gerry cautioned his associates "against pushing the experiment too far. Some people will support a plan of vigorous Government at every risk. Others of a more democratic cast will oppose it with equal determination. And a Civil war may be produced by the conflict." Luther Martin joined Gerry in warning of the "danger of commotions from a resort to the people & to first principles." The people would not ratify the new constitution, he averred, "unless hurried into it by surprise." George Mason declared he would rather chop off his right hand than put his name to a document lacking an enumeration of basic rights similar to those guaranteed in the Virginia Declaration of Rights. He was convinced they had proceeded down the path to monarchy or despotic aristocracy.[71] On the final day of the convention, Edmund Randolph prophesied anarchy and civil war should the delegates reject his proposal for a second general convention and cling to their all-or-nothing strategy.[72] Summing up all the authority of his advanced age and experience as a statesman, Benjamin Franklin appealed to the delegates to bury their differences in the State House and present a unified front to the public in support of the Constitution: "If every one of us in returning to our Constituents were to report the objections he has had to it, and endeavour to gain partizans in support of them, we might prevent its being generally received. . . . Much of the strength and efficiency of any Government in procuring and securing happiness to the people, depends on opinion, on the general opinion of the goodness of the Government, as well as of the wisdom and integrity of its Governors."[73] Hamilton also expressed the hope that everyone present at the convention would sign: "A few characters of consequence, by opposing or even refusing to sign the Constitution, might do infinite mischief by kindling the latent sparks which lurk under an enthusiasm in favor of the Convention which may soon subside. No man's ideas were more remote from the plan than his were known to be; but is it possible to deliberate between anarchy and Convulsion on one side and the chance of good to be expected from the plan on the other?"[74]

Randolph, Mason, and Gerry, to whom those words were addressed, withheld their signatures nonetheless. The remaining thirty-eight delegates signed the Constitution.[75] The convention adopted a final resolution before sending the document off on an uncertain journey: "RESOLVED, That the preceding Constitution be laid before the United States in Congress assembled, and that it is the Opinion of this Convention, that it should afterwards be submitted to a Convention of Delegates, chosen in each State by the People thereof, under the Recommendation of its Legislature, for their Assent and Ratification."[76] The delegates could not bring themselves to compose a message to the people, as proposed by Daniel Carroll from Maryland. For now, the Constitution would have to speak for itself.[77]

The Constitution before Congress and the State Legislatures

Richard Henry Lee's Amendments and the "Appearance of Unanimity"

For reasons both legal and political, the Constitution was sent to Congress. Even with its dwindling credibility, Congress could not be circumvented without risk. Nathaniel Gorham, a delegate to the convention and a member of Congress from Massachusetts, foresaw serious consequences should the Constitution be ratified by only nine or ten states. If Congress then refused to acknowledge the Constitution and voluntarily relinquish its power, the new government would be forced to call in troops to "overset Congress."[78] It was thus important to induce Congress to participate in the process of adopting the Constitution, and to prepare the way for a smooth transition from a confederation of independent states to a national system of government.

The secretary of the Philadelphia Convention, William Jackson, handed the Constitution and accompanying documents to Charles Thomson, secretary of Congress, on September 19, 1787, in New York City. On the following day, the Constitution was read to the congressional delegates, and Wednesday, September 26, was assigned for its consideration. From September 26 to 28 a short but fierce debate took place—behind closed doors as always.[79] The dissenters in Philadelphia had already found allies at the highest level of the Confederation. By casting doubts on the legitimacy of the proceedings and by offering amendments, they put the Constitution's proponents in a difficult position. On their part, the nationalists tried very hard to make sure that everything seemed formally correct and unanimous. In the end, they shrewdly maneuvered their way into a "compromise" that benefited them much more than their opponents.

Eleven states were officially represented when Congress convened on

September 26 to discuss the "new frame of government." The seats allocated to Rhode Island remained vacant; Maryland had no voting rights because only one of its delegates attended. Ten of the thirty-three Congressmen present had also participated in the Constitutional Convention and—except for William Pierce from Georgia, who had left the convention early—signed the Constitution. Convention participants formed the majority in three state delegations, comprised half of the representatives from Connecticut, and had one member each in deputations from three other states. This willingness to sit in convention and congress distinguished the nationalists from critics like Richard Henry Lee, who had refused a commission to attend the convention in Philadelphia after expressing doubts "that the same men should in New York review their own doings at Philadelphia."[80] Seven of the ten delegates were later appointed to state ratifying conventions, where they all voted in favor of the Constitution.

The Constitution's supporters, led by James Madison, had two objectives. They hoped to forward the Constitution to the states with a positive recommendation and a request to appoint conventions as quickly as possible with as little opposition as possible.[81] From the vantage point of the opposition, comprised of the three New York delegates, Virginians Richard Henry Lee and William Grayson, and Nathan Dane from Massachusetts and Abraham Clark from New Jersey, the nationalists were proceeding much too impatiently, thus preventing a dispassionate and impartial evaluation. The minority realized they could not stall—much less reject—the transmittal of the Constitution. Nevertheless, one of the most prominent leaders of the Revolution, Richard Henry Lee proved to be particularly well prepared and intent on exposing the Constitution's weaknesses. He was aided by the fact that George Mason had sent him a written report on the deliberations of the Philadelphia Convention, replete with a list of objections to the Constitution.[82] Lee believed the majority was determined "to push the business on with great dispatch before it has stood the test of reflection and due examination."[83] Together with Dane, he took the view that the convention had exceeded its authority as defined by the February resolution of Congress and Article XIII of the Articles of Confederation. Congress did not have the jurisdiction to debate a proposal whose very purpose was the elimination of the existing constitutional order. On September 26 and 27, Richard Henry Lee and Nathan Dane offered motions that Congress should take notice of this fact and inform the state executives accordingly.

Madison interpreted these motions, which reflected disagreement in Congress, as a "very serious effort . . . to embarrass [the Constitution]."[84] The proponents of change were now forced to defend themselves against charges they had breached the Articles of Confederation, while defending Congress's right to act on the Constitution and to declare its approval. They pointed out that the congressional resolution did not merely authorize a reform of the Articles of Confederation, but acknowledged the need for a "firm national government." During debate with Richard Henry Lee, Madison conceded that convention delegates had not remained "exactly in the line of their appointment." He even allowed himself to be provoked into making the admission that Congress had often exceeded its authority in the past, including the Impost of 1781 and the Northwest Ordinance of 1787. Then as now the decisions were justified by what Madison and his colleague Henry Lee called "the great principle of necessity or the salus populi." Whether or not Congress endorsed the Constitution was of symbolic import only and bore no legal significance. It was the people who would pass the final judgment on the work composed at Philadelphia. Madison and Henry Lee thus openly acknowledged the revolutionary character of the impending transition.

Richard Henry Lee implored his associates not to resort to the "doctrine of the salus populi," the last refuge of tyrants: "If men may do as they please, from this argument all constitutions [are] useless."[85] Nevertheless, his motion to transmit the Constitution with a negative comment to the state executives was postponed by 10 states to 1 (New York). Lee then switched tactics: If Congress had the jurisdiction to act on the Constitution, he reasoned, no one could prevent him from proposing substantial changes. The list of amendments he presented to his colleagues proceeded from the premise that the Constitution did in fact contain "a great many excellent Regulations" yet in its current form posed an extreme threat to civil liberties.[86] The first nine amendments were grouped together in a "Bill of Rights," including such fundamental guarantees as freedom of religion, freedom of the press, the right of assembly, the right to free and frequent elections, and the protection of citizens against "unreasonable searches, seizures of their papers, houses, persons, or property." Lee also envisaged replacing the office of Vice President with an eleven-member Executive Council which should perform some of the duties assigned to the Senate. Other proposals aimed to reduce the authority of the judicial branch, increase the number of seats in the House of Representatives, where the "democratic interest" would chiefly reside, tighten regulations for legislative procedures in Congress, and establish proportional representation in the Senate.[87] The advocates of the Constitution were opposed to an exhaustive debate on these issues. The opposition to the Constitution and the amendments would be recorded in the Journals of Congress, from where they would find their way into the newspapers. A Constitution as amended by Congress might even end up competing with the

Philadelphia plan, resulting in utter confusion. The convention gave the right to discuss the Constitution, but Madison and his colleagues much preferred that Congress refrain from exercising this right. To extricate themselves from this dilemma, they opted for the "silent passage" of the Constitution, as suggested by the delegate from New Jersey, Abraham Clark.[88] They decided to forgo a positive recommendation; in return, all objections and amendments were to be struck from the Journal. The Constitution would be forwarded to the state legislatures without any approving or disapproving comment.[89] In the final wording of September 28, the Federalists, as the proponents of the Constitution began to call themselves, made certain that this compromise was designated as a *unanimous* resolution: "Congress having received the report of the Convention lately assembled in Philadelphia. Resolved unanimously, That the said report with the resolutions and letter accompanying the same be transmitted to the several legislatures in order to be submitted to a convention of delegates chosen in each state by the people thereof in conformity to the resolves of the Convention made and provided in that case."[90] It was true that all eleven delegations present, as well as Maryland's single representative, David Ross, had voted for this procedure, but the Federalists' insertion of the word "unanimous" into the resolution was intended to suggest to the public that Congress had been in complete agreement on the form and substance of the Constitution.

This move shifted the momentum to the Constitution's supporters, giving them a head start in the race for ratification. Informing Washington about the proceedings of Congress, Madison was enamored by the "circumstance of unanimity," which would have a soothing effect on the community. In his answer, Washington agreed that the "appearance of unanimity" would be important, since few people were permitted to "peep behind the curtain."[91] "The people do not scrutinize terms," Carrington wrote to Jefferson. "The unanimity of Congress in recommending a measure to their consideration, naturally implies approbation; but any negative to a direct approbation would have discovered a dissension, which would have been used to favor divisions in the states." Indeed, most observers shared the impression of the British consul Phineas Bond, who interpreted the resolution of September 28 as "a complete adoption of the Constitution."[92]

For a time, the public remained ignorant of the facts surrounding the congressional resolution. The newspapers confined themselves to brief reports; the *Pennsylvania Herald,* in an article published on October 6, was the only newspaper even to hint that a debate had taken place. Not until the second "Centinel" essay in late October did readers learn that the Constitution's proponents had not succeeded, despite "two days of lively debate," in persuading Congress formally to approve the document.[93] In the meantime, Richard Henry Lee had sent an expanded list of his amendments, now including the idea of a "Second Convention," to Elbridge Gerry, George Mason, William Shippen Jr., and Samuel Adams. In his correspondence with Shippen, he intimated that the amendment proposals "may be submitted to the world at large."[94] Lee was convinced that it would suffice if a few important states, like Massachusetts, Virginia, and New York, banded together: "If such amendments were proposed by a Capital State or two, & a willingness expressed to agree with the plan so amended; I cannot see why it may not be effected."[95]

On October 16 Lee explained his opinions of the Constitution in a letter to Governor Edmund Randolph, again enclosing a copy of his amendments. Traveling back from New York City to Virginia, he distributed the amendments to Antifederalists in Philadelphia, Chester, and Wilmington.[96] On November 16 the Winchester *Virginia Gazette* finally published the amendments, accompanied by Lee's charge that Federalists in Congress had willfully misled the public by inserting the word "unanimous." During the winter, Lee's letter to Randolph and the amendments were printed by thirteen newspapers in seven states. They also appeared in a pamphlet anthology published in Richmond, and in the December issue of the Philadelphia *American Museum*.[97] However, the demand for proportional representation in the Senate was dropped from versions submitted to the press. It would surely have harmed the opposition in the smaller states, who stood to gain from the Senate compromise. At that time, George Mason's "Objections to the Constitution," first published on November 21, 1787, were also circulating, first in manuscript and then in print, in most of the states.[98] A strategy of amendments to be discussed at a second general convention was thus emerging which might lead to a complete revision of the work created in Philadelphia. In any case, Richard Henry Lee and George Mason had transformed the vague desire for revisions into concrete, tangible demands.

The State Legislatures Call Ratifying Conventions

The deliberations in Philadelphia had shown that the nationalists were primarily out to do away with the dogma of state sovereignty and break the supreme power of state legislatures. This aim had not escaped the public's attention and was soon the subject of intense debate. Richard Henry Lee's brother, Arthur, who later also joined the opposition, expected the states to furiously resist the new order, "because in fact their powers and abuse of them, are the root of the evil that is to be remedied." When the plan was published, the shift in power from the states to the central government was impossible to overlook. French diplomats de la Forest and Otto surmised that the states would have to "make a great sacrifice of sovereignty," thereafter resembling "corporations rather than Sovereign assemblies."[99] The question was whether the state legislatures would defend their privileges, or whether the Federalists' appeal to popular sovereignty would be the potent means needed to break their resistance and prevail over their vested interests.

By the mid-1780s, the movement toward a concentration of power in the state legislatures had passed its pinnacle and opposing forces were gaining ground. The Massachusetts Constitution of 1780 not only established a bicameral legislature, it also placed great emphasis on the veto power of a directly elected governor and the independence of the judiciary. Soon after, efforts to restrain the power of the legislatures were set in motion in other states as well. Typical was the criticism by "Marcus" leveled at state legislatures, "where eloquence is treated with contempt, and reason overpowered by a *silent vote.*"[100] The preamble to a law enacted by the North Carolina legislature in November 1787 stated that poor voter participation had produced inept candidates, whereas "men of Integrity and Abilities have often . . . declined offering their Services to their Country."[101] On the national level, the deliberations in Philadelphia were indicative of growing discontent with the theory and practice of legislative supremacy.[102] Ironically, this reversal could not be achieved against the will of the legislatures, but rather required their cooperation.

In dealing with the Constitution, the legislatures were confronted with factual and legal problems for which there were no precedents. The Philadelphia Convention had left open all formal details regarding the calling of ratifying conventions, including dates, delegate selection, modus operandi, and jurisdiction. By agreeing to conventions, would the state legislatures not be violating the Articles of Confederation, not to mention their own constitutions? If conventions were convened, could their decision-making powers be restricted through resolutions and instructions? Did the conventions have the authority to suggest amendments, or were they required to approve or reject the Constitution *in toto*? In addition to these questions of a jurisdictional nature, there were also matters to be considered from a tactical and strategic standpoint. Should the conventions be called quickly or be postponed as long as possible? Could the states coordinate their actions and pursue a common plan of ratification? The greatest question looming above the entire affair was whether the various factions and parties were capable of reaching a consensus, or whether the Constitution would merely be the source of more infighting and rivalry.

STORMY BEGINNINGS IN PENNSYLVANIA

The Pennsylvania Assembly had shared the State House in Philadelphia with the Constitutional Convention from September 4 to 17. The Constitution's supporters in Pennsylvania were determined to call a ratifying convention before the legislative session ended in late September. The Republicans, who had committed themselves to strengthening the central government and revising the Pennsylvania constitution, still held a clear majority in the unicameral legislature at that time. However, the elections scheduled to take place in October could bring a shift toward the Constitutionalists, who identified with the radical constitution of 1776 and were suspected of having Antifederalist leanings. Besides, postponing the matter until after the elections would have meant that the ratifying convention could not convene until the summer of 1788 at the earliest. The Republicans were determined to exploit their favorable political situation while it lasted and set an example for other states to follow. The morning after the signing ceremony at the Constitutional Convention, the Pennsylvania delegates delivered a copy of the Constitution to the legislature. During his presentation of the document, Benjamin Franklin encouraged the representatives to offer the ten miles square of land needed for the future capital. The prospect of regaining the seat of government lost in 1783 whipped up the enthusiasm of the spectators in the gallery. The assemblymen resolved to print 6,500 copies of the Constitution—1,500 of which were to be published in German—and distribute them throughout the state.[103] But the Republicans' patience began to wear thin as the conclusion of the legislative session approached with no word from Congress in New York. On September 28, the final day of congressional debate, the Republicans proposed calling a ratifying convention. The date and modalities were open to debate, but not the necessity of initiating the ratification process immediately. Time was running out because the assembly had to pass legislation calling for elections and for a state convention before its scheduled adjournment toward the end of the month. To justify their actions and intensify the pressure, the Republicans produced petitions signed by more than 4,000 people from Philadelphia and surrounding areas demanding the swift calling of a state convention.[104]

The leading Constitutionalists vigorously resisted the passage of a resolution for several hours.[105] They argued that the assembly should wait until Congress officially transmitted the Constitution to the states. Opposition leaders William Findley and Robert Whitehill exercised considerable restraint. They did not categorically dismiss the necessity of constitutional reforms or the calling of a state convention. Yet if the legislature should act without the official transmittal from Congress, they asserted, it would be leaving "federal ground" and quitting the Union. The arguments advanced by the majority, in contrast, were markedly bolder and more radical. Some speakers suggested that Congress had only been consulted out of politeness; others seemed to feel the feeble Confederation had, in effect, already ceased to exist. They stressed that the Constitution deviated "in every principle" from the Articles of Confederation, where, as they were surely all aware, state conventions were not even mentioned. In the present case, Congress and state legislatures were to be regarded as "vehicles to convey information to the people" and had no right to prevent ratifying conventions. If necessary, the people would forge ahead without them: "Recourse is once more had to the *authority of the people*. . . . It is on the principle of self-conservation that we act. . . . We have the power to proceed, independent of Congress or Confederation." Federalist Daniel Clymer denounced the "secret machinations" of certain opponents who lived off the Pennsylvania treasury and would thus like to see the weak Union preserved. He also emphasized that the conventions should "adopt *in toto* or refuse altogether for it must be a plan that is formed by the United States, which can be agreeable to all, and not one formed upon the narrow policy and convenience of any particular state."[106] The Constitutionalists were now convinced their adversaries were acting according to a "concerted plan" designed to cram the Constitution down the people's throats. The final vote, 43 for a convention, 19 against, was even more lopsided than they had feared. Several members of their own party, including all of the representatives from the German-speaking areas, had sided with the majority.[107]

What was left of the opposition then resorted to a desperate maneuver, though one not entirely unheard of in the history of the Pennsylvania legislature, where a quorum of two-thirds was required: they all declined to attend the afternoon session, where time, place, and other aspects of the convention were to be determined, thus rendering the assembly incapable of attaining a quorum.[108] The speaker dispatched the sergeant at arms in a futile attempt to remind the delegates of their duty. He then scheduled a new session for the following morning, the final day of the legislative term. Early the next morning, an express courier arrived with an unofficial version of the congressional resolution of September 28. At that point, public tensions erupted in an act of violence. Backed by a sizable mob, the assembly's sergeant at arms and assistant clerk were sent out on a renewed mission; this time they succeeded in capturing two "secessionists" and hauled them back to the State House. In a scene ripe for a comedy, one of the truant delegates, James McCalmont, offered the speaker five shillings, the fine for an unexcused absence. The spectators reacted with scorn and derision, blocking the exit to the State House and forcing him to stay put. After a short exchange of words, the speaker established that at least two-thirds of the delegates were present as required and took up the agenda. The final resolution specified that convention elections were to be conducted along the same lines as assembly elections, and should take place on November 6. The ratifying convention would convene on November 20 in Philadelphia, "for the purpose of deliberating and determining on the said constitution." McCalmont's pleas for a postponement of the elections were ignored, though he did find fourteen backers for his proposal to hold the convention in Lancaster, located farther to the west.[109]

Following this victory, the Republicans eagerly anticipated the complete collapse of the opposition, crippled by "defectors." But the Constitutionalists drew up an apologia, which they circulated in pamphlet form among the citizens on October 2. This *Address of the Seceding Assemblymen* countered the Federalists' state-of-emergency theory and breathed the spirit of resistance. They denounced the assembly's precipitation and irregular practices, and refuted the right of the Philadelphia Convention to frame a completely new work that subverted the Articles of Confederation and the constitution of the State of Pennsylvania. They used suggestive questions to warn of the high costs and dangerous concentration of power associated with the planned central government.[110] These events had a polarizing effect in Pennsylvania, where they fanned the flames of a heated rivalry long separating the political parties. However, the divisions no longer ran strictly along traditional Republican-Constitutionalist lines, as evidenced by the votes of the ethnic German assemblymen. Whereas in state politics they had been Constitutionalist, in the ratification question many of them sided with the Republicans or Federalists. Instead of the old ideological clash between radicals and conservatives, a new confrontation was looming between the Federalist East with Philadelphia at the center, where most of the Germans were living, and the Antifederalist West. The legislative elections on October 9 proved that the resistance to the Constitution had not been broken: 15 of the 17 "Secessionists" running for reelection were able to defend their seats.[111] Reactions outside of Pennsylvania varied. The Constitution's advocates were pleased that Pennsylvania had assumed the leadership in the ratification movement. Yet they criticized the majority's overly zealous methods, which had spoiled the concept of a smooth transition to the new system of government. The opposition hoped the questionable circumstances surrounding the legislature's resolution would rouse many citizens from their state of apathy and cast doubt on the Federalists' integrity. Fascinated by all these events, French chargé d'affaires Otto anticipated a fierce political battle between the "aristocratic" and "democratic" forces in American society: "The alarm is sounded, the public is on its guard and begin to examine strictly what they would have adopted almost blindly."[112]

MASSACHUSETTS AND CONNECTICUT: FAILED ATTEMPTS TO COORDINATE ANTIFEDERALIST ACTIVITIES

To avoid any further surprises, the most prominent critics of the Constitution contemplated the adoption of a common strategy. Apparently encouraged by Richard Henry Lee, Elbridge Gerry advised his Boston friends to postpone the calling of a ratifying convention until the next term of the Massachusetts legislature. At the same time, he sent a copy of the Constitution to the General Court, presenting his reasons for withholding his signature. George Mason also wanted all other conventions to take place at about the same time, in the spring or early summer of 1788: "By a regular & cordial Communication of Sentiments, confining themselves to a few necessary amendments, & determining to join heartily in the System so amended, they might, without Danger of public Convulsion or Confusion, procure a general Adoption of the new Government."[113] Before these suggestions could reach their destinations, however, five other states initiated measures which seriously impeded the coordination of opposition activities.

The Constitution was surprisingly well received in Connecticut. The Connecticut delegates from the Philadelphia Convention, Roger Sherman and Oliver Ellsworth, reassured their fellow citizens that state interests would be wholly protected and deviations from the Articles of Confederation were of a minor nature. Some towns instructed their representatives to push for an immediate ratifying convention, and the influential Congregational clergy of New Haven County announced their support of the Constitution.[114] When the General Assembly convened on October 11 in New Haven, Governor Samuel Huntington lost no time in presenting to it the Constitution and the letter from Congress. On October 16, the House of Representatives approved a timetable providing for town meetings to elect delegates on November 12 and for the opening of a ratifying convention on January 3 in Hartford. On the following day, the plan was confirmed by the Council, the twelve-member upper house. There were representatives of the agrarian interest in both chambers who in the past had vehemently resisted strengthening Congress, thus earning themselves the moniker "anti-federal men." However, they made no efforts to delay or prevent the ratifying convention.[115] In the wake of social turmoil in neighboring Massachusetts, it seemed wise to keep a low profile. According to one legislator, the "prevailing disposition of the people to support order and good government" left no doubts as to whether Connecticut would ratify the Constitution.[116] Still, radical Federalists like merchant Jeremiah Wadsworth remained somewhat apprehensive. They knew there was resistance in Connecticut, despite the unanimity of the legislature, and sensed a plot of "Democratic[s] and Tories . . . against any change."[117]

Massachusetts Governor John Hancock brought the Constitution and the issue of ratification before the General Court in Boston on October 18. In a speech before both houses, he noted that it was not within the duties of his office "to decide upon this momentous affair." Nevertheless, he praised the Philadelphia Convention's "remarkable unanimity" in striking a difficult balance between the well-being of the nation and the rights of the states.[118] These benign comments reflected the relief felt by the citizens of Boston after Shays's Rebellion was subdued and the Philadelphia plan published. An article in the *Massachusetts Gazette* warned that it was necessary "to have this system carefully revised and corrected, before it will be perfect," while another writer lamented in the Newburyport *Essex Journal* that "a revolution every seven years must be very expensive and *dangerous,* and deprive us of the benefits we might derive from even an imperfect Constitution."[119] Nevertheless, it was widely assumed that the General Court would allow the citizens to reach their own verdict.

On October 19, a joint committee consisting of three representatives and two senators proposed the calling of a ratifying convention and recommended the same election procedures as for choosing state representatives. The following day, the Senate, presided over by Samuel Adams, made some amendments to the report and settled on December 12 as the convention date. In the House debate on October 24, however, Dr. Daniel Kilham from Newburyport and William Widgery, representing New Gloucester, Maine, spoke out in opposition to the Senate resolution. Kilham's remarks did not clearly indicate whether the opposition intended flatly to reject the ratification procedure as a violation of the Articles of Confederation or whether they would be satisfied to see the convention postponed. Either way, Kilham left himself open to charges that he was trying to deprive the people of their right to decide for themselves. One of the Federalists expressed sarcastic remorse before the crowded gallery "that the Dr. was so much against the people's being permitted to think for themselves." Widgery proposed holding a popular referendum in each township analogous to the ratification of the state constitution in 1780. But when Federalists consented to a postponement of the convention until January 9, 1788, 129 of the 161 representatives present voted in favor of the revised Senate resolution.[120] This wide margin belied the relative strength of the opposition in Massachusetts. Many representatives may have disliked the Constitution, but they still favored letting the people decide. A number of representatives from the backcountry who had won elections in May would have supported Kilham and Widgery, had they attended the fall session of the legislature. Furthermore, Gerry's letter of October 18 arrived too late and was not made known to the legislature until October 31.[121] Obviously, the critics of the Constitution did not have a common agenda. That also made it easier for Federalists to insist on Boston as the site of the convention—the dissenters were split between York in Maine and Worcester in the state's interior. Now it was up to the nearly four hundred town meetings to elect delegates to the convention by the beginning of January, the procedure normally required for House of Representatives elections.

Unanimous agreement best describes the situation in Delaware, New Jersey, and Georgia, where ratifying conventions were called between October 26 and November 10.[122] All three states were no strangers to internal conflicts, but they had good reasons for not bickering over the Constitution. Georgia was bracing for a battle with the Creek Indians; New Jersey felt exploited by its economically superior neighbors, New York and Pennsylvania; and the small state of Delaware tended to follow Pennsylvania's example in matters affecting the Union. The legislatures all agreed unanimously, though not without certain individual peculiarities. Georgia decided to combine the election of convention delegates with the ordinary legislative elections slated for December 4, and authorized the delegates, who were to meet in Augusta on December 25, "to adopt or reject any part or the whole [Constitution]." That opened the door, at least in theory, to a partial or conditional ratification. In Trenton, the New Jersey legislature first heard three of the five delegates they had sent to Philadelphia before scheduling the election for November 27 and the opening of the ratifying convention for December 11. The politicians dressed the resolution up as a law, enacted on November 1 after three readings in the assembly and council. In Delaware, finally, the upper house wanted to revise and augment the bill approved by the assembly. Their recommendations included increasing the number of delegates per County from seven to ten and—as was the case in Pennsylvania—offering the new government land for the federal capital. The House of Assembly consented on November 9, thus paving the way for elections on November 26 and the convention on December 3. These states' head start in the ratification process effectively put an end to the concept devised by Lee, Mason, and Gerry for roughly concurrent conventions at winter's end.

COMPROMISES IN VIRGINIA, MARYLAND, AND NORTH CAROLINA

The ratification issue dominated the Virginia General Assembly, which met in Richmond from October 15, 1787, to January 8, 1788. The gentry was uncommonly divided over this question. A group of moderate and undecided delegates provided something of a "buffer" between the Constitution's ardent supporters and bitter opponents, making it difficult to predict the outcome of the deliberations. When Governor Randolph presented a copy of the Constitution to the legislature, he refrained from explaining his reasons for not having signed it in Philadelphia. This silence prompted much speculation, because it was assumed that the governor's position might be crucial to the outcome of the debate in Virginia. George Lee Turberville summed up his first impressions in a letter of October 28 to Arthur Lee: "The plan of a Government proposed to us by the Convention affords matter for conversation to every rank of being from the Governor to the door keeper. . . . The enthusiastic admirers of the thing in toto (fortunately for us) appear the least considerable—a vast consolidated squadron is composed of those who view the plan as an admirable frame wanting only some few amendments to render it desirable—and a pretty considerable band consists of those who hold it as the engine of distruction—& never think or speak of it but with detestation and abhorence—the extremes are certainly erroneous."[123] Numerous local committees had come out in favor of a ratifying convention soon after the publication of the Constitution; no one openly opposed the idea of calling a convention.[124] When that question came up on the agenda, even Patrick Henry, viewed by most as the opposition leader, conceded "that it transcended our powers to decide on the Constitution; that it must go before a Convention."[125] However, the debate over the date and authority of the convention provided Antifederalists with a welcome opportunity to test the strength of their influence, while taking a few swipes at the Constitution.

Federalists presented their resolutions for calling a convention to the House of Delegates on October 25.[126] Patrick Henry responded with a counterproposal to allow the convention to ratify, reject, or amend the Constitution. This suggestion was unacceptable to Federalists because it gave the impression that the legislature considered the Constitution in need of reform. Henry's proposal might have won had Mason lent it his support, but he sided instead with the moderates, who advocated forwarding the Constitution to the people with no indication of either legislative approval or disapproval. The final version provided "that the proceedings of the Fœderal Convention . . . ought to be submitted to a Convention of the people for their full and free investigation discussion and decision." This wording implied the power to propose revisions. The voting rules and regulations governing the elections scheduled for March 1788 were more liberal than those for choosing House delegates. Exempting convention delegates from "those legal and constitutional restrictions" that applied to legislators, the General Assembly provided that local and state officials as well as delegates to Congress were eligible. This waiver allowed, for example, Congressman James Madison, Governor Edmund Randolph, and the judges of the High Court of Chancery to sit in the convention.[127] Delegates were not restricted to running for the county of residence, but could be elected from a county in which they owned property. Several took advantage of this easing of the election rules. George Mason, for instance, was elected for Stafford County instead of his home of Fairfax County, which was overwhelmingly Federalist. The convention was originally set to begin on the last Monday in May, but Senate Antifederalists managed to secure an additional week's time to campaign. The long preparation time until June 2, 1788, was also welcomed by most Federalists, who were unsure of their own support. They looked forward to improved prospects once a few other states had ratified.[128]

The failure of both houses to set the pay for convention delegates gave Antifederalists an opportunity for another "side blow" in late November. In addition to the compensation, Antifederalists demanded the appropriation of special funds to establish contact with the conventions in other states. This proposal was referred to a legislative committee, which went one step further and allocated money for Virginia's participation in a possible second General Convention. However, a slim majority in the lower house blanched at such a blunt allusion to the often-discussed second convention. The final version of the "Act Concerning the Convention," passed on December 12, did in fact emphasize the "essential importance" of interstate cooperation, but avoided any reference to a second convention.[129] At the request of both houses, Governor Randolph sent copies of this act and the October resolutions to the executives of every state. The legislature did not accede to the demands of several Antifederalists, however, who wanted to send a circular to every state proclaiming Virginia's support of amendments. The General Assembly thus concluded its balancing act between Federalism and Antifederalism. If the situation in the legislature was representative of the Old Dominion as a whole, it was easy to predict a rough and winding road ahead for the Constitution. In late December, the debate was again fueled by the publication of Governor Edmund Randolph's reasons for not signing the Constitution. Federalists reacted with relief and Antifederalists with disappointment to the fact that Randolph was less critical of the Constitution than they anticipated, and that he even emphasized the necessity of Union and a strong central government.[130]

The legislature in neighboring Maryland had Virginia's lead to follow in their assembly in Annapolis on November 23. The Constitution's adversaries, led by the popular Samuel Chase of Baltimore, wanted to emulate the Richmond resolutions as far as possible. The conservative Senate and Federalist-dominated House of Delegates, on the other hand, pushed for an earlier convention date and more restricted qualifications for delegates. The ratification issue had already played a role in the September legislative elections. Accused of Antifederalist leanings, Chase had publicly stated his intention of voting for a convention in the lower house. At the same time, he avoided any expression of unconditional support for the Philadelphia plan. Following his reelection, he drew up a proposal for resolutions which would allow the convention delegates broad power to consider the Constitution. Federalists countered with a petition calling on the legislature to authorize "assent and ratification" only.[131] This dispute dragged on in the lower house and led to wrangling between the two chambers. The House of Delegates first followed Virginia's example, granting the convention leeway for a "full and free investigation and decision," but was forced to make important concessions in the course of the debate. In the end, the convention was instructed "to take into consideration the aforesaid constitution, and if approved of by them or a majority of them, finally to ratify the same." To the Senators, who insisted on confining the convention delegates' authority to "assent and ratification," this commission was not restrictive enough. The election and convention dates put forward by the Senate were January 16 and March 3, 1788; the House, under the influence of Chase and his supporters, suggested April 7 and 24, in order to move the Maryland ratification proceedings closer to those in Virginia. Both voters and candidates would have to fulfill the same property qualifications that applied to the lower house. The Senate wanted to establish considerably stricter standards, but their demands fell on deaf ears in the House.[132] A majority of the Senators also clung to their timetable and voter-eligibility preferences until December 1, finally relenting to avoid an unnecessary extension of the term of the legislature. The representatives then ordered the printing of 2,000 English and 300 German copies of the Constitution and accompanying convention resolutions.[133]

Virginia's neighbor to the south, North Carolina, was known for its paper-money policy and anti-Tory sentiments, but also for its "deference to the political opinions of the Old Dominion."[134] Federalists like Archibald Maclaine and Hugh Williamson, a congressional delegate and signer of the Constitution, were anticipating a strong opposition. The driving force would likely be the leaders of the Piedmont and backcountry, who had been embroiled in political dispute with the Tidewater faction for years.[135] In the legislature, however, the Constitution's foes were not yet presenting a unified front. A radical group around Senator Thomas Person resisted any discussion whatever of the ratification procedure and was already prompting contingency plans to be made if the legislature failed to call a convention. The majority agreed nevertheless to a neutral formulation on December 6, similar to what had been decided in Maryland. As to elections (March 28–29) and the date of the convention in Hillsborough (July 21), they gave themselves enough time to wait to see how Virginia would act. Every county was to be allotted five delegates, while borough towns were allowed one each. The delegates had to be in possession of a freehold to be eligible. It was also agreed that 1,500 copies of the Constitution and 300 copies of the legislative resolution should be circulated.[136] In the estimation of French consul Jean-Baptiste Petry, Antifederalists purposefully kept a low profile so as not to harm their prospects of reelection. The true strength of the opposition would not be revealed until the convention itself.[137]

FEDERALIST SUCCESSES IN NEW HAMPSHIRE AND NEW YORK

The president of New Hampshire, General John Sullivan, had dissolved the legislature at the end of September 1787 to give the Constitution's supporters a chance to better their representation in a special session slated for December.[138] Thanks to this move, resolutions were subsequently adopted by the General Court that benefited Federalists in several ways. The early election date for delegates to the state convention, January 14, and the opening of the convention on February 13 made it difficult for Antifederalists to mobilize in remote areas and establish contacts with potential allies in other states. A proposal to double the number of delegates compared with the lower house was rejected. The General Court declared delegates exempt from the ban on "dual officeholding" otherwise valid in New Hampshire. This permitted incumbents like the president, treasurer, and judges, who had openly declared their Federalist sympathies, to stand for a seat in the ratifying convention.[139]

By the time New York considered the Constitution, five states had already ratified. Oblivious to the bitter criticism of his opponents, who accused him of secret Antifederalist machinations, Governor George Clinton declined to call a special session of the legislature, preferring to wait until the regular session scheduled to meet on January 11.[140] In his opening address before both houses, he maintained a stance of public impartiality. He restricted himself to presenting the Constitution without commenting on it directly, heaping praise instead on the stability of the state of New York and its nearly completed recovery from the ravages of war.[141] During the long period between the publishing of the Constitution and the legislative debates, this issue had divided the parties in New York more than anywhere else. Whereas Clinton supporters, the "Clintonians," were strongly Antifederalist, their intrastate adversaries, occasionally known as "Hamiltonians" in reference to their most prominent member, were uncompromisingly Federalist. The fierce clashes between the two sides in the newspapers pointed to a preliminary showdown in the legislature. Since the publication of the first *Federalist* essay, written by Alexander Hamilton and printed on October 27, 1787, in the *Independent Journal,* Federalists carried on a relentless propaganda campaign in favor of unconditional ratification. The Antifederalist *New York Journal,* however, bluntly urged the legislature not to call a ratifying convention.[142] A similar line was taken by two New York delegates to the Constitutional Convention, John Lansing Jr. and Robert Yates, in a letter directed to the governor (but actually intended for the general public), in which they defended their early departure from the convention.[143] Although the Clintonians' popularity among voters had waned since 1786, they were still confident they could muster a majority in both houses of the legislature. The Federalists, on the other hand, were concerned about the "unfavorable Complexion" of the Senate.[144] According to the January 3, 1788, edition of the *New York Journal,* the January session of the legislature was "conceived by every class of people to be the most important one that the state of New York has ever experienced since the first establishment of its sovereignty and independence."

On January 31—the Massachusetts convention had just entered its critical phase—the New York Assembly was finally preparing to take up the ratification issue. On behalf of Federalists, Assemblyman Egbert Benson, the state's attorney general, presented a neutral proposal based on the congressional resolution of September 28, 1787. Antifederalist Cornelius C. Schoonmaker countered with a preamble containing severe criticism of the Philadelphia Convention: instead of recommending revisions to the Articles of Confederation, they had devised a new constitution, "which if adopted, will materially alter the Constitution and Government of this State, and greatly affect the rights and privileges of the people thereof." This method of prejudicing the citizens against the Constitution was, in Benson's opinion, a "very odious idea." The legislature could do nothing in this matter other "than merely to comply with the recommendations of Congress." Benson went on to emphasize that he was fighting for the rights of the people just as resolutely as the self-appointed "champions of the people" on the other side of the House.

Assemblyman Samuel Jones professed support for Schoonmaker's preamble, but was quick to point out that he was not at all opposed to a ratifying convention. He was convinced that the people, "as the sovereign of the land," would have to pass judgment on the Constitution themselves. After a prolonged debate, a slim majority voted to reject both the critical preamble and Jones's proposal to insert the words "for their free investigation, discussion, and decision" in the text. Federalists had achieved their goal of avoiding any allusion to amendments. The assembly subsequently adopted Benson's resolution after extending voting privileges to all "free male citizens" over 21. For the first time, state constitutional property qualifications were suspended, thereby allowing all free adult males to vote. Convention and legislative elections were to be held concurrently from April 29 to May 3; the beginning of the convention was set for June 17 in Poughkeepsie. The number of polling places was to be increased, and voting was to be by secret ballot. On the following day, February 1, Senate Antifederalists behind Abraham Yates also failed in an attempt to initiate changes to the resolution or to adjourn. They could not counter the argument that the legislature had no choice but to submit the Constitution to the people as stipulated by Congress. Yates's collaborators, John Williams and Reuben Hopkins, even played into Federalists' hands by openly criticizing the extended voting rights. Senators James Duane and Nathaniel Lawrence retorted that a decision of this magnitude should be reached by the widest possible consensus. Williams quickly offered assurances that it was beyond him to question anyone's right to vote. By a margin of 11–8, the Senate agreed to the resolution as presented by the assembly.[145]

Just as Melancton Smith had predicted, the Clintonians were outmaneuvered by their opponents.[146] Things might have been easier for Schoonmaker, Yates, and their friends if Governor Edmund Randolph's official letter of December 27, 1787, accompanying the Virginia act of December 12 had reached Clinton in time. For reasons unknown, this letter recommending interstate cooperation was delayed for two whole months and was not available to the New York Assembly until their closing session on March 10.

That Federalists could not summon a majority at will was proven by an extraordinary debate that ensued over the oaths of allegiance and of office prescribed by the New York constitution. The discussion had originated early in the session in the Senate, when Antifederalists tried to change the text of the oath of office so that legislators should "Swear never to consent to any Act or thing which had a *tendency* to destroy or *Alter* the present *constitution of the state.*" Before the issue of ratification was taken up, Federalists, led by Philip Schuyler, succeeded in eliminating this phrase, which obviously was intended to "operate against the proposed new constitution."[147] When the assembly began considering the oath of office on February 16, Egbert Benson and Richard Harison proposed transferring the officeholders' allegiance from the state of New York to the Union. They were worried that convention delegates might use the oath even in its original form as a weapon against the Constitution, which could be construed by Antifederalists as violating the state constitution. According to Benson's understanding, the "power of sovereignty" to which allegiance was owed had already been conferred on the United States: "He confessed that he did not know what allegiance he owed New York, as an individual state." Harison agreed that an oath of office was only meaningful if taken in support of the "Federal Government." Samuel Jones held an entirely different view: "He asked who was the sovereign of the states?—Was it not the people—of which the legislature was the representation? Was not this a more explicit oath than when bound to the United States in Congress assembled?" However, the oath would not prevent him from submitting to the wishes of the people, "if ever the majority should think it proper to change the government." This argument apparently swayed several of the assemblymen who had previously sided with Federalists, as Harison's proposal garnered only 9 of the 45 votes cast.[148] Federalist politicians had successfully steered the Constitution through the legislature, but the Clintonians were still powerful and there remained plenty of time to mobilize the people against ratification.

THE SOUTH CAROLINA LEGISLATURE DISCUSSES THE CONSTITUTION

The South Carolina House of Representatives was the only state legislature to deal with the actual substance of the Constitution. The discussion was initiated on January 16, 1788, by Constitutional Convention delegates Charles Cotesworth Pinckney, John Rutledge, and Pierce Butler, who wanted to refute criticism of the Constitution. Pinckney took the offensive by arguing that experience during the postwar period had shown a "total change of system" to be inevitable. It was time to supplant the "league founded in paternal and persuasive principles" with a "firm, national government" with substantial authority and a "proper distribution of powers." Only time would show whether or not a large territory could be governed according to republican principles. Rawlins Lowndes, by contrast, considered it irresponsible and frivolous to risk political survival for the sake of an experiment. Americans lived under excellent constitutions, he said, which they should hold as sacred. This wealthy plantation owner and former governor of South Carolina told the house that he had only reluctantly agreed to take on the Federalist phalanx. He was acting on behalf of the backcountry delegates, who had asked him to defend "the cause of the people." Once he had stood up as the voice of opposition, however, he found so much to say that Federalists were kept busy for three days responding to his criticism of the Constitution. He decried the reduction of the states to "mere corporations," the supremacy of the President and Senate, and the right of the central government to levy taxes. His main complaint concerned the economic and political disadvantage of the South under the Constitution. In the new Congress, Lowndes alleged, the trading and shipping interests of the northern states would take precedence over the agricultural South. The disdain with which northerners had come to regard the importation of slaves posed a threat to one of the South's vital interests: "Without negroes this state would degenerate into one of the most contemptible in the union. . . . Negroes were our wealth, our only national resource." Though Federalists managed to win Lowndes over on certain points, he argued that the Constitution remained "the best preparatory plan for a monarchical government that he had read." He hoped his grave would some day bear the inscription, "Here lies the man that opposed the constitution, because it was ruinous to the liberty of America."[149]

In reality, the aged Lowndes, who had initially opposed the Revolution and was known for his dislike of everything new and unknown, did not constitute a serious challenge to the Constitution. He rather provided the cues Federalists had been waiting for, giving them an opportunity to dispel widespread fears among the populace in a calm, superior manner. They emphasized that the Constitution would bring more advantages than disadvantages to the South, and the institution of slavery was not threatened in any way in the foreseeable future. Not surprisingly, the debate was generally viewed as a victory for Federalists. Still, the backcountry's opposition to the Constitution remained very much alive. Toward the end of the debate, one of their representatives, James Lincoln, could not resist taking the floor. As expected, his main concern was not slavery, which was of minor significance to the backcountry, but rather the preservation of liberty. The more arguments he heard in favor of the Constitution, he solemnly declared, the more he was convinced of its "evil tendency. It totally changes the form of your present government . . . from a well formed democratic, you are at once rushing into an aristocratic government. . . . Let the people but once trust their liberties out of their own hands, and what will be the consequence? First, an haughty imperious aristocracy, and ultimately a tyrannical monarchy."

Even before the debate on January 16–18, committees in both chambers had begun drafting a convention resolution. Despite similarities in the two versions, a common text was not adopted until mid-February. It called for a convention, "for the purpose of Considering and of Ratifying or Rejecting the Constitution." Delegates would be elected on April 11–12 by all citizens eligible to vote for members of the House of Representatives. During the debate over a suitable convention site, the old conflict resurfaced between the Lowcountry and the Upcountry. The Lowcountry delegates' choice of Charleston, the capital, prevailed by one vote. The distribution of 500 copies of the "Acts and Ordinances" among the parting delegates signaled the beginning of the election campaign.[150]

RHODE ISLAND: REFERENDUM INSTEAD OF RATIFYING CONVENTION

Rhode Island was the only state that refused to call a convention in 1787–88. A reader of the *United States Chronicle* in Providence warned in vain that the "General Assembly of this State have *no Right* to refuse calling a Convention of the People . . . as the People at large have *a Right* to judge of the Propriety or Impropriety of adopting [the Constitution], however the present members may be opposed to it."[151] Under the domination of the Country Party, the legislature merely distributed 1,000 copies of the Constitution in early November 1787, "that the Freemen may have an opportunity of forming their sentiments of the said Proposed Constitution." At the beginning of its spring term, the legislature called on the state's "freemen" and "freeholders" to approve or reject the proposal in town meetings on March 24.[152] Antifederalists were as motivated by their objections to the antidemocratic and extra-constitutional nature of state ratifying conventions, as they were by the knowledge that a referendum was sure to produce the desired results. A convention, on the other hand, could easily fall under the control of a few eloquent speakers from the coastal cities, Providence and Newport.

A petition of the Providence town meeting severely criticized the actions of the majority party and listed all the reasons that spoke for the superiority of the convention method. The petitioners admitted that ideally the citizens should gather together at one site to discuss issues concerning the Constitution and that this practice was still quite common in republican city-states. However, political life in America was based on the fundamental principle of representation. This included Rhode Island, where laws were discussed and enacted by the legislature, not in public assemblies or town meetings. It followed that for decisions beyond the competence of the legislature, delegates should be appointed to a special convention. This would enable communication and a balancing of interests among various regions and social classes, whereas town meetings tended to judge on the basis of purely local considerations. Convention delegates could view matters from a broader perspective and were capable of considering the welfare of the other states and the common good of the Union in their deliberations. Since town meetings could only vote yes or no, Rhode Island was forfeiting its own right to suggest amendments, as had been done in Massachusetts. Furthermore, there was no way for Congress and the other members of the Union to recognize the results of town meetings: "They can only attend to the Voice of a Convention duly authorized to act on the Subject, and to bind all Individuals in the State, in Virtue of having been appointed by their Representatives for this Purpose, agreeably to the Line pointed out by the Federal Convention." The entire procedure was thus flawed and only served to delay the calling of a convention, which would ultimately prove inevitable. In the meantime, the petition claimed, Rhode Island would be forgoing its right to participate in the revision of the Constitution and the creation of a new government.[153] The Newport town meeting lashed out at the legislative resolution even more harshly, calling it "unconstitutional, unprecedented, and invalid. . . . For if the People alone have a right to frame a New Constitution, What right has the Legislature to *restrict* them to any Particular *mode* or *time*?"[154] For the time being, however, Federalist remonstrations had no impact on the Country Party, which continued unwaveringly along its Antifederalist course.[155]

THE SOVEREIGNTY OF THE PEOPLE PREVAILS OVER LEGISLATIVE SUPREMACY

Although the thirteen legislatures had acted independently of each other, their decisions revealed a pattern influenced by broader moods and currents on a national level. Federalists were the driving force in every state. For them the Constitution represented an agenda, a goal, and a source of motivation. But Antifederalists did not block the calling of conventions, with the exception of Rhode Island. Whoever dared to question the validity of the convention method risked being accused of undemocratic thoughts and actions. Following a conversation with Dr. Daniel Kilham, John Quincy Adams, who was studying law in Newburyport at the time, noted in his diary: "He [Kilham] has made himself rather unpopular, by opposing the submission of the federal Constitution, to a State Convention, and I think he is perfectly right, in preferring his independency to his popularity."[156] A contributor to the *Pennsylvania Gazette* found the legislative tactics of the Clintonians in New York reprehensible: "It is bold conduct, thus early after a struggle for liberty, for their new rulers to attempt to restrain the people from determining upon their own affairs."[157] Antifederalists also invoked the higher authority of the people. Not even the Rhode Island General Assembly claimed to have the final say in the matter, preferring to leave that up to the "freemen" in town meetings. In this way, the concept of the sovereignty of the people, at an early stage in the constitutional debate, triumphed over the practice of legislative supremacy. Hardly anyone had the courage to challenge what Noah Webster called the "fundamental maxim of American politics, which is that 'the sovereign power resides in the people.' "[158] By voting for state conventions, not only Federalists but also the Constitution's adversaries had consented to the ratification procedure, as recommended by the Philadelphia Convention and implicitly approved by Congress.

2

Public Discourses and Private Correspondence

There has been an extraordinary revolution in the sentiments of men, respecting political affairs, since I came to America; and much more favorable in the result than could then have been reasonably expected.

DAVID HUMPHREYS TO THOMAS JEFFERSON, NOVEMBER 29, 1788

So wonderfully are men's minds now changed upon the subject of liberty, that it would seem as if the sentiments [which] universally prevailed in 1774 were antediluvian visions, and not the solid reason of fifteen years ago.

RICHARD HENRY LEE TO SAMUEL ADAMS, AUGUST 8, 1789

Public Moods and Public Opinion

The Importance of Public Opinion in a Republican Society

The success of the American Revolution was to a large degree attributable to the mobilization of the "common people" and their inclusion in the political process. From then on, decisions could only gain acceptance if the electorate was convinced of their purpose and if they had majority support in republican institutions. Therefore, public opinion became a vital element of American politics. In contrast to Europe, where public opinion slowly evolved in opposition to the established ruling powers, and where it had at best a corrective influence, public opinion in America constituted a driving force of political development. This experience led to a preoccupation with the forms in which it manifested itself and the instruments that could be used to influence, shape, and manipulate it. Annual elections ensured that changes in mood were registered quickly and translated into legislative mandates. As literacy grew, the public began to feel more competent and capable of expressing its views, concerns, and desires. An open press, which in principle offered all citizens the opportunity to express their views, helped reveal the nuances of public opinion. However, the Revolution had also shown that the press could be easily exploited to channel the people's thoughts and feelings in a particular direction. The Enlightenment concept of public opinion as the rational basis of political action was extended to include an approach which regarded public opinion as an object or product of education—or even manipulation.

A "Revolution of Sentiment": Curse or Blessing?

The American revolutionaries had been forced to acknowledge that the people were susceptible to changing moods and that the "public mind" was subject to fluctuations. The conflict with England and the Loyalists had unleashed a powerful democratic stimulus that pushed for equality, shared responsibility, and self-determination. By 1784, however, an unmistakable countermovement could be observed, driven by a desire for authority, security, economic certainty, and national respectability. It was characterized by disappointment over unfulfilled expectations following the Revolution and reservations about the people's ability to govern themselves.[1] Jeremy Belknap believed in the principle that all power is derived from the people, "but let the people be taught (and they will learn it by experience, if no other way) that they are not able to govern themselves."[2] John Stevens saw a direct correlation between the percentage of the populace participating in governmental decisions and the "most shocking outrages and enormities of every kind" experienced since the Revolution. Government was once again perceived as a necessary control mechanism for the dark side of human nature: "Men unhappily need more government than he [*sic*] imagined," mused Maryland Governor Thomas Johnson in the face of Shays's Rebellion.[3]

A number of beliefs held by the revolutionaries were called into question, among them the necessity of annual elections and dependence of the governments upon public opinion. Critics agreed that the political pendulum had swung too far in the direction of democracy and should now settle back toward the middle. "Our government should, in some degree, be suited to our manners and circumstances, and they, you know, are not strictly democratical," the Confederation's secretary for foreign affairs, John Jay, pointed out to George Washington.[4] Former Loyalist and now Philadelphia merchant Tench Coxe wrote that "the relaxation of government that attends revolutions on popular principles" should not become a permanent condition, but rather give way to the habits of good order and regularity.[5] Occasionally, a writer would apologize for the naiveté with which he himself had embraced the Revolution's ideals: "For my own part, I confess, I was once as strong a republican as any man in America. Now a republic is among the last kinds of government I should choose. I should indefinitely prefer a limited monarchy, for I would sooner be subject to the caprice of one man, than to the ignorance and passions of a multitude." This public, albeit anonymous confession by Noah Webster corresponded to the conviction uttered in private by John Pintard, "that we must have an Energetic government for it must be evident to all by this time that our Utopian Ideas were too fine spun for Execution."[6] John Quincy Adams got a taste of the general disillusionment in a conversation with a certain Captain Wyer: "He was he says an enthusiast for liberty in 1775, but finds it all a farce." And in Rhode Island, congressional financial agent William Ellery felt "almost sick of our democracy. We have lost that public virtue which is the support of a republican government."[7] Such sentiments should not be viewed simply as a reaction to the economic problems and social unrest of the 1780s. They were rather the expression of a profound conflict of values and attitudes that had been unleashed by the Revolution and, with the coming of independence, had entered a new phase. Economic crisis and Shays's Rebellion were mere catalysts which served to accelerate this conflict and turn it into a widespread movement.

The social elite, for the most part, strongly welcomed and encouraged the new climate of opinion. Stephen Higginson had never witnessed "such a great change in the public mind as has lately appeared in this State [Massachusetts] as to the expediency of increasing the powers of Congress." To lawyer Theodore Sedgwick it appeared as if the people had finally come to their senses, "and the first evidence is their discernment of their true friends."[8] A sober approach to economic realities was clearly gaining favor: "The minds of the People are now disposed to hear reasoning upon the subject of Trade, from those who have been long engaged in it."[9] Commenting on reports from South Carolina, Henry Van Schaack compared the enthusiasm for the new Constitution in the South with the "spirit of 1775." However, he confided to Theodore Sedgwick that he had found this mass enthusiasm "infernal" at the time of the Revolution, "and now, my good friend, it appears to me to be a good one. What changeable creatures we are!"[10] In a letter written to Lafayette in May 1788, George Washington confirmed the general change of mind and expressed cautious optimism: "Should every thing proceed with harmony and consent to our actual wishes and expectations;—I will confess to you sincerely, my dear Marquis; it will be so much beyond any thing we had a right to imagine or expect eighteen months ago, that it will demonstrate as visibly the finger of Providence, as any possible event in the course of human affairs can ever designate it. It is impracticable for you or any one who has not been on the spot, to realise the change in men's minds and the progress towards rectitude in thinking and acting which will then have been made."[11]

The leading opponents of the Constitution observed the mood swing with considerably different feelings. Their reaction to this "betrayal" of revolutionary ideals ranged from incredulity to sarcasm and resignation. "We have lived under these constitutions, and after the experience of a few years, some among us are ready to trample them under their feet," wailed "Alfred" in the Philadelphia *Independent Gazetteer.* An "Impartial Examiner" from Virginia reminded his compatriots of the common efforts that had led to the victory over England: "By no means can I conceive that the laudible vigor, which flamed so high in every breast, can have so far evaporated in the space of five years . . . the ardent glow of freedom gradually evaporates;—the charms of popular equality, which arose from the *republican plan,* insensibly decline." According to the Baltimore *Maryland Gazette,* the word "Republicanism" had had a good ring to it a few years earlier, but now the weakness of republics was "the everlasting theme of speculative politicians." Compared to the Revolutionary fervor of the years 1774–76, there had indeed been a "mighty change . . . in the political opinions of many people."[12] No one followed this development more pensively than Richard Henry Lee. In May 1787, he had contrasted the relentless demands for a stronger central government with the revolutionaries' erstwhile distrust: "Whence this immense change of sentiment in a few years? for now the cry is power." In October, he was under the impression that the multitudes had lapsed into a "temporary insanity," similar to what had occurred at the low point of the Revolutionary War. Faced with the fait accompli eight months later, he still groped for an answer: "It will be considered, I believe, as a most extraordinary Epoch in the history of mankind, that in a few years there should be so essential a change in the minds of men. 'Tis really astonishing that the same people who have just emerged from a long & cruel war in defence of liberty, should now agree to fix an elective despotism upon themselves & their posterity!"[13]

Both sides, therefore, recognized the change in sentiments, but they assessed it quite differently. These attitudes collided in the controversy surrounding the Constitution, prompting the people to reflect on the matter critically and air their views. Federalists were determined to capitalize on the situation, which might be temporary, to bring about fundamental reforms. Antifederalists, on the other hand, strove to revive the "spirit of 1776" to defend the accomplishments of the Revolution which they felt threatened. Strong emotions were elicited by the calls for more stability under a national government, as opposed to appeals to Revolutionary values and ideals. Because many people were torn by these issues, they tended to perceive the ratification debate as an oscillation of sentiments from one pole to the other.

The Ratification Debate as the Constitution's Ordeal of Fire

Like the Revolution, the battle over the Constitution was a fight to obtain the support of public opinion. Federalists were the first to recognize this fact and worked to prepare the citizens for the upcoming changes. Shortly after the adjournment of the Philadelphia Convention, a confidante of Washington's, David Humphreys, offered an optimistic assessment of the situation in Connecticut: "Indeed the well affected have not been wanting in efforts to prepare the minds of the Citizens for the favorable reception of whatever might be the result of your Proceedings. I have had no inconsiderable agency in the superintendence of two Presses, from which more News Papers are circulated, I imagine, than from any others in New England. Judicious & well-timed publications have great efficacy in ripening the judgment of men in this quarter of the Continent." At the beginning of October, as the Constitution stood before the "judgment seat" of public opinion, the General answered: "Much will depend however on literary abilities; and the recommendation of it by good pens, should it be openly, I mean publicly, attacked in the gazettes."[14] James Madison believed John Adams's *Defence of the Constitutions* had arrived in America just in time to serve as a "powerful engine in forming public opinion." He explained to Jefferson a short time later that by "public opinion" he meant the judgment of the majority.[15]

Some contemporaries regarded the constant fixation with the "thermometer of public opinion" as opportunistic. Writing in the Northampton *Hampshire Gazette* of October 10, 1787, "Justitia" complained about the mild treatment afforded Shays's supporters by the State of Massachusetts: "There appears to be an influence, in the counsels of the land, that is paramount to law, and the Constitution. . . . The grand inquiry with such men is not, what is the law? what says the constitution? but how stands the thermometer of public opinion? and when that is known, their determination is known." Virginia assemblyman Archibald Stuart admitted self-critically: "We are all contending for popular applause and he is the Cleverest fellow who bellows most against taxes and distressing the good citizens of the country who are so dear to us all."[16] Even those like Gouverneur Morris, who thought little of the common man's ability to think rationally, could not ignore public opinion, living as they did in a country "where Opinion is every Thing."[17] Hamilton also did all he could "to cultivate a favourable disposition in the citizens at large." At the ratification convention in Poughkeepsie, he surmised that in the long run every regime, even a despotic one, was largely subject to the people's opinion. Still, in liberal republics, the will of the people was in fact "the essential principle of the government; and the laws which control the community, receive their tone and spirit from the public wishes."[18] This observation did not so much express theoretical deference to the principle of the sovereignty of the people than the recognition that a popular desire for reform was a prerequisite for the realization of fundamental change under the prevailing political and social conditions in the United States.

The extreme importance of the ratification debate is derived from the fact that for the first time since the Revolution the question of a true national government was again on the agenda. Issues involving constitutional law had always touched a vital nerve among the settlers of the New World. Innumerable sources document their reverence for written constitutions. Viewed by society as contractual agreements, they had evolved from colonial charters into the documents of the Revolutionary period. Americans could not conceive of an orderly, civilized society without a constitution. So it was surely correct when one observer remarked in the *Georgia State Gazette* in June 1788: "There is not, I believe, under the sun, a people who are so trembling alive when any thing is said about government as the Americans."[19] The subject of the Constitution was thus approached with great seriousness and almost religious fervor. "The Formulation of a Constitution, or Fundamental Law for a State, your Petitioners consider as the most arduous as well as the most important Work to which the People can be called," the citizens of Providence declared with gravity.[20] It was the privilege of Americans freely to choose their own form of government, and, according to the *Newport Herald,* they had to prove themselves worthy of the task: "For what is the most perfect Constitution of any nation in Europe? but a crude system, arranged without design, and forced upon the people without their choice."[21] Virginian "Cato Uticensis" believed the proposed Constitution to be "one of the most serious and awful subjects, that ever was agitated by a free people." Since the days of Noah, conjectured "Observator" in Connecticut, the history of the world had not seen a people "so great in numbers, so far separated and extended as to situation and territory, and so different as to their interests, ever taking so rational measures to unite their wealth and power, and to establish a permanent government."[22] Alexander Hamilton summed up all these feelings in his introduction to *The Federalist:* "It has been frequently remarked, that it seems to have been reserved to the people of this country, by their conduct and example, to decide the important question, whether societies of men are really capable or not, of establishing good government from reflection and choice, or whether they are forever destined to depend, for their political constitutions, on accident and force . . . a wrong decision of the part we shall act, may, in this view, deserve to be considered as the general misfortune of mankind."[23]

Young John Preston from Smithfield, Virginia, found the matter so important, "that I can justly term it incomprehensible—I tremble & fear." The fear of uncertainty was eased by the tantalizing thought that the Union could some day pass laws "like Rome, to all the world besides."[24] Still, this was a responsibility not easily accepted even by the most experienced and staid politicians. Richard Henry Lee regarded the establishment of a new system of government as an endeavor "that involves such immense consequences to the present time and posterity, that it calls for the deepest attention of the best and wisest friends of their country and of mankind." In the case of Melancton Smith, this represented a physical and mental strain that was nearly more than he could bear: "But the establishing a good government for a great Country is an object of such moment I cannot give it up—It is a matter of too much magnitude. I view it as affecting the whole system of things for ages far remote."[25] Even the debate itself became sanctified: "That calm deliberation, which ought on such solemn occasions, to mark the character of freemen, should now be religiously observed."[26]

The educated classes of society had been prepared for challenges like the constitutional debate by the theological disputes of the colonial period, the juristic and political conflicts with England, and the rhetorical training in colleges and law offices. The specific contribution of the Enlightenment is revealed in the fact that government was now regarded as a scientific matter, as a "system" which must be approached by way of historical studies, rational analysis, and open discussion. The classic expression of this awareness can already be found in a circular sent by Washington to all state executives in 1783: "The foundation of our empire was not laid in the gloomy age of ignorance and superstition, but at an epocha when the rights of mankind were better understood and more clearly defined, than at any former period: Researches of the human mind after social happiness have been carried to a great extent: The treasures of knowledge acquired by the labours of philosophers, sages and legislators, through a long succession of years, are laid open for use, and their collected wisdom may be happily applied in the establishment of our forms of government."[27] From this aspect, the debate on the Constitution appeared to be a struggle in the quest for progress and perfection: "Government, to an American, is the science of his political safety—this then is a moment to you the most important. . . . Deliberate, therefore, on this new national government with coolness, analize it with criticism; and reflect on it with candour."[28]

Federalists would have preferred that their fellow Americans had not taken this advice so seriously, and had adopted the Constitution without undue hesitation. They did not duck the challenge to defend its worth, however, especially not in this case, where they believed themselves well matched with their opponents in every respect. Tactical considerations also mandated that they take up the gauntlet. There was nothing the public disapproved of more than attempts to stifle the "spirit of free investigation" and impede the exchange of thoughts, opinions, and information. Rarely did an author openly express the conviction that the multitude was "very ill qualified to *judge* for themselves what government will best suit their peculiar situations."[29] In most cases, the people's democratic right to have a voice in government decisions was expressly emphasized: "All men, in the same society, have a right to enquire into all opinions, to examine all subjects, to represent all grievances, to shew what laws are pernicious or defective and to lay before the public their sentiments agreeable to truth."[30] In the estimation of one of the Constitution's foes, Samuel Bryan of Pennsylvania, the educated elements of society bore special responsibility for the common weal. In the first "Centinel" letter, he called on them "to come forward, and thereby the better enable the people to make a proper judgment; for the science of government is so abstruse, that few are able to judge for themselves." His New York peer "Cato," on the other hand, feared it was the new Constitution itself that would render the science of politics "intricate and perplexed" and "too misterious for you to understand, and observe."[31] Generally, free men were believed capable of reaching a proper decision if they were provided with the necessary information and were willing to give matters of national importance priority over their "little personal and local interests."[32] James Madison, who at this time in his life was leery of the public ability to make wise decisions, was one of the few to cast doubt on the ultimate wisdom of the people. To him, the great number of diverging views on the issue of the Constitution was sad proof of the "fallibility of human judgment, and of the imperfect progress yet made in the science of Government."[33]

Federalists and Antifederalists basically agreed that the plan for a new form of government required thorough discussion. Everyone who was capable of contributing to the process of deliberation had not only the right, but also the obligation, to take part in the public discussion: "It is a duty incumbent on every man, who has had opportunities for inquiry to lay the result of his researches on any matter of publick importance before the publick eye."[34] This was the only way for the debate to fulfill its purpose of eliminating mistakes and misunderstandings, increasing knowledge and seeking truth. "If the constitution is good, it can receive no damage from examination, but will, like silver, by rubbing appear brighter and brighter, and the people be led to accept of the same with more unanimity," wrote "Lycurgus" in the Boston *American Herald*. William Ellery of Newport agreed that the "Freedom of debate strikes out truth, as the collision of flint and steel produces light."[35] Jefferson also regarded public discussion as the best means of unearthing the Constitution's strengths and deficiencies. From his diplomatic post in Paris, he strove to contribute to this dialogue as much as possible through extensive letter writing. In the end, he confided to one of his correspondents that the discussions and reflections had largely alleviated his concerns about the potentially harmful effects of the reform.[36] As long as he lived, he never ceased to defend the "free right to the unbounded exercise of reason and freedom of opinion."[37]

At the conclusion of the ratification proceedings, Federalists were convinced the Constitution had received the treatment it deserved. "Since the World began, I believe no Question has ever been more repeatedly & strictly scrutenized or more fairly & freely argued, than this proposed Constitution," was the word Jefferson received from Philadelphia in July 1788.[38] According to the New York *Daily Advertiser,* the new charter had withstood this acid test brilliantly: "The Constitution has, comparatively speaking, undergone an ordeal [by] torture, and been preserved, as by fire."[39] It had "emerged from the fiery ordeal of discussion . . . with additional purity and lustre," one orator proclaimed on Independence Day in 1789.[40] And according to a comment published in the *Pennsylvania Gazette* at the beginning of 1790, the more carefully the Constitution was dissected, "the more the goodness of it has appeared." At the same time, the people had become better educated and more aware: "The new Constitution has diffused political knowledge by the discussions it has occasioned. Compare the present state of the public mind of America, on the subject of Government, with what was its condition previous to the war, and you will be struck with the contrast." The debate over the Constitution had been the key which unlocked new dimensions and opened new horizons of political thought.[41]

The Public Mood from a Regional Perspective

A number of observers noted differences in mood and mentality between the North and the South that diverged from old, often stereotypical images. It was astonishing to some that the citizens of New England, known for their "democratic" posture, were adamantly calling for authority, order, and a stable government. Mathew Ridley of Baltimore was not the only one who wondered how it could be "that the Cold Climate of New-England, and Religious Independency can so assimulate, as to make a Hot-Bed of Governmental Experiments?" It seemed to Edward Carrington of Virginia as early as October 1787 that the proposed Constitution had received a warmer reception in the "Eastern States" than anywhere else. Washington was also surprised "that the men of large property in the South should be more afraid that the Constitution will produce an Aristocracy or a Monarchy, than the genuine democratic people of the east." Madison also took notice of this phenomenon. It was remarkable, he told Jefferson, that the Constitution's adversaries in New England were so infrequently made up of "the men of letters, the principal officers of Govt. the Judges & Lawyers, the Clergy, and men of property." In the South, by contrast, the elite was evenly divided. There were also indications that southerners were not going to follow their radical political leaders, despite the latter's claims to "popular ground." The case of Virginia seemed to prove "that the body of sober & steady people, even of the lower order, are tired of the vicissitudes, injustices and follies which have so much characterised public measures, and are impatient for some change which promises stability & reason." This popular desire coincided with the sentiments of the northern democratic mindset, much of which had not survived the shock of the agrarian uprising.[42]

In the overall course of the ratification debates, each state experienced its own public-opinion curve. Normally, the level of public interest reached its peak during the election campaigns and conventions, then subsided. Pennsylvania was the only state where Antifederalists managed to maintain—even increase—the intensity of the resistance after ratification. Not until early in the summer of 1788 did Federalists discern the long-awaited weakening of the opposition in the Pennsylvania backcountry. However, as late as September 1788 a party convention of Antifederalists met in Harrisburg. In Virginia, the barometer of public opinion was uncommonly erratic. After the initial positive reaction to the Philadelphia plan, the number of critics grew on an almost daily basis in late 1787. The pro-Constitution forces detected an easing of "anticonstitutional fever" in January 1788, but during the election campaign the "demoniac spirit" again spread from a select few to the general population. Madison considered the outcome of the balloting impossible to predict right up to the end. Speculation and wild predictions continued between the March election and the meeting of the convention in June.[43] Federalists felt temporary relief after the adoption of the Constitution, but Antifederalist victories in the legislature late in the year again gave them cause for an "unusual degree of anxiety."[44] Finally, in January 1789 there was an irrefutable "encrease of federal sentiments," and in mid-1789 Archibald Stuart was relieved to note that "party spirit" had been banished for good.[45]

Federalists in New York got off to a promising start with the masterful *Federalist* essay series and with their clever tactics at the assembly session in early 1788. But soon they found themselves on the defensive, their clear domination of New York City notwithstanding. Their overwhelming defeat in the elections in the spring of 1788 were attributed to the fact that the "popular tide" had turned against them. Their own propaganda work, and particularly the adoption of the Constitution in June in New Hampshire and Virginia, brought about a "Change of Sentiment" which facilitated ratification in Poughkeepsie in July. Even after this, however, the influence of Antifederalists—who considered themselves to be truly federal and republican—remained substantial. In November 1788, Hamilton again complained that his compatriots had been seized by a "rage for amendments." The legislative elections of 1789 installed Federalist majorities in both houses nonetheless. "A strange alteration this, to be made in one year, in the minds of the people of the State," concluded Richard Platt. For all that, the attempt to oust Antifederalist George Clinton as governor failed.[46]

The developments in Massachusetts were no less capricious. After the strength of the opposition in the winter of 1787–88 had made ratification very difficult, Antifederalism was regarded as defunct on several occasions over the course of 1788. But it flared up again and again in 1789 during the legislative and gubernatorial elections, as well as during the amendment deliberations in Congress. Whether the public mood was really so volatile, or whether the participants only perceived it as such, remains an open question. Even on the basis of all the available sources, historians find it difficult to reconstruct the "American mind" during the ratification struggle. For the contemporaries, who were torn between their own preferences, fragmentary information, party propaganda, and wishful thinking, it was almost impossible to get a coherent, realistic view of the overall situation.

Public Participation in the Ratification Debate

The debate was of course most intense in the cities, which had the density of population and the newspapers. But even in smaller towns and in rural areas, the proposed Constitution captivated the population, was "the principle topic of conversation in every company," and pushed "all lesser matters" aside.[47] The political front sometimes cut across family lines, as shown by the Lees in Virginia, the Shippens in Philadelphia, and the Banckers in New York. Philosophical and literary societies discussed the Constitution at their meetings, and clubs were founded to debate constitutional issues. In January 1788, William Cranch reported to John Quincy Adams from Boston: "We lads who are students in the law in town have form'd ourselves into a club, meeting once a week, for the purpose of cultivating and encouraging forensic and ex tempore disputations."[48] The Richmond "Political Society" devoted several evenings of public discussion to the Constitution in November and December 1787. The speakers included Patrick Henry and George Nicholas, and invited guests were Gouverneur Morris and Robert Morris from Pennsylvania, who were in town on business. James Breckinridge, who studied law at the College of William and Mary, attended one of the Society's meetings: "The subject was pretty fully discussed the sense of the house was taken and a great majority were in favor of the ratification."[49] There is evidence of similar activities in Philadelphia (Society for Political Enquiries; Federal Club); New York (Philological Society); Newark (Society for Promoting Useful Knowledge); Danville, Kentucky (Political Club); Poughkeepsie (Constitutional Society); Wilmington, North Carolina (Federal Club); and Charleston (Free and Easy; Ugly Club). Discussions that were less highbrowed, though just as earnest, also occurred in coffee houses, taverns, and public squares. On religious and civic holidays, the ministers and other speakers drew inspiration from the Constitution as well as from the Bible.

Women had the worst lot during this period of feverish debate. Already having little direct voice in public affairs, politics intruded into their usual social activities as well: "A general anxiety for the Event, suspends the love of pleasure. All the Men are immers'd in Politicks;—and the Women say 'Life is not Life without them.' "[50] Two active female participants in the ratification debate were the historian Mercy Otis Warren and Ann Gerry, the wife of Elbridge Gerry, known in Boston as the "anti-federal ladies."[51] Other women were also forming their own political opinions. Some examples of this are the correspondence between John Adams's daughter, Abigail Adams Smith, and her mother Abigail and brother John Quincy Adams, as well as the letters exchanged between John Jay and his wife Sarah, and between Samuel B. Webb and his fiancée Catherine C. Hogeboom. Abigail Adams fiercely defended her husband John against public criticism: "Some of his Sentiments I presume will be very unpopular in our Country, but time and experience will bring them into fashion, every day must convince our Countrymen more & more, of the necessity of a well balanced government and that a Head to it, is quite as necessary as a body & Limbs."[52] Sarah Jay followed the public debate closely and, while visiting friends in Elizabethtown, reported the positive reception her husband's "Citizen of New-York" pamphlet had received there.[53] After Samuel Webb's bride-to-be took exception to the condescending expression "Petticoat Philosopher," he obviously felt an apology was in order: "You need not fear of my reproving you with the term female politician, I do not hold your Sex in that trifling point of view, Men generally do,—I can readily conceive, that your sensations are lively when you think your friends or Country in danger—and I know not why you may not speak your opinions as well as those who term themselves the Lords of the Creation."[54] Robert Morris's wife, Mary, also addressed political issues, "as you know that I am something of a politician."[55] Abigail Adams Smith found even Governor Clinton's fourteen-year-old daughter "as smart and sensible a girl as I ever knew—a zealous politician, and a high anti-Federalist."[56] In a few cases, newspaper articles appeared under female pseudonyms, such as "Maria," who criticized the "pomp" of the ratification celebrations in Boston.[57] The often-mentioned presence of "many ladies" in the galleries of the ratifying conventions is a visible proof that American women, especially in the cities, did not remain unaffected by the general politicization of 1787–88.

There was less access to news reports in rural areas, and the opportunity for an exchange of ideas was only given on certain occasions, such as town meetings, court days, visits to church, and militia training. This says little about the people's level of interest, however. The farmers in the outlying areas usually had their definite opinions, which they expressed by voting for and instructing delegates. It was somewhat easier for the residents of New England to formulate and advance their demands because they lived in cohesive settlements and had a tradition of town meetings. The main political unit in the middle and southern states was the county or parish. Of course there were areas where the people went about their daily work without giving much thought to politics. "In this County we have few Politicians, nor do the People seem to concern themselves much about the New fœderal Constitution," was the word from Botetourt County in Virginia in February 1788.[58] According to Silas Lee, the Constitution was hardly ever mentioned in the vicinity of Penobscot in Massachusetts: "The people in general appear to be totally unacquainted with it and equally indifferent as to its establishment."[59] Even so, it would be incorrect to conclude from these pockets of apathy that a general lack of knowledge or interest prevailed among farmers in the backcountry. A good example to the contrary was the western town of Pittsfield, Massachusetts. Henry Van Schaack noted a "disposition for information" and the political will "to do that which is right" at a neighborhood meeting he organized there in December 1787. Van Schaack was so consumed by the question of the Constitution himself, "that I can neither think or talk of any thing else." Incidents around Carlisle in western Pennsylvania had shown that passions ran high in rural America. Federalists knew all too well that their greatest threat came from the backcountry and frontier.[60]

The Climate of Public Opinion and Pressures to Conform

John Quincy Adams's letters and diary furnish an excellent example of the effects of public opinion on individuals. The sensitive Harvard graduate's first reaction to the Constitution had been extremely critical. He believed it violated the Articles of Confederation and was inconsistent with key provisions of the Massachusetts constitution. Even worse, it was "calculated to increase the influence, power and wealth of those who have any already . . . it will be a grand point gained in favour of the aristocratic party." Although his legal mentor, Theophilus Parsons, was a Federalist, as were most of his friends and acquaintances, Adams considered himself a "strong antifederalist" well into 1788. His health was even affected by the awareness that he had chosen the "weaker side": "My nerves for two or three months have been somewhat disordered, and my mind has been totally incapable of much application."[61] After Massachusetts voted to ratify in February 1788, he viewed continued opposition as incompatible with republican principles: "In this Town [Newburyport] the Satisfaction is almost universal: for my own part, I have not been pleased with this System, and my acquaintance have long since branded me with the name of an antifederalist. But I am now converted, though not convinced. . . . In our Government, opposition to the acts of the majority of the people is rebellion." He assured his cousin, fellow student William Cranch, that he would have voted for the adoption of the Constitution at the Boston convention, "not from the arguments and characters which favoured that side, but from those which appeared on the other."[62] A visit to the first session of the New Hampshire convention served to confirm his change of heart: "I am now a strong *federalist*—Not that I am convinced the plan is a good one; but because I think opposition would be attended with more immediate and perhaps greater evils."[63] In March, he was surprised but relieved to note that his father had praised the Philadelphia plan in the third volume of his *Defence of the Constitutions*. Nevertheless, his conscience was still bothered as late as April: "The revolution that has taken place in sentiments within one twelve months past must be astonishing to a person unacquainted with the weaknesses, the follies, and the vices of the human nature." But it was the fate of the once highly respected General James Warren that prevented him from "relapsing" into Antifederalism: "Among all those who were formerly his [Warren's] friends he is extremely unpopular, while the insurgents and antifederal party (for it is but one) consider him in a manner as their head."[64]

John Quincy Adams's path from a principled opponent of the Constitution, to a self-doubting critic, and finally to a reluctant supporter, was not an isolated case. This development can rather be seen as representative of a large number of young Americans distressed by the popular repudiation of the radical republican tradition they had grown up with and internalized. Two additional examples may suffice here. In March 1788, William Nelson, a thirty-year-old lawyer from Virginia, wrote to William Short in Paris: "The theories of republicanism (at least according to my ideas) are degraded as the phantasies of enthusiastick minds,—as metaphysical exercises for youthful genius; but too chimerical for practice.—My God! is it possible that thou hast given reason merely as an ornament, & not as a light wch. we are to follow in pursuit of philosophical & political truth. Is sound argument at variance with fact?"[65] In the fall of 1788, Bostonian Peter Thatcher regretted the "erroneous sentiments with respect to government which I formerly entertained and which I expressed in the convention for forming the constitution of government of this commonwealth. . . . I had formed my ideas of government from books and observations made in a period when imagination naturally too warm was incapable of judging cooly upon facts."[66]

New Ideas Regarding the Nature and Benefits of Public Opinion

The ratification debate heightened an awareness of the power of public opinion and the importance of influencing it in a republic. "A Native of Boston," Jonathan Jackson, advised his compatriots to acquaint themselves with an art form that was already highly esteemed in Europe: "It is this—a previous preparation of the publick mind for publick measures, by convincing the people as much as possible, beforehand, of the expediency of them."[67] Others, like David Howell of Rhode Island, were more fascinated by the elemental force of public opinion, which they experienced during the ratification proceedings: "Under all governments where the people have any considerable influence . . . there is a pervading influential principle superior to all constitutions and laws on paper—I mean, the spirit of the times. . . . There is a majesty in the people, and a sovereignty in their voices, that prostrate all other authority."[68] George Washington after his election as president was keenly aware of the importance of public opinion and the need to respect its power: "In a government which depends as much in its first stages on public opinion, much circumspection is still necessary for those who are engaged in its administration. Fortunately the current of public sentiment runs with us."[69] James Madison preferred a government that could deflect public opinion, or prevent it from creating a potentially "tyrannical" majority. The new administration had hardly demonstrated its new power, however, when he began to take a more differentiated view of the relationship between public opinion and government: "Public opinion sets bounds to every Government, and is the real sovereign in every free one." Nevertheless, he believed that government could take a role in shaping opinion: "As there are cases where the public opinion must be obeyed by the Government, so there are cases, where, not being fixed, it may be influenced by the Government." Government and public opinion could influence each other. The goal was a government "deriving its energy from the will of the society, and operating by the reason of its measures, on the understanding and interest of the society."[70] Madison's collaboration with Thomas Jefferson in the development of the Republican Party began on the basis of these philosophical and ideological underpinnings.

The Print Media: Books, Pamphlets, and Newspapers

Books and Almanacs

As the only intercolonial and interstate means of communication, the press had contributed to the formation of an American identity ever since the Stamp Act crisis of the mid-1760s. Publishers had the benefit of the society's astonishingly high rate of literacy. In contrast to the Revolution, the ratification struggle was a purely internal, well-organized, and reasoned effort of forming an opinion and arriving at a decision through the electoral process. For this reason, the ratification debate takes a predominant position in the annals of the great "campaigns of minds," considered by President Woodrow Wilson to be equally as grueling and severe as "campaigns of arms."[71] Or, in the words of President Franklin D. Roosevelt, the Constitution "was born in invective, pamphleteering, and plain politics."[72]

Certain similarities to a military campaign were indeed impossible to ignore, and it was no coincidence that martial expressions found their way into the vocabulary of both parties. Hamilton sent his first *Federalist* essay to Mount Vernon along with a word of concern that the "artillery of the opposition" was already having an effect. His co-author Madison commented on the first essay in the Antifederalist "Brutus" series with the words: "A new Combatant . . . with considerable address & plausibility, strikes at the foundation."[73] All forms of printed matter known at the time were put to use. As during the Revolution, they complemented each other. All told, the material written and published in the years 1787–89 "probably forms the greatest body of political writing in American history."[74] The printers' active participation in these events left an imprint on the field of journalism itself. The debate over the Constitution provided a glimpse of the future confrontational roles of the government and opposition press.[75]

Up to the 1760s American literature had a starkly religious character. With the advent of the Revolution, however, political writings were catapulted into the limelight, and the subjects of government, law, and constitutional theory became a central focus of intellectual pursuits. The circle of authors grew; they usually remained anonymous and often were hidden from view behind the collective works of committees and legislative bodies. The literature of the Revolutionary period reached its quantitative peak in 1776. After that, the length and severity of the war, coupled with constant paper shortages, placed tight constraints on the writers' creativity. Production did not revive until the mid-1780s, soaring to new heights in 1787–88.

Books were normally the least effective method of influencing a running political debate. They took too long to write and put into print, for one thing. Whenever books were quoted, it usually involved "classic" (though not so very old) authors like Locke, Blackstone, Montesquieu, and Hume. Montesquieu's *De l'esprit des lois* was regarded as "a Kind of Bible for Politicians." According to a tongue-in-cheek remark by Richard Peters, however, this political bible suffered the same fate as the original book of books: "Every one finds a Text to suit his own Purposes. If indeed the Text does not exactly fit, convenient Interpretation must do the Business."[76] The first volume of John Adams's *A Defence of the Constitutions of Government of the United States,* which arrived in America in the spring of 1787, fueled the desire for reforms. Instead of defending the existing state constitutions, the author emphasized the need for thorough revisions. Adams's call for "balanced governments" furthered the campaign for the establishment of an energetic federal government and the strengthening of the executive branch in the individual states. The general public learned about his ideas through excerpts, editorials, and reviews in the newspapers. The reaction was not altogether positive. Some readers were put off by Adams's high praise for the British constitution, and even more so by his conviction that a "natural aristocracy" was essential to a republican government.[77] Unfortunately for Adams, he used the term "well born" to describe the meritorious who, in his judgment, should govern.

The ratification debate also generated its own books. Of lasting value among these were the two volumes of *The Federalist.* Directed to "the People of the State of New-York," the essays by Alexander Hamilton, John Jay, and James Madison, which were signed "Publius," had appeared in four New York newspapers between October 27, 1787, and April 2, 1788.[78] Because the essays were unusually long and—in some people's opinion—too difficult to digest for average readers, few of them were reprinted outside of New York. This was apparently what prompted the publishing of the *Federalist* volumes, edited by John and Archibald M'Lean in March and May 1788. The second volume contained eight additional letters that had not appeared in the newspapers. Both volumes together comprised over 600 pages; 500 copies of each volume were printed. A Federalist committee assumed half of the publishing costs, remitting £144 New York money to the M'Leans. *The Federalist* was sold by printers and to subscribers. Yet by May 1789, several hundred copies remained still unsold. Though the identity of the authors had been revealed only to a few, anyone interested in politics was able to make an educated guess at the names of those involved. Some readers immediately realized the originality, scholarly quality, and historical importance of this contribution to the public discourse. The polished and pointed arguments contained in *The Federalist* were known and used by supporters of the Constitution throughout the Union. Reading the text in Paris, Thomas Jefferson lauded *The Federalist* as "the best commentary on the principles of government which ever was written."[79] At the time of the debate, however, the "Publius" essays and the book version had to compete with hundreds or even thousands of other publications which were less erudite and elaborate but reached a broader audience.[80]

An opportunist in the service of Federalists was Thomas Lloyd, who took shorthand notes of the deliberations at the Pennsylvania ratifying convention. At the beginning of February 1788, he published a book which bore the title *Debates of the Convention of the State of Pennsylvania* but which contained in its 150 pages only selected orations by two of the most prominent proponents of the Constitution, James Wilson and Chief Justice Thomas McKean. Federalists exploited the book far beyond the state's borders. Indeed, the Pennsylvania *Debates* were better adapted to short-term propaganda use than *The Federalist,* whose full impact did not become evident until much later.[81] Also available for sale in the spring of 1788 were the *Debates, Resolutions, and Other Proceedings, of the Convention of the Commonwealth of Massachusetts.*[82] Publishers Thomas Adams and John Nourse used newspaper reports to compile this volume of speeches by delegates from both sides. Inspired by the success of the debates from Pennsylvania and Massachusetts, advocates for ratification also published debates from Virginia and the first North Carolina convention. Both books arrived on the market quite late, yet were useful to the ongoing ratification process and beyond.[83]

The extent to which politics began to affect popular literature can be seen in *Bickerstaff's Boston Almanack, or, The Federal Calendar, for the Year of Our Redemption, 1788,* which was published by Ezekiel Russell in December 1787. Russell embellished the title page of the almanac with a woodcut of "The Federal Chariot" which he interpreted for his readers: "The FRONTISPIECE represents the truly patriotick WASHINGTON and FRANKLIN, triumphantly seated in the FEDERAL CHARIOT drawn by 13 FREEMEN, figurative of the happy UNION now forming by these States.—The heroick WASHINGTON holds in his hand the grand FABRICK of AMERICAN INDEPENDENCE, the FEDERAL CONSTITUTION, offering it with paternal affection to his *freeborn Brethren* the SONS of COLUMBIA." On the facing page, Russell reprinted the text of a widely circulated song which had first appeared in a Boston newspaper under the title "The Grand Constitution: or the Palladium of Columbia: a New Federal Song."[84]

Pamphlets and Handbills

Pamphlets had advanced the cause of the Revolution and preserved the feeling of national identity after the war.[85] They were addressed to the general populace or to a specific author and discussed current political issues. A good pamphlet was supposed to make the readers aware of the foremost problems facing society, while stimulating and guiding the public mind. The author should present logical arguments, avoid long-winded digressions, arouse constructive passions, and "thrill the nerves."[86] None of the pamphlets written for or against the Constitution, however, was as persuasive or sold as many copies as Thomas Paine's *Common Sense,* from 1776.[87] Pamphlets were usually distributed nationally, even reaching the backcountry where newspapers were not normally available. The authors, for their part, often had to bear the printing costs themselves, and sometimes help with distribution.[88] The Federal Farmer's forty-page *Letters to the Republican,* long attributed, though probably wrongly, to Richard Henry Lee, was one of the most sophisticated and influential pamphlets from the Antifederal side. It came out in New York in November 1787, was reprinted four times as a pamphlet, and thousands of copies were circulated around the country.[89] Also widely known and effective from the Antifederalist point of view were James Warren's *Republican Federalist;* William Findley's *An Officer of the Late Continental Army;* Mercy Otis Warren's *Observations on the New Constitution . . . ,* by "A Columbian Patriot"; Melancton Smith's *Federal Republican*, written under the "Plebeian" pseudonym and printed in Philadelphia; and the pamphlet edition of Luther Martin's *Genuine Information.* Limited to Pennsylvania and a few adjacent areas, on the other hand, was the satire written by tailor William Petrikin from Carlisle ("Aristocrotis": *The Government of Nature Delineated*), as well as the *View of the Proposed Constitution,* by John Nicholson, Pennsylvania's comptroller general.[90]

Philadelphia merchant Pelatiah Webster and Noah Webster from New York distinguished themselves as Federalist pamphleteers. Writing in October 1787 under the pseudonym "A Citizen of Philadelphia," Pelatiah Webster responded to criticism from the legislative minority in Pennsylvania, and in November attacked the author of the "Brutus" essays.[91] Noah Webster's thirty-five-page *Examination into the Constitution* ("A Citizen of America") and Charles Pinckney's *Observations on the Plan of Government* were the first detailed commentaries on and defenses of the Constitution in pamphlet form.[92] A new, authoritative interpretation was then provided by James Wilson, whose speech at the Pennsylvania ratifying convention on November 24 appeared a few days later as a pamphlet. Thousands of copies at a price of one shilling apiece were sold.[93] Confederation Secretary for Foreign Affairs John Jay, who wrote only five *Federalist* essays, succeeded in reaching a remarkably large audience with his nineteen-page pamphlet *An Address to the People of the State of New-York.* The pamphlet was published on April 15, 1788, under the pseudonym "A Citizen of New-York," but Jay was quickly identified as the author. Similar to the reasoning in his *Federalist* essays, Jay derived the necessity of a "national government" from the weaknesses inherent in a confederation and implored New Yorkers to join together with other states as a "Band of Brothers." New Yorkers were encouraged to trust in themselves and give the Constitution a fair chance until time and experience dictated appropriate amendments. The treatise was said to have had a "most astonishing influence in converting Antifederalists, to a knowledge and belief that the New Constitution was their only political Salvation."[94] Even an "anti fœderal Mind," marveled Washington, must be impressed by the work's calm and patient tone, provided the reader "is not under the influence of such local views as will yield to no arguments—no proofs."[95] Other important contributions were made by John Stevens Jr. ("A Farmer, of New Jersey": *Observations on Government*); John Dickinson (*Letters of Fabius*); Alexander Contee Hanson ("Aristides": *Remarks on the Proposed Plan of Federal Government*); and James Iredell ("Marcus": *An Answer to Mr. Mason's Objections*).[96] In Philadelphia, the center of American publishing, the first editions of six pamphlets had been issued by April 1788. Next in importance were New York and Boston, though pamphlets were also published in Maryland, Virginia, and the Carolinas. Besides these political essays, there were also speeches and sermons that had been delivered on Independence Day or following ratification and were judged worthy to appear in print.[97] A particularly popular method of disseminating information and propaganda was pamphlet anthologies of material that had already been published and proven successful. This category included *Various Extracts on the Federal Government,* published by Augustine Davis on December 15, 1787, in Richmond, and *Observations on the Proposed Constitution,* put in circulation by New York Antifederalists who had combined the extremely effective *Dissent of the Minority of the Pennsylvania Convention* with the first nine "Centinel" essays, both originating from Pennsylvania.[98]

Especially suitable for election campaigns were broadsides, broadsheets, and handbills, which could be produced quickly, cheaply, and in large quantities. Consisting of one to six pages, they mainly contained articles reprinted from newspapers or excerpts from pamphlets. Texts often appeared first in newspapers, followed soon thereafter as a broadsheet. Philadelphia merchant Tench Coxe's early "American Citizen" essays provide a good example of this. The first three came out in the Philadelphia *Independent Gazetteer* on September 26, 28, and 29, 1787. On October 21, Hall and Sellers offered a four-page "broadside anthology" containing a fourth essay in addition to the partially revised first three. Also included were James Wilson's speech in the State House yard in Philadelphia on October 6 (originally printed as an extra edition of the *Pennsylvania Herald* on October 9) and two other pro-Constitution pieces.[99] Pennsylvania Antifederalists followed the same practice, publishing—just to name a few—the *Address of the Seceding Assemblymen,* the *Dissent of the Minority,* and numbers IV and V of "An Old Whig" essays almost simultaneously in newspapers and as handbills in English and German.[100] A broadside comprising the first two "Centinel" essays and James Tilton's "Timoleon" was printed in New York and circulated in Pennsylvania and Connecticut as well.[101] During the New York election campaign, the Republican (i.e., Antifederalist) committees employed broadsheets to inform the people of their objections to the Constitution and to urge them to vote for Antifederalist delegates to the state convention. These publications had a tremendous impact because they were directed to the common man.[102] This was also the case in Boston, where an anti-Constitution handbill caused a stir: "Last Wednesday morning [November 14], hand-bills were posted up in every part of this metropolis, dropped in the streets, and liberally distributed among our Political Fathers [the legislators]—They were read with avidity by all ranks of people."[103]

The debate over the ratification of the Constitution differs from the debate over Independence in the sheer volume of printed matter and improved methods of distribution on the one hand, and in the crossover between the various types of publications on the other. Newspaper reports appeared as handbills and were included in pamphlet anthologies; broadsheet texts resurfaced in newspapers; broadsides and newspaper essays were based on excerpts from pamphlets; a series of essays or a speech might come out in book form. The most important and original disquisitions on the Constitution were simultaneously circulated throughout the Union as newspaper articles, handbills, and pamphlets—or as part of a pamphlet anthology. Tench Coxe was particularly adept at exploiting all the possibilities offered by the printing press. He maintained close ties with leading Federalists in several states, was interested in scholarly pursuits, wrote well, and had the financial means necessary to express his enthusiasm in literary works. In a little more than a year, he wrote around thirty sizable essays in support of the Constitution. This was supplemented by smaller contributions to various newspapers and by an extensive private correspondence. Benjamin Rush praised Coxe as "extremely active and useful in spreading federal knowledge and principles in Pennsylvania as well as in other parts of the United States." His literary hyperactivity was not conducive to his business pursuits or his health: "My profession was too often postponed—and I am now suffering very seriously for it—and my health was nearly sacrificed by the sedentary habits I was led to."[104] Like Coxe, a number of private citizens devoted large portions of their time and energy to the battle over the Constitution. The collective endeavors of these contemplative, committed, and prolific citizens comprise a large part of the debate over the Constitution.

Newspaper Authors and Pseudonyms

The six pamphlets that appeared in Philadelphia between September 1787 and April 1788 seem modest compared with the eight Philadelphia newspapers churning out twenty-two numbers per week. One of the most important venues for the "collision of opinions" were the newspapers, and these publications were regarded as a "Political Barometer."[105] Though the publishers occasionally put pen to paper themselves, more frequently newspapers served as a forum for others to voice their opinion. Indeed, many gifted and less gifted writers availed themselves of this opportunity. "Those who cannot write and those who can, All rhyme, and scrawl, and scribble to a man!" exclaimed "Philopoemen" in the New York *Daily Advertiser,* at once amazed and disgusted.[106] Essays were usually anonymous or were signed with a pseudonym. One advantage of a pseudonym was that thoughts and ideas were judged on their own merits. The author's name and identity were kept out of the picture, so as not to prejudice the readers. To be sure, there were also less noble reasons for this practice. For instance, one person could write under several aliases, making it appear to the public as if a large segment of the population was in agreement on that particular issue. Above all, he could attack his opponents and government officials without fear of retribution.[107]

The serious essayists carefully chose their pseudonyms. They were meant both to characterize the message and stimulate positive associations. The authors therefore liked to adorn themselves with classical names, along the lines of "Cato," "Brutus," "Publius," "Cincinnatus," "Poplicola," and "Timoleon," thus establishing themselves as enemies of despotism and champions of true republican virtues. "Cato" had a double connotation, also alluding to the ideology of the English opposition in the early eighteenth century, made known in America mainly through the *Cato Letters* by John Trenchard and Thomas Gordon. Other designations designed to capitalize on this "Country" tradition and the more recent European radicalism were "An Old Whig," "A Real Whig," "A True Whig," "A Plebeian," "Algernon Sidney," "Harrington," "Hampden," "John Wilkes," and "John DeWitt." To avoid being labeled anti-Union, critics often used compounds with "federal," as in "Federal Farmer" and "Federal Republican." In fact, outside of Pennsylvania the term "Republican" was coming to denote hostility toward Federalists. The opposition was not above professing democratic sympathies through such pseudonyms as "A Democratic Federalist" or, simply, "Democratic." The pen-name "Caesar," which masked the name of a pro-Constitution writer, purportedly even Hamilton himself, would have been unthinkable for an Antifederalist.[108] As an author, Hamilton usually identified with Greeks and Romans, who, according to Plutarch, had accomplished much for the state without being immediately rewarded for their efforts. One of these was Publius Valerius (Poplicola), whom Plutarch compared with Solon. Federalists were particularly fond of the names of legislators from the classical period ("Solon," "Lycurgus") and terms that emphasized national identity, such as "America," "Americans," "An American," "An American Citizen," "A Citizen of America," and "A Citizen of the United States." The readers made note of whether the essayist proved worthy of his alias: "When the author takes a signature, he should behave accordingly. Cato should shew a grave, senatorial wisdom . . . Caesar should imitate the magnanimity of his Roman namesake."[109] Representatives of both sides tried to appeal to the larger public through such names as "Farmer," "Freeman," "Independent Freeholder," "Planter," "Countryman," "Mechanic," "One of the People," and "One of the Middling Interest." Writers also took the pose of being above party when they chose pseudonyms like "A Man of No Party," "An Impartial Citizen," an "Impartial Examiner," or a "Conciliator." On a less sublime level were humorous, mocking, and fanciful pen-names, like "A Foe to Scribbling Dunces and Pseudo-Patriots," "A Pamphlet-Monger," "Crazy Jonathan," "A Turk," "A Lunarian," and "Federalissimo"—all the way up to the monstrosity "Flaccinancinehilipilification."

The practice of using pseudonyms was eventually challenged on two fronts. Prominent adversaries of the Constitution, among them Richard Henry Lee, George Mason, Elbridge Gerry, and Luther Martin, spoke out for amendments under their own names. Benjamin Franklin and John Vaughan therefore pressured leading Federalists to follow suit so their words would not be drowned out by the torrent of mediocre anonymous contributions. John Jay's response, nevertheless, epitomized the traditional view: "If the Reasoning . . . is just, it will have its Effects on candid and discerning minds . . . if weak and inconclusive my name cannot render it otherwise."[110] In the same vain, "Valerius" told Richard Henry Lee that errors remained errors, even if embellished with "dignified names."[111] Be that as it may, others began to emulate the Antifederalists' example. Virginian Alexander White purposefully signed his own name in order that his foes could not complain "of being attacked by an anonymous writer."[112] At the same time, several publishers aroused controversy by rejecting submissions whose style and content they considered overly polemical. To many readers, the demand of Federalist printers that Antifederalists authors either sign articles or at least leave their names with the publisher constituted an attempt to suppress dissent and an infringement of the freedom of the press.[113] That view did not stop the public from engaging in the search for the identities of unnamed penmen like some kind of parlor game. The writers often "gave themselves away"—not entirely by accident—through their choice of a pseudonym or through stylistic mannerisms. This had dire consequences for author Benjamin Workman, who lost his job as a tutor at the University of Pennsylvania when Federalists identified him as "Philadelphiensis." In Boston, the Reverend Jeremy Belknap rejoiced: "Mr. Hopkinson has done admirably well in exposing the antifederal Writers in Philadelphia. . . . If ours were to be as publickly known they would turn out to be bankrupts and insolvents, or equally dirty characters."[114]

The Importance of Newspapers for the Breadth and Intensity of the Debate

The debate over ratification illustrated the immense growth in popularity and influence the press had enjoyed since the Revolution. During the conflict with Britain, patriotic printers had demonstrated the effectiveness of newspapers as a "popular engine," an instrument for activating, influencing, and articulating the will of the people. A new generation of publishers was now benefiting from this gain in prestige, having been initiated into this "Art which preserves all other Arts" by such great printers as Benjamin Franklin, Isaiah Thomas, and John Holt. Following the war, printers energetically pushed for self-employment and financial independence. Their services were in particular demand because, after separation from Great Britain, commercial and investment enterprises relied on them more than ever to provide precise economic data and information. It was thus no coincidence that newspapers began to spring up along the post routes connecting the coast with the backcountry. In addition, the public's interest in politics, which had subsided near the end of the war, resurged in the mid-1780s in the face of economic difficulties and heightened social tensions.

For its part, the press had no cause to join in the lamentations about "hard times." Enterprising printers and information-hungry readers combined to turn the production and sale of newspapers into an expanding—albeit not overly profitable—business. This dynamic is evidenced by the increased number of newspapers, as well as their advancement into the country's interior and the transition of many papers in the cities from weeklies to biweeklies, or even to dailies. At the conclusion of the War of Independence there were thirty-five newspapers, almost all weekly publications. From the end of 1783 to the beginning of 1788, the total number of newspapers (including two in Vermont) had soared to eighty, six of which were appearing daily.[115] This jump seems impressive even when related to the growth of the white population for the same period, from approximately 2.2 million in 1776 to 3.2 million in 1790. During the period from September 1787 until New York's ratification in late July 1788, eighty-nine newspapers and three monthly magazines appeared in the thirteen states and Vermont.[116] The regional distribution shows that New England and the middle states with thirty-two and thirty-one papers, respectively, were better supplied than the less densely populated South, with twenty-six. The impetus provided by the dispute over the Constitution together with the economic upswing can be seen in the fact that another thirty-five journals, including thirteen in the southern states, were founded between September 1788 and December 1790. Around the turn of the century, 242 newspapers were in circulation, and by 1810 the United States had more newspapers per capita than even the most developed European countries.[117]

Only fourteen of the newspapers and magazines involved in the debate over the Constitution had been in existence since the colonial period. Whereas another fourteen had originated during the Revolution era, the vast majority had not been founded until after the war. More than half of the total ninety-two periodicals were still printed in coastal cities. Of the thirty-seven published in the interior, thirty-one had been established after 1783 in rising communities like Litchfield, Exeter, Northampton, Keene, Albany, Trenton, Carlisle, Fredericktown, and Winchester. As the first newspaper west of the Alleghenies, the *Pittsburgh Gazette* was launched in December 1786. The history of the *Kentucke Gazette*'s founding is instructive for the situation on the frontier. In December 1784, the delegates from the Kentucky District of Virginia resolved "that the freedom of the press is highly subservient to Civil Liberty and therefore such measures ought to be taken as may be most likely to encourage the introduction of a Printer into the District." A committee was chosen in 1785 to search for a printer. Finally, two years later, inexperienced John Bradford agreed to give it a try—after he had been promised "public patronage" and a piece of land in Lexington. In order to survive economically, he may have sold—like a colleague in Keene, New Hampshire—"writing paper, quill pens, blank deeds, justice writs, summonses and executions, ink, powder and books."[118]

The coastal cities from Boston to Charleston remained the Union's political, commercial, and cultural centers. Increases in population, new wants and necessities, and more sophisticated readers all contributed to a growing market that spurred new enterprises and permitted several newspaper editions per week. In urban areas, this growth was accompanied by greater specialization, leading to "commercial newspapers" especially designed for the business world and monthly magazines of a literary or political nature. The competition for subscribers and advertisers unquestionably contributed to a widening of political divisions. Both parties in Philadelphia, the Constitutionalists and the Republicans, had "their" newspaper. The same was true of Boston, New York, and Rhode Island. Moreover, newspapers were now becoming a commodity that could change hands—and political orientation—for monetary gain. In January 1788 Philadelphia's 42,000 inhabitants had the choice of three weekly newspapers, two biweeklies, one thrice-weekly, and two dailies: the *Independent Gazetteer* and the *Pennsylvania Packet.* These were supplemented by two monthly magazines, Mathew Carey's *American Museum* and William Spotswood's *Columbian Magazine.* In New York City (33,000) there were two biweekly and three daily newspapers (the *New York Journal, Daily Advertiser,* and *Morning Post*), as well as Noah Webster's *American Magazine.* Yet another weekly and biweekly were added in the course of 1788. With a mere three weekly and two biweekly publications, Boston (18,000) was somewhat behind. Baltimore (13,500) counted two biweeklies; Portsmouth (4,720) had two weekly papers and one biweekly; and Charleston (16,300) had two biweeklies and one daily. Three weekly newspapers were published each in Albany (3,500), Richmond (3,760), and Winchester (1,650) with their large surrounding rural areas.

Exact circulation figures are difficult to come by for the years 1787–88. The *Albany Gazette,* a weekly, reported a circulation of over 800 in December 1788. The *Wilmington Centinel* and the Philadelphia *Federal Gazette* each began with 400 subscribers. Antifederalists in Carlisle held up the prospects of 1,000 subscribers for anyone willing to found an additional newspaper sympathetic to their cause. Mathew Carey managed to accumulate 1,600 subscribers in May 1789 to his *American Museum,* including prominent citizens in all thirteen states. He was easily able to sell 3,000 copies per edition, but he bitterly complained about the "careless and irregular" payments of the subscribers.[119] Urban newspapers like the *Independent Chronicle* and *Massachusetts Centinel* in Boston or the *Pennsylvania Packet* and *Pennsylvania*

Gazette in Philadelphia, leading publications both in terms of quality and circulation, had between 2,000 and 4,000 subscribers. John Fenno set up the *Gazette of the United States* in September 1789 in New York City with 600 subscribers, "about one third of the requisite number."[120] The transition to a daily was usually accompanied by a drop in readership, due to the roughly 300 percent increase in subscription prices. For this reason, when the *New York Journal* became a daily, it continued to publish a separate "country" edition on Thursdays, which was popular among backcountry readers.

The ratification debate seems to have significantly boosted newspaper circulation. The large number of "extraordinary" issues, along with the printers' willingness to attempt biweekly and daily ventures, are indicative of the surge in readership. On many occasions, printers explicitly noted an increase of circulation. One must also bear in mind that a single copy passed through many hands, that newspapers were laid out in taverns, coffee houses, and post offices, and that they were often read aloud to a considerable number of listeners. The publisher of the Portland *Cumberland Gazette,* Thomas B. Wait, was informed by readers from the backcountry of Maine that "Our principal publick intelligence is through the medium of your paper; which since the promulgation of the Federal Constitution, is read with greatest avidity."[121]

Both sides used the press for propaganda purposes during election campaigns, hastening the advance of this medium into otherwise "newspaperless" parts of the country. Nevertheless, the geographical distribution of newspapers was lopsided in even the most "well-read" state, Connecticut, with its nine publications. While Windham and Tolland counties were forced to make due without a single newspaper, the 38,000 citizens of Hartford County could choose between two, the *Connecticut Courant* and the *American Mercury.* Both had a circulation of over 1,000 and together were read in about 40 percent of the homes in Hartford County every week.[122] The situation differed not only between cities and backcountry, but also between North and South. While for each edition of a newspaper in New England there were on average 26,500 inhabitants, the ratio in the South, at 1 to 105,200, was considerably higher.[123]

Numerous comments attest to the great importance Americans placed on the principle of freedom of the press. In the *Virginia Independent Chronicle,* a correspondent praised the "usefulness of the press in a free state. It gives all the people an opportunity to learn and to be wise, to choose or refuse, in an important affair; indeed it is the noblest exhibition, the new world has yet witnessed."[124] Richard Henry Lee called the newspaper "the happiest Organ of communication ever yet devised—the quickest & surest means of conveying intelligence to the human Mind." Samuel Adams was said to prefer insult at the hands of "scribblers" to any restriction of the freedom of the press. According to Benjamin Rush, newspapers formed "the principles, and direct the conduct of the greatest part of mankind in all countries."[125] "Newspapers will become more important to our friends in the [back] country than they ever have been before," predicted the *New York Journal* on May 29, 1788. "NEWSPAPERS are the GUARDIANS of FREEDOM."

The difficulties involved in transporting newspapers were partially relieved through a system of private or semiofficial channels of news distribution. This system was contingent upon the free delivery of newspapers from printer to printer by way of post roads established during the colonial period and expanded by Congress. This gave individual printers access to a wealth of information provided by colleagues near and far. The hubs of this network were the seaport cities, which were population centers and the points of arrival for foreign newspapers. From there, the news spread in waves along the main postal route from Wiscasset, Maine, to Savannah, Georgia. Though mail usually required 13 days to travel from Massachusetts to Virginia, the swift "New York Packet" could manage the Boston–New York line in a mere 37 hours. Since few of the sixty-nine post offices operating in 1788 were located in the western parts of the country, printers in the interior established their own information and delivery service to supplement the government's postal system. Charles Webster of the *Albany Gazette* had sent a rider every week since 1785 "from his office through Kings district and into New England, as far as Sheffield and Great Barrington, at which last mentioned place he will meet and exchange papers with the several post riders from Boston, Hartford, New London, Springfield, New Haven and Litchfield."[126] Matthias Bartgis, who rose to become a newspaper czar of sorts in the areas settled by German immigrants between York, Pennsylvania, and Winchester, Virginia, initially advised his subscribers to form groups and take turns picking up the papers from the printers. He then organized a distribution system from Fredericktown to the Shenandoah Valley, "for the purpose of conveying my English and German Newspapers to Funk's-Town, Hager's-Town, Sharpsburg, Sheperd's-Town, Martinsburgh, and Winchester."[127]

Two examples may suffice to illustrate the efficiency of this method. James Wilson's "State House" address of October 6, 1787, the source of several formulations destined to become standard pro-Constitution arguments, first appeared on October 9 and 10 in the *Pennsylvania Herald*. From Portland, Maine, to Augusta, Georgia, a total of thirty-seven newspapers in twenty-seven locations reprinted the text partially or fully. The earliest reprints appeared in Pennsylvania itself, yet it still took until November 3 for Wilson's comments to reach the readers of the *Pittsburgh Gazette*. By that time, the speech had already arrived in eight other states: New York (reprinted first in the *Daily Advertiser* of October 13); Maryland (Baltimore *Maryland Gazette,* October 16 and 19); Rhode Island (*Newport Herald,* October 18); Connecticut (*Connecticut Courant,* October 22); New Jersey (*Trenton Mercury,* October 23); Massachusetts (*Massachusetts Centinel,* October 24); Virginia (*Virginia Independent Chronicle,* October 24); and South Carolina (*Columbian Herald,* November 1). The final reprints were in New Hampshire and Vermont in the North (*New Hampshire Gazette,* November 9 and 16; *Vermont Gazette,* November 12) and Georgia in the South (*Georgia State Gazette,* Augusta, December 22 and 29). All along the way, the earliest reprints were picked up and spread by other newspapers.

The Antifederalist counterpart to Wilson's address was Elbridge Gerry's letter to the Massachusetts legislature, in which he justified his refusal to sign the Constitution in the Constitutional Convention and put forward proposals for amendments. After the Massachusetts legislature ordered the letter printed in the *Massachusetts Centinel* in Boston on November 3, 1787, it was reproduced in forty-two periodicals in eleven states within two months. By November 21, ten reprints had appeared in Massachusetts alone. Gerry's letter reached New Hampshire on November 6 (*New Hampshire Spy,* Portsmouth); Rhode Island on November 8 (*United States Chronicle,* Providence); Connecticut on November 12 (*American Mercury; Connecticut Courant*); New York on November 13 (*Daily Advertiser; New York Packet*); Pennsylvania on November 16 (*Pennsylvania Packet; Pennsylvania Mercury*); Maryland on November 20 (Baltimore *Maryland Gazette*); New Jersey on November 28 (*New Jersey Journal,* Elizabethtown); Virginia on December 5 (*Virginia Independent Chronicle*); Georgia on December 6 (*Gazette of the State of Georgia,* Savannah); and North Carolina on December 17 (*North Carolina Gazette,* New Bern). The last reprints were published in the backcountry of Pennsylvania and Maryland, where Matthias Bartgis included the text in the December 26 edition of his papers in York and Fredericktown.[128]

This system of disseminating information did not always function smoothly. In fact, it nearly collapsed entirely in the wake of a few administrative changes in the post office in early 1788. At the beginning of the year, Postmaster General Ebenezer Hazard, a fervent Federalist, demanded postage fees for transporting newspapers from printer to printer. At the same time, he gave post riders preference over stagecoaches when awarding postal contracts, for reasons of cost efficiency. However, the riders often refused to carry the heavy bundles of newspapers during the winter, even when offered special incentives. In fact, post riders sometimes sold newspapers at taverns and inns along their routes. This resulted in delays and disruptions in newspaper delivery, giving rise to severe political criticism. The proponents of the Constitution, with their dense network of private correspondents, were less affected by these irregularities than their adversaries. Antifederalists were even more incensed by the fact that an uncanny number of their letters tended to get lost in the mail, or were opened, or needed months to reach their destinations. They complained that their newspapers were not being received and that their circulation of major essays opposing the Constitution was being suppressed. The opposition saw these events as precursors of life in America after ratification of the Constitution, as a premonition of censorship and restrictions of the freedom of the press. In July 1788, George Washington complained to John Jay that Hazard's incompetence had furnished Antifederalists with ostensible grounds "for dealing out their scandals, & exciting jealousies by inducing a belief that the suppression of intelligence at that critical juncture, was a wicked trick of policy, contrived by an Aristocratic Junto."[129]

Despite these deficiencies and obstacles, the newspapers were a crucial factor in the national debate. The press ensured that the most important arguments on both sides were made known throughout the Union. Some texts were reprinted up to fifty times, meaning they appeared in two-thirds of all newspapers in the country. Yet even the number of reprints cannot adequately illustrate an article's degree of dissemination. For example, the "Brutus" essays were commented on by writers in Exeter, Albany, and New Haven, though they were not published in newspapers at those locations. This was possible because some people read newspapers from other towns, and because articles were cut out or quoted and circulated in letters.

Research into the distribution of initial publications and reprints provides additional insight into a newspaper's reputation and influence. "National" publications had subscribers in several states, published a high percentage of original material, and made the most sustained effort to keep the public informed on the ratification proceedings. Their articles tended to be reprinted most frequently. Eleven newspapers can be grouped into this category, based on a comparison of reports on the ratification debate, as well as the publication of important series of essays and other much-read contributions—individual essays, reports on elections, conventions, and celebrations, even poems and songs. The country's leading newspapers were the *Connecticut Courant* in Hartford, the *Massachusetts Centinel* in Boston, the *Maryland Gazette* in Baltimore, the *Pennsylvania Packet, Pennsylvania Gazette,* and *Independent Gazetteer* in Philadelphia, the *Daily Advertiser, Independent Journal,* and *New York Journal* in New York City, the *Virginia Independent Chronicle* in Richmond, and the *Columbian Herald* in Charleston. These newspapers set the standards for quality and controlled the tone and tempo of the debate. They were followed by a few regional publications covering several states, such as Isaiah Thomas's *Worcester Magazine* in New England. The rest were either limited to their own state or intended for a local audience, often resorting to republications of material from other sources. The press was a well-structured, multichanneled system of information distribution. Familiarity with this system is essential to understanding the progression and dynamics of the debate over the ratification of the Constitution.

By the end of October 1787, seventy-five newspapers across the Union had reprinted the Constitution.[130] From then on, the press was present every step of the way, animating the dispute and sustaining public interest. In this process, newspapers themselves underwent a substantial change. Though their size remained the same (normally one octavo sheet folded into four pages, with three or four columns per page), their preoccupation with the Constitution reduced their reporting on other news events. Lengthy political essays and accounts of ratifying conventions and ratification celebrations filled the front pages, to the detriment of "European Intelligence," which had formerly occupied that position. The section on "American Intelligence" from page 2 was greatly expanded, consisting primarily of ratification news for months on end. Among other things, newspapers carried lists of convention candidates, reported on town meetings devoted to debating the Constitution, and published the names of elected delegates—often providing the exact number of votes received by each candidate. The last page traditionally had been reserved for public proclamations, the publication of laws and ordinances, advertisements, and marginal notes. Now, however, pro-Constitution publications dedicated that space to "Federal Poetry" extolling the virtues of the new system of government, applauding its creators, and singing praises to the future glory of the "American Empire." Every gap was filled with "squibs," brief reports on the progress of the debate. The Antifederalist editors did their best to stem this tide by publishing critical essays and letters as well as satirical or sarcastic comments. Those citizens interested in other subjects, who were growing weary of this constant fare of politics, were informed by Thomas Greenleaf of the *New York Journal:* "As the parole of the day is NEW CONSTITUTION, the countersign STATE CONVENTIONS, and the RAGE of the season, is, Hallow, damme, Jack, what are you, boy, FEDERAL or ANTI-FEDERAL?—Constitution must be the burthen of the song, until some dreadful news attract the public attention."[131]

The Party Press and Partisan Printers

American printers never missed an opportunity to emphasize their independence from political parties and their openness to diversity of opinion. Typically, publishers like John Hayes of the Baltimore *Maryland Gazette* promised "to support the dignity of the press, by an impartial admission of pieces, on both sides of those great political questions, that are intimately connected with the public welfare."[132] Many newspapers displayed a commitment to this ideal in their names (*Independent Journal; Independent Gazetteer*) or in a motto along the lines of "Open to all parties, but influenced by none" (*Freeman's Journal; Newport Mercury; Providence Gazette*). John Carter of the *Providence Gazette* drew a distinction between a printer's private opinion and his public function: "As a Citizen, he professes to be a Fœderalist; but as a Printer, neither fœderal nor antifœderal."[133] The epithet "partial" only applied to the party organs of one's adversaries; each side characterized its own papers as "impartial," "neutral," or "independent." Some printers tried to introduce voluntary self-control as a means of forestalling party criticism. The editor of the *New Hampshire Gazette,* for example, pointed out that he felt obligated to the community in which he lived: "Attacks upon individuals, party quarrels, satire aimed at religious denominations of every name, immorality and obscenity, are foreign from promoting any real benefit, or proper amusement, therefore he must be excused from presenting them to the public eye."[134] However, such steps did not remain unchallenged. Bearing the title "News-Paper-Freedom," a submission to the *Federal Gazette* of March 13, 1788, accused the printer of exercising the despotic might "which, from time immemorial, has characterized his illustrious predecessors; and, vested with the sole power of judging what is, and what is not proper for the perusal of the people, he examines, scrutinizes, determines upon, accepts, corrects, or rejects the favours of his correspondents."

Upon close examination, only twenty-one newspapers stayed truly impartial throughout the course of the ratification debate. Even if one counted the ten papers that cannot be adequately assessed today due to a lack of surviving copies, the fact remains that newspapers which were equally accessible to both friends and foes of the Constitution and refrained from making one-sided judgments were an exception to the rule. An examination of the remaining sixty-one periodicals reveals a clear bias in favor of the Federalists. Based on the selection of original and reprinted articles, as well as the content of sparse editorial comments, sixteen newspapers can be classified as distinctly Federalist, and five as distinctly Antifederalist, thirty-seven as moderately Federalist, and three as moderately Antifederalist. Though the moderate publications did in fact print a limited number of contributions from the opposing side, they left no doubt as to their position on the Constitution. When publishing one Antifederalist submission, the *New Hampshire Recorder* inquired of its readers whether such attacks on the "GRAND FŒDERAL CONSTITUTION" were not more inclined "to alarm the fears of the People, rather than to answer any good or valuable purpose."[135]

The sixteen Federalist and five Antifederalist newspapers that were most heavily involved and deeply committed were also the main catalysts of the debate. The leading Federalist publications were the *Pennsylvania Gazette* in Philadelphia, the *Independent Journal* and *Daily Advertiser* in New York, the *Massachusetts Centinel* in Boston, and the *Connecticut Courant* in Hartford. The five patently Antifederalist papers were the *Freeman's Journal* and the *Independent Gazetteer* in Philadelphia, the *New York Journal*, the *American Herald* in Boston, and the *United States Chronicle* in Providence. The debate over the Constitution led to the emergence of a national Party press which was to develop its full potential during the following decade in the dispute between Federalist and opposition Republican newspapers. A look at some specific newspapers and their editors will be useful.

Eleazer Oswald and the Independent Gazetteer

The Philadelphia *Independent Gazetteer*'s intense involvement in the debate was closely linked to the personality of its owner and publisher, Eleazer Oswald. In 1770, Oswald emigrated from England to New York and became apprenticed to John Holt, the publisher of the *New-York Journal*, and in 1772 he married Holt's daughter. After serving in the Continental Army from 1775 to 1779 under the command of Colonel John Lamb, he published the Baltimore *Maryland Journal* with William Goddard from 1779 to 1781. He then moved to Philadelphia, where he established the *Independent Gazetteer* and reopened the London Coffee House. He also helped his widowed mother-in-law operate the *New-York Journal* until it was sold to Thomas Greenleaf in early 1787.[136] During the ratification debate, Oswald was variously referred to by his Federalist enemies as the "typographical Cain of Philadelphia," an "Incendiary," a "restless firebrand, driven by the devil," a "seditious turbulent man," a "mad political demoniac," and an "Ishmaelitish Printer."[137] Yet until 1787, Oswald had supported the state Republicans close to Robert Morris, James Wilson, and Benjamin Rush, and he even observed neutrality for a time following the publication of the Constitution. His personal aversion to Chief Justice Thomas McKean, a Pennsylvania Constitutionalist who became a leading Federalist, and to Mathew Carey was surely a factor in his turn to Antifederalism. McKean had charged Oswald with seditious libel in

1782, but was unable to obtain a conviction. The clashes between Carey, who had left Ireland in 1784 to escape British prosecution and censorship, and Oswald, known for his animosity toward the Irish, culminated in a duel in 1786. A resulting serious injury did not prevent Carey and his *Pennsylvania Herald* from continuing to compete successfully against Oswald commercially. In early 1787, Carey founded a nationally circulating monthly, the *American Museum,* soon earning himself the reputation of a "Federalist to Enthusiasm."[138] That apparently made it easier for Oswald to put aside his year-long feud with Francis Bailey, whose *Freeman's Journal* functioned as the Republican's party organ. By November 1787, the *Independent Gazetteer* and the *Freeman's Journal* both were under the Antifederalist banner. Their greatest rivals were John Dunlap and David C. Claypoole, publishers of the *Pennsylvania Packet.* Dunlap was a dynamic, entrepreneurial printer adept at transforming political connections into successful business ventures. The *Packet,* the first American newspaper to become a daily, was known for its journalistic merit and large circulation. The only other publication of comparable quality was the *Pennsylvania Gazette,* a weekly owned by David and William Hall together with William Sellers. The *Packet* and the *Gazette* printed a large number of original Federalist essays, many of which were reprinted in other states. It was only a question of time before commercial and political rivalries merged to create a spiral of escalating tensions.

Oswald made little effort to disguise his departure from the doctrine of neutrality: "It is cried with vehemence, 'Printers are partial.' . . . But a printer, as a printer, has no choice so long as parties are not decided; he admits every good essay; and if it should happen to appear partial, pray . . . do not stigmatize the printer, but take one paper of each sort."[139] William Spotswood of the *Pennsylvania Herald* described for Jeremy Belknap in Boston the unenviable situation of a truly neutral printer in Philadelphia, "where parties carry their political opinions to a degree bordering on ill nature, if not worse. . . . My study was to have steered an impartial line. This I found impracticable in Philadelphia, as the existence of a newspaper in Philadelphia depends solely on the printer's avowing himself and his paper devoted to some party."[140]

Newspapers in Pennsylvania were flooded with contributions from both parties. Benjamin Rush advised his friend Henry Muhlenberg with regard to the German-language publication *Gemeinnützige Philadelphische Correspondenz:* "I hope you do not neglect to fill your Gazette with fœderal essays—Anecdotes—and intelligence. Hall and Seller's paper is filled every week with them all."[141] In the *Independent Gazetteer,* "Tom Peep" reported that the "aristocratic Junto" had supposedly set up an account for donations to keep the press campaign alive even after ratification in Pennsylvania. James

Wilson ("James de Caledonia") was allegedly concerned about the progress made by "the democratic party (to which to be sure he gave another name)," demanding "that the press ought to be kept groaning with pieces, paragraphs, anecdotes, and skits of all kinds in favor of the new form of government."[142] No amount of denials were able to dispel suspicions of a centrally controlled Federalist propaganda machine.

As the struggle for ratification neared its climax, Oswald could no longer bear simply to observe events from within the confines of his print shop and behind the counter of his London Coffee House. He participated in a late attempt to consolidate and coordinate the opposition across state borders. In the summer of 1788, he traveled to Richmond, Virginia, on behalf of the New York Republican Committee. Equipped with letters and important news, he established direct contact with the Antifederalist faction at the convention, led by Patrick Henry and George Mason. After this episode, he was so hated by Philadelphia Federalists that they seized on a minor infraction he committed in a legal dispute with a former partner to throw him in jail for a month on charges of "contempt of court." That did not silence the *Independent Gazetteer,* which in the meantime had become a major source of political agitation. While Oswald composed articles in his jail cell railing against violations of civil rights and restrictions on the right to free speech, his equally temperamental wife, Elizabeth, saw to it that the paper continued to roll from the press.[143] When she asked Benjamin Franklin to intervene on behalf of her imprisoned husband, he demanded in return "that your prudent counsels might prevail with him to change that Conduct of his Paper by which he has made and necessarily provok'd so many enemies."[144] After his release from prison, Eleazer Oswald's life remained turbulent. A passionate supporter of the French Revolution, he fought as a colonel under General Dumouriez in the battle of Jemappes in 1792. The next year, Robespierre's Welfare Committee sent him to Ireland on a secret mission to probe into anti-British sentiments among the populace there. After his return to the United States, he fell victim to the yellow fever epidemic in 1795.

Thomas Greenleaf and the New York Journal

A close associate of Oswald's was Thomas Greenleaf, whose *New York Journal* added life and color to a city otherwise firmly under the control of the Hamiltonians. Greenleaf, a native of Abington, Massachusetts, had been trained by Isaiah Thomas, the era's most prominent and successful printer, who at the high point of his career employed 150 people at five printing presses. Greenleaf published the *Independent Chronicle* in Boston until, in 1785, he became manager of the *New York Journal,* under the direction of

Eleazer Oswald. He married a great-niece of Governor Clinton, and in January 1787 he purchased the *Journal* from John Holt's widow.[145] A little later he proudly reported there had been "large and respectable additions to the list of subscribers," and as the debate over the Constitution heated up, the *Journal* began appearing daily in November. But even the daily newspaper and weekly "Country" edition together could not offer enough space for all the contributions flooding Greenleaf's office. His overt criticism of the Constitution provoked the ire of the business world, which rallied to the attack in various competing papers. One of these was Francis Childs's *Daily Advertiser*, which, as the name indicates, was normally devoted to advertisements and business news. Just as Greenleaf maintained intimate connections with the Clintonians, Childs was closely allied with the city's Federalist politicians. Benjamin Franklin had taken him under his wing following the death of Childs's father and helped him to establish his press.

Federalists were determined to discredit Greenleaf as a "party printer." His friends dismissed such charges, maintaining that the *New York Journal* was merely providing a much-needed counterbalance to the torrent of Federalist publications: "Where there is no opposition, there is no argument."[146] Finally, when Greenleaf dared to ridicule the resplendently staged New York Federal Procession held on July 23, 1788, his adversaries resorted to more drastic steps. No sooner had New York ratified the Constitution than a mob raided his print shop, demolishing the printing press and other furnishings.[147] The destruction rendered a continuation of the daily edition of the *Journal* utterly impossible. However, the Clintonian-controlled New York legislature secured Greenleaf's economic survival by naming him the state printer. This was a highly desirable position in every state because the volume of official business was large enough to ensure a basic income.[148] Like various other Antifederalist printers, Greenleaf joined one of the "Democratic Societies" in the 1790s, whose radical agitation presaged the rise to power of the Jeffersonian Republicans.[149]

Benjamin Russell and the Massachusetts Centinel

Like Thomas Greenleaf, Benjamin Russell had served an apprenticeship under Isaiah Thomas. In contrast to Greenleaf, however, Russell devoted his newspaper as well as his superior literary and satirical abilities to the cause of the Constitution. He was the first printer to insist that authors provide their names along with submissions for possible anonymous publication. This departure from established usage, designed to intimidate the opposition, provoked a wave of protest from the Constitution's opponents. The Philadelphia *Freeman's Journal* warned the public against the "endeavours of certain characters amongst us to insult the understanding of the public, by preventing that freedom of enquiry which truth and honour never dreads, but which tyrants and tyranny could never endure."[150] On those rare occasions when Russell printed an item critical of the Constitution, he diluted its effect by carrying several opposing articles in the same number. In a striking visual metaphor, he portrayed the Constitution in the *Massachusetts Centinel* as a temple whose columns represented the states of the Union. Whenever a state ratified, the corresponding column was raised into position. In the end, only the shattered ruins of two columns remained as testimony to Antifederalist sentiments in North Carolina and Rhode Island.[151] This appeal to the senses was underscored by poems of Russell's own composition. When New York finally adopted the Constitution, Russell wrote:

> Eleven Stars, in quick succession rise,
> Eleven Columns strike our wondering eyes;
> Soon, o'er the whole, shall swell the beauteous Dome,
> Columbia's boast, and Freedom's hallowed home.[152]

Russell was also involved in the caucus of Boston tradesmen, who strongly favored ratification. In February 1788 he attended the Boston ratifying convention, taking stenographic notes of the debates, which were published in the *Centinel.*

Party Newspapers and Party Quarrels in the Backcountry

Rural areas were also infected with partisan fever. Since Federalists often dominated in cities and towns, the overwhelmingly Antifederal citizenry in the hinterland felt neglected by the local press. In Carlisle, Pennsylvania; Albany, New York; and Wilmington, North Carolina, attempts were made to found competing papers. While such endeavors met with failure in Carlisle, Caleb D. Howard took up the battle against the Constitution in March 1788 with his *Wilmington Centinel.*[153] Albany Antifederalists were also able to find a suitable printer in Solomon Southwick after a protracted search. Supported by Governor Clinton, the *Albany Register* managed to stay in business, reaching a weekly circulation of 1,500 around the middle of the next decade. Two Federalist "country printers" were John Babcock and Ezra Hickock, who moved their *Northern Centinel* from Lansingburgh to Albany, the seat of the New York legislature, in February 1788. Their relocation was based on a perceived duty "to prepare the minds of the readers for the reception of the Constitution."[154] They paid obvious tribute to their political preferences by renaming the *Centinel* the *Federal Herald.* Around this same time, there were four other papers that expressed a partisan bias directly in their masthead:

the *Middlesex Gazette, or Fœderal Advertiser* in Connecticut; the *Federal Post* in Trenton, New Jersey; the *Federal Gazette* in Philadelphia; and the *Herald of Freedom, and Federal Advertiser,* founded in September 1788 in Boston. The owner of the *Federal Gazette* candidly professed his political conviction by informing readers in the first number: "To the great cause of LIBERTY and of the FEDERAL GOVERNMENT, this paper shall be particularly devoted."[155]

Printers were subjected to pressure to conform to the views held by the majority or by powerful economic interests. All anti-Constitution newspapers told of threats and attempts at intimidation. Philadelphia Federalists accused Mathew Carey's editor, Alexander J. Dallas, of intentionally misconstruing their speeches in the ratifying convention and exposing them to ridicule. They punished the *Pennsylvania Herald* by canceling subscriptions and withdrawing advertisements, despite the dependable service it had consistently provided. Federalists were still not placated when Dallas was fired by William Spotswood, who had purchased the paper from Carey. In February 1788, the *Herald* was forced to discontinue publication.[156] In Providence, thirty-three subscribers informed Bennett Wheeler of the *United States Chronicle,* "in a friendly manner," that "Such Personal Invectives must be Discontinued for the future or you Must Discontinue Sending us your Paper." His neighbor, John Carter of the *Providence Gazette,* which was committed to balanced reporting, fared no better: "Six of the Gentlemen who signed a Paper addressed to him have since called and erased their Names." He firmly resisted the humiliation "of publishing a Paper under the Influence of what might perhaps be termed Instructions or Directions."[157] Still, Federalists managed to ensure the demise of the *Pennsylvania Herald* and drove the *American Herald* out of Boston. Economically boycotted and branded as a "rabble-rouser," Edward-Eveleth Powars moved his press to Worcester, where he hoped to breathe the "pure air of the country."[158]

Though opponents of the Constitution had more limited means of economic pressure at their disposal, they were not entirely innocent themselves. In June 1788, the Rhode Island legislature rescinded an agreement granting the *Newport Herald* a fee for the publication of laws and ordinances. Publisher Peter Edes's untiring crusade against the Country Party's paper-money policy had strengthened the Federalists' morale while infuriating the majority. The unflappable *Herald,* popularly known as the "scourge," immediately turned the legislature's decision into a public-relations campaign: "An exclusion of pay will not prevent the publication of the Acts, as the publisher of the *Herald* will do it gratis, from this consideration, that a general information of governmental proceedings, constitutes a grand palladium against encroachments."[159] In Carlisle, opposition spokesmen blatantly informed the owners of the *Carlisle Gazette,* George Kline and George Reynolds, of their intention to destroy their printing press should they continue their "one-sided" depiction of local disputes. This was a resurgence of the intimidation tactics from the Revolutionary period, leaving political opponents with no choice but to fall in line or be run out of town.[160]

The Newspapers' Influence on the Form and Progress of the Debate

Federalists attributed a great deal of their success to the newspapers. John Fenno's *Gazette of the United States* proclaimed on January 1, 1789, that never in the history of the printing press had "their benign influence been more conspicuous, than in the production of that light, information, & harmony of sentiment, which have led this great & various people to the Adoption of the Federal Constitution." On the other hand, the opposition felt one of the main reasons for their defeat was the press advantage enjoyed by the other side. According to Powars of the *American Herald,* Federalist propaganda had been extremely effective because it had unceasingly poured forth from "a number of infamous service papers, which are and have been under the entire influence and controul of a most contemptible and unprincipled part of the community."[161] To a "Lover of Truth and Decency" the smear campaign conducted against opposition politicians like Elbridge Gerry was proof "that aristocratical and wicked men . . . convert presses, which ought to be decent and free, into vehicles of private resentment and scandal."[162] In the Philadelphia *Independent Gazetteer,* a correspondent from Virginia fumed: "Of all the arts practiced by the advocates of the proposed system of arbitrary power, that of stopping all real information, and publishing a great deal of misinformation, they have been the most successful in."[163] An informant of John Lamb's, Hugh Ledlie, believed the citizens of Connecticut had not received balanced information, "for it is evident everything was published that was in favor of the new Constitution, but on the contrary, everything hugger-muggered and suppressed that was truly alarming against it." In Aedanus Burke's estimation, the proponents of the Constitution in South Carolina comprised less than one fifth of the population, yet "the whole weight and influence of the Press was in that Scale. Not a printing press, in Carolina, out of the city [Charleston]. The printers are, in general, British journeymen, or poor Citizens, who are afraid to offend the great men, or Merchants, who could work their ruin. Thus, with us, the press is in the hands of a junto, and the Printers with the most servile insolence discouraged Opposition, and pushing forward publications in its favour, for no one wrote against it." Lamb was informed by the leader of the New Hampshire Antifederalists, Joshua Atherton: "The presses are in a great measure, secured to their [the Federalists'] side." Samuel Bryan, the author of the "Centinel" essays, added to the criticism, complaining in late 1788 that most printers in Pennsylvania had been much more inclined to publish material for the Constitution than against it.[164]

All told, there can be no doubt that the 7 to 1 ratio of newspapers in favor of the Constitution made a significant difference. In states where the Federalist press was nearly unopposed, such as Connecticut, New Jersey, Delaware, South Carolina, and Georgia, ratification obviously went smoother than in states with a counterbalance of critical publications. Still, one must take care not to overestimate the influence of the press. Pro-Constitution organs like Thomas's *Worcester Magazine,* Webster's *Albany Gazette,* and Kline's *Carlisle Gazette* were obviously unable to change the opinions of the solidly Antifederalist population in the surrounding region. Similarly, extensive efforts undertaken by Antifederalist printers in Boston, New York City, and Philadelphia failed to prevent the vast majority of these urban voters from supporting the other party. Finally, the fate of the Constitution hung in the balance in New Hampshire and Virginia, even though there were no staunchly Antifederalist printers in either state.

Initially at least, it was Antifederalists who used the press to attack the Constitution and to put pressure on Federalists. A careful observer of public opinion like James Madison perceived in October 1787 a discrepancy between the public mindset and the tenor of the press: "Judging from the News papers one wd. suppose that the adversaries were the most numerous & the most in earnest. But there is no other evidence that it is the fact."[165] A year later, "Alfred" expressed his observation in the *Massachusetts Spy* "that where the press is free, a few interested and virulent scribblers may keep up the appearance of a general fire, and sound perpetual noise of threatening and abuse, while the body of the people wait only for a cool and dispassionate inquiry."[166] The press probably did not harm Antifederalists as much as they claimed, and even helped them to activate a latent distrust of strong government and a spirit of opposition inherent in the population. One can therefore agree—certain reservations notwithstanding—with the publisher of the Baltimore *Maryland Journal,* William Goddard, that everyone was able to inform himself and freely express his opinion on either side of the argument.[167] The undeniable predominance of Federalist newspapers in the seaboard cities was offset to some extent by the distribution of opposition broadsides and pamphlets in rural areas. Voters were inundated with information and propaganda from both sides, which sometimes seemed to leave them more baffled than enlightened. "At Present many people are halting between two opinions," is the way John Smith described the situation in Long Island as late as June 1788.[168] The interrelationships between the public and the press were thus complex. However, three points are worthy of special emphasis. First, the press played a major role in the emergence and proliferation of a climate of reform, without which the transition to a new system of government would not have been possible. Second, a predominantly Federalist press strengthened the belief that the Constitution was the right solution to the problems of the Confederation. And third, Federalist newspapers became noticeably more self-assured and confident as the ratification proceedings progressed, while stalwart opposition publications came under increased pressure and took on a defensive posture. The press thus added to the momentum in favor of adoption of the Constitution that was created by each succeeding state ratification.

The debate over the Constitution exposed the conflict between the eighteenth-century ideal of a homogeneous community of citizens and the reality of an increasingly fragmented, self-seeking, conflict-oriented society. Despite their affirmation of the necessity of discussion and debate, the idea of a loyal opposition providing an alternative to the majority agenda was still suspect. On the other hand, Antifederalist printers did not suffer the same fate as their Loyalist colleagues during the Revolution, who were driven out of the country or left voluntarily. Most of them remained faithful to their political views and supported the Republican Party in the decades that followed. For the Constitution's adversaries, there was an inescapable paradox inherent in the transition from Antifederalism to national opposition. Though they began with the intention of defending state sovereignty against centralism and consolidation, their interstate political and publishing activities contributed to the nationalization of political life in post-Revolutionary America. Like their counterparts, Antifederalists also appealed to a national audience, thus unwittingly contributing to the construction of a common American identity.

After a brief respite, the party squabbles and press feuds erupted again in the 1790s. Following the pattern set during the dispute over the Constitution, newspapers and party organs in the individual states joined together on the federal level, establishing a highly competitive national system of communication, information, and propaganda.[169] The question as to the proper manner and limits of conducting political dispute within the new frame of reference was the essence of the conflict that culminated in 1798 with the Alien and Sedition Acts. The Federalists' ultimately thwarted attempt to gag the opposition confirmed that the warnings issued in 1787–88 regarding the threat of encroachments on freedom of the press and speech were not entirely unfounded.[170]

Networks of Private Correspondence

The Importance of Letter Writing

In addition to the official letters exchanged between Congress and the states, the congressional delegates and their state legislatures, and among the states, respectively, there was also a network of private and business contacts binding the Confederation together. In view of the limited mobility of eighteenth-century citizens, letter writing was a practical necessity, though to many people it meant much more than that. Leonard Gansevoort, a congressional delegate from New York, called letter writing a gift, "which the Almighty has been pleased in his wise providence to dispense to us for the purpose of cultivating the social Virtues and rendering the flames of Friendship, of fraternal Affection, and the Ties of Duty flowing from them alive."[171] The pedagogical and literary aspects of this activity are clearly revealed in a passage from a letter in which Peter Van Schaack, one of the wealthiest landowners in the Hudson Valley, implored his son Henry to provide him with more detailed accounts of the people and proceedings at the ratifying convention in Poughkeepsie: "I wish you was a little more circumstantial—You give me indeed a Prospect of the Convention but it is a distant one. . . . You point out a Valley but do not describe the Verdure with which it is covered, the Serpentine Stream with which it is intersected, the Trees which diversify it, the Flowers which enrich its Banks—nor the Woods which with baleful Vegetation obstruct the Growth and Beauty of the Fruit. You seem always to write in a Hurry as if it was Time lost. Mind not what any one tells you of my coming down, but write on, for suppose one Letter should be wrote while I am on the Road: would this be Labor in vain?"[172]

It is still a pleasure today to read the letters of 1787–88, which evince erudition, a sense of literary style, and great subtlety and insight. The range of expression varies from the deliberate manner of a George Washington to the precise logic and language of a James Madison, the matter-of-fact business tone of commercial firms, and the clumsy yet impressive idiom of men whose style and orthography reflect only a basic literacy. Major Samuel Nasson, sent by Sanford, Maine, to the ratifying convention in Boston, admitted "the want of a proper Education—I feel my Self too Small on many Occations that I allmost Scrink into Nothing—Besides I am often obliged to Borrow from Gentlemen that had advantages which I have not—this to a Greater Soul you must know is such a Burden that cannot Bear." This deficiency did not prevent him from playing a prominent role in the political life of his town.

A man of similar breeding was his neighbor from New Gloucester, William Widgery, who proudly informed their common acquaintance, George Thatcher, that he was conducting "a corrispondence both East and West and I find it very advantages to me on many occasions."[173]

Interpreting the Constitution in Letters

Letter writers who dealt with the Constitution and ratification were usually pursuing two objectives: the exchange of thoughts and observations on constitutional issues and the coordination of political activities with an eye to adopting, rejecting, or amending the Philadelphia plan. Their correspondence did not always remain private. Some letters were printed in newspapers anonymously, though with the authors' consent, while others found their way into print without their permission.[174] The ordinary shortcomings of the mail service were amplified by the politically motivated curiosity of many contemporaries, who did not stop short even of opening or pilfering mail addressed to third parties. However, this had little impact on the general fondness for letter writing and the need to communicate, rooted as they were in the conviction that it was possible and desirable to reach an independent conclusion even in—or especially in—complicated matters such as those at hand. To the mind of experienced Virginia lawyer and politician Edmund Pendleton, honesty mattered more than infallibility: "Thus you have my judgement in Favor of the Constitution upon its General principles," he wrote to his nephew Nathaniel, "it may be erroneous & probably is in some things, but it is candid, & unbiassed by self Interest other than in common with my fellow-Citizens."[175] The fact that he went on to criticize the inadequate separation of the legislative and executive branches in the very next paragraph only underscores an important advantage of private correspondence: candid feelings and doubt were more freely expressed under the seal of secrecy than in public.

It is thus not surprising that some of the most thorough interpretations of the Constitution can be found in letters. Even though pamphlets and newspaper essays often appeared in letter form, they still resembled legal briefs in which a rigid line of argumentation is pursued with no room for "ifs" and "buts." By contrast, many letter writers displayed a better awareness of complex realities, along with more tolerance for the fact that the various parts of the Constitution could be interpreted in different ways and might have unexpected effects. Letters afforded Madison the opportunity to test the viability of his thoughts and ideas through dialogues with friends. The correspondence between Madison and Jefferson, initiated by Madison in late October 1787 with a detailed report on the Federal Convention, is an example of the subtlety and insights contained in letters. Madison again defends the proposal rejected by the convention for a right of Congress to veto all state laws, and he develops some of the main concepts later to appear in the "Publius" essays. Jefferson responded on December 20 with an enumeration of those aspects of the Constitution he favored and those he questioned. From then on, their discussion mainly centered around a bill of rights, the lack of which was Jefferson's foremost concern. Some of Jefferson's criticism became known publicly in a roundabout way and had a significant influence on the debate in the South. Although this indiscretion hampered Madison's efforts to secure an unconditional ratification, he continued his private constitutional discussion with Jefferson.[176] Also noteworthy from the Federalist point of view was an exposition by Timothy Pickering, a Federalist delegate to the Pennsylvania ratifying convention, in which he attempted to allay the concerns of his New York acquaintance and son-in-law of John Lamb, Charles Tillinghast. This letter, written on Christmas Eve in 1787 and over twenty pages long in the original version, combined a basic criticism of the "Federal Farmer" pamphlet, sent to Pickering by Tillinghast, with interesting thoughts on the issue of a standing army and the powers of the federal judiciary.[177]

Antifederalist letter writers often had to cope with conflicting feelings. They generally conceded that reforms were inevitable and necessary and acknowledged the Constitution's positive aspects. At the same time, they had serious reservations about accepting an unfamiliar, untried system of government which promised to impose important restrictions on the states and the people. Harvard graduate and lawyer William Symmes felt he had only managed "a light sweep on the surface of things" in the analysis of the Constitution he undertook at the behest of merchant Peter Osgood, a fellow citizen of Andover, Massachusetts, and a member of the Massachusetts House of Representatives. Yet Symmes's letter contained one of the most thoughtful, subtle critiques of the Constitution known. Symmes believed the accumulated powers of the president, Congress, and judiciary exceeded all reasonable limits and signified "a great, almost a total, & probably a final change. . . . So great a revolution was never before proposed to a people for their consent." Elected by the citizens of Andover to attend the Boston convention, he abandoned his resistance to ratification after Federalists agreed to recommend amendments. Osgood's brother Samuel, who had also studied at Harvard and since 1785 had served on the three-member Confederation Board of Treasury, reflected on the Constitution just as arduously—albeit not as profoundly—as Symmes. After several sleepless nights, he hit upon the document's greatest flaw: the ten miles square district in which the federal capital was to be established, and where Congress would have exclusive jurisdiction, threatened to create an "inexhaustable Fountain of Corruption." There the government would be isolated from the citizens, who would have "very little Knowledge of its Operations, until by Bribery and Corruption, & an undue Use of the public Monies, Nabobs are created in each state; & then the Scenery will be changed, the Mask will be laid aside."[178]

Just how torn Antifederalists were can be seen in a letter from Philadelphia merchant Charles Pettit, who had lost a bid for a seat at the ratifying convention and, much to the distress of his friends, had since withdrawn from the political arena. In June 1788 he gave opposition leader Robert Whitehill to understand that he no longer regarded complete rejection of the Constitution as an option: "I am among those who find much to approve in the proposed Constitution, and who think it may be so amended as to make it a better plan than we shall be likely to agree upon again if it should be wholly rejected. . . . Wholly to reject the New Plan and attempt again to resort to the old would therefore be worse than vain: it would throw us into a State of Nature, filled with internal Discord."[179] Some evidence would suggest that Pettit's business and investment interests were influential in the formulation of this moderate stance. In any case, he attended the Antifederalist Harrisburg convention in September 1788, and he did allow himself to be nominated by Antifederalists as a candidate for the U.S. House of Representatives—only to come up short again.

Correspondence over an Extended Period

The best opportunity for a regular exchange of views was provided by family or business relations. As the case of the Adams family shows, family ties did not guarantee agreement in political matters. The division ran even deeper in the numerous branches of the Lee family in Virginia. Brothers Richard Henry and Arthur fought for amendments as Antifederalist essayists. Opposing views were held by another brother, Francis Lightfoot Lee, and relatives Henry and Charles Lee.[180] Henry Lee was an enthusiastic correspondent of Washington, Madison, and Hamilton, to whom he wrote a total of twelve letters during this period. Philadelphia doctor William Shippen Jr., a brother-in-law of Richard Henry Lee's, sought to resolve his own ambivalence through correspondence with his son Thomas Lee Shippen, a law student in London. Family patriarch William Shippen Sr. had become a "perfect Antifederalist" in the wake of a conversation with Richard Henry Lee. Thomas, on the other hand, indicated in his first letter that he was overpowered by the document itself, as well as the reaction of the British: "It appears to me the most stupendous fabric of legislative contrivance that the wit of man has ever devised. . . . The people here extol [the Constitution] as the master piece of policy, and the Convention as a Roman Senate—We stand six inches higher at least than we did." Soon after, however, he learned "that the greater part of the true whigs, the liberty men of England, are opposed to the form of government which has been proposed." Now it appeared to him that the plan was "full of virtues and full of faults, and that it is hard to say which preponderate." In the meantime, his father was moving in the opposite direction, declaring to Washington that *The Federalist* had turned him into an "enthusiast in favor of our new Constitution."[181]

In New York City, Evert Bancker was at the center of a web of family correspondence which included his son Abraham B. Bancker in Ulster County, together with Evert's brother Adrian Bancker and Adrian's son Abraham Bancker in Richmond County. As delegates to the ratifying convention in Poughkeepsie, cousins Abraham and Abraham B. Bancker did their best to satisfy Evert Bancker's thirst for information. The latter was much more pleased with his nephew, who shared his Federalist credo, than with his own son, who kept company with opponents of the Constitution like Charles Tillinghast and Peter Van Gaasbeek. Evert wrote his cousin that "I am sorry to be informed that one of my own Blood should be Antifederal."[182] Boston merchant and shipowner Joseph Barrell had the same problem with his brother Nathaniel, who as a member of the Sandemanians, a fringe religious group, had not participated in the struggle for Independence and was now heading to the Massachusetts ratifying convention as an Antifederalist delegate. Joseph was determined to accept his brother's reasons of conscience and not renounce him, but he warned Nathaniel that "you will meet the most pointed opposition from all your friends here, as an Antifederalist." This word of caution may have been one of the reasons why Nathaniel ended up voting for the Constitution.[183]

A harmonious worldview was more likely to be found where the correspondence was based on a long-standing friendship. Evidence of this can be seen in the more than fifty letters exchanged between Jeremy Belknap and Ebenezer Hazard. The two friends had known each other since 1779, when Hazard, a Boston native, traveled to New Hampshire to gather material for his *Historical Collections* and met Belknap, who was working on his *History of New Hampshire* in Exeter. From then on, Hazard acted as an intermediary between Belknap and his publishers in Philadelphia and New York. In 1787–88 Belknap was pastor of the Long-Lane Congregational Church in Boston, which provided the site of the Massachusetts convention, while Hazard was the Confederation's Postmaster General. Beyond providing testimony of a close personal friendship, their letters are among the best sources of information on ratification in Massachusetts and New York.[184] Equally valuable are the thirty-one letters written by William Ellery from Newport to Benjamin Huntington, a congressional delegate from Connecticut who was later elected to the U.S. House of Representatives. Ellery had been a signer of both the Declaration of Independence and the Articles of Confederation. During the dispute over the Constitution, he oversaw the Union's financial affairs as a congressional commissioner in Rhode Island. His Federalism was tempered by his knowledge of Rhode Island's democratic traditions and his insights into the character of its inhabitants. Despite Ellery's strong aversion to the inflationary politics of the Country Party, the detailed background reports he sent to Huntington painted a realistic picture of political life in Rhode Island.[185]

Political Correspondence on the State Level

The clearest use of private correspondence for political objectives occurred where conflicting interests and political differences were institutionalized in the form of factions or parties. Successful political operations were dependent on a functional system of intrastate communication. Letters played a vital role due to the vast distances involved. Whatever went beyond public information or propaganda and required confidentiality—essentially the selection of candidates, the mobilization of "opinion leaders," and the development of strategies and tactics—had to be imparted through private correspondence, often delivered by courier. Following the Federalists' defeat in the Massachusetts gubernatorial election in April 1789, Samuel Henshaw wrote Theodore Sedgwick that all available means would have to be exploited in the political battle ahead. Recent experience had shown, however, "that we can do infinitely more by private Letters than by News paper publications. . . . Let your Friends be very cautious to whom they write, and by whom they send—and let the carrier be charged not to lisp to any person whatever the design of his riding."[186]

One of the main problems was always establishing and maintaining the flow of information between the coast and the interior. The early election date in Pennsylvania, on November 6, 1787, rendered it virtually impossible for the opposition to mobilize their forces in the state's western regions and conduct an organized campaign. Later, Antifederalists also had great difficulty coordinating the activities of their legislative faction in Philadelphia with those of their colleagues in the backcountry. Similar problems surfaced in South Carolina, even though more time had been allowed to prepare for the elections there.

By contrast, Antifederalists in New York, where the election was not held until late April 1788, made superb use of all available means of communication. They founded committees in each county to select and contact candidates, organize the election campaign, and exchange information with each other. During the decisive months leading up to the election, they established an efficient triangle of correspondence between John Lamb's Committee in New York City, Albany Antifederalists Jeremiah Van Rensselaer, and the Ulster County faction led by Peter Van Gaasbeek, with statewide leadership provided from New York City by Governor Clinton, Melancton Smith, and Samuel Jones. A specially formed correspondence committee directed by John Lansing bore most of the responsibility for reporting from the convention. From May 1788 on, Lamb's New York Federal Republican Committee actively sought interstate cooperation in obtaining amendments to the Constitution. A mixture of private and committee correspondence thus emerged which was reminiscent of developments during the Revolution but now marked the transition to a national party organization and political culture.[187]

It was often the case that citizens in neighboring states supported each other, such as William Tilghman in Maryland and Tench Coxe in Pennsylvania. In the South, this interstate communication was facilitated by the bonds of blood and friendship linking many families in Virginia with the surrounding states of Maryland and North Carolina.[188] A similar situation in the North was represented by the Van Schaack family, New York landowners whose largest estates were in Columbia County on the upper Hudson River, though some family members also lived across the border in Massachusetts. Peter Van Schaack from Kinderhook, New York, and Henry Van Schaack from Pittsfield, Massachusetts, encouraged each other to fight for the Constitution. The importance of their correspondence is magnified by the fact that Henry was a confidante of Theodore Sedgwick, an influential Massachusetts politician who represented Stockbridge, a community near Pittsfield, at the Massachusetts convention.

National Correspondence

Those who maintained diverse and geographically dispersed connections benefited from them in two ways. First, they learned to think in "continental" or national dimensions. Second, they could take advantage of their large circle of friends and acquaintances—relationships which had often been formed at the university or during the war—to guide and coordinate activities in the debate over the Constitution. It is not surprising that this group contains a large number of congressmen. Despite its limited decision-making power, the Confederation Congress remained the Union's primary hub of information and the central meeting place. The congressional delegates possessed a great deal of political experience and were well informed on the situation in other parts of the Union by virtue of their personal and official association with each other. A few exceptions notwithstanding, congressional service widened their intellectual horizons, gave them "continental vision," and made them more receptive to proposals for innovation and reform.

One letter writer stood head and shoulders above the rest, however, and he was not a member of Congress, but the commander in chief during the War of Independence and president of the Federal Convention: George Washington. Following his return from Philadelphia, he labored untiringly behind the scenes for ratification. His basic conviction was contained in a letter written on September 24, 1787, to three former Virginia governors, enclosing the Dunlap and Claypool broadside of the Philadelphia plan: "I wish the Constitution which is offered had been made more perfect, but I sincerely believe it is the best that could be obtained at this time—and as a constitutional door is opened for amendment hereafter, the adoption of it under present circumstances of the Union is in my opinion desirable."[189] Whoever stopped over at Mount Vernon while traveling through Virginia—regardless of political persuasion—was treated to gracious hospitality and a heavy dose of Federalist doctrine.[190] Still, Washington mainly used his letters to encourage supporters of the Constitution, to offer guidance to the undecided, to win over adversaries, and to ask correspondents in foreign countries for understanding. Between September 1787 and March 1789, he sent at least 137 letters to sixty-six different people in which the Constitution was accorded more than a casual mention.[191] He wrote to people in eleven of the thirteen states, as well as in France and Great Britain. The largest number of recipients lived in Virginia (12), Pennsylvania (11), Massachusetts (9), New York (6), and Maryland (5). Only Delaware and Rhode Island were not represented. Most of those who received letters also replied, and a considerable amount of mail was received from unsolicited sources near and far. Washington had particularly close contacts with Madison, to whom he wrote seventeen letters and from whom he had received no fewer than forty-three by the end of 1789. Since Madison occasionally copied excerpts from his own mail for Washington, the General was also able to participate indirectly in the extensive correspondence of his compatriot from Virginia.[192] Another important standing contact was General Benjamin Lincoln in Boston, who had quelled Shays's Rebellion and was lieutenant governor of Massachusetts from the spring of 1788 to the spring of 1789. Up until his inauguration as president, Washington exchanged about twenty letters with General Lincoln. Reports from New York were mainly sent by former aide-de-camp Alexander Hamilton, as well as by Henry Knox and John Jay, the Confederation's secretary at war and secretary for foreign affairs. Gouverneur Morris wrote from Philadelphia, President John Langdon from New Hampshire, James McHenry from Maryland, and Jonathan Trumbull Jr., Washington's secretary from 1781 to 1783, from Connecticut. The General's main sources of information on events in his own state were Governor Edmund Randolph and David Stuart. Now and then, the name of one of the Constitution's adversaries turns up on the list, among them Patrick Henry, Richard Henry Lee, George Mason, and James Monroe. Correspondents abroad included Jefferson, Paine, Lafayette, Rochambeau, Catharine Macaulay Graham, and Sir Edward Newenham. Though he remained at Mount Vernon, because of his correspondence Washington was thus one of the best-informed and most active men in America. His influence on the process of ratification was profound.[193]

The role of "clearing houses," hubs in the news network where information was gathered and disseminated, was also assumed by James Madison, Henry Knox, and Tench Coxe. Madison's output of correspondence—160 letters to twenty-four addressees from September 1787 to December 1789—is even more astounding in light of the fact that he authored at least twenty-nine "Publius" essays during the same period, gave several speeches at the ratifying convention in Richmond, conducted an arduous election campaign against James Monroe for a seat in the U.S. House of Representatives, and pushed the amendments through the new Congress. Some of his letters were composed at the seat of Congress in New York, some in Virginia's capital city Richmond, and others at his family plantation in Orange County. Most were addressed to Washington (43), Randolph (21), Jefferson (20), Coxe (11), Pendleton (10), Hamilton, and Rufus King (8 each). He received the most mail from Carrington in Virginia (24) and Coxe in Philadelphia (23). Other productive correspondents were Virginians Archibald Stuart and John Dawson (an Antifederalist), as well as congressional delegate John Brown, who was especially concerned about affairs in his home district in Kentucky. Unike Washington, Madison did not cultivate the image of a statesman who stood above political parties. Instead, he battled it out in the political arena, though without great enthusiasm and sometimes even reluctantly. His letters reveal a theoretician well versed in history and philosophy, a single-minded organizer, and a skillful tactician with the psychological ability to put himself in his adversaries' position.

Madison's excellent connections in the South were matched by the northern-oriented correspondence of Henry Knox, who was born in Massachusetts and soon made a name for himself as a military theoretician. He had run the London Book Store in Boston prior to the Revolution, a meeting place for British officers. Promoted to general and artillery commander during the war, he had access to the Boston aristocracy and an exclusive circle of politicians, the Boston Stone House Club. In 1783, he initiated the founding of the Society of the Cincinnati, and became its first secretary. Two years later, he was named secretary at war in New York.[194] During the debate over the Constitution, he corresponded with over forty people; seventy-three of his letters have been preserved. His friend Henry Jackson sent him twenty-seven letters from Boston. Less frequent but sometimes more substantial reports from Rufus King, Benjamin Lincoln, Nathaniel Gorham, and Stephen Higginson provided a constant flow of information from Massachusetts. Particularly among Knox's correspondents in the other major New England states, Connecticut and New Hampshire, were Jeremiah Wadsworth and John Sullivan, the heads of local Cincinnati chapters. Through Knox their collected knowledge reached Washington, who closed the circle by keeping Madison informed.

Tench Coxe did not belong to the narrow circle of Pennsylvania's leading citizens. Nonetheless, he managed to keep abreast of political and economic affairs in both his own state and the Union through numerous informants. His political persuasion was largely determined by commercial interests, as seen in his development from Tory merchant to propagandist for the Constitution to Jefferson supporter.[195] His prolific journalistic endeavors during the struggle for ratification were complemented by a dense network of private correspondence, from which sixty-four letters to twenty-four recipients have been preserved. This number increases substantially if the business letters posted by Coxe & Frazier are included, where the Constitution is often praised in dry business terms. Other commercial enterprises that maintained Union-wide communications included Brown & Benson in Providence and Levi Hollingsworth and Stephen Collins & Son in Philadelphia. The sympathies of businesses specializing in trade definitely lay with the new Constitution, which promised to unify the domestic market and put American firms on an equal footing with European competitors. Accordingly, they placed their well-established channels of news distribution at the Federalists' disposal. As one can see, Federalists commanded a network of private correspondence that covered the whole Union.

Of course, communication on a national level was not a monopoly of the Constitution's supporters. The most active correspondent for the opposition, Richard Henry Lee, sent thirty-four Constitution-related letters to twenty recipients by the end of 1789. The list includes names from Massachusetts (Samuel Adams, Elbridge Gerry, James Sullivan), New York (John Lamb), Maryland (Samuel Chase), and Pennsylvania (William Shippen Jr.). Lee's fellow congressman from Massachusetts, Nathan Dane, was also an avid correspondent. Though he concentrated while attending Congress in New York City mainly on his home state, some of his letters traveled as far as Pennsylvania (William Irvine) and Virginia (William Grayson). While at home in Beverly, Massachusetts, he wrote an extremely important letter to Melancton Smith and Samuel Jones, the leaders of the New York convention. As a moderate critic, Dane was one of a group who also exchanged ideas with Federalists (King, Strong, Gorham, Sedgwick). George Mason seems less provincial, too, if one considers that his correspondents included Washington, Richard Henry Lee, and Arthur Lee, Randolph, Jay, Jefferson, Gerry, Lamb, Robert Yates, Charles C. Pinckney, and John Francis Mercer. In addition, he provided his son John, who had established himself as a merchant in France, with long-distance advice in matters of economics and finance. Still, Mason and Richard Henry Lee did not exploit the scope of their influence as early or intensively as Washington, Madison, and Knox. This is even more true of Elbridge Gerry and Patrick Henry, whose correspondence during this period was light and geographically limited. It was this obvious lack of an efficient system of communication and news dissemination that moved Governor George Clinton and General John Lamb to take steps in the spring of 1788 to establish permanent contact with opposition leaders in the individual states. This initiative was too late to prevent ratification of the Constitution. Nevertheless, it may have been instrumental in getting New York to adopt amendments similar to Virginia's. As an early form of party activity on the national level, its significance transcends the ratification debate.

3

The Debate over Basic Principles

The power under the Constitution will always be in the People. It is entrusted for certain defined purposes, and for a certain limited period, to representatives of their own chusing; and whenever it is executed contrary to their Interest, or not agreable to their wishes, their Servants can, and undoubtedly will be, recalled.

GEORGE WASHINGTON TO BUSHROD WASHINGTON, NOVEMBER 10, 1787

The vast Continent of America cannot be long subject to a Democracy, if consolidated into one Government—you might as well attempt to rule Hell by Prayer.

THOMAS B. WAIT TO GEORGE THATCHER, NOVEMBER 22, 1787

The Antifederalist Critique of the Constitution

Fundamental Consensus and Conflicting Approaches

It is fascinating to observe the seriousness and devotion with which Americans from all walks of life applied themselves to complicated constitutional issues. The crisis apparently worked like a stimulant that enabled the people of the thirteen states to focus their intellectual powers on essential questions of government and society. They sought advice in the Bible, in the long history of mankind, and especially in their own colonial and Revolutionary experiences; all known authorities on constitutional and public law were consulted, from Plato and Aristotle to Coke, Grotius, Hobbes, Locke, Blackstone, Vattel, Beccaria, Burlamaqui, Montesquieu, Rousseau, and Hume. The scope of the deliberations was not limited to the requirements of the day and the immediate future; consideration was given to the long-distant future as well. This dialogue on the basic tenets of social, economic, and political relationships, and the limits of governmental power did not conclude with the ratification of the Constitution and the adoption of the Bill of Rights. It can be traced through the entire history of the United States and will undoubtedly continue on into the future.

It has been correctly pointed out that the rival parties in 1787–88 drew from a rich intellectual storehouse of common beliefs and values. It was generally acknowledged that a republican form of government was best suited to the social circumstances and liberal spirit of the American people, and that this principle should be permanently laid down in a written constitution. It was also unquestioningly accepted that sovereignty rested with the people, that the will of the majority should be duly respected in a republic, and that it was the duty of every legitimate government to protect the rights and liberties of the citizens and serve the common good. Any regime that violated these principles could, according to the Declaration of Independence, the Virginia Declaration of Rights, and other state charters, be changed or abolished. Hardly anyone seriously considered suppressing the expression of public opinion in the press, in elections, or in the legislatures, nor disbanding the Union. Although it was uniformly agreed that the frailties of human nature mandated the existence of government, virtually everyone also agreed in principle with the calls for restrictions on the government's authority, the separation of powers, and the institution of checks and balances. John Stevens Jr. ("Americanus") summed up these self-evident "sacred truths" as follows: "That all power originally resides in the people; that the object of all free government should be the happiness of its subjects; that the governments are not instituted to promote the advantages of those, who govern, but to secure the prosperity of those, who are governed; that all men are by nature free, and that one man is not superior to another than, that by consent of all, he is raised above all; . . . that the people have an indefeasable right to institute, amend, or annihilate governments, when it seemeth good unto them."[1]

For all that, the debate over the Constitution clearly proved that this basic republican consensus left plenty of room for alternative interpretations and hypotheses and in no way eliminated political strife or factional disputes. Federalists and Antifederalists engaged, as has been correctly pointed out, in "one of history's most fundamental reexaminations of the nature of republics."[2] The differences between the Constitution's supporters and critics are often portrayed in simplistic, black-and-white terms. They can best be visualized as a scale representing the citizens' various reactions to the Constitution. At one end of the scale we find those who believed the Philadelphia plan did not go far enough and who would have preferred the establishment of a stronger central government. The opposite end of the scale is characterized by those who flatly rejected any changes whatsoever to the Articles of Confederation. The area in between ranged from unconditional approval of the Constitution to insistent yet constructive criticism of individual provisions and a demand for corrective amendments prior to adoption. Toward the middle, the positions grew more similar, even overlapping in some instances.

Few Antifederalists disputed the need for reforms, while a number of Federalists were dissatisfied with particular provisions. There were times when someone would publicly endorse the Constitution even though he privately had even greater reservations than those expressed by the critics. A good example of this is John Adams, who remained skeptical even after the Constitution had gone into force and he had been elected vice president:

> The great decisions and distributions of powers on which depend that delicate equipoise, which can alone give security to liberty, property, life, or character, have not been attended to with necessary accuracy. . . . It is and ever has been amazing to me, that the people of America who boast so much of their knowledge of government, and who really understand so well the principles of liberty, should have so far forgotten the institutions of their ancestors, and have been so negligent of this indispensable ballance in all the State constitutions as well as in that of the united states. Untill we shall correct our ideas under this head, we never shall get right: and we shall be tormented with a government of men and parties instead of being blessed with a government of laws.[3]

Conversely, even so profound a critic as the "Federal Farmer" had to concede that the Constitution contained "many good things"—a remark that was immediately rebuked by the Antifederalist "Countryman from Dutchess County" (Hugh Hughes).[4] There were some who stopped short of taking a clear stance, or purposely attempted to hold a middle ground. "In this Case, as in almost every other," George Turner, assistant secretary-general of the Society of the Cincinnati, wrote to Winthrop Sargent, "there is a middle walk to be trodden, as the directest Road to Truth. For my part, I like the Outlines of the Plan—and, being a Friend to Energy of Government, I approve of most of the Powers proposed to be given: But as a Friend to the natural Rights of Man, I must hold up my Hand against others."[5] Some people found solace in the postulate that government, in the words of the British Enlightenment philosopher Richard Price, was always "the choice of evils." "Of two evils I would choose the least if neither can be avoided," wrote Kentucky judge Caleb Wallace.[6] John Breckinridge had never been so much "at a loss to decide absolutely on any Question as on that one. I am for it, and against it. I sufficiently despise the present [Constitution—i.e., the Articles of Confederation] and think the one proposed, has some Fundamental Objections." Virginian William Nelson's feelings toward the plan were just as divided. He wept "over the corpse of dying republicanism," and confessed: "As a lawyer, I always liked [the Constitution]; tho' as a citizen I was averse to it."[7] An inclination toward Federalism did not prevent David Howell ("Solon, Jr.") of

Rhode Island from regarding the Constitution more "as a system of government than as a system of liberty."[8] Many Federalists concurred with Edmund Pendleton, the president of the Virginia ratifying convention: "As to the merits of the Constitution, tho' I wish some amendments, yet I think those not mistaken who pronounce it more perfect than any now subsisting."[9]

Neither side had an official line or party platform binding its supporters to certain principles or objectives. The citizens looked to leading essayists for examples or took inspiration from key documents, like the Pennsylvania *Dissent of the Minority of the Pennsylvania Convention* and the "Publius" essays. But nothing prevented anyone from expressing individual and divergent views: "I think for myself, and intend to do so, and I allow all men the same privilege," averred John Wilson in South Carolina."[10] This insistence on independent judgment permitted an incredibly wide range of opinions and varying—at times even conflicting—approaches.

For historians, this plethora of opinions creates a considerable methodological problem.[11] If their documentation is taken from the two poles of the scale, the image of a society divided by irreconcilable worldviews and ideologies emerges. Should the focus be shifted toward the middle of the scale, the differences become blurred, creating the impression of an all-encompassing sociopolitical consensus. Depending on the particular emphasis and the material selected for substantiation, one can demonstrate either unity or division, accentuate either the "conservative" or "radical" elements of the debate. Antifederalists can be easily made to appear as narrow-minded and naive. Yet it must be stressed that neither camp could claim a monopoly on rationality, and that both sides demonstrated a coherent reasoning and a general underlying unity. The concepts and theories presented to the public on the subject of government and constitutions were sufficiently different to be regarded as alternatives by contemporaries. At the same time, it is inaccurate to portray the debate as just thirteen separate or disparate controversies. The Union-wide distribution of key essays and speeches, along with the mountain of evidence in private letters, provides sufficient proof that Americans were participating in a national debate.

The Threat to Basic Values and Political Stability

The political language used by both sides was greatly indebted to the thought and mode of argumentation of British oppositional ideology. The Country tradition was based less on a well-rounded theoretical system than on a collection of political maxims and doctrines, moral precepts, and propagandistic formulas which had gradually flowed together to form a generally recognized political language. Its complexity was chiefly the result of a long course of development and transformation, having progressed from early Florentine-style "classical" republicanism over Harrington's utopia of an agricultural state of armed freeholders to seventeenth- and eighteenth-century British party controversies. It was a language that had been constantly adapted to the particular historical situation of the opposition, regardless of whether it was employed by the Whigs of the Restoration period or the Tories following the Glorious Revolution. Along the way, it had acquired the dual character it possessed in the late eighteenth century, as both an ideological framework and a pragmatic program of opposition.

The American variety of this philosophical and linguistic construct was characterized by a tension between egalitarian-participatory ideas and conservative-elitist tendencies. However, this incongruence remained concealed for a time behind a united front against the colonial rulers and their local representatives. When this unifying element dissolved at the end of the war, diverging interests and priorities led to the emergence of factions and parties in the patriotic camp. These divisions increasingly shaped state politics during the "critical period." However, neither the friction between various state parties nor the subsequent debate over the Constitution can be adequately described by the traditional contrasts of Tories versus Whigs and Court versus Country or by a modern liberalism/republicanism dichotomy. Just as had previously been the case in England, individual components of the opposition ideology were recombined to form new patterns of argumentation and infused with elements of everyday language. The terminology of republicanism was flexible enough to satisfy the rhetorical needs of both parties. Antifederalists took the simplest route by transposing the language of the Revolution and the War of Independence almost directly to the new domestic conflict. They felt justified in this, having again been saddled with the job of resisting centralist and oligarchic tendencies.[12] Federalists, on the other hand, blended republican precepts with Locke's natural law and social contract theories as well as with the enlightened economic principles that had enabled the Whigs to transform England from an agricultural country to a trading power after 1689. Though this lent the Federalists' political philosophy more agility, it also put them at risk of being associated with the English Court Party of the Walpole era, infamous for its patronage and corruption.

Taken as a whole, Antifederalists were oriented toward the established lines of seventeenth- and eighteenth-century British oppositional ideology, based on the theories of Harrington and Bolingbroke and popularized by Trenchard and Gordon in their *Cato Letters*. They viewed themselves as the true champions of republicanism and never tired of alluding to the maxims, postulates, and principles of the Revolution.[13] Their criticism was directed at the behavior and philosophy of Federalists, on the one hand, and the structure of the planned system of government on the other. Their foremost complaint involved the delegates to the Philadelphia Convention, whom they accused of not complying with the instructions given to them by state legislatures and the congressional resolution of February 1787, which only provided for a revision of the Articles of Confederation. The Constitution represented a breach of the Articles of Confederation, the most obvious manifestation of which was the departure from the principle of unanimous agreement by the state legislatures. "The same reasons which you *now* urge for destroying our *present* federal government," fumed Luther Martin, "may be urged for *abolishing the system* which you now propose to adopt; and as the *method prescribed* by the *articles* of confederation is *now totally disregarded* by you, as *little regard* may be shewn by you to the *rules prescribed* for the amendment of the *new system*."[14] This chain of illegitimate actions was rendered all the more serious by the fact that there was no need for such a revolution in government. "Centinel" praised the "jealousy of innovation in government" based on experience and regretted that the Revolution had evidently done away with the "great reluctance to change" which protected mature societies against the "artifices of ambition." In a similar vein, "Samuel" lamented in the Boston *Independent Chronicle:* "This Constitution does not wear the complexion of uniting the nation—but of dividing it. Had we not much better keep on our old ground? . . . Why should we be fond of another revolution so soon? Why should we be fond of such an innovation?" "A Farmer" from Maryland was bothered by the "phrenzy of innovations" that seemed to have seized Americans, and the "Impartial Examiner" cautioned: "A wise nation will . . . attempt innovations of this kind with much circumspection."[15]

The vast majority of the populous recognized the need for an increase in the powers of Congress with respect to economic and financial matters. However, they did not agree with the Federalists' dismal depiction of the existing situation and dismissed as scare tactics their predictions that anarchy and civil war would ensue if the Constitution were rejected. "Alfred" conceded that the expectations created by the Revolution had not yet been fulfilled, but he was not convinced "that America is in that deplorable, ruined condition which some designing politicians represent."[16] It appeared to a "Citizen" writing in the *New York Journal* of November 24, 1787 that the internal and external security of the Union were not threatened: "From abroad, we have nothing to fear . . . at home we are in a state of perfect tranquility—for, although there are defects in the existing articles of confederation, yet the governments of the different states have energy sufficient to command obedience to their laws, and preserve domestic peace." According to "Candidus," the actual sources of the undeniable problems lay much deeper: "Upon the whole, we are too apt to charge those misfortunes to the want of *energy* in our government, which we have brought upon ourselves by dissipation and extravagance. . . . I will venture to affirm, that the extravagance of our British importations,—the discouragement of our own manufactures, and the luxurious living of all ranks and degrees, have been the principal cause of all the evils we now experience."[17] Richard Henry Lee agreed: "I fear it is more in vicious manners, than mistakes in form, that we must seek the causes of the present discontents."[18] To the minds of Antifederalists, more important than the elimination of institutional defects were moral rejuvenation and a return to the "public and private virtues" of patriotism, self-sacrifice, courage, diligence, frugality, modesty, honesty, uprightness, and self-discipline—qualities that had been much too quickly forgotten after the Revolution. Only through a gradual process of recovery, they maintained, could the material and moral effects of the war be overcome.

It was of little use for Federalists to underscore their own unremitting patriotism or the exceptional abilities possessed by the members of the Philadelphia Convention. Even esteemed personages can err, was the answer, and America needed a government of laws, not of great men. The criticism culminated in the assertion that the Federalists' actions jeopardized the basic values on which civic and social life had been founded since the Revolution. Their disregard for the existing constitutional law and hasty acceptance of innovation was said to undermine the citizens' confidence in the stability of the political organism and make any future system seem tentative: "What security can be given that in seven years hence, another Convention shall not be called to frame a third Constitution? And as ancient Greece counted by olympiads, and monarchies by their Kings reigns, we shall date in the first, second or third year, of the seventh, eighth, or ninth Constitution." [19] The result would be anarchic. If a constitution, this "most solemn and important compact," was no longer secure, "where is the ground of allegiance that is due to government? Are not the bonds of civil society dissolved?"[20] This apprehension was all the more serious as Antifederalists doubted their adversaries' promise that future constitutional changes could be achieved in a peaceful way: "The consequence will be that, when the constitution is once established, it never can be altered or amended without some violent convulsion or civil war."[21]

The Dispute over Terms and Party Labels

The political-ideological dimension in the choice of party names was interwoven with the larger debate over the Constitution and represented a major factor in gaining favor with the public. The Constitution's proponents had managed to stake a claim to the expression "federal," with its positive connotations, at a very early stage. The word occupied a central position in their terminology, and the derivative "federalism" was incorporated into their ideology. The expression "national government" had been replaced by "federal government" during the Philadelphia Convention; now one also spoke of the "federal union" and "federal constitution," as well as "Federalists" and a "federal party" promoting ratification in every state. Just as the Union had led the states during the war, now the government of the "Federal Republic" must be given authority over state legislatures.[22] The latter designation was attributed by Mercy Otis Warren to James Wilson. She scornfully remarked that the framers of the Constitution had not had the courage "to denominate it a Monarchy, an Aristocracy, or an Oligarchy, and the favoured bantling must have passed the short period of its existence without a name, had not Mr. *Wilson,* in the fertility of his genius, suggested the happy epithet of a *Federal Republic.*"[23] The opposition realized, of course, that the choice of name was no insignificant matter and could influence the outcome of the debate. Their political adversaries had succeeded, wrote "Sidney" in the *New York Journal,* in finding and capitalizing on "epithets" and "ketch-words": "Of late they have covered themselves under the term federal, while they were undermining and annihilating the confederation." "Veracitas" in Maryland confirmed the success of this strategy. The Constitution's supporters had labeled their opponents "antifederal" and "contrived by vile arts to make the epithet odious and unpopular. Thus, by the force of sound alone, they are drawing to their standards, numbers of giddy thoughtless persons, and some too, whose understandings entitle them to a rank superior to that of a blind follower."[24]

The opponents of the Constitution subscribed to the original meaning of the word "federal" but felt the Philadelphia plan had turned the situation on its head. They were the ones who now actually deserved the name "Federalists," since they were defending the traditional concept of a confederation against the centralist Philadelphia plan. Under the heading "definitions" the Boston *American Herald* wrote, on December 10, 1787: "A FEDERALIST is a friend to a Federal Government—An Antifederalist is an Enemy to a Confederation—Therefore, the Friends to the New Plan of CONSOLIDATION, are Anti-Federal, and its Opponents are firm, Federal Patriots."[25] "Terms of distinctions, on a difference in political sentiments," were often arbitrary, insisted a "republican" (i.e., Antifederalist) pamphlet in New York: "Thus . . . the term FEDERALIST, is applied to a man who is for destroying the Confederation. . . . That of ANTI-FEDERALIST to the one who is for preserving it."[26] In one of his ironic "Countryman" essays, De Witt Clinton, the governor's nephew and secretary, called for an exchange of party designations after having discovered during a conversation with his neighbor "that those who are for abiding by the confederation and strengthening it, so as to make it lasting, are called Antifederalists; and the other party who are for throwing it aside, and having nothing farther to do with it, but are for making of us into one solid government, are called federalists."[27] The opposition believed this was a perversion of the political positions involved in the debate, giving the public a distorted view of their plans and objectives.

All attempts to reclaim the word "federal" and confer such fitting titles as "nationalists" or "consolidationists" ("consols") on the other party failed. The Federalists' propaganda helped to ensure that their chosen designation stuck during the entire course of the dispute. The triumph of the word "federalism" elicited the following sarcastic—yet telling—remark from Virginian David Thomas in a letter to his nephew in Philadelphia in March 1789: "How does Fedralism go on in your State? does the people know the meaning of the word Fedralism, it is a very pretty word, it has a beautiful sound, it charms all the learned, the wise, the polite, the reputable, the honorable, and virtuous, and all that are not caught with the alurements of its melody, are poor ignorant asses, nasty dirty;—reserved for future treatment agreeable to their demerit . . . the whole American world is in an uproar, there is nothing too mean dirty and infamous for the most worthy personages to carry the sound, which carries away the people any where to obtain Fedralism whose happiness and felicity can not be compared to any state below heaven itself."[28] While the proponents of the Constitution were soliciting support under the "Federalist" banner, the opposition tried desperately yet vainly to rid themselves of their odious reputation as a destructive anti-party hostile to the Union. Those Antifederalists who did not reconcile themselves with the Constitution only gradually succeeded in getting the public to adopt the more expressive, positive, and effective designation "Republicans," or "Democratic Republicans."

Consolidation Instead of Federalism

The Antifederalists' analysis of the Constitution revealed significant structural deficiencies in three closely related areas: in the delimitation of powers between the central government and the states; in the relationship between the central government and the individual citizens; and in the organization and mechanisms within the central government itself. Antifederalists were not willing to sacrifice the principle that all states in the Union were sovereign and equal for the sake of the additional authority needed by Congress. They believed the Articles of Confederation embodied the true spirit of the Declaration of Independence and federalism. Patrick Henry proclaimed this conviction in a dramatic fashion at the beginning of the Virginia ratifying convention. Taking aim at the preamble's wording "We, the People," he insisted that "States are the characteristics, and the soul of a confederation. If the States be not the agents of this compact, it must be one great consolidated National Government of the people of all the States."[29] To substantiate their claims that a "true" confederation was comprised of independent states bound together to regulate a limited number of common affairs, Antifederalists were particularly fond of quoting Montesquieu. In *De l'esprit des lois,* the famous Frenchman had designated this construction as the ideal solution to the structural weaknesses of republics. Small republics supposedly fell victim to external forces, whereas large republics were just as likely to destroy themselves from within. As a "société de sociétés," a federative republic, by contrast, combined the intrinsic advantages of a republican form of government with the outward strength of a monarchy: "Composé de petites républiques, il jouit de la bonté du gouvernement intérieur de chacune; et à l'égard du dehors, il a, par la force de l'association, tous les avantages des grandes monarchies."[30]

The critics claimed several main points in the Constitution deviated from this model. It did away with the balance of power in favor of a central government which from then on would have nearly unlimited control over taxation and the military, the pillars of governmental power. This would necessarily lead to a "consolidation" of the Union, characterized by relentlessly growing centralism and the continual erosion of the authority of state governments. Eventually, the independence and vitality of the states would be so diminished that they would be reduced to mere administrative provinces or disappear entirely. Yet another of Montesquieu's pronouncements was believed to apply to the "consolidated republic" comprising the United States: territories of this size could only be ruled by despotic means, not liberal principles. "Un grand empire suppose une autorité despotique dans celui qui gouverne. Il faut que la promptitude des résolutions supplée à la distance des lieux où elles sont envoyées; que la crainte empêche la negligence du gouverneur ou magistrat éloigné; que la loi soit dans une seul tête; et qu'elle change sans cesse, comme les accidents, qui se multiplient toujours dans l'État à proportion de sa grandeur."[31] Further support for this theory was discovered by "Alfred" in the Earl of Shaftesbury's *Characteristics* from 1737: "Vast empires are in many respects unnatural: but particularly in this, that be they ever so well constituted, THE AFFAIRS OF THE MANY *must, in such governments* TURN UPON A FEW; and the relations be less sensible, and in a manner lost between the magistrate and people, in a body so unwieldy in its limbs, and whose members lie so remote from one another, and distant from the head."[32] "Agrippa" pointed to the "ablest writers on the subject" for verification "that no extensive empire can be governed upon republican principles, and that such a government will degenerate to a despotism, unless it be made up of a confederacy of smaller states, each having the full powers of internal regulation."[33]

Should an attempt be made nonetheless to control the Union centrally along republican lines, insurmountable difficulties would soon arise. Antifederalists felt that a legislative body should reflect the makeup of the constituency as precisely as possible, or at least be accessible to all social classes and interest groups. This was still feasible in the individual states, with their relatively homogeneous populations and economies, though even here some oversized and unwieldy entities had developed. An elected legislature for the entire Union would either be too small to properly represent the interests of each region, state, social class, and ethnic or religious group, or too large to be functional. On the authority of Montesquieu and Cesare Beccaria, "Brutus" made his opinion in this regard very clear in his first letter, dated October 18, 1787: "The territory of the United States is of vast extent; it now contains near three million of souls, and is capable of containing much more than ten times that number. Is it practicable for a country, so large and so numerous as they will soon become, to elect a representation, that will speak their sentiments, without their becoming so numerous as to be incapable of transacting public business? It certainly is not. In a republic, the manners, sentiments, and interests of the people should be similar. If this be not the case, there will be a constant clashing of opinions; and the representatives of one part will be continually striving against those of the other." The legislature would either be unable to draft any fitting laws at all, or would enact laws favoring a certain part of the Union to the detriment of the rest: "The United States include a variety of climates. The production of the different parts of the union are very variant, and their interests, of consequence, diverse. Their manners and habits differ as much as their climates and productions; and their sentiments are by no means coincident. The laws and customs of the several states are, in many respects, very diverse, and in some opposite; each would be in favour of its own interests and customs, and, of consequence, a legislature, formed of representatives from the respective parts, would not only be too numerous to act with any care or decision, but would be composed of such heterogeneous and discordant principles, as would constantly be contending with each other."[34]

The fundamental republican principles of accountability, adequate representation, and effective supervision by the constituency could not be fulfilled by a consolidated government, Antifederalists insisted. To exert its powers, such a government would eventually have to resort to force, thus revealing its true despotic nature. Had Americans fought against tyranny at the hands of the Crown and Parliament only to submit to the yoke of another distant and inaccessible central government? The critics rejected Federalist claims that the federal government would possess only limited and clearly defined powers and that the states would retain all necessary authority to regulate their internal affairs. As opposed to the Articles of Confederation, the Constitution did not contain a corresponding clause guaranteeing the power, jurisdiction, and rights of the states except those "expressly" delegated to Congress. In fact, Antifederalists were convinced the imprecise language and ambiguities supported their interpretation. A contributor to the *United States Chronicle* found "that almost every section of each article, admits of a double construction, and requires an interpreter to explain them." "Denatus" considered the Constitution "incomprehensible and indefinite" in its entirety, adding that God alone could comprehend it and gauge its future effects. This was reason enough to make extreme caution advisable: "The constitution of a wise and free people, ought to be as evident to simple reason, as the letters of the alphabet." For "Impartial Examiner," as for most Antifederalists, "the idea of two sovereignties existing within the same community" was "a perfect solicism." In the proposed new system, therefore, only the national government would be sovereign. The states might continue to exist for a while, but experience was said to show that questions of constitutional interpretation tended to be settled in favor of the central authority.[35]

Besides being unclearly defined, the powers of the new government seemed overly extensive. The right of taxation put the "power of the purse" in the hands of Congress, which could dry up the states' financial resources, forcing them into a state of dependence. "Everyone who has thought on the subject, must be convinced that but small sums of money can be collected in any country, by direct taxes; when the fœderal government begins to exercise the right of taxation in all its parts, the legislatures of the several states will find it impossible to raise money to support their governments. Without money they cannot be supported, and they must dwindle away, and . . . their powers absorbed in that of the general government."[36] The "general clauses" seemed to encourage the unrestrained acquisition and expansion of power. Congress was authorized to levy taxes "to pay for the Debts and provide for the common Defence and General Welfare of the United States"; it could also enact all laws "which shall be necessary and proper for the carrying into Execution of the foregoing Powers"; and the Constitution, the laws of the United States, and all treaties were to be "the supreme Law of the Land . . . any Thing in the Constitutions or Laws of any State to the Contrary notwithstanding."

Each of these provisions alone would have been cause for concern, but in combination they threatened to unleash a lust for power that would pour forth in every conceivable incarnation, pillaging the states and the citizens.[37]

When viewed from this angle, even seemingly innocent clauses in the Constitution took on a dangerous aspect. One of the points of contention mentioned most often and most emphatically was Article I, section 4, which gave Congress the power to regulate the "Times, Places and Manner of holding Elections for Senators and Representatives" if a state legislature failed to arrange for scheduled elections to take place. The opposition suspected this provision was only a front for malicious designs, and even supporters saw a potential for abuse. Antifederalists scared themselves and the public with extreme scenarios, suggesting, for example, that Congress might require elections for all representatives from Pennsylvania to be held in Pittsburgh, in effect depriving most citizens of their right to vote. And the manipulations would not end there: once the initial steps had been taken down this path of arbitrary rule, the same provision could be misapplied to extend the legislative period of Congress indefinitely and eventually abolish elections altogether. These dark premonitions, the source of considerable public anxiety, were rooted in fears that the representative system would be subverted by the well-known propensity of legislative bodies to perpetuate their own existence. One only needed to observe the history of the British Parliament, which had extended its term to seven years by means of the "Septennial Act" of 1716.[38]

The broad powers allotted to the central government were combined with provisions explicitly restricting the states' powers. Antifederalists argued that these restraints were designed to render it impossible for the states to pursue independent economic and fiscal policies, meaning that in difficult times they would be entirely at the mercy of the central government. The new administration could use legal and military means to dictate its conditions to the states. For support it could turn to the Supreme Court and its system of lower federal courts, which would ensure the uniform application of the laws and strict control over state legislation. There were widely differing opinions among members of the opposition as to the future structure of the judicial branch and the extent of its discretionary powers. Some adversaries of the Constitution correctly predicted that the federal courts would take it upon itself to interpret the Constitution, and that state as well as federal laws would be subject to judicial review. For "Brutus" it was "obvious that these courts will have authority to decide upon the validity of the laws of any of the states, in all cases where they come in question before them." With regard to the Supreme Court, "Brutus" asked his readers "whether the world ever saw, in any period of it, a court of justice invested with such immense powers, and yet placed in a situation so little responsible. . . . [If] the legislature [i.e., Congress] pass any laws, inconsistent with the sense the judges put upon the constitution, they will declare it void; and therefore in this respect their power is superior to that of the legislature."[39]

Should the influence of the national legal system not suffice, there was always the army as a last resort, which Congress would be permitted to raise and maintain. A standing army in times of peace was the worst nightmare of British Country pamphleteers, and the warning against standing armies as the "powerful engine of despotism" was a common theme in Antifederalist writings. The mere existence of such an institution corrupted the citizen's virtues and lowered their morale.[40] History had shown that this instrument of force was more often deployed against the opposition at home than against outside enemies, and that its true function was the suppression of regional uprisings. "Troops when once in pay and service," admonished "Honestus" in the June 18, 1788, issue of the *Wilmington Centinel*, "make no distinction if employed against a foreign enemy or their own relations." The Constitution's foes invariably had European absolutism in mind, the rise of which had been closely tied to the creation of standing armies. The Philadelphia plan left the decision as to whether a state was in compliance with its obligations or whether coercion was in order entirely up to federal organs, particularly the judicial branch and the president. This led to the conclusion that the states would be totally subjugated to the random impulses of the national government. They would still have their militias, of course, considered the only suitable form of military in a system of rule founded on republican principles. This offered little consolation, however, as the president commanded not only the army and naval forces but the militia as well, "when called into the actual Service of the United States." This meant he could mobilize the militia in one part of the Union to deploy it against the real or imagined actions of a renegade state in another part.[41]

The cumulative effect would inevitably be the "melting down" or fusion of the states and the end of their existence as autonomous political entities. They may continue to exist nominally for a time, but the new Constitution struck at the core of "true federalism." Antifederalists were not put off by charges they were placing particular interests above the good of the nation. James Winthrop was quick to respond: "It is vain to tell us that we ought to overlook local interests. It is only by protecting local concerns, that the interest of the whole is preserved."[42] In this view, the Constitution threatened to recast political life from the bottom up. As a result, the American states, those shining stars of the Revolution, would soon plummet like comets: "Scarce has peace secured them the independence they sought, when a mighty revolution is to annihilate their separate and independent sovereignties, and to embrace them in the wide arms of one general government."[43]

Centralism and Civil Rights

Antifederalists were of the opinion that the Constitution not only threatened the existence of the states, it also endangered individual and collective liberties, those "popular privileges" whose defense had been a primary goal of the war against England. A prominent feature of the new Constitution was the power of the federal government to levy taxes directly, instead of going through the states. Despite this exposure to the whims of federal prerogative, the people themselves would have very little influence over the central government, as compared with their influence over the state legislatures. Antifederalists understood "good government" to mean a government that was close to the people, that was contingent on their explicit and ongoing approval and subject to their permanent supervision: "The only balance, which it was of consequence to attend to, is that between the governors and the governed," declared a contributor to the *Virginia Independent Chronicle.*[44] Key words in the Antifederalist vernacular were thus "consent," "accountability," "responsibility," and "control." The workings of government should be transparent and comprehensible, and the participation of the citizens should be as extensive as possible. The state legislatures, with their large number of representatives, their provisions for annual elections, rotation in office, and the recall of delegates, approached this ideal, which was nourished by the "agrarian myth" of an original, unspoiled English constitution.[45] Some Antifederalists were convinced that the degree of public participation could still be improved, even in a state like Pennsylvania, with its exemplary "popular government": "Let Pennsylvania pursue with energy and propriety the ray of light, which beams through the mass of her constitution; let her establish country meetings of *freeholders,* to whom one third of the legislature may refer a contested law for the revision of the great body of the people *by actual vote*—establish county seminaries of learning and similar institutions to promote true patriotism and true knowledge, and she will last the envy of mankind until time shall be no more."[46] Remarks like this bear witness to a faith in the forms and elements of direct democracy, which was precisely where leading Federalists believed to have found the source of political and economic instability.

Just as the government of a large territory was thought to be unresponsive to the various interests and customs of each region or group, a national legislature would not be truly representative of the people it served: "The legislature of a free country should be so formed as to have a competent knowledge of its constituents, and enjoy their confidence. To produce these essential requisites, the representation ought to be fair, equal, and sufficiently numerous, to possess the same interests, feelings, opinions, and views, which the people themselves would possess, were they all assembled; and so numerous as to prevent bribery and undue influence, and so responsible to the people, by frequent and fair elections, as to prevent their neglecting or sacrificing the views and interests of their constituents, to their own pursuits."[47] These criteria were based on the assumption that "power is a very intoxicating thing, and has made many a man do unwarrantable actions," as "Amicus" wrote in the Charleston *Columbian Herald*.[48] Samuel Bryan cited John Dickinson's *Letters From a Farmer in Pennsylvania*, published in 1767–68 ("a perpetual jealousy respecting liberty is absolutely requisite in all free States"), and Montesquieu's dictum "that slavery is ever preceded by sleep."[49] Bryan and his friends agreed that the maxim, "The prerogatives of princes may easily, and do daily grow and increase,"[50] was not reserved to monarchies and aristocracies, but could serve as a warning to the citizens of a free country as well. "The natural course of power is to make the many slaves to the few. This is verified by universal experience," pronounced William Findley at the Pennsylvania ratifying convention.[51] Vigilance and a healthy distrust of power were not only imperative, they constituted the lifeblood of republicanism.

But what good was vigilance when the national government was beyond the reach of normal citizens, and when its authority was virtually unrestricted? Though they may have been at variance over certain issues, there was complete agreement among Antifederalists that the Constitution did not fulfill the basic conditions of a "full and equal representation." The initial House of Representatives was to have 65 delegates, each of whom would represent far more than 30,000 inhabitants, mentioned in the Constitution. How was such a small body supposed to reflect the enormous diversity of interests in the United States? If the principle of annual elections were done away with, one could no longer speak of accountability, in the traditional sense of the word. There would be House elections every two years, but senators would only be elected (by state legislatures, not the people) every six years. There were provisions neither for rotation in office nor recall between elections. To the opposition this signaled the beginning of a trend toward longer and longer terms, eventually leading to mandates for life tenure, if not a hereditary nobility. The small size of Congress, its distance from the voters, and the extent of its powers would hasten the development of an aristocratic or despotic regime: "Instead of seeing powers cautiously lodged in the hands of numerous legislators, and many magistrates, we see all important power collecting in one centre, where a few men will possess them almost at discretion."[52] In Britain, the king and his ministers had used patronage and bribery to manipulate the lower house of Parliament, even though it contained considerably more representatives than the future American Congress.[53] This deep-seated fear of corrupting influences also explains many critics' aversion to the ten-miles-square district conceived as the site of the new federal capital. It promised to become the symbol of a government estranged from the people, a government which placed the luxury and immorality of courtly life above agrarian-republican austerity.[54]

The contrast between the government and the governed corresponded on the societal level to the struggle between "the few" and "the many." This was a manifestation of the fundamental conflict between the rich and the poor already theorized by Aristotle and Polybius, reflecting as well the ambitions of an aristocratic elite determined to rise above the broad middle class. Alluding to the philosophy of Sir William Temple, a "Farmer" from Maryland spoke of "a constant warfare" existing in every society between "aristocracy and democracy, that is the *rich* and the *poor*."[55] Another critic quoted from Cesare Beccaria's *Essay on Crimes and Punishments* to illustrate how the few always strove "to keep down the common people and encrease their own power."[56] Antifederalists upbraided John Adams for his theory of the "well born," though they did not deny the existence of a class of Americans set apart by birth, property ownership, and education. "Centinel" (Samuel Bryan) regarded this class of citizens as a threat that should be kept in check as much as possible instead of honoring them with public offices and legislative seats. The true purpose of government was to protect the weak from the oppression of the powerful and to put every man upon the same level of civil liberty: "A republican, or free government, can only exist where the body of the people are virtuous, and where property is pretty equally divided."[57] From this perspective, Bryan understood and portrayed the movement for a national government as a vast conspiracy of the "few" against the "many." Another opponent of the Constitution, referring to himself as "An Anti-Fœderalist," disputed "that such mighty talents are necessary for government as some claim." The "Watchman" from the opposition's more radical fringe called on his "brothers and sisters" in western Massachusetts to "keep the power in your own hands, and let nothing be established that may deprive you of your liberties and make you unhappy."[58]

It was not difficult for Antifederalists to situate the Constitution in this antagonistic worldview. Elections in larger constituencies favored the "aristocracy" over the "middling classes," so that they were automatically over-represented in Congress. Samuel Chase tried to make this clear to delegates at the Maryland ratifying convention: "Mechanics of every branch will be excluded by the general voice from a seat—only the gentry, the rich and the well born will be elected. Wealth creates power. . . . In fact no order or class of people will be represented in the House of Representatives—called the Democratic branch—but the rich and the wealthy. They will be ignorant of the sentiments of the middling (and much more of the lower) class of citizens, strangers to their ability, unacquainted with their wants, difficulties and distress and need of sympathy and fellow feeling."[59] It was feared that members of Congress would band together with the other branches of government to create a powerful, hostile, remote apparatus that would ever more restrict the rights of the citizens. To secure its dominance, this government would need a constantly growing force of civil servants and a standing army. The funds required for the bureaucratization and militarization of the central administration would be squeezed out of the public in the form of taxes. Federal measures of coercion would meet with attempts at resistance and unleash a spiral of violence ultimately resulting in a state of utter lawlessness. Then Americans themselves would have brought on the fate originally ordained for them by rulers in London: "The revolution which separated the United States from Great-Britain, was not more important to the liberties of America, than that which will result from the adoption of the new system. The former freed us from a foreign subjugation, and there is much reason to apprehend, that the latter will reduce us to a federal domination."[60]

The Necessity of a Bill of Rights

The lack of a declaration of fundamental rights immeasurably increased many citizens' distrust of the Constitution. At the same time, it lent the opposition a useful propaganda tool. James Wilson was the first to explain publicly that a bill of rights was unnecessary because the Constitution was devised according to a completely different principle from the state constitutions. The Constitution did not grant the federal government comprehensive powers. Instead, the federal government was given limited powers that were especially enumerated and clearly defined. All other powers and rights were "reserved" to the states and the people. Therefore they need not be explicitly named and guaranteed.[61] Federalists also argued that basic rights were already sufficiently guaranteed in the state constitutions, and that a bill of rights made no sense in the republican framework of the new system of government. "Bills of Rights were introduced in England when its kings claimed all power and jurisdiction, and were considered by them as grants *to the people*," the "Landholder" explained. "They are insignificant since government is considered as originating from the people, and all the power government now has is a grant *from the people.*"[62] Noah Webster even went so far as to mock the idea of a federal bill of rights: "A Bill of Rights against the encroachments of an elective Legislature, that is, against our own encroachments on ourselves, is a curiosity in government."[63] In the 84th *Federalist* essay, Alexander Hamilton stated another standard Federalist position, that in America bills of rights were not only unnecessary but even dangerous: "They would contain various exceptions to powers which are not granted; and on this very account, would afford a colourable pretext to claim more than were granted." Hamilton went further than most Federalists when he argued that the most important civil rights could never be clearly defined: "What signifies a declaration that 'the liberty of the press shall be inviolably preserved'? What is the liberty of the press? Who can give it any definition which would not leave the utmost latitude for evasion? I hold it to be impracticable; and from this I infer that its security, whatever fine declarations may be inserted in any constitution respecting it, must altogether depend on public opinion, and on the general spirit of the people and the government."[64]

These arguments could not bear close legal scrutiny by the practiced Antifederalists. The doctrine of "reserved powers" was contravened by Article I, section 9, which guaranteed the right of habeas corpus and prohibited the granting of titles of nobility. These restrictions were pointless if one accepted James Wilson's theory, since the Constitution neither authorized the government to interfere with habeas corpus nor to grant titles of nobility. Contrary to the emphatic reassurances offered by Federalists, the federal government's powers were not limited and precisely defined. Quite the opposite, a number of nearly boundless "implicit" powers could be derived from the general clauses and the necessary-and-proper clause. It was conceivable, for instance, that Congress could restrict the freedom of the press by way of taxation laws and postal regulations. With a little skill, surmised "Brutus," any law could be justified as "necessary and proper": "The powers, rights, and authority, granted to the general government by this constitution, are as complete, with respect to every object to which they extend, as that of any state government—It reaches to every thing which concerns human happiness—Life, liberty, and property, are under its controul. There is the same reason, therefore, that the exercise of power, in this case, should be restrained within proper limits, as in that of the state governments."[65] The one and only possible remedy, according to the "Old Whig," was a declaration of fundamental rights, "to which we might appeal, and under which we might contend against any assumption of undue power and appeal to the judicial branch of the government to protect us by their judgment."[66]

Antifederalists insisted most adamantly on the right of the accused to appear before a jury of peers. The Constitution specified this privilege in criminal trials but not in civil proceedings—allegedly because legal practices in the various states were too divergent. Opponents of the Constitution concluded, therefore, that the right to a trial by jury was abolished in civil cases.[67] Other matters of overriding importance to the critics were the protection of the right to assembly, freedom of speech, freedom of the press, and freedom of religion. Antifederalists were more likely than their adversaries to underscore the relationship between republican values and Christian beliefs, besides emphasizing the importance of religious education for the community. Some even criticized the Constitution for prohibiting a religious oath, which meant it would be impossible to reserve government offices for Protestants, or at least Christians.[68]

In general, a declaration of "certain unalienable and fundamental rights" was deemed indispensable for protecting the people against the abuse and usurpation of governmental power while upholding minority rights and reminding the governing and governed alike of the basic principles of republicanism. Bills of rights had both a protective and an educational function: "We do not by declarations change the nature of things, or create new truths, but we give existence, or at least establish in the minds of the people truths and principles which they might never otherwise have thought of, or soon forgot. If a nation means its systems, religious or political, shall have duration, it ought to recognize the leading principles of them in the front page of every family book."[69]

As much as Antifederalists valued a bill of rights, this was not regarded as an alternative to revising the body of the Constitution itself. If the proposed system were not restructured and the authority of the national government reduced to a level commensurate with republican liberty, the simple addition of a list of general principles would make little difference. "A Declaration of Rights alone will be of no essential Service," Samuel Chase wrote to John Lamb. "Some of the powers must be abridged, or public liberty will be endangered, and in time destroyed."[70] Antifederalists, therefore, continued to argue for substantive changes in the Constitution in addition to a bill of rights.

The Flawed Structure of the Central Government

Involvement in any detailed analysis of the Constitution touched on a sensitive issue among Antifederalists: radical opponents used such a clause-by-clause review as a means to affirm their flat "no" to the Philadelphia plan, while moderate opponents saw it as an opportunity to suggest structural reforms and amendments that would make the Constitution acceptable. This created the impression that the opposition would eventually come to terms with the new state of affairs. The radical critics advocated a simple form of administration they referred to as "popular government," "simple, responsible government," or "purely democratical system."[71] The need to protect the minority did not change the fact, however, that in such a system the majority would always prevail. Besides, there were great differences in what "democracy" and "democratic" were understood to mean, just as there was a wide range of theories on the risks and advantages of a democratic system. A considerable number of Antifederalists had as great a fear of excessive democracy as the most fervent supporters of the Constitution. Most Antifederalists believed the democratic element should be given its proper place in the grand design of the central government. Yet there were also those who dismissed as outdated the common distinctions between monarchical, aristocratic, and democratic forms of government and the resulting theory of a "mixed constitution." "William Penn" explicitly restricted himself to exploring a "democracy, or government, of the people, which I am confident is the only one under which liberty can be obtained or preserved."[72] This signified a departure from the principles of the British Constitution, still viewed as exemplary by many Americans in its "original," "pure" form.

The proponents of radical Antifederalism tended to prefer the unicameral system, which had lost favor in recent years. But a unicameral legislature and the separation of powers were not sufficient alone to assure "simplicity" and "responsibility" in government. Since every government was susceptible to corruption and the abuse of power, precautionary measures were necessary, in the form of internal checks and balances. Still, a "simple, responsible government" remained the ideal of all critics, regardless of whether their arguments were more traditionally, moderately, or radically democratic. "Centinel" was of the opinion that the best form of government for free citizens was one "which holds those entrusted with power, in the greatest responsibility to their constituents."[73] Lawyer Peter Stephen Du Ponceau believed Americans could be ruled "without being restrained too much, and the simpler the machine of government, the more easily it is put in motion."[74] A popular government, in which every segment of the citizenry was adequately represented and which rested upon the permanent consent of the people, seemed to Antifederalists appropriate for the agrarian-egalitarian character of American society. Yet Antifederalists could only envision the realization of these ideals on the local or, at best, state level. An administration's complexity necessarily grew with the size of its territories and the duration of the country's existence, as could be seen in Europe. Some states in the Union already appeared too large and heterogeneous to be ruled "simple." This was evidenced by the separatist movements plaguing North Carolina, Virginia,

Pennsylvania, New York, and Massachusetts. A suitable "popular government" for the entire country was almost unthinkable. "Thirteen complicated forms all under one form of government, still more complicated, seems to bid defiance to all responsibility (the only test of good government)," wrote the "Farmer" from Maryland.[75] Proper representation in a national legislature would require hundreds—and within a few decades even thousands—of delegates, an utterly hopeless endeavor. Yet if not even the House of Representatives could be trusted, which according to republican ideology was supposed to defend the interests of the "middling classes," then the entire government would be beyond the control of the people.

Hence, a national government could neither be analyzed nor judged in accordance with the principles of "simple government." In fact, to help reduce the threat posed by a national government that could act directly on the people without the mediation of the states would require a design that was especially complex and sophisticated. The relative success of a similar system in England was generally attributed to the fact that the government of king, lords, and commons was a natural reflection of the social order. America, by contrast, lacked the social fundament of "standing orders," on whose lasting, diverse interests a complicated system of this type could be founded. Antifederalists strongly doubted that a purely functional separation of powers not mirrored in society could fulfill its purpose. A "Farmer" from Maryland categorically denied the possibility of a "fixed and permanent government that does not rest on the fixed and permanent orders and objects of mankind." Patrick Henry was no less emphatic at the Virginia ratifying convention in Richmond: "In the British Government there are real balances and checks—In this system, there are only ideal balances."[76] Basically, the proposed administration could only be maintained by increasing and perpetuating existing social disparities in the United States; in other words, by furthering the feudalization of American society. This was precisely what Antifederalists believed to be the likely development facing the nation under the new Constitution. The constitutional and sociopolitical circumstances in England held no appeal for them, nor did the British Empire's accumulation of power. The central government was certain to become an aristocratic instrument of oppression in America as well, despite the artificial division into executive, legislative, and judicial branches.

Antifederalists subscribing to the principle of simplicity naturally feared the president would turn out to be another monarch, a "prince under a republican cloak." This gave rise to the proposal that the president be furnished with an executive (or privy) council instead of a vice president, who was not only redundant but perhaps even dangerous in his role as president of the

Senate. Yet close scrutiny of the complex government model had to lead to the opposite conclusion, namely, that the president was too weak to stand up to the "aristocratic" Congress.[77] Similarly, there were those who dismissed the House of Representatives as insignificant and impotent, whereas others were alarmed by its virtually unlimited powers, particularly as regards taxation and other economic matters. The most common complaint involved the allegedly inadequate separation of powers. The Constitution did not restrict the president to executive duties, but rather allowed him to intervene in the legislative process by way of a partial veto. This overlapping of powers was especially conspicuous in the Senate, which in addition to its function as the second chamber of the legislature also carried out important executive duties through its confirmation of appointments and its ratification of treaties. It had even been assigned a role in cases of impeachment, which had better been reserved for the judicial branch. Many Antifederalists therefore regarded the Senate as the greatest hazard, and a collaboration between the president and the Senate was the most likely scenario: "The president general is dangerously connected with the senate; his coincidence with the views of the ruling junto in that body, is made essential to his weight and importance in the government, which will destroy all independence and purity in the executive department."[78] Only if the Senate were primarily judged as the embodiment of federalism, since it represented the states, could one perceive its positive aspects. This was most appreciated in the small states.[79]

Antifederalists had at best mixed feelings toward the judicial branch. On the one hand, they supported its wide jurisdiction for protection against the usurpation of power by other arms of the government, by the federal government against the states, and for infringements of fundamental rights. On the other hand, the judges, with their appointments "during good behavior" and their guaranteed salaries, were even further removed from popular control than the executive and legislative branches. Under such circumstances, the Supreme Court could become too powerful and force its will upon the administration and Congress. Yet it could just as easily become subservient to the president and Senate, thus fostering a transition to authoritarian rule.[80] The establishment of the Supreme Court and inferior federal courts threatened to expand federal jurisdiction and undermine the state courts, unduly delaying appeals and driving up costs. Common citizens would be forced to fight for their rights far from home and at considerable expense. Counted among the questionable "Blessings of the New Government" by a contributor to the *Independent Gazetteer* were therefore "Appeals to the supreme continental court, where the rich may drag the poor from the furthermost parts of the continent."[81] The beneficiaries of this institution were the wealthy and influential, who could pressure their adversaries to capitulate under threat of lengthy and expensive proceedings. This prospect must have been especially frightening to those who owed money to British or American creditors but whom state legislatures had so far shielded.

All told, the proposed system of government seemed to Antifederalists to be an odd, ill-conceived edifice, a "consistent piece of inconsistency," as General Samuel Thompson put it at the Boston ratifying convention.[82] It neither conformed to the conventions of a true confederation nor fulfilled the conditions of an English-style "mixed government." Their fear of this "dark, intricate, artful, crafty, and unintelligible composition," and their contempt for what they regarded as "the new leviathan," a "heterogeneous phantom" and "many-headed monster," or "13 horned monster," suggests that the Constitution's adversaries were intellectually unprepared for a complex, partially national, partially federal form of government.[83] Their aversion to sophisticated and mixed systems collided with the view that a certain measure of complexity was unavoidable in light of the economic progress and "aging" of American society. The majority of critics surely recognized the need for a stronger Union, but were unable to break away from the ideal of a "simple government" and the traditional concept of federalism—particularly when the only alternative appeared to be the unpopular British model of government and society and the British colonial system that prevailed before the Revolution. This dilemma contributed to the mood of pessimism and resignation which increasingly came to characterize Antifederalist commentaries.

Slavery and the North-South Conflict

In addition to the inconsistencies already mentioned, there were some basic disagreements which weakened the Antifederalist position. Opponents of the Constitution organized resistance in the South by charging that it mainly served northern interests. They warned that New England and the middle states would use their majority in Congress to conclude unfair trade agreements and dominate and monopolize the profits from the South's staple exports. In Virginia, this fear, propagated most fervidly by George Mason, overshadowed at times all other aspects of the debate.[84] Antifederalists in the North, on the other hand, warned against economic handicaps and losses thought unavoidable due to concessions to the southern states. Particularly where taxes were concerned, the South had obviously faired far better than the North. Direct taxes were to be levied proportionately on the basis of population, yet five blacks counted the same as only three whites. Since there were considerably fewer slaves in the North than in the South, the tax burden on the North increased accordingly. Furthermore, free blacks residing in the

North counted as full persons and not as three-fifths of a person. At the same time, all southern farm produce was forever exempt from export duties.[85]

In the same breath in which they complained about this unfairness, northern Antifederalists also warned about the threat to republican virtue posed by an overly close association with the South, which was known for lax morals, extravagance, and aristocratic manners.[86] Such an argument called the viability of the Union in general into question. If the interests of the North and South were really as divergent as many Antifederalists claimed, this would cast doubt on the feasibility of the Confederation itself. Supporters of the Constitution skillfully countered this argument by pointing to the economic unity of America and the fundamental identity between the interests of every region. The North and South complemented each other ideally and jointly contributed to the good of the nation precisely because of their differing economic structures: "The American regions supplement each other.... The prosperity of agriculture in the southern states... will depend on the shipping of the middle and eastern states."[87] According to the *Massachusetts Centinel,* the fact that Antifederalists in both regions felt cheated by the Constitution was the best testimony to its fairness. Northern critics, said the *Centinel,* claimed "that in the new Constitution, the southern states have preeminence." Yet the complaint could be heard in the South "that in almost all things the eastern states out-wit and unhinge us." This only went to show "*how easy it is to find sticks to make a fire, on which to sacrifice an innocent creature.*"[88]

It was the issue of slavery that rendered the problem of regionalism particularly volatile. Several states had already enacted laws designed to eliminate slavery gradually.[89] Prominent Americans like Benjamin Franklin, John Jay, and Benjamin Rush held leading positions in anti-slavery societies and corresponded with similar organizations in Europe. Religious denominations, above all the Quakers, Baptists, and Methodists, demanded more stringent measures against the evils of the foreign slave trade and slavery itself.[90] Dedicated reformers regarded the Philadelphia compromise on slavery as a bitter setback. This was one of the favorite targets of the opposition to the Constitution in the northern and middle states. They interpreted the three-fifths clause, the fugitive-slave clause, and the provision forbidding a congressional nationwide ban on the importation of slaves before 1808 as constitutional guarantees for the continuance of this inhuman and unchristian practice. In speeches and in writing, slavery was soundly denounced for religious, moral, and political reasons. It violated the laws of nature and the Christian duty to love one's neighbor, thus raising the threat of divine retribution; it was contrary to the truth contained in the Declaration of Independence that all men were created equal, and exposed the Americans' opportunism to the rest of the world; it not only impinged on the rights and dignity of the victims, it also undermined the morals of slave owners; finally, it weakened the political and military might of the country tolerating this practice by making it vulnerable to civic unrest and foreign intervention. As expressed by "Brutus," slavery was contemptuous of "every idea of benevolence, justice, and religion, and . . . all the principles of liberty, which have been publickly avowed in the late glorious revolution. . . . What adds to the evil is, that these [southern] states are to be permitted to continue the inhumane traffic of importing slaves, until the year 1808—and for every cargo of these unhappy people . . . they are to be rewarded by having an increase of members in the general assembly." As the number of slaves in the South grew, so did the South's representation in Congress, while its share of taxes dropped proportionally.[91]

In Massachusetts, "Adelos" distanced himself from a Constitution "which at its first breath will be branded with eternal infamy, by having a stamp of slavery and oppression upon it."[92] One of the fiercest attacks on the slavery provisions came from Joshua Atherton at the first session of the New Hampshire ratifying convention: "We become consenters to and partakers in the sin and guilt of this abominable traffic, at least for a certain period, without any positive stipulation that it shall even then be brought to an end. . . . We will not lend the aid of our ratification to this cruel and inhuman merchandise, not even for a day. There is a great distinction in not taking part in the most barbarious violation of the sacred laws of God and humanity and our becoming guarantees for its exercise for a term of years. Yes, sir, it is our full purpose to wash our hands clear of it."[93] Writing in the *New York Journal,* Hugh Hughes was just as adamant in his condemnation of "Trade in Blood, and every Vice, of which the Avarice, Pride, Insolence and Cruelty of Man is capable. A Trade, which, if ever permitted, will entail eternal Infamy on the United States and all that they have ever said or done in Defence of Freedom."[94]

Of course, pronouncements of this sort were also used for propaganda purposes, since it could be assumed that many northern citizens, including those dedicated to the Federalist cause, abhorred the institution of slavery. There were also critics in the South, like "Philanthropos" and "Othello," who called for the liberation of slaves and their "colonization" in Africa.[95] However, this view was shared at best by a minority of the Constitution's adversaries, since not just the great planters but also numerous small and midsized farmers in the South had built their existence around the availability of unfree labor. Antifederalism in unison with the defense of slavery was much more common here, as the debates in South Carolina and Virginia reveal. The concern that the system of slavery was endangered by the Constitution was even regarded as an important reason for rejecting its ratification. South Carolina Antifederalist Rawlins Lowndes warned his colleagues in the state assembly that people in the North "don't like our slaves, because they have none themselves, and therefore want to exclude us from this great advantage. . . . Without negroes this state would degenerate into one of the most contemptible in the union. . . . Negroes were our wealth, our only national resource."[96] In the Virginia ratifying convention, George Mason attacked the Constitution for not protecting slavery while it protected the slave trade until 1808: "Instead of securing and protecting us, the continuation of this detestable trade, adds daily to our weakness. Though this evil is increasing, there is no clause in the Constitution that will prevent the Northern and Eastern States from meddling with our whole property of that kind. . . . It is far from being a desirable property. But it will involve us in great difficulties and infelicity to be now deprived of them. There ought to be a clause in the Constitution to secure us that property, which we have acquired under our former laws, and the loss of which would bring ruin on a great many people." Patrick Henry assisted Mason, asking the delegates "why it was omitted to secure us that property in slaves, which we held now? He feared its omission was done with design. They might lay such heavy taxes on slaves, as would amount to emancipation; and then the Southern States would be the only sufferers."[97]

Somewhat overstated, though not entirely fallacious, were the claims of Federalist "Crambo" in the *Massachusetts Centinel* that one of the motives for southerners' resistance to ratification was the fear "that they shall be deprived of the liberty of killing a Negro when they please. . . . They feared that this Constitution would in time give liberty to their slaves—or prohibit their purchasing others, when they have worked these to death."[98] Two years later, a letter writer in North Carolina described the same circumstances in a more sedate manner: "The People in the Southern States who have any property, hold it mostly in Lands and Negroes, and if divested of their Negroes their Lands will become useless or rather burthensome to them, they will not be able to cultivate or pay the taxes on them, and the most opulent and considerable families would in a short time be reduced to indigence and extreme poverty."[99]

When viewed from a local perspective, it is understandable that northern Antifederalists attacked the Constitution for protecting slavery, while southern Antifederalists attacked it for endangering slavery. On the national level, however, this harmed their credibility and weakened their position.[100] Federalists backed the Philadelphia compromise and held it up as further proof of their ability to harmonize regional differences through a national agenda: "Regard was necessarily paid to the peculiar situation of our southern fellow-citizens; but they, on the other hand, have not been insensible to the delicate situation of our national character on this subject."[101] The decision temporarily to abstain from any intervention in the slave trade was a concession essential to the preservation the Union. This point was summarized by James Madison in the Richmond convention: "Great as the evil is, a dismemberment of the union would be worse."[102] All this obscured the fact that there were great differences in the way Federalists interpreted the compromise. In the northern and middle states, it was heralded as "one of the beauties of the Constitution" and a preliminary step toward the ultimate abolition of slavery.[103] In the South, by contrast, Federalist supporters were assured that slavery could continue unabated even after a prohibition of the foreign slave trade. Charles Cotesworth Pinckney maintained that the Constitution did not authorize the federal government to deal with the system of slavery in any way, shape, or form: "We have a security that the general government can never emancipate them, for no such authority is granted. . . . The general government has no powers but what are expressly granted by the constitution." In this connection, Pinckney, one of the signers of the Constitution, offered a pragmatic reason for dispensing with a Bill of Rights: "Such bills generally begin with declaring, that all men are by nature born free, now we should make that declaration with a very bad grace, when a large part of our property consists in men who are actually born slaves."[104]

The Danger of Aristocracy and Elite Rule

In January 1788, Madison saw no better means "of serving the federal cause at this moment than to display the disagreement of those who make a common cause against the Constitution."[105] That was surely true from a tactical standpoint. Melancton Smith was correct in a more profound sense, however, when in the *Plebeian* pamphlet he referred to a remarkable unity characterizing the criticism of the Constitution: "It would be easy to shew, that in the leading and most important objections that have been made to the plan, there has been, and is entire concurrence of opinion among the writers, and in public bodies throughout the United States."[106] There were both practical and theoretical reasons for this accord. The common preference for a strengthened confederation and for constitutional forms allowing for the active participation of the citizens corresponded, on a basic level, to an emotional, almost instinctive aversion to Federalists and their policies. Antifederalists knew their opponents well from past political conflicts, were quite aware of the Federalists' superiority in certain respects, and predicted that if Federalists gained power on a national level, they would use it as against the interests of the "common people." The election of delegates in large districts favored widely known or wealthy candidates, resulting in the exclusion of the "middling classes" to whose cause Antifederalists were dedicated. An attack on the "overly democratic" state constitutions which served as the last bastion of the opposition would likely be the next link in the growing chain of tyranny. An aristocratic regiment consisting of the president, Congress, and the Supreme Court could join forces to isolate itself from the states and people, thus permitting "energetic" government action in the broadest sense of the word.

As these fears and premonitions intensified, terrifying scenarios began to emerge. The "better sort" would satisfy their lust for power and fame to the detriment of the common man; the cost of their aspirations for national glory would be devastating wars and a massive national debt; to raise the money needed for arms and interest payments, taxes would soar and be collected by force if necessary; the concern for the common weal would give way to private profit-seeking and unbridled egoism, leading to the complete subjugation of the middling and lower classes to a phalanx of merchants, lawyers, and creditors. The final result would be corruption, moral decline, and government by and for a narrow elite. America was on the verge of imitating all the mistakes already endured by Europeans. Moderate Antifederalists had no principled objections to a "commercial society" based on growth and prosperity, but did not want to sacrifice state sovereignty and republican virtues to this end. They insisted the common good fared best in a country with a relatively homogeneous population, a broad sharing of economic and political power, and an equitable distribution of property. The new Constitution ran contrary to all of these convictions and values. Still, most critics realized they were not strong enough to reject the Constitution summarily. They presented counter-suggestions aimed at significantly increasing the economic, fiscal, and military powers of the Confederation Congress.[107] There had to be a way to find a compromise between this idea and the Philadelphia plan. The goal was a complete revision of the Constitution along with the addition of a bill of rights.

The Federalist Defense and Interpretation of the Constitution

The Best Possible Constitution

Federalists viewed themselves as the dynamic, forward-looking element of American society. They did not long for a return to prewar conditions, aiming instead to tame the social forces of the Revolution and to devise constructive goals for the latent energy resting in the population: "The American war is over: but this is far from being the case with the American revolution. On the contrary, nothing but the first act of the great drama is closed. It remains yet to establish and perfect our new forms of government; and to prepare the principles, morals, and manners of our citizens, for these forms of government, after they are established and brought to perfection."[108] Federalists were indeed the revolutionaries of 1787–88, regardless of whether they had exuberantly followed the call to arms a decade earlier or, as their critics were wont to maintain, with extreme reluctance. They knew they would have to break with all established modes of thought and political language to succeed: "Our projected revolution evidently required the utmost wisdom and caution. Deeply-rooted opinions and principles do not change so easily and speedily."[109]

Ironically, Federalists intended their revolution to achieve stability, order, security, and predictability. To accomplish this, though they had little faith in the political wisdom of the common man, they were forced by the social and political realities of Revolutionary America to respect the sovereignty of the people and to win the majority to their side. The Philadelphia plan gave Federalists a clear, positive agenda to rally around, and they did. But this is not to say that many Federalists did not have private reservations. Some of them found the Constitution too centralist, or lacking the necessary internal balance of power; others thought the national government was still too weak to contain the destructive forces inherent in republics and federations. Concerns of this nature troubled Ezra Stiles, president of Yale College: "I think there is not Power enough yet given to Congress for firm Government." "Civis" also found the new system wanting: "Its frequent elections, with the uncontrollable power of the people over all the three branches, will, I am afraid, involve it in various convulsions; and its being too limited and confined, may be productive of many inconveniences." In the sixth "Landholder" essay, Oliver Ellsworth came to the conclusion that "The danger of the constitution is not aristocracy or monarchy, but anarchy."[110] Despite these doubts, Federalists were unified in their support of ratification. Only practical use could show whether or not the Constitution truly contained material flaws. And if any such defects should manifest themselves in the future, they could be remedied by way of amendments.[111]

The Need for a New Constitution

Federalists did not in the least doubt the necessity for fundamental changes, and they considered the work of the Federal Convention to be the only realistic alternative to the weak Congress. Their criticism of the Articles of Confederation, described by John Adams as a "rope of sand," was extremely harsh, often overshooting its mark. By constantly deriding the Confederation as impotent and bankrupt, they created a kind of self-fulfilling prophecy that dealt the final deathblow to the floundering government. The prudent French chargé d'affaires, Louis Guillaume Otto, realized there could be no turning back in the face of so much public turmoil—there was now no alternative to creating a new system: "In effect it was impossible to carry out a more violent coup to the authority of Congress, than in saying to all America, to the entire Universe, that this body is inadequate to the needs of the Confederation and that the united States have become the laughing-stock of all the powers. This principle repeated over and over again by all the Innovators seems as false as their spirits are excited; the united States held the place among nations which their youth and means assigned them; they are neither rich enough, populated enough, nor well established enough to appear with more luster and perhaps one ought to reproach them only for the impatience of anticipating their future grandeur."[112] The characteristic tone of the Federalist commentaries to which Otto was referring had already been common at the time of the Philadelphia Convention: "It seems to be generally felt and acknowledged, that the affairs of this country are in a ruinous situation. With vast resources in our hands, we are impoverished by the continual drain of money from us in foreign trade; our navigation is destroyed; our people are in debt and unable to pay; industry is at a stand; our public treaties are violated, and national faith, solemnly plighted to foreigners and to our own citizens, is no longer kept. We are discontented at home, and abroad we are insulted and despised."[113] A writer in Connecticut lamented the declining moral standards: "The pages of history nowhere describe a government that has been so famous a nurse of all kinds of vices as that of the American states since their independence. . . . I believe the Grecian states never half-equaled us in overreaching, in injustice, in knavery, and of mutual jealousy and distrust."[114] This exaggerated perception of reality led to a black-and-white worldview which saw no middle ground between the Constitution and chaos. At the same time, this ominous feeling of crisis and this now-or-never mentality generated a sense of urgency; paired with an awareness of the uniqueness of their historic situation, this urgency gradually took hold of many Americans. The Federalists' concern for the present and future was real, and by no means baseless. It was founded on historical comparisons, the study of classical as well as modern political theory, and on their Protestant-Puritan heritage with its propensity for introspection and self-doubt.

History offered many examples of successful revolutions that resulted in decline and a gradual slide back into oppression. The main source of reference at the time was the seventeenth-century British civil war, which had regressed from the execution of King Charles I to the military dictatorship of Cromwell, to the restoration of the Stuarts. What would have happened, Hamilton mused in *Federalist* No. 21, if a Caesar or a Cromwell had been leading the Massachusetts farmers instead of Daniel Shays?[115] "Harrington" posed the question in the *Pennsylvania Gazette:* "Shall the United States become a theatre, on which the crimes of the Caesars and Cromwells of past ages are to be acted over again?"[116] The British and the Tories had prophesied that the colonies, when left to their own devices, would live in a state of permanent conflict and eventually use their arms against each other. "This is the moment of crisis which is to verify, or contradict the European prediction, that the American states will be crushed under the weight of their independence, by the troubles and divisions which shall arise amongst them," declared a "True Friend" in the *Virginia Independent Chronicle.*[117]

Warning signals were also sounded in connection with the theory of the cyclical development of constitutions, originally conceived by Aristotle and important for eighteenth-century political thought in a version developed by Polybius. Anyone observing the United States from this angle during the "critical period" had to conclude it was at that stage of development where democracy regressed into ochlocracy or demagoguery on its inevitable slide toward despotism.[118] Puritanism included both a sense of calling and a fear of failure. The constant fear of straying from the path of Providence and getting lost in the wilderness was given liturgical-literary expression in the jeremiad, a ritual of self-castigation combining a desire for repentance with the hope of redemption. Almost all known sermons from the ratification period attributed the postwar symptoms of crisis to a sinful disdain for the will of God. Shortly before the beginning of the New Hampshire ratifying convention, pastor Samuel Langdon urgently pleaded with the members of both legislative chambers to heed the lessons learned from the transgressions of the ancient peoples of Israel: "Their constitution both in government and religion was excellent in writing, but was never exemplified in fact. . . . If I am not mistaken, instead of the twelve tribes of Israel, we may substitute the thirteen States of the American union."[119] Even beyond the pulpit, almost all public summations of developments over the preceding five years took the form of secularized jeremiads. Amidst all these exhortations and appeals, Federalists were not demanding a radical spiritual revival, but a remedy of a more institutional and administrative nature: the adoption of the Constitution would place the nation's political and economic life on sound footing and all would soon take a turn for the better. Moral rejuvenation did not have to precede this change, but rather would be a consequence of it along with countless other blessings. This recipe for solving the crisis was congruent with the Enlightenment's faith in the power of reason and the superiority of scientific methods and systems.

Behind these exertions stood the conviction that the Articles of Confederation, like most state constitutions, contained profound flaws which could not be eliminated by treating their symptoms. Under the pressure of war, the latest advances in the "science of politics" had not been properly taken into account. For a time, the citizens' patriotism and courageous sacrifice had helped to offset the constitution's deficiencies. However, the apparent decline since 1783 proved that the threat of British arms had done more to preserve the Union than the Articles of Confederation. In the long run, the United States could not survive without a true national government: "When we call ourselves an independent nation, it is false: we are neither a nation, nor are we independent. Like thirteen contentious neighbors, we devour and take advantage of each other, and are without that system of policy which gives safety and strength, and constitutes a national structure."[120] The Confederation contained two major flaws: first of all, it allowed the states to retain their full sovereignty, in effect subjugating the Union to the good will of state legislatures. Second, it apportioned the responsibility for important national affairs to Congress without giving it the means to fulfill its obligations. The essence of the problem was thus an inability to convert powers granted on paper into tangible political action. Congress had the right to borrow money, for instance, but was unable to pay interest on loans because it could neither raise taxes nor force the states to pay their requisitions; Congress was expected to defend the country's borders, but was not allowed to raise and maintain an army; it was permitted to conclude treaties with foreign powers, but could not force the states to respect those treaties. This situation must inexorably lead to bankruptcy, a dissolution of the Union, and civil war.

The Advantages of a Federation

Federalists regarded the Union as the most important legacy of the Revolution. A good deal of their literature was devoted to illustrating the practical advantages of the Union, the "utility of the UNION to your political prosperity."[121] The first fourteen *Federalist* essays were largely dedicated to the purpose of indelibly impressing on their readers' minds the identity of Union and Constitution. A well-founded, federally structured Union would bring benefits in the three major areas of domestic security, foreign relations, and the economy. If centrifugal tendencies were not checked, perpetual conflicts among the states and sections would ensue, eventually escalating into military action. The territorial disputes between Pennsylvania and Connecticut, between New York and Massachusetts, and between Maryland and Virginia, as well as separatist movements in Maine, Vermont, Kentucky, and Tennessee, proved that the seeds of future discord had already been sowed. The states' economic development was more likely to increase the threat of violence than deter it. Hamilton drew examples from history to show that "commercial republics" did not necessarily behave more peacefully than monarchies or despotic regimes.[122] The threat of war would result in the formation of separate confederacies which would attempt to protect their regional interests through alliances with foreign powers. For a taste of what was to come, one only had to look to the Southwest and their threats to seek British help against Spain. Internal clashes could thus serve as an excuse for foreign intervention, once again making North America a battleground for European politics. And even if the states managed to limit their conflicts and reduce squabbling between political parties, the security of the Confederation's borders would still be at risk. Powerful nations seeking to increase their dominance were always tempted to use the instability of a weak state as a pretext for starting a war. Only a sound federation could act with enough self-confidence in the international arena to be treated with respect by potential adversaries.

The economic advantages of a strong Union followed from the political-military benefits. Without the vigorous support of a firm central government, a trading nation could never effectively defend its commercial interests. British restrictions preventing American ships from calling at the ports of important Caribbean islands demanded firm retaliation. Yet actions by Congress were futile as long as individual states continued to undermine them by making their own self-serving policies. This was yet another case where the doctrine of state sovereignty stood at odds with efforts to shore up the Union.[123] By investing the federal government with sweeping authority over matters involving taxation, customs, and commerce, significant progress could be achieved in the area of domestic trade. Of underlying importance were thus a single currency and a free domestic market, along with the creation of a network of roads and canals to improve the infrastructure, and import duties set by the national government to raise revenue and to force foreign powers to open their markets to American goods. Federalists portrayed the future as an alternative between a prosperous federation and heavily armed regional confederacies backed by European powers, isolating themselves behind borders and trade barriers. This would increase the costs of government, professional armies would become commonplace, and material gains would fall victim to mutual distrust.[124]

Of course, all of these frequently repeated arguments were based on the assumption that the Confederation really was on the brink of ruin and could only be saved by a new constitution. Federalists insinuated time and again that their foes were knowingly or carelessly prepared to accept the demise of the Union. It is true that some opponents of the Constitution regarded the breakup of the Union as a lesser evil than the loss of liberty at the hands of a "consolidated" republic. Patrick Henry, for one, openly proclaimed that Virginia could well stand on its own two feet.[125] That said, the fact remains that Antifederalists did not advocate disunion or deny the benefits of the Union. George Mason even declared that no one was "more completely federal in his principles than he was. . . . From the east of New-Hampshire to the south of Georgia, there was no man more fully convinced of the necessity of establishing some general government."[126] However, when Antifederalists proposed simply revising the Articles of Confederation, their own arguments against the Constitution were used against them: was it not too dangerous to grant additional authority and jurisdiction over the states to a body like the old Congress, where there was no separation of powers and no internal checks? Were republican rights and freedoms not significantly better protected by a federal government divided into executive, legislative, and judicial branches, including a directly elected House of Representatives?[127]

Federalists had a clear edge in this aspect of the debate over the Constitution. It was obvious to nearly everyone that a strong central government could bring about improvements in foreign policy, domestic security, and commerce. America's international reputation had suffered; its economy was in depression; its workers and farmers were hurting. A powerful change in government was needed to reestablish momentum, restore optimism, and put the nation back on its path to greatness and prosperity. Why hesitate when an effective means of resolving the crisis was within arm's reach? Federalists combined pragmatic, interest-oriented reasoning with the emotional appeal of a "rising empire" on the North American continent.[128] The crisis was an historic opportunity which must be taken advantage of or everything would be lost. Isaac Stearns wrote to Nathaniel Gorham that, though he did not claim to possess prophetic vision, an inner voice was telling him "we may

Date the rise or fall of these States, from the Day that we adopt, or reject, the Federal Constitution now under consideration."[129] "'To be or not to be' is now the question! The moment is at hand when America will rise respected and affluent, or sink into contempt, anarchy, and perhaps a total dissolution of our short existence as a nation," declaimed the author of a letter from North Carolina.[130] "This is the period to try men's souls!" was another popular quotation often used as a motto for Federalist essays. In this way, the people were told that they were facing a monumental decision, "comprehending in its consequences nothing less than the existence of the UNION, the safety and welfare of the parts of which it is composed, the fate of an empire in many respects the most interesting in the world."[131] The more Federalists succeeded in impressing this sense of urgency upon the population, the better the chances of ratification. But they still had to provide convincing proof that the new order was consistent with the principles of federalism as well as respect for the individual and collective rights of the citizens.

The Compatibility of Federalism with a Strong Central Authority

While the Federal Convention was still in progress, Henry Knox wrote of his conviction "that the national government ought to possess full and complete powers within itself, unconstrained by the concurrence of any state or corporate body to deliberate, decree, and execute." Should this not be possible, there was no other choice than "the abolition of the State governments or the annihilation of all hopes founded on our existence as a nation."[132] A short time later, Federalists were busy publicly defending the Philadelphia plan with vigor and enthusiasm, though many of them were still plagued by nagging doubts about whether they had really found the right mixture of general and particular powers. A slight echo of Antifederalist concerns about the erosion of state sovereignty could occasionally be discerned. Far more common, however, was the opposite fear that the states had retained too much influence and would be able to undermine all endeavors undertaken by the national government for the common good. For this reason, Hamilton would have preferred to see the Union divided into provinces or districts of approximately equal size and without true legislative powers.[133]

Jonathan Jackson ("A Native of Boston") believed the continent needed a "new arrangement," just as his fellow citizens must be "properly organized." Inspired by David Hume's treatise on *The Idea of a Perfect Commonwealth*, he proposed dividing the Union into ten states with 300,000 inhabitants each. Each state was to be composed of twenty districts, and each district of two counties. As Hume had suggested, this organizational framework was to be combined with a system of direct elections in which the participation of voters was limited to the lower levels. The highest ministerial positions were to be filled by means of an "intricate ballot," a complicated procedure reminiscent of Venetian doges. The best means of ensuring the superiority of the central government, in Jackson's estimation, was a veto over state legislation like the one Madison had pursued at the Philadelphia Convention. The rejection of this proposal had left Jackson with grave doubts about the efficiency and stability of the entire plan.[134] Pelatiah Webster, too, would not have minded if the states had been "melted down" into a "great commonwealth."[135]

James Madison started from a similarly centralizing position, but during the debate over the Constitution he moved in a different direction. The historical studies he had been immersed in since 1786 had taught him that the greatest threat to the federal system of government did not come from the central administration but from the jealous attempts of its member states to preserve their independence and authority. Regardless of whether one examined the leagues of states in ancient Greece, such as the Amphyctionic League and the Achaean League, or the German Empire and United Netherlands of the late eighteenth century, the tendency of individual members always existed "to encroach on the authority of the whole."[136] The results were invariably the same: conflicts between separate cities or states; regional revolts and uprisings; third-party intervention; dissolution, anarchy, and conquest by foreign powers or rulers. These historical and contemporary case studies seemed to coincide exactly with what Americans had experienced since the Revolution. This seemed to be the path they would be forced to follow to the bitter end if remedial action were not taken immediately. There was no known system of federal rule—not even the Swiss Confederation extolled by Montesquieu, Turgot, Mably, and other republican theoreticians—that could serve as a model for Americans. Yet such historical comparisons were by no means fruitless, as they exposed the flaws in other systems and provided lessons on how to avoid them: "The uniform conclusion drawn from a review of ancient and modern confederacies, is, that instead of promoting the public happiness, or securing public tranquillity, they have, in every instance, been productive of anarchy and confusion; ineffectual for the preservation of harmony, and a prey to their own dissentions and foreign invasions . . . I most earnestly pray that America may have sufficient wisdom to avail herself of the instructive information she may derive from a contemplation of the sources of their misfortunes, and that she may escape a similar fate by avoiding the causes from which their infelicity sprung."[137]

Madison and Hamilton determined that the cardinal error inherent in a confederation was the inability of the central government to approach the citizens directly: "The great and radical vice in the construction of the existing Confederation is the principle of LEGISLATION for STATES OR GOVERNMENTS, in their CORPORATE OR COLLECTIVE CAPACITIES and as contradistinguished from the INDIVIDUALS of which they consist." As long as the general government could only indirectly approach the citizens by way of the states, its authority and ability to assert itself were more than doubtful. Stern words and appeals to moral, religious, and patriotic principles were of little avail; if society could really function on this basis, government would be redundant from the start: "Why has government been instituted at all? Because the passions of men will not conform to the dictates of reason and justice without constraint. Has it been found that bodies of men act with more rectitude or greater disinterestedness than individuals? The contrary of this has been inferred by all accurate observers of the conduct of mankind."[138] The use of military force under the auspices of executive authority did not constitute a viable solution to this dilemma. Even if the national government had the jurisdiction to institute such measures, the Union would more closely resemble a permanent battlefield than a smoothly functioning system of government. The situation changed dramatically, however, once the central administration could act directly on the people: "The government of the Union, like that of each State, must be able to address itself immediately to the hopes and fears of individuals; and to attract to its support those passions which have the strongest influence on the human heart." Then the "compassionate, benevolent power" of the federal bureaucracy, foremost embodied in tax inspectors and judges, could ensure that federal laws and regulations were respected, thus rendering more severe means of force essentially superfluous.[139]

Yet if the Union government was supreme, and if its actions no longer required the approval of all the states, could the Union still be considered a "confederated republic" as defined by Montesquieu? Hamilton did not perceive any contradiction to the often-quoted passages from *The Spirit of the Laws,* since the French philosopher had only peripherally and vaguely dealt with the structure of a federal republic.[140] Other Federalists distanced themselves from Montesquieu altogether, claiming a completely new federal system of government had been conceived in Philadelphia. James Wilson denied that the American federal republic resembled any of Montesquieu's configurations. At the Pennsylvania ratifying convention he argued that the new Constitution established "a system hitherto unknown."[141] John Stevens ("Americanus") pointed out that the "learned Frenchman" had based his theories on the knowledge and experience available to him at the time: "Had he been an American, and now living, I would stake my life on it, he would have formed different principles."[142]

In *Federalist* No. 39, Madison analyzed the Constitution with regard to five aspects: the foundation on which it was created, the sources of governmental authority, its manner of asserting this authority, the scope of its authority, and the provision for amendments. Items one and four could be regarded as "federal," only item three as "national," and the second and fifth were "mixed." Thus, the Constitution did, indeed, represent something entirely new and unprecedented: a government "partly national and partly federal," a republican system based on a blend of national and federal elements.[143] Rather than eliminating the states, the federal government was dependent upon their existence and incorporated them into the new order in various ways. The state legislatures elected the Senate and regulated the election of representatives; the states played a complex role in choosing the president, and they had an important role in both procedures for amending the Constitution. Of course, they would have to relinquish a portion of their coveted sovereignty for the common good, and the Constitution rerouted the flow of political power in the direction of a national entity. Still, the federal government could not exist or function without the states and their political institutions. Was it not absurd to assume a roof could remain hovering in the air if the walls collapsed?[144] In a long letter to Jefferson in Paris, Madison listed the "great objects" which Federalists were trying to attain: "(1) To unite a proper energy in the executive and a proper stability in the legislative departments, with the essential character of republican government. (2) To draw a line of demarcation which would give the general government every power requisite for general purposes, and leave to the states every power which might be most beneficially administered by them. (3) To provide for the different interests of different parts of the Union. (4) To adjust the clashing pretensions of the large and small states."[145]

Federalists considered it particularly important to emphasize that the federal government and the states would have two different spheres of operation. The first comprised all overarching matters relating to the well-being of the public at large (which is what was meant with the phrase "general welfare"); the second, the states' internal affairs. Each of the two authorities could act freely within its own sphere. The objection that this constituted an *imperium in imperio,* as raised by Antifederalists in accordance with contemporary thought, was dismissed by Federalists in a simple yet ingenious manner: neither the central government nor the states were sovereign; sovereign power was vested solely in the citizens of the thirteen states, in whose discretion it lay to delegate a certain set of powers to the Union and another set to the states. It was ridiculous to claim the central government would "devour" the states, insisted Timothy Pickering: "Do not the *people* constitute the *states*? Are not the *people* the *fountain* of *all power*? & Whether this flow in 13 distinct streams,—or in one large stream, with thirteen branches, is not the *fountain* still the same? and the *Majesty* of the *People* undiminished?"[146]

Wilson's "reserved powers" theory gave the impression that the areas of federal and state activity were clearly distinct from each other. He said in his October 6 speech that "congressional authority is to be collected, not from tacit implication, but from the positive grant expressed" in the Constitution. But in the Pennsylvania ratifying convention, on November 24, he admitted that only a principle had been established "that whatever object was confined in its nature and operation to a particular state ought to be subject to the separate government of the states, but whatever in its nature and operation extended beyond a particular state ought to be comprehended within the federal jurisdiction." It was "impracticable to enumerate and distinguish the various objects to which it extended."[147] Those Federalists with political experience and a legal background knew full well that the wording of the Constitution left much room for interpretation. The true distribution of power would only gradually evolve. Hamilton believed the citizens would for a time be more committed to the state legislatures, which were close by and familiar, than to the federal government. In the long run, however, their loyalty would be conferred on whichever institution best cared for their needs, and this could only be a well-organized central government.[148]

Initially, Madison was also not bothered by the thought that the center would eventually absorb all political power. In Philadelphia, he hypothesized that such a trend would have no "fatal consequences": "Taking the reverse of the supposition, that a tendency should be left in the State Governments towards an independence on the General Government and the gloomy consequences need not be pointed out."[149] Under the pressure of the public debate, he nevertheless allowed, in *Federalist* No. 51, that the states had a protective function which augmented the traditional separation of powers: "Hence a double security arises to the rights of the people. The different governments will control each other, at the same time that each will be controlled by itself."[150] In 1792, he praised this "double security" as "the best legacy ever left by law-givers to their country, and the best lesson ever given to the world by its benefactors."[151] This learning process, which in the span of five years elevated the makeshift solution of 1787 to the greatest achievement of the Revolution, distinguished Madison from most of his former Federalist colleagues and placed his political theories in the vicinity of the Republicans' anti-centralist views. The dispute over national-versus-state sovereignty had forced Federalists into the defensive, as they found themselves at odds with public opinion and the authority of important writers. They probably were not entirely convinced by their own ideas and were struggling to construct a theoretical foundation for the "partly national, partly federal" government. Only the future could reveal whether the centralist and particularist forces were capable of maintaining the balance needed for the survival of the whole system.

The Compatibility of Republican Liberty with a Strong Central Authority

Federalists generally had a more positive attitude toward governmental authority than most opponents of the Constitution, being less concerned about protections *against* the government than about the security and support a government owed *to* its citizens. Federalists denied the existence of a fundamental antagonism between the two principles of order and freedom: "There is no quarrel between Government and liberty; the former is the shield and protector of the latter. The war is between Government and licentiousness, faction, turbulence, and other violations of the rules of society, to preserve liberty." It was understandable that Americans had overemphasized the principle of liberty during the Revolution; now it was time for the country to regain its equilibrium and to pursue another equally important objective: "I mean a principle of strength and stability in the organization of government, and vigor in its operations."[152]

It was precisely the fierce opposition to the Constitution that convinced Benjamin Franklin that Americans would never allow themselves to be tyrannized: "And thus the Happiness of its People is less in danger from an Excess of Power in the Governors, than from the Defect of due Obedience even to their own Laws, in the Governed."[153] In response to the skepticism of Philip Mazzei, Madison explained that the problem in America was the need to redress the "defect of energy & stability," whereas people all over Europe were suffering from "too much government."[154] Fellow congressman Nathan Dane also believed a backlash was unavoidable, and feared it might go too far in the other direction: "We have experienced the evils of a Government popular in its principles and too popular, on many occasions at least in its administration—we are coming back and I have for sometime felt anxious that the political pendulum may stop in the proper medium, and in that point only . . . we are in the mean Stages of society, in which protection and obedience, property, law, and liberty are all to be respected."[155]

Forfeiting some of one's liberties so as to better enjoy the others was an essential aspect of the social contract. To provide benefits and ensure the "greatest possible good to the greatest number of people," the national government had to be endowed with the necessary authority.[156] The distrust of power must not be allowed to impede or even paralyze the essential activities of government. Carried to extremes and directed against a freely elected government, this "republican jealousy" became a destructive force. "Why should we be alarmed with visionary evils?" was the standard question posed by James Wilson and repeated by Federalists everywhere.[157] The central administration, Pelatiah Webster explained, must have "a supreme power, superior to and able to controul each of its parts. . . . The supreme power of government ought to be full, definite, established, and acknowledged." In light of the frailties of human nature, the possibility that governments might occasionally exceed their authority could never be ruled out. Nonetheless, it was pointless "to withhold the necessary powers of government, from the supreme rulers of it, least they should abuse or misapply those powers." Far more dangerous was a weak government incapable of operating an efficient and just administration and lacking the energy "which is absolutely necessary for the support of the State, and the security of the people." The capacity to do good always presupposed the potential of abuse. According to Oliver Ellsworth, it was not excessive governmental authority that was responsible for the plight of American farmers. The opposite was true: "You are oppressed for want of power which can protect commerce, encourage business and create a ready demand for the productions of your farms."[158]

The Constitution merely ensured that the federal government was granted the authority and coercive power necessary to live up to its responsibilities. This included, in particular, the right to levy imposts and customs duties, to regulate trade between the states and with foreign countries, and to maintain an army and navy. Federalists rejected any attempts to constitutionally limit or more precisely define these requisite powers. To Hamilton's mind, logic dictated that the central government be given the unrestricted right to impose taxes: "Money is, with propriety, considered as the vital principle of the body politic; as that which sustains its life and motion and enables it to perform its most essential functions. A complete power, therefore, to procure a regular and adequate supply of it, as far as the resources of the community will permit, may be regarded as an indispensable ingredient in every constitution."[159] It was probable that for many years to come, the essential funds would be raised primarily through duties on imports and taxes on certain consumer goods.[160] But no one could look far enough into the future to allow for every possible contingency.

It was Hamilton's conviction that the "enumerated powers" merely provided an outline of the goals and purpose of the federal government. The means of achieving those goals, by contrast, could not be listed individually and must be left to the discretion of the government. If the right of taxation were recognized as imperative to the survival of the Union, then it must not be restricted. It would be equally ill conceived to place constraints on the federal government in the area of defense: "The authorities essential to the common defense are these—to raise armies—to build and equip fleets—to prescribe rules for the government of both—to direct their operations—to provide for their support. These powers ought to exist without limitation: Because it is impossible to foresee or define the extent and variety of national exigencies, and the correspondent extent & variety of the means which may be necessary to satisfy them." A sentence in *Federalist* No. 34 reveals the essence of Hamilton's views on military power and government: "I acknowledge my aversion to every project that is calculated to disarm the government of a single weapon, which in any possible contingency might be usefully employed for the general defense and security."[161] Federalists criticized the militia, the "republican soldiers," as woefully inadequate, and announced to the astonished citizenry that a small standing army was both indispensable and politically acceptable. Ample security was provided by the stipulation that Congress could appropriate money for the military for no longer than two years—twice as long as in Great Britain.[162]

Federalists saw the national judiciary as a unifying force that would help to extend federal authority into the states. Judge James Sullivan viewed this institution as "the mainspring of the whole machinery"; Charles Pinckney referred to the judiciary as the "key-stone of the arch, the means of connecting and binding the whole together, of preserving uniformity in all the judicial proceedings of the Union."[163] It was believed that lower federal courts would prove especially advantageous in states like Rhode Island, where the legal system was a mockery of justice. Federalists believed that paper money, soft currencies, and regulations favoring debtors were a threat to property rights and individual liberties. The elimination of these evils would represent a significant contribution to the general welfare. The Constitution, and the strength of the federal government, were guardians of the citizens' well-being: "The stronger we make our government, the greater protection it can afford us, and the greater will our safety be under it." The Union would then be more than a simple conglomeration of states, having acquired a dynamic character which generated power: "The Thirteen States all united and well cemented together, are a strong, rich and formidable body, not of stationary maturated power, but increasing every day in riches, strengths, and numbers." The true goal of the Constitution was thus not to limit power but to create it.[164]

Of course, remarks of this kind were not well suited to dispelling the concerns of skeptics. Instead, the emphasizing of such terms as energy, efficiency, stability, order, and authority only added to the fears of the opposition. An unfortunate contribution to these fears was made by Pennsylvania Chief Justice Thomas McKean, who saw fit to declaim at the ratifying convention "that a despotism, if well administered, is the best form of government invented by human ingenuity."[165] A storm of protest ensued, putting Federalists in an extremely difficult situation. With even greater insistence than before, Antifederalists and others asked for assurances that the Constitution would not endanger liberty. In their response, Federalists pointed to three safeguards for republican liberties: the principle of representation, the complex structure of the federal government, and the great territorial extent and variety of the Union.

REPRESENTATION

Federalists dismissed the talk of an "aristocracy" as ludicrous. Even a superficial reading of the Constitution sufficed to prove that the new system more than satisfied all the demands of republican theories: it was democratic through and through. "Its origin is the voice & its end the good of the people," proclaimed David Ramsay. Hamilton referred to the proposed system as a "representative democracy," while Wilson described its fundamental principles as "purely democratical." All the governmental powers could be traced "to one great and noble source, THE PEOPLE." Tench Coxe called the people "the fountain of power and public honor." The will of the people pervaded every article of the Constitution and would always have the last word. The new order thus rightfully deserved the name "true democracy."[166] These democratic qualities resulted from the "elective principles" on which the federal government was based: "The uniform experience of history demonstrates that government founded on elective principles or on the broad basis of the people, never will violate the laws of justice and good order, unless the people are so stupid as to neglect their rights, or so corrupt as to countenance the conduct of a wicked administration."[167] The House of Representatives was to be directly elected, the Senate and the president would be chosen by the people indirectly. The majority would prevail on all levels, and Americans would thus be the first people in history to live under a government thoroughly dedicated to the principle of representation: "The world has left to America the glory and happiness of forming a government where representation shall at once supply the basis and the cement of the superstructure."[168]

Officials of the federal government were trustees acting on behalf of the people, from whom they came and to whom they would return when their term of service ended. The electorate could and must have a certain amount of faith in these public servants; otherwise it would be impossible for them to carry out their duties. In Madison's opinion, they deserved this trust more than state legislators. Politicians acting on the national scene would be generally more experienced and better educated, would have to convince a larger constituency of their talents and abilities and to pass through a kind of filtering process at the local and state levels which ensured that only the fittest would reach the top. This "regular uninterrupted gradation" represented, in John Stevens' estimation, "a perfection in Republican Government, heretofore unknown and unprecedented."[169] In *Federalist* No. 35, Hamilton dismissed the idea of an "actual representation" of all social classes as utterly unrealistic. With few exceptions, tradesmen and laborers would always vote for merchants: "They know that the merchant is their natural patron and friend; and they are aware that however great the confidence they may justly feel in their own good sense, their interests can be more effectually promoted by the merchant than by themselves." Furthermore, elections in expanded districts served as impediments to corruption, since it was basically impossible to manipulate a majority of eligible voters spread out over such large areas. This would ensure, explained Jonathan Jackson, that power would be delegated only to those "who by nature, education, and good dispositions, are qualified for government." Annual elections and rotation requirements would then not only be unnecessary, they would be downright ridiculous, insisted Noah Webster in a review of the "Federal Farmer" pamphlet in the May 1788 issue of the *American Magazine*. Legislative terms of two, four, or six years would have to be the minimum if the public were to truly benefit from the mandates granted to members of Congress and the president. The decision as to whether or not they should be allowed to continue their public service was perfectly safe in the hands of the voters.

This line of argumentation made it possible for Federalists to use the words "democracy" and "democratic" just as naturally as their critics. However, these terms had different connotations for each side. Federalists did not believe a democratic government had to be close to the people and subject to their direct control. In fact, the quality of governance increased proportionately to the distance from the people. Direct democracies were nothing more than mob rule. "In proportion as you approach in a Constitution of government to a complete democracy," wrote John Adams to Henry Marchant of Rhode Island, "by the same degree your people must become Savages."[170] The *Albany Gazette* of November 8, 1787, put it even more succinctly: "A Government too popular borders on tyranny." Representative democracies even on the state level still tended toward instability and tyranny of the majority. Only at the highest, national level did the principle of representation guarantee both security and justice. A "State Soldier" from Virginia openly proclaimed: "The more independent a government is therefore of the people, under proper restraints, the more likely it is to produce that justice."[171] Precisely, the small size of Congress and the relative distance from its constituents would prove beneficial. A large representative body was prone to demagogy, susceptible to rapid changes of mood, and more closely approximated a mob than a legislative assembly. According to a conviction expressed in the *Connecticut Journal*, "An overabundant representation is an evil which this country has long complained of."[172] Besides, the national legislature was not supposed to defend local and regional interests at all costs, but rather to devote all its energies to the common good of the Union. Chosen by the people and thoroughly informed about the nation's problems by way of exhaustive discussions with fellow congressmen, only these national legislators were competent to assume this great responsibility. In this way, Federalists managed to align their hierarchical-elitist views with the sovereignty of the people, representation, and majority rule. The people formed the base of the political pyramid and were the source of all power. However, the most important decisions were best taken at the top by a select group who were as knowledgeable as they were patriotic.

COMPLEX GOVERNMENT

The deliberations on the Constitution in Philadelphia had been influenced by a desire to restore some of the balance and restraint of the British Constitution and the imperial system. It was not against these constitutional precepts that the war had been fought; it had been waged against a Parliament that claimed a power to legislate in American matters, "in all cases whatsoever," and an administration far removed by corrupt practices from the "true" British Constitution. Many agreed with Hamilton's opinion "that the British Government was the best of the world: and that he doubted much whether any thing short of it would do in America."[173] Pierce Butler admitted to a friend from England that in many respects the convention had taken as its example the "Constitution of Britain, when in its purity." Writing as an "American Citizen," Tench Coxe hailed "the constitution of England, as it stood on paper," as "one of the freest at that time existing in the world."[174] Many an American longed for a return to the—at least in theory—well-regulated affairs under the "mixed constitution," which some even regarded as the basis of England's phenomenal rise to the status of world power.

Leading Federalists were careful not to overdo the comparisons between their own plan and the English Constitution. There was still too much resentment toward England and everything English. Instead of emphasizing the similarities, Federalists preferred to concentrate on those elements that distinguished the American Constitution from the British model. In newspaper articles and pamphlets, they pointed to significant differences from British constitutional theory, and in particular from the "degenerate" political practices of the English government: "Compare the *Fœderal Constitution* with this *highly extolled government,* and you will find its excellencies eclipsed, like the faint lustre of the *moon,* by the dazzling splendor of the *sun.*"[175] The American Constitution was "vastly superior," "surely more popular," and contained "all the theoretical and practical advantages of the British constitution without any of its defects or corruptions."[176] Madison flatly rejected what he said was a frequent "impropriety," the characterization of the British government as a republic. The term "republic" was reserved for a system of rule "which derives all its powers directly or indirectly from the great body of the people; and is administered by persons holding their offices during pleasure, for a limited period, or during good behavior."[177] As opposed to the British system, the American Constitution satisfied precisely these requirements.

It was true, Tench Coxe argued, that the American president and the British king had similar powers. However, the president did not command the "immense patronage" of a supreme head of an established church, and he lacked the "enormous influence" the Crown wielded over Parliament. His office was not hereditary; he had to be elected and to run for reelection every four years. Candidates who were unsuitable by nature thus had no chance of election, and any officeholder who proved to be incompetent or unworthy of the position could be removed in the usual manner at the end of the term or through impeachment proceedings. In Coxe's view, therefore, the president was the first servant of the people and not a substitute monarch: "As he is created through the Electors by the people at large, he must ever look up to the support of his creators. . . . Whatever of dignity or authority he possesses *is a delegated part of their majesty and their political omnipotence, transiently vested in him by the people themselves for their own happiness.*" Unlike the members of the British upper house, senators were not hereditary but elected by the state legislatures, and did not constitute a separate social class removed from the citizenry: "As our President bears no *resemblance to a king,* so we shall see the Senate have no similitude to nobles . . . not being hereditary, their *collective* knowledge, wisdom and virtue are not precarious, *for by these qualities alone are they to obtain their offices;* and they will have none of the *peculiar* follies and vices of those men *who possess power merely because their fathers held it before them.*" Finally, the House of Representatives was in a much better position to express the will of the people than the British lower house, where a great number of delegates championed the rights of "rotten borroughs," while large cities like Manchester and Liverpool only had a few spokesmen each.[178]

The Philadelphia plan thus corresponded to the ideal of a mixed constitution founded on democratic-republican principles. At the hub of the system, the office of the president radiated the authority and dignity of a monarchy. The holder of that office had the ability to execute federal laws with the necessary energy and to act quickly and decisively in times of crisis. Congress represented the interests of the people and of the states. The democratic principle reached its pinnacle in the House of Representatives, vested with the sole power to initiate tax bills. It was protected against uncontrolled, eruptive bursts of emotion through the process of "filtration" described by Madison, and it was kept in check by the Senate, the president, and the courts. The independent judges appointed for life ("during good behavior") would ensure that the principles and provisions of the Constitution were adhered to on the federal and state levels. If the English system provided a degree of freedom hitherto unknown, how much more liberal and secure must life be under the republican Constitution of the United States! It was just as complex as the British Constitution, without the need for balancing the interests of the monarch, the nobility, and the people. Instead, it divided the powers according to their function into an executive, legislative, and judicial branch. Federalists were confident that this innovative, "artificial" separation of power would withstand the test of time. They pointed out that "complex" state governments like those in Massachusetts, New York, and Maryland were already functioning according to this principle and were comparable to the federal Constitution.

The fact that various Antifederalists alternately argued that the president, the Supreme Court, and Congress were overly powerful and hence a threat to liberty only proved to Federalists that the Philadelphia Convention had succeeded in creating a well-balanced system. Each of the three branches possessed only the authority it needed to do its job and protect itself against domination by the other two. Of decisive importance here were both the separation and cooperation of the three arms of government. As actual practice in the various states had shown, a total separation was neither possible nor desirable. The three branches should not paralyze each other, they should mesh like the cogs of a wheel. Accordingly, watch and machine metaphors were exceedingly popular among the Constitution's supporters.[179]

This complex system of divided, balanced, and interconnected powers constituted, in Madison's view, the best guarantee "against a gradual concentration of the several powers in the same department," but was not intended to prevent the president and Congress from governing energetically. There was a dynamic character to Madison's concept that "ambition must be made to counteract ambition." The energy generated by this rivalry between the branches of government would fully serve the common good and the betterment of the Union. The federal government as a whole would always remain under the control of the people and within the limits set by the Constitution.

THE EXTENDED REPUBLIC

The concept of separation of powers and checks and balances was only partially successful in countering the objections and allaying the concerns of the opposition. Was it not possible for a particular social class, political party, or ambitious special interest to gain control of all components of the machinery of government and transform this cleverly devised apparatus into an instrument of oppression? In answer to this question, Madison provided his third major contribution—in addition to his historical analysis of the structural flaws inherent in past confederacies and his theory of representation through selection and filtration—to the debate over the Constitution. He believed the Union's vast size and diversity, regarded by Antifederalists as an insurmountable obstacle to the creation of a republican central government, was precisely what guaranteed that no single clique, faction, or party would ever be able to acquire absolute power. Factions and parties, he explained in *Federalist* No. 10, were rooted in human nature and the manifold sentiments and abilities of the people. Anyone wanting to banish them from political life would first have to eliminate the condition that enabled them to exist in the first place, republican liberty, or to imbue all people with the same opinions, interests, and passions. The first solution would be as unwise as the second was impracticable and utopian. Hence, the best procedure would be to accept parties as the natural product of conflicting interests and to integrate them into the political system: "The regulation of these various and interfering interests forms the principal task of modern legislation and involves the spirit of party and faction in the necessary and ordinary operations of government."[180]

The greatest danger was that a majority might coalesce into a single party and exploit the government, "to sacrifice to its ruling passion or interest both the public good and the rights of other citizens." Whereas a minority's designs on power were kept in check by the convention of majority rule, the republican system had no built-in impediment to a majority's arbitrary use of power. This was all the more true—and in this regard Madison differed from Montesquieu—of a "pure democracy," such as might be found in a small city-state where the citizens gathered in the marketplace to decide public issues. Here the passions and interests of the majority rapidly manifested themselves and were immediately transformed into political decisions. This situation improved as soon as the direct democracy was replaced by a representative republic. Yet a vast territory offered the best remedy, in Madison's opinion: "Extend the sphere and you take in a greater variety of parties and interests; you make it less probable that a majority of the whole will have a common motive to invade the rights of other citizens; or if such a common motive exists, it will be more difficult for all who feel it to discover their own strength and to act in unison with each other. . . . Hence, it clearly appears that the same advantages which a republic has over a democracy in controlling the effects of faction is enjoyed by a large over a small republic—is enjoyed by the Union over the States composing it. . . . In the extent and proper structure of the Union, therefore, we behold a Republican remedy for the diseases most incident to Republican Government."[181] The liberties and rights of the citizens were thus best protected by extending the Union's territory. Within certain geographical limits, economic, ethnic, religious, and cultural diversity were not obstacles but rather advantages to a republican form of government.

In *Federalist* No. 51, Madison again dealt with this key issue regarding the relationship between government and society: "Whilst all authority in [the federal republic of the United States] will be derived from and dependent on the society, the society itself will be broken into so many parts, interests and classes of citizens, that the rights of individuals, or of a minority, will be in little danger from interested combinations of the majority. . . . In the extended republic of the United States, and among the great variety of interests, parties, and sects which it embraces, a coalition of a majority of the whole society could seldom take place on any other principles than those of justice and the general good. . . . It is no less certain than it is important, notwithstanding the contrary opinions which have been entertained, that the larger the society, provided it lie within a practicable sphere, the more duly capable it will be of self-government."[182]

Madison broke new ground with his "extended sphere" theory, far removed from the teachings of Montesquieu and Hume, to whom he was otherwise so much indebted. Hume had postulated that a vast country could, in fact, form a republic (commonwealth) and was better adapted to this form of government than any other. However, preconditions for this "Perfect Commonwealth" were the division of the country into smaller and smaller segments, as well as indirect elections limiting the citizens' unmediated participation in government to the local level. Madison's point of departure, on the other hand, was the territorial and social structure already established in the United States, and he supported the direct election of the House of Representatives in large voter districts. Whereas Montesquieu believed the main threat to small, self-governing communities came from external sources, Madison stressed the inner weakness induced by the principle of direct democracy. Joining several such entities to form a union would not suffice to eliminate their key disadvantage: political instability. Only an extended republic with a strong central authority and a federal structure offered adequate protection against both the danger of despotism, as described by Montesquieu in respect of large empires, and the threat of anarchy, which affected republican confederations just as much as small city-states.[183]

Republican Virtue and the Constitution

It is difficult to assess the actual influence Madison's innovative ideas had on his contemporaries—or even his own supporters, for that matter. Some considered his theories too elaborate and complicated, while others dismissed them as an after-the-fact justification for decisions that had been taken in Philadelphia for purely pragmatic reasons. Madison had made a large number of fundamental contributions during the Federal Convention, and he was one of the most active leaders in the struggle for ratification. Even so, he remained an independent thinker who attempted to consider matters from a distance.[184] Many Federalists tended to be intolerant of opponents, were less prepared to make compromises, and viewed political and constitutional issues pragmatically. They had nothing against a complete supremacy of the central government; in fact, that was exactly what they were striving to accomplish. In actuality, they considered no one but themselves to be truly competent to govern, and the federal government was their natural domain. At the same time, they did not necessarily see themselves as a "party" as such. They simply believed they understood and represented the common good. It cannot be clearly ascertained from their writings whether they endeavored to attain political and social harmony by balancing opposing forces in accordance with Madison's theories, or whether they rather subscribed to the traditional view that the interests of all social classes, economic interests, and regions were actually complementary, and interim periods of discord were merely the result of the acts of agitators and demagogues.

An additional unresolved question was whether a lasting political entity could be founded solely or primarily on the pursuit of self-interest and group interests. A number of Federalist essays downplaying the value and necessity of "civic virtue" pointed in this direction. Noah Webster went the furthest in this respect by attempting to replace Montesquieu's fundamental republican principle of "virtue" with the principle of "property": "Wherever we cast our eyes, we see this truth, that *property* is the basis of *power;* and this being established as a cardinal point, directs us to the means of preserving our freedom. . . . The system of the great Montesquieu will ever be erroneous, till the words *property or lands in fee simple* are substituted for *virtue,* throughout his *Spirit of Laws. Virtue,* patriotism, or love of country, never was and never will be, till men's natures are changed, a fixed, permanent principle and support of government."[185] At the same time, Federalists reserved the right to resist arbitrary rule violently in the event all security precautions failed: "If the representatives of the people betray their constituents, there is then no source left but the exertion of that original right of self-defence, which is paramount to all positive forms of government."[186] Yet how were republican virtues supposed to prevail in times of constitutional crisis if they fulfilled no practical purpose under "normal" circumstances? Did this not prove that a republican society required an underlying spiritual foundation, an ethical-moral consensus which transcended material interests.

In general, Antifederalists placed greater value on the role of "virtue" in sustaining a republican political system. However, they did occasionally make concessions. A local "Cato" in Charleston acknowledged that virtue may suffice to hold Plato's imaginary republic together, "But in other Republics, and in modern times, I deny that Virtue alone is adequate to tumultuous operations." In a similar vein, men like William Findley in Pennsylvania and James Winthrop ("Agrippa") in Massachusetts sought to prove that "virtue" and "commerce," civic morals and the pursuit of material gain, were not mutually exclusive.[187] For their part, Federalists conceded that a republic was always in danger no matter how well it was constituted. If the love of liberty and willingness to make sacrifices were abandoned, even the best constitution would gradually lose its effectiveness until nothing remained but a form without content. However, there was hope in the fact that civic virtue was as much the result of good government as it was its source. This manner of thinking helped Federalists to distance themselves from a purely functional, mechanistic view of government and unconditional faith in the Constitution that at times pervaded their writings.

Past and Future

Nothing appealed to eighteenth-century Americans more than historical precedents and arguments clothed in historical images. History was considered the most instructive branch of practical philosophy at colleges and an instrument of social and political criticism. To the Enlightenment era, the "Histories of all Ages & Nations" seemed like open books waiting to be read and exploited.[188] Reform proposals now needed to be legitimized by historical references rather than religious ones. Contemporary sources continuously stressed the importance of historical knowledge in everyday life.

The past was a "faithful monitor" revealing the "experience of human nature" and the "accumulated experience of the ages."[189] Mostly, the implication was that one should and must learn from past mistakes. According to a pamphlet that appeared in New Hampshire in advance of the Constitutional Convention, "The states of Greece and Rome were overturned by their licentious abuse of liberty.—The states of Holland were obliged to deviate from republican principle, in order to prevent the dissolution of their government. We ought, then, to take warning from the misconduct of other republics in the abuse of liberty, and avoid similar practices."[190] "The history of monarchy is the history of crimes," lectured New York Antifederalist Abraham Yates. The Virginia legislature based its demand for a second constitutional convention on the principles "which have been established by the melancholy example of other nations in different ages." Madison regarded the sum total of all classical, medieval, and modern confederations he had been studying since 1786 as instructive failures.[191]

During the ratification debate, both the Constitution's supporters and adversaries made selective use of historical facts, each in their own way, and came to different conclusions. This had little to do with the historical sources they used. The material available to both sides was essentially identical and—prior to the existence of critical historiography—equally problematic and unreliable. Rather, the contrasting interpretations were rooted in each party's ideological predispositions, as a result of which the Constitution evoked dissimilar associations and images. Some Antifederalists blamed the republics' downfall solely on a loss of virtue. More often, however, they attributed it to the unrestrained greed of "the few" for power and property. Greece and Rome provided the best examples of the destructive effects of this phenomenon, though it was prevalent throughout history.[192] Federalists, by contrast, pinpointed direct democracy as the source of all evil: a lack of counterbalances and constraints destroyed the inner cohesion of republics and subjected their citizens to mob rule and anarchy.

The diverse "ancient and modern confederacies," generally consisting of small republics, most closely resembled the situation in the United States. It was therefore assumed that comparisons with these systems would prove the most fertile. Here again, contrasting premises produced contrasting results. Antifederalists agreed with Montesquieu, Beccaria, Rousseau, and the Abbé de Mably that only small states could form republics and that a confederation represented the best way for them to survive and prosper. It followed that Americans had been fundamentally correct to adopt the Articles of Confederation, despite its considerable weaknesses: "Thus it appears from the first authorities, that we have chosen the form of government best adapted to the extent of our country, and the genius of the people. It is composed of states of the same nature of the republican kinds, and in its constitutions is superior to any confederation on earth."[193]

If such unions ultimately failed, it was because of the aristocratic inclinations of their leaders in conjunction with the lack of vigilance and the moral depravity of the citizens, or they were conquered by an overwhelming foreign power. In any case, the democratic and federal principle was not the cause of their demise. The fall of the United Netherlands, brought on in 1787 by conservative circles collaborating with the absolutist regimes of neighboring countries, provided a dramatic illustration of this. The Swiss Confederation, on the other hand, seemed to offer the best example of a successful, smoothly functioning union. "If these small republics, in the neighbourhood of the warlike and intriguing Courts of Paris, Vienna, and Berlin, have kept their freedom and original forms of government, is it not reasonable to suppose, that the same good sense and love of freedom, on this side of the Atlantic, will secure us from all attempts within and without?" conjectured a "Newport Man."[194] At the Virginia ratifying convention, Patrick Henry elaborated on how Switzerland comprised democratic and aristocratic cantons but had nevertheless been held together for more than four hundred years by the "Swiss spirit": "They have encountered and overcome immense difficulties with patience and fortitude. In this vicinity of powerful and ambitious monarchs, they have retained their independence, republican simplicity and valour."[195] Several other writers for the opposition joined in the praise of Switzerland, among them Luther Martin, Samuel Bryan, George Bryan, and Arthur Lee. The "Democratic Federalist" also suggested that Americans emulate the "glorious example" of the freedom-loving, virtuous, and modest Swiss. Like the United States, the Swiss confederation was a republic whose cantons were organized around a "federal government." Surrounded and eyed with envy by Europe's most powerful nations, it had managed to defend its independence and prosperity over the centuries with nothing but a militia, "and has never been known to have a standing army, except when in actual war."[196]

The Federalist's conception of history dispensed with both the myth of the small republic and Montesquieu's ideal of a "confederated republic." Proceeding from case to case, Madison and Hamilton showed how each confederation was doomed to fail from the start because it was constructed on false principles. Even classical confederations of cities like the Achaean and Lycian leagues apparently had only been able to survive for relatively long periods of time because they had already formed representative organs and strong, unified executives that extended beyond Montesquieu's conception of a "confederated republic." In a direct dispute with Patrick Henry, Madison also refuted the idyllic depiction of Switzerland: "Even there, dissensions and wars of a bloody nature, have been frequently seen between the cantons. A peculiar coincidence of circumstances contributes to the continuance of their political connection. Their feeble association owes its existence to their singular situation."[197] The bitter lessons learned by the United States during the "critical period" merely served to confirm the universal truth that a confederation of republics could not survive, or could only survive under unusually favorable circumstances. This contention distanced Federalists from a tradition of political thought extending back to the Renaissance and strongly influencing all of seventeenth- and eighteenth-century European republicanism.[198] When confronted with the argument that history had also established that large territories could not be governed along republican principles, some Federalists promptly switched from historical criticism to the complete rejection of historical comparisons. At the very least, they denied that any criteria or standards derived from history and experience could apply to the Constitution. Thus it was simply not possible "to draw perfect parallels between an ancient and a modern state"; or so little was known of past confederations "that they must now be considered rather as subjects of curiosity, than of use or information."[199]

There were also much more radical, categorical disclaimers. On December 24, 1787, "Examiner" wrote in the *New York Journal:* "As there never existed a nation since the world was made, who were circumstanced as we are, so it is impossible for us to derive any information or advantage from the sources of former experience." An extra edition of the *Virginia Independent Chronicle* began with the statement that historical arguments were pointless, "for this is a new case, without its resemblance in history, and unknown to the theorists, of ancient and modern times."[200] This signaled the emergence of a new concept, one that contrasted the notion of the universality of all human experience with a belief in the historical uniqueness of a country and its inhabitants. America was a distinct nation, the Americans set their own standards, and the Constitution represented a new turn of events in world history. In this context, the admiration expressed by John Adams, in the form of a question, almost seemed modest: "What would Aristotle and Plato have said, if anyone had talked to them, of a fœderative Republick of thirteen states, inhabiting a Country of five hundred Leagues in extent?"[201] Caleb Strong ("Alfred") went further still: "No people yet known in history, have appeared on the great theatre of human affairs, with such illustrious magnanimity as those of the United States of America."[202] Before Major William Pierce, the featured speaker at a Fourth of July celebration in 1788, turned to the new Constitution and the country's bright future, he reviewed the history of the world for his audience and concluded: "With what contempt does an American look back and trace over such scenes of past folly!"[203] The Constitution seemed to burst the dam that had restrained mankind from surging to higher and higher levels of perfection. From this point on, predicted James Wilson, the "revolutions in government" would be of a different quality, having been purposefully inaugurated as "progressive steps in improving the knowledge of government, and increasing the happiness of society and mankind."[204]

The cyclical perception of history, very common among Antifederalists as well as some Federalists, was giving way to a new belief in linear progress or progression in stages. How could the tiny Alpine republic of Switzerland maintain its allure in this context? Even if the Swiss confederation represented the consummation of republican ideals, it would remain an unsuitable model for the considerably larger, wealthier, and much more dynamic North American continent. This view made it possible to attack Antifederalists on two fronts. Their high regard for the insignificant European republics and confederations made them appear old-fashioned. It also weakened their credibility, since most of them realized themselves, or at least suspected, that the future held more in store for the United States than simply imitating the virtuous and frugal Swiss. In a forceful way, this point was made by a writer in the *Hampshire Gazette* of July 9, 1788: "The republick of Switzerland in Europe, has long been celebrated for its virtues, and impartiality to its citizens; but that government, when brought in comparison with the Grand Federal Columbian Republick, which is now on the eve of its establishment in America, for extensiveness of empire, for the encouragement and promotion of those arts and sciences . . . must bear but a small comparison."

The Rising American Empire

If Federalists acknowledged the success of any historical model, it was the union between England and Scotland in 1707. Roger Sherman posed the rhetorical question whether the events in America couldn't be seen as a parallel to the "so much dreaded union between England and Scotland, where the Scots, instead of becoming a poor, despicable, dependent people, have become more secure, happy, and respectable." For Hamilton, Scotland's incorporation into Great Britain "subdued its fierce and ungovernable spirit, and reduced it within those rules of subordination, which a more rational and a more energetic system of civil polity had previously established in the latter kingdom."[205] In comments like these, Federalists intentionally or unintentionally revealed the standards by which they wished to be measured. They took the "westward course of empire" metaphor seriously, which implied that the center of world power, having migrated from Asia to Greece, Rome, and then England, would some day shift to the American continent. "I have no doubt but in time this western empire will exceed in wealth, dignity and greatness, the most famed nations of ancient or modern date," proclaimed a letter writer from Portland, Maine. Antifederalists lacked a proper appreciation for the "future greatness of the AMERICAN EMPIRE," complained another correspondent. "United under one common energetick head, America will become the envy and admiration of the nations of the world."[206] Hamilton had already touched on the idea of an "empire" in his first *Federalist* essay, and by the eleventh essay he had become even more explicit: "Let the thirteen States, bound together in a strict and indissoluble Union, concur in erecting one great American system superior to the controul of all transatlantic force or influence and able to dictate the terms of the connection between the old and new world."[207] On a popular level, empire prophesies turned up in various poems and songs, a typical example being "THE GRAND CONSTITUTION: OR, The PALLADIUM of COLUMBIA" from the *Massachusetts Centinel:*

And riches and honour flow in with each tide,
Kamschatka and China with wonder shall stare,
That the Federal Stripes should wave gracefully there.

Here Plenty and Order and Freedom shall dwell,
And your Shayses and Dayses won't dare to rebel—
Independence and culture shall graciously smile,
And the Husbandman reap the fruit of his toil.

Our Freedom we've won, and the prize let's maintain
Our hearts *are all right—*
Unite, Boys, Unite,
And our EMPIRE *in glory shall ever remain.*[208]

The reserved response to such proclamations by the Constitution's adversaries was largely due to the concurrent existence of two conceptions of an empire. The Antifederalists' restraint was based on the pre-Revolutionary understanding of this term, with its aggressive-expansionistic and despotic connotations. They often admonished their compatriots to place "domestic peace and justice" before "national glory."[209] To the "Farmer" from Maryland and "John DeWitt" from New England, "empire" and "republic" designated two mutually exclusive configurations. They agreed that America should assume its appropriate place in the circle of world powers; however, the United States was created as a "fœderal union," not as a "Universal Empire."

An empire of the type envisioned by Federalists would be preoccupied with military pursuits, constantly attacking other countries to satisfy its thirst for expansion and glory.[210] Seeming justification for this concern could be found in the claim by "Caesar" that ratification would signal the beginning decline of Europe's political might. A submission to the *American Herald* warned that a "*monstrous, unweildy Empire,* more extensive than that of the Roman at its height; and in point of freedom, not exceeding the *Republic of Venice,*" would emerge from the ruins of the thirteen sovereign states.[211]

Since 1776, however, when John Adams's *Novanglus* letters appeared, a different, "patriotic" conception of an empire had begun to take hold which envisaged a peaceful, trade-oriented, culturally flourishing "American Empire." Antifederalists were not altogether willing to surrender the use of this term to their rivals. "Agrippa" drew a distinction, for example, between a centralized empire held together by political constraints and military force, and an "American Empire" which allowed the individual states to retain their sovereignty and whose "bond of union" was founded on mutually beneficial commerce.[212] The precondition for the establishment of this peaceful empire, according to the Federalists, was the adoption of the new Constitution: "We shall then behold America with extended arms, inviting the numerous, oppressed and distressed inhabitants of Europe; we shall see them flocking to America; our woods and waste lands will become at once valuable, and in great demand . . . every European ship which should enter our ports, would, by properly laid duties, assist in paying off our debts;—our taxes will considerably diminish—our national character will rise—arts and sciences will be cultivated with redoubled ardour—every kind of business will increase—in a word, this continent will soon become, under the new government, the delight and envy of the European world."[213]

Since such dreams were deep in the heart of virtually every American, it was extremely difficult for Antifederalists to present their gloomy predictions. Even allusions to the fall of other great empires were summarily rejected: "If we consider the progress of Empires that have hitherto subsisted in the world, we shall find the short duration of their most glorious periods, owing to causes which will not operate against that of North-America.—Those Empires were formed by conquest . . . ; when the bond of union, force, was weakened, they returned to their original and natural separation. . . . America hath an advantage decisive of its duration. This great continent was chiefly peopled by British subjects whose language and national character were the same . . . so that the seeds of decay sown in the very formation of the ancient Empires will have no existence here."[214] This vision of national greatness was effective and seductive. Federalists called on their fellow citizens to think in continental terms, to join in the creation of a trade empire that would ensure domestic prosperity and earn America a seat at the table of the world's great powers. This was a convincing agenda, worth fighting for and very appealing to the middle classes and all citizens throughout the Union who had not yet made a firm commitment to radical Country doctrines.

4

Party Formation and Convention Elections

What a miserable business is this of annual elections! how unstable the exercise of government, and what compliances are even good men obliged to stoop to, if they mean to keep in place! But it is republicanism, and it is treason to say a word against it.

JEREMY BELKNAP TO EBENEZER HAZARD, MARCH 10, 1787

It has been a generally received maxim, that frequent and free elections are the greatest security against corruption in government, and the oppression of the people. Have the United States, hitherto, suffered any inconvenience from annual elections? Have their delegates been too often shifted, or too frequently recalled? This, I believe, will not be pretended.

"CORNELIUS," *HAMPSHIRE CHRONICLE*, DECEMBER 11, 1787

Party Spirit and Party Leaders

State Parties and the Debate over the Constitution

The growing popular participation in government and the economic turbulence of the "critical period" fostered the development of factions and parties in the thirteen states. Political and social issues such as the treatment of the remaining or returning Loyalists, the devaluation of paper money, the speculation with state and federal securities, the protection of debtors, and the geographical differences between East and West tended to divide the states.[1] The debate over the Constitution brought the partisan rivalry of the "critical period" to a head, and it paved the way for the first national party system of the United States. The ratification campaign required enormous organizational efforts on the part of both sides. Federalists and Antifederalists were able to draw from their experience with legislative and gubernatorial elections, yet in most states improved planning and coordination can be observed along with the intensive and specific application of all available propaganda techniques. It was easier for politicians in the generally Federalist coastal areas to organize election campaigns, since they lived in close proximity to one another, were linked by business and social contacts, and had recourse to more and better sources of information. Antifederalists attempted to offset this disadvantage by forming committees whose job it was to establish regular channels of communication between the coast and the backcountry, as well as between the anti-Constitution activists in various states. "Centinel" pointed the way in Pennsylvania: "Societies ought to be instituted in every county and a reciprocity of sentiments and information maintained between such societies. . . . Nothing but such a system of conduct can frustrate the machinations of an ambitious junto." William Petrikin reported from Carlisle in February 1788 that new "Societies for the purpose of opposing this detestable Fedrall conspiracy" were being founded almost daily in the backcountry. In March, the Country societies waged a campaign against the final adoption of the Constitution, and in September they dispatched delegates to Harrisburg to take part in a nominating convention for the first federal elections.[2] Governor Clinton and his followers in New York City founded the "Society of Gentlemen" in the fall of 1787 for the purpose of dispatching political literature to the counties and across state borders. This was the precursor of the Federal Republican Committee under the direction of General John Lamb, headquartered in the customs office in New York City. By the end of April 1788, Antifederalist committees had been established in twelve of the thirteen New York counties. At the same time, the Lamb Committee tried to stay in touch with leading opponents in other states in order to block unconditional ratification. These institutions in Pennsylvania and New York can justifiably be regarded as the nucleus of a permanent party organization. Oddly enough, the initial concrete steps toward the foundation of a national party pursuing national objectives were thus taken by the champions of state sovereignty known for their staunch aversion to political nationalization. Yet bowing to the harsh exigencies of their uphill battle against ratification, they pragmatically resorted to forms of cooperation which transcended state borders.

Parallel to the improvement of their organizational structures, both supporters and opponents of the Constitution refined their political-ideological stances. Both parties had a political agenda without ever having explicitly approved one as such. The Constitution with its famous preamble can be deemed the first national manifesto of the Federalist Party. Similarly, the *Dissent of the Minority of the Pennsylvania Convention,* published on December 18, 1787, may be described as the unofficial Antifederalist platform because of its fundamental message and its wide circulation. The dispute over the Constitution finally gave competent organizers, theoreticians, and speakers the opportunity to prove their worth as party leaders on the national level. At least in some states, the legislative factions of the "critical period" had already come to resemble "true" parties, with established leadership, organizations, and programs buttressed by a power base in the electorate. There is also some evidence that the ratification controversy was not based on interests alone, but that already established party affiliation now represented a separate motivating factor. Thus "Landholder" claimed that the Pennsylvania Constitutionalists (advocates of the democratic State Constitution of 1776) only rejected the federal Constitution so vehemently because it had been crafted by their adversaries.[3] The opposition to the Constitution in Pennsylvania was "evidently the opposition of a State-Party," concluded Timothy Pickering. "The politics of the state have been constantly vibrating as the one or the other party gained an ascendancy in the government."[4] The distinction between Antifederalists and Federalists now quickly supplanted the previous contrast between Constitutionalists and Republicans—much to the advantage of the latter group. According to Charles Swift, the Constitution was "strongly opposed by many (not all) of what was called the Constitutionalist Party. I say what was called because the distinction now is 'Federal or Antifederal.'"[5] From Montgomery County, New York, Federalist Abraham Van Vechten reported: "I am sorry to add, that in common those who bestow the greatest Attention on the new Constitution seem to regard it more with an Eye to party Interest, than as a System of future Government submitted to their impartial Discussions. . . . Your Irish Landlord is a violent Antifederalist . . . but unfortunately in the Transport of his Zeal he does not hesitate to declare that he scorns even to read the new Constitution."[6] There were reports from North Carolina that the critics of the Constitution were taking advantage of the opportunity to avenge themselves on their adversaries for past political defeats, "and because one is *federal* the other *will be anti.*"[7] French Consul Jean-Baptiste Petry confirmed the general congruence between Up Country and Antifederalists, Low Country and Federalists in South Carolina.[8]

However, the division into friends and foes of the Constitution seldom occurred precisely along the lines of the old state parties. Party considerations often took a backseat to the citizens' interest in deriving the greatest possible advantages from the transition to a new form of government. Dispirited by the popularity of the Constitution in Connecticut and Maryland, the number of Antifederalists shrank to the extent that effective opposition was no longer possible. Oliver Ellsworth observed a mixture of continuity and change in Connecticut, where the contrast between "federal" and "antifederal" had first been applied to state politics: "The opposition here is not one half so great to the federal government, as it was three years ago to the federal impost; and the faction, such as it is, is from the same blindfold party." In another "Landholder" essay, he described the opponents of the Constitution as "unfederal from the beginning."[9] Federalists were also assured of victory in New York City, "for Persons of very distinct and opposite Interests have joined on this Subject."[10]

The Meaning of Party for Federalist and Antifederalist

Henry Knox counted the Philadelphia Convention among the "fortunate circumstances in the affairs of men," yet also pinpointed it as the source of the "germ of opposition": "The gentlemen, who refused signing [the Constitution] will most probably conceive themselves obliged to state their reasons publickly. The presses will groan with melancholy forebodings, and a party of some strength will be created."[11] In Massachusetts, Henry Gibbs predicted the Constitution would be "well approv'd by the thinking & disinterested part of the Community but I expect there will be a party of an opposite Character in this & all the States violently to oppose it."[12] Friends and foes of the Constitution were often unable to resist the temptation to equate their views with those of the American people at large, or at least the "republican and honest part of the community," while discrediting their adversaries as "internal enemies," "enemies to their country," and "enemies of America."

Considering the ideological heritage of the Revolution, it is not surprising that the aversion to parties was asserted. But some expressed the hope that the Constitution would lead to the end of parties. At the Pennsylvania ratifying convention, Thomas McKean praised the Constitution's tendency "to break our parties and divisions," and the *Pennsylvania Gazette* expressed a desire to do away with parties altogether: "It is expected the new government will abolish party, and make us, once more, Members of one great political Family."[13] Writing in the *Massachusetts Centinel* after six months of heated debate, "Pythias" thought it lamentable "when a country becomes divided by a spirit of party at so early a period as now dawns upon America."[14] In June 1788, a contributor to the *New York Packet* admonished: "Whenever the spirit of party reigns, the public weal generally falls a sacrifice to it."[15] James Buchanan even took the view that party was the "most Infamous word in the English Language."[16]

Others expressed a reluctant acceptance of factions and parties in the debate over the Constitution and after. "The spirit of party will, generally, ever predominate"; or "Faction, Sir, is the vehicle of all transactions in publick bodies . . . the prevalent faction will always be right."[17] It was becoming increasingly common to speak of parties in a neutral, business-like manner, and participants on both sides eventually became less reticent about referring to themselves and their adversaries as a party. Describing the session of the Virginia legislature for fall 1788, Joseph Jones informed Madison: "The parties fœds and antis have in most transactions been pretty distinguishable."[18] Remarks were even occasionally heard to the effect that the opposing camp also contained honorable and principled people, and that neither party was as bad as the propaganda suggested.

Not only were Americans quite aware of the frequent correlation between state politics and the position on the Constitution, they also closely followed the emergence of national parties. They often perceived the Union-wide political rivalry as a repeat of the great drama of the Revolution. Even before the Constitution had been published, a letter submitted to the *Pennsylvania Gazette* advised: "The former distinction of the citizens of America . . . into whigs and tories should be lost in the more important distinction of fœderal and anti-fœderal men. The former are the friends of liberty and independence—the latter are the enemies of liberty, and the secret abettors of Great-Britain."[19] It was an idea that caught on quickly; by March 1788 the dichotomy between "Fœderalist and Antifœderalist" was "as familiar to the ear as Whig and Tory formerly was."[20] Toward the end of the year, Virginia Congressman Edward Carrington noted that Federalist and Antifederalist had become "established terms throughout the United States."[21] Orthographic uncertainties spawned such spellings as Fedrall, Feadreal, Fadiral, AnteConfœderalist, AnteFeddural, Federial, Fœderalest, and Feodralist. The growing popularity of the two expressions is evidenced by ironic renderings of the names (antifiddlers, Featherals) and shortened forms (Feds, Antis, Antes, Anties, Anti party). Even the passions of the Revolutionary era seemed to have been revived, if not surpassed. "Tories were never detested with half the Zeal, as Antifederalists are now," reported John Francis from Philadelphia.[22] Framed in more modern terms and personalized, the antithesis was described as a clash between WASHINGTONIANS and SHAYITES.[23]

There was considerable disagreement, however, as to just who had assumed which of the former roles in this new act of the Revolution. In New York, William Smith noted a similarity "between those who term themselves federal and Anti Whiggs."[24] St. George Tucker was convinced that Whigs would be undone in the event of a Federalist victory, in which case he "must turn Cat in pan once more & be a Tory."[25] Patrick Henry counted himself among the "Friends of Liberty" and the "whiggish Americans."[26] And James Sullivan, who voted for the Constitution in Massachusetts, labeled many of the critics as "old revolutionaries." At the same time, it seemed to him that some of the more radical Federalists were driven by a "habitual hatred to the old Whigs."[27] The opposition turned the tables in their propaganda, insisting it was they who were protecting the "liberty of the country" against "downright Tories," "lukewarm Whigs," and "advocates of despotism."[28]

In reality, there were members of both the Federalist and Antifederalist Parties who had remained neutral during the struggle with Great Britain, had taken the "wrong" side, or had hesitated. In 1790, John Adams deeply regretted that so many of his former radical companions had rejected the Constitution, and that now the "old tories" and the "youngsters" had banded together against the "old whiggs" of the Samuel Adams and Richard Henry Lee school, who had made good revolutionaries but were inept at crafting laws and a constitution.[29] Antifederalists not only portrayed themselves as the upholders of the revolutionary tradition, they also liked to emphasize that their party's social base differed entirely from that of their adversaries. In Maryland the "great and Rich" were said to be "generally in favour of the Federal Government; but many in the middle ranks of life, who are the more Industrious part of the Community, are opposed to it."[30] In Massachusetts, Silas Lee agreed that the "most reputable characters" leaned toward Federalism but "the middling & common folk are on the opposite."[31] Antifederalist propaganda reinforced this perception and portrayed the debate over the Constitution as a struggle between the wide middle class and the power-hungry, rich-and-mighty few, who were out to establish an aristocracy. Samuel Adams was plagued by concerns that the movement to establish the Constitution was in fact motivated by such aims. The "seeds of aristocracy" had been sewn during the battle against Britain and were now threatening the very roots of the free American system, he wrote in a letter to Richard Henry Lee, adding: "The few haughty Families think *They* must govern."[32]

It was easier for French chargé Otto than for most Americans to move beyond the conceptual categories of the Revolution. He wrote that those in favor of the Constitution were called Federalists and their opponents Whigs, but these names had no "direct relation to the object in question." On the other hand, he also conceived that the dispute was dividing the American people and splitting the diverse social and economic interests of the country.[33] A North Carolina bookseller named Sterling even went so far as to claim the "Demon of discord" could not have devised a more effective method of dividing the people than the Federal Convention: "Every American citizen is now either federal, or Antifederal, and looks with a jealous Eye on the conduct of his Neighbour, who will not be allowed to Steer a middle course."[34]

John Quincy Adams and his sister Abigail Adams Smith found this development disturbing. John Quincy entered in his diary on April 7, 1788, that Federalist and Antifederalist had become "the only distinctions at this day. . . . We have not yet sufficiently settled to have stated parties; but we shall soon I have no doubt obtain the blessing." Two months later, his sister wrote from New York City: "Federalist, or Antefederalist, is the question—and pray upon which side of the important question do you Stand? . . . It ever has been and ever will be the Case that upon every Subject there is a diversity of opinion. . . . Thus we must ever expect to see—One Party rejoice at the ill success of its opponents—and Using all the means in its Power to render the opposite disregarded, disrespected and all their measures frustrated."[35] Upon his return from London, Abigail's father, John Adams, noted with suspicion the secret "chain of communication" that opponents of the Constitution had established across state lines.[36] With the English example fresh in his mind, he resigned himself to the inevitability of a national two-party system: "We shall very soon have parties formed; a court and country party, and these parties will have names given them."[37]

Many Americans shared this dread. They had misgivings about political parties, yet they anticipated that the national division would outlast the ratification debate, making party strife a permanent fixture in politics. This concern was justified and borne out, because Federalism and Antifederalism were more than mere names: they stood for divergent attitudes, values, mentalities, and worldviews. In their extreme manifestations they were opposite poles to which Americans gravitated. Both sides were sincere in their conviction that they were defending fundamental principles and values. "Impartial Examiner" felt the opposition was acting "on the broader scale of true federal principles," in contrast to Federalists with their reliance on the "sound of names."[38] As "Centinel" saw it, the objections to the Constitution were the product of a "philanthropy and liberality that reflects lustre on humanity. . . . They embrace the interests and happiness of the whole union."[39] A letter-writer in Poughkeepsie was convinced that no one displayed more "candor, fairness, consistency and patriotism" than the opponents of the Constitution: "They have opposed Federalists with that spirit, freedom and openess, which the consciousness of rectitude naturally inspires."[40] In the view of "Federal Farmer," however, Federalists and Antifederalists constituted two wings between which "the solid, free, and independent part of the community" was situated. If names were needed to characterize accurately the "general politics" of the two parties, the best choice was "republicans and anti-republicans."[41] This alternative originated in New York, where Governor George Clinton's followers had begun calling themselves Republicans even before 1787. It was no more suitable than reviving the terms Whig and Tory, but it implied that the opposition was not dedicated to the republican principles of the Revolution.

Federalists and some Antifederalists took similar stances opposed to the phenomenon of political parties, but there were some significant distinctions. The proponents of the Constitution were more likely to display the stereotypical anti-party attitude, combing through the history of the ancient republics of Rome, Carthage, the city-states of the Renaissance, and modern Europe seeking proof of the destructive influence of party spirit. They reserved the terms "faction" and "party" for their adversaries, while they preferred to call themselves "friends of government" or "friends of the country." Many Federalists were counting on the new Constitution to weaken—if not eliminate—political opposition. "For the moment the Federal Constitution begins to operate, their influence must and will disappear like a vapour," commented Henry Jackson on the fate awaiting Massachusetts Antifederalists.[42] William Gardner comforted himself over the unfavorable composition of the New Hampshire legislature: "However after the much wish'd for federal government is in motion, it will not matter much who are sent to our [General] Court, as their wings will be pretty well clip'd."[43] The Pennsylvania opposition could not accept the new system, explained Thomas Hartley, one of Tench Cox's confidants, "because it operates against their power."[44] Rhode Island Federalists fought for ratification in the hope that it would finish the political dominance of their agrarian adversaries once and for all.[45]

The proponents of the Constitution also found it difficult to come to terms with opposition on the national level. Washington, at least, allowed that the opposition to the Constitution might "ultimately be productive of more good than evil; it has called forth, in its defence, abilities . . . that have thrown new lights upon the science of Government, they have given the rights of man a full and fair discussion, and have explained them in so clear and forcible a manner as cannot fail to make a lasting impression." Nevertheless, the General assumed that criticism would cease the moment the new Constitution went into effect.[46] Hamilton considered it the primary duty of the new administration more effectively to control the state parties and eradicate the spirit of opposition through successful governance. In July 1788 he confided to Madison that some amendments might be necessary, because "they will satisfy the more considerate and honest opposers of the constitution, and with the aid of time will break up the party."[47] Madison took an unusual position for a Federalist. He hoped the Constitution would create an "extended Republic," in which factions and parties could exist without danger and where their energies could be applied constructively. He arrived at this view largely by way of his profound interest in the principles of freedom of religion and separation of church and state. They taught him that a peaceful competition in ideas was possible and benefited the common good. This made any attempts to suppress parties as unconscionable and unnecessary as they were futile.[48] Madison, then, like Adams, did not expect parties to disappear under the Constitution.

This was both a defense of competition between parties and an appeal to the antagonists to keep the political struggle within certain limits. A "Republican" in Maryland upheld the principle of a legitimate, loyal opposition: "When once a government is agreed to by those who are to be affected thereby, it becomes the duty of every one to carry it into execution, and to procure it to be administered in a manner the most to the ease and advantage of the people."[49] Benjamin Harrison, who had voted against ratification in Virginia, assured Washington afterwards: "It has ever been my line of conduct, to combat every system of government that my judgment disapproved, with firmness, and decency; but being over ruled, to acquiesce, and endeavour by a prompt obedience to the laws, to carry the opinions of others into execution."[50] Upon the publication of their reasons for voting against the Constitution, three Massachusetts delegates were quick to qualify their remarks to ensure that no one was given the impression "that we mean to be disturbers of the peace, should the states receive the constitution; but on the contrary, declare it our intention, as we think it our duty, to be subject to 'the powers that be,' wherever our lot may be cast."[51]

When many Antifederalists referred to "parties," they were referring to economic and social special-interest groups. Antifederalists did not expect the Constitution to eliminate parties; they wanted the heterogeneous interests and parties to be represented in Congress. They also justified political parties as the means to resist tyranny and the abuse of power. Antifederalists believed they should organize themselves against an aristocratic party allegedly already in existence and actively pursuing political objectives.[52] The dissenters seized on isolated past remarks according parties a watchdog function in the government. Franklin, for example, had explained to the readers of his *Internal State of America 1786* that there would always be parties wherever there was freedom: "By the collusion of different sentiments, sparks of truth are struck out, and political light is obtained. The different factions, which at present divide us, aim all at the public good; the differences are only about various modes of promoting it."[53] At the Massachusetts ratifying convention in early 1788, even a pro-Constitution delegate conceded that "competition of interest . . . between those persons who are in and those who are out of office, will ever form one important check to the abuse of power in our representatives."[54] In the same tradition, Jefferson wrote from Paris praising the opposition to the Constitution. Though he preferred not to see them strong enough to derail the reforms, he thought they ought to be able to push through necessary amendments and revisions.[55] Antifederalist essayists placed increasing value on the distinction between a harmful, self-seeking form of party spirit detrimental to the interests of the people, and a noble form serving the cause of liberty. This was the simplest answer to their adversaries' attempts to dismiss their objections as the effusions of party spirit.

The Federalists' constant attacks also elicited more speculative responses, now approaching a theoretical justification for the existence of parties and opposition. "Atticus" in Massachusetts saw the contention between the two state parties (which he called "aristocracy" and "democracy") in a positive light: "Parties are the materials of which the most perfect societies are formed. . . . The most opposite interests rightly blended, make the harmony of the state. . . . *Parties give life to the moving powers of the State,* and when properly checked and balanced, are productive of much good. . . . *Parties always keep alive an attention to public measures. . . . Parties produce great attendance and carefulness respecting elections. . . . Parties keep any one interest from swallowing up the rest.*" To this list of useful functions of two-party competition, however, he appended the warning that there must always be a "third power sufficient to check the exorbitances of each."[56] A critic of the Constitution in Maryland offered his readers a "most difficult and necessary lesson: That on the preservation of parties public liberty depends. Whenever men are unanimous on great public questions, whenever there is but one party, freedom ceases and despotism commences. The object of a free and wise people should be so to balance parties, that from the weakness of all you may be governed by the moderation of the combined judgments of the whole, not tyrannized over by the blind passions of a few individuals."[57]

It is no coincidence that the most interesting comment came from New York, a major center of national opposition. The text is the product of brainstorming by a group of active Antifederalists. Their point of departure had been the distinction between the destructive "spirit of faction" and a perfectly natural difference of opinion over political issues:

> The spirit of faction is an unreasonable and violent passion. . . . The man of this temper is always wrong, even though he takes the side that is right; but men may differ in sentiments, and be very active and zealous in supporting the side of the question they espouse, from the conviction of their mind, that the party they take is that of truth, and that the public prosperity and happiness will be promoted in the attainment of the object they pursue. . . . Such diversity of opinions do not injure good government, it tends to bring truth to light, to keep the minds of people in exercise, and make them acquainted with, and watchful of their rights—indeed party spirit itself, in some measure, contributes to this end. Difference of

> views, and ideas, do indeed prevail in the state, they always have been, and always will; these, no doubt, partly flow from a spirit of party, and partly from different ideas men have, and their different modes of reasoning on subjects . . . the integrity of no man ought, therefore, to be called in question, merely because he is zealous in using means to accomplish the end he has in view, unless these means are dishonest or dishonorable.[58]

The Spectrum of Approaches and Political Decisions

The political and ideological division and competition between Federalists and Antifederalists was much more complex than these two party labels may suggest. The advocates of a strong, hierarchically organized national government contrasted with proponents of a decentralized system dedicated to republican virtues, state sovereignty, and the greatest possible protection of individuals against government authority. There were also moderates on both sides willing to compromise. The situation becomes even more complicated if the chronological aspect is added. It sometimes occurred over the course of the debate that a moderate critic turned into a fierce opponent of the Constitution. More common still was the opposite case: radical opponents toned down their criticism before eventually coming out in favor of ratification.

Despite these complexities, there are reliable indicators that make it possible to locate the actors on a political scale. Strong Federalists felt the Philadelphia plan contained the minimum authority needed to control majorities in some of the states with egalitarian tendencies. They therefore strictly rejected any revisions of the Constitution that would have strengthened the position of the states or individuals and weakened the power of the national government.[59] Moderate Federalists viewed the Constitution as a successful compromise and signaled to the opposition their willingness to accept some amendments, including a bill of rights. However, any revisions would have to be effected after ratification as provided for in Article V. The social views of this group were, in general, more moderate than those of their radical associates, who regarded the common man with a mixture of condescension, contempt, and fear.[60]

The strong Antifederalists demanded, in addition to a bill of rights, "structural" amendments, which in effect meant scaling back the power of the central government. Not content to wait until after ratification, they were only prepared to accept the Constitution once it was amended. Their preferred method of accomplishing this was a second federal convention called to revise the Constitution.[61] Anyone who had reservations about the Constitution but deemed strong opposition too dangerous was bound to move to the moderate Antifederalists sooner or later. For many in this group, the main concern was a bill of rights—more substantial changes could wait until later. They were also more willing to believe the Federalists' assurances that amendments would be enacted should the Constitution be unconditionally adopted. In light of the fact that the political scales were fairly balanced in several states, the moderate Antifederalists held the key to the fate of the Constitution.[62] Politicians who had strong popular support but continued to straddle the fence on ratification also played a vital role. They had the power to influence voters and convention delegates.[63]

For every rule that can be used to explain the varied and complex patterns of behavior, there are a number of conspicuous exceptions. Each personal decision was based on the interplay of numerous factors, such as an individual's background and character, his level of education, occupation and financial circumstances, political experience and ideological precepts, concern for his reputation and career, the advice of friends and relatives, and, of course, the wishes and demands of the constituents. Speculation on personal and immediate material gain usually took a back seat to long-term considerations based on such factors as the welfare of a particular state, a specific region, occupational groups and social classes, or the Union as a whole. It is true that prominent Antifederalists typically did not enjoy the same social status as their Federalist counterparts. The members of the "great families" continued to regard men like George Clinton, Melancton Smith, Patrick Henry, Samuel Chase, Luther Martin, Samuel Adams, and Abraham Clark as parvenus. Politically, however, the leading Antifederalists, with their extensive legislative experience and successful careers in public office, were equal to the "well born" in every respect. The resentment stirred up against "upstart unprincipled characters"[64] during the dispute over the Constitution ignored the fact that a new political power had emerged after the Revolution, led by the *homines novi* and within which the disparities in property ownership between the leaders and the electorate were diminished. What was still lacking, however, was social homogeneity between the parties. This explains the fierceness of the debate, as well as the surprising degree of oscillation between the political parties in the 1790s. The latter phenomenon should not be misconstrued as unrestrained opportunism. Close examination reveals that basic convictions remained stable as a rule and that certain personal traits and dispositions usually augured political turnarounds long in advance of their actual occurrence. One must also consider the fundamental political-institutional transition from a confederation to a national system of government and the intensification of regional conflicts. Following the adoption of the Constitution, the South was generally more Republican, the North more

Federalist, a circumstance which was not without influence on politicians in the respective regions. The partisan rivalry of the 1790s confirms that, far from being a one-way street, political leadership in a republic is the product of the immutable, reciprocal relationship between the entitlements of the élite and the will of the electorate.

Election Campaigns

Direct Participation and Communication

The citizens' participation in the debate over the Constitution was not limited to voting, though this was thought to be the single most important political act. At the time of the convention elections, between 50 and 80 percent (depending on the region) of the approximately 640,000 white Americans over twenty-one fulfilled the property qualification required for suffrage, meaning there were between 320,000 and 512,000 eligible voters. Various estimates agree that around 150,000 citizens cast votes for convention delegates.

The election campaigns were launched in various parts of the country by spontaneous or hastily organized town and county meetings. The prevailing atmosphere was one of satisfaction and jubilation over the successful conclusion of the Philadelphia Convention, with the meetings always culminating in a call for immediate ratification. Newspapers eagerly reported on these rallies, creating the impression that an uncontested grassroots movement was underway to adopt the Constitution. To this end, methods were borrowed that had proven especially effective in the struggle against England. Of particular importance were public readings of the Constitution, the drafting and signing of resolutions and petitions, and the adoption of instructions to town and county delegates.

These methods of direct participation were put to use right from the outset of the struggle for ratification. The Constitution was solemnly read aloud in public meetings; listeners were encouraged to express their opinions and sign petitions; delegates received political guidelines in the form of instructions. The citizens of Philadelphia and vicinity were the first to react: soon after the Constitution was made public, the Pennsylvania legislature received petitions which by September 29 had been signed by more than four thousand citizens from the city of Philadelphia, Philadelphia County, and Montgomery County. The signers had concluded that the Constitution was "wisely calculated to form a perfect union of the states, as well as to secure to themselves and posterity, the blessings of peace, liberty and safety," and should therefore be adopted without delay. On September 21, a "respectful number of the citizens of Germantown" gathered under the leadership of the physician Charles Bensel. Following a reading of the text, it was unanimously resolved "that we do highly approve of the proposed Constitution of the United States, and that we will concur with our fellow citizens in Philadelphia in praying the legislature immediately to adopt the measures recommended by the late Honorable Convention, for carrying the same into execution." The wording of the petitions was nearly identical in each case, which indicates the existence of a well-orchestrated campaign designed to get a head start on the opposition.[65] Not until December 12 did Robert Whitehill manage to respond with a petition signed by 750 residents of Cumberland County, "praying . . . that the proposed constitution should not be adopted without amendments and, particularly, without a bill of rights." In the spring of 1788, around six thousand Antifederalists, primarily from the western part of the state, submitted petitions to the Pennsylvania legislature demanding that it refuse to acknowledge the state's ratification.[66] Moving in exactly the opposite direction, Federalists in Rhode Island and North Carolina began a petition drive in 1788 to persuade their legislatures to call ratifying conventions. The initiators of these campaigns—John Nicholson in Pennsylvania, merchants from Providence and Newport, and James Iredell in North Carolina—wanted to demonstrate that the respective legislative majorities did not reflect the "true" will of the people.

In several of New Jersey's thirteen counties, public meetings adopted resolutions and instructed their legislators "to use their utmost endeavors to have a convention appointed for this state, without delay, agreeably to the recommendations of Congress, for the purpose of considering and ratifying said Constitution."[67] In Connecticut, the Constitution's proponents allegedly drew up a blacklist containing the names of everyone who refused to sign a petition they had circulated.[68] At least eight Federalist town or county meetings occurred in Virginia by October 1787. The freeholders of Fairfax County caused a Union-wide stir on October 2 by formally directing their delegates, George Mason and David Stuart, to push for a ratifying convention in the state legislature. Federalists hailed this move as Mason's just reward for refusing to sign the Constitution.[69] In Baltimore, Federalists used similar tactics to put pressure on Samuel Chase.[70] The diary of a Moravian in Salem, North Carolina, shows that on November 3 a meeting was held in Richmond County, "in which an assembly member from our county tried to learn the opinion of the whole people concerning the proposed new Constitution for the land. It appeared that nearly all were in favor of it."[71] A few days later, the grand jury of Edenton County approved a "presentment" penned by James Iredell and Hugh Williamson and addressed to the state legislature. It combined praise of the Constitution ("a proper jealousy of liberty mixed with a due regard to the necessity of a strong authoritative government") with an urgent request for an early convention date.[72] Opportunity to discuss the Constitution was also provided on court days and at other regularly scheduled events, such as the annual conference of the Philadelphia Association of Baptist Churches in New York and the conference of Congregationalist ministers from New Haven County in Connecticut, both of which endorsed the Constitution.[73] The impact of these gatherings was magnified by the efforts of newspaper publishers. Forty-six papers in ten states printed the Philadelphia petition of September 20 alone. The twenty Federalist meetings known to have taken place prior to the first convention elections were mentioned nearly four hundred times in the press.[74]

Not all events were characterized by a peaceful, relaxed atmosphere and a desire for harmony. There were also parades and demonstrations that assumed a threatening, militant aspect. One popular method of venting anger was burning politicians in effigy. There were reports of such activities having taken place in New York, Pennsylvania, and North Carolina. Alexander Hamilton was afforded this dubious honor in New York, as were Federalists Thomas McKean and James Wilson in Pennsylvania and Antifederalists Willie Jones and Thomas Person in North Carolina. Aedanus Burke received word from the backwoods of South Carolina "that in some places the people had a coffin painted black, which, borne in funeral procession, was solemnly buried, as an emblem of the dissolution and interment of publick liberty."[75] In other places, mobs gathered to make bonfires out of copies of the Constitution. Federalists usually responded to provocations of this kind by burning Antifederalist pamphlets. All of these rituals were borrowed from the traditional repertoire of British opposition politics and had been used during the Revolution to intimidate colonial officeholders and Loyalists.[76] Nevertheless, only on rare occasions did the symbolic bloodshed precipitate real acts of violence. The most disturbing reports came from the Pennsylvania backcountry, where Antifederalists had organized "societies" and "associations" to resist the establishment of the new system of government at all costs. On Christmas day 1787, Charles Nisbet, a Presbyterian minister and president of Dickinson College, reported from Carlisle that Antifederalists "flatter the People with a Community of Goods, & a general Release of Debts in Case they will take Arms to oppose [the Constitution]. . . . I need the Prayers & Pity of good Christians, as the hottest Opposition is in these Western Counties. Mobbish Meetings were held here last Night, to draw up

Letters of Thanks to the Minority of the Convention, & in these Meetings the Speakers exhorted the People to take up Arms in Defence of their Rights."[77] However, such threats were eventually abandoned in the face of the smooth progression of ratification in the other states and the steady growth of the pro-Constitution majority within Pennsylvania itself.

Propaganda, Polemics, and Conspiracy Theories

Before the actual election campaign had even begun, both sides endeavored to supply a wide audience with written information and propaganda material. This was accomplished with the help of printers and their distribution systems, as well as private correspondence and, increasingly, the newly created organizations intended to coordinate petitions within states, and sometimes interstate. The activists sometimes came to the aid of groups of supporters in other parts of the Union who asked for pamphlets and newspapers. Letters were often stuffed with newspaper clippings and other material. The impact of the propaganda campaign waged by both sides in Pennsylvania, Massachusetts, and New York was thus generally felt across the nation. The first wave of Federalist literature originated in Philadelphia, where Wilson, Benjamin Rush, Tench Coxe, Francis Hopkinson, Noah Webster, and Pelatiah Webster filled newspapers and wrote pamphlets with essays and had them distributed by supporters. The public discussion was still in its infancy in Maryland when Coxe began offering newspaper articles, pamphlets, and good advice to his friend William Tilghman: "I send you a couple of handbills prepared here by the friends of the new Constitution for circulation thro Penna, which I hope may be of use in Maryland. If you have a press at Chester Town, it may be useful to reprint them in your newspapers." Tilghman responded with a request for more information "on this important business," and thanked Coxe in advance for "any good publications on either side of the question." Coxe also sent material to Madison, Hamilton, and Rufus King, asking them to seek publishers in the northern and southern states.[78]

The Antifederalists' effort was also marked by determination and organization. The most important publications by the Pennsylvania opposition were distributed from Massachusetts to Georgia.[79] Antifederalists in the Pennsylvania backcountry received newspapers and pamphlets from Philadelphia, then forwarded them to party sympathizers in the southern states. One of Coxe's correspondents, Thomas Hartley, was informed while on a trip through Maryland in January 1788 that a certain Dr. Ewing from Philadelphia was working "to install his Principles and extend the Influence of the antifœderalists." Hartley was concerned that the tireless efforts of a "designing few" were starting to show results and that the western shore of

Maryland had already "caught the System of the Minority in Pennsylvania."[80] Around this same time, a pamphlet edition of the *Dissent of the Minority of the Pennsylvania Convention* appeared in Richmond, Virginia. The French consul reported from Charleston that the minority in Philadelphia was sparing neither trouble nor expense "to flood This state and its Neighbours with Its pamphlets and writings Against This Constitution." Charles Cotesworth Pinckney agreed: "Pamphlets, speeches, and protests of the disaffected in Pennsylvania" had allegedly been put in circulation to confuse and prejudice the citizens. As John Brown Cutting learned, the Virginia opposition was also stirring up public sentiments against the Constitution in the backcountry of the Carolinas.[81] In New York, the *Dissent of the Minority of the Pennsylvania Convention* made the rounds in newspapers and pamphlets, as well as part of a pamphlet anthology sent to all county branches of the city's Antifederalist committee (which called itself the Federal Republican Committee). The two sides would later strongly disagree over whether the Pennsylvania *Dissent* had actually reached Boston in time for the beginning of the Massachusetts ratifying convention. In Pennsylvania itself, the essay inflamed the citizens in the western counties to the extent that they started forming anti-ratification committees. Federalists were outraged by its "wilde & pernicious tendency," and Tench Coxe responded with no less than six essays refuting the assertions made in the *Dissent*.

Antifederalists matched Federalists in the propaganda battle in several states, and perhaps outdid them in New York, Virginia, and North Carolina. As far as the distribution of anti-Constitution literature was concerned, the diligence of New York's Clintonians was unsurpassed on either side. The Federal Republican Committee in the municipal customs office, led by John Lamb, functioned as a redistribution center and clearinghouse for opposition literature of every kind. Based on the Clintonian party organization, Lamb's Committee came close to being the first national party headquarters. With the aid of local "republican" committees, it succeeded in spreading large quantities of the most persuasive publications in New York and in neighboring states. While some of the material was the work of New York Antifederalists, such as "Brutus," "Cato," "A Countryman," "A Plebeian," and "Federal Farmer," other essays were imported from Boston ("*A Columbian Patriot*"; *Republican Federalist*), Philadelphia ("An Old Whig"; "Centinel"; *Dissent of the Minority*), and Maryland (Luther Martin's *Genuine Information*). Governor Clinton had subsidized the printing of "Genuine Information" by Eleazer Oswald, a friend of Lamb's in Philadelphia.[82] Since November 1787, Lamb, Abraham Yates, Hughes, and Smith had been forwarding packets of pamphlets and broadsheets, primarily the "Centinel" and "Federal Farmer," to prominent adversaries of the Constitution in New Jersey, Connecticut, Rhode Island, Massachusetts, and New Hampshire. Lamb was commissioned by the Federal Republican Committee in May 1788 to post identical letters in seven states and again enclose a large number of publications, this time mainly concentrating on Mercy Warren's "A Columbian Patriot," Smith's "A Plebeian," and Martin's *Genuine Information,* as well as the lengthy pamphlet *An Additional Number of Letters from the Federal Farmer to the Republican.*[83]

Federalists were outraged over this "outside interference." In the *New Haven Gazette,* which published no contributions from the opposition, one correspondent railed: "A piece called the CENTINEL is circulating with great industry in this state [Connecticut], in the same covered, secret, and insidious manner as British proclamations, pardons, and manifestos were in the days of yore. . . . These pieces are sent in large packets from a neighbouring state [New York] which is draining us of £35,000 annually by her impost."[84] Jeremiah Wadsworth hoped they would be able to thwart the efforts of the Constitution's foes, despite the "devils in NY & Pensa. from whence they daily receive pamphlets & news papers full of Wrath Slander & evil Speeking." He praised the *Federalist* essays as the ideal antidote. In Boston, Nathaniel Gorham determined that the opposition had received letters from New York, "which have done damage."[85] The *Newport Herald* warned readers in late May 1788 about the activities of a certain "J[oh]n L[am]b" from New York, who had had the audacity "to transmit to his E[xcellenc]y the G[overno]r a large packet of pamphlets against the proposed Constitution."[86] Even though some of the parcels had apparently landed in the wrong hands or were otherwise intercepted, the campaign by the New York Federal Republican Committee did not miss its mark. Lamb was soon near the top of the Federalists' list of most-hated opponents. Philip Schuyler had come to know this veteran of the New York Sons of Liberty during the war as a "very turbulent and troublesome" individual.[87] Be that as it may, it was partly to the credit of people like Lamb that the Constitution was subjected to intense scrutiny and debate, instead of simply being thrust upon an ill-informed citizenry.

The traditional ideological framework of Republicanism was at once helpful and detrimental to both sides. On the one hand, it provided points of reference which facilitated the meaningful structuring of their collective experiences; on the other, it impeded acknowledgement of historical change and innovation. Just as had been the case in England, a potentially explosive rift was emerging between the language of politics and social reality.[88] The conventional political vocabulary not only exacerbated existing political-ideological differences, it also distorted the true nature of the conflict by exaggerating its social dimension. This was particularly dangerous because parts of the "lower" and "middling sort" of the people harbored social resentments which could easily be ignited by the imprudent or malicious use of language. Neither the critics nor the supporters of the Constitution were altogether immune to such temptations. The bitter animosity which often surfaced during the election campaigns was due to the feeling on both sides that crucial values were at stake. These vicious verbal attacks were the consequence of the mistrust and apprehension that escalated to the point that adversaries seemed capable of the most abominable acts against property, public order, or liberty and republicanism, including "conspiracies" among opponents.

The most prominent Antifederalist conspiracy monger was Luther Martin, a Maryland delegate to the Constitutional Convention, whose *Genuine Information* discussed events in the convention and in whose writings the Constitution was decried as the work of a "Monarchical Party" bent on the annihilation of republican liberty.[89] Such notions assumed particular virulence in Pennsylvania, where Antifederalists became convinced that Robert Morris was at the center of a secret plan to overthrow the state constitution before advancing on the Union behind the shield of the Philadelphia plan. Martin's "revelations" provided the perfect grist for their mill. "Centinel" (Samuel Bryan) praised Martin for having "laid open the conclave, exposed the dark scene within, developed the mystery of the proceedings, and illustrated the machinations of ambition. His public spirit has drawn upon him the rage of the conspirators, for daring to remove the veil of secrecy . . . all their powers are exerting for his destruction; the mint of calumny is aciduously engaged in coining scandal to blacken his character, and thereby to invalidate his testimony."[90] There was also a thriving market for such speculations in New York. Congressional delegate Abraham Yates, who held views similar to those of Luther Martin and Samuel Bryan, interpreted the framing of the Constitution as a large-scale conspiracy by the rich and powerful to undo the achievements of the Revolution and the republican system of government. Yates, a shoemaker long subjected to condescension from the likes of the Schuylers and Jays, perceived the history of New York since the colonial period as the history of aristocrats determined to suppress the "middle sort." His "Rough Hewer" and "Sydney" articles, together with his work for the Antifederalist committees in New York City and Albany, ensured that this became a generally accepted interpretation among Clintonians. In 1789, Yates combined the conspiracy and aristocracy theories in a history of the Revolution and postwar period, arriving at the conclusion that Federalists had "turned a Convention into a Conspiracy, and under the Epithet Federal have destroyed the Confederation."[91]

Republican ideology lent itself to this historical approach, based as it was on the conviction that to preserve their freedom a people must be constantly vigilant. Richard Henry Lee alluded to the "silent, powerful, and ever active conspiracy of those who govern" in the introductory remarks to his plan for amendments.[92] Not surprisingly, the opponents of the Constitution began to suspect at a very early stage in the debate that the Union was under siege. John Smilie was even more explicit. In his estimation, the country had been beleaguered ever since the war ended by "a set of men from N. Hampshire to Georgia who could not bear to be on the same footing with the other citizens. . . . If this Constitution is adopted, I look upon the liberties of America as gone."[93] "David" expressed the conviction in the Boston *Independent Chronicle* that Federalists had publicly condemned Shays's Rebellion while secretly rejoicing "*at the opportunity of establishing, under pretence of necessity, a tyrannical rule in the room of our free, and happy constitution.* . . . These men are chagrined at the return of peace. They have long been in the sentiment, that we could not live under a free government, and their last chance is, to bring the people to a loss of their confidence, in those who have led them through the revolution, and sat down with them in a land of freedom."[94] A writer calling himself "John DeWitt" also referred to the supporters of the new Constitution as "ambitious men throughout America, waiting with impatience to make it a stepping stone to posts of honour and emolument . . . men who openly profess to be tired of republican governments."[95]

This specter of conspiracy fed on the conviction that the course of history was determined by clashes between the rich and the poor, and that social tensions increased as a country became more highly developed. A contributor to the New York *Morning Post* warned: "In all ages, the bulk of mankind have been consigned to slavery. . . . The wealthy and powerful combine together to make a property of their fellow citizens; and few governments have ever existed, in which a conspiracy has not been formed against the liberties of the people." The Albany Antifederal Committee feared the federal government would be a "powerful engine in the hands of the rich, to oppress and ruin the poor. . . . Is it for the sake of the poor and common people, that the rich and well born are so indefatigable? . . . Sacred as well as profane history afford abundant examples to prove that the most strenuous assertors of liberty, in all ages after having successfully triumphed over tyranny, have themselves become tyrants, when entrusted by the people with unlimited and uncontroulable powers."[96] A "Farmer and Planter" from Maryland adjudged the Constitution to contain little good but "a great deal of evil," warning: "Aristocracy, or government in the hands of a very few nobles, or RICH men, is therein concealed in the most artful plan that ever was formed to entrap a free people. . . . Look around you and observe well the RICH MEN, who are to be your only rulers, lords and masters in the future! Are they not all for it? Ought not this to put you on your guard? Does not riches beget power, and power, oppression and tyranny?"[97] Federalists conceded that every society was characterized by a natural struggle between the haves and have-nots, even acknowledging that the adverse social effects of economic progress might eventually cause the New World to resemble the "overpopulated" countries of Europe. Yet they maintained that the new Constitution, with its "mixed" features, was eminently suited to preserve a social balance to the benefit of all members of the community.[98]

There were also those who responded to these class-based conspiracy theories as baseless and inflammatory. A Baltimore "Mechanick" rejected the provocative slogans used at the time of the state legislative elections in September 1787: "Let them not call upon the poor to unite against the rich, or the rich to unite against the poor, the mechanic against the merchant, or the merchant against the mechanic, who have all one common interest in choosing sensible, honest, independent men."[99] The author of a letter published in the *Hudson Weekly Gazette* resented the constant vilification of the "rich and well born" by Antifederalists in New York: "Are we to understand by this that the objectors are not well born, or that anti-federalists are not rich, not invested with high state offices, not in the receipt of state salaries?" In Boston, resistance was also mounting to the allegations of aristocratic plots: "My fellow citizens, let reason counteract the crafty insinuations of malicious spirits." On this side of the Atlantic, there was "such a fluctuation of property, as will not give room for a permanent superiority in fortune." The Constitution did not apportion any special rights to citizens with "extensive property," in marked contrast with Great Britain, where "dignity and wealth are held to be universally concomitant."[100]

Writing in the *American Museum* of February 1788, Noah Webster offered a psychological explanation for the conspiracy theories. He suggested that the critics perceived imaginary threats because they were too preoccupied with the friction between the people and absolutists in Europe: "The Americans have seen the records of their struggles; and without considering that the objects of the contest *do not exist in this country,* they are laboring to guard rights which there is no party to attack. They are as jealous of their rights, as if there existed here a King's prerogative, or the power of nobles, independent of their own will or choice, and ever eager to swallow up their liberties. But there is *no man* in America, who claims any rights but what are common to *every man;* there is no man who has an interest in invading popular privileges, because his attempt to curtail another's rights, would expose his own to the same abridgement. . . . The jealousy of people in this country has no proper object against which it can rationally arm them; it is therefore directed *against themselves,* or against an invasion which they *imagine* may happen in future ages." Webster had hit upon the psychological mechanism behind the suspicion, even paranoia. Instead of judging the Constitution against the backdrop of political realities in post-Revolutionary America, Antifederalist rhetoric tended to dwell on the countless past and present political calamities that had befallen Europe, which was then projected into America's future.[101]

But Webster's rational analysis could not defuse the potentially explosive atmosphere created by party "electioneering" and propaganda. His own political allies were too caught up in the rhetorical warfare themselves to avoid the temptation to fight fire with fire. They charged that Antifederalists were not merely clinging to their government jobs and looking for elegant ways to avoid repayment of debts, but were up to far worse abominations. Jonathan Williams from Boston was convinced that all opponents of the Constitution were Tories, who "now are and allways have been Enemies to the freedom of the Country." Henry Gibbs of Salem expected that there would be opponents to the Constitution in Massachusetts, "& in all the States," who would "violently oppose" the Constitution.[102] One popular element of this reverse conspiracy theory was the often repeated supposition that the dissenters were endeavoring to split the Union into separate confederacies. Antifederalists were even suspected of secretly collaborating with the British, determined to promote their own glory at the expense of the Union. For Henry Knox, 80 percent of Massachusetts Antifederalists were "paper money and tender law people and insurgents [Shaysites]—who are under the influence of people pushing for a reunion with Great Britain."[103] In the *Hampshire Gazette,* "Monitor" distinguished "four classes of opposers": (1) the open or secret friends of Great Britain; (2) the "lawless, disobedient and licentious, whose highest wishes are to live uncontrouled without restraint"; (3) reckless public debtors; (4) the ambitious "lovers of novelty, whose restless, fickle and unstable temper provokes them to an unsatiable fondness for innovation and changes—divisions and subdivisions of states, counties and towns."[104]

Even moderate critics were suggestively linked to images of chaos, anarchy, and civil war and denounced as traitors. One of those so accused protested that he had only taken the liberty of publicly pointing out the weaknesses of the Constitution: "Am I, for this, to be called the enemy of the country? Am I to be condemned as a man that would destroy government and introduce anarchy and confusion?"[105] Deaf to such remonstrances, Federalists continued to charge that treasonous factions and juntos were at work, weaving an interstate intrigue to defeat the Constitution. The activities of the

Lamb Committee and the Union-wide distribution of Antifederalist pamphlets only served to confirm their suspicions. In light of the fact that the conspiracy motif also turned up in private correspondence, it can hardly be dismissed as a mere propaganda ploy. Even such rational thinkers as Washington and Madison were not above such speculations.[106]

In the emerging republican culture of the late 1780s, the use of a polarizing rhetoric drove the political camps farther apart than was warranted by their political differences. One observer offered a fitting description of this phenomenon: "From every mouth issues Constitution! Constitution! the enthusiasm of some of its pillars is such, that they fancy in their dreams that they see the finger of God himself writing it at large on the surface of the Heavens . . . the opposition, on the contrary, views it drawn up in letters of fire, blood, and despotism, through a black cloud, pregnant with horrors, and ready to burst on the cursed heads of its inventors. Heavens, what a contrast!"[107] Both parties soon realized, however, that elections could not be won solely by demonizing one's political adversary. The election campaigns also contained more sophisticated appeals to individual and group interests, a method of attracting voters which was better suited to the social foundations of the evolving pluralistic society.

Interest Groups

Most of the propaganda was simply directed to "the people" in general in a particular state, county, or town. In the course of the election campaigns, however, it became more common to target social, ethnic, or religious groups—the manifestation of a heightened awareness of the segmentation of the social structure. The Constitution's adversaries portrayed this segmentation in a very general manner as a barrier to centralizing tendencies, and Madison saw in it the ideal foundation on which to establish the new government. The appeals to "special interests" also suggests the recognition that a majority could not be attained in a republican system without alliances, coalitions, and compromises across social classes and occupational groups, which, in fact, became the rational basis of post-Revolutionary American politics.

It is not surprising that farmers were wooed by both parties, as they constituted a large majority of the population. Even so, not all information sent in their direction was of a complimentary nature. One author, himself claiming to be "A Countryman," emphasized that his articles were not addressed to "the people" or "the citizens of Maryland," but rather to the "country people in particular," who both needed and deserved such special attention. He then proceeded to deny that farmers were capable of properly assessing the proposed Constitution: "Shall any among you, my dear countrymen and fellow Americans, object against what we do not fully understand? . . . Can you and I then be critics and judges of such a profound work as our national government? Shall we have the arrogance to arraign it at the tribunal of our scanty knowledge, and condemn it as wrong?" He suggested it would be wiser to elect educated men to the conventions and otherwise limit themselves to signing petitions "for a redress of grievances."[108]

Though not all Federalist articles were this condescending, it is true that the opposition was generally more adept at finding the right tone when addressing the rural population. One special group was composed of tenant farmers on large estates in New York along the Hudson River. Despite their often hostile relationship with their "manor lords," they were generally considered to have conservative leanings. In their election campaign, Antifederalists therefore stressed the need to improve the tenants' self-image and ease their political dependence on large landowners. This required a careful balancing act, since some manor lords were themselves Antifederalists. The tenants in Albany County were addressed by an opponent of the Constitution claiming to be one of their own: "My farm is subject to rents and services. These are moderate, nor do I complain that they are exacted with rigor; but such I believe are the natural effects of all tenures, that they produce a kind of dependence, for I have often given my assent to the will of my landlord in supporting his political importance, without inquiring into the propriety of it." The tenant system as such was not called into question, most farmers only wanted to see their own rights better protected. Recent experience led the writer to conclude "that my landlord . . . may be for a mode of government very convenient for a great man, but not for the common farmer; in fact, that he may have an interest to support, at the expence of my own. . . . If you wish the proposed constitution properly amended before it is adopted, then let us join our interest in voting for such persons whose sentiments and principles agree with our own." Signed by "A Tenant," the essay concluded with the assurance that secret ballots offered protection against any repressive measures on the part of the landlords.[109]

These direct appeals to the interests and sentiments of tenant farmers surely contributed to the amazing landslide victory of Antifederalists in New York. Still, Governor Clinton and his political allies were not entirely confident of the farmers' continued support. In the end, Abraham G. Lansing preferred to accept the evil of unconditional ratification rather than risk adjourning the convention, which would have given Federalists another opportunity to court rural voters. A majority of tenants might then fall victim to the "Baneful Manor Interest" after all and withdraw their support for subsequent amendments.[110]

Both parties set their sights of their propaganda on the urban middle class comprised of tradesmen, manufacturers, small-scale merchants, and storekeepers. Federalists often painted a rosy picture of the advantages the new Constitution would bring to all segments of society. In the largest towns, by contrast, tradesmen and small businessmen were accorded special attention or spoke out themselves. The most famous example of the latter instance were the Federalist "Mechanicks of the North-End" in Boston, who waged their own campaign with the help of printer Benjamin Russell and succeeded in influencing the outcome of the elections. A writer calling himself "An Elector" enjoined artisans to vote for the Constitution, in the adoption of which all their "hopes of business, employment and adequate pay" lay.[111] The "Mechanicks of the North End," proposed a Federalist ticket for the convention, "convinced that our salvation—and the salvation of our families—depend upon the establishment of a government by which the commerce of our country may be put on a regular and advantageous footing."[112] Other, similar appeals bore such signatures as "One of the Middling Interest," or simply "A Mechanick." Responses in the Boston press were not long in coming. Antifederalists predicted a decline in business and trade should the new Constitution come into force, and "One of the Common People" insisted that a bill of rights should at least be added. The Boston *American Herald* warned the mechanics to beware of "Designing Men" who were only out "to make Tools of you, who have once and again suffered by interfering in public matters."[113] This thinly disguised recommendation to stay out of politics most likely elicited the opposite of the intended response from the self-confident "Mechanicks of the North-End."

Like Russell's men in the *Green Dragon* tavern, Federalist workers in New York City and in the Rhode Island towns of Newport and Providence held their own election meetings.[114] The "middling sort" in Baltimore was at least as actively involved in state and national politics. During the ratification campaign, "Sydney" sent a Federalist message "To the Working People of Maryland": "We common people are more properly citizens of *America* than of any particular state. Very many of our sort, die in different parts from where they were born. . . . The Constitution will . . . enable us to borrow money, in other countries, on reasonable terms, to pay workmen, for improving our lands and houses, that we may make better crops."[115] In the *New Hampshire Gazette* of June 12, 1788, a "Federal Mechanic" implored the ratifying convention to remember the working people and not adjourn for the second time.

Throughout the Union, skilled tradesmen participated in the preparations for ratification celebrations and marched in the parades in large numbers. The success of Federalism in the cities was due in no small part to the willingness of the working classes to embrace national interests and equate their own well-being with the fate of the Constitution.

Throughout the debate, Antifederalists remained very much in the minority in Baltimore. That did not prevent them, however, from waging a fierce battle for the sympathies of mechanics and laborers in the post-ratification election campaigns for seats in the state legislature and national Congress. While James McHenry's party was determined to keep them in the Federalist camp, Samuel Chase and his acolytes sought to regain their political influence by winning over this large block of voters. Newspapers were soon filled with contributions along the lines of "To the Manufacturers and Mechanics of Baltimore," "To the Tradesmen, Mechanicks, and Manufacturers," and "A Federal Mechanic." Chase's supporters, who were now fighting for amendments, were not entirely convinced of the harmony that Federalists claimed existed between merchants and tradesmen. In actuality, insisted "A Citizen," only the more affluent tradesmen had joined forces with the merchants against farmers, "labouring People," and the general class of the poor and uninformed.[116] "An Old German" vouched for Chase: "Manufacturers and mechanics! neglect this man, and you'll neglect your own interest! The aristocratic party, the great and the rich men, never loved him. . . . I should be glad to know, how it comes to pass that those very men, who formerly cared nothing about manufacturers and mechanics, are so suddenly converted, and such great friends to them."[117]

As the pseudonym "An Old German" indicates, efforts were also undertaken to influence and mobilize ethnic and religious groups. Marylanders of German descent, generally admired for their respect for law and order, industriousness, and virtuous ways, represented an important constituency. The opinion expressed by "An Old German" met with considerable resistance from some of his peers, who wrote to Baltimore papers under such aliases as "A Real German," "A Young German," or simply "A German," denying the Chase party the right to speak for all Germans. In Baltimore city and county, Germans were thought capable of tipping the scales, "if they stick together." Following the convention elections, opponents of the Constitution complained that the "peaceable and reputable" Germans had been forcibly prevented from voting.[118] Federalists had no need to resort to such tactics in and around Fredericktown, where they had been quick to secure the support of the German community through clever candidate selection. The best choice should have been Dr. Thomas instead of Abraham Faw, explained a local Federalist to General Horatio Gates, especially considering that Faw had hitherto supported the Chase faction: "However, that Faw being a German and as this kind of people forms a very numerous and industrious part of the community, it is well enough I think and not inconsistent with policy, that they should be indulged in having one of their class for to represent them."[119] Antifederalists responded by making sure at least one German name appeared on every "County Ticket" on the western shore of Chesapeake Bay. There was a similar situation in some of the western counties in Virginia and North Carolina.

A group of Germans in New York City spoke out in favor of the Constitution prior to the elections there,[120] while committees from both sides worked to attract Scottish voters. Federalists were convinced they had the backing of most "Scotsmen" in the city and presented a long petition containing mostly Scottish names. This prompted the Anti-Federal Committee of Albany to publish a broadside signed by forty-one citizens of Scottish descent, to illustrate "that they are decided against adopting the New Constitution, unless the intended amendments are made a condition of adopting."[121] The largest foreign-language contingent in New York was Dutch; they had always tended to endorse Clinton's farmer-friendly politics and largely shared his views on the Constitution. Just as German-language articles, and even entire newspapers, appeared in Maryland and Virginia, leaflets in Dutch were circulated in New York counties.[122]

The ethnic and religious mix in Pennsylvania was particularly receptive to group-oriented political strategies.[123] Yet much to the chagrin of Antifederalists, the outcome of the election there had already been determined before their campaign had gotten off the ground. They were also handicapped by Benjamin Rush's close connections with influential Germans like Henry Melchior Muhlenberg, the father of the Lutheran Church in America, and his son Frederick Augustus Muhlenberg, a minister and legislator. Pennsylvania Constitutionalists (the party that supported the state constitution) had alienated other religious groups, especially Quakers, by their rigid insistence on the Test Oath.[124] It was thus relatively easy for Federalists to sweep the ethnic groups, in greater Philadelphia at least, where they entered the debate well prepared and caught their opponents off guard with their unexpectedly aggressive propaganda activities. Nevertheless, the battle for the support of the Germans, Irish, Scotch-Irish, Quakers, Presbyterians, and Baptists had still not been settled in Pennsylvania, as evidenced by the new round of squabbling which broke out in 1788 during the run-up to elections for seats in the state assembly and in Congress. Similar situations existed elsewhere, such as the intense competition to gain favor with Quakers in Rhode Island and Baptists in Massachusetts and Virginia.

The delegations of entire regions were at stake in Maine and Kentucky, which were in the process of splitting away from Massachusetts and Virginia, respectively. Of special importance to voters there were constitutional provisions for or against their desired independence. Frontier voters had to decide whether the economic and military protection afforded by a strong central authority would endanger their desire for independence. Federalists and Antifederalists alike offered support to the residents of these districts in their quest for independence. Federalists won a 2-to-1 majority in Maine, while Antifederalists were even more successful in Kentucky (10–2), where they took advantage of the "Mississippi trauma" still affecting many citizens in the wake of the Jay-Gardoqui negotiations.

The Clergy between Hope of Salvation and Fear of Degeneration

The clergy had had a decisive influence on public opinion during the Revolution and were still held in high esteem. Many of them represented and amplified the voice of the people who felt that this was a time of crises. In New England, in particular, the pulpit was often used on Sundays and holidays to scourge the signs of moral and political degeneration. A majority of American clergymen favored the Constitution, for a variety of reasons. Although ministers had less direct influence on political decisions than they did on the public's general frame of mind, their ability to extract knowledge from the three sources of reason, revelation, and experience put them in a position "to warn the people against encroachments of power on the one hand, and the evils of anarchy on the other."[125] They reacted with particular sensitivity to the postwar symptoms of crisis, which they perceived as divine admonitions. In their sermons, they often drew parallels to the people of Israel, who had neglected to show gratitude for God's help during the exodus from Egypt and their liberation from Babylonian oppression. In the traditional form of the Jeremiad, preachers lashed out at the arrogance of individual citizens, the state legislatures' appalling abuse of the gift of self-government, the disregard for civil authority, and a general loss of faith, morals, and common virtues. The feeling of decline was widespread and cut across denominational boundaries. This was especially distressing when viewed against the premise that America was God's chosen land, where the work of creation would culminate in the establishment of a thousand-year reign of peace.[126] If the people did not soon repent, it was feared God would hold up America "as a monument of what an impious and ungrateful people may expect from his hands."[127]

The dissatisfaction with their own social position and a loss of status following the Revolution surely contributed to the clergy's critical assessment of the state of affairs. Their sympathy with the constitutional reform movement was also heightened by the fact that the churches were experimenting with new forms of organization at this time, with an eye toward interstate cooperation. Methodists, Presbyterians, and Baptists framed charters establishing, for the first time, representative and governing councils on a national level. In the process, they experienced firsthand the difficulties involved in balancing the necessity of a strong "ecclesiastical government" with the congregation's right of self-determination. The pursuit of unity also led to interdenominational contacts and the desire for national churches.[128] It is not surprising that ministers of all faiths were thoroughly convinced of the need for "political reconstruction," committing themselves to this purpose despite their considerable theological differences. In their estimation, this renewal could only spring from self-restraint, obedience to rightful authorities, and observance of the law. This would heal society's wounds and restore devotion to the common good. By propagating these ideas, the clergy paved the way psychologically and spiritually for the transition to a new form of government.

Federalists skillfully translated the clergy's goodwill into voter and delegate support. In Boston, they were able to convince Baptist minister Samuel Stillman to stand for a convention seat. "He is a high Federal Man and charmed with the proposed plan," reported Henry Jackson. "He being at the head of the *Baptists* in this State and of great influence among them it is thought policy to choose him one of the Deligates by which means we shall gain that whole *Sect* in favor of [the Constitution]." In a letter from Boston, dated February 9, 1788, Federalist Benjamin Lincoln assured Washington: "It is very fortunate for us that the Clergy are pretty generally with us; they have in this State a very great influence over the people."[129]

If religious councils entered the debate at all, it was usually to endorse the new system of government. Baptists from the middle states, who had joined together to form the Philadelphia Association, sent an open letter to all parishes in October 1787, urging them to back ratification. The Constitution promised "to rescue our dear country from that national dishonor, injustice, anarchy, confusion and bloodshed, which have already resulted from the weakness and inefficiency of the present form."[130] In New Hampshire, the Association of Christian Ministers called on all Americans to pray "that there may be no delay in clothing Congress with all necessary powers to act in character as the Federal Head of a sovereign, independent nation."[131] The Congregational clergy of New Haven County, Connecticut, discussed and unanimously approved the Constitution at their annual meeting in late September 1787.[132] Presbyterians in New Jersey and members of the Dutch Reformed Church in New York established days of fasting and prayer for the good of the Union.[133] A correspondent in the *New Haven Gazette* considered ratification inevitable, "since the ministers and christians, of all denominations are now engaged in praying for it, and there is good reason to believe, that no prayers have as yet been offered up against it."[134] The opposition in the middle states and New England decried the one-sided intervention of the clergy, who should rather concern themselves with religious matters. In the February edition of the *American Magazine*, Noah Webster responded by accusing the critics of a "grave mistake": Ministers had the duty "to inform the minds of people on all subjects and to correct their morals; so that they have a direct influence on government."[135]

The clergy, however, did not unanimously favor the Constitution. There were protests in Connecticut against the "sinful Omission in the late federal convention, in not looking to God for direction, and of omitting the mention of the name of God in the Constitution." Congregationalists, Baptists, Methodists, and Quakers were troubled by the toleration of the slave trade, slavery, and by the right of slave owners to demand the return of escaped slaves. In the opposition-led west of Massachusetts, New York, and Pennsylvania, ministers often shared the opinion of their congregations.[136] The resistance was even stronger in Virginia and North Carolina, where Anglicans and Presbyterians were divided, while Baptists presented a united front against the Philadelphia plan. The General Committee of Virginia Baptists answered their own question as to whether the Constitution contained adequate safeguards for the "secure enjoyment of religious liberty" with a resounding no.[137] Baptist ministers in North Carolina conducted an Antifederalist campaign, passing "circular letters" from congregation to congregation. An observer complained that the backcountry Baptists were so fanatical and ignorant that they were desecrating the Lord's temple with "vile declamations against the Constitution."[138] For his part, Madison took the Baptists' concerns seriously and placed them at the forefront of his push for amendments.

Forty-four clergymen participated in the state ratifying conventions, thirty-two of whom voted for ratification, compared with twelve who voted against it. In Massachusetts, only three Baptists and one Congregationalist out of seventeen ministers sided with the opposition. This led to a rumor in the newspapers that the legislature's Antifederalist majority planned to punish the clergy with special poll and property taxes, "for taking so active a Part in Favour of the intended new Constitution, and introducing Politics into their Sermons, instead of adhering strictly to the Gospel."[139] Federalists received uniform support from the three Congregationalists at the Connecticut convention, as well as the three Presbyterians and one member of the Dutch Reformed Church who participated in New Jersey. In the South, however, Baptists, Anglicans, and Presbyterians were almost equally represented on both sides of the controversy. Apart from the 32-to-12 majority among the clergy, the Constitution's advocates were particularly gratified to have the directors of important educational institutions on their side, such as the Reverends James Manning in Providence, Ezra Stiles at Yale, and John Witherspoon at Princeton.[140]

Post-Revolution Voting Procedures in the United States

Since the Revolution, voting had become routine for Americans, with annual elections for legislatures, but also for governors and lieutenant governors. Some members of the political elite were concerned about these constant elections, maintaining that they placed extreme demands on the candidates and freeholders and contributed to the polarization of the electorate. The reform movement was thus partially driven by an aversion to annual elections as a source of endless turmoil and an obstacle to consistent governance. As early as 1785, Mathew Carey had called on both parties in Pennsylvania to build a coalition to rid the state of the "evils of annual elections" and the corresponding "weathercock state of legislation and government." In the *New Jersey Gazette,* a year later, "Eugenio" established a connection between the depressed economy and the short intervals between election days: "The more frequent legislatures are changed, and the more easily law is altered, the more precarious does the credit of paper, founded on acts of the legislature become."[141] Jeremy Belknap also bemoaned the "miserable business" of annual elections, although he was not oblivious to the jealous devotion of most citizens to their right to vote and to the balloting practices in place since the Revolution. It is therefore not surprising that the Constitution's move away from annual elections was cause for considerable alarm.

Though voting procedures had not been fundamentally revised since the colonial period, they had been modernized in several ways. Elections now took place at regular intervals, whereas the dates had formerly been left up to the discretion of governors appointed by England. Religious discrimination had become a rarity and eventually disappeared altogether. Graded property qualifications for candidates and electors in elections could still be found in most states. They had often been reduced, however, to increase the number of eligible voters. Laws governing suffrage, which differed from state to state, still officially excluded one-fifth to one-third of all free white men over twenty-one from participation in legislative elections. But, especially in the North, these laws were not strictly enforced. New York went so far as to institute general male suffrage for the elections to the ratifying convention. All other states based their voting rights for this occasion on the relatively liberal qualifications used for elections to the lower house. By comparison, only around 10 percent of adult males were entitled to vote in parliamentary elections in England.

Voter turnout had also improved since the Revolution. Depending on the significance of the particular election—gubernatorial elections often elicited a greater response than legislative elections—voter participation climbed to over 40 percent of eligible citizens in the late 1780s, even reaching 60 percent in some areas.[142] This development was fostered by more consistent scheduling of elections and better organization. Polling stations grew in number and stayed open longer, or the ballot boxes were circulated by county sheriffs. The citizens' desire to take part in elections was further enhanced by improved security and by the transition from open to secret balloting. The rise of political parties considerably intensified election campaigns while at the same time focusing the public's attention on the issues at hand. They also rendered the selection process more open by allowing the constituents in some places to participate in the nomination of candidates. Voter turnout climbed by increments in some states, while in others it shot up after 1786, due to the economic crisis and the increased use of party propaganda. Voter participation was high for the elections to ratifying conventions in most states. The only exceptions were Pennsylvania and Maryland: the Antifederalist campaign had taken too long to build up steam in the first instance and there was too little competition in the second. In Rhode Island, Federalists in Providence and Newport boycotted the referendum that had been called for instead of a convention.

Participation was above average in Connecticut, by contrast, and New York even set a record at 43.4 percent. The figures tend to understate the popular interest. Even in divided states there were certain regions that were so solidly Federalist or solidly Antifederalist that there was no real competitiveness in the elections. Numerous friends of the Constitution in New York City and in Maryland, for instance, were apparently prepared to vote but saw no need to in view of the great lead enjoyed by their candidates. It is difficult to glean exact figures from the fragments of information available. The estimate of 160,000 active voters is, if anything, perhaps a little high.[143] A turnout of these proportions would mean that one-fourth of all free white males in the thirteen states went to the polls. This is still within the normal range, yet clearly shows that the people regarded the adoption of the Constitution as a vital issue.

Election procedures were closely linked to the development of political parties and the press, all of which were in a stage of transition to modern, democratic forms. This can be seen in the gradual elimination of property requirements (land ownership and/or tax payment), in the debate over voter instructions, and, in particular, in the criticism of unbalanced and unfair representation voiced in several states. The conviction had become more prevalent that individual citizens should be represented in legislative bodies, not traditional corporate units like towns, counties, or parishes, which failed to take the size of the population into account. The principle of "representation by numbers" was not yet firmly established in 1787. As rapid population growth in the interior threatened the dominance of older, eastern establishments, the coastal residents in control of legislatures began to resist the equitable redistribution of seats. This prompted the backcountry delegates to mount an assault against the dominance of the more established regions under the motto "One elector—one vote."[144]

Federalists must have been thankful this idea was not yet in wide use. "Fair" representation in the state ratifying conventions would have considerably impeded, if not prevented, the adoption of the Constitution. In South Carolina, for example, the 149 delegates who voted for the Constitution only represented 39 percent of the white population, whereas the 73 delegates opposing the Constitution represented 52.2 percent. The commercially oriented Charleston district alone was allocated 109 delegates; the entire Upcountry, by comparison, only received 86. In Georgia, delegates representing only 13 percent of the population were in a position to control the ratifying convention. The malapportionment of delegates was less in most other states. Still, a more nearly equal representation could have made the Federalists' task even more difficult than it was.[145] On the whole, however, and by the standard of the times, the ratification elections were seen as representative of the will of the people. The argument that suffrage requirements kept too many white males from the ballot boxes and that women were not at all allowed to vote did not come up in the debates—or at least cannot be found in the historical record.

Town Meeting Democracy, County Politics, and Gentry Culture: The Elections in Massachusetts, New York, and Virginia

MASSACHUSETTS

The variety so typical of political life in the United States was also a defining element of the election system. The framers of the Constitution had wisely abstained from dictating to the states a uniform method of appointing convention delegates. A closer look at the situation in Massachusetts,

New York, and Virginia may serve to illustrate the regional differences that had developed since the colonial period and had not been eradicated by the Revolution. In the North, it was the New England town, the "American Polis,"[146] that constituted the main political unit on which the representative system was based. Of the approximately 700 incorporated towns in existence at that time, 520 were located in New England. Just as the official name "Commonwealth of Massachusetts" indicates, the state regarded itself as an alliance of essentially autonomous communities. Often founded on a covenant, these towns had become a model of self-administration and independence during the colonial era. Under the influence of Puritanism they had spawned a unique form of "communal élan" which supported individuals while subjecting them to a variety of constraints for the common good. The former "peaceable kingdoms" had not survived the social fragmentation of the eighteenth century unscathed.[147] They, too, had been forced to deal with the growing conflict between communalism and individualism. Since commercial activity was the main breeding ground for this new individualism, the social and intellectual transformation occurring in the communities was naturally more advanced in the coastal areas and along trade routes. The course of the election campaigns and the results in each district were heavily influenced by these economic and ideological disparities.

The state constitution of 1780 combined the right of representation reserved for towns as corporate units with the rights of individuals, while according special protection to "property rights." Every town with more than 150 eligible voters was entitled to send a delegate to the House of Representatives. Additional seats were added as the number of "ratable polls" exceeded 300. Toward the end of the century, several relatively large towns had four representatives each; the city of Boston was allotted twelve. This was approaching proportional representation and—in a departure from standard practice—was actually based on a formula that favored western areas. In the Senate, where each county had up to six senators, depending on its tax base, property ownership was given its due representation. The maximum number of seats was set at forty. Some towns showed little interest in the proceedings in far-away Boston, others balked at the expense associated with sending delegates to the capital. The significance attached to the debate over the Constitution can be seen in the fact that the ratifying convention, with over 350 delegates, was the largest representative body ever assembled in Massachusetts up to that date. There were three times as many delegates from the Maine district as had been present at the preceding General Court meeting.[148]

The system of town meetings, founded on the ability of autonomous communities to debate and arrive at a consensus, was seen by many citizens as an alternative to party politics. In the course of the election campaign for ratifying convention seats, however, it became more and more apparent that the towns were not acting in isolation, having been drawn into the swirl of partisanship. Neither during the selection of candidates nor in personal appeals to voters did the squabbling factions stop at the borders of their own town. Only in Boston were candidates appointed by way of caucuses and printed lists of nominees.[149] That did not prevent leading proponents of the Constitution from concluding written and oral agreements to ensure that "good men" were put up for election in other locations as well. Henry Van Schaack was quick to warn his associates of the anti-lawyer sentiments in large parts of the west and urged them to proceed with great circumspection: "Cool, temperate but firm men ought to be held up." Theodore Sedgwick, his correspondent, agreed that the matter should be treated with "great care and caution." Both mustered supporters in Pittsfield and Stockbridge and met with representatives from other western communities to prepare for the respective town meetings.[150] In the eastern section of the state, Federalist influence spread from such strongholds as Boston, Cambridge, and Newburyport to the surrounding areas. Speakers were sent into neighboring towns, where they handed out leaflets and made extensive use of the published version of the last speech Benjamin Franklin made in the Constitutional Convention "to inculcate moderation & a due respect to the opinion of others." Their endeavors were reinforced by enthusiastic young citizens like James Bridge, who subsequently asked former schoolmate John Quincy Adams if he could picture him riding sixty miles "to influence our late Elections in favour of federalists in this county? . . . That I voted myself and sollicited the votes of others, that I publicly harangued the audience?"[151]

During this same period, Antifederalists were hardly resting on their laurels. Yet the idea of organizing statewide efforts through such channels as committees of correspondence apparently did not occur to them in the wake of the turmoil caused by Shays's Rebellion. In Maine, Samuel Nasson, William Widgery, and Samuel Thompson exhorted towns to appoint delegates. Thomas B. Wait, the publisher of the *Cumberland Gazette,* canvassed Maine spreading his Antifederalist credo. There seemed to be agreement with neighboring communities in Massachusetts and Connecticut that the Constitution was unacceptable in its present form.[152] In the central and western parts of the state, many citizens felt a lingering sense of solidarity stemming from the popular uprising. Here the opposition worked quietly but effectively to transform the pent-up wrath into hostility toward the Constitution. Prior participation in the rebellion was less an obstacle to candidacy than it was an asset.[153] Where Shaysism had not been a factor, Antifederalists had openly to attack the Constitution to win votes. They could not rely on lingering Shaysism to elect delegates.

There is also some evidence that coordinated partisan activity and political literature tended to arouse opposition and resistance. Some people associated the use of propaganda and zealous outside interference with corrupt election practices in Britain, which they strongly felt had no place in their "commonwealths." An article in the *American Herald* likened Rufus King's campaign style to that of members of the British House of Commons, whose best argument was the money in their pockets.[154] As the Pittsfield town meeting drew closer, Henry Van Schaack thought it wise to temper the enthusiasm of his friend Theodore Sedgwick, whose assistance he had recruited: "It would be best you should not give your attendance on Town Meeting days for fear the idea should go abroad that the [supporters?] wanted [i.e., needed] advocates from abroad." Even the Antifederalist fervor of John Bacon, who went door-to-door in Stockbridge commending himself as a candidate until he was "converted" by Sedgwick, must have seemed suspicious under these circumstances.[155] According to Sedgwick, "Some Great Barrington politicians have falsely & weakly suggested, that Mr. B & myself were acting in concert."[156]

The town meetings followed a general pattern, with a certain amount of room for local variation. The time, place, and purpose of the meeting were announced by the selectmen of the towns. At the outset of the meeting itself, the citizens first chose a "moderator," whose job it was to ensure that the event was conducted in an orderly manner. The Constitution was then read aloud, followed by an exchange of arguments for and against it. At this juncture, the citizens often revealed their sentiments for and against ratification in an open vote. In the simplest cases, this was immediately followed by the selection of delegates. Voting was conducted either openly or by secret ballot. In the latter case, the ballots were placed in a hat in the middle of the room, then counted by the moderator and selectmen. The winner had to receive a majority of votes. If a community was entitled to send more than one representative, the candidates had to receive a majority or additional polls were taken.[157] The agenda could also be organized in such a way that the delegates were elected before the open vote on ratification. It was left to the discretion of the citizens whether or not they wanted to enjoin the delegates to act in accordance with the majority opinion.

In many instances, the towns took more time to examine the Constitution before arriving at such a momentous decision. Toward this end, a committee was appointed at the first meeting to review the Philadelphia plan and present a report at the second meeting. Of course, this two-to-three-week interval offered ample opportunity for increased "electioneering" and tactical maneuvering. In some cases, a party managed to have a third meeting called to amend or revoke a previous resolution or repeat the election proceedings. The committee reports often formed the basis for instructions issued by the town meeting to their convention delegates.

The report of the committee appointed by the town meeting in Harvard, Worcester County, was representative of the prevailing mood in the interior: "We are of opinion, that the proposed Constitution will, if adopted, effectually destroy the sovereignty of the States, and, in all probability, will soon bring the good people of the United States under Despotism." After hearing this report, the Town Meeting chose Josiah Whitney, Esq., as its delegate and instructed him "to give your negative vote" on the Constitution, and at the same time work for a system of government "vested with such powers as are sufficient for the purpose of legislation." The committee report outlined the central points of contention: the Philadelphia plan contained no bill of rights; the term for senators was too long; the power of Congress to regulate the election of senators and representatives was objected to; the taxation power of Congress was too broad; the powers of the presidency were "dangerous to a free people"; the judiciary was too powerful and might endanger property; no religious test was demanded of officeholders; the sovereignty of the states was threatened by the supremacy clause. A reform of the Articles of Confederation was deemed preferable to adopting the Constitution. This manifesto, which was published in the Boston *American Herald* on January 21, 1788, approached a threshold of radicalism beyond which few Antifederalists dared to tread in public.[158] The only towns that went further were those that refused on principle to elect a delegate.[159] The tenor of most reports was more moderate, and in many instances their instructions allowed delegates some leeway to use their own discretion and reach compromises. The town of Southborough, for example, also recommended "that the Constitution by no means be Set up as it now Stands, without Amendments." Yet the committee members left it up to their delegate, Captain Seth Newton, and to the ratifying convention to determine the nature and extent of revisions, "fully confiding in their Wisdom and Integrity that they will, at the Same time Guard the Liberties of the people, and Secure to Congress all those powers which are necessary to Secure and maintain the federal Union."[160] Bernardston and Leyden in Hampshire County advised Agrippa Wells "not totally to reject the abovesaid Constitution, being of the opinion that by proper amendments, it may be adopted to secure our liberties and answer the Design of the general Union." In revising the Constitution, Wells was to bear in mind the objections expressed by Elbridge Gerry and by the legislative minority in the Pennsylvania Assembly.[161]

In fact, questions concerning instructions became the central issue during the Massachusetts elections, which were held in the town meetings from November 1787 to early January 1788. Federalists would have preferred communities to abandon instructions altogether. In those areas where Federalists commanded an absolute majority and were convinced of the reliability of their candidates, they restricted themselves to providing only a brief, general statement in favor of the Constitution. If they found themselves in the minority, they concentrated on preventing strict instructions requiring delegates to reject the Constitution. They did not fundamentally deny communities the right to issue instructions, but argued that they should not be restrictive. In the *Worcester Magazine,* "Propriety" questioned whether the duties of convention delegates could be equated with those of ordinary legislative representatives: "The design of the Convention . . . is for the Members to Give all the Information they can, to each other, respecting the proposed federal government—to HEAR all that can be said for and against it—then to CONSIDER what is best; and finally to determine according to the best information they shall have received from hearing this weighty and important business thoroughly debated." The author hoped such considerations might move the towns to refrain from insisting on instructions, or even rescind those already issued.[162]

Some commentaries hinted that binding directives were not entirely appropriate in a modern representative system of government. "Marcus" criticized the (Antifederalist) instructions given to the delegates of Sandwich: "If a town decides upon the question, and their decision is binding upon their delegates, *they* can answer the purposes of carriers only, or be the mere mechanical echo of a party; and the design of the Convention . . . is intirely frustrated."[163] Federalists turned Thomas Bourn from Sandwich, Barnstable County, into a national figure when he resigned his convention seat after the town tried to compel him and fellow delegate Thomas Smith, by a vote of 73–3, to vote against the Constitution. The reasons he offered for his resignation were soon carried in all Federalist newspapers: "It is true my sentiments at present, are not in favour of the Constitution. Open to Conviction however, they may be very different when the subject is fairly discussed by able and upright men. . . . Under the restrictions with which your delegates are fettered, the greatest ideot might answer your purpose as well, as the greatest man."[164]

Friends of the Constitution in Northampton and Easthampton on the

Connecticut River merely offered a few "suggestions" to delegates Caleb Strong and Benjamin Sheldon after expressly declining to give them instructions:

> The Object of your Mission, Gentlemen, is of the highest Magnitude in human affairs. . . . Be not unduly influenced by any local consideration—Let your minds be impressed with the necessity of having an equal, energetic, federal Government —'Tis the welfare & dignity of the Union, as well as of Massachusetts that you are to consult—and while you are tenacious of the rights & privileges of the PEOPLE, be not afraid to delegate to the federal Government such powers as are absolutely necessary for advancing & maintaining our national Honor & Happiness. But, Gentlemen, We mean not to give you positive instructions relative to your voting for or against the reported Constitution—When assembled you will have the collected wisdom of the State before you—will hear all that can be said on the Subject and consequently be able to form a judicious opinion—And having the fullest confidence in your political wisdom, integrity & patriotism, We chearfully, on our part, submit the all important Question to your decision—And We beseech the All Wise Governor of the World to take the Convention under his holy Influence, that the Result may be, THE BEST GOOD OF THE PEOPLE, OF THE UNITED STATES OF AMERICA.

At the behest of Federalists, this imposing "address" was adopted by several towns along the Connecticut River, thus helping Federalists to encroach on opposition territory in the west. Ignorant of the text's source, even Greenleaf's *New York Journal* recommended "this cautious mode of proceeding" as an example worthy of emulation.[165]

Binding instructions had been a point of contention for some time, and far beyond New England. At the height of the paper money controversy in Maryland, in February 1787, Samuel Chase defended the right of voters to instruct their delegates: "If they are your representatives, they are bound by your instructions, or you destroy the very idea of election, and of delegated power. To represent, is to speak and act agreeably to the opinions and sentiments of the persons represented, in the same manner as they would do, if personally present." Prior to the legislative elections in the fall of 1788, Chase reiterated that he felt obligated as a representative "to give up my private sentiments . . . to those of my constituents, and to execute their wishes, and not my own, or to resign my seat."[166]

Reaction to this republican position was typically justified by references to "historical" rights, and were not long in coming. Direct responses were offered by James McHenry and Alexander Contee Hanson, who encouraged the citizens of Maryland to move away from instructions and toward "information, remonstrances, or advice."[167] Noah Webster addressed the question of instructions in March 1788. With impeccable logic, he demonstrated that the will of the people as a whole, which formed the foundation of all laws and constitutions, could only be derived from a meeting of all citizens or an assembly of their elected representatives. Even taken together, the declarations of intent issued by town or county meetings did not represent the "collective sense" of the state: "For not being possessed of the best general information, the people often form wrong opinions of their own interest." The minutes of state legislatures clearly revealed that local meetings had provided the impetus for many of the most damaging measures taken, such as the emission of paper money and the protection of debtors. Fettering delegates by instructions was not only misguided in a practical sense, it also violated the "very doctrine of representation in government. . . . The design of choosing Representativs is to collect the wisdom of the State; the Deputies are to unite their Councils; to meet and consult for the public safety: But positive instructions prevent this effect; they are dictated by local interests, or opinions formed on an imperfect view of facts and arguments. . . . They make the opinions of a small part of the State a rule for the whole; they imply a decision of a question, before it is heard; they reduce a Representative to a mere machine, by restraining the exercise of his reason; they subvert the very principle of republican government."[168]

Nearly all Federalists adopted this position during the dispute over the Constitution. In Massachusetts, New Hampshire, Rhode Island, Virginia, and the Carolinas, they dedicated a large portion of their energy to preventing or undermining binding instructions against ratification.[169] In some cases, they were apparently convinced that this end justified nearly any means. Theodore Sedgwick used filibusters to protract town meetings until there was nearly no one left but his own supporters. At the following meeting he made sure there was majority support for the Federalist candidate—with the help of ineligible voters, if necessary. In Great Barrington, he employed such methods to wrest a duly awarded convention seat from Dr. William Whiting, a Shays activist previously convicted of seditious libel. In an awkward complaint by Antifederalists, the selectmen were implicated in the affair: "It was aboundantly Evident that the Selectman & their pertizans ware determined to Imbarris the Meeting & if possible to nulify Every thing which had been done."[170]

At other places, Federalist candidates collected the ballots themselves, abruptly called special meetings to revoke instructions, or added pro-Constitution delegates where a single Antifederalist had been chosen. With the help of tactics such as these and, in particular, their successful anti-instruction campaign, Federalists managed to minimize losses in western Massachusetts. They were much stronger in Boston and along the seacoast. The Boston elections took place on December 7, 1787, at Faneuil Hall after several lists nominating convention delegates had been published by both parties in the newspapers. In all, 763 votes were cast, with former governor James Bowdoin receiving the most, 760. The twelve delegates Boston was entitled to elect turned out to be mostly prominent public officials, merchants, and lawyers. Only three among them—Governor John Hancock, Samuel Adams, and Charles Jarvis—were suspected of harboring Antifederalist feelings. In order to put pressure on Adams and the other "doubtful" candidates, 380 Boston tradesmen gathered two days before the opening of the Massachusetts convention, on January 7, 1788, in the Green Dragon Tavern, where they issued a warning that a vote against ratification would be "contrary to the best interests, the strongest feelings, and warmest wishes" of the town's working people.[171] In Cambridge, Federalists Francis Dana and Stephen Dana were chosen by an overwhelming majority, whereas the prominent Antifederalists Elbridge Gerry and James Winthrop received only one vote each, "and these it is presumed were put in by everybody guesses who," as the *Massachusetts Centinel* scornfully commented.[172] Another Antifederalist leader and publicist, James Warren, lost in Milton in Sussex County.[173]

Yet despite all their electioneering efforts, Federalists constituted a minority when the Massachusetts convention met on January 9, 1788. The large number of delegates (over 350), coupled with the delicate nuances of language used in many of the towns' instructions, rendered an accurate assessment of the political landscape exceedingly difficult. Federalists felt encouraged by the fact that "the weight of ability, property and probity, is decided in favor of the Constitution." At the same time, they were aware of the presence of some "men of integrity and candor" among their opponents, "who declare they come not decided, but are ready and desirous of being informed."[174] If they could succeed in winning over about twenty of these delegates, they might be able to wrestle the Constitution from the brink of defeat.

NEW YORK

In comparison with New England's town meeting model, the elections in the middle states, and especially in New York, seem quite modern. In these areas, voting districts were drawn up along county lines and each county was apportioned a certain number of delegates. The greatest drawback here was that the redistribution of seats to accommodate demographic changes was undertaken by legislatures only at very great intervals or not at all. There were also complaints about the small number of polling stations, which meant that voting could become a very arduous procedure, particularly during inclement weather. Some improvements had already been instituted in this regard, and voters were normally willing to travel a certain distance anyway, since elections were also a social event at which one might meet old friends and acquaintances. Overall, the manner of elections in New York was more adapted to the needs and mentality of a free-market society in which individual values were placed above corporate ones. Like their counterparts in neighboring Pennsylvania, New Yorkers were accustomed to the fact that the principle of competition also prevailed in public life, and a political party could only gain control of political institutions if it had the firm backing of the electorate. Consequently, Hamiltonians and Clintonians vied to establish a close rapport with their constituents, seeking to persuade and mobilize the electorate through meetings, speeches, articles in the press, petition campaigns, etc.[175] The combined legislative and convention elections in the spring of 1788 were overwhelmingly regarded as the most decisive event in the state's history up to that point. Nowhere did Federalists and Antifederalists wage a more fierce battle for voters than in New York, where state and national politics became inseparably connected. New England native Samuel Blachley Webb, now a New York merchant, explained to a business partner in Boston the difference between Boston and New York: "With you 'tis all fair and quiet, but with us 'tis all confusion. Parties for different sides appear publicly and sometimes blows ensue."[176]

The election owed its intensity to a combination of strong personal commitments and advanced political organization. After a lengthy period in which the debate had been primarily carried out in the press, the announcement of the convention date in early February 1788 whipped both sides into frenzied activity. The elimination of property qualifications for voting and the concurrence of legislative and convention elections reinforced the general feeling among the populace that a historic event was unfolding. Holding both elections simultaneously was not merely practical, it also made sense politically. In the view of Federalists, it symbolized the permanent fusion of New York's fate with that of the Union; Antifederalists, on the other hand, saw the legislature and the convention as two fortifications in their double line of defense against the Constitution. To Henry Oothoudt, a judge and Antifederalist candidate for a convention seat, the election campaign in Albany County appeared to set new standards for political activism: "I do believe since the settlement of America such exertions have not been made upon a business of any kind as the present upon the New Constitution. Those who advocate the measure are engaged from morning untill evening they travel both night and day to proselyte the unbelieving Antifederals." The weekend before, the city of Albany was said to have been nearly devoid of the "Better Kind of People," all of whom were supposedly visiting surrounding communities to preach the gospel of the new Constitution.[177]

Examples from other counties confirm that Albany was not an aberration. A letter to London by Peter Van Schaack reveals the pleasure he derived from his energetic efforts in Columbia County on behalf of the Constitution: "A frame of government held out to the people at large for discussion, is a phenomenon in political annals. You cannot conceive what agitation it has occasioned; it was a war of tongues, but a few bloody noses have been the consequence. I have mounted the rostrum several times, and harangued the multitude on law, government and politics. . . . Public speaking is much in vogue, and were you here you would be reminded of the days of ancient Greece and Rome."[178] The Federalists' hopes in Westchester County were revived when Philip Van Cortlandt, the son of the lieutenant governor, cast his reservations to the wind and charged into the battle "as out of a Gothic Cloister. . . . The Air so strongly impregnated with federalism has infused into his nostrils the aromatic, his whole frame infected with the contagion has called him forth to Action and has transported him from extreme inaction to increasing exertion. He is making Interest to be returned a Delegate."[179] Abraham Bancker was too proud to come right out and ask the voters of Richmond County (Staten Island) for their support, though he did maintain daily interaction with constituents.[180] In New York City, Federalists not only had the advantage of such famous candidates as Alexander Hamilton, John Jay, James Duane, and Robert R. Livingston, they also benefited from the tireless efforts of Samuel Blackley Webb, who became so involved in the election campaign that he neglected his business obligations.

As impressive as all this activity may have been, it was still eclipsed in most counties by the exertions of Antifederalists. "We are in close action from morning to night," the chairman of the Anti-Federal Committee of Albany, Jeremiah Van Rensselaer, reported to John Lamb in New York City.[181] At his estate in Columbia County, Robert Livingston was perturbed by the constant comings and goings of Antifederalist messengers sent to "poison" the minds of his tenants. In Ulster County, Peter Van Gaasbeek traveled from town to town, conferred with allies, and wrote letters to anyone who appeared open to Antifederalist ideas.[182] The opposition activists spurred each other on in the southern part of the state, where the political wind seemed to be blowing in their faces: "*For Shame*—you must *Stir yourself* meet your Friends some where—agree upon a good list—hold them up—persevere—even to the end—Characters you know—go through the County—don't lie Idle."[183]

The most striking feature of the New York elections was the high level of party organization, not the passionate commitment of individual figures. This became particularly obvious during the candidate-selection process. In most counties, Federalists and Antifederalists created election committees, which established contact with possible candidates and selected those with the most potential. They then presented their lists of suggested candidates to party members in other parts of the district and called together representatives from each precinct for a nominating convention. At these conventions, the Constitution was discussed and often put to a vote. The primary purpose of the meetings, however, was to draw up a definitive list of candidates, which was then published along with an election announcement designed to get their candidates' campaigns off to a flying start. The Federal Committee of Albany presented its ticket on March 16, offering voters this choice: "Shall we continue to be UNITED with the other STATES? or, Shall we rashly oppose them? Therefore, we strongly advise, That you vote every Individual on the List." This statement was signed by the thirteen committee members and twenty-four other citizens of the city of Albany.[184] Three weeks later, the seven Antifederalist candidates were also put forward: "From an apprehension that the Constitution, if adopted in its present form, would deprive the people of their dearest rights and liberties, a Number of Gentlemen, from different parts of this county, met for the purpose of nominating and recommending Delegates for Convention, and unanimously resolved on the following Gentlemen." In response to the claims of their adversaries, Antifederalists listed their most important objections to the Constitution "in as few words as possible." The twenty-six signers considered it wiser to call a second general convention to amend the Constitution rather than to ratify the plan, with its numerous "material and radical defects."[185]

In Columbia County, the Federalist ticket was adopted on March 11 at a "Meeting of a number of very respectable citizens . . . from each district, held at Claverack." The opposition met at the same location a week later. According to the *Hudson Weekly Gazette,* the second nominating convention was attended by "a number of very respectable citizens from a majority of the districts of this county, though perhaps not the first characters in point of property, yet as such in point of attachment to the liberty, independence and happiness of America." The selection of candidates in Dutchess, Ulster, and Montgomery Counties followed the same pattern.[186] However, the proceedings were not always conducted in an open and seemly manner. For example, a party might put several tickets in circulation at the same time to divide their adversaries and confuse the public. When Robert R. Livingston accused Federalists in Ulster County of inaction, Thomas Tillotson replied: "We prefered secret to open measures in order that the other party might divide before we came foreward with our nomination." He conceded that the Federalists' prospects looked "very gloomy" in that particular Clinton stronghold.[187] Opponents of the Constitution also resorted to trickery to win votes in New York City. Shortly before the election, they distributed ballots which at first glance looked identical to those used by Federalists. Clinton's name led the list, but the list was folded in such a way as not to be noticeable.[188] Antifederalists had already taken care to ensure that the governor had a place on the Ulster ticket. Getting Melancton Smith on the Dutchess County ticket proved somewhat more difficult, as a few local dignitaries felt they had been snubbed. Federalists—disguised as "Many Antifederalists"—added fuel to the fire by reawakening latent doubts about Smith by suggesting that he was an outsider and that his opposition to the Constitution was not firm.[189]

Still, these problems were minor compared to the complications facing Federalists in many districts. In Columbia County, for example, their preparations were hampered by a family feud between various members of the Livingston clan, which raged on despite efforts by Philip Schuyler to intervene. John Livingston withdrew his candidacy following disagreements with Federalists in the city of Hudson and ignored the pleas of his relatives to reconsider. Unsuccessful attempts were also made to replace Henry Livingston with the more popular Peter R. Livingston, John's brother and the brother-in-law of Chancellor Robert R. Livingston. Even Peter Van Schaack nearly lost heart in the face of so much contention: "A Family that can so disjoin themselves upon so momentous an Occasion whilst they have shewn they will coalesce in any Point of County Politics must not be relied upon. Our Opponents forego all these partial Considerations and floate to one Standard."[190] Considerable damage was also sustained in the westernmost county of Montgomery when Abraham Van Vechten petitioned to have his name removed from the ticket three weeks before the election. His Federalist friends, who had taken great pains on his behalf, were vexed: "We are apprehensive that the Consequence of his declining at this Crisis, will Create Confusion amongst the Election." The situation looked worse still in Ulster County, where Federalists were incapable of capitalizing on discord in their adversaries' camp.[191]

In general, "local electioneering" within the confines of one's particular precinct or county prevailed, despite considerable efforts to coordinate activities between counties and unite local pursuits in a statewide campaign. In early February, for example, opponents of the Constitution from Orange and Ulster Counties met in the town of Montgomery to express their "unanimous disapprobation of the system" before solemnly delivering up the Constitution to the flames. Antifederalist delegates from Ulster and Kings conferred with one another on the question of which of the two districts should best be represented by Clinton.[192] The greatest sources of motivation and inspiration were both parties' election committees in New York City and Albany, who spared no trouble or expense to prop up their less organized supporters in the surrounding counties. It was the duty of the Albany committees to disseminate printed matter, most of which originated in New York City, throughout the backcountry. Express rider services created specifically for this purpose helped improve both the flow of information to the citizens and the coordination of the election campaign. Abraham Yates even began to fear they might be doing too much. Federalists might use the extensive traffic between counties as an excuse to claim that resistance to the Constitution was strictly a "party affair." He worried that if he returned to the campaign trail and revived old contacts, he would strengthen this Federalist argument.[193] Despite this concern, the Antifederalist committees of Ulster and Albany later initiated the establishment of correspondence committees in every county to promote a regular exchange of ideas.[194]

Whereas the opposition doubled their efforts as election day grew near, Federalists seemed to be losing momentum everywhere but in New York City and vicinity. When the polling stations opened on April 29, observers were on hand from the county committees to keep an eye on the official inspectors and rule out voter intimidation or other means of manipulating the outcome. Jeremiah Van Rensselaer had impressed upon the Antifederalist representatives in each precinct: "Pray attend the Poll constantly until it is closed to see that all Matters are properly conducted. We rely on your Exertions." They were to take particular care to ensure that landlords did not exert political influence over their tenants, who had allegedly been directed to fold their ballots in a certain way: "If they do, you will direct the anti Voters to do the same."[195] Over-vigilance also posed certain hazards, as a Hudson man discovered when he was jailed after falsely accusing a member of the board of supervisors of exchanging ballots.[196] The *Daily Advertiser* in New York City instructed the electorate on how to make proper use of their right to vote: simply handing back the printed list of candidates was not enough—the names of preferred candidates had to be marked. Those persons who received the most votes would be declared the winner.[197]

In New York City, Federalists won a landslide victory. Samuel Blachley Webb vividly described this triumph in a letter to his fiancée: the citizens "laid aside their usual business, and paid their whole attention to the important business before them, all was conducted with perfect order and regularity, it was not a contested Election, the Friends to an Energetic Fœdral

Government were so unanimous, that no danger was to be apprehended,—a small attempt was made by the Governors expiring party, in the first day, after which we heard no more of them, out of about 3,000 votes, I much doubt if they have two Hundred." Nathaniel Hazard gushed that "Never were so many Votes given in at any Election in this City and County, as for the State Convention; nor were the People ever so *unanimous* I may say, as on this Business."[198] Thanks to the industrious party committees, the remaining twelve counties also registered a record turnout, this time mainly to the advantage of the opposition, however. Peter Wynkoop reported from Kinderhook in Columbia County that Federalists and Antifederalists had both gone to great lengths: "No pains has been spared in collecting the Votes—upward of 700 have been taken for Delegates."[199] Considerably more votes were cast for convention delegates than for legislative candidates—one and the same person in many cases.[200] This was partially attributable to the retention of property qualifications for voters in the legislative elections, though the heightened interest surrounding the issue of the Constitution was also clearly a factor.

The five-day elections were followed by a period of extreme tension: the law mandated that the ballot boxes be kept sealed for four weeks. A group of county supervisors especially sworn in for this service commenced counting the ballots on May 27. They announced the results and issued election certificates to the delegates, then destroyed the ballots and related documents. Federalists began struggling with their fate long before the results had been officially announced. "In this state, as far as we can judge the elections have gone wrong," Hamilton warned Gouverneur Morris and Madison on May 19.[201] Pennsylvania Congressman William Bingham blamed the New York Federalists for the result: "If the Friends of the fœderal System had been more active in disseminating their opinions, and had taken an earlier period for impressing them, they would not have at present to lament their unsuccessful Efforts in procuring a Majority in the Convention of this State—they confided too much in the good sense of the People and in the Belief that their Interests were too intimately connected with the Adoption of the proposed Government to admit the possibility of their rejecting it."[202]

The true scale of the Federalists' defeat exceeded even their most pessimistic predictions. Their opponents carried nine of the thirteen counties and controlled forty-six of the sixty-five convention seats. The voters' strong party identification can be seen in the complete absence of split delegations. Either all Federalist contenders were chosen or every candidate on the "republican" list won by approximately the same number of votes. "Our antagonists are much Crest fallen and have very little to say," sneered Abraham G. Lansing in Albany.[203] All the same, Federalists were not yet ready to throw in the towel, especially considering that their most important leaders were elected to the convention on the New York City ticket. Hamilton was confident that some of Clinton's supporters would be daunted by the consequences of rejecting the Constitution and would not want to risk breaking away from the rest of the Union. "As Clinton is truly the leader of his party, and is inflexibly obstinate I count little on overcoming opposition by reason. Our only chances will be the previous ratification by nine states, which may shake the firmness of his followers; and a change in the sentiments of the people which have been for some time travelling toward the constitution, though the first impressions made by every species of influence and artifice were too strong to be eradicated in time to give a decisive turn to the elections."[204] Peter Van Schaack was also counting on a swing in the public mood. This time the "popular tide" had been against them, he consoled his friends, but "what was *right* and *good*" would prevail in the end.[205] The Antifederalists' victory was aided by their position as the ruling party in New York behind a governor who enjoyed the widespread backing of the rural population. Antifederalists had also developed an exceptional organization, and they were determined not to let this slip away. The Federal Republican Committee in New York City, with branches in the counties, represented a partisan infrastructure with great promise for the future. John Lansing hoped that Antifederalist delegates from all over the state might meet together a day or two before the convention to develop unified amendment proposals and draw up a plan of operation "which would promote our object and systamize the Business."[206]

VIRGINIA

The elections in Virginia reveal a society searching for a balance between the pull of tradition and the forces of change. The public attitude of many Americans was still shaped by the image of an elite class of plantation owners who drew their strength from slave labor and the political compliance, or "deference," of small farmers. It was said in the South itself that the states from Maryland to Georgia had only emerged from the Revolution with a republican façade: "For however democratic they may be in their Constitution, they are in their exercise and operation, almost, if not altogether, perfectly aristocratic."[207] To Antifederalist James Mercer it was unthinkable that the "High Toned Gentry" of Virginia could ever become "sound Republicans": "They but deceive themselves if they think so, like the Lady in the Fable they will catch Mice if ever one comes their way."[208]

In reality, the situation was not as static as it seemed. The Virginia gentry's patriarchal style of leadership and their social predominance had been subjected to challenges ever since the middle of the century. The mainsprings of this development were of an economic, religious, and political nature. The gradual transition from a purely tobacco-based economy to grain production favored the middle class, whose material existence was less dependent on slave ownership. This shift, on the other hand, rendered Virginia equally as vulnerable to militant forms of small-farmer protests as states like Massachusetts and New Hampshire. Furthermore, a spiritual reawakening had been gathering momentum among lower- and middle-class whites since the 1740s. This primarily Baptist movement not only threatened the privileges of the Anglican Church, it declared war on the "courtly" gentry culture in general. The crusaders of this "evangelical" religion challenged the elite's self-perception and values by replacing their carefree lifestyle and chivalrous concept of competition with rigid moral constraints and the ideal of brotherly communion. Their message was spread orally, which lessened the influence of the written word, the basis of gentry culture. The third challenge was represented by the radical Whig ideology. Adopted by the gentry themselves during the struggle against England, its egalitarian dogma now threatened the very foundation of their stronghold on domestic politics. By subscribing to the theory of a social contract as a voluntary pact among individuals of equal rank, the gentry had succeeded in forming a Revolutionary alliance with the evangelical movement and securing for themselves a leading role in the War of Independence. However, the right to have an equal say in political decision making implicitly applied to all free citizens, a conception that eroded the hegemony of the plantation owners. In addition, the severity of the South's struggle against England had rendered the "common man" less willing to recognize an authority based on social class alone. The convergence of these various factors had resulted in a transformation of political attitudes and patterns of behavior.[209]

To prevent this development from getting out of control, the gentry would have to forgo its dependence on established rights and privileges, responding to public opinion on a scale previously unthinkable. The paternalism and condescension commonly used by the members of the upper class when addressing "middling" constituents would have to give way to mutual respect and real competition for votes. Paradoxically, one of the elements of the gentry's own code of competition, their propensity for internal rivalry, turned out to be an advantage. Their nearly equal division between the two camps of Federalists and Antifederalists meant that prominent representatives of the gentry were able to maintain their dominion over both sides. This helped avoid a social confrontation and kept the door open for future accord.

The preeminent political role played by the "Old Dominion" during the Revolution and the framing of the Constitution was perplexing to many citizens of New England. "How happens it that the Southern States produce such gigantick politicians?" Thomas B. Wait inquired of George Thatcher. The southerners were generally less well educated than the northerners: "The great body of their people are certainly not so well informed as we yankees—not because they are inferior in point of understanding, but because their States are unfortunately divided into Counties, instead of towns—by which means they are deprived of the inestimable privileges of Town Schoolmasters for Boys and Girls, and Town Teachers of Morality and Religion."[210] This reference to the greater disparity between the various levels of education in the South was surely justified. The poor schooling available to the rural population and inhabitants of the relatively small number of large communities contrasted sharply with the elite education conferred on the gentry, who had the means to hire private tutors for their sons and enroll them in universities abroad. A considerable number of politicians and judges in Maryland and Virginia had perfected their knowledge of law at the London Inns of Court. This mixture of wealth, education, and leisure gave southern "gentlemen" an unparalleled advantage and unlocked doors to public office. There was thus a vast social chasm between the constituents and their representatives, and the outcome of elections was more closely linked to the public persona of the candidates than was the case in other regions.

Still, the political circumstances in the South were in a state of flux and were beginning to resemble those in the North. Since the end of the Revolution, the voters had taken increased interest in such issues as the relationship between church and state and efforts to solve the economic crisis. They insisted on being better informed and were more adamant about making their wishes known. In response, the gentry increased the flow of information through speeches, articles in the press, and broadsheets, while slowly turning their attention to political party organization. They were nevertheless unable to prevent *homines novi* such as Patrick Henry from rising out of the middle class to enter legislative bodies, where they made the public arena more spirited yet less predictable.

The election campaign in the "Old Dominion" was launched on October 31, 1787, by a legislative resolution calling a ratifying convention, and it continued unabated right up to the elections themselves in March 1788, "on the first day of the court to be held for each county, city, or corporation."[211] At this time, Virginia and the District of Kentucky had eighty-four counties, each of which could send two delegates to the convention, analogous to their representation in the state legislature. State officials as well as delegates to Congress were freed from legal restrictions and allowed to run for a convention seat, heightening thereby the prestige and excitement of the elections. The opposition took an early lead on the propaganda front with the help of controversial and widely disseminated proclamations by George Mason and Richard Henry Lee, whereas Federalists were forced to make due with printed matter shipped in from other states. From his vantage point at Mount Vernon, Tobias Lear (George Washington's personal secretary) had the impression that Antifederalists were showing more verve and initiative: "Every exertion has been made by the enemies, while the friends of the Constitution seem to have rested the issue upon the goodness of their cause."[212] The General himself—having declined to be a candidate for the ratifying convention—was infuriated by the style and content of opposition publications, which had obviously been crafted to appeal to the people's emotions and prejudices instead of their sense of reason. He was also incensed by the aggressive campaign tactics of his neighbor, George Mason, about whom David Stuart remarked that he should have contented himself with simply publishing his *Objections*, "without taking the pains to lodge them at every house."[213] In Fredericksburg, James Duncanson cursed the "worthless antifederalists" who were going to such great lengths "to poison & prejudice the lower order of People."[214]

Federalists particularly chafed at Patrick Henry's relentless "sermons" against the Constitution in the southern part of the state, where Edward Carrington lamented that so many people had joined the "wrong" side "that the people must be misled for want of the necessary information."[215] Madison learned from the Reverend John B. Smith in Henry's home district of Prince Edward that the tireless agitator had "descended to lower artifice & management upon the occasion than I thought him capable of." He had reportedly extended his influence to the Kentucky district and alarmed the settlers "with an apprehension of their interests being about to be sacrificed by the Northern States."[216] There were also local politicians in Kentucky who energetically supported the opposition. Harry Innes petitioned the county courts to promulgate a notice he had penned in order to make it accessible to all voters before the election. Its main point was that the happiness and greatness of the western territories would be destroyed forever if the Constitution were adopted: the North was planning to scrap plans to invest in the navigation of the Mississippi and to redirect the funds intended for development of the region to the federal tax coffers. Furthermore, a centralized militia would leave them exposed to Indian raids. To Madison this form of propaganda was akin to hurling the "torch of discord" into the volatile masses.[217]

Federalists were forced grudgingly to acknowledge their adversaries' successes in several parts of the state. This triumph was the work of "men high in popular estimation," explained the *Pennsylvania Packet*, "some of them of first rate talents, indefatigable in spreading their objections, and artful in addressing them in such language, and in such a mode, as is most likely to captivate and delude the vulgar."[218] Included in this reference was surely John Leland, leader of the Virginia Baptists, who, like Madison, resided in Orange County, and who baptized more than three hundred converts in 1788. The appeal of Virginia-style Antifederalism was evidently based on a mixture of regional pride, Revolutionary ideology, and evangelist preaching.[219]

The proponents of the Constitution were by no means content to watch from the sidelines. They were quite able and willing to make themselves heard and defend their position. In February 1788, St. John de Crèvecoeur gained the impression while traveling through the Union that Virginia was the only state "in which the parties pro & con seem to run very high." To John Dawson it appeared that the efforts of all sides were fairly well matched: "The approaching elections are the subject of general conversation in this state at this time, and uncommon exertions are made by all parties to have elected those persons whose sentiments agree with their own."[220] The nature of the parties was described by James Madison in a letter to Thomas Jefferson dated December 9, 1787. The first group, whose supporters included Washington and Edmund Pendleton, strove for ratification without amendments; the second group, featuring such prominent members as George Mason and Governor Edmund Randolph, demanded additional guarantees for the rights of the states and the citizens; the third group, led by Patrick Henry, initially joined the chorus of those calling for amendments, though their real goal was changes in the very essence and structure of the proposed system of government, which, in effect, would have meant either returning to a confederation or splitting the Union into separate regional alliances.[221]

The selection of candidates was more closely linked to party agendas than had been usual before this time in Virginia. "A Planter" championed traditional criteria and values, explaining that the voice of nature and the language of reason demanded that those who had previously proven themselves "the *most worthy*" be chosen as representatives in matters of national importance, "men of acknowledged abilities, and of tried integrity;—men, who have, already, rendered important services to the state."[222] Personal reputation and past accomplishments in this election were not, however, the only points considered. Voters wanted to know a candidate's stance on the Constitution and whether he intended to vote for or against ratification. The informal nomination proceedings fostered tactical maneuvering and intrigue. Confidential discussions and letters were the best means of encouraging promising candidates and discouraging those who had little chance of winning, or were unreliable. A politician's prospects could be ruined by rumors he had no serious intentions of fulfilling a voter mandate. The dovetailing of national and state politics forced candidates to consider whether it would jeopardize their chances of victory in the upcoming General Assembly elections if they took a definite stance for or against the Constitution. This led to intense behind-the-scenes wrangling which felled even such prominent candidates as Arthur Lee.[223] The parties' main objective was a popular county delegation prepared to pursue a clear political agenda. For their part, Federalists felt the need to come up with a few Revolutionary War heroes. The citizens preferred "military men," John Mark pointed out in a letter to General Horatio Gates, "being well assured if the New Plan of Government is not adopted we must Sink, therefore every exertion should be made to Send Gentn. that would use their Utmost and best endeavours to have the Government recommended."[224]

In the Antifederalist camp, there was great consternation regarding the nomination of George Mason, whose views were not popular in his home county of Fairfax. The dilemma was solved by having Mason stand for election in Stafford County. Just to be on the safe side, James Mercer suggested having Mason run in both counties, "for such a Man shou'd not be risqued at so important a crisis."[225] Stafford County did elect the famous owner of Gunston Hall. A suitable slot on a ticket could also have been reserved for Richard Henry Lee, had he not withdrawn from consideration at a very early stage—much to the chagrin of his friends.[226] George Nicholas had an entirely different approach than Mason and Lee. His respect for the will of the constituents went so far that he committed himself to voting for ratification, "however contrary it may be to his own opinions."[227] By contrast, Judge Henry Tazewell refused the Antifederalists' offer of a nomination, even though he shared their views. He felt a majority of county residents favored the adoption of the Constitution, and he wanted to avoid "warm conflict with old friends."[228]

All sides concurred that the battle for convention seats was far more severe than any known assembly elections. There were direct confrontations between proponents and adversaries of the Constitution in fifty-five of the eighty-four Virginia counties—a high percentage compared to earlier elections. Along the Rappahannock River and in the Northern Neck, Antifederalists only nominated candidates if they believed they had a serious chance of winning. Federalists proceeded in the same manner in the area controlled by Patrick Henry's "demagogues" south of the James River. The unprecedented intensity of the debate is evidenced not only by the parties' increased use of pamphlets and newspapers, the candidates were also forced to conduct organized campaigns if they wanted to have any chance of victory. Robert Carter, for example, who had already retired from public life in 1775, informed the voters of Westmoreland County in a notice posted on the court building in late November 1787 "that he offers himself a Candidate on this very interesting and important occasion—And he herein Solicites the favor of their Votes at this place on the Court day in the Month of March Next." He asked his friend James Bland to provide him with the names of all freeholders who had voted in the last legislative election, so he could address each one individually. Since his health did not permit him to realize this idea, he circulated a subscription list in February 1788 for people to sign, "who wish my attendance at the approaching convention." Despite Carter's efforts, the voters finally elected Henry Lee and Bushrod Washington.[229]

James Madison regarded such canvassing as beneath his dignity and admitted to an "extreme distaste to steps having an electioneering character."[230] He would have much preferred to remain in Congress and leave this business to his friends and relatives in Orange County. In certain instances prominent citizens received enough votes in absentia, or the voters spontaneously elected a candidate of their own choosing. This is precisely what happened in York County: on election day, the freeholders spurned both the Federalist and Antifederalist candidates, proceeding as a group to Williamsburg instead, where they beseeched George Wythe and John Blair to accept convention seats, men who were considered "still open to conviction" and "well qualified to determine wisely." In response to the chorus of "Will you serve? Will you serve?" Judge Wythe leaned out the window of his house and said simply, "Surely, how can I refuse?" The crowd then escorted Wythe and Blair back to the site of the assembly and unanimously elected them to be convention delegates. This incident reveals the curious manner in which traditional deference to leading citizens could be combined with the freeholders' new sense of self-confidence and desire to regulate their own affairs.[231] Madison, on the other hand, would probably have lost if he had not returned to campaign in Orange County.[232]

The climax of the campaign, of course, was the actual voting, which normally took place on the particular county's court day. Public elections in Virginia always amounted to a ritualistic confirmation of community spirit, and as such resembled a mass celebration. The personal element, which had always given Virginia politics a special flair, came to bear in discussions between candidates and constituents, as well as in the tradition of voting by voice. Though the written word obviously possessed great power, it was no substitute in this part of the country for an inspiring election address. In fact, the art of speech making had experienced a renaissance in the Revolutionary era, as audiences grew and the eloquence of lawyers was complemented by the simple yet stirring rhetoric of evangelical revivalists.

For James Madison, whose convention seat remained uncertain to the end, there was no escaping the necessity of "stump oratory." The "absurd and groundless prejudices against the fœderal Constitution" showed no signs of abating until he followed the urgent advice of friends and traveled to Orange County himself, where he took the podium amid snow flurries on a chilling, windswept day. James Duncanson witnessed the mood swing: "Your friend Maddison came in the day before the Election in Orange, and when the People assembled converted them in a speech of an hour and three quarters, delivered at the Court house door before the Pol opened, so that he and James Gordon were chosen by a large majority." Francis Taylor also confirmed in his diary that a great feeling of satisfaction pervaded the community after Madison's defense.[233] Conversely, Antifederalist John Dawson explained to the citizens of Spotsylvania County the "fatal Tendency" of the Constitution in "so masterly a Manner" that he received a large majority of votes, despite the fierce resistance of his adversaries.[234]

In the assumption that his nephew in Philadelphia was wholly unaware of the meaning of "to hold a pole," David Thomas sent him this wry description of voting Virginia style:

> The Candidate stands upon an eminence close to the Avenue thro which the people pass to give in their votes, viva voce, or by outcry. There the Candidates stand ready to beg, pray, and solicit the peoples votes in opposition to their Competitors, and the poor wretched people are much difficulted by the prayers and threats of those Competitors, exactly similar to the Election of the corrupt and infamous House of Commons in England. At the last Election I was drag'd from my lodging when at dinner, and forced upon the eminence purely against my will, but I soon disappeared and returned to my repast; and as soon as they lost sight of me they quit voting for me. Such is the pitiful and lowliv'd manner all the elected officers of Government come into posts of honour and profit in Virginia, by stooping into the dirt that they may ride the poor people; and would you have your Uncle to divest himself of every principle of honour to obtain a disagreeable office I hope not.[235]

This direct contact between candidates and voters at polling places was also problematic for other reasons. The convention elections in Amherst County, noted Antifederalist William Cabell, "were more hotly contested on the hustings and at the polls than any previous thereto." The fact that he and his son Samuel J. Cabell eventually won the elections likely had as much to do with the generosity of the wealthy plantation family of Union Hill as it did with their politics. In any case, when the dust had settled, father and son Cabell treated everyone present at Lucas Powell's Tavern to ninety-eight gallons of grog ("toddy") and ten gallons of rum. Had Federalists won, the celebration would presumably have been more austere.[236]

Be that as it may, special emphasis was placed on direct contact with the candidates during the convention elections. These exchanges were used to probe the candidates' ideological precepts and pressure them into committing themselves for or against the Constitution. Since established membership in a particular party was unknown, there was simply no other way to compel representatives to observe the will of the constituents. Detailed instructions like those in New England were rare in the South.[237] The citizens were usually content with solemn promises in the form of pledges. Edward Carrington was not fond of this practice: "Most of the elections in the upper & Middleparts of the south side of James River, have been made in Phrenzy, and terminated in deputations of weak & bad Men, who have bound themselves to vote in the negative, and will in all cases be the tools of Mr. H[enry]."[238] Kentucky Antifederalists had planned a special district assembly to solemnly instruct the entire delegation prior to their departure for Richmond. This idea was abandoned, however, when most of the winning candidates declared during the elections that they were open to ratification.[239] Nevertheless, there were contenders on both sides who agreed to oral pledges. Carrington himself lost in Powhatan County to Assemblyman Thomas Turpin, who promised on election day to vote for adoption after originally inveighing against the Constitution. He later enraged his constituents by voting against it after all. In the next election, he lost his seat in the assembly and never regained it.[240]

In early April, Federalist Charles Lee informed his brother Richard Henry Lee that—except from Kentucky—the names of the elected delegates were now generally known, "and the sentiments of almost all of them have been declared."[241] Well-informed politicians kept private lists, and newspapers divided the delegates into Federalists, Antifederalists, and neutral (or "doubtful").[242] The positions of the candidates were known. These enumerations indicated that supporters and critics of the Constitution were evenly matched east of the Blue Ridge Mountains, that the Southside had overwhelmingly voted against, and that the Northern Neck had clearly voted for ratification. According to one account, in the *Virginia Centinel* of April 9, only three counties—Loudoun, Louisa, and Spotsylvania—would send split delegations to the convention, while the outcome in seventeen counties was still doubtful. The Shenandoah Valley gave Federalists an overall edge, but it was thought the delegates from the western part of the state, about whom little was known at that juncture, might help the opposition make up the difference. Both sides had succeeded in securing convention seats for their leaders, which promised interesting debates. Federalists were buoyant, convinced their rivals were sending "weak and desparate characters" into the fray alongside a handful of respected politicians like George Mason and Patrick Henry. Edward Carrington gleefully noted that the tide of passion had swept a throng of "weak & obscure men" to the convention.[243]

Madison was also confident "that in point of characters the advantage will be on the federal side," crediting his party with a general "superiority of abilities."[244] However, George Nicholas sent a word of warning from Charlottesville that the Federalist majority would probably be too slim simply to brush aside the opposition's objections and dictate the decision. They would have to prepare for a compromise along the lines of Massachusetts. Nicholas was looking even farther ahead: following the successful conclusion of the convention, it would lie in the hands of the state legislatures whether or not the new system of government got off to a good start. Madison should therefore be prepared to serve in the Virginia Assembly and help ensure that only "federal men" were elected.[245]

COMMON FEATURES

Regional differences and diverging historical traditions notwithstanding, the elections in these three key states also bore some important similarities. In contrast to legislative elections, the campaign for convention seats was based on a single issue presenting clear alternatives to the voters. This focused their attention on the matter at hand and away from the candidates' person, which in turn fostered a commitment to a particular worldview or ideology. The Constitution also provided a basic agenda with which the people could either agree or disagree, creating at all events clear divisions. This encouraged voter participation and placed unusually severe demands on the candidates. "Campaign fever" acquired unheard of intensity. The use of highly developed and large-scale propaganda techniques naturally increased the need for more coordination and improved party organization. Another unifying element was the fusion of state—and even local—conflicts with national interests. This interdependence between the various levels of government, which is precisely what makes a federal system so intricate and breathes life into it, could already be seen before the new Constitution had gone into force.

It should be noted that the elections were generally calm, fair, and orderly despite the strong emotional element. There was of course plenty of room for improvement compared with modern standards. Some incidents proved that Americans were not known as a "restless people" for nothing. Late on election day in Philadelphia, for example, a mob incited by Federalists marched on the residences of opposition assemblymen and party leaders. Stones were thrown and threats were made to lynch the "damned rascals" for their resistance to ratification. Three days later, the assembly condemned "this violent riot and most outrageous assault" as a "breach of the privilege of its members" and offered a reward of 300 dollars for information leading to the arrest of the perpetrators. The act went unpunished just the same, leaving the skeptical William Shippen to wonder if Pennsylvanians had just been given "a foretaste of this blessed Constitution."[246] The most common complaints involved the manipulation of town meetings, the intimidation of candidates, and the obstruction of voters at the polling places. The victims of these irregularities were often the opponents of the new system, though Federalists also had grounds for complaint on more than one occasion. Several members of the opposition posed as supporters of the Constitution in Maryland, for example, to con desperately needed votes from unsuspecting citizens. Samuel Chase, Luther Martin, and William Paca violated a provision of the Maryland electoral law which stipulated that a candidate could only run for office in his home county.[247] Antifederalists challenged the results of the election in the city of Baltimore, claiming the moderators had not been sworn in and citizens "without any property" had been allowed to vote. In Baltimore County it was also alleged that ballots had been accepted from "apprentice boys, servants and slaves." On the third day of the elections, a mob partially comprised of drunken foreign sailors armed with clubs was reported to have taken control of the ballot boxes and prevented many peaceable constituents from casting their votes.[248]

The most serious incidents occurred in Delaware and in the North Carolina counties of Hertford and Dobbs. The disputes that arose during the Delaware elections had less to do with the Constitution than with the mutual aversion that had characterized the relationship between the so-called Whigs and Tories ever since the Revolution. The commotion began when Tories spread the rumor that Whigs were planning to prevent ratification. The tensions were exacerbated by the double election combining the appointment of convention delegates with the always turbulent allocation of legislative seats. Whigs won in New Castle County and Tories in Kent County for the simple reason that the opposition party in each case abstained from nominating candidates. When efforts to establish a "Union Ticket" in Sussex County failed, Tories abruptly changed the location of the polling station to a more suitable venue and surrounded it with several hundred armed guards. To avoid bloodshed, Whigs refrained from casting votes. Consequently, fewer than 700 ballots were counted instead of the usual 1,000 to 1,100. Whigs then passionately yet futilely petitioned the convention and the state legislature several times to invalidate the results of both elections.[249]

North Carolina Federalists broke up an election meeting in Hertford organized by Baptist preacher Lemuel Burkitt, whose prophecies of loose morals in the nation's future capital had infuriated advocates of the new plan. They also caused a tumult in front of the courthouse the following day, but were unable to prevent Burkitt from winning a convention seat.[250] Dobbs County Federalists resorted to even more drastic measures. When the vote count showed that every one of their candidates, including former governor Richard Caswell, had received fewer votes than even the least popular Antifederalist, Baptist Abraham Baker, they snuffed out the torches, violently disrupted the proceedings, made off with the ballot box in the ensuing confusion, and burned the remaining ballots. Their ringleader, a rich and influential landowner, commented on the riot, in which several opposing candidates and the sheriff had been injured, with the words: "Well done Boys Now we'll have a new Election." Indeed, Governor Samuel Johnston granted their petition and ordered new elections. When the opposition boycotted the second round, the Federalist candidates all won hands down. The ratifying convention subsequently acceded to a written protest signed by 248 Dobbs County residents and stripped Federalists of their seats. As a result, Dobbs County was not represented at the North Carolina convention.[251] The negative press generated by the "Dobbs County Riot" was a source of embarrassment to Federalists and harmful to their image as law-abiding citizens. "Thank God, we have had nothing like it in any other county," sighed Archibald Maclaine.[252]

Incidents of this kind were generally of local importance and had little overall impact on the distribution of convention seats. Considering the explosive atmosphere surrounding the elections, it is astounding there were so few acts of fraud and violence. Neither side had gained any notable advantage by unscrupulous means, and at least a portion of the questionable results was annulled. All conventions established committees to hear complaints about the elections, read witness accounts, and present a report on their findings. In the Dobbs County affair and a few other controversial cases, the convention succeeded in invalidating the election certificates issued by local supervisors or sheriffs, thus excluding the disputed candidates from participation in the ratification debate. Since the rulings of these committees and conventions were also decided by majority vote, abuse was still possible. Nevertheless, the formal investigations did provide meaningful protection against fraud and deception. It can thus be assumed that the final results in every state accurately reflected the will of the people within the bounds of constitutional provisions and election laws valid at that time.

Election Results

Federalist Victories

There is no one explanation for the election results. Interpretations focusing on a single factor, such as the conflict between the coastal regions and the backcountry, between the commercially and agriculturally oriented segments of society, between creditors and debtors, aristocratic conservatives and radical democrats, or nationalists and particularists, cannot do justice to the complexity of the issue. In fact, all these elements played a role in the dispute. But no simple dichotomy can by itself adequately explain the distribution of votes and convention seats. At the same time, the historical realities are not so enigmatic as to force historians to capitulate altogether. The quantitative research undertaken in recent years has facilitated the distinction between relevant and irrelevant factors. In particular, specific regional and local influences, as well as the various economic and political circumstances in the individual states, should not be neglected in favor of a "monolithic" approach. The elections took place in thirteen states and in hundreds of towns and counties. Local personalities, issues, and economic interests all played important roles. It therefore seems advisable to first examine the various state election results.

At least nine of the thirteen states had to ratify the Constitution for it to come into force. However, election results indicated that ratification was only relatively certain in seven states: Pennsylvania, Delaware, Georgia, Connecticut, New Jersey, Maryland, and South Carolina. Close races in Massachusetts, New Hampshire, and Virginia made it impossible to predict the outcome of those conventions. Citizens in Rhode Island, New York, and North Carolina, on the other hand, had so solidly voted against the Constitution that its adoption in any of these three states appeared highly unlikely.

DELAWARE, NEW JERSEY, AND GEORGIA

The three counties of New Castle, Kent, and Sussex had broken away from Pennsylvania under the name of Delaware in 1776. The economic future of this small state nevertheless remained firmly tied to the economies of Pennsylvania and Maryland. Philadelphia was the main trading port on the Delaware River, the most vital commercial route for the states of Delaware and Pennsylvania. Bolstered by its two prosperous neighbors, Delaware had survived the "critical period" with its economy intact. Its population had developed a feeling of sovereignty and a desire for more independence, as expressed by the transformation of New Castle and Wilmington into free ports and the search for prospective waterways between the Delaware and Chesapeake Bays.[253]

One can thus not claim that Delaware's clear support of the new Constitution was rooted in a fear of losing control over its own destiny in a confederation. Indeed, all signs pointed to increased economic and political cooperation between the states and a strengthening of the authority of the Confederation Congress. The Delaware legislature had been steadily pursuing this course since 1781 despite internal opposition. It supported all of the impost and reform proposals in Congress and joined Maryland in efforts to increase the congressional influence of the "landless" states over the appropriation of the western territories. In the Constitutional Convention, it resolutely insisted on equal voting rights for large and small states in the central government. Once this demand had been met by the equal representation of the states in the Senate, citizens of Delaware had little reason to oppose the Constitution. Of course there were critical voices, but Richard Henry Lee failed miserably in an attempt to kindle the spirit of opposition in Wilmington while crossing Delaware on a trip from New York to Virginia.[254] In the view of Delaware residents, the Constitution hardly diminished the state's status, while promising considerable economic benefits. Particularly welcome was the prospect of reduced taxes, which the central administration could offset through duties on imports, thus imposing a greater burden on surrounding states more than on Delaware. The election of delegates to the state ratifying convention took place at a time when the Federalist victory in Pennsylvania was as good as assured. The election was dominated by local rivalries and disputes rather than debate over the Constitution. Since both Whigs and Tories were fervent supporters of the Union, all thirty seats went to friends of the Constitution. Eleven days after the election, on December 7, 1787, the convention in Dover ratified the Constitution without opposition, making Delaware the "first state" in the new Union.[255]

A swift acceptance of the Constitution seemed expedient to the citizens of New Jersey, too, where the economy had labored under the deficiencies of the Articles of Confederation. The potential advantages of the state's central geographical location had been nullified by the want of a good harbor and the lack of an urban center of commerce. Dwarfed by New York to the north and Pennsylvania to the south, bereft of the possibility of expanding to the west, and divided into two distinct economic, religious, and cultural regions, the state of New Jersey had to fight for its existence. East Jersey lay in the shadow of New York, while West Jersey with its large number of Quakers gravitated toward Philadelphia. All progress in agriculture and manufacturing was for naught as long as the modest profits from these enterprises continued to be consumed by customs duties owed to the neighboring states, through which nearly all imports and exports had to pass. To allay annual costs of 40,000 pounds sterling for import duties, New Jersey politicians had persistently pressed for a strengthening of Congress and uniform trade regulations. If import duties were levied by the central government, this would not only reduce New Jersey's financial contributions to New York and Pennsylvania, it would also allow Congress to pay public creditors, including those in New Jersey.[256]

Finally, the hope that government forces would improve military protection was no small matter to the citizens of this war-torn and vulnerable state. Even skeptics like Abraham Clark did not deny the possibility of such tangible benefits and thought it better to swim with the tide of public opinion. Regional factions that had been fighting bitterly over the paper money issue between 1784 and 1786 temporarily united during the deliberations over the Constitution. Not a single anti-Constitution candidate ran in the elections held between November 27 and December 1, 1787; even the radical-agrarian, pro-paper-money residents of East Jersey solidly supported ratification. Eight counties elected their three allotted delegates by voice vote; the other five used ballots. In some districts the sheriff circulated the ballot boxes to the various polling places to enable more citizens to vote. Unlike most other states, New Jersey carefully distinguished between legislative and convention seats. Consequently, there was only one lower-house representative and one senator among the winning candidates.[257] On December 11, thirty-eight of the thirty-nine delegates met in Trenton to discuss the new plan of government. Though some reservations and concerns were voiced, the Constitution was unanimously ratified one week later.[258] This did not put an end to the fierce internal conflicts, however, which returned to their previous level soon after this harmonious intermezzo. Whereas voter turnout for the convention elections was not particularly high, due to a lack of opposition, 44 percent of all white males participated in the first congressional elections held at the beginning of 1789.[259]

In addition to economic stagnation and the erosion of their currency, it was mainly the constant threat of attacks by the Creek Indians that convinced Georgia citizens of the need for an "efficient hand of a powerful government."[260] The rapidly growing population of the state was relentlessly expanding the area of settlement, making friction with the Spaniards and Indians inevitable. The ratification debate was strongly influenced by the fear of a major attack by an alliance of Creek Indian tribes, a situation which for the first time forced Georgia politicians to reconsider their pointedly loose and rather uncooperative relationship with the Union. George Washington was aware of their predicament. In January 1788 he wrote that if a weak state "with powerful tribes of Indians in its rear and the Spaniards on its flank, [does] not incline to embrace a strong *general* government, there must, I should think, be either wickedness or insanity in their conduct."[261]

Indeed, Georgia desperately needed the support of Congress and the other states, so it could hardly afford to delay—let alone resist—ratification. It is therefore all the more astonishing that the Constitution was criticized privately as well as publicly and the citizens were warned of its long-range effects. Weapons, ammunition, and Union troops were welcome, but not a powerful central government that would rigorously collect taxes, meddle in such "internal affairs" as the slave trade, and impede westward movement by negotiating treaties with the Indians and Spaniards. The adoption of the Constitution was thus inspired more by practical considerations than ideological conviction. Ratification only thinly masked the concerns of slaveholders and the resentment felt by the inhabitants of the rapidly growing backcountry toward any form of outside government intervention whatsoever.[262]

Despite—or perhaps because of—the tense situation, a surprisingly large number of voters turned out for the combined legislative and convention elections on December 4, 1787. In the city of Savannah, in Camden County, 401 votes were cast, a record-setting 59.2 percent of the eligible population. The only other known figures are from Burke County in the northwest, where 270 citizens (18.7 percent) voted. Each of the eleven counties could choose three delegates. Nearly two-thirds of those elected were members of the state legislature, congressmen, Federal Convention delegates, or holders of public office. Seven representatives were not in attendance when the convention in Augusta ratified the Constitution on the final day of 1787 by a vote of 26–0.[263] Anyone who concluded from the unanimous election results that new government enjoyed uncritical support in the region was in for a bitter disappointment. Most Georgians would soon disagree with the foreign and domestic politics of the Washington administration and join the Republican opposition. The President was supposed to have declared in 1791 that the United States was "at peace with all the world except the state of Georgia."[264]

Delaware, New Jersey, and Georgia were small or sparsely populated states hardly capable of standing alone. Each state had individual, specific reasons for its support of a strong federal government. Their unanimous ratification of the Constitution thus does not allow any reliable conclusions to be drawn regarding their internal affairs or future political direction. Furthermore, the example provided by these states clearly demonstrates that there was not necessarily a correlation between agrarian radicalism, insistence on the right to issue paper money, and Antifederalism. All three states had primarily agriculturally oriented economies and large Country factions that could have offered resistance to ratification. In each case, however, the affinity between Country ideology and Antifederalism took a back seat to more pressing needs.

PENNSYLVANIA

Ratification was also a foregone conclusion in Pennsylvania, Connecticut, Maryland, and South Carolina, where Federalists secured comfortable election victories. On November 6, 1787, elections were held in Pennsylvania's eighteen counties and the city of Philadelphia. Each county could select up to six delegates, depending on its population, while five seats were allotted to the city of Philadelphia. The divergent political preferences in east and west Pennsylvania again manifested themselves, as they had in the preceding legislative elections on October 9. Yet the political scales, roughly balanced before, had meanwhile shifted markedly in favor of Federalists. The spirited election campaign waged by the Constitution's proponents had won over the entire eastern section of the state, including those regions earlier dominated by the state party Constitutionalists. The final distribution of convention seats in Philadelphia and the seven eastern counties bordering on the Susquehanna and Delaware Rivers was 39–1 in favor of Federalists. The lone Antifederalist was John Whitehill, a member of the six-man delegation from Lancaster County, with its high ethnic German population.[265]

In and around Philadelphia, all ten of the convention seats went to supporters of the Constitution. Of the greatest significance numerically were not so much the merchants, entrepreneurs, lawyers, and bankers who were normally aligned with the state Republican Party and Robert Morris, but the tradesmen, artisans, and mechanics who had long formed the basis of the Constitutionalist Party. This time, however, they joined forces with area farmers to back Morris's party. While the top five Federalist candidates were amassing from 1,157 to 1,215 votes, their opponents received from 132 to 150.[266] The local patriotism was heightened by the prospect of luring the seat of the central government back to Pennsylvania, or even to Philadelphia itself. There were also other reasons for the Federalist leanings among the urban middle class. Tradesmen had never forgiven Constitutionalists for attempting to restrict their right to vote in 1786, and, correspondingly, their representation in the legislature. From an economic standpoint, the federal government was expected to introduce more favorable customs duties to stave off European competition and boost exports. Increased exports were also a central issue for farmers, whose support was crucial to a Federalist victory in the east.[267]

The nearly unanimous Federalist delegations from eastern Pennsylvania stood in stark contrast to the results in the central and western counties, where over two-thirds of the convention seats went to opponents of the Constitution (22–7). The voting patterns of the German-speaking population indicate that regional factors weighed more than ethnic or religious affinities. The further west the German communities were situated, the greater their aversion to ratification. In a similar vein, the Antifederalism of the Scotch-Irish says less about their ethnic background than about the mindset in the west, where most of them had settled. The opposition earned easy victories in Berks, Dauphin, Cumberland, Bedford, Fayette, and Westmoreland Counties. Though Federalists prevailed in population centers like Carlisle and Pittsburgh, these gains were more than offset by the overall results in their respective counties. Important contributions to the success of the opposition were made by Robert Whitehill in Cumberland, William Findley in Westmoreland, and John Smilie in Fayette.

It is interesting to note that Antifederalists nominated prominent politicians for convention seats, whereas Federalists claimed that they deliberately refrained from including public officeholders and elected representatives on their tickets to avoid conflicts between their oath of loyalty to the existing constitution and their vote for the new system.[268] These lesser-known candidates nevertheless achieved respectable results in the central and western parts of the state, carrying Luzerne, Northumberland, and Huntingdon Counties while running even with the competition in Franklin County and Washington County on the Ohio River. The opposition asserted that their vote was held down by lack of information; their supporters had boycotted the elections in some areas to protest against the early convention date. Antifederalists were in fact able to regain some of the lost ground in the subsequent legislative elections. The two-thirds Federalist majority at the ratifying convention (46–23) was thus not entirely indicative of the Constitution's level of support among the citizens of Pennsylvania. Only 13,000 of the 70,000 eligible voters had cast ballots—6,400 fewer than in the preceding assembly election, and 7,400 fewer than in the one that followed. At 16.7 percent, voter participation was around 8 percent below average. The Federalist candidates had allegedly received only 6,800 votes, slightly more than half.[269] To be sure, the Federalists' position was somewhat precarious despite their overwhelming majority at the convention. They expected their adversaries to protract the debate as long as possible to give backcountry leaders more time to organize resistance to the proposal.

CONNECTICUT

The outcome of the elections in Connecticut represented the culmination of a rapid political development that had begun in 1786. Until then, the agrarian opposition, whose ranks had swollen as a result of disputes over army officers' retirement pay, imposts, and the Society of the Cincinnati, had nearly drawn even with the ruling élite, united by the bonds of tradition and family. In October 1786, the Connecticut legislature had refused to appropriate funds requisitioned by Congress and ignored the proposal for a commercial convention in Annapolis. One year later, however, the state legislature expressed decisive approval of the Constitution and ratifying proceedings were instituted without dissent. In the convention elections on November 12, 1787, between two-thirds and three-fourths of the ninety-eight towns voted pro-Constitution. Some Antifederalist delegates later changed sides, so that the Constitution was easily adopted by a vote of 128–40.[270]

There were several reasons for this abrupt change of direction. Shays's Rebellion in Massachusetts not only alarmed the wealthy, it was also disquieting to small-scale farmers, who were still heavily influenced by the stern clergy with their reverence for law and order.[271] Despite the sundry measures taken by the government to reduce the effects of the slumping economy in 1785–86, the limitations of independent state action had become evident. As was the case with New Jersey, most imports to Connecticut had to pass through New York, at an annual cost to Connecticut consumers of between 20,000 and 40,000 pounds sterling. Smaller sums for the same purpose went to Rhode Island and Massachusetts. These "tributes" to other states' treasuries were desperately needed for improvements to the state's economic infrastructure and the discharge of public debts—a problem that was particularly acute in Connecticut, which had assumed a disproportionately high share of Continental bonds. If the central government were to regulate trade, levy import duties, and finance the public debt, the tax burden on the citizens could be significantly reduced. Federalists relentlessly bombarded the public with these arguments in an extensive propaganda campaign.[272] Any concerns about state sovereignty were dismissed by references to the equality of state voting in the Senate and the constant level of representation Connecticut would have in the new Congress as opposed to the old one. Roger Sherman's assurances that the Constitution did not fundamentally change the manner of government and that the new system was "partly national [and] partly federal" also had a soothing effect on the population.[273]

Under these circumstances, the areas from which the agrarian opposition had previously drawn its support were reduced to a few isolated pockets in the north along the Massachusetts border, in the southern sections of Tolland and Windham Counties, and on the coast in New Haven County. Antifederalist sentiment in these trading and commercial districts was largely attributable to the influence of James Wadsworth, who had utilized his charisma and his position as state auditor to establish a kind of "power base" in the region. The erosion of the opposition's support is exemplified by the fact that the majority of towns that in 1784 had rejected the limited impost plan put forth by Congress in 1783, now accepted the proposed Constitution. Even the radical agrarian communities that had demanded the emission of paper money during the economic crisis were not firmly Antifederalist.

Although some towns did not send a full contingent of delegates to the convention, and a few sent none at all, 168 delegates were elected out of a possible 175. The figures available indicate that attendance at town meetings was unusually high and voter participation exceeded the average for general elections. Of the seventy-nine communities whose minutes of the town meetings have been preserved, twenty-four met more than once to continue the debate or hear committee reports. The proposed Constitution was officially put to a vote in fourteen towns, with seven approving and seven rejecting ratification. Three towns from each side bound their delegates to vote in a prescribed manner. Although there were few official instructions or votes on the Constitution in most communities, only a few days after the elections it was widely known which towns would send "federal men" and which would send "antifederal men" to the deliberations in Hartford.[274]

To ensure there would be no unpleasant surprises at the convention, Federalists gathered an impressive array of prominent politicians in the state capital, including Philadelphia delegates Roger Sherman, Oliver Ellsworth, and William Samuel Johnson, followed by the governor and lieutenant governor, five judges from the state supreme court, and six members of the governor's council, known for its elitist disposition. Council member James Wadsworth was the only high-ranking representative of the decimated opposition. The outgunned Antifederalists could thus do little more than temper the nearly unrestrained zeal of the "aristocrats," lament their own organizational deficiencies and ineffective use of propaganda, and seek solace in the belief that the majority of freemen still strongly opposed ratification.[275]

MARYLAND

There was also wide public support for the Constitution in Maryland. In late 1787 the two state parties had roughly balanced representation in the House of Delegates—the site of heated disputes over paper money and the protection of debtors since 1785. Soon after publication of the Constitution, it became apparent that the Chase-Ridgely faction would not be able to derail ratification even with the help of the supporters it had won to break the supremacy of the plantation owners. The established elite spared no effort on behalf of the Constitution, in the hope that this would relieve the intense political pressure they were under on the home front. This time they could count on the support of the state's commercial interest, the merchants, artisans, and tradesmen, whose power had increased as a result of the growing importance of the trading and manufacturing sectors. On the other side, the opposition's propaganda campaign was not as focused and effective as the reputation and experience of its leaders, including Samuel Chase, Luther Martin, William Paca, John Francis Mercer, Thomas Johnson, and Governor William Smallwood, would have expected. The bulk of the effort was borne by Luther Martin, evidently the only member of the group dedicated to organizing a statewide election campaign.[276]

There were strategic and personal reasons for the restraint shown by the other prominent opponents of the Constitution. To avoid being labeled obstructionists, they called less for rejection than for specific amendments, secretly hoping to delay a decision until the Virginia convention. In addition, private financial difficulties doubtlessly compelled them to keep a low profile. They were already the object of intense criticism by Federalists, who missed no opportunity to denounce their involvement in speculation and scandals. Equally conscious of the public's approval of the Constitution and their own tarnished reputations, leading Antifederalists resorted to deceptive measures. In a departure from earlier practice, they spoke out against issuing instructions to candidates or otherwise binding them to vote in a certain way. They hoped this would allow them to "smuggle" some of their allies into the convention. This plan was thwarted, however, by the vigilance of their rivals. Already months before the elections, Federalists exhibited an unusual preference for democratic principles—albeit limited to the special case of the ratifying convention: it should be left to the voters to declare themselves unequivocally for or against the Constitution; the job of their chosen delegates would then be simply to proclaim and formally affirm the will of the people.[277] Anyone who dared to oppose this concept, even a Federalist like George Lux in Baltimore County, risked having his name unceremoniously struck from the list of candidates.[278]

The opposition was involved in a singular debacle in the city of Baltimore. Samuel Sterett and David McMechen had solemnly promised the city's voters to advocate ratification without prior amendments. Not until election day did Sterett acknowledge his Antifederalist leanings, under the cross-examination of a citizens' committee. Even though the polling stations were already open, Federalists quickly nominated James McHenry and Dr. John Coulter as candidates and—apparently not without resorting to dubious means—helped them to clear victories over Sterett and McMechen. Samuel Chase switched his candidacy at the last minute from Baltimore to Anne Arundel County. Following a whirlwind campaign, he was swept to victory, along with John Francis Mercer, Jeremiah Townley Chase, and Benjamin Harrison, despite strong competition from the Carolls. A leaflet distributed shortly before the election and containing a political platform condensed to a few key phrases had had a major impact on voters: "BILL OF RIGHTS—LIBERTY OF CONSCIENCE—TRIAL BY JURY—NO EXCISE—NO POLL TAX—NO STANDING ARMY IN PEACE, WITHOUT LIMITATION—NO WHIPPING MILITIA, NOR MARCHING THEM OUT OF THE STATE, WITHOUT CONSENT OF THE GENERAL ASSEMBLY—NO DIRECT TAXATION, WITHOUT PREVIOUS REQUISITIONS." In Daniel Carroll's estimation, the dark determination on the faces of many voters as they approached the ballot boxes showed "they were really frightened by what they had just heard."[279] Four additional seats were procured for Antifederalists in Baltimore County by the well-oiled political machinery of the Ridgely clan. The opposition also won an uncontested race in Harford County, where Martin and Paca had sought refuge. Nevertheless, only 12 of 76 convention seats, representing eighteen districts and two cities, went to Antifederalists.

Federalists were surely not incorrect in their assumption that resistance to the Constitution was largely motivated by the fear of insolvency and losses from speculative investments. Still, if all debtors and speculators had voted Antifederalist, the results would unquestionably have been much closer. By the end of the campaign, Chase and Ridgely's followers had shrunk to a small band of determined supporters in counties on the upper end of Chesapeake Bay, which until then had always sent proponents of paper money to the state legislature. All the same, these centers of opposition were some of the most populous sections of the state.[280] A contributor to the Baltimore *Maryland Gazette* claimed only 6,000 citizens had voted, two-thirds of whom resided in Baltimore and the seven surrounding counties. In all other counties, fewer than 200 votes were needed, on average, to secure a seat at the convention.[281] If these figures are accurate, it would mean that only 15 to 20 percent of adult white males, and about 25 percent of eligible voters, participated in the election. The known statistics in individual districts range from 20.9 percent of eligible voters in Baltimore County, to 48.8 percent in Montgomery County. The city of Baltimore was on the upper end of this scale, at 43 percent. Had the need arisen, Federalists could have drawn considerably more people to the polls in most counties. In Washington County, 1,000 Federalist-minded voters allegedly kept themselves ready, "but the Unanimity of the People in the more central parts, rendered such Assistance entirely unnecessary."[282] For comparison, one may consider the hotly contested general elections in the fall of 1788, which produced a voter turnout of 33 percent on average (14,000 voters), even approaching 60 percent in some districts. Despite the continued existence of its elite social structure and relatively strict property qualifications, Maryland recorded voter participation that was among the highest in the Union around the turn of the century.

In the case of the convention election, there was simply too little competition in many parts of the state. The eastern shore counties, under the moderate-conservative influence of the Methodists, all went to the Federalists. The opposition only attempted to put up a fight in Kent and Talbot Counties, but lacked effective leadership. In most other counties, no opponents of the Constitution even stood for election. Any critics who ventured to speak out on the lower end of the western shore were also quickly rebuffed. The elections were ultimately decided in the region along the Upper Potomac, whose legislators had always sided with the debtors in the past. But when Frederick County defected to the creditors in 1786, Montgomery and Washington Counties soon followed suit. Shortly before the convention elections, "Mentor" reported from Montgomery that "the merchants and traders of George-Town exerted all their influence to persuade the farmers and planters of the county to agree to the new government . . . without any alterations."[283] German settlers had no small say in political affairs in the western districts and were supplied with German-language versions of the Constitution as well as the most important arguments for or against ratification. Courted by both parties, they showed a clear preference for Federalists.[284]

Of even more significance was perhaps a long-term trend that had altered the economic and political character of the entire region. The enticing abundance of rich farmland in the area around the Potomac had led to a dramatic increase in migration from the east. Improvements to inland waterways also brought added value and facilitated trade both across borders and within Maryland itself. As the farmers gradually shifted their activities to urban markets, they became more receptive to the commercial mentality of the coastal inhabitants. The same transition could be observed along the Potomac and in the Shenandoah Valley of neighboring Virginia. Another reason why the farmers leaned toward Federalism was their assumption that the nation's future capital would be situated on the Potomac. Hence, the easy victory for the Constitution's advocates was attributable not only to the plantation-owning aristocrats' preference for a strong central government and a stable union, it was also the result of economic development that transformed Maryland from a purely agricultural state into a commercial, market-oriented society.

Federalists were not as confident as one might have expected in view of their 64–12 advantage. Their ranks may have been filled with a number of respected politicians, most notably senators and members of the governor's council, but they would have to manage without the aid of Charles Carroll, one of their most knowledgeable and esteemed leaders.[285] Furthermore, the orators chosen to represent the opposition could hardly be said to possess less eloquence, finesse, and experience than their own speakers. They therefore resolved to avoid long-winded discussions and smother all attempts to delay a decision.

SOUTH CAROLINA

South Carolina was the state with the system of representation that most drastically distorted the will of the constituents. All efforts by citizens from the more heavily populated western counties to achieve fair representation in the state legislature had been thwarted by the powerful Lowcountry elite. Consequently, the Antifederalists' defeat was not due to poor organization, the ineffective use of propaganda, or a lack of diligence. The deciding factor lay in the ability of residents in and around Charleston to outvote the rest of the state at will. At times the east-west divide was mitigated by discord between various political factions within the Lowcountry plantation owners and merchants, and by the tendency of numerous parishes in the central areas to side with farmers in the west.

On the issue of the Constitution, however, the coastal residents stuck together, despite their diverse interests. Key improvements expected of the new system included a rejuvenation of the trade and credit, funding of the national debt in a manner favorable to South Carolina, and improved federal military protection. In exchange, plantation owners were prepared to accept temporary increases in personal debt along with the potentially costly economic hegemony of the northern states. The few members of the Lowcountry elite who opposed the Constitution for private or ideological reasons usually did not campaign for election on the coast, running instead in the western districts where they also had property. The most widely known of these, Rawlins Lowndes, turned down a convention seat offered by his home parish of Saint Bartholomew, on account of the pro-Constitution sentiments in Charleston.[286]

Because at least half of the communities in the central part of the state this time sided with the Lowcountry, the multitude of small tobacco growers, farmers, and traders in the Upcountry once again discovered their hands were tied—as was usually the case when important political issues were being decided. The ensuing protest was equally directed against the potential curtailment of their autonomy threatened by the Constitution and the condescending treatment they were continually subjected to by their fellow Carolinians from the east. Disputes over financial policies were of lesser significance, since the proprietors of the huge Tidewater plantations were often more heavily in debt than the settlers in the west. As a result, the landowners advocated extensive protective measures which Federalists in other parts of the Union generally found too radical.[287]

The only known statistics were kept in Charleston, where 424 citizens went to the polls, 22.3 percent of the adult white males. All voted Federalist. Apart from the above-average participation, this result can be considered representative of all parishes in the three coastal districts of Charleston, Beaufort, and Georgetown. They were allotted a total of 151 delegates, compared with only 86 for Upcountry residents. The Charleston district alone, home to 11.3 percent of South Carolina's white population, sent 109 representatives to the convention, nearly half of the total number.[288]

A comprehensive overview of the entire state can only be derived by examining the voting patterns at the convention itself, though this picture is somewhat skewed due to defections to the Federalist camp. In the very first test of strength, which in all likelihood most closely reflects the original election results, 89 delegates voted for and 135 against the opposition's proposal for adjournment. Of the 135 Federalist votes, 111 came from the Lowcountry, 9 from the central parishes, and 15 from the Upcountry. The other 72 Upcountry representatives voted for adjournment, and were supported by 9 delegates from the coast and 8 from the interior.[289] The disproportionate relationship between the population and the apportionment of convention seats can be seen in the fact that the 135 Federalists represented approximately 20 percent, the 89 Antifederalists around 80 percent of the white population.

Further evidence of this regional imbalance can be seen in the number of slaves in the east and the tax burden. The roughly 30,000 white residents of the Lowcountry owned around 78,000 slaves, over 70 percent of all blacks in South Carolina. In most parishes, whites constituted no more than 25 percent of the population. This same region, however, generated over 75 percent of the state's tax revenue. It follows that the distribution of convention seats more closely reflected slave ownership and tax contributions than the number of eligible voters in a particular district. By the time the final vote was taken on ratification, the Federalist majority had further expanded its ranks. Even then, the 149 delegates who ultimately approved the Constitution spoke for only 39 percent of the eligible voters. The clear 149–73 Federalist victory thus obscures the fact that nearly two-thirds of the citizens of South Carolina opposed the unconditional ratification of the Constitution.[290]

CONTESTED STATES

Besides New Hampshire, this category includes the key states of Massachusetts and Virginia, home to nearly a third of the Union's total population. These two states were capable of existing as independent nations or breaking away to form a confederation of their own. Like Pennsylvania and New York, they were used to playing a leading role and dictating the conditions under which they were prepared to serve the Union. The argument that there was no alternative to ratification may have been decisive in small and weak states, but it was less effective here. The main thrust of Antifederalist propaganda, on the other hand, namely that the Constitution was dangerous to the states and to individual liberty and that it needed revisions before final approval, struck a chord.

The election results in Massachusetts basically ran along the political-ideological fronts established during the "critical period." Federalist delegates prevailed in most towns in the east and in the Connecticut River Valley, which had endorsed conservative financial policies and called for the rigorous suppression of the agrarian uprisings. The majority of central districts, whose residents advocated debtor relief and shared the concerns of the rebels, rejected the proposal. Nevertheless, the geographic patterns of the election results were too variegated to be attributed to these issues alone.

Due to the Constitution's importance and the state's payment of the expenses for convention delegates, approximately 100 more convention delegates were elected than members of the House of Representatives, whose session began in May 1787.[291] Federalists enjoyed the greatest success in Boston and other communities along the coast. The ticket agreed to by Boston's north and south caucuses included Governor John Hancock, Samuel Adams, and Charles Jarvis, politicians whose stance on the Constitution was known to be skeptical if not critical. However, since they had been nominated and elected by constituents who clearly favored the Philadelphia plan, it was assumed they would follow the lead of the city's nine other delegates and vote for ratification. The remaining Antifederalist hopefuls were reduced to watching the proceedings from the sidelines. Neither James Warren from Plymouth nor Elbridge Gerry and James Winthrop, who were soundly defeated in Cambridge, managed to win a seat at the convention. This did not stop the opposition from achieving respectable overall results in the east. Federalists were forced to concede that Gerry's letter to the General Court had had a major impact. This could be seen in Bristol and Middlesex Counties, in particular, where a large number of residents expressed reservations modeled on Gerry's objections. Antifederalists secured sixty seats in the seven eastern counties, about half as many as their rivals. This minor victory was all the more significant in view of the opposition's clear dominance in the west. The three counties of Worcester, Hampshire, and Berkshire sent at least three times more foes of the Constitution to Boston than friends. The Antifederalist delegates included more than thirty men who had actively taken part in Shays's Rebellion or in local uprisings.[292] Most of the western Federalists came from the Connecticut River Valley and the frontier. The former region was influenced by connections to centers of trade on the lower reaches of the Connecticut River, while the latter was swayed by Theodore Sedgwick's prestige. All told, more people voted pro-Constitution than might have been expected given events in recent years.

In the east and west together, Antifederalists had a good twenty-seat majority. The outcome of elections in the three counties of the District of Maine had little effect on this ratio: though residents along the coast preferred Federalists by a margin of 22–5, seventeen of the nineteen delegates elected by towns farther inland came from the opposite party. Available figures indicate voter participation stood at 27 percent of the approximately 89,000 adult white males. This was only slightly lower than the turnout for the gubernatorial elections in 1787, when voter interest had surged from 10.3 to 29.3 percent in the midst of the agrarian unrest. Only around 25 percent of the eligible citizens voted in the population centers of Boston, Charlestown, and Marblehead, whereas the smaller western communities of Sheffield, Great Barrington, and Worcester recorded impressive turnouts of 43.2, 44.9, and 45.7 percent, respectively. The election results fairly accurately reflected public opinion, as the mode of choosing delegates guaranteed both parties an equal chance. On the whole, the final figures heading into the ratifying convention spoke against the Federalists, but the quality of the leading Federalists and the location of the convention in Boston were in their favor.[293]

Interests of a purely economic nature cannot explain the outcome of elections in New Hampshire any more than in Massachusetts. They were intricately interwoven with political, ethnic-religious, and ideological motives, not to mention the influence of prominent politicians. Constitutional principles were important to the electorate as well. New Hampshire had posted the highest voter turnout of all thirteen states in gubernatorial elections since 1784. The town meetings held in January 1788 to elect convention delegates were—probably because of the weather conditions—not as well attended as the regularly scheduled March meetings. Nevertheless, about one-third of the approximately 25,000 white adult males participated, with heated debates and narrow votes being the rule at several locations. The tedious process of framing a new state constitution in 1783 had already shown just how deeply rooted the anti-centralist Country mentality was. Now the townships again had no intention of waiving their right to critically review and, if necessary, reject constitutional proposals.[294]

All towns with at least 150 taxpayers were allotted a convention seat; for every 300 "ratable polls" beyond that, they received an additional seat. Accordingly, Portsmouth was apportioned three delegates, Londonderry two, and the rest of the communities one apiece. In the state's interior, small towns and "places" often joined together to elect and finance a delegate jointly. The 106 delegates who attended the ratifying convention in Exeter constituted the largest political forum ever convened in New Hampshire up to that time. The minutes of the seventy-seven town meetings that have been preserved indicate that citizens at most locations carefully evaluated the Constitution with respect to such republican virtues as self-determination, shared responsibility, and civil rights. Besides choosing delegates, the town meetings attempted to determine the general views of the populace, and appointed committees to prepare instructions.

At least nineteen town meetings rejected ratification. Some merely resolved "not to accept the Constitution," while others gave their delegates precise instructions, as was the case in Marlborough: "Where as We have this Day Chosen You and Appointed You to Represent us in Convention to Accept or Reject the New Proposed Federal Constitution if you Can have our Bill of Rights Secured to us and a Firm Test of the Protestant Religion . . . it Will be Satisfactory otherwise Reject the Whole." The town meeting in Conway was particularly perturbed by the lack of a procedure for proposing revisions before ratification: "As we Repose full Confidence in you and as we find a great many good things in the Proposed Constitution Blended with what we cant approve of and as there is not any alterations to be made in said Constitution we Desire you to act all in your Power to hinder the Establishment thereof."[295] Towns with Federalist majorities were usually satisfied just to appoint delegates and express their general approval of the proposed Constitution, though they sometimes explicitly directed their representatives to support ratification.[296]

The various regions etched out by rivers and mountain ranges were characterized by divergent political preferences. The Constitution was clearly favored in the better developed area near the mouth of the Piscataqua River, including Portsmouth, Dover, and Durham. It is worth noting that the arch rivals for the office of president, John Langdon of Portsmouth and General John Sullivan from Durham, both campaigned and were elected as Federalists. The opposite pole was represented by the Merrimack River Valley and the next county to the west, Hillsborough, the site of Joshua Atherton's hometown of Amherst. The Merrimack communities had been pursuing an agenda in the state legislature that ran counter to the Piscataqua region's commercial interests. They now supplied the bulk of Antifederalists at the convention. Ethnic-religious affiliation was also a factor: the Irish-Presbyterian settlements on both sides of the Merrimack formed a solid block against the Constitution. The center of paper-money agitation since 1786 was the remote and agriculturally oriented Hillsborough district. Most of the towns there that had petitioned the legislature in favor of paper money now instructed their delegates to oppose ratification.

Antifederalists also had the upper hand farther to the west, in Cheshire County. However, many towns along the Connecticut River favored the Constitution. This was partially due to the importance of the river as a channel of trade, as the Constitution was expected to be a boon for commerce. Commercial agriculture was of minor importance at best, since the farmers hardly produced enough to meet their own needs. The same was true of Grafton County, which stretched north from Cheshire County all the way to the Canadian border. The strong Federalist support there had less to do with the Connecticut River than with the influence of Superior Court Chief Justice Samuel Livermore of Grafton County. Few people dared to contradict this Princeton-educated "frontier aristocrat." He was personally acquainted with most delegates and managed to convert even those from towns hostile to the Constitution. The specter of a British invasion from Canada and Nova Scotia also turned many a citizen into a fervent supporter of the Union. Strafford County, finally, which bordered on the District of Maine to the east, was almost equally divided between advocates and critics of the Constitution. To all appearances, the same could be said of the state of New Hampshire as a whole. But in the end, if all of the delegates sent to Exeter adhered to their instructions, the Constitution would come up more than ten votes short.[297]

An analysis of the elections in Virginia reveals the single most important factor there to have been regionalism. With few exceptions, the outcome of the elections followed a geographic pattern shaped by legislative disputes and the rise of political parties in the 1780s.[298] Whereas Federalists and Antifederalists had roughly equal support in the state on the whole, political views in the various regions differed widely. The opposition secured forty-nine of the sixty-four convention seats at stake on the Southside and in the Piedmont. Citizens in these parts stood firmly behind Patrick Henry and his debtor-friendly politics. Advocates of the Constitution controlled the banks of the James, York, Rappahannock, and Potomac Rivers. Try as they might, Antifederalists could not win even a third of the fifty-four seats available there. If the entire territory west of the Blue Ridge Mountains is added to this balance, Antifederalists had a narrow twelve-seat advantage over their adversaries. It would thus be left to the backcountry areas to tip the scales in one direction or the other: the Shenandoah Valley, the Alleghany counties (now West Virginia), and the Kentucky District.

The vast majority of settlers in Kentucky voted against the Constitution, out of fear of losing their free access to navigate the Mississippi River and because they suspected the new federal government might be an obstacle to their quest for statehood. A group of land speculators was even secretly investigating the possibility of an alliance with Spain.[299] In the Shenandoah Valley, by contrast, every single convention seat went to a Federalist. The major factor in this case was the extensive trade with Maryland and beyond, which could only benefit from uniform federal economic policies. In addition, area residents hoped the central government would invest more than the individual states in the development of inland waterways, particularly the Potomac. In political matters, the seven Alleghany counties had traditionally agreed with the Southside, whose distinguishing social feature, like their own, was the predominance of small farmers with few slaves. As opposed to their southern neighbors, however, they had begun around 1787 to push for the fulfillment of the peace treaty by allowing British creditors to collect their prewar debts. Only then would Britain evacuate the western forts. These fortifications were needed by the settlers for defense against Indian raids and were the key to continued expansion in the direction of the Ohio Valley. The

Constitution would put an end to violations of the peace treaty by both sides and create a government capable of energetically pursuing the process of territorial expansion. Consequently, some Alleghany delegates pledged right from the outset to vote for ratification; others hesitated but were eventually won over. Several Tidewater counties that had previously always sided with the debtor faction in the legislature this time went with the Federalists. As a result, the pro-Constitution votes in western Virginia and the Shenandoah Valley outweighed the Antifederalist majority in Kentucky, slightly tipping the scales in favor of ratification. It was of little consolation to the opposition that they had received almost 60 percent of all votes cast.[300]

Voter participation remained within its usual range in Virginia. The known figures in seven districts indicate that 26.5 percent of adult white males went to the polls, with Frederick County posting the lowest turnout at 6.2 percent and Essex County the highest at 29.9 percent. The inhabitants' interest in politics had climbed overall since the Revolution but was down somewhat compared with the general elections of 1787 and 1788. One can once again observe that the competition in contested regions caused a surge in voter participation. In all three states in this group, the distribution of convention seats fairly accurately reflected the will of the people. Malapportionment slightly favored Federalists in Virginia and New Hampshire but helped the opposition in Massachusetts. A count of convention seats shows that proponents of the Constitution had an edge in Virginia, while their adversaries led in Massachusetts and New Hampshire. In every case, however, the outcome of the conventions was too close to call.[301]

Antifederalist Victories

RHODE ISLAND

Rhode Island continued its resistance to constitutional reform by refusing to call a ratifying convention, preferring instead to hold local referenda in which the citizens could choose between approval and rejection of the Constitution. This method admittedly served the political interests of the Country Party, but was also compatible with the state's popular tradition of town-meeting democracy. Since the outcome of the voting was a foregone conclusion, Federalists resolved to boycott the referenda in their strongholds of Providence and Newport. Of the over two thousand eligible voters in these two cities, which together had ten representatives in the lower house (all other towns only had two each), only thirteen people voted on March 24, 1788. Two votes were cast for the Constitution in Newport, none in Providence. The Newport town meeting nevertheless appointed a committee "to draft instructions for the deputies of this Town . . . to Obtain a Resolution for Calling a Convention [and] to instruct the Deputies to use their influence for Obtaining a repeal of the tender and limitation Laws."[302]

Supporters of the Constitution clearly abstained from voting as a sign of protest at other locations as well. There were twenty-one towns besides Providence and Newport, out of thirty altogether, that registered fewer than ten votes for the Constitution. Federalists only prevailed in Bristol (26–23) and in Little Compton, which by a margin of 63–57 called for the convening of a ratifying convention. Compared with the gubernatorial elections in 1787, the final result of 2,711 votes against and 243 for the Constitution indicated participation had dropped by 10 percent (or 1,200 voters), to 24.4 percent.[303] Even without the boycott, Federalists would scarcely have carried more than six towns and one-third of the population. There was a general consensus in most areas that the Constitution should be rejected. In Richmond, for instance, sixty-nine of the seventy-seven eligible voters attended the town meeting, and all but one voted—*viva voce* as at every location in the state—against ratification.

It is not hard to understand why most Rhode Island farmers opposed the Constitution. First of all, the text's centralist tendencies ran afoul of the prevalent concept of democracy, which was based on direct, unmediated participation in the process of political decision making. Also, the treatment of the slavery issue aroused the ire of the zealous anti-slavery movement led by Rhode Island Quakers.[304] Most important, however, was the fiscal policy of the state legislature, which had been at the center of heated debate for three years. Joining the Union at that point would have threatened the Country Party's program to eliminate the state's war debt and provide farmers with some relief from their heavy tax burden—in some cases, even from the burden of their private debts.[305] As in Newport, though from the opposite political perspective, several Antifederalist towns drew a connection between the referendum and the paper-money issue. All 177 citizens in attendance at the meeting in Foster rejected the Constitution, taking advantage of the opportunity to instruct their legislative delegates "to use the[ir] Influence in the Hon. General assembly at their next Session that no alteration be made but that the Tender of the paper Currency Remain as it now stands."[306]

Nearly every community that approved of the Country Party's economic policies voted against the Constitution. The adversaries controlled all sixteen towns in the state's interior and at least half of the fourteen coastal communities. Like their counterparts in other states, most Rhode Island Antifederalists were less interested in leaving the Union than in gaining time and effecting amendments. Still, one may infer from the Country propaganda that at least a handful of politicians were seriously considering the possibility of turning their state into a free port of transit for shipments of goods from abroad. This role could ensure the survival of even a small independent territory and generate—through smuggling among other means—considerable revenues.[307]

NORTH CAROLINA

Elections for convention delegates were held in North Carolina on March 28 and 29, 1788, just a few days after the Rhode Island referendum. Antifederalists had waged an aggressive campaign. Despite the sparse flow of information in the area, there is nothing that would indicate the inhabitants of North Carolina were less well informed than the residents of other large states. What was lacking in homegrown material during the month-long campaign was made up for through imported broadsides and shipments of newspapers from New York, Pennsylvania, and Virginia. The Hillsborough convention was of particular interest to the people of North Carolina because the volatile issue of the location of the state's capital was to be considered in addition to the question of ratification.[308] Election fever was most prevalent in counties in which both sides nominated candidates. Voter turnout was unusually high at these locations, as evidenced by the few available figures: 372 citizens had cast votes in Dobbs County when Federalists suddenly made off with the ballot box to ward off a sure defeat. That corresponds to around 40 percent of adult white males and over 50 percent of taxpaying freemen. If Timothy Bloodworth's comments are correct, publicly championing the Constitution was punished by voters: "Many of our Leading Characters have lost their Election by declaring their Sentiments in favor of the new System, while others shared the same fate through suspicion."[309]

The fifty-eight counties were allotted five delegates each, to which six representatives were added from the "borough towns" of Salisbury, Hillsborough, Halifax, Edenton, New Bern, and Wilmington. Voting patterns show that the rivalry between the Tidewater and the Piedmont was the essential element of the election results, and that the dividing line between the country and coast parties became even more marked than was normally the case in the state legislature. Federalists won no less than 63 of their 83 seats in the fifteen counties and five cities along the northeast stretch of coastline between the Albemarle and Pamlico Sounds. However, they lost in the adjoining counties to the west as well as parts of the Cape Fear region. Opponents of the Constitution even claimed victories along the coast in Onslow, New Hanover (home to Timothy Bloodworth), and Brunswick Counties.

Friends of the Constitution were a rare breed in the Piedmont and on the Tennessee frontier. Some support came from the German settlers, who helped to ensure that five seats, at least, went to Federalists in Mecklenburg, Lincoln, and Burke Counties.[310] At all events, the spirit of Federalism thrived almost exclusively in the Tidewater, where farmers, planters, lawyers, merchants, and artisans had developed commercial interests, and for whom it was easier to establish contact with the trade centers of Philadelphia and Charleston. In addition, the Tidewater faction had always resisted the Piedmont's paper-money policies. This fiscal conservatism had apparently alienated the wealthy yet debt-laden plantation owners in the Cape Fear area and elsewhere, with their heavy reliance on paper money.

In the state's midsection and the vast western regions, where smaller farms were the rule, advocates of the Constitution fought a losing battle, due to both local and "foreign" influences. Along the Virginia border, they not only had to compete against such local leaders as Willie Jones (Halifax), Thomas Person (Granville), and William Lenoir (Wilkes), but also against the influx of Antifederalist ideas and propaganda from Patrick Henry's Virginia Southside. The charisma of these leaders and their popular style of government created a political-ideological wall that Federalists—already saddled with a negative image as the "lawyers' party"—had as yet been unable to penetrate. Just as the northern section of the state was influenced by Virginia, the southern counties were infected with the spirit of opposition by the backcountry of South Carolina. Finally, the settlers on the frontier shared the Kentuckians' fears of being cut off from navigating the Mississippi River. The large-scale speculators, who anticipated that ratification would greatly boost the value of their cheaply acquired landholdings in Tennessee, resided for the most part in the Tidewater and voted accordingly. Not until after the Constitution had gone into force did local inhabitants, themselves not adverse to speculation, begin to realize the potential of increased land values. In any case, the western regions were the first to desert the Antifederalist cause and add their voices to the call for a second ratifying convention. The driving force here seems to have been the German settlers, who had a particularly large presence in these counties.[311] The elections for seats at the Hillsborough convention were not influenced by concerns of possible exclusion from the Union and total isolation. As a result, they are most likely to provide an accurate picture of the citizens' views at the climax of the debate over the Constitution. Antifederalists garnered more than twice as many seats as their adversaries and entered the convention with a safe majority of over 100 delegates.

NEW YORK

The opponents of the Constitution celebrated their greatest victory in New York, where they soundly defeated some of the country's most renowned nationalists. The outcome of the preceding assembly elections had led Federalists to believe they had a chance of winning, with Philip Schuyler's home county of Albany providing the swing vote in favor of ratification. Instead, they were forced to watch their sphere of influence shrink to New York City and the surrounding counties: Westchester, Richmond, and Kings. An awareness of the magnitude of the issue at hand and the introduction of general suffrage for free white adult males combined to produce the highest turnout ever registered in a New York election during the Confederation period. More than 24,000 citizens, 43.4 percent of the eligible voters, went to the polls. The highest percentage was recorded in Columbia County, including the city of Hudson (63.5 percent), followed by Albany County (52 percent), New York City (48.4 percent), and Montgomery County (42.4 percent). Slightly lower, but still high compared with previous elections, was the turnout in Dutchess (35.4 percent), Queens (34.7 percent), Ulster (27.9 percent), and Westchester (25.2 percent) Counties. The only complete aberration was Orange County, at 10.6 percent.[312] The supporters of the Constitution could find some solace in the fact that they had fared relatively well in such Antifederalist-dominated counties as Montgomery, Columbia, Albany, and even Dutchess, a Clintonian stronghold. These votes were ineffectual, however, due to the state's majority-take-all system. Even so, the Federalist counties and New York City managed to send more delegates to Poughkeepsie than their level of support among the total population would seem to have warranted.[313] Yet there could be no denying that Antifederalists had achieved a spectacular victory, taking nine of the state's thirteen counties and 46 of the 65 convention seats.

There were manifold reasons for this result; above all, the elections in New York were a party affair, and the most unified and determined party won. The large Antifederalist vote was just as much a tribute to Governor George Clinton as it was a rejection of the Constitution. It signaled widespread approval of the Clintonians' agenda: economic independence based primarily on lucrative import duties; fiscal policies oriented toward the needs of the property-owning middle class; a good rapport with farmers; a hatred and distrust of former Loyalists; resistance to aristocratic-oligarchic tendencies; an aversion to the elite class of merchants and lawyers; and support for the principle of a viable middle-class republic and a loosely knit, decentralized confederation.[314] Federalists were convinced that Clinton was calling the shots and knew how hard it would be to overcome his opposition. Nevertheless, they believed they had a chance if the Constitution were judged by its intrinsic value rather than from partisan perspectives and if it were discussed at Poughkeepsie in a fair and open manner: "But if blind prejudice, predetermined opposition, and 'silent negatives' are to be characteristic of our Convention, our reputation as a Sovereign State will be deservedly lost forever!"[315]

IMPLICATIONS OF THE ELECTION RESULTS

A review of the overall election results confirms how divided Americans were over the Constitution. The fact that "only" about 160,000 voters went to the polls should not be misinterpreted. The sources show clearly that the actual level of involvement in the constitutional struggle was much higher: a considerable number of citizens did not vote, either because they felt sure that the election results would reflect their political opinion anyway, or because they knew that their participation was useless (as in the case of Federalists in Newport and Providence). There were landslide Federalist victories in five states: Delaware, New Jersey, Georgia, Connecticut, and Maryland. In Pennsylvania, the proponents of the Constitution had less popular support than the distribution of convention seats would suggest, and the Federalist majority in South Carolina, because of malapportionment, did not reflect the will of the majority of the people. The people of the remaining six states either were almost evenly split or they emphatically rejected the Constitution. If South Carolina is added to this group, these seven states comprised 62.9 percent of the white population. Had the issue been decided on the basis of the election results alone, five states, containing 41.9 percent of the population, would have voted against unconditional ratification: Massachusetts, New Hampshire, Rhode Island, New York, and North Carolina. In that case, the Constitution would not have been adopted by the requisite number of nine states. A second convention or something more dramatic might have been the result.[316] A search for decisive factors reveals four main components which shaped the vote results with varying intensity and in unique constellations: state-specific interests, regional and sectional interests, interests specific to certain social classes or groups, and political-ideological views and attitudes. There is little evidence, however, of a generational conflict. The notion that Federalists appealed to the young, dynamic, and cosmopolitan element of the American population is not borne out by statistics.

In several cases the election was obviously determined by the state's specific situation and the collective interests of its citizens, not individual or partisan preferences. This was particularly true of uncontested states like

Delaware, New Jersey, and Georgia, where any potential disadvantages of the Constitution were perceived to have been outweighed by economic and security considerations. Equality in the Senate ensured their influence in national politics. Connecticut and Maryland were in similar positions, which partially explains why the opposition there was so weak. Rhode Islanders went in the opposite direction out of fear the Constitution would spell the end of the state's popular fiscal policies. In a similar way, New York Antifederalists, under the stewardship of Governor Clinton, customs collector John Lamb, and other state officials, firmly believed they were acting in the best interests of their constituents. New York profited economically more than all of its neighbors—in some cases even at the expense of its neighbors—from the status quo. The majority of citizens therefore saw no compelling reason to experiment with a new system of government.

The election results also reflected the natural partitioning of the Union into northern, central, and southern sections, as well as the coast versus backcountry conflict and the geographically influenced, trade-related structures in individual states. Repulsed by slavery provisions of the Constitution, many northerners became Antifederalists. New Englanders could not comprehend why Virginia should receive as many as 5½ seats in the House of Representatives for its 170,000 slaves, with a tax break thrown in for good measure. Conversely, reservations against the proposal in Virginia and the Carolinas were largely based on concerns that the South would become economically dependent on the North and might eventually be deprived of its involuntary labor force. The 1787–88 elections were thus influenced by the paradoxical circumstance that both slaveholders in the South and anti-slavery groups in the North worked against the Constitution. Moreover, reliable statistical evidence indicates that the same economic factors affected the election results in various ways in different parts of the country. The ownership of government securities and involvement in trading and banking transactions were more conducive to ratification in the New England states, for example, than in the rest of the Union. The impact of speculation depended on the distribution of state versus federal securities and the level of war debt in the various states. Land speculators generally favored the Constitution in New England and the South but not in the middle states. Heavy private debts were more likely to increase resistance to the Philadelphia plan in the southern states than in the middle and northern sections of the Union, where this factor only had an appreciable effect on elections in states that did not issue paper money.[317]

Of extreme importance were small territorial divisions within states. Several of these regions, which transcended political boundaries in some cases, had more or less led an independent existence since the colonial period. The increased specialization brought on by economic development and market relations only strengthened this trend. By the time of the convention elections, a clear pattern had emerged: with few exceptions, attributable to special influences, those regions that tended to support the new system were either centers of foreign trade and commerce themselves, or were linked to commercial centers on the eastern coast by means of well-developed roads and waterways. The economic benefits of Federalism were more tangible to inhabitants of the large river valleys and estuaries, the source of growing amounts of farm and industrial products sold to urban centers or exported. That was not enough in New York, however, to win over the counties along the Hudson River. Still, there were many more friends than foes of the Constitution in several of the most important river communities, like Hudson and Albany.

By contrast, the opposition was more successful in the remote areas of the interior, where farming was generally the rule. There were special reasons for the Antifederalist sentiments in Kentucky and Tennessee. These settlers used their votes to reinforce their demands for better channels of transportation—meaning, in this case, unobstructed navigation of the Mississippi River. If frontier regions like the Allegheny counties in Virginia and the Georgia backcountry joined the Federalists' cause, it was because of the westward push and corresponding conflicts with Indian tribes. By and large, Jackson Turner Main's observation is correct that the areas moved by the economic spirit of the East sent Federalists, and the isolated sections of the interior sent Antifederalist delegates to the conventions.

A striking feature of the convention elections was the almost unanimous tendency of the urban lower and middle classes to vote Federalist. All cities on the coast and most large towns in the interior expressed general—if not overwhelming—approval of the Constitution. Artisans and laborers nominated few of their own kind, backing instead representatives of the urban elite with whom they otherwise had not been on particularly friendly terms during and after the Revolution. Their support was not based on deference, much less subservience, to their social superiors, nor were they the victims of political manipulation—they were simply guided by an awareness of the convergent interests of all segments of the population involved in commerce and trade and shipbuilding. They favored ratification because they thought the Constitution would improve both their and the country's economic future. Especially in the cities, where the disparities between the social classes were the most pronounced, there was widespread agreement on this particular issue. Significantly, whenever mob activity occurred, it was directed at the Country factions' leaders and propagandists, not the property owners and urban establishment. The middle class was devoted to preserving the Union and had uniform economic objectives which they aggressively pursued in the political arena. Typical of their mindset is an appeal by "Sydney" to the "Working People of Maryland": "We common people are more properly citizens of America than of any particular state. Very many of our sort die in different parts from where they were born."[318] One may with some justification describe the urban middle class as the "dynamic element" of the ratification debate.

There was less agreement among the members of the upper class. Merchants, businessmen, lawyers, government officials, and intellectuals could be found on both sides of the political front, though their numbers were substantially greater behind Federalist lines. When it came to economic policies, export merchants, for example, seldom saw eye to eye with traders and manufacturers focusing on the domestic market. The one side pressed for Union-wide regulations while the other believed—albeit with diminishing steadfastness—in the acumen of state legislatures. Government officials could be either disciples of the new system or opponents, depending on their party affiliation or how their state had fared under the Articles of Confederation. Among the members of the "professions"—lawyers, doctors, ministers, college instructors—there were always a few nonconformists who swam against the current of public opinion. Most contemporary reports convey the impression that the "commercial interest" was strongly—particularly in the northern and middle states—disposed toward ratification. The great majority of merchants, bankers, artisans, and tradesmen were Federalist. Anyone who had invested a considerable share of his assets in government securities or land speculation in the West was also more likely to favor ratification than other citizens. The exact influence of all these factors on voting behavior varied by region depending on prevailing economic, political, and institutional circumstances. As a result, there is no absolute correlation between commercial interests and stance on the Constitution; only the statistical probability of a vote for or against ratification can be established.

From a purely numerical standpoint, the fate of the Constitution lay in the hands of farmers—an interest group transcending state borders. In some states—Delaware, New Jersey, Georgia—they uniformly voted for ratification; in others—Rhode Island, North Carolina—they were nearly as unanimous in their rejection of the Constitution. Voting patterns confirm that in most states farmers in the vicinity of cities and along important trade routes generally endorsed the Philadelphia plan; their counterparts in remote areas untouched by economic development generally did not. With the help of small farmers in Massachusetts, New Hampshire, New York, Pennsylvania,

North Carolina, and Virginia, the opposition nearly succeeded in derailing constitutional reforms which they and others felt were nothing short of a revolution. The tax burden was an important factor for many voters. This prompted New England farmers as well as southern planters to oppose the Constitution that prohibited paper money and had vast new taxing power. In fact, southern planters in general were much less predisposed to think in terms of one nation than the middle and upper classes in the North. At the same time, advocates of the Constitution were predominant among the wealthy planters with more than a hundred slaves, at least in Maryland and Virginia.[319]

The examination of economic motives should not create the impression that voting behavior was entirely or even primarily guided by self-interest. Naturally, some voters who otherwise tended to support the reforms were forced to rethink their position if ratification meant incurring direct financial penalties. Yet the sources illustrate again and again that replacing the old system of government with a new one was perceived as an exceptional event which partially rescinded the laws of basic self-interest. The intrinsic political character of the debate over the Constitution was the most evident in areas where well-structured party organizations competed for control of the government. The Constitution was quickly seized upon as an issue and placed at the center of their power struggle. The motivation and propaganda activities of the parties increased accordingly. In areas less developed politically, the Constitution itself became the catalyst and focal point of party organization. Voters no longer merely based their decisions on private—or even collective—economic interests. Many now also considered the political-ideological principles of their party affiliation. This competition between the parties gave the debate a new dimension. To vote for or against the Constitution meant more than just passing judgment on the virtues of the proposed system. It also expressed a commitment to certain values and precepts regarding the structure of society, thus establishing the principles on which future Americans would build their nation. It was not a matter of creating new principles and values as much as redefining existing ones. These ideologies were at the core of the conflict between Federalists and Antifederalists and increasingly served as the driving force behind political developments.

Federalism and Antifederalism were not systematically devised, precisely formulated ideologies. Nevertheless, the people were conscious of the values and attitudes each party represented. The perspectives from which the Constitution was judged were determined by upbringing, experience, and social environment. A receptiveness to thinking on a national plain was determined by such factors as education, interests and contacts that traversed state lines, travel, civil and military service on behalf of the Union, and urban life. Life in the country, which followed the rhythm of the seasons and revolved around family and farm, planting and harvesting, formed a mentality that placed more value on local needs in a narrower frame of reference combined with the fierce defense of one's right to self-determination. Once again the determining effect of social environment is undeniable.

The election results prove that Federalists had been wise to avoid a referendum. At the ratifying conventions they could still overcome the setbacks they had suffered at town meetings, polling places, and rostrums, thus avoiding the unforeseeable consequences of the Constitution's defeat. The main question now was whether the state conventions could succeed in mitigating the polarizing effects of the election campaigns and opening the door to compromise and cooperation.

5

State Ratifying Conventions

Concenter'd HERE *th' united wisdom shines,*
Of learned JUDGES, *and of sound* DIVINES;
PATRIOTS, *whose virtues, searching times have try'd,*
HEROES, *who fought, where* BROTHER HEROES *dy'd,*
LAWYERS, *who speak, as* TULLY *spoke before,*
SAGES, *deep read in philosophic lore;*
MERCHANTS, *whose plans, are not to realms confin'd*
FARMERS—*the noblest title of mankind,*
YEOMEN *and* TRADESMEN—*pillars of the State:*
On whose decision hangs COLUMBIA'*s fate.*

Thus, the various orders which constitute the great Family of the Commonwealth, concur to form the august, the honourable Convention now sitting in this metropolis; To this enlightened and respectable body, the eyes not only of their constituents, but of AMERICA, *and the world are turned.—And from the rays of intelligence which beam from every quarter of the assembly, we fondly anticipate the most learned, candid and patriotick discussion of the great subject of the Constitution.*

THE CONVENTION, *MASSACHUSETTS CENTINEL*, JANUARY 12, 1788

Whatever veneration might be entertained for the body of men who formed our Constitution, the sense of that body could never be regarded as the oracular guide in expounding the Constitution. As the instrument came from them it was nothing more than the draft of a plan, nothing but a dead letter, until life and validity were breathed into it by the voice of the people, speaking through the several State Conventions. If we were to look, therefore, for the meaning of the instrument beyond the face of the instrument, we must look for it, not in the General Convention, which proposed, but in the State Conventions, which accepted and ratified the Constitution.

JAMES MADISON, CONGRESSIONAL ADDRESS, 1796

The Conventions as Social and Cultural Events

Organization, Procedures, and Public Participation

Sixteen ratifying conventions were held between November 20, 1787, and May 29, 1790, stretching from Concord, New Hampshire, in the North to Augusta, Georgia, in the South. They represented the climax of the debate on the state level and, taken together, were the focal point of the struggle for a new system of government. The length of the deliberations and the number of delegates involved varied widely from state to state. Delaware's delegates needed only five days to adopt the Constitution. In contrast, it took nearly a month for the conventions of Pennsylvania, Massachusetts, and Virginia to complete their intense and sometimes even dramatic deliberations. New York can boast of having been the most thorough. Its delegates scrutinized the document in Poughkeepsie for forty days before adopting it. The conventions in Delaware, New Jersey, and Georgia were small, from 25 to 40 delegates, and even populous states like New York and Pennsylvania made due with 65 and 69 delegates, respectively. By comparison, the conventions in Virginia, North Carolina, South Carolina, Connecticut, and Massachusetts resembled mass meetings, with between 170 and 360 elected members. On average, in all states, there was one delegate for every 180 free citizens. Again, however, there were considerable discrepancies, ranging from a ratio of 1 to 55 in South Carolina, to 1 to 620 in Pennsylvania. Yet these differences were offset by basic similarities which make it possible to examine these conventions as a single event. It was in the conventions that, in Madison's words, the people "breathed life" into the Constitution.

While the opportunity to participate actively in the ratifying conventions was regarded as a great honor by most delegates, it also involved for some a good deal of hardship. Some delegates left ill family members or pregnant wives behind, not to mention neglected businesses and farms. The journey to the convention alone, usually undertaken on horseback, was arduous, especially in large states like Virginia, North Carolina, and Georgia. Winter travel in New England, although cold, was made easier by using sleighs that could more safely cross frozen waterways. The strains of this long and difficult passage were easier to bear if one met up with delegates from other districts along the way and they continued the trip together. Upon arrival at the convention site, the delegates might be lodged in taverns, boardinghouses, or made-over barns, and many a participant had to share a bed with a colleague. When Federalists and Antifederalists were forced to sleep under one roof, the resulting tensions adversely affected social intercourse and leisure activities.[1] Expense allowances were normally minimal and barely sufficed to provide room and board in a coastal city. Since the costs incurred were not reimbursed until near the end of the convention, less-affluent delegates often found themselves strapped for cash, thus providing them with additional motivation to bring the deliberations to a swift conclusion.

Not everyone was eagerly anticipating the conventions. A good number of citizens could still recall the dubious gatherings of the postwar period that had unsettled the legislatures with their threats, raucous protests, and radical demands. In some commentaries there was thus a note of concern that the events might get out of hand and end in disorder. In the opinion of Nathaniel Freeman, a lawyer and private tutor, the Massachusetts convention, with its nearly 360 delegates, was an "unwieldy assembly" that was not conducive to calmly considering important constitutional issues: "As the great subject of the federal Constitution is advancing to a decision the anxiety of suspense in both parties is brought to the highest pitch . . . in the heat of animosity of party, arguments will not be able on either side to stem the torrent of prejudice. Passions will usurp controul over dethroned reason, and, perhaps, the deliberations of our Convention end in such a tumultuous rage as to disgrace the boasted intelligence of man."[2] In Virginia, James Duncanson was also worried that the convention might not remain peaceful, "for you never saw your Country Men so much agitated, not even at the time of Cornwallis's Invasion, every Man warm for and against the measure, & nothing but debate and altercation in all companies." According to Duncanson, Richmond was "exceedingly crowded" and turmoil was feared.[3] This concern was not limited to Federalists. In the ranks of the opposition there were also those who would have preferred to dispense with the conventions altogether and leave the decision up to state legislatures and town meetings.

This uneasiness was magnified by wide disparities in the authority ascribed to the ratifying conventions, despite the similar resolutions that had called them into being. General agreement only existed regarding the right of the conventions to adopt or reject the Constitution *in toto*. Whether or not they were also empowered to propose amendments, defer a decision, or attach conditions to ratification was a matter of dispute within the two political camps. Answers to these questions were based more on tactical considerations than on an objective reading of the original mandates. When on November 9, 1787, the Pennsylvania Assembly tried to establish a quorum for the convention of two-thirds of the elected delegates, analogous to the assembly's own rules, Federalists pointed to the "higher authority" possessed by the ratifying convention. According to this principle, the state legislature did not have the right "to lay down rules and regulations for that convention, because that body stands on superior ground to what we occupy, inasmuch as they are bound to no forms by a previous constitution." Pennsylvania Federalists maintained that the delegates had been appointed by the "supreme original authority of the people at large" and thus stood above the state government, which was bound by the existing constitution. During the actual deliberations, however, the Federalist majority interpreted the convention's jurisdiction as narrowly as possible so as to close the door on any thoughts of revisions the opposition might be harboring. James Wilson denied the delegates even the right to discuss amendments, much less record them in the official journals and in the Form of Ratification sent to Congress. The Constitution must be viewed as one proposal, they argued, to be accepted or rejected in its entirety. In response to an objection by William Findley and Robert Whitehill that the Philadelphia plan must be inspected piece by piece and weak points eliminated, Benjamin Rush replied metaphorically that the Constitution resembled a house: they had the choice of either moving into it or, should they find it unsuitable, returning the key to the owner. "We are come to stamp the system with the authority of the people, or to refuse it that stamp," Thomas Scott agreed. Now it was Antifederalists who hoped that elevating the importance of the convention might be beneficial to their fight for adjournment or amendments. Robert Whitehill brushed aside all examples taken from English or American history: "Precedent, sir, cannot be adduced on this occasion, for a similar situation never has occurred before in the history of the world, nor do we know of any body of men assembled with similar powers to investigate so interesting a subject. The importance and singularity of the business must place it beyond any former rule."[4]

The citizens came down squarely on the side of the Federalists—at least in Philadelphia. "One of the Gallery," claiming to be the voice of the common man, questioned the sense of protracted debates when the voters of Pennsylvania had long made up their minds. The will of the constituents in each county was what counted, not the delegates' private opinions: "The present Convention, therefore, is not a deliberative body. The members are to be considered only as tickets containing the votes of the counties for the adoption or rejection of the proposed Constitution."[5] The enthusiastic supporters of the Constitution in Pennsylvania did not seem to notice that such theories stood in direct contradiction to nearly everything Federalists had said up to that point regarding the danger of instructions and the benefits of a representative system.

The positions were reversed two months later at the Massachusetts ratifying convention, where Federalists found that ratification was impossible without at least proposed amendments. Confident of their ability to muster a majority against the Constitution, Antifederalists wanted to prevent their adversaries from proposing changes which might weaken wavering delegates' resolve to reject the plan. "We have no right to make amendments," pronounced General Samuel Thompson on February 2, 1788. Two days later, Charles Jarvis stated the position of the pro-Constitution delegates: "If we have a right, sir, to receive, or reject the Constitution, surely we have an equal authority to determine in what way this right shall be exercised . . . we are convened in the right of the people, as their immediate representatives, to execute the most important trust which it is possible to receive, and we are accountable in its execution, to God only, and our own conscience." This stance eventually prevailed. The nature of the debate had changed entirely, Fisher Ames observed on February 5, "and the inquiry is now, not what the Constitution is, but what degree of probability there is that the amendments will hereafter be incorporated into it."[6]

At the Maryland convention in April, Federalists did not follow the precedent set by Massachusetts, where out of desperation Federalists agreed that "recommendatory amendments" could accompany an unconditional ratification. In fact, the stance of the Maryland Federalists was even more restrictive than the Pennsylvania majority had been. With an eye to South Carolina and Virginia, they refused to engage in any discussion whatsoever of the contents of the Philadelphia plan, or of amendments, in order to avoid the appearance of weakness. They expressed the conviction that the convention was not authorized to suggest changes, and that even discussing the subject constituted a violation of their mandate. At best, they were willing to debate the issue of amendments after the adoption of the Constitution. Yet the convention would then not be functioning as an institution per se; rather, each participant would be acting merely in his capacity as a citizen of the United States. Federalists later retracted even this offer when it became evident that some of the proposed amendments went further than they wished.[7] Other states refused to follow Maryland's example, however, and the authority of the conventions, as in Massachusetts, to suggest revisions was the generally accepted interpretation. The right to stipulate conditions under which a state would join the new Union, on the other hand, continued to be disputed, but was nowhere accepted.

Disputes not only arose in connection with complex legal and procedural issues. There were other problems of secondary importance that nonetheless bore heavily on the people. Newspapers occasionally complained that some of the conventions were lasting too long and costing too much, thereby placing an unnecessary burden on taxpayers still suffering from the effects of the economic depression. Such comments were sometimes motivated by a desire to put pressure on delegates and bring about a swift resolution. Pennsylvania's outlay of between $200 and $300 per day can hardly be deemed extravagant, and the entire convention in Massachusetts cost around £4,500 ($11,250).[8] Several states took advantage of the fact that legislators and convention delegates were often the same people, scheduling legislative sessions to follow the convention deliberations. This prevented the representatives from having to make—and the state from having to finance—repeat trips to the capital. The Virginia convention, together with a special session of the assembly, cost the state £5,500, while South Carolina had to expend £10,000 altogether in 1788 for the convention and both sessions of the legislature.[9] Depending on the length of their journey, North Carolina delegates received a compensation of between $15 and $55 (£6–£22). The expenses for the two conventions in that state, including printing the Constitution and the Form of Ratification, must also have come to about £10,000. While these figures may seem modest, they are hardly insignificant if one considers that the total expenses incurred by the government and administration of North Carolina in 1788 amounted to just £20,370.[10] A frugal newspaper reporter in Maryland declared that the Federalists' uncompromising rush to ratification had saved the state at least £4,000.[11]

There was a general mood of joyous expectation among the citizens at the convention sites and in the press, augmented by a festive atmosphere and an awareness of the uniqueness and momentousness of the occasion: "The fate of America is now suspended, as it were, in a balance, and awaits its final doom from you and the conventions of the different states; with whom it rests, either to entail misery on millions yet unborn or to transmit your dear-bought liberties, inviolate, to your latest posterity. That real patriotism may guide your councils is the sincere wish of A Plain Citizen."[12] The citizens of Boston felt much the same as those in Philadelphia: "May the Great Idea fill the minds of every member of this honourable body, that Heaven on this auspicious occasion favours America, with an opportunity never before enjoyed by the sons of men, of establishing a form of government *peaceably* and *deliberately,* which will secure to these States all those blessings which give worth to existence, or dignity to man, PEACE, LIBERTY and SAFETY!"[13] Antifederalists took the occasion just as seriously as their rivals: "Never had 'the good people of this Commonwealth' a matter before them which had involved in it questions of so high a nature as at present . . . for if you adopt the proposed system, you give your explicit approbation to the breaking in upon the continental constitution, and overthrowing the same in a way totally unconstitutional."[14] The delegates were welcomed nearly everywhere by public addresses and poems similar to the following:

> Fathers and countrymen!
> . . . .
> On your debates depends th' impending fate
> Of all that freemen prize as good and great:
> Your wisdom, unborn millions must adore,
> Or curse your names as they each deed explore;
> For should the glorious plan, before you, fall,
> We must attend a tyrant's lordly call.[15]

The *Massachusetts Centinel* reminded the delegates on January 12, 1788, that not only the eyes of their constituents were upon them—all of America and the rest of the world were closely monitoring the events as well.[16] A man with an eye for detail, Tench Coxe composed a lengthy essay for every important convention, delineating the specific problems and future prospects of the particular state. He described the delegates' contribution as "the most dignified temporal act of human nature."[17] The duration of the debates was often excused as an honest attempt to find a lasting solution to the difficult issues facing the country. Accordingly, the *Virginia Gazette* defended the Richmond convention, which by June 19, 1788, had been in session for over two weeks: "Their constituents and posterity will applaud the assiduity and attention they have shewn to this interesting subject."[18]

The delegates themselves, who often labored under the heavy burden of their responsibility, sensed the air of expectation among the citizenry. As the day of the final vote at the Boston convention grew nearer, Tristram Dalton found the tension almost unbearable: "I tremble at the approach, and dread the feelings I shall have when the Names and Answers are called and marked!"[19] It was not merely an empty phrase when South Carolina delegate Alexander Tweed ended his speech by alluding to future generations: "We sir, as citizens and freemen, have an undoubted right of judging for ourselves; it therefore behoves us, most seriously to consider, before we determine a matter of such vast magnitude. We are not acting for ourselves alone, but to all appearance for generations yet unborn."[20] A number of delegates intimated that they felt almost overwhelmed by the enormous responsibility of passing judgment on the Constitution. New York delegate Abraham Bancker described his feelings in a letter from Poughkeepsie on July 12, 1788: "I am apprehensive you will find me among the Minority. Wherever I shall be I hope I shall so determine as that I shall be able to answer to my Constituents for my Conduct, and finally to the righteous Judge of all Mankind, at that Awful Tribunal before which I am Sure to appear, to answer for the deeds done in the Body."[21] It was around this same time that Nathaniel Hazard and Mathew Carey began to mull over the idea of gathering the forms of ratification and proposals for amendments from every state convention and preserving them for posterity to further the study of constitutional history, as well as to enable future scholars to arrive at a fair assessment of the day's far-reaching events.[22]

The conventions adopted procedures, both worldly and spiritual, to assure an orderly discussion of the issues. After appointing a president, secretary, sergeant-at-arms, printers, messengers, and doorkeepers, each convention established a committee to draw up rules. These committees on rules and regulations were guided by parliamentary procedures used in the state legislatures. It was the responsibility of the president of the convention to ensure that the deliberations proceeded smoothly and that "order and decorum" were observed. He had the authority to censure unruly delegates and, if necessary, to propose their expulsion. The delegates were obligated to be punctual and conduct themselves in a civilized manner. They had to ask the president for leave to speak and were only allowed to address the convention while standing in front of their seat. It was forbidden to interrupt a speaker or refer to other delegates by name. Proposals could only be submitted if they had the support of at least one other member. While these rules of order differed only slightly from state to state, the more tactically important rules of procedure varied widely, depending on which party was in the majority. Key questions that could decisively influence the outcome of the conventions included the number of delegates required to attain a quorum, whether a proposal of adjournment was to have precedence over other proposals, and when and in what form votes should be taken. The settlement of these issues often led to the first test of strength between Federalists and Antifederalists.[23]

In several states it was hoped that the presence of the clergy might induce flashes of inspiration and help calm riled spirits. A suggestion put forth by Benjamin Rush in Philadelphia to open the convention with a prayer fell on deaf ears, however. Antifederalists viewed the idea as an unnecessary departure from established procedure and doubted that a minister acceptable to all confessions could be found. Federalists were also reluctant to support Rush out of fear his proposal might be construed as an indirect criticism of the Federal Convention in Philadelphia, which had rejected a similar proposal put forward by Benjamin Franklin. As a compromise, invitations were accepted to attend a commencement celebration at the university and a service at the Lutheran church.[24] The Boston convention, by contrast, agreed to Samuel Adams's proposition "that the Convention will attend morning prayers daily, and that the gentlemen of the clergy of every denomination, be requested to officiate in turn." Federalists were quite enthused about the idea, hoping the prayers might help temper the virulent partisan spirit in evidence at the outset of the deliberations.[25] The clerical atmosphere was heightened when the event was forced to move to Jeremy Belknap's church, a Congregationalist meeting house in Long Lane, owing to the large number of participants.[26] The New Jersey convention asked Presbyterian pastor James Francis Armstrong to open each day's session with a prayer.[27] In Connecticut, as in Massachusetts, a lack of space necessitated the relocation of the convention to a church, where the parish minister, the Reverend Nathan Strong, fervently called down the Lord's blessings upon the delegates.[28] The nearly three hundred North Carolina delegates were forced to meet in a church as well. Unconcerned by provisions in their state constitution mandating the separation of church and state, the Virginians elected the Reverend Abner Waugh unanimously as "Chaplain to the Convention" and ordered him "to attend every morning to read prayers."[29] There had apparently been a similar arrangement in Poughkeepsie, as the convention explicitly conveyed thanks to two ministers at its conclusion. In those states where the services of the church were not requested, the presence of the clergy among the delegates and spectators still lent the proceedings a dignified air.

Even the rules of conduct in tandem with ecclesiastical support could not prevent some disagreeable scenes. In Philadelphia, delegates William Findley and Stephen Chambers expressed their "perfect contempt" for each other, resulting in tumult on the floor and calls for adjournment. Provocative interventions from the gallery elicited angry reactions from Antifederalists at several points during the debates.[30] Boston had a scandal of its own when a fierce argument between Elbridge Gerry and Judge Francis Dana nearly turned violent and the session had to be adjourned amid great commotion.[31] Samuel Holden Parsons, the president of the Society of the Cincinnati in Connecticut, used the convention there to settle accounts with his arch enemy, William Williams, whom he had previously accused of being a follower of Daniel Shays in a bitter dispute waged in the newspapers.[32] In Poughkeepsie, John Lansing accused Alexander Hamilton of suggesting in the Constitutional Convention that the states be eliminated. Hamilton denied the charge, while condemning Lansing for divulging confidential information.[33] A duel was narrowly averted, as was the case in the Virginia convention between Patrick Henry and Governor Edmund Randolph. In general, however, the delegates observed protocol, enabling the conventions to proceed calmly and without interruption. Newspaper accounts repeatedly stressed that the debates were characterized by full attendance and extraordinary punctuality. Across the Union, the turbulent election campaigns had given way to a benign "spirit of moderation" which both sides strove to maintain. In an almost beseeching tone, John Jay lauded the high degree of "temper and deliberation" displayed at the convention in Poughkeepsie, including the "assiduity and regularity" with which the participants went about their business.[34] The *Virginia Independent Chronicle* in Richmond was also full of praise for the Virginia delegates: "The calm, cool, and deliberate manner in which this important subject has been investigated, will be a lasting monument of national gratitude to those venerable statesmen, who have so eminently distinguished themselves in forming this new plan of government."[35]

The immense consequence of the ratifying conventions was underscored by the unusually high level of public interest in the proceedings. Not merely political forums, the conventions were also social events that added color and excitement to the drabness of everyday life. In its call to the states to hold ratifying conventions, Congress, whose own proceedings were not open to the public, had never specified that the meetings must be open to the public. Nevertheless, the citizens took it for granted that their presence would be accepted at the deliberations. Ever since the Massachusetts lower house had been equipped with a gallery in 1766, it had been regarded as a matter of course that the normal workings of government should be conducted before the eye of the constituents.[36] In view of the circumstances, it is not surprising that the secrecy surrounding the Federal Convention of 1787 had been regarded by many as a departure from republican norms. Some Antifederalists described that convention as a dark conclave. Only at the very beginning of the ratification process—yet again in Philadelphia—was the question of public participation briefly discussed. There were some doubts, reported the *Pennsylvania Herald* somewhat indignantly on November 21, 1787, as to whether the doors of the convention should be open to spectators. However, the article continued, the nature and occupation of that body left no other choice, "for the plan of the federal government is to be submitted to the people, yet as it would be highly inconvenient, if not impracticable, to lay it before the citizens at large, it is agreed to submit it to a part of the whole. Whatever therefore is transacted by the convention is, in fact, transacted by the people, and to exclude them from hearing what passes is in effect excluding them from a share in their own act." The writer also suggested that the "secret proceedings" and remoteness of the Federal Convention were responsible for the fierce resistance the Constitution had subsequently encountered. Two days later, the delegates, meeting at the State House, unanimously resolved "that the doors of the Convention be left open during the session." This example was followed by all other states without further discussion.[37]

The people did not hesitate to exercise their right to obtain unfiltered information. The state houses and court buildings were often incapable of accommodating such large masses of spectators; the facilities either had to be enlarged or the conventions moved to more suitable locations in churches and theaters. Politically interested citizens and curiosity seekers came from near and far, creating considerable lodging problems at the convention sites. "There is a great conflux of gentlemen from all parts of the state to attend and hear the deliberations," observed Ezra Stiles in Hartford.[38] The appeal of the Boston convention extended across state lines, attracting around four thousand spectators from all over New England. The perpetually filled gallery of the Long-Lane Congregational Church held from six hundred to eight hundred people. Anyone hoping to gain admission had to be in line at least an hour before the doors opened. Prompted by reports in the newspapers, John Quincy Adams rode to neighboring New Hampshire in February with several friends to get a firsthand impression of the goings-on in Exeter. He found the city overcrowded, and it was nearly impossible to get a seat in the spectators' section at Mr. Mansfield's Meeting House, despite what Adams considered the poor quality of the speeches.[39]

Like Noah Webster and Samuel Blachley Webb, many a New Yorker was unable to resist the temptation to travel up the Hudson to Poughkeepsie, where Baron von Steuben had also betaken himself to size up the situation. The courthouse only offered seating for two hundred spectators, however, a number of which were occupied by society ladies, according to the *New York Journal*.[40] The conspicuous presence of women at the conventions was also noted in Annapolis and Richmond. This provided an additional diversion for spectator Alexander White: "We have every day a gay circle of Ladies—to hear the debates—and have the pleasure of believing them all Federalists."[41] In the South, the greatest number of observers, among them Robert and Gouverneur Morris, sought out the convention in Richmond. Every day hundreds of people jammed into the New Academy, a spacious wooden structure erected as a theater. Private debates raged in the gallery as well as in the taverns; newspaper reports were studied and discussed and bets were taken on the size of the majority this or that party was likely to obtain. Over a thousand people witnessed the spectacular final vote: "Awful and solemn was the pause which preceded the question . . . could the mind be otherwise than tremulously anxious?—to describe my feelings exceeds my power of description. But if I felt before, how can I convey to you those sensations which filled my mind after the decision; in presence of upwards of a thousand spectators, with minds agitated by contending and opposite opinions—the dignified humility of the majority—the tempered patience, manly firmness and virtuous demeanor of the minority . . . finished a scene, which thus stood completed the most grand and solemn I ever beheld."[42]

Spectators were expected to show at least as much consideration and self-control as the delegates themselves. In accordance with common legislative practice, the gallery was obliged to remain absolutely silent and refrain from ostentatious displays of approval or disapproval. A reader of the *Massachusetts Gazette* thought it necessary to remind his fellow citizens of this principle, for the proceedings in Philadelphia seemed to have set a dangerous precedent. On December 10, the Federalist-dominated gallery had enthusiastically applauded a three-hour address by Chief Justice Thomas McKean. The Antifederalist minority did not believe this was a spontaneous reaction, suspecting this "gross insult and disrespect" to be part of a larger plan to intimidate the opposition. That did not sound like the voice of the people, delegate John Smilie cried into the packed auditorium, adding that he would not let any "appearance of violence" prevent him from performing his civic duties, even if the gallery were armed with bayonets. Turning to the president, McKean scoffed: "The gentleman, sir, is *angry*—because other folks are *pleased.*"[43]

That incident, indicative of the tense atmosphere in Philadelphia, was reported on by the *Pennsylvania Herald* and eagerly exploited by Antifederalists. Writing in the *Massachusetts Gazette* under the name of "Agrippa," James Winthrop assailed the "heroes of aristocracy" in Pennsylvania for having sought applause from the rabble, completely unashamed of this blatant "violation of decency."[44] Antifederalist speakers who had been disturbed by "shuffling and stamping of feet, coughing, talking, spitting, and whispering" at the Hartford convention also questioned the spontaneous nature of the interruptions.[45] Boston spectators violated the rules as well, by applauding the rejection of a proposal put forth by the opposition. Antifederalist reactions to this affront led to a "momentary agitation," but calm was soon restored.[46] When a similar incident occurred in Charleston, opponents of the Constitution demanded that the gallery be cleared. Judge Nathaniel Pendleton, however, shrewdly excused the "intemperate conduct of the spectators" as an innocuous display of unbridled patriotism.[47] It was obvious everywhere that city dwellers feverishly anticipated the adoption of the Constitution and could barely control their enthusiasm. In this atmosphere, the addresses and sermons delivered on Independence Day in 1788 took on an admonishing undertone directed toward recalcitrant citizens who had still not embraced the Constitution.[48] In Poughkeepsie, Federalists made a point of inviting their aloof adversaries to a common banquet on the 4th of July.[49] There was also no dearth of private celebrations, receptions, and other events. The representatives of the backcountry found themselves welcomed with open arms everywhere they went—provided the strict instructions they had been issued by their constituents were open to discussion. The most generous city in this regard was Charleston, where the citizens threw "lavish entertainments" for their guests.[50] The little town of Hillsborough, North Carolina, on the other hand, had little to offer in the way of amusements. Local citizens and convention delegates alike therefore must have been quite relieved when a theater group turned up in the city at the right moment to help everyone pass the time.[51] Normally, only the residents of large cities like New York were accustomed to such attractions. In that metropolis, the pastoral play *The Convention or The Columbian Father* and Samuel Low's comedy *The Politician Out-Witted* had been performed in the spring of 1788 to put citizens in the right frame of mind for the upcoming convention in Poughkeepsie.[52]

Participants, Factions, and Social Contrasts

The nearly two thousand delegates who served in state conventions may have been representing the entire Union, yet they were hardly any more representative of the nation's population—even if women and slaves are not considered—than the Federal Convention had been. Several of the original fifty-five participants in the latter event, incidentally, were also involved this time around. At least one of the delegates in the Constitutional Convention had been elected to the ratifying convention in every state. By all accounts, the conventions constituted a meeting ground for the most prominent politicians, lawyers, planters, and merchants from each county or town in every state, thus lending the occasion a rather elite air. The Litchfield *Weekly Monitor* was perhaps only slightly exaggerating when it described the Hartford convention as an "assembly of chosen philosophers and patriots," the likes of which had never before been seen in Connecticut. Even staid Ezra Stiles deemed the event "the grandest assemblage of sensible and worthy characters that ever met together in this state." A "Connecticut Farmer" examined the published voting list and determined that the following persons, among others, had voted yes to the Constitution: two governors, one lieutenant governor, six members of the governor's council, four superior court judges, two ministers, eight generals, eighteen colonels, seven majors, thirteen captains, and various county court judges and justices of the peace. Among the forty delegates who voted no were one member of the governor's council, two generals, four colonels, three captains, one lieutenant, and an assortment of local judges.[53]

The participants in the larger Massachusetts convention were not quite as illustrious, though 51 of the 358 delegates did bear the title "Honorable," according to notes taken by Ezra Stiles. This indicated they were members of either the governor's council or the senate. Stiles also counted around eighty officers, eighteen ministers, at least a dozen doctors, and a handful of lawyers. The *Boston Gazette* was convinced the body was "undoubtedly composed of the first characters that Old Massachusetts could depute from among her sons."[54] The New Hampshire delegates included thirty-nine judges, thirty-eight officers of the Continental Army or militia, and fifty-six members of the state legislature or Congress.[55] The Pennsylvania convention was made up mainly of lawyers, businessmen, and various assemblymen who were basically professional politicians.[56] Of the sixty-five New York delegates, forty-five were in the 1787–88 session of the state assembly, in the state senate, or in Congress. In addition to the Confederation's secretary for foreign affairs, the state governor, and the chancellor, the convention in Poughkeepsie included all three former participants in the Federal Convention, all three justices of the state supreme court, all five members of the Council of Revision, and four county judges.[57] It is no wonder one participant declared that nowhere else had the Constitution been "fairer canvassed, abler defended, and more powerfully opposed" than in the State of New York.[58]

To an even greater extent than in New England and the Middle Atlantic states, the conventions in Maryland and Virginia represented a cross-section of the social and political elite. Gathered in Annapolis were three present or past governors, four members of the governor's council, ten senators, and thirty-five assemblymen and senate electors. The majority of delegates belonged to the relatively small group of lawyers, merchants, and planters who had dominated Maryland politics since 1776.[59] Of the one hundred seventy Virginia delegates, Forrest McDonald identified five as merchants, twenty-nine as lawyers, three as ministers, and six as doctors. Rounding out the participants were a number of wealthy planters and an unusual number of officers who had served in the War of Independence or were still active in the militia. As in most other states, the deliberations were also attended by the governor, state and county judges, former delegates to the Federal Convention, and congressmen. Forty-six of the convention delegates were elected to the state legislature in October 1788.[60] Ordinary farmers and artisans were present in considerable numbers only at the large conventions of Massachusetts, South Carolina, and North Carolina, as well as in both sessions of the Rhode Island convention. Yet even these "simple folks" fulfilled important functions in their home towns or districts, where their special abilities or accomplishments had earned them the voters' trust. Thus, the "filtration process" elaborated by Madison in the "Publius" essays had already had a measured effect on the selection of candidates for the ratifying conventions, bringing forth a host of respectable and competent delegates.

CONFRONTATION IN NEW ENGLAND

Property, education, talent, and experience were not equally divided between the two parties. Indeed, Federalists had a distinct advantage in this regard. At some conventions an enormous social gap was evident between the advocates and opponents of the Constitution. This disparity did not go unnoticed by the participants themselves, though they drew different conclusions from it. Federalists believed the support of so many intelligent, accomplished, and affluent personages said more about the merits of the Constitution than any theoretical arguments could have. If the judgment of these leaders was so important in everyday political affairs, how much more indispensable must it be when complex constitutional issues were being resolved, requiring extensive legal and historical knowledge? Federalists also strongly questioned the credentials of their adversaries, in whose ranks there appeared to be a large number of less intellectually endowed, less prosperous, and less successful individuals. The opposition's speakers allegedly lacked both the necessary expertise and the moral integrity to decide on important matters affecting the citizens' general welfare and future prosperity. By openly flaunting their higher social status, Federalists only confirmed the suspicions of their opponents that the new system of government was designed to serve the interests of the privileged upper classes and restore the social structures of the colonial period.

The social disparity varied, with the widest gaps being in the New England states and the narrowest in Virginia. At the Massachusetts convention, the contrast was so striking that both sides made an issue of it. Immediately after publication of the election results, Federalist Christopher Gore gleefully declared that there was just one serious rival in the opposition camp, namely Samuel Adams, amid a mere handful of capable people. After the first meeting of convention delegates, Jeremy Belknap noted that the opposition had several "noisy leaders" but "the best men, the best speakers" were on the side of ratification. The Antifederalist Party, asserted Nathaniel Gorham, was an assemblage of paper money and debtor-protection advocates, former Shays rebels, separatists from Maine, and an assortment of "honest doubting people." They were up against a "phalanx of sensible men and good Speakers," including such notables as Governor John Hancock and his predecessor James Bowdoin, three state supreme court judges, fifteen senators, almost twenty ministers, ten to twelve lawyers, three generals, and various other respected public figures. As the deliberations progressed, the sense of social confrontation became more pronounced. Henry Jackson commented in a letter to Knox: "It is astonishing to see the weight of respectability, integrity, property and ability on the side of the proposed constitution. And on the other side the—Characters that oppose it—my god the contrast—Harry, it is too much to think of." This contrast soon became a burden to Federalists, however, as it confirmed the opposition's "prejudices" and fueled their propaganda machine. An immense obstacle, a slightly rankled Rufus King informed Madison, was the general distrust of "men of property or Education." It was impossible to allay the critics' suspicion "that some injury is plotted against them—that the system is the production of the rich and ambitious, that *they* discern its operations and that the consequence will be the establishment of two orders in the Society, one comprehending the opulent and great, the other the poor and illiterate. The extraordinary Union in favor of the Constitution in this State of the Wealth and sensible part of it, is a confirmation of their opinions and every exertion hitherto made to eradicate it, has been in vain."[61]

The fear of being outclassed and looked down upon was best articulated at the Massachusetts convention by Antifederalist delegate Amos Singletary, the owner of a mill in Sutton:

> These lawyers, and men of learning, and monied men, that talk so finely and gloss over matters so smoothly, to make us poor illiterate people swallow down the pill, expect to get into Congress themselves . . . then they will swallow up all us little folks, like the great Leviathan, Mr. President, yes, just as the whale swallowed up Jonah. A sigh of relief went through the ranks of Federalists when the very next speaker, a plain farmer, spoke out in favor of ratification. Delegate Jonathan Smith from Lanesborough in Berkshire County began by asking the president to bear with him, for he earned his living with a plow and was not accustomed to public speaking. He just wanted to say a few words to remind his "brother ploughjoggers": "They that are honest men themselves are not apt to suspect other people . . . these lawyers, these monied men, these men of learning, are all embarked in the same cause with us, and we must all swim or sink together . . . now is the time to reap the fruit of our labour."[62]

Nevertheless, the socioeconomic disparity is clearly evident in the final vote: around 40 percent of Federalists, but only 12 percent of the opposition delegates, were merchants, lawyers, large landowners, doctors, or ministers. Antifederalists had a clear majority of farmers and men of unspecified standing, at 58 percent to 38 percent. The fact that the occupations of 89 of the 168 dissenters cannot be determined speaks for itself. Delegates with high social, military, or economic status voted for the Constitution by a three to one ratio, while their less well-situated colleagues rejected it by a two to one ratio. Government securities were almost exclusively in the hands of 58 Federalist delegates.[63] Behind the façade of camaraderie and cooperation erected by Federalists for reasons of political expediency, their air of social superiority persisted. This can be seen, for instance, in Henry Jackson's remark about the "*poor devils*" who had to pay for their journey home out of their own pockets, as well as in Caleb Gibbs's comment to Washington that the "feeble speakers of the Rabble" had taken a beating. Neutral observers were more inclined to admire the opposition's determined resistance, "which was made against the Combined force of the whole body of the literati in the State."[64]

The social fronts were similar at the conventions in Connecticut, New Hampshire, and Rhode Island. In Hartford, at least half of the Federalists, but only one-fifth of their adversaries, were members of the educated and propertied classes. Twenty-two of the twenty-three delegates who had attended college voted for adoption. Antifederalist Hugh Ledlie attributed his party's defeat to the fact that the other side not only had better writers and speakers, they also had more citizens "of superior rank, as they call themselves."[65]

President John Sullivan regarded the debate in Exeter as a clash of "men of property and of good Sense" against a mixed bag of "arrant Toreys, friends to paper money, Tender Laws, Insurrections, persons in debt distress, and poverty, either real or Imaginary; men of blind piety, Hypocrites, and Bankrupts; together with many honest men cowed by Instructions to vote against the Constitution at all Events." While Federalists boasted "all the Men of abilities, integrity and property and influence," their opponents were simply "dumb & obstinate." After a visit to the second session of the New Hampshire convention in Concord, Tobias Lear thought it "pretty well ascertained that at least ¾ of the property, and a larger proportion of the abilities in the State are friendly to the proposed system. The opposition here (as has generally been the case) was composed of men who were involved in debt."[66] The fifty-seven-member Federalist delegation contained a higher percentage of merchants, lawyers, wealthy landowners, doctors, and ministers, but a lower percentage of farmers than the forty-seven-man group who voted against the Constitution. The contrast was even more striking in such areas as education and experience. Nineteen percent of Federalists were college graduates, compared with only 4 percent of Antifederalists; 26 percent of the first group, but only 6 percent of the latter, had served more than one term in the state legislature; all six congressmen in attendance and twenty-seven of thirty-eight officers voted in favor of the proposed system.[67]

In Rhode Island, Federalists almost uniformly represented the "Mercantile Interest." "Our Federal Delegates are many of them men of abilities and good speakers; this circumstance justifies us in the hope that ignorance and obstinacy will give way to Eloquence and fair reasoning," Henry Knox was told by a friend from Providence after the convention elections in February 1790. Yet in South Kingston the opposition retained the upper hand, their ranks peopled with "many of Desparate Circumstances and the principle heads of the Paper money faction," according to former deputy governor Jabez Bowen. Henry Marchant ascribed the later approval of the Constitution in Newport primarily to the fortunate circumstance that the "largest fœderal Interest, and little Influence of the Country Anties" had prevailed. The ratification of the Constitution, William Vernon related to Jeremiah Wadsworth, "gave inexpressible pleasure to the Persons of property, and a fatal stab, to Paper Money robbers and Legislators."[68] That several Antifederalist delegates were involved in trade and in speculative investments apparently went unnoticed or, more likely, was considered immaterial. The sole criterion of any relevance was whether a delegate belonged to the Merchant or Country Party, that is, whether he represented the interests of the merchants and tradesmen or those of the farmers.[69]

SOCIAL HOMOGENEITY AND HIERARCHY IN THE MIDDLE AND SOUTHERN STATES

Socioeconomic stratification was also a factor at the conventions in the middle and southern states. Even in cases where the levels of education, occupation, and income were similar, observers were aware of differences in social rank. Antifederalists stressed their dedication to the solid rural middle class, whom they resolved to protect from the arrogance of the elite and the licentiousness of the urban rabble. Federalists, by contrast, made no secret of their self-perception as members of a "natural aristocracy" uniting knowledge, high moral standards, concern for the common good, and respect for property ownership; they questioned the intelligence, integrity, and solvency of all those who dared to oppose the Constitution.

This "elite vs. middle class" dichotomy came closest to describing the situation in South Carolina. There, Federalists were, in the words of John Vaughan, "all the men of Virtue, sense and property who have had the means of information"; lined up against them were "the violent, ignorant, and those who have been deprived of the means of information." Henry W. DeSaussure confirmed that the greater share of "leading Characters" joined the campaign for ratification, leaving the opposition nearly bereft of capable leaders. Taking a different political perspective, Arthur Bryan distinguished between the pro-Constitution "Aristocracy" and the oppositional—yet unfortunately rather apathetic—"second class of people." In the words of Aedanus Burke, the new system enjoyed the support of "all the rich, leading men, along the Seacoast, and rice settlements; with few exceptions, Lawyers, Physicians and Divines, the merchants, mechanicks, the Populace, and mob of Charleston." These were aided by the former Tories and their followers, in addition to all British citizens residing in Charleston, from the consul to the printers' apprentices to the street-sweepers.[70] At the convention, a majority of delegates from the business and trade sector were on the side of Federalists (18–5), as were the lawyers, doctors, and ministers (23–4), as well as planters (87–31). Antifederalists had a greater number of planters and small farmers (27–15).[71]

Though less glaring, social disparities were also perceivable at the Pennsylvania convention. Over half of the Federalist delegates, but only one-fifth of their adversaries, were merchants, manufacturers, large landholders, lawyers, doctors, or ministers. The artisans, innkeepers, and small businessmen were evenly split for the most part (33 percent to 30 percent), while a wide majority of small farmers opposed the Constitution (48 percent to 13 percent).[72]

Any analysis of the New York convention in Poughkeepsie is hampered by the fact that nineteen of the delegates originally elected as Antifederalists either changed sides toward the end or abstained from voting. If estimates are based on the figures at the outset of the event, the social disparity does not seem particularly striking. Fifteen of the nineteen Federalists in attendance and twenty-three of the forty-six Antifederalists were lawyers, judges, merchants, or large landowners. While the first group contained considerably more wealthy citizens, most of the Antifederalist delegates also made a comfortable living as civil servants, farmers, or businessmen, and fourteen of them held government bonds worth over $100. The dividing lines become more pronounced, however, if we examine the final vote: most of the defectors came from the ranks of the affluent, educated, and business-oriented delegates. A total of twenty Federalists and twelve Antifederalists can be described as members of the upper class. After two college graduates and thirteen investors in government securities had changed sides, the ratios in these two categories shifted to 8–1 and 22–8 in favor of Federalists.[73]

Such difficulties notwithstanding, it was inaccurate for Antifederalists to discredit their rivals as aristocrats, referring to them even in their private letters as "*the mighty*" and "the *better sort*."[74] Yet their feeling of social inferiority was real and must therefore be included in any historical assessment of the process of ratification.

Antifederalists at the convention in Annapolis also felt overwhelmed by their adversaries, apart from their numerical inferiority. Even though they held important government offices themselves (Luther Martin and William Paca), were prosperous lawyers (Samuel and Jeremiah Townlee Chase, John Francis Mercer, and William Pinckney), had large estates and many slaves (the Chases, Martin, Paca, Benjamin Harrison, and Nathan Cromwell), and were among the state's foremost entrepreneurs (Charles Ridgely and Samuel Chase), most of these men could never entirely shed the stigma of an intruder in society's upper echelons. This perception was intensified by the fact that a good number of them were in difficult financial straits and in disrepute as a result of dubious speculative ventures. At the ratifying convention they faced the united front of the planter-commercial elite. Almost all Federalist delegates were slave-owning planters, and many of them augmented their incomes through activities as lawyers and entrepreneurs. There could be little doubt as to which of the two sides was held to have the advantage in social prestige and moral integrity.[75]

Critics of the Constitution appeared the most self-confident in North Carolina and Virginia, though certain remarks by North Carolina politicians revealed that differences in social status and education were perceived here as well. Timothy Bloodworth affirmed that the "Attorneys, Merchants, and Aristocratic Part of the community" almost unanimously favored ratification. Federalists themselves considered most of their opponents to be much too ignorant to grasp the "true Nature of Government."[76] In actuality, there was little difference between the two factions at the conventions in Hillsborough and Fayetteville. Property, as measured by land and slave ownership, was equally divided for the most part. There were proportionately more Federalists in the groups with twenty or more and fifty or more slaves, yet the size of the farms and plantations was nearly even.[77] Leading Antifederalists like Willie Jones and Thomas Person had no reason to shy from comparisons with their wealthy adversaries from the coast. Commercial enterprises, which were most likely to be in the hands of proponents of the Constitution, had only slowly begun to increase a politician's influence and enhance his reputation in this solidly agricultural state. As in other areas, Federalists may have felt inclined to look down on the opposition in North Carolina as well. Their opponents, however, had no intention of looking up to them, and simply followed the dictates of their own conscience.

The Richmond convention was also characterized by relative social equality. The gentry—owners of large plantations, land speculators, college graduates, and former military officers—predominated in the upper and middle classes, and even most "unknown" representatives were members of the social elite in their counties. The greatest influence was exerted by law school graduates, seventeen of whom were Federalists vis-à-vis twelve Antifederalists. As to comparative wealth, mainly measured by the amount of land and the number of slaves in a delegate's possession, Robert E. Thomas and Forrest McDonald were unable to ascertain any significant differences between the two parties. Norman Risjord, on the other hand, applied his "multivariant analysis" to convention participants as well as legislators serving in 1788 and discovered a correlation between rising affluence and Federalism, though other factors such as occupation and military service played a more important role. Politicians engaged in commercial activities, college graduates, and Continental Army officers showed an above-average inclination to sympathize with Federalists, but again it was a matter of degree. Regional and other formative influences were apparently more decisive in determining who voted for or against the Constitution than social class.[78] This conclusion is consistent with the observation of contemporaries, who were more struck by the similarities between the opposing parties at the convention than their differences. It is true that Federalists like James Madison and Edward Carrington were convinced the lion's share of talent and prestige were on their side, but this notion was not corroborated by the accounts of neutral and independent observers. Both parties were roughly evenly matched and worthy of "equal respect and deference," according to Governor Edmund Randolph. Robert Morris, a prominent visitor from Pennsylvania, noted that the deliberations in Richmond were "supported with Ability & pursued with Ardour on both Sides." Accordingly, both parties treated each other with "the utmost moderation and temper," bringing the convention to a conclusion "in friendship & Amity."[79]

Two conclusions can be drawn from the above. First of all, the social composition of the various conventions was not uniform but, rather, differed by degrees, from the stark social contrasts in Massachusetts to the minute disparities in Virginia. Only in New England did the debate over the Constitution resemble a clash between the rich and the poor, the educated and the uneducated, the powerful and the weak. On the other hand, there were forces at work that disconnected perception and reality, deepening the divisions. Federalists claimed to have the support of the men of education and wealth. For their part, Antifederalists were never entirely able to shed their insecurity and overcome their resentments, and they attacked their opponents as the "mighty," even when they were equals in all respects. This should not be construed to mean the social contrasts only existed in people's minds—

there were real differences. Overall, however, the social element was less important than contemporaries made it seem and was by no means the sole determinant.

The Role and Influence of Rhetoric

The oratorical abilities of the delegates had a considerable effect on the outcome of the deliberations. The spoken word was still a powerful force despite the growing importance of printed matter. Verbal communication in the form of addresses and sermons was a fundamental element of Anglo-American culture, and the practice of debating had gradually shifted its focus in the course of the eighteenth century from the theological to the political sphere.[80] Public speaking had been popularized during the Revolution, taking the country by storm. Even after the war there were plenty of opportunities to hone this skill. College life culminated in commencement celebrations at which the speakers and participants regularly conversed in Latin and Greek. Practical examples of formal speaking were provided by the clergy's sermons and public addresses, patriotic speeches on special occasions like Independence Day, the instructions of judges, the summations of attorneys, and the debates in the thirteen state legislatures. All across the Union, students and local residents founded discussion groups reminiscent of "enlightened" circles and clubs in European cities. Political discourse was not a privilege of the educated upper class in America. Common citizens were not ashamed to step forward and express their opinions at town meetings and county conventions, in election campaigns, and in "publick Houses."[81] At the same time, Baptist and Methodist revivalist preachers did not hesitate to include politics in their sermons and even had the audacity to admit slaves to their gatherings. Not everyone was enthused about this development, as evidenced by the growing number of warnings against rabble-rousers and demagogues.

Many people considered training in rhetoric to be the best preparation for a career as a lawyer or politician. During the convention in Poughkeepsie, a solicitous father impressed upon his son: "Be attentive . . . to telling a Story in a graceful and Short and intelligible manner. Study Oratory and Eloquence which often is very useful in a republican Government especially."[82] South Carolina convention delegate Pierce Butler was pleased with his son's progress in Latin at a school in England. He bade the boy's teacher to pay special attention to "his reading and repeating aloud, to enable him to suit his Voice to the Subject and the Audience—Among my many anxieties for him is that of His distinguishing himself as a publick Speaker. . . . If in the Senate of this little Republic he may take a lead, or, still more flattering, in the Senate of the United States, it will be some little reward to You."[83] The debate over the Constitution together with the prospect of a large forum of national politics clearly fed many a son's ambition and encouraged scholarly pursuits. Edward Rutledge Jr. took lessons in Latin and applied himself to the study of law, "as it is the only one, in this country, that leads to riches and honour."[84]

Robert C. Johnson, son of famed Connecticut politician and signer of the Constitution, William Samuel Johnson, now president of Columbia College in New York City, was inspired by the deliberations at the New York convention. His spirited report from Poughkeepsie was intended to show his father that he had resolved to improve his ways and apply himself to his studies from then on:

> I scarcely ever experienced more perfect pleasure, than from attending to *some* of the Speakers in convention; a pleasure that was only clouded by the reflexion, how little progress in the art of Speaking, have I yet made. . . . I esteem the Speaker as such an enviable character, so far exalted above evry other, that no study can be too intense, no labor, no self denial too great, if the object can but be obtained. . . . To be a good Speaker, is the great object of my wishes, Evry thing else is but secondary in my mind—& I wish to have evry Study subservient to that point—there is no labor no fatigue that I am not, at present, willing to undergo.[85]

Henry Van Schaack, who also attended the Poughkeepsie convention, received the following admonition from his father:

> You should occasionally recur to the Specimens you have in your Reading met with of antient Oratory, "the Thunder of Demosthenes & the Splendid Conflagration of Tully"—Human Nature is the same in all Ages—Habits & Manners vary—Which of our present Orators wod. have resembled those of Antiquity had they lived in those Days, or which of the antient Orators according to the Doctrine of Transmigration of Souls are at present in the convention at Poughkeepsie?[86]

William Pierce's "Character Sketches of Delegates to the Federal Convention," in which considerable attention is paid to the delegates' rhetorical abilities, shows the high value placed on this skill. Of Hamilton, for example, Pierce writes that he combined "a clear and strong judgment" with the "ornaments of fancy, and whilst he is able, convincing, and engaging in his eloquence the Heart and Head sympathize in approving him. Yet there is something too feeble in his voice to be equal to the strains of oratory;—it is my opinion that he is rather a convincing Speaker, than a blazing Orator. . . . His language is not always equal, sometimes didactic like Bolingbroke's at others light and trippling like Stern's. His eloquence is not defusive as to trifle with the senses, but he rambles just enough to strike and keep up the attention." In Pierce's view, James Madison combined in his person the profound politician and the scholar, "and tho' he cannot be called an Orator, he is a most agreeable, eloquent, and convincing speaker." Pierce reserved the best grades for the oratorical performances of Rufus King and Gouverneur Morris.[87]

Hence, forceful and convincing argumentation was not enough; the characteristics of a good orator also included a clear voice, a secure, elegant delivery, cleverness and wit, and the effective yet inconspicuous use of gestures. Furthermore, anyone aspiring to speak in support of or against men like Hamilton, Madison, Rufus King, James Wilson, and Gouverneur Morris, participants in the Federal Convention in Philadelphia, needed at least a basic knowledge of law, history, and literature. For William Tilghman, being elected to the Maryland convention meant immersing himself in a subject "to which I have not hitherto devoted much study." He therefore asked Tench Coxe to name the principles "which have struck you as being most forcible, either in support of the Government, or by way of answering the objections urged against it."[88] Coxe recommended consulting books, reading pamphlets and essays, studying the records of debates already in print, and committing his own speeches to writing well in advance of the convention.

It goes without saying that college graduates, especially lawyers and judges, were better prepared for disputations of this kind than merchants and artisans, not to mention farmers. They had experience in public speaking, for one thing, while discussions on constitutional issues and the political system had been included in their studies and were a part of their daily professional life. Besides being particularly well versed in the theories of Locke, Blackstone, and Montesquieu, they were also quite capable, as the debates would show, of quoting from the works of Machiavelli, Sidney, Coke, Harrington, Hobbes, Pufendorf, Grotius, De Lolme, Vattel, Burlamaqui, Beccaria, Hume, and Adam Smith. They further exhibited a familiarity with classical authors, who were read at the universities, with seventeenth- and eighteenth-century literature, and with more modern historians like Edward Gibbon. To be sure, their knowledge was not always profound and their quotations occasionally had more to do with oratorical embellishment than with argumentation. Nevertheless, the debates at most conventions were held on a level that permitted only a small percentage of the delegates to take part in the proceedings. How many people were competent to expound on the Delphic amphictyony, the Roman decemviri, the history of Magna Carta, the Polish electoral monarchy, and the duties of the Dutch governor? Consequently, a handful of select persons invariably bore most of the burden of criticizing or defending the Constitution. The list of speakers from the record of the Pennsylvania convention contains the names of only twelve of sixty-nine delegates—nine Federalists and three Antifederalists. The *New Hampshire Spy* counted fourteen "principal speakers" from among the more than one hundred participants in the Exeter convention, and only twenty of the one hundred seventy delegates in Richmond spoke.[89]

Whereas the opposition managed to hold their own for the most part in Pennsylvania, Virginia, and New York, their low social status and lack of education was sorely felt at other conventions. They were repeatedly forced to pit inexperienced speakers against Federalist luminaries. In Massachusetts and South Carolina, criticism of the Constitution was often limited to expressing doubts and asking questions, merely providing Federalists with cues for drawn-out rebuttals and expositions. Those who did summon the courage to expound on their views often began by asking their listeners for forbearance, explaining that they had little experience as politicians or were "simple men." William Symmes Jr., a talented lawyer from Andover, Massachusetts, introduced himself with the following gesture of humility:

> Mr. President, in such an assembly as this, and on a subject, that puzzles the oldest politicians, a young man, sir, will scarcely dare to think for himself; but if he ventures to speak, the effort must certainly be greater.—This convention is the first representative body in which I have been honoured with a seat, and men will not wonder that a scene at once so new, and so august, should confuse, oppress, and almost disqualify me to proceed.

Nathaniel Barrell followed his example:

> Awed in the presence of this august assembly—conscious of my inability to express my mind fully on this important occasion—and sensible how little I must appear in the eyes of those giants in rhetorik, who have exhibited such a pompous display of declamation:—Without any of those talents calculated to draw attention—without the pleasing eloquence of Cicero, or the blaze of Demosthenian oratory, I rise, Sir, to discharge my duty to my constituents, who I know expect something more from me than a silent vote.[90]

Antifederalist delegate Alexander Tweed in Charleston, a man with a "circumscribed scale of talents," freely admitted that he could not compete with speakers "whose profound oratory and elocution would, on the journals of a British house of commons, stand as lasting monuments of their great abilities."[91]

Federalists generally looked on the backcountry delegates' attempts at public speaking with contempt. The minute a member of this group developed a fondness for the Constitution, however, their educated peers were suddenly enthralled by the simple language of the common man. They lavished praise on the conciliatory message sent by Massachusetts delegate Smith to his "brother plough-joggers": "It gives us great pleasure to hear some of the honest, sensible, independent yeomanry speak in favour of the Constitution. Their feelings, their natural language, their similes, are highly entertaining. . . . Is not this true natural eloquence and forcible reasoning?"[92]

Frequent remarks in letters and diaries confirm the receptiveness of eighteenth-century citizens to the aesthetic and emotional appeal of rhetoric. Even so, caution is advised when assessing the true significance of this skill in the process of ratification. To be sure, the comparison of leading speakers with such classical orators as Cicero and Demosthenes was more than an empty phrase. It was an expression of sincere admiration accompanied by the desire to follow in the footsteps of the most famous republican statesmen of antiquity, an ambition which appeared eccentric to European observers. According to the *Pennsylvania Packet,* James Wilson captivated the audience at the ratifying convention with a speech "which the celebrated Roman orator would not have blushed to own." The *Connecticut Courant* proclaimed that Oliver Ellsworth's and William Samuel Johnson's contributions to the debates in Hartford were "equal to any of the Roman senators and will deserve as famous a place in modern history as theirs did among the ancients."[93] Hamilton's clear logic and eloquent delivery were thought most reminiscent of Cicero, while Patrick Henry embodied the intensity and captivating pathos of Demosthenes.[94] Gifted speakers like Francis Dana could move the audience to tears and distract the stenographers from their work.[95]

It was not unusual for listeners to revive their enthusiasm during subsequent attempts to describe their experiences and feelings. "Rufus King shines among Federalists with a superior lustre. His speeches are clear, cool, nervous, pointed, and conclusive. Parsons distinguishes accurately and reasons forcibly," raved Jeremy Belknap in a letter to Ebenezer Hazard.[96] George Benson of Rhode Island was careful not to miss a single speech by esteemed Federalists at the Boston convention: "The soft and persuasive addresses, of a [Caleb] Strong,—the Cogent and nervous reasoning of a [Theophilus] Parsons—the perspicuous and emphatical Arguments of a [Theodore] Sedgwick and the irresistible Eloquence of a [Rufus] King—a Torrent of good Sense, embellished with all the Charms of the most engaging and winning Manners—. . . to hang on their Lips is a Luxury which absorbs all my attention." It was an indescribable pleasure to attend the "feast of reason" that was the ratifying convention.[97] James Breckinridge was surprised to find that the proceedings in Richmond exceeded even his high expectations: "They have been elaborate, elegant, eloquent, & consequently entertaining and constructive."[98] The opening address in Poughkeepsie, in which Chancellor Robert R. Livingston poked fun at the "Phantom Aristocracy," was judged a "stream of delicate satire and truly Attic eloquence." Despite being unable to walk due to a leg injury, Samuel Blachley Webb went to great lengths to avoid missing a single contribution by Hamilton, Livingston, or John Jay. The discussions were "truly interesting, and important," he wrote to Catherine Hogeboom, "and if an elegant display of oratory founded on truth and reason can have its due weight over Art and ill founded prejudice, this convention will yet adopt the proposed Constitution."[99]

Except for isolated dissatisfaction with the level of the debates in New Hampshire and North Carolina and with the determined silence of pro-Constitution delegates in Annapolis, the conventions were almost uniformly described as impressive, elegant, and informative. There was also general agreement that Federalists tended to have the best speakers. It is difficult to determine, however, to what extent they were able to use this advantage to win over opposing delegates. The leading Federalist speakers in Pennsylvania, namely James Wilson, Thomas McKean, and Benjamin Rush, all had certain foibles that weakened their effectiveness and tarnished the otherwise stellar image of the majority faction. Rush's religious ardor was just as disturbing as McKean's observation that a "well administered despotism" was the best form of government.[100] During the debate over the necessity of a bill of rights, Wilson denied the existence of the Virginia Declaration of Rights as well as the institution of trial by jury in Sweden. William Findley then gleefully quoted from Blackstone's commentary on jury trials in Sweden, adding that if his son were to reveal such a lack of knowledge after only six months' study of law he would deserve a good thrashing. The Shippens were surely not alone in the malicious delight they took in the public mortification of that "eminent lawyer." Such debacles weakened the impact of Wilson's and McKean's otherwise splendid contributions, while providing Findley, John Smilie, and Robert Whitehill with an opportunity to shine as erudite and witty adversaries. In William Shippen's estimation, the minority made the most of the situation: "Never was there a finer field for the display of eloquence and abilities, than the opposition to this system affords." He declared Findley had earned great respect and proven himself superior to Wilson and every other participant in the convention.[101] Be that as it may, the oratorical performances of all those involved merely served to cement the two sides' positions. When the final votes were counted, it became evident that no shift had occurred and Federalists had merely succeeded in maintaining the numerical advantage they had taken into the deliberations.

The proceedings in Boston were unquestionably dominated by pro-Constitution speakers like King, Caleb Strong, Nathaniel Gorham, Francis Dana, Theophilus Parsons, Theodore Sedgwick, and Fisher Ames. Their only serious rival was Elbridge Gerry, who had been invited to speak as an expert but soon left the convention, when Federalists limited him to direct responses to their specific questions. Federalists accused opposition delegates of soliciting outside help with the preparation of their speeches. By trying to put a positive spin on the difference in quality between the two parties, Antifederalist essayists indirectly acknowledged their lower standard. "Helvidius Priscus," for instance, accused the "aristocratick faction" of missing no opportunity "to depreciate the abilities of that part of the convention . . . who are opposed to the arbitrary system. . . . On the other hand, there seems to be modesty of benevolence and the boldness of truth, in the short, unadmired speeches which, in the garb of simplicity, utter the native dictates of good sense, uncorrupted by the splendour of wealth."[102] John Quincy Adams, by contrast, concluded after reading newspaper reports that, far from dealing with key issues in a profound manner, opposition speakers had not even touched on such important points as the separation of powers, representation, mandatory rotation of offices, and "the indefinite powers granted to the administration."[103]

Despite this Federalist dominance in the debate, their early optimism that they could convert many of the "moderate and silent members" of the opposition by the sheer force of their eloquence soon gave way to a more realistic estimation of the situation. It had become apparent that their dazzling rhetoric changed few minds. Joseph Crocker summed up the situation two weeks into the proceedings: "The honest, wise & judicious are steadfast in Accepting; the Friends to Anarchy & Confusion in nonacceptance."[104] Still, there are indications that Federalist efforts were not entirely in vain and actually moved a few delegates to rethink their positions. The turning point, however, came when Governor Hancock, in collaboration with Federalists, presented a list of recommendatory amendments to be appended to the Form of Ratification. The amendments would be submitted for consideration of the first federal Congress under the Constitution. Those delegates who had begun to waver in the course of the debates were now given an opportunity to change their stance with a clean conscience and without losing face.

Antifederalist protagonists also found themselves mismatched in Connecticut and New Hampshire. James Wadsworth and Joshua Atherton struggled valiantly but were clearly not equal to their dual role as party leaders and experts on the Constitution. The *New Haven Gazette* quoted an observer from Hartford who claimed Wadsworth's arguments had "exceedingly injured the cause of the opposition—they have been weak and, in some instances, urged with great spleen."[105] Atherton's address was criticized for finding fault with every single paragraph of the Constitution without revealing a recognizable overall approach. It was due more to his ineptness than to the Federalists' powers of persuasion that opposition delegates began to question their instructions, the result being that the convention adjourned to prevent a defeat of the Constitution.[106] In Charleston, eloquent speeches by the Rutledges and Pinckneys did appear to weaken what resistance remained. The Federalists' supplications fell on deaf ears, however, at the first convention in North Carolina, where they were up against an overwhelming and undivided majority. Their main accomplishment was preventing the final, irreversible rejection of the proposal.

The high points in oratory were the conventions in Richmond and Poughkeepsie. Those conventions suggest the power of the spoken word. To all appearances, the Virginia convention boiled down to an oral duel between James Madison and Patrick Henry, two distinctly different personalities and temperaments with contradictory speaking styles. Madison's delivery was extremely matter-of-fact, sedate, rigidly organized, and scholarly, just as it had been at the Federal Convention. Eschewing flashy rhetorical flourishes, he relied entirely on the clarity, logic, and enlightened rationality of his ideas. John Marshall stated afterwards that if eloquence, being "the art of persuasion," included the ability to convince listeners through rational argumentation, then Madison was the most eloquent man he had ever known. The Chief Justice was no doubt mainly referring to the ratifying convention in Richmond, where he had supported his esteemed companion to the best of his own ability.[107]

Madison's historical studies, his notes from the Federal Convention, and his co-authorship of the "Publius" essays had provided the best conceivable preparation for the ratifying convention. Sometimes reasoning like a lawyer, at other points lecturing like a college professor, Madison gleaned precedents and instructive examples from history. The advantages of the new Constitution were laid out in a dispassionate, meticulous manner; the objections against the proposal were presented, dissected, and refuted. In poor health and under immense stress, Madison at times spoke so softly that his voice was barely audible in the gallery and in the back rows of the hall.[108]

Patrick Henry's speaking style could not have been more different. Edmund Randolph could still picture him years later: "In Henry's exordium there was a simplicity and even carelessness. . . . A formal division of his intended discourse he never made. . . . He transfused into the breast of others the earnestness depicted in his own features, which ever forbade a doubt of sincerity. . . . His was the only monotony which I ever heard reconcilable with true eloquence . . . [the] chief note was melodious, but the sameness was diversified by a mixture of sensations which a dramatic versatility of countenance produced. His pauses, which for their length might sometimes be feared to dispell the attention, riveted it the more by raising the expectation. . . . His style . . . was vehement, without transporting him beyond the power of self-command. . . . His figures of speech . . . were often borrowed from the Scriptures. The prototypes of others were the sublime scenes and objects of nature. . . . His lightning consisted in quick successive flashes, which rested only to alarm the more."[109] Henry mainly appealed to the emotions in the popular preaching style of Virginia revivalists, adapted for political purposes. Patrick Henry's foes regarded him as a dangerous demagogue who deliberately affected the gestures and mannerisms of the common man. Even his more well-disposed critics conceded "that the mere intensity with which he regarded the ends of public liberty was likely to mislead his judgment as to the means by which it was to be secured and upheld."[110]

A forum of 170 delegates and several hundred spectators was the perfect sounding board for Henry's superb speaking ability. His speeches were a passionate appeal not to endanger the freedom they had won in the Revolution. He was less disturbed by the individual details of the Constitution than about what he saw as the flawed conception of a system of government that would eliminate the sovereignty of the states and seriously threaten civil liberties: "I conceive the republic to be in extreme danger. If our situation be thus uneasy, whence has arisen this fearful jeopardy? It arises from this fatal system—it arises from the proposal to change our government:—A proposal that goes to the utter annihilation of the most solemn engagements of the States. A proposal of establishing 9 States into a confederacy, to the eventual exclusion of 4 States. . . . If a wrong step be now made, the Republic may be lost forever. If this new Government will not come up to the expectation of the people, and if they should be disappointed—their liberty will be lost, and tyranny must and will arise." Henry then turned his attention to the preamble, directing his wrath at the framers of the Constitution: "Sir, give me leave to demand, what right had they to say, *We, the People.* My political curiosity, exclusive of my anxious solicitude for the public welfare, leads me to ask, who authorized them to the language of, *We, the People,* instead of *We, the States?* States are the characteristics, and the soul of a confederation. If the States be not the agents of this compact, it must be one great consolidated National Government of the people of all the States. . . . The people gave them no power to use their name. That they exceeded their power is perfectly clear."[111]

Henry seemed to have all the advantages on his side in his verbal confrontation with Federalists. He masterfully exploited the entire range of his abilities, playing one rhetorical trump card after another. This exhibition continued for three weeks, during which time he put his listeners through an emotional wringer. He asked leave to speak as many as eight times in a single session; his longest speech went on for seven hours. Henry set new standards for eloquence, acknowledged James Breckinridge, who midway through the convention saw the Federalists' hopes being doused by a virtual flood of rhetoric. No one in the world was better suited in an assembly of that kind "to carry his point & lead the ignorant people astray. . . . Madison's plain, engenious, & elegant reasoning is entirely thrown away and lost among such men."[112]

Madison limited himself to rebuttals of Henry's tirades, speaking in a conciliatory and respectful tone. He responded to the sweeping criticism of the proposed system in Henry's introductory remarks with the observation that "a candid examination of history" proved "that turbulence, violence, and abuse of power, by the majority trampling on the rights of the minority, have produced factions and commotions, which, in republics, have, more frequently than any other cause, produced despotism." The United States, he continued, were by no means immune to this threat: "Perhaps, in the progress of this discussion, it will appear that the only possible remedy for those evils, and means of preserving and protecting the principles of republicanism will be found in that very system which is now exclaimed against as the parent of oppression."[113]

Antifederalists relied on Henry's ability in order to provide a counterweight to the Federalists' strengths, perhaps even tipping the scales in their favor. William Grayson figured his party had won over one delegate during the debate on presidential powers and was poised to gain a few more as they approached the issue of the judicial branch properly.[114] Federalists were also convinced that minor shifts in delegate support were likely—in their favor, of course. Archibald Stuart believed that Madison's cool reasoning, resolute bearing, and profound earnestness could not help but kindle the light of understanding in every listener. At all events, only about a dozen delegates were undecided and at least three of these were needed to obtain a majority.[115]

The dramatic climax was a speech by Patrick Henry toward the end of the convention. As he conjured up the "awful immensity of the dangers" posed by the Constitution, a thunderstorm darkened the sky outside and lightning struck the ground within a few feet of the academy building. Seemingly in concert with the forces of nature, Henry warned the delegates that their actions were beheld by "those intelligent beings which inhabit the aetherial mansions, reviewing the political decisions and revolutions which in the progress of time will happen in America." At that moment, the wind thrust open the windows, creating such havoc that, after a short exchange of arguments, the session had to be adjourned. Stunned by this spectacle, the participants and spectators hurried home.[116]

The final vote indicates that Federalists won seven of the "doubtful delegates" and Antifederalists five. All other participants steadfastly clung to the positions they had taken during the election campaign. This result represented neither a defeat for Henry nor a victory for Madison, though Federalists were determined to portray it in that light. It merely demonstrated the limited force of even the greatest rhetoric. The power of the spoken word remained just one factor among many.[117]

The adoption of the Constitution in New York was immediately cast as a triumph of Alexander Hamilton's oratorical skills. "Little Hamilton shines like a Star of the First magnitude," gushed Richard Platt upon the delegates' return from Poughkeepsie.[118] Audiences at the debates reportedly felt they were beholding the "Thunder of Demosthenes & the Splendid Conflagration of Tully" during Hamilton's prolonged speeches. Newspapers dubbed him "the American Cicero," an appellation that also appeared in a number of private letters. Samuel Blachley Webb exalted Hamilton as "one of the most remarkable genius's of the Age, his Political knowledge exceeds I believe, any Man in our Country, and his Oratorical abilities have pleased his friends and surprised his Enemies." Philip Schuyler's admiration also knew no bounds: "His sentiments are so true, his judgment so correct, his elocution so pleasing, so smooth, and yet so forcible that he reaches the heart and carries conviction, where every avenue to conviction is shut up."[119]

Indeed, like the oratorical duel between Patrick Henry and James Madison, the contest between Hamilton, Jay, and Chancellor Livingston on one side and the Antifederalist majority behind Governor George Clinton and Melancton Smith on the other stands out from the colorful conglomeration of events that made up the debate over the Constitution. And there is little doubt that Federalists won: Livingston's charm and Jay's statesmanlike sagacity contrasted favorably with Clinton's rigid doctrinairism, while Hamilton's brilliance and masterfully tempered vehemence outshone Smith's plain, dry, syllogistical delivery. The "force of Argument & Elocution" spoke against the [Antifederalist] majority, Abraham Bancker assured his uncle Evert.[120] Yet anyone who, like Philip Schuyler, hoped for a rapid "conversion" of Antifederalist delegates had underestimated their principled commitment and resolve. The longer the convention went on, the more it became apparent that the effects of great rhetoric were severely limited. Hamilton's well-chosen words bounced off the wall of mistrust that had been built up over the years, an apparently impenetrable barrier despite Hamilton's passionate affirmation of his commitment to republican principles. What his friends regarded as the "force of Argument and Elocution" seemed more like the "power of Oratory and Deception" to his foes.[121] Just as Federalists accused Clinton of piecing his speeches together from newspaper essays, the opposition berated Hamilton for quoting from the "Publius" essays for hours on end. After ten days of debate, Christopher P. Yates assured Congressman Abraham Yates: "In point of Argument we stand firm we have as yet lost no ground."[122]

On the other side of the aisle, Abraham Bancker was also forced to admit the futility of all rhetorical efforts: "With persuasive Arguments and the Exposition of Facts clear and perspicuous as the Sun in it's Meridian Altitude, we have not in my Humble Opinion, come a whit nearer embracing this salutary Expedient, than we were a Week ago—How unhappy is it for us that So much good reasoning Should be lost upon a stiffnecked and refractory Set of people . . . the fact is simply this Most of the Members whom we term Antifederal, were elected by People of that Class or in other Words People, who from their Ignorance & Credulity were calculated to promote faction and oppose good Government . . . as long as [Governor Clinton] Stands at the head of a formidable Opposition, No Arguments however rational, however founded in fact, will have any other tendency than to irritate and exasperate the determined Party."[123] There was as yet no reason to assume, John Jay wrote on June 30, "that either Party has made much impression on the other." Hamilton's own remarks a few days later were hardly more encouraging: "Our arguments confound, but do not convince."[124] If a claim published on July 11 in the *Morning Post* is to be believed, a strong impression had in fact been made on Antifederalists, "but they are too proud to confess it."[125]

Although the intellectual and oratorical dexterity displayed by leading Federalists may have contributed to the gradual erosion of confidence and unity among the opposition delegates, more important still was the delaying effect of the interminable speeches, which gave Federalists a chance to step up the pressure on their adversaries behind the scenes. In the end, it was the adoption of the Constitution in New Hampshire and Virginia along with threats of secession from New York City and some southern counties that forced Governor Clinton, Melancton Smith, and others to rethink their position. Isaac Roosevelt, a Federalist delegate and senator, was thus correct when he noted that the debate "only Served to delay a Rash decision and give time to reflection, and finally Caused a Division of Sentiments."[126] This reality could not shake the conviction of the Constitution's proponents that the sheer force of Alexander Hamilton's rhetoric had transformed an overwhelming Antifederalist majority into a 30–27 Federalist triumph.

Ideology and Politics in the Conventions

The First Phase: Pennsylvania to Connecticut

By quickly calling a ratifying convention and electing delegates, Pennsylvania Federalists got a head start over their rivals and never looked back. Moreover, in November 1787, the Federalist majority in the state legislature thwarted attempts by the opposition to prescribe a convention quorum of two-thirds of the delegates, the same quorum as in the assembly. Experience in September had shown that such regulations gave the opposition an ideal instrument by which to bring the deliberations to a standstill by boycotting or leaving meetings.[127] The proceedings of the Pennsylvania convention began on Wednesday, November 21, 1787, when sixty delegates assembled in Philadelphia's State House.[128] At that time, a surprisingly large percentage of the arguments for and against the Constitution had already been disseminated by the American press. Everybody knew, however, that the decisive political battles would be waged in the ratifying conventions. Therefore, these bodies now moved to the center of public attention. The strategy and the tactics used by the parties to consolidate their support, win over the small number of undecided delegates, and create division in the opposing camp became almost as important as the content of the debates.

Finding themselves in a clear minority position in Philadelphia, Antifederalists hoped only to delay the deliberations, but they lost the dispute over crucial rules of procedure at the very outset of the convention. Federalists agreed to discuss the Constitution section by section, but rejected the minority's proposal to constitute the convention as a committee of the whole, along the lines of the Pennsylvania Assembly, to enable a "more free and candid discussion." That would have given the opposition the opportunity to discuss the entire document twice, once in a committee and once in a convention, and separate votes could be required on individual points. James Wilson and Benjamin Rush justified their party's stance by pointing out that the Constitution formed a cohesive unit which must be taken as a whole. Hence, no amendments could be suggested and the convention would have to accept or reject the Constitution in its entirety. A committee of the whole was consequently deemed a waste of time and money. In yet another departure from legislative procedure, Antifederalist delegates were refused the right to have their reasons for voting against the measure included in the minutes. In this case as well as others, Federalists benefited from the fact that both the president of the convention, Frederick A. Muhlenberg, and the secretary, James Campbell, were members of their party.[129]

The convention entered into a discussion of the Constitution on November 28, proceeding "article by article." Progress was very slow. In order to shorten the convention and prevent the proceedings from getting bogged down, the majority voted to add afternoon sessions starting on December 1.[130]

The Antifederalists' main points of contention were the "consolidating" tendency of the plan, the combining of legislative and executive powers in the Senate, the advantages given to the upper stratum of society to the detriment of the "lower and middling classes of men,"[131] and the lack of a bill of rights. In their opinion, the proposed system would reduce the states to mere provinces and create an aristocracy of the wealthy, which would only be able to preserve its power by encroaching on civil liberties and suppressing the majority. "Every door is shut against democracy," lamented John Smilie on December 8.[132]

Federalists insisted that popular sovereignty would not be diminished in the least; the Constitution represented an "ordinance and establishment of the people." The new system of government was founded not on a contract, but "upon the power of the people . . . from their ratification, and their ratification alone, it is to take its constitutional authority." If democracy were defined as a form of government "in which the people retain the supreme power, and exercise it either collectively or by representation," then the future constitutional order was "in its principle . . . purely democratical." Wilson reiterated his "reserved powers" theory to prove that the Constitution would neither threaten the existence of the states nor the rights of the people. The central government allegedly had nothing to do with such matters as freedom of speech, religion, and the press, which explained why a bill of rights was redundant at best, probably even harmful. In Wilson's view, the new system constituted a historical leap forward. "Revolutions in government" had previously always been associated with war and violence; from this point on they could be regarded as "progressive steps in improving the knowledge of government, and increasing the happiness of society and mankind." Federalists predicted future greatness for America, politically as well as economically, artistically, and scientifically—provided the Constitution were ratified: "By adopting this system, we become a NATION; at present we are not one."[133]

Speaking for the opposition, John Smilie suggested there might be room for compromise if the majority agreed to discuss a bill of rights and other amendments. Federalists saw no need for conciliatory gestures, however, much less concessions. From December 4 onward they became increasingly impatient, demanding an end to the article-by-article discussion in order to proceed with the final, overall assessment of the Constitution.[134] By this time, both sides knew there was no hope of converting opposing delegates. They were essentially posturing for the benefit of their constituents, the other states, and posterity. Proud of the leading role played by Pennsylvania, Federalists were determined to bring about a quick decision to make an unequivocal statement and give the ratification movement momentum. Amendments, even if presented in the form of recommendations for consideration after the states had ratified the Constitution, were rejected out of hand because that would have suggested the Constitution was in need of improvement. For their part, Antifederalists sought to inspire public resistance by showing how their defiant struggle in defense of liberty was crushed by a tyrannical majority. They made a final attempt to postpone the vote on December 12, more than twenty days after the opening of the convention. Robert Whitehill presented fifteen amendments along with a petition bearing the signatures of 750 citizens from his county of Cumberland proposing the fifteen amendments to the Constitution and an adjournment to give the people an opportunity to examine the suggestions. As expected, the proposal was rejected by a vote of 46 to 23 and the Constitution was immediately approved by the same margin. On the following day, the Form of Ratification that had been drawn up by a committee was signed by the 46 Federalist delegates and formally promulgated in front of the State House:

> In the Name of the PEOPLE of Pennsylvania.
>
> BE IT KNOWN UNTO ALL MEN,—That We, the Delegates of the PEOPLE of the Commonwealth of Pennsylvania, in General convention assembled, have assented to and ratified, and by these Presents DO, in the Name and by the Authority of the same PEOPLE, and for ourselves, assent to and ratify the foregoing Constitution for the UNITED STATES of AMERICA.[135]

The convention spent the last two days discussing the issue of a national capital, before offering Congress a ten-miles-square tract of land along with the use of state buildings. After forwarding these resolutions together with the state's ratification to Congress on December 15, the delegates authorized the printing of 5,000 copies of the Constitution and the Form of Ratification

(3,000 in English and 2,000 in German), and formed a committee to oversee the publication of the convention's Journal. Finally, the convention thanked President Muhlenberg and adjourned *sine die.*[136]

The boundless delight of the Constitution's supporters was dampened on December 18, however, when the *Dissent of the Minority,* signed by twenty-one of the twenty-three Antifederalist delegates, appeared in the *Pennsylvania Packet* and as a broadside. More than just a fierce partisan polemic, the *Dissent* also contained the first comprehensive, critical analysis of the Constitution. Its most controversial aspect was the reproduction of the fifteen proposed amendment that the majority had excluded from the minutes of the convention. These amendments included the guarantee of habeas corpus rights and the continued use of juries in civil cases; the affirmation of freedom of conscience, speech, and religion as well as the right to bear arms and the right to hunt and fish on public lands; the superior authority of the states in matters involving militias, and a ban on standing armies in peacetime; the restriction of the central government's right of taxation to import-export duties and other duties; annual elections for the House of Representatives, better representation, and the elimination of the power of Congress to regulate elections; a stricter separation of powers in conjunction with a "constitutional council" to advise and assist the president; rendering void any treaty contrary to the Constitution of the United States or the constitutions of the several states; narrower limits of federal jurisdiction; and the inclusion of a clause taken from the *Articles of Confederation* stating "that the sovereignty, freedom, and independency of the several states shall be retained, and every power, jurisdiction, and right which is not by this constitution expressly delegated to the United States in Congress assembled."[137]

Instead of calming the population and reconciling diverse interests, the Pennsylvania convention only served to roil political spirits. Federalists had soundly defeated their adversaries in the legislature, in the election of delegates, and in the convention, yet they could not silence them. On the contrary: the *Dissent of the Minority* sent a signal which reverberated far beyond the borders of Pennsylvania, inspiring the critics of the new system of government to increased vigilance and activity. For the friends of the Constitution in other states, Pennsylvania's rush to ratification was a dubious blessing. It is quite possible that the process of adoption would have been smoother and less clamorous if Philadelphia Federalists had been more tactful and conciliatory.

In Delaware, New Jersey, and Georgia, where ratification was a foregone conclusion, the delegates spent more time on procedural and ceremonial matters than on the actual discussion of the Constitution. The deliberations in Dover and Trenton lasted all of three days, and both conventions underscored their Federalism by offering to furnish land for the new seat of government at no cost. The final results were 30 to 0 in Dover on December 7 (five days earlier than the Pennsylvania ratification, making Delaware the "first state"), and 38 to 0 in Trenton on December 18. In Augusta, it took four days to obtain a quorum; on the fifth day, a Saturday, the Constitution was debated "with a great deal of temper" before being unanimously approved by the twenty-six delegates present on the following Monday, December 31, 1787. The rest of the time prior to the conclusion of the meeting on January 5, 1788, was dedicated to drafting two different Forms of Ratification, ordering the printing of two hundred copies of the journal, and settling expense-related questions.[138]

There was an Antifederalist faction at the much larger Connecticut convention held on January 3–9, 1788, in Hartford, but it was too weak in terms of both numbers and ability to offer organized resistance.[139] Following Pennsylvania's example, it was agreed the Constitution could be discussed "by single articles, sections, paragraphs, or detached clauses and sentences," yet it had to be voted on as a whole.[140] Criticism was mainly directed at representation and taxation provisions allegedly favoring the South, the extensive federal jurisdiction, and the right of Congress to interfere in election procedures. Other concerns related to the omission of religious qualifications for officeholders and the need for a bill of rights. Clearly ruffled by the Federalists' press campaign against the "Wrongheads," the main opposition speakers, James Wadsworth, Eliphalet Dyer, and Joseph Hopkins, performed poorly. They had allowed themselves to be flustered by the self-confidence of their adversaries and the hostile behavior of the spectators. "The objections and the objectors were weak; the strength lay on the other side," commented Enoch Perkins, who was on hand to take stenographic notes for the printers in Hartford.[141] The *Connecticut Courant* did not even bother to convey the objections to its readers: "Suffice it to say that all the objections to the Constitution vanished before the learning and eloquence of a [William Samuel] Johnson, the genuine good sense and discernment of a [Roger] Sherman, and the Demosthenian energy of an [Oliver] Ellsworth."[142]

Federalist speakers explained how the new order would politically and economically benefit the North in general and Connecticut in particular. Ellsworth and Sherman, delegates to the Philadelphia Convention, argued with the authority of men who had been present at the creation of the Constitution. They insisted no system of government could be effective without "coercive power." In the future, this power would be founded on constitutional law rather than on military strength, and would act upon individual citizens rather than on states. Indirect taxes would suffice to cover the Union's financial needs for the foreseeable future; and the states' existence was in no way threatened. Richard Law asked the delegates and the audience to think of the new central government as a "vast and magnificent bridge built upon thirteen strong and stately pillars."[143] The Federalist leadership, knowing that the Connecticut convention was being closely monitored by the other New England states, suppressed any reservations or desire for revisions that surfaced in their own camp. Governor Samuel Huntington conceded several months later that members of the majority had felt some changes were in order, "but deemed it too dangerous to hazard delays under a tottering constitution, until every difficulty should be removed so as to obtain a constitution which would meet the entire approbation of all the states in the Union."[144]

After five days of debate the opposition had run out of ammunition and showed signs of dissolution. The final blow came when Federalists warned that obstinate critics might have trouble retaining their public offices or acquiring new ones. Two prominent Antifederalists, councillor William Williams and House delegate Joseph Hopkins, promptly abandoned ship, taking several wavering delegates along with them. As a result, the final vote of 128 to 40 on January 9 was even more lopsided than the election results would have suggested. The ratification document signed the next day resembled Pennsylvania's in both form and content.[145] Members of the losing party declared their willingness to accept the convention's decision but left the scene "heavy-hearted and discouraged." Besides their concerns about the future of the state, they probably realized that Federalists would not soon forget their opposition vote and would seek political revenge.[146]

Crisis and Turning Point: Massachusetts

The Massachusetts convention began on the same day, January 9, 1788, that Connecticut became the fifth state to adopt the Constitution. The news from Hartford caused a stir in Boston but did not help settle the issue there as much as Federalists had hoped.[147] Accompanied by a flood of newspaper articles, pamphlets, and speculation in private correspondence, the Massachusetts convention lasted for almost a month. Due to the large number of delegates (358 had been elected) and their various instructions, it was difficult for both sides to gauge their own strength or that of their opponents. Each party therefore dedicated the first few days to feeling out the opposition and assembling and organizing their own supporters. Federalists demonstrated their skill in tactical maneuvering right from the start by getting two men of their choice, Lieutenant Governor Thomas Cushing and George R. Minot, appointed to the key positions of convention vice president and secretary. Since neither side was interested in an early test of strength, there was a mutual desire to stall for time. It was agreed that the Constitution should be discussed slowly and thoroughly point by point. Referring to other sections during the debate on a particular article in order to put them in relation to each other was expressly allowed. Prior to the final vote, individual speakers were to be given the opportunity, if desired, to praise or criticize the document as a whole.[148]

Federalists encountered their first real challenge when Antifederalist leader William Widgery proposed on January 12 that Elbridge Gerry be invited to attend the convention to answer questions concerning the framing of the Constitution. Although the motion does not appear in the journal, "a majority appeared against it." The motion was renewed on January 14. Federalists objected strenuously and took certain precautions to prevent their foremost critic from presenting his personal opinions about flaws in the Philadelphia plan. But the motion was adopted when some Federalists joined the opposition in order to avoid a test of strength. Gerry accepted the invitation out of a sense of obligation, then sat idly by for three days while the Constitution's adversaries vainly attempted to come up with a suitable question for him. When he was finally asked, on January 18, to comment on representation in the future Congress, Federalists insisted that both question and answer be submitted in writing. The following day, Gerry attempted to enter the debate of his own accord, eliciting fervent protest from his adversaries and a call to order from the president. A heated argument with Judge Francis Dana ensued, which would have ended in a brawl if more level-headed delegates had not separated the antagonists. After the session adjourned, Rufus King ruminated over possible repercussions or even the likelihood of another ugly scene—but Gerry decided not to return.[149] He wrote a letter to Cushing defending his actions and complaining about the rude treatment he had received at the convention.[150] In reality, he was probably relieved that his participation in the affair had come to an abrupt end. For as much as he disapproved of the Constitution, he did not feel at ease in the company of former sympathizers and followers of Daniel Shays. For their part, Federalists were glad to be rid of a potentially dangerous rival.[151]

Since no one seemed to be in a particular hurry, the debate crept forward. A reader of the *Cumberland Gazette* feared the proceedings might take an entire year if they continued at that pace.[152] The opposition returned over and over to the familiar tenets of republican ideology, dwelling on every deviation from this doctrine by the Federal Convention, no matter how insignificant. In their attempts to respond to the objections, Federalists strayed further and further from traditional thought, which only served to create more mistrust.

Even Minot felt the rejection of established values had gone too far, recording in his diary:

> The most serious principles in government were argued away to nothing, by able casuists, & the mouths of the opponents being shut, they were ashamed to say that they were not convinced. Annual elections, rotation in office, qualification of officers, standing armies, & declarations of rights, were all shewn to be too trivial to be insisted upon. And it was demonstrated that to withhold any powers of taxation, or of any other kind from government, but they should abuse them, was an unreasonable principle of jealousy which would prevent any government at all."[153]

The Antifederalists' fear of a future government vested with the "power of the purse and the sword" was magnified by their aversion to slavery and the feeling that the Constitution was partial to the South. Federalists replied that there could be no government without military strength and the authority to levy taxes, that the North would benefit more economically from a strong Union than the South, and that the Constitution's provision to allow the slave trade to be prohibited by Congress after 1808 was an initial step toward abolishing slavery.

The most important events took place not at the convention but outside and behind the scenes.[154] With Gerry out of the way, Federalists concentrated on bringing two other potential adversaries in line, Governor John Hancock and Revolutionary patriot and president of the state senate, Samuel Adams. The means and methods of persuasion and coercion used were carefully tailored to each individual. On the eve of the convention, the Boston tradesmen had gathered nearly four hundred sympathizers at the Green Dragon Tavern for their largest caucus ever. The purpose of the meeting was to discuss ways of preventing Samuel Adams from openly opposing the Constitution. Paul Revere was chosen to present Adams with the written declaration of the tradesmen's and mechanics' desire to see the Constitution ratified.[155] This was an outrage in Minot's view, for it prevented Adams from speaking freely on the issue. The grassroots pressure was maintained throughout the convention. Henry Jackson wrote to Henry Knox on January 20 that Adams would probably keep still, "as the meeting of the mechanicks of the Town and their proceedings must and will have an influence over him." Four days later, Adams announced at the convention that he still had "difficulties and doubts" with the Constitution but was determined "rather to be an auditor, than an objector."[156]

Flattery and promises were used to win over John Hancock, who was bothered by the Constitution every bit as much as by his gout. Leading Federalists, including clergymen, whom Hancock held in particularly high regard, made repeated visits to his sickbed and coaxed him into believing the future of the United States lay in his hands. If he would help smooth the way for the Constitution, he was told, James Bowdoin and his supporters would back his bid to be reelected governor. Moreover, he had good prospects of becoming vice president of the United States, or even president if Virginia failed to ratify.[157] Persuaded by such prospects, Hancock agreed to appear at the convention and present as his own compromise offer of an amendment plan secretly crafted by Federalists. A move of this sort had become imperative after the opposition began a push on January 23 to bring the proceedings to a more rapid conclusion. Federalists had made no significant inroads, despite their diligence in debate and their attempts to pressure individual delegates outside the convention. It was evident that they did not have a majority to ratify the Constitution. They were now forced to make concessions to Hancock and to Antifederalists.[158]

The idea of combining the adoption of the Constitution with suggestions for amendments to be submitted to the first federal Congress and the other states had been expressed privately on several occasions and could also be inferred from Gerry's comments. The first concrete remarks to this effect were contained in a letter posted to Benjamin Rush on November 10, 1787, from David Ramsay in Charleston. Ramsay observed that the resistance could better be overcome "if the first state convention after accepting [the Constitution] in its present form would nevertheless express their approbation of some alterations being made on the condition that Congress & the other States concurred with them. I think this would cause no delay nor would it endanger the acceptance of the constitution. . . . I would not make these alternations conditions of acceptance: I would rather trust to the mode of alteration proposed in it than hazard or even delay the acceptance of the proposed plan."[159]

Pennsylvania Federalists had not pursued this possibility because they commanded a majority at the ratifying convention. In Boston, by contrast, the instrument of "recommendatory amendments" had been held in reserve in the event the approval of the Constitution should be seriously threatened. Rufus King informed Madison on January 16 that revision proposals could not be ruled out; three days later, John Avery concluded that a slim majority could only be obtained if the friends of the Constitution joined forces with the proponents of amendments: "My Wishes are that they adopt it and propose Amendments which when agreed upon, to transmit to the several States for their Concurrence—That Amendments should be made, seems to be the prevailing Opinion."[160] In the January 26 *Massachusetts Centinel,* an

Antifederalist (probably James Sullivan) spoke out in favor of accepting the Constitution under certain conditions.[161] For Federalists, "conditional ratification" was out of the question, but they took the newspaper article as a first sign of conciliation. By this time, they had founded their caucus, a group of party leaders that met regularly between sessions of the convention to discuss policies and strategies. While the caucus worked out an amendment plan without formal conditions, King, Jackson, Gorham, and Lincoln gently prepared their correspondents in New York and Virginia for the news that ratification could only be obtained with recommendatory amendments. At the convention, they avoided any direct confrontation with the opposition for the time being: "From motives of Policy we have not taken any Question which has divided the House, or shown the strength of sides."[162] Lincoln related on January 27 that their opponents were determined "to hurry over the business and bring on as soon as possible the main question—however this they are not permitted to do."[163]

At the end of January, Governor Hancock was finally induced to present the amendments at the convention. Had Federalists officially submitted the proposal themselves, it would likely have met with resistance, due to the prevailing climate of suspicion. Even if their plan worked, they only anticipated a slim majority of twelve to fifteen votes. King believed the convention's defining moment had arrived: "Our Business approaches to a crisis and the result is still uncertain." A veil of confidentiality was essential: "All this is scarcely known out of our caucus, wherein we work as hard as in convention."[164] On January 30, Hancock felt well enough to assume the seat of convention president. To pave the way for the governor's grand performance on January 31, Federalists made a surprise proposal to put the matter to a vote and General William Heath made a conciliatory address. Presented in the form of questions, his remarks guided the listeners' thoughts in the desired direction: "If we should ratify the Constitution, and instruct our first members to Congress, to exert their utmost endeavours to have such checks, and guards provided as appears to be necessary in some of the paragraphs of the Constitution . . . is there not the highest probability that every thing which we wish may be effectually secured?" This was Hancock's cue to announce his intention to intervene that afternoon. The spectators in the gallery remained glued to their seats, for fear of missing anything important, and had their lunch brought in.[165] At the beginning of the afternoon session, Hancock introduced the amendments one by one and urged the delegates to give them careful consideration. James Bowdoin and Samuel Adams, who by now had been brought into the plan, immediately spoke warmly in favor of approving the "Hancock Proposal." Adams pointed out that the objections to the Constitution were similar across the Union all the way down to Virginia, and stressed that Americans must not be divided. He suggested that if Massachusetts set an example by endorsing the proposed revisions, the other states would surely follow without delay.

At first, the coup seemed to be working—yet the opposition refused to budge. In the meantime, they, too, had organized themselves, and were holding secret meetings and benefiting from the advice of experienced politicians as well as capable essayists like James Warren and James Winthrop.[166] In their opinion, the convention was not authorized to recommend amendments, and even if it did, it was highly improbable that they would ever be added to the Constitution. Federalists had intended for the Hancock proposal to be taken as a compromise offer and not as an admission of a need for changes. Nevertheless, General Samuel Thompson made no secret of the satisfaction it gave him and his associates to see the "gentlemen" finally acknowledging that the Philadelphia plan was flawed. Once again, the outcome of the deliberations—and with it the fate of the Constitution—hung in the balance as support for ratification rose and fell like the mercury in a thermometer. After Antifederalists had estimated that they had over 200 votes at the end of January, Gorham predicted, on February 3, that Federalists would win by a margin of 185–160, but conceded the opposition was still confident of a 10-vote advantage.[167]

Federalists were now willing to go to almost any lengths to secure the required number of "proselytes." "We are not idle by Night or Day—and sacrifice everything but moral Honesty to carry our point," wrote Tristram Dalton.[168] Relatives, business partners, even creditors were recruited to put moral—and probably financial—pressure on "stubborn" delegates. The "*poor devils*" in the opposition were stunned by the news that the state treasury was empty and enough money to reimburse the delegates' expenses could only be scraped together if the Constitution were accepted.[169] Yet most of those who changed their minds at the last minute, such as Nathaniel Barrell, Charles Jarvis, John Winthrop, Charles Turner, and William Symmes, were Antifederalists of above average wealth and prestige from coastal areas.

When the convention formed a committee to consider Hancock's proposed amendments on February 2, it was composed of two delegates per county, Antifederalists believed the seats had been evenly divided. In reality, Federalists had a majority.[170] Of the twenty-five members of the committee, fifteen recommended the adoption of the slightly modified Hancock plan on February 4. On the following day, Antifederalists strove to ward off defeat by proposing an adjournment. The motion was only supported by 115 of the 329 delegates in attendance, however. On Wednesday, February 6, Samuel

Adams made an attempt to contribute to the proposed compromise, perhaps to mediate or possibly to upset the deal. But he was forced to withdraw his proposal.[171] The delegates then proceeded with the final vote, approving both the committee report and the Constitution by a vote of 187–168.

The nine proposed amendments were added to the resolution of ratification and introduced by the following passage: "And, as it is the opinion of this convention, that certain amendments and alterations in the said Constitution, would remove the fears, and quiet the apprehensions of many of the good people of this Commonwealth, and more effectually guard against an undue administration of the federal government, the convention do therefore recommend, that the following alterations and provisions be introduced into the said Constitution."

The first amendment provided that the states would retain all powers not expressly delegated to the federal government by the Constitution. To many citizens, this article alone amounted to a bill of rights. The other suggestions were designed to define more precisely the mode of representation and the right of Congress to intervene in state elections, confine Congress's power to levy direct taxes to emergency situations, prohibit Congress from creating trade monopolies, limit the authority of the federal judiciary, and guarantee the continued use of the grand jury in criminal cases and the petit jury in civil cases. Furthermore, it was to be forbidden for Congress to allow foreign potentates or countries to grant titles of nobility or similar titles to the holders of government offices. Finally, the Form of Ratification bound future congressional delegates from Massachusetts to exert all their influence to bring about the adoption of these proposed amendments in accordance with Article V of the Constitution.[172]

Despite a continued undercurrent of distrust, the convention ended on a conciliatory note. Several of the delegates who had voted against ratification formally declared their willingness to respect the majority decision and work to ensure that peace, accord, and respect for the law and the Constitution were upheld. William Widgery vowed "to sow the seeds of union and peace among the people he represented," and thanked the people of Boston for not unduly influencing the convention. His resistance to the Constitution notwithstanding, Abraham White pledged to do everything in his power "to induce his constituents to live in peace under, and chearfully submit to it." Delegate Daniel Cooly also promised to encourage acceptance of the decision to ratify, while Dr. John Taylor "found himself fairly beaten—and expressed his determination to go home, and endeavour to infuse a spirit of harmony and love among the people." On the final day of the convention, even Samuel Nasson voiced his support of the new system of government, and Major Benjamin Sawin conceded "that the Constitution had had a fair trial." Of the leading Antifederalists, only Amos Singletary and General Samuel Thompson refrained from issuing conciliatory statements.[173]

Those representatives who had been sent as opponents but changed their minds in the course of the convention had no reason to hang their heads in shame: they could point to their successful struggle for amendments as proof of the fulfillment of their instructions. Outwardly at least, Federalists showed respect for their adversaries and included them in the celebrations, which began with the reading of the ratification proclamation by the sheriff of Suffolk County from the balcony of the State House. They were following George Washington's advice, who had warned that based on the experiences in Pennsylvania, the friends of the new system could overcome the opposition, "yet they would never be able, by precipitate or violent measures, to sooth and reconcile their minds to the exercise of the Government; which is a matter that ought as much as possible to be kept in view."[174]

The actions of Federalists in Boston have often been the object of criticism, beginning with comments by Secretary Minot himself. He titled his diary entries on the convention "Bad measures in a good cause," and prefaced them with the remark: "Never was there a political system introduced by less worthy means, than the new constitution for the United States." Law student John Quincy Adams was incensed by the behavior of his master, Theophilus Parsons, who after returning from Boston had bragged about the artifice to which Federalists owed their victory: "Mr. Parsons makes of the science of politics the science of little, insignificant intrigue, and chicanery, these principles may possibly meet with success sometimes; but it is my opinion that fair, open and candid proceedings, add an influence, as well as a lustre to the most brilliant capacity."[175] The opposition in New York later used the Boston convention as an example of what "Federal Chicanery" was capable of.[176] Historical accounts have also occasionally left the impression that ratification was achieved through illicit means.

Yet one should take care not to jump to the conclusion that the bounds of legitimate political persuasion had been exceeded just because some of the methods employed were of a questionable nature. Legislative delegates were accustomed to rough and tumble competition: tactical maneuvering and trickery, traps, deception, and intrigue were the order of the day in state politics. Aside from the fact that more than usual was riding on the outcome of the ratification debate, there was nothing out of the ordinary about the Massachusetts convention in terms of the conduct of the participants. Perhaps the degree of organization, as exemplified by the party caucuses, and the determination with which the politicians went about their business were new.

The alleged bribery of Antifederalist delegates was the only serious charge made in Boston, but an investigation turned up no evidence of wrongdoing. The claims were soon revealed to have been based on mere rumor; the instigator of the affair was identified, and an apology was rendered.[177]

The political maneuvering of Federalists in the Boston convention should not be allowed to detract from the event's immense importance and its positive aspects. It represented the first attempt by friends and foes of the Constitution to reach a compromise. Antifederalists were defeated only by a narrow margin after forcing Federalists to make concessions. The Massachusetts convention changed the face of the ratification debate. Until then, the central issue had been solely whether the Constitution should be approved or rejected; from this point on, the focus increasingly shifted to the terms of adoption and whether it should be made contingent upon the promise of future amendments. Fisher Ames's observations on the concluding phase of the deliberations in Boston also applied to the Union at large: all subsequent ratifying conventions would have to deal with the question of what amendments were essential and what guarantees should be demanded.[178]

Although the one side would have preferred a clearer margin of victory and the other more firm guarantees, both parties had reason for optimism. Federalists had, of course, emerged victorious, having turned a minority into a majority and ensured the continuation of the process of ratification. By proposing amendments, they had succeeded in softening the resistance without sacrificing the core elements of the Constitution. Madison regarded the amendments as a "blemish," but felt they had been linked to the act of ratification in the "least Offensive form" possible.[179] Other Federalists hailed the favorable outcome of the Massachusetts convention as "perhaps the most important event that ever took place in America," and thanked "overruling Providence" for saving the United States from ruin.[180] For their part, the opposition had not only demonstrated their strength, they had also provided a worthy display of republican sentiments. Moreover, the convention had instructed the Massachusetts representatives in Congress "to exert all their influence, and use all reasonable and legal methods" to obtain a ratification of the proposed amendments. No one better understood what that meant than Thomas Jefferson in faraway Paris. After hearing about the decision in Boston, he continuously encouraged the imitation of the "Massachusetts mode of ratification" and the "glorious example of Massachusetts." In a letter written to Thomas Lee Shippen in June, Jefferson said he constantly prayed the remaining states might accept the Constitution, "as Massachusetts has done, with standing instructions to their delegates to press for amendments till they are obtained. They cannot fail of being obtained when the delegates of 8 states shall be under such perpetual instructions."[181]

The Interlude: New Hampshire, Maryland, South Carolina

Massachusetts's example was duly noted by its northern neighbor, New Hampshire, though its full impact was not immediately felt. Federalists in Exeter, where the ratifying convention began on February 13, first had to come to terms with the distressing revelation that they had the solid support of only thirty of the over one hundred delegates in attendance. The rest were either undecided or had received instructions to oppose unconditional ratification. Yet it became clear just how heterogeneous the Antifederalist majority actually was when Federalists managed to fill the offices of president and secretary as well as the seats in the elections and rules committees with representatives of their own choosing. The rules subsequently passed provided an initial indication of Federalist strategy. Of particular significance were rules 7 and 10, which established that voting on the issue of ratification must be conducted by name, and a proposal for adjournment was to take priority over other measures. The idea was to avert defeat by postponing the convention if necessary.[182]

Federalists had taken a defensive position in their decision to discuss the Constitution article by article and paragraph by paragraph. The opposition's key speaker, Joshua Atherton, bore down on the text and "picked all the holes in it he possible could."[183] His criticisms were the six-year terms for senators and two-year terms for members of the House; the numerous congressional powers listed in Article I, section 8; the jurisdiction of the federal judiciary; the compromise on slavery; and the lack of religious qualifications or oaths for officeholders. Delegates speaking in defense of the plan—John Langdon, John Sullivan, Samuel Livermore, and John Pickering—were aided by letters and newspaper reports from Boston. Before moving on to weightier matters, however, they first had to deal with such curious concerns as the observation that the Constitution would allow a Turk, Jew, Catholic, or—even worse—a universalist to become president of the United States. Antifederalists, incidentally, were also receiving support from Massachusetts: John Quincy Adams had come to Exeter accompanied by Dr. Daniel Kilham, who a few months before had unsuccessfully opposed the calling of a ratifying convention by the Massachusetts legislature. Both stayed with New Hampshire politician Nathaniel Peabody, who was not directly involved in the convention but, much to the Federalists' chagrin, never missed an opportunity to strengthen the resistance of individual delegates to the adoption of the Constitution.[184]

After a week of deliberations Federalists had managed to balance the scales through a mixture of persuasion and coercion. When the convention proceeded with the general discussion on February 21, the advocates of ratification estimated that forty-five delegates were on their side along with eleven others who might disregard their instructions and vote "yes." A number of delegates indicated that they could use a temporary adjournment to ask their constituents for more favorable instructions. The idea of a brief delay was dropped for practical reasons, however, and the situation seemed too precarious to risk a final vote. The only alternative was a long-term adjournment to give interested delegates time to campaign for a Massachusetts-style ratification and seek new instructions. This would also accommodate a desire privately expressed by several delegates to wait until after the approaching New Hampshire general elections. They were afraid of losing their seat in the legislature if they approved the Constitution against the will of their constituents. Besides, postponing the decision for a few months would allow them to follow the developments in other states and gain more insight into the probable fate of the Constitution.[185]

John Quincy Adams dismissed the motion to adjourn as "the offspring of the fears of the federal party." He believed that Antifederalists offered little resistance because they, too, were apprehensive about reaching a final, irrevocable decision.[186] At all events, the vote taken on February 22 was extremely close. Only 56 of the 107 delegates present supported the proposal to adjourn to Concord on the third Wednesday in June. Both publicly and privately, the rigid instructions were named as the main impediment to ratification. The *New Hampshire Gazette* reported that a large number of delegates wanted to postpone the decision due to "their being tied up to instructions, to vote against the constitution, of which they could not divest themselves without incurring the displeasure of their constituents."[187] In light of the instructions binding so many delegates to act against their will, wrote President Sullivan, it was better "to have an adjournment that they might go home & obtain liberty to act on their own judgment." He agreed with most other Federalists that the situation would be much improved in June, when the Constitution was likely to be adopted without further ado.[188]

Outside of New Hampshire, the initial reaction was mainly one of disappointment and skepticism. The dissatisfaction was intensified by the false rumor that the convention had only resolved to adjourn after first voting 54 to 51 against the Constitution.[189] Gradually, however, the view prevailed that Federalists had been wise to choose a temporary postponement over an uncertain final vote. Tobias Lear reported to Mount Vernon that, had the members of the opposition "acted like good politicians," the Constitution would have been doomed in New Hampshire.[190] Indeed, if New England were taken as a whole the results could have been much worse. The Constitution had been in danger of being rejected in both Massachusetts and New Hampshire, and after the Rhode Island referendum on March 24, which went 2,714 to 238 against the Constitution, no one seriously expected that state to ratify soon. A defeat in three of the four New England states would surely have put an untimely end to the envisaged "revolution in government." It was due to the tactical skill of Federalists as well as the political incompetence and poor coordination on the part of their adversaries in Massachusetts and New Hampshire that the crisis was eventually overcome. Moreover, Boston and Exeter had shown that when the moment of truth arrived in the ratifying conventions, many critics did not have the resolve to reject the Constitution entirely, desperately seeking temporary solutions, compromises, and stopgap measures instead.

After their setbacks in New Hampshire and Rhode Island, Federalists were determined to avoid any further delays. The first to feel the effects of this new resolve were the opponents of ratification at the Maryland convention. Their arrival in Annapolis on April 21 was preceded by rumors that they were plotting to stall for time in the hope of obtaining either an adjournment or amendments. This in turn threatened to have an unfavorable influence on the discussions in Virginia and the Carolinas.[191] The conspicuous absence of the opposition leaders on the first day of the Maryland convention tended to confirm the suspicions of the majority. Federalists immediately formed a caucus (the first ever recorded in Maryland) and resolved to ratify the Constitution as quickly as possible and without concessions of any kind.[192] Before Samuel Chase, William Paca, and Luther Martin arrived in Annapolis on the fourth day of the convention, the majority had already approved rules and resolutions establishing that voting could be held on acceptance or rejection of the Constitution only and that there would be no article-by-article discussion. Federalists justified these measures by pointing to the thorough public discussion that had already taken place and the unequivocal instructions they had received from their constituents. Following the second reading of the Constitution, Chase finally took the floor on April 24, presenting twenty-seven objections in a speech lasting two-and-a-half hours. The conclusion of his remarks was greeted by a profound silence: Federalists chose not to respond to the opposition's arguments at all and simply waited for the storm to blow over. Luther Martin was unable to come to Chase's aid, having lost his voice due to a cold. President Thomas Johnson had no choice but to adjourn the morning session. A spiteful Federalist could not resist commenting that Martin's ailment had saved "a great deal of time and money to the state."[193]

The next assault on the Constitution was mounted that afternoon by William Paca, who advocated recommendatory amendments and asked the president for a brief delay to give delegates time to compile a list of suggestions. Although most Federalists were not enthralled by this idea, Johnson granted the request because he admired Paca and was beginning to doubt the political wisdom of the Federalists' tactic of stifling all debate. When Paca presented his amendments the next day,[194] Federalists insisted that there could be no discussion of amendments as long as the main issue remained unsettled. After listening to the opposition's objections, Federalists called for a final ballot and ratified the Constitution on April 26 by a vote of 63 to 11. Paca voted with the majority to demonstrate his willingness to compromise, and to keep the idea of amendments alive. Federalists honored this gesture by agreeing to appoint a thirteen-member committee to review Paca's amendments along with any other changes desired.

The nine Federalists and three Antifederalists on the committee first drew up thirteen amendments on April 27, which, taken together, amounted to a declaration of fundamental rights. The members of the opposition then proposed to add another fifteen revisions, some of which would have significantly reduced the powers of the president and Congress. Faced with stiff Federalist resistance, Chase whittled the list down to three amendments he considered essential: that a state militia could not be sent outside the state without the consent of the legislature; that Congress was to be prohibited from changing election dates; and that the collection of direct federal taxes was to be suspended if a state raised the money itself and remitted it to the central government. When this supplementary proposal was rejected by a vote of 8 to 5, Chase announced his intention to present all of his original suggestions to the convention. This in turn gave Federalists the excuse they needed to abandon the thirteen joint proposals and cease participation in the amendment committee. The convention reconvened on April 28 and, following a short discussion, refused to debate the thirteen original amendments in conjunction with the three put forward by Chase. Paca and a number of Federalists led by Governor Johnson wanted to continue the search for a compromise, but a proposal to adjourn the convention *sine die* was approved by a margin of 47 to 26. Nothing more could be done at this point other than sign the Form of Ratification and announce the results.

Following the example of the Pennsylvania minority, Antifederalists, including Paca, published a dissent in the Annapolis *Maryland Gazette* on May 1, in which they harshly criticized the actions of the majority and listed all twenty-eight amendments submitted to the committee. The authors maintained that the public should have the opportunity to reach its own conclusions: "We consider the proposed form of national government as very defective, and that the liberty and happiness of the people will be endangered if the system be not greatly changed and altered." The *Address of the Minority* was reprinted in both Baltimore newspapers five days later, and by early June it appeared in seven others outside of Maryland. The amendments themselves were even more widely circulated, though in a form which made it unclear whether they had been accepted or rejected by the Maryland convention.[195] Since the public response was more subdued than they feared, Federalists refrained from submitting to the press a rebuttal they had already drafted.[196] Antifederalist John Francis Mercer composed an "Address to the Members of the Conventions of New York and Virginia," warning them not to draw false conclusions from the majority's wide margin of victory in Maryland and their refusal to adopt amendments. According to Mercer, four-fifths of the citizens of Maryland wanted "considerable Alterations and Amendments, and will insist on them." This text also never appeared in print, however, and was probably passed along privately to George Mason and Patrick Henry by Mercer's brother James.[197]

The Maryland convention was surely not one of the prouder moments in the ratification process. Using the supposed will of the people as an excuse to refuse any and all discussion made a mockery of the very principle of representation and debate. As to Samuel Chase and his supporters, it is doubtful whether they really intended for their amendments to be taken seriously—they seemed to be more interested in causing a Pennsylvania-style sensation than striving for the partial success that was surely within reach. The radical adversaries of the Constitution regarded recommendatory amendments as a temporary solution at best; many even suspecting them to be a trick designed to weaken and divide the opposition. Federalist tactics probably gave alarm to many as to what might happen if the new government went into effect.[198] Their actions are only comprehensible if viewed against the backdrop of the overall Federalist strategy. After the process of ratification had begun to stall in New England, southern Federalists felt they must avoid any further delays at all costs. Moreover, ratification in Maryland might, as George Washington saw it, clear the way for the final adoption of the Constitution: "If they are decisive and favourable, it will most assuredly raise the edifice."[199]

Hence, Maryland Federalists railroaded the Constitution through the convention, sacrificing political decency to the overriding goal of reestablishing the momentum of the ratification process. The appointment of Thomas Lloyd as convention stenographer and the advance announcement of a book version of the debates show that this was not planned from the start. It evidently cost Federalists a great deal of effort and expense afterwards to prevent Lloyd from publishing his manuscript, which consisted almost entirely of Antifederalist speeches.[200] The Federalist fear, after the setback in New Hampshire, can be seen in the fact that even such leading figures as Washington and Madison condoned the actions of the Maryland majority without reservation.

David Ramsay of South Carolina felt the same way, confiding in Benjamin Lincoln at the end of March that he was "more anxious since the adjournment of New Hampshire convention. . . . I counted on the support of New Hampshire & am since doubly anxious for the vote of our State to be in favor of it."[201] When more than two hundred delegates slowly began to arrive in Charleston in the second week of May, it appeared as if Federalists would have a slim majority of twenty to thirty votes. The convention was held at the Stock Exchange due to a fire at the State House. Despite a lack of seating, this location was chosen over the Baptist Church, which had also been offered. Governor Thomas Pinckney was elected president, and the Committee of Rules and Order fixed the quorum at eighty delegates plus the president. On May 14, an article-by-article debate began which was to culminate in a vote "for the acceptance and ratification of the whole."[202]

The following six-day discussion was less a political debate than a question-and-answer session in which the skeptics and opponents of the Constitution were instructed on its virtues by Federalists, with the assistance of former delegates to the Constitutional Convention. The leading opposition speakers were Judge Aedanus Burke, the physician Peter Fayssoux, and the plantation owner and slave trader John Bowman. Their criticisms were the departure from the principle of rotation in office; the powers of the president (whom Burke described as a "prince under a republican cloak"); the economic predominance of the northern states; the lack of a bill of rights; and the absence of religious tests and oaths. Federalists responded by emphasizing the necessity of a stable system of government. Chancellor Rutledge declared the "doctrine of rotation" had spread across America like a brushfire, creating unnecessary mistrust and making life difficult for elected officials. By way of comparison, Charles Pinckney and David Ramsay pointed to the extensive powers of the governor of New York and the Maryland senate as examples worthy of emulation. The "soul of the Constitution," according to Pinckney, was section 10 of Article I, which prohibited the states from coining money, emitting paper money, making anything but specie legal tender, or interfering with the obligation of contracts; nor could the states levy duties on imports or exports without the consent of Congress. Federalists argued that the best measure of a society's productivity was its export figures, and here the South far outshone the North. From the standpoint of "productive wealth," 100,000 slaves were equal to 400,000 free Pennsylvanians. Moreover, the southern states had superior growth potential in the West. Declarations of fundamental rights like the Magna Carta were redundant in a "popular government," and religious qualifications for office and oaths constituted an unlawful restriction on the freedom of conscience. Antifederalists were repeatedly told that the objections to the Constitution and the proposed amendments varied widely from state to state and were even mutually exclusive in some cases.

Federalists controlled the debate, especially since the opposition leaders, by their own admission, had not conferred with each other in advance of the proceedings, let alone worked out a common strategy. Outward influences also contributed to the dwindling resistance. Aedanus Burke later commented that the site of the convention in Charleston, "where there are not fifty Inhabitants who are not friendly to [the Constitution]," gave Federalists their greatest advantage. Wealthy merchants and others opened their doors to the delegates for the duration of the event and dazzled backcountry representatives with elegant entertainment. It was no secret, wrote one journalist, that the "town gentlemen" had invested a fair amount of money in large quantities of wine and several banquets to convert Antifederalist delegates.[203] The deciding factor was probably the news of ratification in Maryland, which arrived in Charleston on May 18. This moved the most active and astute Antifederalist, Dr. Fayssoux, publicly to renounce his opposition to the Constitution. He justified his decision in the *State Gazette* by explaining that Maryland's vote had completely and decisively changed the situation. He was prepared to sacrifice his own principles for the sake of peace and tranquility in the Union, "and as I consider this as the constitution under which we must live, I shall desist from a line of conduct in opposition, which as it will tend only to irritate and inflame men's minds, would in my opinion be criminal."[204] Fayssoux was surely not alone in his view that Antifederalists were now fighting a hopeless cause.

The advocates of ratification hastened the erosion of the opposition's support by making concessions on the issue of amendments. President Thomas Pinckney had introduced Governor Hancock's circular letter on the outcome of the Massachusetts convention at the beginning of the deliberations, thus indicating that a similar arrangement might be possible in South Carolina as well. After voting 135 to 89 on May 21 against a motion to postpone the debate until the opening session of the new state legislature in October, Federalists proposed, of their own accord, forming a committee "to draw up such amendments to the Federal Constitution as they think ought to be recommended to Congress for adoption."[205] Antifederalists had little choice but to accept the offer, as their remaining followers were growing impatient to return home.

Prominent critics seem to have voluntarily abstained from joining the nine-member committee, which presented its report to the convention on May 23. Burke introduced a supplementary proposal to limit the president to one term, fearing that the possibility of reelection was apt "to perpetuate in one person during life the high authority and influence of that magistracy [and] in a short time to terminate in what the good people of this state highly disapprove of, an hereditary monarchy." This idea was rejected, meeting the same fate as the demand for a more extensive bill of rights, a proposal to grant the states sole authority over the militia, and an amendment prohibiting the acceptance of presents, offices, honors, and titles from foreign governments.

What remained roughly resembled the Massachusetts amendments: Congress was only to intervene in election procedures if states were negligent of their duties; all authority not expressly delegated to the central government was reserved to the states; Congress could only collect direct taxes if income from duties and other indirect sources was insufficient and requisitions were not complied with; finally, an addition to Article VI was agreed upon to placate all those who considered religious oaths indispensable.[206] After approving these recommendations the convention ratified the Constitution by a margin of 149 to 73. Reverend Francis Cummins had decided at the very last minute to vote for the Constitution, feeling that it was better than the Articles of Confederation and there was a distinct possibility amendments would be enacted. As an additional motive, Cummins mentioned his trust in General Washington, who had signed the Constitution, and "whose unsullied and patriotic character, is equal, if not superior, to any in this world." Following the balloting by name, with fourteen delegates absent, a number of Antifederalists declared their loyalty to the Constitution, promising "that they would exert themselves to the utmost of their abilities to induce the people quietly to receive, and peaceably to live under the new government."[207]

The convention met one last time on May 24 for the signing ceremony and authorized the printing and distribution of 1,200 copies of the Constitution along with the amendment proposals. The delegates then took leave of each other in a spirit of conciliation. Although some Antifederalists harbored resentment against the "defectors" and threats were heard from the backcountry, the situation generally remained calm. Avoiding the mistakes of the majorities in Pennsylvania and Maryland, South Carolina Federalists took the wind out of their critics' sails by remaining amicable and making voluntary concessions. They had yielded on several minor points, Edward Rutledge informed his friends in New York and New Hampshire: "We had prejudices to contend with and sacrifices to make. Yet they were worth making for the good old cause."[208] Observers in Congress noted that South Carolina had essentially copied the amendment recommendations of the Boston convention. As the actions of both the majority and the minority showed, the "Massachusetts ideas about Some future alterations" were beginning to catch on.[209]

Efforts at Interstate Cooperation and Coordination

Much has been written about the Federalists' superior strategy and cooperation on a national level. Yet it would be incorrect to assume that all of their actions were guided by a common will and directed by a central political organization. Their strength lay precisely in their independent initiatives, their freedom to think for themselves, and their keen powers of perception, the sum total of which enabled them to make the right move at the right time in the state in question. Of extreme importance were of course their vast networks of private correspondence, their contacts in and through Congress, and George Washington's role as an intermediary behind the scenes. Yet since the Constitutional Convention in Philadelphia there had been no further meeting of Federalist leaders on a national scale to discuss strategies and issue instructions. What Federalists did have was the benefit of a clearly defined goal: consecutively obtaining a majority in each state to ratify the Constitution with as few concessions to the opposition as possible. The closer they came to achieving their objective, the easier it was to act decisively and to choose the best tactical means and methods.[210]

The opposition, on the other hand, never really arrived at an exact understanding of what their goal was. The fact that they had not one but several options contributed to their political undoing: they could reject the Constitution in toto and try to return to the, in some way or other revised, Articles of Confederation; they could demand a second general convention to rework the Philadelphia plan; they could make their state approval of the Constitution contingent upon certain conditions to be fulfilled by Congress; or they could choose to accept recommendatory changes that would be implemented at a later date in accordance with the amendment provisions in the Constitution. Whereas the first option was made unlikely by the adoption of the Constitution in Massachusetts, the other three were still viable when the battle over ratification entered the decisive phase in the summer of 1788. If there was to be any semblance of joint action, Antifederalists would have to plan their next moves before the opening of the Virginia convention in early June. The first to grasp this opportunity were the New York Antifederalists, who had been involved in the nationwide distribution of political literature since the previous winter and had already founded committees of correspondence in their own state.

At the beginning of May, Governor Clinton took the initiative by writing a letter to Governor Edmund Randolph in which he lauded a suggestion by the Virginia legislature in December to improve communication and cooperation among the states and offered his assistance.[211] Clinton seems to have been prepared to accept Virginia's leading role, but only a short time later the New York Federal Republican Committee under the direction of General John Lamb, which by now was organizing the election campaign for the convention in Poughkeepsie, seized control of the movement to amend the Constitution before it was ratified. On May 18 to 20, Lamb sent a circular letter on behalf of the committee to prominent adversaries of the Constitution in six states, in which he defined "previous amendments" as the common goal of the opposition. To achieve this, it was imperative "that those States who have not yet acceded to the Plan should open a Correspondence, and Maintain a Communication—That they should understand one another on the Subject and unite in the Amendments they propose." Of particular importance was the collaboration between Virginia, New Hampshire, and New York, whose conventions would take place at approximately the same time. Instead of suggesting detailed amendments, Lamb referred to the proposals contained in the enclosed *Federal Farmer* pamphlet. The continent and the world must be shown, he wrote, "that our Opposition to this Constitution does not arise from an Impatience under the Restraint of good Government from local or State Attachments, from interested Motives or Party Prejudice—but from the purer Sentiments of the Love of Liberty, an Attachment to Republican Principles and an Adherence to those Ideas which prevailed at the Commencement of the late Revolution."[212]

Although some of Lamb's letters were long delayed and others never arrived, the response was generally positive, and expressions of goodwill poured in from all parts of the Union. In Richmond, where Eleazer Oswald, acting as courier of the New York committee, delivered Lamb's letters on June 7, prominent Virginia Antifederalists formed a Republican Society chaired by George Mason.[213] Lamb's initiative also lifted the spirits of the Pennsylvania opposition after their disappointing petition campaign in the spring, and they discussed how they might contribute to the amendment crusade.[214] For South Carolina's Antifederalists, the appeal from New York came too late to turn the situation around. The Charleston convention was already over when Lamb's letters finally reached Rawlins Lowndes, Aedanus Burke, and Thomas Sumter after four weeks in transit. Had the plan been conceived earlier, Lowndes answered on June 21, "I doubt not it might have produced very good Effect in this Country. A Strong Systematic Opposition wherein the Opinions and Sentiments of the different States were Concenter'd, and directed to the same specific Objects, would have had a Weight, which the Advocates for the Constitution must have submitted to."[215]

Joshua Atherton and Nathaniel Peabody received Lamb's communication in time for the New Hampshire convention's second session in Concord. Delighted over the long-awaited offer of cooperation, Atherton promised to do everything in his power to help establish a common amendment policy: "Permit me to hope you will lead the Way, and delineate the Method of a Correspondence between the States, who have not yet resigned their Lives, Liberties, and Properties, into the hands of this new and unlimited Sovereignty: Your central Situation, and great Importance as a State, gives us a Right to expect it of you, while nothing shall be wanting, here, to second such a desireable Event."[216] The next letter of the Federal Republican Committee, dated June 6, did not contain the desired list of amendments, however, and it arrived only shortly before the final vote was taken in Concord.[217]

The Climax: New Hampshire, Virginia, New York

Joshua Atherton had remained confident to the end, for the mood swing prophesied by New Hampshire Federalists after the Exeter convention, and promoted through an extensive propaganda campaign, did not fully materialize.[218] New town meetings had been held in the interim, even new elections in some cases, and the delegates' instructions had been confirmed, revised, or eliminated.[219] Five participants in the Exeter convention did not return, including at least two Antifederalist sympathizers. Four communities sent new delegates to Concord, two others were represented for the first time. This fluctuation, though minor, rendered it impossible to predict the fate of the Constitution. The convention opened on Wednesday, June 18, first looking into several allegations of election irregularities. The opposition suffered its first defeat when two of their members were eliminated as "not legally elected."[220] The next day, before a packed gallery, the delegates resumed the discussion interrupted in February. There was nothing new to be said, however, just "the same hard worn out, dry arguments . . . until both sides were quite tired out."[221] An Amendment Committee was formed on June 20 at the instigation of Federalists. With characteristic skill, they managed to obtain a one-vote majority in the committee of fifteen and to elect a Federalist as chair. The committee adopted the nine Massachusetts amendments with only one substantial change, then added three suggestions of its own: to permit a standing army in times of peace only if approved by a three-fourths majority in both Houses of Congress; to protect freedom of religion and speech against encroachment by the federal legislature; and to prohibit Congress from disarming the citizens unless they were engaged in open rebellion.[222]

The committee report read by John Langdon was accepted without objection. Antifederalists declared they were prepared to vote for ratification on condition that the new Constitution would come into force in New Hampshire only after it had been altered in accordance with the convention's specifications. Federalists considered the idea entirely unacceptable. Livermore offered a counterproposal that the Constitution be adopted and the amendments forwarded to Congress as recommendations. Both proposals were shelved after a heated debate. On Saturday, June 21, Atherton's request for an adjournment to an indefinite point in the future was rejected. The Livermore proposal was then put to a vote and approved by a majority of 57 to 47. Four delegates abstained from voting to avoid a breach of their Antifederalist instructions.[223] It was another Federalist victory masterminded by meticulous planning and behind-the-scenes maneuvering. Atherton believed "that they did not carry their Point by Force of Argument and Discussion; but by other Means, which were it not for the Depravity of the humane Heart, would be viewed with the warmest Sentiments of Disapprobation." His only comfort was the hope that the New York convention might yet succeed in "chaining and reducing within proper Bounds this young Lion, fostered by so many States, and permitted to run rampant trampling under Foot all our Bulwarks of Liberty." Should the Constitution go into effect, Antifederalists would have to ensure that a majority in Congress could block the legislative process until amendments had been implemented. He suggested several other amendments to Lamb and declared that the New Hampshire legislature would pursue these objectives as well. In any case, he wished to continue the correspondence with New York's Federal Republican Committee.[224]

New Hampshire Federalists lost no time in sending notice of the ratification by express rider to Alexander Hamilton in Poughkeepsie, who immediately relayed the news to Congress in New York City and to the Virginia convention in Richmond.[225] As the ninth state to ratify the Constitution, New Hampshire had the honor of "placing the Key Stone in the great Arch," thus fulfilling the conditions for the Constitution to come into force.[226] Yet Federalists realized that without New York and Virginia the Federal Dome would remain a mere skeleton. Another hard reality was that adopting recommendatory amendments had now become established practice. Their inclusion in the Forms of Ratification in several states had given them publicity and legitimacy that would later make them difficult to ignore. As useful as they were for tactical purposes, actually incorporating these proposed amendments into the Constitution was an entirely different matter. New York, Virginia, and North Carolina could at the least be expected to follow Massachusetts's example, as South Carolina and New Hampshire had now done. Boston Federalists had thus unwittingly created a process that might result in the adoption of amendments to which they were strongly opposed.

When word from New Hampshire arrived in Richmond on June 27, the Constitution had already been ratified and the delegates were preparing to leave the city. Federalists regretted having missed the opportunity to make the "Old Dominion" the all-important ninth state, yet they were proud to have added their pillar to the Federal Edifice without knowledge of the events in Concord. The convention had opened on June 2 by unanimously electing Edmund Pendleton president. After various other posts down to the chaplain and printer had been filled and the usual formalities involving commissions settled, the committee of the whole took up the debate on June 4. Much to everyone's surprise, George Mason's suggestion that they proceed without undue haste and discuss the Constitution article-by-article and paragraph-by-paragraph met with no resistance. Unlike the situation in Maryland, Federalists here were not certain they had a majority and were therefore eager to debate.[227]

The confidence of the "federal party" among the 170 elected delegates received an unexpected boost when Governor Edmund Randolph spoke out in favor of unconditional ratification, thus publicly confirming the change of heart he had first intimated in December 1787.[228] In his very first address, on June 4—much to everyone's astonishment—he pronounced the quest for "previous amendments" pointless since so many states had already adopted the Constitution.[229] The impact of Randolph's speech was strengthened by the news of unconditional ratification in South Carolina. Though alarmed by these "unlucky circumstances," the opposition remained undaunted, as William Grayson informed fellow congressman Nathan Dane in New York, through whom he maintained contact with Elbridge Gerry in Massachusetts: "The district of Kentucki is with us, & if we can get over the four Counties, which lye on the Ohio between the Pennsylvy. line & Big Sandy Creek, the day is our own."[230]

The news of Randolph's "conversion" and its effect on the opposition spread quickly. "The Governor has expressed himself in Favour of the general Union, which hath occasioned a Pensiveness, not to say Gloominess, in a part of the House, whose sentiments do not accord with his," was the word sent from convention delegates to Peter Singleton in Princess Anne County.[231] "The Governor's declaration we here consider as the clinching nail," pronounced a letter writer from Richmond in the *Pennsylvania Mercury;* the *New York Journal,* by contrast, spoke of "Randolph's treachery and dissimulation."[232] George Washington was delighted, commenting on June 8 from Mount Vernon to John Jay in New York: "The beginning has been as auspicious as could possibly have been expected."[233]

The two parties at the convention at first resembled a pair of boxers cautiously testing their opponent in the early rounds of a fight. The drawn out speeches, as everyone knew, were just as much intended to gain time as to defend a particular position. Speakers, especially Patrick Henry, digressed from the subject under debate to dwell on subsidiary subjects or on general points and principles. Madison accused the opposition of stalling to bring about a "postponement of the final decision to a future day."[234] The heat and the approaching special session of the legislature at the end of the month to discuss court reform seemed to speak for an adjournment. Madison's foremost concern was the Antifederalists' attempt to gain favor with undecided delegates, a pursuit they dedicated considerable energy to between debates and outside of the convention. The critics were inflicting most of their damage "out of doors" and not in the deliberations themselves, he complained to Rufus King on June 13.[235] Other recipients of Madison's pessimistic letters were Hamilton in Poughkeepsie and Washington at Mount Vernon, the latter also being informed on June 13 that the whole affair was "in the most ticklish state that can be imagined."[236] To the mind of moderate Antifederalist Theoderick Bland, the dispute had by now been reduced to the question of "anterior" or "posterior" amendments. At the moment, both parties were claiming an advantage of three to eight delegates. As is often the case when two sides are equally matched, the outcome was determined by behind-the-scenes "management" aided by a few "fortuitous events."[237]

In the meantime, Eleazer Oswald had arrived in Richmond bearing Lamb's letter of May 18 and was included in the deliberations of the Antifederalist Republican Society. Parallel to the open debate on the floor, this steering committee began to compile a list of fundamental rights and "substantial" amendments.[238] The dispiriting turn of events at the outset of the convention was partially offset by Oswald's announcement that the New York "Republicans" would likely enter the Poughkeepsie convention with a commanding majority. In the four days of consultations between Lamb's emissary and Mason, Henry, and Grayson, it was agreed that the opposition in Virginia and New York must present clear conditions for ratification. Lamb's suggestion that the adversaries of the Constitution keep in constant contact and extend their cooperation also met with approval.

The letters Oswald was to take back to New York nevertheless conveyed the concern that the advocates of "previous amendments" would remain a minority in Richmond. In the event they should fail, Grayson took a dim view of the prospects of further collaboration and therefore wanted to keep the exchange of information on an unofficial and strictly confidential level. Henry, on the other hand, believed the probable defeat of the amendment movement in Virginia would only render it even more necessary "to form the Society you mention. Indeed it appears the only remaining Chance for securing a Remnant of those invaluable Rights which are yielded by the new Plan." North Carolina would have to be included in the considerations and the system organized in such a way "as to include lesser Associations dispersed throughout the State. This will remedy in some Degree the Inconveniences arising from our dispersed Situation."[239] Henry apparently had been given this idea by Oswald's report on the correspondence committees in New York and the county societies in Pennsylvania. Finally, Mason enclosed in his letter to Lamb the Republican Committee's tentative list of amendments.[240]

Oswald left Richmond on June 11, stopped in Philadelphia along the way to inform George Bryan and James Hutchinson of the latest developments, then delivered the letters to the Federal Republican Committee in New York City on June 16. Lamb's son-in-law Charles Tillinghast, secretary of the Federal Republican Society, forwarded them to Poughkeepsie the following day, where the New York convention was just getting underway.[241] At Governor Clinton's request, Robert Yates answered Mason's letter on June 21 in his capacity as chairman of the newly formed Correspondence Committee. He thanked him for indicating a willingness to cooperate and expressed his satisfaction "that your Sentiments with respect to the Amendments correspond so nearly with ours, and that they stood on the Broad Basis of securing the Rights and equally promoting the Happiness of every Citizen in the Union." At the same time, however, he informed Mason of the Committee's wish to refrain from any official correspondence between the two conventions for the time being. The informal method was deemed preferable, due to "the doubtful Chance of your obtaining a Majority—and the Possibility that we will compleat our Determination before we could avail ourselves of your Advice." Yates underscored his party's determination to push through "previous amendments," but did not specify how these revisions were to be integrated into the Constitution.[242]

Yates's remarks amounted to an admission that the coordination efforts had come too late. The system of communication was working, yet the vast distances to be covered meant the dissemination of information always lagged behind the rapidly unfolding events. Another problem was the nagging question of whether interstate cooperation was even appropriate. Many Antifederalists thought it unwise to stress such contacts because they could be misconstrued as a conspiracy. Concerns of this kind were just as detrimental to the establishment of an effective national opposition as the myriad practical considerations.

In the meantime, Antifederalists in Richmond were desperately fighting to save the situation. Their criticism again focused on the omission of a bill of rights, the inadequate system of representation, and the authorization of Congress to levy direct taxes, which they believed would sound the death knell of state sovereignty. At the center of Henry's brilliant, fiery, and driving orations was the concept of "true federalism," something he saw embodied in the Articles of Confederation. The new plan of government, by contrast, lacked sufficient checks and balances as well as clearly defined powers. The fate of liberty was sealed if the people's well-being was dependent on the virtuousness of their leaders. Consolidating the states was incongruent with the "American spirit," the principle of republican simplicity, and the love of freedom, fostering instead a lust for power, glory, and wealth. Henry's second line of argumentation combined Virginian patriotism with the specific needs of the southern states to resist the threatened predominance of the North. The serious danger inherent in the power of Congress to pass, by a simple majority, measures regulating commerce and trade was illustrated again and again by the Jay-Gardoqui negotiations, which were alleged to have nearly deprived the southern states of their access to the Mississippi. These remarks were particularly designed to raise the ire of the Kentucky delegation, whose support both parties considered crucial.[243]

Unlike the opposition, Federalists were able to spread the weight of defending their cause across several shoulders. In addition to Madison, they had sent such experienced orators as Governor Randolph, George Nicholas, Edmund Pendleton, John Marshall, and Henry Lee. Yet it was Madison who delivered the most thorough and lucid speeches, despite infirmity probably brought on by stress. By June 6 he had already prepared a response to Henry's allegations, picking them apart point-for-point within the context of a basic defense of the Constitution, providing evidence of misinterpretations, unsound logic, and a deficient knowledge of history. The next day he analyzed the defects of confederations in general and the American confederation in particular, informing Henry that the Constitution was not a matter of achieving "national splendor and glory," but rather of ensuring domestic security and prosperity, the only way the United States could earn the world's respect. On June 11 he responded to James Monroe's provocative remarks from the previous day by insisting that the right of Congress to collect direct taxes was as essential, practical, and safe as it was economically viable. The new manner of taxation, he asserted, was far superior to the old requisition system, which left financial contributions up to the discretion of the particular state:

"In the general council, on the contrary, the sense of all America would be drawn to a single point. The collective interest of the union at large, will be known and pursued. No local views will be permitted to operate against the general welfare." Just as the people were currently paying taxes both to local and state institutions, they should be free to allow the "concurrent collection of taxes" by the state and the Union: "The people at large are the common superior of the state governments, and the general government." A "uniform and steady course of legislation" would benefit precisely the hardworking farmers and artisans, who until then had lived in constant danger of being cheated by shrewd profiteers.

As regards the need for a bill of rights, Madison reiterated on June 12 that the variety of churches and faiths in America guaranteed the freedom of religion better than any written declaration of basic rights. He addressed the issue of navigation on the Mississippi a day later, dispelling the fears of the Kentucky delegation by stressing that the northern states had a vested interest in safeguarding the free access to the river: "For, if the carrying trade be their natural province, how can it be so much extended and advanced, as by giving the encouragement to agriculture in the western country, and having the emolument of carrying their produce to market?" Besides, he said, continued emigration from the coastal states would soon give the West considerably more sway in the institutions of the central government. Yet what counted in the final analysis was not proclaiming navigation rights to the Mississippi, but exercising those rights. By creating the necessary conditions to make this possible, the Constitution would succeed where the weak Confederation had failed. Madison then proceeded to deal with such issues as regulating the compensation of members of Congress, the danger of multiple office-holding, the ability of Congress to regulate election procedures, the relationship between the militia and the federal army, the exclusive jurisdiction of Congress in matters pertaining to the federal capital as well as the slave trade, and the rights of slave owners. The importation of slaves was already prohibited in Virginia, he noted, and in twenty years Congress could extend this ban to include the entire Union. Until then, however, it could not assess a tax in excess of $10 per slave. Without this compromise allowing states to temporarily import slaves, there could have been no agreement in Philadelphia: "Great as the evil is, a dismemberment of the Union would be worse." Slavery itself was secure. Because of the connections between representation and taxation, no tax could be laid on slaves, "as will amount to a manumission." And the fugitive slave clause was a substantial improvement over the current situation, which did not provide for the return of slaves who escaped to other states.[244]

When the debate over the judiciary began on June 19 with a speech by Edmund Pendleton,[245] Antifederalists summoned their strength for what was shaping up to be the decisive battle. They claimed that the broad jurisdiction of the federal courts would bring material harm to thousands of Virginians and undermine the state's own legal system. Mason and Henry appealed to the fear of many Virginians that if the Constitution went into effect and the Peace Treaty were enforced, they would be summoned by British creditors to appear before federal courts, perhaps even the Supreme Court itself. Moreover, Antifederalists prophesied that the Indiana Land Company would revive its former claims and demand compensation for land in the western part of the state it had allegedly purchased from the Iroquois in 1768, claims the Virginia legislature had declared invalid in 1779. This scenario was intended to alarm the delegates from counties in the backcountry, who had begun to play a key role as the debate wore on.[246]

The grand finale of Madison's series of masterful expositions was his oration of June 20 on the judicial power of the national government, intended to repel the final offensive mounted by the opposition. A recurring theme in Madison's speech was faith in the ability of the citizens to choose suitable men for the important duty of administering justice: "Were I to select a power which might be given with confidence, it would be the judicial power. This power cannot be abused, without raising the indignation of all the people of the states." He conceded that the scope of original and appellate federal jurisdiction was not yet precisely defined, but insisted that Congress would be more likely to restrict rather than extend this authority and would see to it that 99 percent of all cases remained in the state courts. Madison offered no hope of immediate relief for debtors, though he did see prospects for long-term improvement: "Industry and œconomy is their only resource. It is in vain to wait for money, or temporise. The great desiderata are public and private confidence. . . . The circulation of confidence is better than the circulation of money. . . . The establishment of confidence will raise the value of property, and relieve those who are so unhappy as to be involved in debts."[247]

Antifederalists had been overwhelmed "by the deep reasoning of our glorious little Madison," gushed the author of a letter published in the *Pennsylvania Mercury* on June 26. Madison's reassuring words had apparently left quite an impression on the western delegates. Right up to the end, both parties competed fiercely for the votes of the delegates from Kentucky and a handful of "doubtful delegates" from other counties. Gouverneur Morris, who attended the convention as a visitor, suspected Antifederalists of resorting to "certain dark modes of operating on the Minds of Members."[248]

When it came to the use of unseemly methods—allegations which were never proven—Federalists surely did not take a back seat to their adversaries.

Madison anticipated that the opposition would "bring forward a bill of rights with sundry other amendments as conditions of ratification," and, if refused, would seek an adjournment. To forestall such a move and to placate skeptics in their own camp, Federalists planned "to preface the ratification with some plain & general truths that can not affect the validity of the Act: & to subjoin a recommendation which may hold up amendments as objects to be pursued in the constitutional mode."[249] From comments on June 23, Madison gathered that the resistance was weakening and Antifederalist leaders were beginning to despair: "Col. Mason in particular talked in a style which no other sentiment could have produced. He held out the idea of civil convulsions as the effects of obtruding the Government on the people."[250]

On June 24, Federalist George Wythe moved that the committee of the whole should ratify the Constitution and recommend amendments to be considered by the new Congress. Countering this proposal, Patrick Henry demanded that the convention approve amendments and submit them to the other states for examination before conducting the final vote on ratification.[251]

In his response to Henry's proposal, Madison at times put aside his previous restraint, passionately appealing to the delegates not to destroy, so near completion, the work of creating a free system of government that had begun in the Revolution and was admired by all the world: "It is a most awful thing that depends on our decision—no less than whether the thirteen States shall Unite freely, peaceably, and unanimously, for the security of their common happiness and liberty, or whether every thing is to be put in confusion and disorder!" No one, he emphasized, could expect the eight states that had already ratified to repeat the entire process. On the other hand, should the Virginia convention solemnly proclaim that the states were to retain all rights not delegated to the federal government and, moreover, recommend a few amendments to be dealt with by Congress in the prescribed manner, its wishes would surely be heeded. Yet these amendments must not shake the very foundations of the Constitution, he warned, nor should they be made a condition for ratification.[252]

The day after Madison's passionate appeal the convention rejected an Antifederalist resolution to submit a declaration of rights and amendments to the other states, by a vote of 88 to 80. When the expected motion to adjourn did not materialize, a final vote took place. Eighty-nine delegates voted for ratification, seventy-nine against.[253] In the end, only three of fourteen Kentucky delegates, but fifteen of sixteen delegates from the Allegheny counties sided with the Federalists. The latter group's nearly unanimous endorsement of the Constitution, which had been anything but certain, ultimately paved the way for unconditional ratification. Only a handful of delegates voted contrary to the wishes of their constituents—all but one of these voting in favor of the Constitution. Two delegates, one from each party, were absent on the final ballot. As good republicans, Antifederalists kept their poise in spite of their disappointment and helped to ensure that the session could be closed "with due decorum and solemnity." Henry declared he respected the decision of the majority, being a "quiet citizen," but would fight to regain the lost liberties "in a constitutional way."[254]

The convention then appointed two committees, one to prepare a Form of Ratification, the other to prepare recommendatory amendments. The Form of Ratification, written by five Federalists, emphasized the "essential rights" of the states and the people and expressed the conviction "that whatsoever imperfections may exist in the Constitution ought rather to be examined in the mode prescribed therein than to bring the Union in danger by a delay with a hope of obtaining Amendments previous to the Ratification." On June 26, the engrossed document was read in the convention and signed by President Pendleton.[255]

The second committee, consisting of eleven Federalists and nine Antifederalists and chaired by George Wythe, compiled the most extensive list of amendments to the Constitution of any convention up to that time. Although Federalists held the majority, the committee based its work upon the declaration drafted around June 9 by George Mason's Republican Society.[256] The forty amendments reported by the committee were divided into two groups of twenty each, the first of which constituted a bill of rights, while the second restricted the power of the federal government, clarified ambiguous clauses, and altered the structure of the proposed government. The committee of the whole accepted the list of twenty fundamental rights without discussion on June 27, but was less receptive to the structural amendments. Federalists were disturbed by provisions requiring a two-thirds majority in the Senate for commercial treaties and a two-thirds majority in both houses of Congress for navigation laws to regulate commerce or the maintenance of a standing army. Nor did they approve of limiting the president's term of office to eight years within a sixteen-year period. They were particularly opposed, however, to two other amendments. One would have denied the federal courts jurisdiction over all cases originating before ratification of the Constitution. This would have prevented Britons and Loyalists from suing for the recovery of debts, reviving questions about the fulfillment of the terms of the Peace Treaty with England. The other corresponded to the fourth Massachusetts amendment, providing that Congress could only collect direct taxes if the states failed to meet their quotas requisitioned by Congress.

There was serious objection to this last provision, which was disturbingly reminiscent of the requisition system under the Articles of Confederation. A motion by a group of Federalists, including Randolph, Madison, and Marshall, to strike this amendment from the list was defeated 85 to 65. Joining forces with Antifederalists to vote down the motion were, among others, President Pendleton, two of his colleagues from the state supreme court, and Henry Lee.[257] This last controversy resolved, the convention ordered that the Form of Ratification and the amendments should be forwarded to the Confederation Congress as well as to each state executive or legislature. Convention printer Augustine Davis was ordered to produce 4,300 copies of the documents, 50 for each Virginia county. Finally, the delegates thanked Edmund Pendleton for the "able, upright, and impartial discharge" of his duties as president of the convention. In this way, the two parties managed to preserve a semblance of solidarity and enable Pendleton to close the convention "in friendship & Amity."[258]

While the conciliatory actions of some Federalists were based on principle, others were motivated by tactical considerations. Their apparently conciliatory behavior toward those who favored amendments was promptly rewarded by the opposition's decision not to publish an alarming address to their constituents, which they had already drafted. Patrick Henry calmed some agitated delegates, discouraging open resistance or acts of violence.[259] Madison admitted in a letter to Washington that a number of the proposed changes to the Constitution were "highly objectionable," but they had to be accepted.[260] "Hot federalists" of the likes of Francis Corbin had nothing good to say about this turn of events, and even Madison was not safe from their wrath: "This whole business was ludicrous and is absurd in the Extreme. . . . I myself scouted Every Idea of proposing any amendments—trusting alone to those which Experience might Suggest. I wish our friend Madison had not been of the Committee—I am sure he blushes when it is talked of."[261] Yet what counted the most was that the most important and influential state in the Union would be part of the new government under the Constitution.

Federalists had benefited from experiences in other states, where recommendatory amendments had been deemed permissible and unobjectionable, as well as from Governor Randolph's unexpectedly strong commitment to their cause, and, finally, from the competence, patience, and determination with which Madison defended the Constitution. Another factor which should not be underestimated was the weight of George Washington's prestige. Although the General remained at Mount Vernon, everyone knew where he stood on the issue of the Constitution, and his presence was felt at every discussion. The likelihood that Washington would become the first president of the United States made it easier for some delegates to set aside their reservations and vote for ratification. The opposition had not succeeded in establishing the need for "previous amendments" and a general revision of the Philadelphia plan. Just the same, they had forced Federalists into a debate over the need for a bill of rights and for structural changes. This division in their adversary's camp, along with their own relative strength in the Virginia Assembly, gave Antifederalists hope that subsequent amendments might be adopted with the help of Massachusetts, New York, and several other states. At all events, Antifederalists left the convention safe in the knowledge that they had put up a fierce struggle and averted utter defeat.

The news of the decision in Virginia reached New York City by an express rider on July 2, between 2:00 and 3:00 a.m., and reached the Poughkeepsie convention on the same day around noon. After the message delivered from Concord on June 24, this was the second shattering blow to the Antifederalists' faith in their ability to prevail.[262] Outwardly, the Constitution's opponents accepted this pair of setbacks with equanimity, creating the impression of unshakable solidarity. In reality, however, word that the ninth state had approved the Constitution had already shaken their confidence and was threatening the unity of their party. The news from Richmond was the turning point Hamilton and Jay had been desperately waiting for, although it would take three more weeks for New York to join the fold.[263]

At the convention that had commenced in Poughkeepsie, eighty-four miles north of New York City, on June 17, there was more partisan maneuvering than had been the case at any of the previous conventions. Nowhere, except Rhode Island, did the critics of the Constitution have better prospects than in the State of New York. Since two-thirds of the delegates were sympathetic to their cause, they had no trouble electing Governor Clinton as president and Judge Henry Oothoudt as chairman of the committee of the whole, while Abraham B. Bancker and John McKesson were appointed secretaries. The greatest danger, from the standpoint of the nineteen Federalists, was that all discussion might be smothered in the opening stages of the convention, and the deliberations terminated by a speedy decision against ratification. In fact, that would have been the Antifederalists' safest route to victory. But there were other matters to be considered. For one thing, Antifederalists believed they owed the public and their opponents a fair debate; for another they still lacked clear objectives. The majority was evidently hoping to use the debate as a means of determining just how the fundamental revisions of the Constitution they had promised their constituents could best be arranged. Consequently, they also had no objections to a paragraph-by-paragraph discussion, their only stipulation being the right to suggest and discuss changes at each step along the way.[264]

This agreement greatly eased the pressure on Hamilton and his associates. They had been spared the ordeal of an immediate rejection or an adjournment and now had at least two weeks to appeal to their adversaries' better judgment while waiting for the intervention of "external circumstances."[265] Some of the more astute Antifederalists, both inside and outside the convention, sensed that the opposition had now ventured upon a slippery slope which could lead to the defeat of their party. "I apprehend some Injury from a long delay by diminishing our Numbers and perhaps from Operations on the Hopes or Fears of a few," John Lansing confided to Abraham Yates. His younger brother, Abraham G. Lansing, agreed: "We will eventually be injured by delays, notwithstanding the decided majority." Besides the "Federal Chicanery" and the influence of other states, he was also concerned about the growing impatience of Antifederalist delegates kept away from their farm work during the growing season. David Gelston in New York City was also of the opinion that it would have been better to adjourn the convention "immediately after reading the Constitution." The prevailing sentiment in Poughkeepsie, however, was that the unity and harmony among Clintonians would crush any hopes Federalists might harbor of saving the day, and "neither Sophistry Fear or Influence" could help them now.[266]

The discussion got off to a very slow start, having proceeded only as far as the eighth section of Article I after two weeks, but at least both sides contributed to an atmosphere of politeness and civility. Melancton Smith announced that he was willing "to make every reasonable concession, and indeed to sacrifice every thing for a Union, except the liberties of his country." Fellow Antifederalist John Williams had nothing against a thorough examination of the Constitution to determine whether it protected civil liberties and fundamental rights: "If it be so, let us adopt it.—But if it be found to contain principles, that will lead to the subversion of liberty—If it tends to establish a despotism, or what is worse, a tyrannical aristocracy, let us insist upon the necessary alterations and amendments." Governor Clinton declared "that the dissolution of the Union is, of all events, the remotest from my wishes." Hamilton advocated a consolidated republic, Clinton a federal republic, yet "The object of both of us is a firm energetic government: and we may both have the good of our country in view; though we disagree as to the means of procuring it."[267]

Between debates, Hamilton, Livingston, and Jay began to search for weak links in the opposition's armor by taking individual critics aside. Jay was the most adept at piercing the reserve of Antifederalist delegates, who almost always went about in groups, to avert attempts to sow division between them.[268] Every nuance of opinion they unearthed fed the Federalists' hopes that some of their opponents, at least, might yet come around. Even after New Hampshire's ratification, both parties were in uncommon agreement that the convention was not getting anywhere and that they were still far from reaching a decision. Hamilton was anxiously awaiting word from Madison, whom he repeatedly reminded that the prospects for success in Poughkeepsie were entirely dependent on a favorable outcome in Virginia. His last appeal, dated July 2, contained the admonition that there was now, more than ever before, reason to assume "that our conduct will be influenced by yours. . . . Some of the leaders appear to me to be convinced by circumstances and to be desirous of a retreat." This did not apply to the Governor, however, "who wishes to establish Clintonism on the basis of Antifœderalism."[269]

No sooner had the long-awaited news of ratification in Richmond arrived than Federalists completely changed their tactics. Until then, they had been tenaciously defending the Constitution against every suggestion for amendments. From this point on, however, they declined to debate the remarks made by Antifederalists, enabling the discussion of the last six articles of the Constitution to be completed by July 7. Their delaying tactics had paid off. The main question now was whether the opposition would be satisfied to recommend subsequent changes, or would insist on attaching conditions to ratification. This put immense pressure on the Antifederalists, who had growing differences of opinion in their caucus in developing a bill of rights and structural amendments.[270] The paper presented by John Lansing on July 10 distinguished between "explanatory," "conditional," and "recommendatory amendments." The first category consisted of a bill of rights, along with clarifications and interpretations of specific clauses. The stipulations contained in the second group prohibited Congress, prior to the convening of a second constitutional convention, from (a) deploying the New York militia beyond state borders for more than six months at a time without the consent of the state legislature; (b) regulating federal elections in the State of New York; and (c) collecting direct taxes from New York residents without first requisitioning the state government. The numerous revisions suggested in the third part of the program were to be dealt with by the first federal Congress, in accordance with the provisions of the new Constitution.[271]

The convention formed a fifteen-member amendment committee, then immediately dissolved it when the eight Antifederalist members declared the Lansing plan to be their "final word." Federalists responded on July 11 with a motion of their own calling for unconditional ratification together with a few explanations and recommendatory amendments. No vote was taken on either plan, however, both being shelved in favor of continued negotiations. In the meantime, more cracks were appearing in the Antifederalist bulwark—yet it continued to hold. On July 16, Federalists resorted to a measure which they always held in reserve for emergencies: Associate Justice John Sloss Hobart from New York City moved for an adjournment until September 2 to give delegates an opportunity to go "home to Consult their Constituents."[272] Antifederalists like Abraham Yates had long been expecting such a move, knowing it would allow the Hamiltonians "to shew their dexterity at Management." Yates feared they would use the interim to put pressure on individual delegates and keep the state in "Continual Convulsion."[273] Antifederalists were losing faith that the public would support their position. Abraham G. Lansing had now reached the point where he preferred the "Virginia Form [of Ratification]" to an adjournment.[274] In any case, Hobart's motion had too many ulterior motives to be endorsed by the majority in Poughkeepsie. When it was rejected on July 17 by a vote of 40 to 22, the convention had reached an impasse.

At this point, Melancton Smith, the Antifederalist floor leader, felt it was time to act. Ever since ratification by New Hampshire he had been secretly searching for a solution that would protect the interests of the states and the Union while allowing Antifederalists to save face. He confided in Massachusetts Congressman Nathan Dane on June 28 that he considered it better to recommend only absolutely essential amendments as a condition for ratification rather than demanding changes of secondary importance. Dane responded on July 3 with an insightful, compelling analysis of the dilemma facing Antifederalists. If New York rejected the Constitution, Dane predicted, civil war would break out, resulting in a system of government that was more authoritarian than any of those previously considered. Their only objective therefore must be "to improve the plan proposed: to strengthen and secure its democratic features; to add checks and guards to it; to secure equal liberty by proper Stipulations to prevent any undue exercise of power, and to establish beyond the power of faction to alter, a genuine federal republic." This could only be accomplished by peaceful means and a willingness to accept compromise. Any state that continued to stand apart and to offer resistance to the new Union was making a serious mistake, Dane warned. Unconditional ratification was the only way for Antifederalists to preserve their ability to influence the amendment process. The first Congress would be the proper place to join forces "in making the best of the Constitution now established."[275] Samuel Osgood, a member of the Confederation's Board of Treasury, expressed a similar opinion in letters to Smith and Samuel Jones. The opposition had already accomplished "a great deal of good," he said, and Federalists were obligated to enact amendments: "There is so little danger in assenting to the plan now, that it has become a matter of no small expediency. Indeed the danger of not obtaining Amendments such as we would wish for, will in my opinion be greatly enhanced by the absence of New York." Smith replied on July 15 that he was prepared to take a stance in favor of ratification at the convention even if it cost him the support of his fellow party members.[276]

Backed by Judge Zephaniah Platt, Smith presented his case on July 17. According to his plan, New York would unconditionally adopt the Constitution but reserve the right to leave the Union if Congress failed to call a second constitutional convention in four years. This proposal again put Federalists, as well as Smith's colleagues (who felt the compromise went too far), in a difficult position. Hamilton inquired of Madison, who had now returned to Congress, whether "*the reservation* of a right to recede" by New York would be accepted by the other states. Madison answered immediately and unequivocally that New York could not be received in the new Union on the basis of a "*conditional*" ratification: "The Constitution requires an adoption *in toto,* and *for ever.* It has been so adopted by the other States. An adoption for a limited time would be as defective as an adoption of some of the articles only."[277] Of greater importance than the open debates were now the "secret conclaves," in which both parties struggled to preserve unity and agree on a policy. The situation became muddled; the convention was divided into four groups, "one of which was for an Adoption with Conditions, one for a given time in order to withdraw if a General convention is not obtained in that time; one for an adjournment and one for an absolute Ratification."[278]

The draft of ratification formulated by John Lansing was debated from July 19 to July 23. It stipulated that New York would adopt the Constitution "upon Condition" that a bill of rights and certain structural amendments were accepted by a second convention of the states. Samuel Jones with the support of Melancton Smith, proposed replacing the words "upon Condition" with "in full Confidence" and leaving out the reference to a second general convention. They agreed that the Constitution was flawed, but felt that Virginia's ratification left them no choice but to drop their insistence on conditions. Continuing to pursue that course "would certainly prove in the event, only a dreadful deception to those who were serious for joining the Union." The Antifederalist leadership agreed that the state must ratify unconditionally. They sought Antifederalist delegates who would either vote for ratification or abstain—either action which might be opposed by their constituents. The Antifederalist vote ended 31 to 29.[279]

The next day, staunch opponents of the Constitution, led by Clinton and Lansing, made a final attempt to ward off defeat by reintroducing Smith's earlier idea of reserving New York's right to withdraw from the Union. Hamilton now played his last trump card by reading Madison's answer to the question he had posed a few days earlier. James Duane, Robert R. Livingston, and John Jay invited the opposition to show a spirit of accommodation, and the convention was adjourned for the day. On July 25, Lansing's proposal was rejected by a margin of 31 to 28, and on July 26 the convention voted 30 to 27 to approve the report of the committee of the whole confirming the adoption of the Constitution with a declaration of rights and recommendatory amendments.[280]

New York's ratification consisted of a Declaration of Rights with twenty-four articles, to which the actual Form of Ratification was attached. The Form stated that the Constitution was adopted "In full confidence" that Congress would abstain from exercising certain powers in New York until another constitutional convention had been convened by Congress. This was followed by an enumeration of no less than thirty-two amendments which were recommended to Congress and for whose adoption New York's representatives were to push with all their might.[281]

After the documents had been signed by Governor Clinton as president of the convention, John Jay introduced a circular letter addressed to the other state executives that had been drafted at the request of the committee of the whole. This circular letter was apparently a part of the deal to get Antifederalists to vote for unconditional ratification. It was adopted unanimously. The document stated that a majority of the convention found several articles of the Constitution "so exceptionable . . . that nothing but the fullest confidence of obtaining a revision of them by a General convention, and an invincible reluctance to separating from our sister States, could have prevailed upon a sufficient number to ratify it, without stipulating for previous amendments." Since the approval of two-thirds of the state legislatures was required to call a constitutional convention, it was suggested that the various legislatures should act quickly to submit the appropriate resolutions to Congress. New York was prepared to initiate such measures forthwith.[282] Before going their separate ways, the delegates unanimously voted to instruct Governor Clinton to exhort the state legislature in its next session, "to cooperate with our sister states in measures for obtaining a general convention to consider the amendments and alterations proposed by them and us, as proper to be made in the Constitution of the United States."[283]

Melancton Smith and his followers had bowed to the force of events. The threat of civil war used to intimidate Antifederalists was very real. The bloody clash between supporters and adversaries of the Constitution on the 4th of July in Albany showed that the public mood had reached the boiling point and more violence was to be feared if the convention failed.[284] By the end of June there was also growing evidence of a possible secession of the southern counties from the state. As the convention appeared to come closer to reaching a decision, New York City Federalists became more explicit about their intention to place the city under the protection of Congress if necessary and to request a separate admission to the Union. An echo of these threats was unmistakable in Hamilton's speeches in Poughkeepsie.[285] Since all of the neighboring states had ratified, the New York legislature could not rely on them to help fight the separatist tendencies. Even if the state should remain intact, there would be substantial setbacks to contend with. The first of these would be the departure of Congress and the forfeiture of the city's lucrative position as the federal capital. Philadelphians had long observed the squabbling in New York with a certain amount of malicious glee, hoping this would improve their prospects of luring back the federal government.[286] From the standpoint of those who truly advocated amendment, it was undeniable that New York could accomplish little outside the Union but could make a great contribution with like-minded people in other states.

Reactions to the outcome of the Poughkeepsie convention varied. There were Federalists who celebrated the decision as a great victory and Antifederalists who openly admitted defeat. The first group included Samuel Blachley Webb and his friends, who spent the night "in loud acclamation of Joy"; Philip Schuyler, who hailed the turn of events as the triumph of "perseverance, patience and abilities" over "numbers and prejudice"; and Edward Carrington, who believed the "Antis" had wanted to reject the Constitution but did not know how to go about it.[287] Except for the unmistakable undertone of spite in these comments, they were entirely consistent with the opinion of Antifederalist delegate Cornelius C. Schoonmaker, who after reviewing the proceedings came to the conclusion "that Federalists have fought and beat us from our own ground with our own weapons."[288] It is interesting to observe the nuances attached to the words victory and defeat. It has already been noted that Melancton Smith's vote in favor of unconditional ratification by no means indicated a principled endorsement of the Constitution. The same applied to Zephaniah Platt, who considered his final vote to be "a Choice of evils." After Virginia's adoption of the Constitution, it had become obvious that the new government would be established and the only remaining course of action was "to get a convention as Soon as possible to take up our Amendments . . . while the Spirit of Liberty is yet alive . . . be assured that we have endeavoured to consider all Sides of the question and their probable consequences and on the whole decided on what we supposed was for the Interest and peace of our State under present Circumstances."[289] Abraham G. Lansing also put a brave face on the situation in a letter to Abraham Yates. Lansing maintained that "upon the whole I believe or *endeavour* to believe that it is best both in a political and private light—for had the Constitution been so adopted [by New York] as that Congress would not accept it—yourself and our Friends would have incurred blame & Censure if any serious commotions had ensued—as we stand our Friends in this quarter are firmly united—and I trust we shall be able to send such Members [to Congress] as will assist in bringing about the reformation we wish."[290]

Leading Antifederalists outside New York, including George Mason and Elbridge Gerry, felt the same way. They believed that joining the new Union had been a wise decision because it would enable New York "to cooperate with the other States to make amendments," thereby improving the chances for "proper & safe Amendments."[291] Realistically minded supporters of the Constitution admitted that they owed their success to Melancton Smith.[292] Moreover, many Federalists were dissatisfied with the manner in which ratification had been achieved. They were particularly unhappy with the circular letter sent by the convention to the other states, calling for a second constitutional convention, which was something to be dreaded. Madison referred to the letter signed by Clinton as a "signal of concord & hope to the enemies of the Constitution every where." Madison would have preferred that New York reject the Constitution than "to purchase an immediate ratification in any form and at any price." This tactic he attributed to the desire to keep Congress in New York City and to preserve the city's chances of becoming the federal capital.[293] The convention in Poughkeepsie had finally added "the eleventh pillar" to the Federal Temple after a prolonged struggle, yet the true import of this act could not be ascertained until the outcome of the battle for revisions and amendments was known.

Bringing Up the Rear: North Carolina and Rhode Island

For most observers of the ratification proceedings, it was a foregone conclusion that North Carolina would "follow in the footsteps of Virginia" and ratify the Constitution.[294] Yet as the Hillsborough convention would show, they were underestimating the Antifederalist majority's independence and their commitment to the will of the voters. Behind such substantial leaders as Willie Jones, Thomas Person, and Timothy Bloodworth, the adversaries of the Constitution marched into the Presbyterian Church, the site of the convention, on July 21 determined not to allow themselves to be divided or outmaneuvered. They would have preferred to follow the example set by Federalists in Maryland and to declare that their instructions prevented them from entering into any discussion whatsoever. James Iredell was forced to summon all his oratorical skills just to ward off a push to put the matter to an immediate vote. In a spirited address, he beseeched the delegates to consider the "extreme impropriety of such precipitancy in so important a business," and coaxed them into agreeing to treat the Constitution in the committee of the whole.[295] The six-day debate that followed was dominated by Federalists, at least as reported. Jones spoke little. The major Antifederalist speakers were Samuel Spencer, David Caldwell, Bloodworth, and Joseph McDowell. Iredell, William R. Davie, Archibald Maclaine, Samuel Johnston, and Richard Dobbs Spaight carried the Federalist side. Further dividing the convention was the volatile issue of the final site of the state capital, an added burden placed on the delegates by the state legislature.[296]

By August 1, a report was beginning to take shape in the committee of the whole very similar to what Antifederalists in Virginia demanded: a twenty-article declaration of rights and twenty-six additional amendments. New suggestions included a provision to prevent Congress from interfering with the paper money and certificates in circulation in individual states. Unlike in Virginia, however, North Carolina was determined to make ratification contingent upon the implementation of revisions. The intention, as Willie Jones readily admitted, was to increase the pressure on Congress. At this juncture, Antifederalists were still assuming that the Clintonians in New York, with whom they were corresponding, would follow the same course. They may also have been advised to try this method by Patrick Henry after his failed attempt to use it in Virginia.[297] Federalists warned in vain that this would mean the voluntary exclusion from the Union, with unforeseeable consequences for the state's economy, security, and internal stability. The convention rejected an alternative proposal put forward by Iredell providing for recommendatory amendments, and on August 2 it voted 184 to 83 to adopt the committee of the whole's report.

Under Willie Jones's leadership, the majority then provided a demonstration of their conciliatory spirit, their devotion to the Union. In a supplementary resolution, the convention called on the state legislature to continue to support the federal government. Should the new Congress impose a general import duty, North Carolina was to follow suit and pass the revenue on to the federal treasury. Moreover, the convention instructed the legislature to withdraw the remaining paper money from circulation as quickly as possible. This shift in the paper-money policy coincided with a legislative resolution a short time later recognizing the validity of the Peace Treaty with England. The state seemed to be saying that its opposition to the Constitution was based on principle and not narrow self-interest.[298] Antifederalists also were careful to emphasize in the final resolution that the convention thought it best neither to ratify nor reject the Constitution. As their remarks reveal, they presumed events would then proceed as follows: Congress would call a second constitutional convention to search for common ground among the suggested amendments. Its report would then be submitted to the states for approval by yet another round of specially elected conventions. Only then would the Constitution be valid and universally binding. Antifederalists publicized their imposing declaration of rights in newspapers and pamphlets to prepare the people for this drawn-out process.[299]

North Carolina's unexpected decision created considerable alarm, especially since the exact details were either entirely unknown or were based on rumor. The Hillsborough delegates were the object of criticism, curses, and contempt as far north as New Hampshire; they were pronounced stupid or accused of having base motives. It was utterly incomprehensible to many Americans that they could refuse to ratify "in this stage of the business."[300] Even Antifederalists regretted this "bold move," since it meant there would be fewer proponents of amendments in the new Congress. The initial furor soon gave way to sober and circumspect reflection on the positive and negative implications of this turn of events. Once the actual wording of the resolutions had become known and Congressman Hugh Williamson had appealed to the people through the press to show more understanding for his fellow North Carolinians, the delegates' actions were seen in a "much less censorial light"—the impression created by the "federal disposition" evinced by the state effected a change in public opinion.[301] Besides, no one seriously believed that North Carolina and Rhode Island could impede the implementation of the Constitution now that eleven states had already ratified. In view of the large number of aspirants for government offices, the other states did not at all mind if North Carolina temporarily relinquished its share. Moreover, the bitter dispute being waged over the future capital of the United States made the move seem almost desirable in view of the finely calibrated balance of political power between the North and South. As long as Rhode Island refused to join the Union, the presence of North Carolina could have given the South an advantage during the important start-up phase of the new system of government. It appeared to some that it might be better if they were later added in tandem, and the anticipated independence of Kentucky and Tennessee could be balanced by the statehood of Maine and Vermont.

Of course, such speculations were hardly comforting to North Carolina Federalists. They felt shut out from Union politics and left to the mercy of an impulsive majority willing to risk the state's reputation, prosperity, and internal security.[302] Federalists interpreted Willie Jones's "doctrine of opposition" as an attempt to prevent federal courts from being turned loose on the citizens of North Carolina for the next five to six years: "He is continually haranguing the people on the terrors of the Judicial power, and the certainty of their ruin, if they are *obliged now* to pay their debts." The conviction was also voiced in the Tennessee district that no people could be forced "to enter into Compact without their own Consent." Moreover, there were plenty of citizens who believed that permanent independence would foster population growth in the state and promote trade.[303]

Unwilling to give up, Federalists did everything in their power to rectify the situation as quickly as possible. They wanted to cultivate the marked shift in public sentiment that had set in when the Constitution came into force, and exert more pressure on the state legislature to call a new ratifying convention. After the elections in the fall of 1788, Governor Johnston teamed up with Iredell, Maclaine, and Davie to initiate a wave of town and county meetings at which petitions were drawn up and forwarded to the legislature. Often signed by several hundred citizens, the appeals lamented the general feeling of public crisis, criticized the irresponsible actions of the Hillsborough delegates, expressed concerns about economic hardship, anarchy, and civil war, and implored politicians to call another convention. Thus, the "public mind," which Davie had described in September as "strangely unsettled and wavering," remained in a state of agitation. According to Maclaine, most people simply could not bear the thought of having to live outside the Union.[304]

The new legislature, flooded with petitions, approved a second convention after vigorous negotiations between the senate and the house of commons. The increasing threat of a war with the Indians seems to have expedited the process, as the representatives from the westernmost portions of the state were suddenly receptive to the Federalist cause. The opposition to the Constitution still held enough sway, however, to delay the convention until November 1789. The practical advantage of this arrangement was that since many of the legislators who would not be in the fall session would also be convention delegates, they would have an immediate opportunity to act on a decision to ratify by calling a special session of the legislature to initiate measures for the state's reentry into the Union.[305]

Federalists used a carrot-and-stick approach during the following period to further weaken the resistance to the Constitution. On the one hand, they stressed the progress made by the federal government, the prestige of President George Washington, and the advantages the citizens would enjoy under the umbrella of the Union; on the other hand, they stepped up the psychological pressure on their adversaries. The specter of secession reared its head, for instance, just as it had in Rhode Island, Virginia, and New York, this time in the form of separatist threats by the Edenton District. Rumors surfaced in the spring of 1789 that, to ensure their economic survival, the entire coastal region would be forced to join the nine Edenton counties.[306] These fears were nourished by a new customs law, enacted on September 1 by Congress, imposing special tonnage duties on foreign ships. Though concerned this measure might apply to North Carolina, Federalist merchants welcomed the opportunity to show their compatriots just how serious the situation was and warn them that Congress was losing patience.[307]

After their bitter experience in Hillsborough, the friends of the Constitution were determined to leave nothing to chance this time around. Iredell and Davie published the Hillsborough debates in book form and distributed them just in time for the August election campaign for convention seats. Also exploited for propaganda purposes was the address sent by the North Carolina State Council to George Washington in May 1789, as well as the president's amiable reply.[308] Yet the most effective weapon of all was the announcement by Madison in the U.S. House of Representatives on May 4, 1789, that he intended to introduce amendments to the Constitution. This move robbed the opposition of the standard argument that Federalists had no serious intention of keeping their promises to revise the Constitution. On June 10, Davie thanked Madison for his initiative, which had "dispersed almost universal pleasure" in North Carolina: "we hold it up as a refutation of the gloomy profecies of the leaders of the opposition, and the honest part of our Antifederalists have publickly expressed great satisfaction on this event." Davie advised Madison that it was "extremely important" for the amendments to be proposed before the state convention met in November.[309]

In all parts of the state except the central Piedmont region, the adversaries of the Constitution were in retreat during the election of convention delegates. Willie Jones did not even seek election. The most marked shift in sentiments occurred in the Tennessee District, whose residents had chosen nineteen Antifederalists and two Federalists a year before. They now sent twenty-one proponents of the Constitution to Fayetteville along with only two dissenters.[310]

When the convention met, however, it became clear to Federalists that they would have to be on their guard right to the end, when the convention voted on November 17 to reject their motion for immediate ratification. But on November 21, the delegates resolved by a vote of 194 to 77 "that this convention in behalf of the free men Citizens and Inhabitants of the State of North Carolina do adopt and ratify the said Constitution and form of Government." Whereas the opposition failed in its attempt to attach conditions to ratification, their proposal to recommend amendments was approved. It was a sign of a shift in the political wind that, of the twenty-six Hillsborough amendments, only eight relatively insignificant proposals remained. The tax amendment, which had been approved by a committee of seven, was eliminated on November 23 in the final session of the committee of the whole.[311] An examination of the list of participants confirms that the outcome of the proceedings in Fayetteville was less attributable to the conversion of Antifederalists than the influx of new delegates. Over half of the representatives in Fayetteville had not been a part of the Hillsborough convention. Most critics had been silenced in advance of the convention or had lost their bid for a seat. But of the fifty-seven delegates who had voted against ratification in 1788 and had returned a year later, twenty-two switched sides.[312]

North Carolina's decision to adopt the Constitution and rejoin the Union was noted with satisfaction across the country. Tench Coxe, in Philadelphia, exuberantly proclaimed that the "wonderful revolution" was nearing its happy conclusion.[313] The resoluteness with which North Carolinians had resisted all threats and enticements for over two years was not without merit. Madison indirectly admitted that this circumstance made it easier for him to propose amendments. He revealed to Governor Samuel Johnston that his plan pursued the dual purpose "of removing the fears of the discontented and of avoiding all such alterations as would either displease the adverse side or endanger the success of the measure."[314] This approach had unquestionably proven successful in North Carolina. Now that there were no further impediments to the state's full political and economic integration into the new system of government, its legislature could implement proceedings to elect delegates to the Senate and House of Representatives. Congressmen from the other southern states were impatiently awaiting their arrival to strengthen their vanguard against the imperious airs of some delegates from the North.[315] For the representatives of the "eastern interest," on the other hand, who supported Hamilton's policies, it was high time Rhode Island was brought into the fold to restore the balance of power.

Federalists in Newport and Providence were driven by a fervent desire to free themselves from the financial stranglehold of their internal political rivals and enjoy the fruits of membership in the Union. At the elections for governor and legislature in April and August of 1789 they were again defeated by the Country Party.[316] It was also becoming apparent beyond the state's borders that criticism and expressions of contempt for Rhode Island were not enough to win its ratification.[317] This tiny yet obstinate state was a constant reminder that the Union was still incomplete, and this disturbed the appearance of harmony. Pessimists feared the situation would create an open wound which might spread the poison of discord and the "principles of wild Democracy." John Adams observed in September 1789 that in view of the "turbulent state of Europe," Americans would be well advised to get their own affairs in order as quickly as possible.[318] A short time later, Tench Coxe again took up his pen to compose the last of his anonymous addresses to the state ratifying conventions. He explained to Madison that he considered the "reformation" of Rhode Island to be "an object of the first magnitude to the United states, and interesting in a high degree to every lover of Mankind."[319]

In the newspaper articles, speeches, petitions, and protests used by Federalists to alter the state's political climate, three compelling reasons for ratification were named over and over. Rhode Island's economic existence was threatened without the protection provided by Congress; as a member of the Union the state could strengthen the forces defending the specific interests of New England; finally, the only way to contribute to the revision of the Constitution was to occupy seats in Congress. The decision facing the citizens was portrayed as a choice between isolation and ruin on the one hand, and integration in a rising empire, the emergence of Providence as the commercial center of New England, and the development of Newport as the Union's naval base on the other. Federalists argued that this would benefit the entire population and not just merchants, artisans, and laborers. The proponents of the Constitution were less forthcoming, however, about their expectation that the federal government and federal courts would support private creditors damaged by the manipulation of currency by the Rhode Island legislature.

Antifederalists retained their misgivings, but leading Country Party politicians nevertheless came to the conclusion that sooner or later ratification was inevitable. Their critics had predicted all along that they would come around once the public and private debts had been discharged. Although they were close to reaching this goal in the summer of 1789, they found it exceedingly difficult to alter their previous political course. For one thing, they were trapped by their own rhetoric, which they had used to turn the democratic instincts of the people against the Constitution. Still fresh in the people's minds was their insistence that Rhode Island was fully capable of surviving on its own and could freely choose when the proper time had come to join the Union. Should party leaders now suddenly recant, they might lose favor with their surprised and disappointed constituents. The trick was to perform a political about-face as delicately as possible, to avoid losing control of the state government and to minimize damage. To make matters worse, certain measures instituted by the Washington administration only served to increase the resistance. Antifederalist skepticism found further confirmation in the heated controversy over the seat of the federal capital as well as Hamilton's funding plan. Under these circumstances, the progress toward rejoining the Union was proceeding so slowly that Rhode Island Federalists were nearly driven to distraction.[320]

The voters at town meetings held true to their convictions, enabling the ruling party to maintain its majority. By the end of 1789, the question of a ratifying convention had come up for debate and been rejected no less than seven times by the General Assembly. Yet by judiciously abandoning their paper-money policies, Country politicians signaled that the time had come to consider seriously the issue of ratification. The surprisingly wide majority by which North Carolina had adopted the Constitution hastened Rhode Island's search for a way out of their dilemma.[321] On January 17, 1790, both houses of the legislature finally agreed to call upon the towns to send delegates to a convention in South Kingstown at the beginning of March. A tie in the upper house was broken by Governor John Collins, who had always leaned toward a strong central government. Antifederalists seemed glad to be rid of the "unpleasant business" and secretly promised not to stand in their adversaries' way.[322] Since no public endorsement of ratification was issued, however, the opponents of the Constitution managed to win the elections on February 8, securing forty of the seventy convention seats.

Oblivious to the remonstrations of the Federalist delegates, the South Kingstown convention did little during the first week in March other than copy a bill of rights and amendments from the ratification documents drawn up by New York and North Carolina, which they then forwarded to the towns for review. That done, they adjourned after agreeing to resume the deliberations in Newport on May 24.[323] In their secret nightly caucuses, Antifederalists had come to the conclusion that they could not risk adopting the Constitution before the general elections in April. They first wanted to ensure that their nominees were installed in key state offices and were in a position to defend their legislative majority, which would allow them to appoint both U.S. senators. Governor Collins was picked as their public sacrifice to the constituents who remained adamantly opposed to ratification. Having made himself unpopular by his pro-convention vote, he was now to be supplanted by Arthur Fenner. The results of the April 15 elections confirmed the wisdom of their strategy. Even so, most towns rejected the amendment proposals as inadequate and instructed their delegates to insist on several other substantial changes, such as the swift prohibition of slavery and the right to recall senators. It appeared that the Newport convention, too, was in danger of adjourning without reaching a final decision, again leaving the fate of Rhode Island in a state of limbo.

At this point, the Federalist majority in Congress finally lost patience and responded to demands for increased pressure on those responsible for the delays. There was no lack of suggestions as to suitable means of compulsion. Merchants and politicians like Jabez Bowen, Henry Marchant, John Brown, George Benson, and William Ellery had compiled a lengthy list of prospective measures. These ranged from threats to deny patronage and private credit to Antifederalists, to a ban on imports from Rhode Island, all the way to a proposal that Congress dismember the state, remove the judges from office, expel all adversaries of the Constitution, and divide the state between Connecticut and Massachusetts. Another long-discussed option was the secession of the coastal towns, a move which could only be risked if the federal government agreed to protect the separatists. A number of these suggestions were fed to the press to intimidate the opposition.[324] To the same end, reports were published on the formation of citizens committees in Pennsylvania dedicated to boycotting products from Rhode Island, a method once employed against Great Britain.[325]

Radical Federalists such as Theodore Sedgwick, Caleb Strong, Fisher Ames, and John Sullivan flatly refused to regard Rhode Island as a "foreign country" under any circumstances. They considered the Union to be "indissoluble and integral," and anyone who thought otherwise was committing treason against the United States. It followed that Congress had the right to take coercive measures against Rhode Island. The zealousness of delegates from the northern states extending down to New York was of course influenced by a desire to strengthen their hold on the Senate with the help of the two Rhode Island votes. Delaware senator Richard Bassett had the impression that the northern states were pulling closer together and "Eastern politics" was likely to become the order of the day: "The Eastern men here are exerting all possible influence to bring [Rhode Island] in, from this motive principally alone, I fear, to give [them] a clearer decided majority."[326]

On April 28, 1790, the Senate formed a committee to study the Rhode Island issue. It soon drafted a sharply worded bill providing for a complete economic blockade of the state. The measure was to be accompanied by a demand for the repayment of $25,000 to the Union by the end of 1790. The small band of politicians opposing this drastic move included Richard Henry Lee and Pennsylvania senator William Maclay. The latter warned his colleagues that threatening such measures was akin to "playing the tyrant." He noted in his diary that the bill could not be justified "on the principles of freedom, law, the Constitution, or any mode whatever." The law was being used "in the same way that a robber does a dagger or a highwayman a pistol, and to obtain the end desired by putting the party in fear."[327] The bill's initiators realized they were treading on thin ice legally, privately referring to the matter as a "pretty bold measure." They nevertheless felt vindicated by the principle that the end justifies the means.[328]

On May 18, 1790, the "Act to prevent bringing Goods, Wares and Merchandizes, from the State of Rhode Island and Providence Plantations, into the United States; and to authorize a demand of Money from the said State" easily passed the Senate. Before the House of Representatives could begin deliberations on the bill, its wording was published in Rhode Island newspapers. "I assure you that the Contents have made a very alarming impression on the antifederal minds," George Benson communicated to Senator Theodore Sedgwick. No previous development had had a more favorable impact from the Federalists' point of view: "We rather enjoy than regret the expected operation of the Prohibitory Bill, as the inveterate Enemies of the Federal Government will then Suffer in the Common Calamity." Another effective maneuver was the publication of unsigned letters from Congress ensuring citizens loyal to the Union that they could count on the protection of the federal government in the event of secession.[329]

The turmoil aroused by the "Prohibitory Bill" came at a convenient time for Country Party politicians, providing them with a plausible justification for the ratification already planned. On May 18 Judge William Channing wrote to Theodore Foster, the brother-in-law of newly elected Governor Arthur Fenner, that the current Rhode Island administration would never have a better opportunity "of effecting their various purposes than by an immediate accession." Foster, who had already been designated by the Country Party leadership to fill one of the seats in the Senate, answered on the opening day of the Newport convention: "Many of Antifederalists wish the Business done but do not love to do it themselves."[330] Federalists helped resolve the dilemma by winning over the towns of Middletown and Portsmouth, thus nearly achieving a balance with Antifederalists.[331] The rest was left up to Jonathan J. Hazard, the Country Party's unchallenged leader. In the hope that Federalists would support his bid for a Senate seat, he worked toward ratification behind the scenes and supplied the requisite number of "defectors" to achieve a slim margin of 34 to 32 in favor of ratification on May 29 after a week of delay tactics. Once again, a bill of rights and twenty-one amendments were attached, though they were not made a condition for the "lost sister's" return to the Union. Fifteen months after the federal government had taken up business, Rhode Island became the last of the thirteen states to adopt the new system of government.[332]

Federalists in Newport and Providence had been apprehensive to the end and could now barely contain their delight. In the words of William Vernon, ratification gave "inexpressible pleasure to the Persons of property, and a fatal stab to Paper-Money robbers and Legislators."[333] Far from going into mourning, Antifederalists immediately dedicated themselves to the business of governance and the upcoming Senate elections. Jonathan J. Hazard was selected as their second scapegoat. In his place, Joseph Stanton Jr., who had always toed the party line, was nominated for a seat in the Senate alongside Theodore Foster. The main beneficiary of Foster's appointment and Hazard's political fall was Governor Fenner. Backed by a coalition of Antifederalists and moderate Federalists, he consolidated his position, and remained in power until his death in 1805.

In Congress, the news from Rhode Island was seen as "a new victory gained by the men of the North . . . it infinitely displeases the States of the South, which will henceforward have two more votes against them in the Senate and whose interests were already too neglected by the Congress."[334] Sedgwick and Strong advised Foster of the "great importance of having your State represented in the Senate," and instructed him on the benefits of Hamilton's finance program: "To the commercial States in general, and to your's which is peculiarly so in particular, the funding of the debt, and thereby providing a medium of commerce, is immensely important."[335]

On June 4 Washington wrote a conciliatory, forward-looking response to Governor Fenner's request for help in resisting the Prohibitory Act: "Since the bond of Union is now compleat, and we once more consider ourselves as one family, it is much to be hoped that reproaches will cease and prejudices be done away . . . we must drive far away the daemon of party spirit and local reproach." John Adams surmised that the successful "renovation" of the Union would restore respect for America and confirm the principles "which are like to produce a compleat Revolution both in Religion and Government in most parts of Europe."[336]

An observer from the European perspective who grasped the momentousness of the occasion was French consul Louis Guillaume Otto. He viewed the Rhode Island decision as the beginning of a new era:

> This ratification, Sir, finally completes the new government of the United States and makes them a more redoubtable mass than they were under the old system. From this moment on the United States can be considered as an homogeneous nation which receives its laws and its impetus from a common center, which is no longer, as before, a Congress of delegates without power and without force, but a government of three well organized branches whose powers are clearly defined by a written constitution, which gives it a great superiority over the English one.[337]

In typical European fashion, he could not resist adding that the central government could make even quicker progress if not impeded by the continued existence of state legislatures.

At the same time, a new wave of exuberant Federalist poetry hit the newspapers. A poem entitled *The American Union Completed,* which appeared in the Boston *Independent Chronicle* and was reprinted in the *Providence Gazette* on June 5, contained many of the typical metaphors and themes found in contemporary political verse:

> 'Tis done! 'tis finish'd! guardian union binds,
> In *voluntary* bands, a nation's minds:
> Behold the dome complete, the pillars rise—
> Earth for the basis, for the arch the skies!
>
> Now the *new* world shall mighty scenes unfold;
> Shall rise the imperial rival of the *old;*
> And *Roman freedom* tread the western soil,
> And a new *Athens* in the *desert* smile.
>
> O happy land!—O ever sacred dome
> Where peace and independence own their home:
> Commerce and tillage, hail the queen of Marts,
> Th' *asylum* of the world, the residence of arts.

The state ratifying conventions had given the freely elected representatives of the people an opportunity publicly to debate the Constitution, weigh its pros and cons, and come to a decision. It was to the delegates' credit that they introduced an element of innovation into the process. The option of suggesting changes opened the door for compromise across party lines without threatening the reform program as such. Originally devised as a vote-getting ploy, "recommendatory amendments" soon became an integral part of the ratification proceedings, thereby acquiring a significance which made them impossible to ignore by the subsequent federal government. This moderate extension of the conventions' decision-making latitude enabled the process of adopting a new Constitution founded on popular sovereignty to be brought to a successful conclusion. Without this innovation, the push for reform would have ground to a halt, stymied by irreconcilable demands. As New York Federalist Adrian Wynkoop pointed out, it was indeed remarkable "that every State, where conventions have met for the purpose, have accepted the Constitution; where too so much opposition to it was made."[338]

Remarkably, once ratification was achieved, Antifederalists turned from opposition to working within the new system. Antifederalists had strenuously tried to use the conventions as vehicles for revisions and amendments, and especially in Massachusetts, Virginia, and New York they made considerable progress in this direction. They continued to seek revisions by the provisions of Article V of the Constitution. They became a "loyal opposition." This is what James Sullivan wanted to convey to John Adams in July 1789 when he defended the Massachusetts minority against charges of treason and subversion. Despite having voted for the Constitution himself, Sullivan denied no one the right to act according to his own conscience. In fact, anyone who did not was a coward and unworthy of the freedom gained by the Revolution:

> There can be no Minority, or Majority, composed of a large number, but what must include some unprincipled men; and as it cannot be fully concluded, that all those of the Massachusetts convention, who voted for the adoption of the Constitution, were Patriots instigated by genuine Love to their Country, so the conclusion on the other side, that all who voted against it, were Enemies to their Country would be equally fallacious. My opinion is . . . that the Minority (with few exceptions) both in convention and out, are as zealously inclined to support the general Government as the Majority are; they wish amendments, but they neither wish them in any other mode than the one pointed out by the Constitution; nor that the effecting them should interrupt the necessary business of the Revenue, or that of organizing the Government.[339]

6

Republican Festive Culture

The Inhabitants of this Earth are singing out now is Salvation come.

JEREMIAH HILL TO GEORGE THATCHER, FEBRUARY 14, 1788

We are all mad—Fœderal mad here.

JAMES BUCHANAN TO TENCH COXE, APRIL 29, 1788

We are in danger of running into excess in regard to processions. . . . It is an implied triumph over minority which always irritates.

SAMUEL A. OTIS TO GEORGE THATCHER, JULY 17, 1788

Celebrating the Constitution

Church Bells, Cannon, and Toasts

In all regions with Federalist leanings, the ratification of the Constitution induced spontaneous outbursts of joy along with the irresistible desire to organize public celebrations. In fact, celebrations spread from the coastal regions to the backcountry and reached a crescendo in July 1788 when Independence Day coincided with the birth of the new Union. These events provided the population with another opportunity for direct participation in public life. The people wanted to express their joy while simultaneously patting themselves on the back. The written and spoken addresses directed by the intellect were now complemented by an appeal to the senses in the form of art, music, and propaganda, as conveyed through sounds, images, emblems, and choreography. The celebrations developed a unique republican style of their own, a "universal language of celebration" fostering American national identity.[1] At the heart of the revelry stood the "Federal Processions" in the coastal cities, magnificent parades uniting all occupational groups and "respectable" classes of society. These events were characterized by a desire for a closer federal union, efforts to promote social harmony and symmetry, and the longing for an effective national government founded on popular sovereignty. Unprecedented in grandiosity, variety, dynamic, and colorfulness, this republican style became the standard for public celebrations in the emerging American nation.

The joyous news of ratification was always first communicated to the populace by the ringing of church bells. Whether their own state or another key state was involved, the bells were often rung for hours at a time, continuing far into the night. The people would pour into the streets at the first sound of bells, the universal method of signaling the passing of both pleasant and sorrowful events. Jeremy Belknap mused on the various tidings imparted through church bells in a letter from Boston: "Fire, death, joy, dinner, public worship, town-meetings, and what not, all set it a-going, and we are often puzzled to know what it is for. When the ringing began for Maryland, on Tuesday last week, people ran to see where the fire was. So it was when Connecticut ratified the Constitution."[2] On learning what had transpired, the people wandered through the streets in excited groups, cheering and congratulating each other. In Boston, "the moment the *Ratification* was declared outdoors, the whole of the Bells in Town were set a Ringing & general Joy & Congratulation took place throughout the Town—every class of people assembled as it were in an instant in State Street, which was crowded with thousands & to express their Joy with one heart & soul, sent three *Huzza's* to *Heaven* which made all nature tremble to the very centre."[3] The most sincere gratitude was owed the returning convention delegates, who were often met on horseback outside town and triumphantly escorted home. John Quincy Adams registered "universal Satisfaction" in Newburyport, but he himself kept a skeptical distance: "A number of very respectable citizens, and a number, who were not very respectable, went out on horse-back to meet the members [of the convention] and escorted them into Town . . . the bells at the different churches were set to ringing, and this noisy expression of joy was continued with some intermissions till 8 o'clock in the evening. The mob huzza'd. . . . I pass'd the evening at home reading and writing."[4]

The militia companies, never absent on such occasions, were immediately drummed together for parades and drills.[5] Scenes of back-slapping, handshaking citizens, as experienced by Otho Holland Williams in Baltimore on his return from the Annapolis convention, occurred in numerous places: "All my old acquaintances received me with pleasure and many who knew me not before seized, and shook, my hands as a patriot Citizen of a Patriotic State."[6] If newspaper accounts are to be believed, each announcement of a further ratification inspired "spontaneous and universal joy," in which the majority of citizens were included irrespective of social standing or class: "Words are too weak to describe, and none but the federal heart can conceive the transport and extacy that instantly glowed in every countenance."[7] According to the *United States Chronicle,* the rejoicing over New Hampshire's ratification spread through Providence like wildfire, "catching from Breast to Breast, till it pervaded the whole town"; and a contributor to the *Winchester Advertiser* described the "sparkling eyes and elated spirits" of his fellow citizens on the occasion of Virginia's ratification. Many private letters and diaries also bear witness to the jubilation, and room was even found in dry business correspondence for a brief depiction of the prevailing atmosphere in a particular city and a few words of congratulation.[8]

The "joyful noise" of the church bells and huzzas was surpassed only by the percussion of cannon shots, compliments of the militia companies, the batteries installed along the coast, and the ships at anchor. Federalists took care to ensure that the cannon were not fired randomly, orchestrating the barrages to reflect the status of the ratification proceedings. The simplest way to satisfy the general fondness for numeric symbolism was to fire off thirteen volleys, for each state added to the new Union. In this way they could remind everyone within earshot that the integration of all thirteen states was the ultimate goal. If a governor hesitated to provide the necessary quantities of gunpowder, the residents helped him along by generously announcing the collection of private donations.[9] This enthusiasm for cannonades was not without peril, as Federalist militiamen in Maryland and South Carolina discovered. Accidents caused by defective or improperly used cannon led to the loss of an arm by a man in Talbot County and even a fatality in Prince Frederick Parish. In an odd way, these men thus joined the thin ranks of the victims of the ratification debate.[10]

The evenings on ratification days were devoted to receptions, banquets, dances, illuminations, and bonfires. Of particular importance were the common meals, in which the skeptics and critics were also invited to take part. Care was taken that these events did not turn into carousals—the "social mirth" and "conviviality" were instead intended to sooth partisan spirits and promote social harmony. "Party differences subsided on the social table," declared a letter from Wilmington following North Carolina's accession to the new constitutional order.[11] Exemplary, disciplined behavior was expected of the celebrants as a sign that the political restructuring of the Union went hand-in-hand with moral rejuvenation. The *Newport Herald* apparently felt the citizens of Rhode Island needed some prompting to adopt the proper attitude: "Let us be united to put away old things, that all things may become new."[12] Thirteen toasts were nearly always on the agenda, with General Washington, the King of France (as the most important foreign ally of the United States), and the members of the Federal Convention invariably being among the honorees. Other toasts were proposed to the prosperity of agriculture, commerce, and manufacturing in America. Also common were calls to Antifederalists in the remaining states to come to their senses and (re)join the Union. Lexington residents emphasized the number fourteen in the hope that Kentucky might soon become "the Fourteenth luminary in the American constellation."[13] The adoption of the Constitution also seemed to reinforce America's role as the herald of liberty and a refuge for the downtrodden: "May the Example of the New World enlighten the Nations of the Old, and may America remain an Asylum for the injured and oppressed of every Country."[14]

Participation in the banquets was occasionally reserved for "the principal *Male* Inhabitants of the Town." By way of compensation, it appears that dances were held expressly for the sake of the women. At least George Washington remarked after being the honored guest of Alexandria's residents on a particular Sunday that the following day had been set aside for "fiddling & Dancing, for the amusement, & benefit of the Ladies."[15] Observed at a ball in New Haven was "the greatest accord of fœderal feelings in both sexes." And a chronicler of the festivities in Norfolk, Virginia, could not contain his enthusiasm for the "Fair Sex, whose animating form, and most bewitching charms, caused the hearts of many batchelors to sigh and lament their wayward fate." He was also impressed by the illumination of the harbor and the ships decked with flags.[16] Like Norfolk, other American cities were brilliantly lit up at night as a part of the ratification celebrations. A description of Edenton, North Carolina, provides further testimony to the importance of symbolism: "In the evening the cupola of the Court House was beautifully illuminated, and twelve lighted lanthorns . . . were suspended to the flag staff, with a dark one for Rhode Island . . . the day concluded with that harmony and concord which federal principles always must command."[17]

The morning after a celebration was often less than amusing for those who had elected to disregard the appeals for moderation. The *Federal Gazette* chortled that various friends of the Constitution in Richmond who had toasted the Massachusetts ratification were "pretty mellow with Madeira." Samuel Blachley Webb, having celebrated the same occasion with local merchants in the Coffee House in New York City, complained to his employer in Boston: "I am much afflicted with Headache this day (owing to drinking and rioting in a good cause)." Several months and celebrations later, a comrade of Webb's, Ebenezer Hazard, admitted he had had his fill of the "*joyful Uproars*. . . . I am sick of them."[18] These were purely private sentiments, however, and in no way dampened the general feeling of elation. The eruptive, spontaneous, and infectious displays of jubilation were symptomatic of a release from extreme emotional stress. For contemporaries, the outcome of the debate was anything but a foregone conclusion. These outbursts of joy must therefore be understood as a welcome release from the uncertainty that had weighed heavily on the minds of the population far into the year 1788.

Boston residents were utterly ecstatic following the long-awaited and hard-fought ratification of their state. The bells rang for three straight days, the population "was over head and ears in joy—bells, drums, guns, processions, etc." After reading Henry Jackson's reports, Henry Knox was convinced his fellow Bostonians had completely lost their minds.[19] Proponents of the Constitution in Baltimore referred to themselves as "fœderal mad" when the news of victory finally arrived from Annapolis. "We are all in a hubbub here," exclaimed Jeremiah Libby from Portsmouth, New Hampshire, the "ninth state."[20] People did not limit themselves to celebrating their own state's ratification; they gleefully marked every step along the way toward the formal adoption of the new system of government. Residents of Providence and Newport were long forced to be content with this manner of vicarious participation. When the bells sounded to announce the triumph of Federalists in Virginia, over 1,000 citizens in Providence immediately formed a parade: "without any previous arrangements . . . the old and the young . . . the rich and the poor, united together in hearty acclamations."[21] Not restricted to certain regions, this rising tide of federalism and national unity soon engulfed the entire Union. The addition of each new state seemed to reaffirm the stance of those that had already ratified, while encouraging the remaining states to follow suit.

Federal Processions in the Cities

As the people's awareness of the historic importance of these events grew, they began to seek more formalized ceremonies to lend style and contour to their outpourings of joy and spontaneous rallies. There was a general desire for something that went beyond the normal framework of festivities inherited from the colonial period. The extraordinary ritual commensurate with the momentousness of the occasion turned out to be the Federal Procession, a great parade uniting the whole urban community. There were certain models for these events in Europe, such as the Lord Mayor Shows in London or glittering coronation ceremonies at the seats of royalty. Other antecedents could be found in the Union's own Revolutionary history, including the famous Mischianza of 1778; the victory and peace celebrations that took place from 1782 to 1784, culminating in the Dauphinade in Philadelphia; and the commemorative activities on Independence Day.[22] Yet inherent in the rituals honoring the Revolution was a certain anti-authoritarian and rebellious aspect which somehow seemed incompatible with the principles of an upstanding, self-governing citizenry. The ratification celebrations, therefore, put more emphasis on regularity, order, and harmony, thus creating an entirely new version of popular, republican festivals.

The idea of a Federal Procession had begun to take shape in the final weeks of 1787. When Pennsylvania adopted the Constitution on December 12, the procession from the site of the convention to the court building was very staid and official, comprising the convention delegates, sundry public administrators and dignitaries, then a few professors and officers of the militia, with the citizens bringing up the rear. After a public reading of the ratification resolution, the onlookers gave three cheers, an artillery company of the militia fired a salute, and the church bells were set in motion. The residents of Philadelphia continued to celebrate on their own, but in a manner too loud and frivolous for Antifederalist William Shippen's taste: "The mob in the streets are huzzaing triumphantly on the great event, perfectly ignorant whether it will make them free or slaves."[23] On the evening of December 13, dock workers and sailors loaded a flag-decorated boat onto a wagon, hitched five horses to it, then led it through the streets, cheering and singing. Spectators found this display both amusing and disturbing. The Antifederalist *Independent Gazetteer* scoffed at what was perceived as an awkward attempt to attract the attention of the citizens, who were unaware "what grandeur is preparing for them and their posterity." As subsequent events would show, however, the seamen had actually hit upon an original idea. Their Federal Ship became a symbol that was copied in numerous towns. In the days that followed, small-scale ratification celebrations took place outside of Philadelphia in towns like York, Lancaster, Northampton, Easton, and Chambersburg.[24]

The concept of a grand federal parade reemerged during the Massachusetts convention and was realized for the first time in Boston. The initiator and driving force was the caucus of Boston tradesmen, which had already made a name for itself through the production of campaign literature, the organization of mass rallies, and Federalist resolutions on the Constitution. Even before the ratification had been officially promulgated by the sheriff on February 7, the caucus decided that a parade comprised of artisans and mechanics was the only suitable means of celebrating this monumental occasion. The tradesmen's guilds were immediately informed of the idea and, working feverishly, managed to plan the parade and get it off the ground within two days.

On February 8, the Federal Procession headed down the snow-covered streets of Boston, silently observed by stupefied passers-by and spectators from the windows of houses along the route. The parade was led by a group of ax-swinging lumberjacks symbolically clearing a path to the American

West. Then came a band, followed by farmers from the neighboring community of Roxbury. They had been politely invited to join in the festivities and were purposefully placed toward the front of the parade with their oxen and horses, to represent the common interests of farming and trade. The greatest share of the 1,500 participants, however, consisted of artisans and laborers organized according to occupation. Marching behind banners and standards bearing the insignia and mottos of their respective crafts and guilds, row after colorful row passed by, featuring representatives from every branch of the shipbuilding industry, from sailmakers to the manufacturers of mathematical instruments, and including blacksmiths, coopers, painters, stonemasons, glaziers, plumbers, forty bakers, fifty shoemakers, fifty-six tailors, twenty-six hatters, eight candle-makers carting a miniature tallow press, one hundred thirty-six carpenters exhibiting decorated tools, cabinet-makers, cartwrights, bricklayers, and more. At the heart of the parade, pulled by thirteen horses, was the *Federal Constitution,* a whaling vessel disguised as a warship, decorated from stem to stern and manned by a captain, officers, and thirteen sailors. Other attractions included a horse-drawn scale model of a shipyard in which shipbuilders were working on miniature boats, and the printers' wagon replete with a press from which songs were printed and distributed among the onlookers. The marchers stopped and cheered whenever they passed the house of a Boston convention delegate.[25]

Finally, the rear of the parade, made up of the members of the organizing committee riding in a sled and the Republican Volunteers militia unit, returned to Faneuil Hall, from where the participants had set out a full five hours earlier. In the meantime, a large number of citizens had joined the procession, causing the number of participants to swell to 4,000. Although provisions for only 1,500 people had been procured, everyone was treated to punch, wine, cookies, and cheese. As a grand finale, a group of shipwrights carefully inspected a decayed barge dubbed the *Old Confederation,* declared it unseaworthy, and cast it to the flames.[26]

Not that the "federal frolicking" in Boston ended there. On February 12, the various divisions of the militia were assembled in a single battalion which paraded in front of the Commander in Chief and engaged in target shooting and other activities. Long-Lane, the street where the convention had taken place, was renamed Federal Street by the town meeting.[27] This was the beginning of a practice often emulated by other towns across the country, giving rise to such names as Federal Hill and Federal Green. Still, it was the procession that had most captivated the people's minds and kindled their imagination. There was widespread agreement that this constituted an "entire new stile," the likes of which had never been seen before, at least not in Massachusetts.[28] Henry Jackson found it impossible "to describe the subblimity & Grandeur of the Column—such Joy—Huzzas—& Shouts, never assend'd Heaven before. . . . every thing was conducted with the greatest order. . . . all the Candor—Love—Harmony, Friendship, & Benevolence of the whole world appear'd on that day to be Centred in this little Spot." Benjamin Lincoln also declared that newspaper accounts would "no more compare with the original than the light of the faintest star would with that of the Sun."[29] That did not stop Benjamin Russell's detailed and enthusiastic depiction of the events in his *Massachusetts Centinel* from being reprinted thirty-eight times in newspapers as far away as Georgia. It thus became the blueprint used by later procession organizers.

Marylanders were equally awed by the events in Philadelphia and Boston. As a result, they resolved to treat themselves to an official celebration at the site of the convention in Annapolis as well as a public festival in Baltimore. The first consisted of an official proclamation of ratification followed by a procession of delegates to Mann's Tavern and a banquet for two hundred invited guests. At the fifth toast of the evening, honoring George Washington, a portrait of the general painted by Charles Willson Peale was unveiled. No less striking was a 3-square-meter transparent painting by Peale embellishing one wall of the ballroom. An allegory entitled *The New Constitution* depicted the genius of America as a woman swathed in a dark blue, star-spangled dress and wearing a headband bearing the word "Perseverance." Her right hand pointed to the fruits of good government—farming, trade and commerce, art, and science—while her left hand warded off disorder and anarchy. The public buildings and harbor were brightly illuminated for the residents of Annapolis, who would not see the work until later. The Federalist delegates assumed the costs of this radiant display out of their own pocket.[30]

A true public festival "allamode de Boston" was staged in the trading town of Baltimore on May 1.[31] The group of organizers, which now included merchants, had the advantage of more time to prepare, more money, and better weather than their northern predecessors, whose conventions had met in the winter. They made no secret of their goal to outdo the "Boston parade of Yankee Dudle keep it up."[32] The procession was to be as comprehensive as possible, uniting tradesmen and farmers with the city's other occupational groups. The 3,000 marchers were arranged without deference to hierarchy to demonstrate that the new Constitution was founded on the principle of universal equality. The organizing committee placed the farmers at the front of the parade and the lawyers, doctors, clergymen, and convention delegates at the rear. Of utmost importance in the design of floats were symbolism, vividness, and dynamism. The members of the over forty participating guilds not only displayed banners, tools, and costumes representing their respective trades, they also brought along entire workshops showing apprentices and masters at work. Everywhere one looked there were variations on the themes "seven"—representing Maryland, the seventh state to ratify—and "thirteen," for the original states of the Union. Particularly noteworthy from among the large number of remarkable displays was the carpenters' contribution, inspired by the "Federal Edifice" metaphor. They had constructed a wooden tower with thirteen floors, thirteen fronts, thirteen columns, thirteen arches, thirteen gables, and thirteen spires, all resting on the shoulders of seven architects. Also popular was a ship christened *Federalist,* constructed especially for the parade and equipped with actual cannon that were fired intermittently.[33] After the celebration, the *Federalist* was declared a gift to George Washington and sailed down the Chesapeake Bay and up the Potomac to Mount Vernon by Captain Joshua Barney. There it was destroyed by a hurricane a few weeks later—a bad omen to the minds of some contemporaries.[34] The procession ended at Federal Hill with its scenic view of Baltimore Harbor. Here a banquet had been laid out for several thousand people amid the banners of the various guilds. Every toast was accompanied by a 13-cannon salute:

1. The Majesty of the People.
2. The late Convention.
3. Congress.
4. The seven States which have adopted the Federal Constitution.
5. A speedy Ratification by the remaining Six, without Amendments.
6. George Washington.
7. His Most Christian Majesty, and our other Allies.
8. The virtuous Sixty-three of the Maryland Convention.
9. The Agriculture, Manufacturies and Commerce of America.
10. The Memory of those who have fallen in Defence of America.
11. The worthy Minority of Massachusetts.
12. May the American Flag be respected in every Quarter of the Globe.
13. A Continuance of Unanimity among the Inhabitants of Baltimore-Town.

A surviving bill of sale shows that 560 pounds of ham, 1,025 pounds of beef, 800 loaves of bread, 22 ox tongues, 199 pounds of cheese, and 36 jars of mustard were washed down with 7½ kegs of beer, 9½ gallons of peach schnapps, and 240 gallons of cider. The festivities cost 600 pounds sterling, not counting the guilds' expenses.[35] Rounding off the day's activities were illuminations, a fireworks display on Federal Hill, and dances in the city.

"Baltimore must have exceeded Boston in Exertions and demonstrations of Joy, there were not Less than five thousand people assembled," proclaimed merchant Henry Hollingsworth triumphantly. Like Mark Pringle, he was convinced that this degree of enthusiasm, combined with the wide majority vote for ratification in Annapolis, would not fail to have an impact on the remaining states.[36]

More and more cities began to emulate the "Processional Idea of Boston."[37] The activities in Baltimore were followed by a celebration in Charleston on May 27 in which nearly 3,000 people took part. Since the South Carolina ratifying convention itself had called for this parade, the delegates—including a number of Antifederalists—were among the revelers, as was every assemblyman and government official. A group of gentlemen planters and farmers, followed by an "Inspection of Rice, Indigo and Tobacco, with a hogshead of Tobacco, drawn by horses," highlighted the economy of the region.[38] The press noted attentively that the fifty-seventh position in the parade was reserved for Charleston students and teachers to sing the praises of a republican education.[39] A little further back were the members of the Charleston City Council, accompanied by their slave servants (a rare allusion to the presence of blacks at the celebrations). Eight white horses, their heads adorned with the names of ratifying states, pulled the ship *Federalist* decorated with the flags of the Union. The patriotic atmosphere was enhanced by a band and several militia units at the front and rear of the parade.

For the banquet on "Federal Green," the butchers donated an ox, which was roasted on a spit and "to which the People sat chearfully down, without distinction." Charleston physician and historian David Ramsay had prepared an oration, but was unable to deliver it because the crowd "was so great that it could not be spoken with convenience."[40] Obviously, this hitch had no influence on the public mood: "A joyful spirit of Republicanism seemed to pervade every breast; the utmost order and good harmony was preserved, and the day closed with hilarity."[41]

A procession of the highest order was staged by the citizens of Portsmouth, New Hampshire, on June 26 to celebrate their state's becoming the crucial ninth state to ratify. Once again it was a ship, the *Union,* that captured everyone's attention in this shipbuilding and port community. The flag-covered vessel rolled through the narrow streets with its sails hoisted and a sailor at the top of the mast searching the seas for the ship *Virginia.* In addition to the nine horses pulling the float, there was a tenth fully harnessed horse symbolizing Virginia chomping at the bit to be hitched up to the others. The "Order of Procession" listed over seventy positions, including potters, tinners, coppersmiths, brassmiths, and goldsmiths, clock-makers, and jewelers. Printers operating a new press built by Benjamin Dearborn distributed songs praising the Constitution under the motto:

> A Government of Freemen never knows
> A Tyrant's shackles on the Press t'impose.

Schoolgirls had made a globe in geography class featuring New Hampshire in the center of the Union and Rhode Island "on the western horizon, mourning." Transporting their work were two boys in uniform marching with the students and teachers. Following the parade, there was a cold buffet on Union Hill, accompanied by nine very typical New England toasts, including:

> 5. May America be as conspicious for Justice, as she has been successful in her struggles for Liberty.
>
> 6. May the flag of American commerce be displayed in every quarter of the globe. . . .
>
> 8. May America become the nurse of manufactures, arts and sciences, and the asylum of the oppressed in every part of the world.
>
> 9. Let peace liberty and safety be the birthright of every American.

The evening was dedicated to the entertainment of a "large company of ladies and gentlemen," who had gathered around the State House in a semicircle to enjoy the music pouring forth from the candle-lit balcony.[42]

The 4th of July, 1788, gave Philadelphia a welcome occasion to restore its reputation as America's foremost city in this category as well. Ratification by the ninth and tenth states, New Hampshire and Virginia, had instilled in the residents of this metropolis the desire to prepare a "true Gala day," a procession that would surpass any similar celebration previously held in America.[43] The arrangements committee was chaired by the ingenious and enthusiastic author of "The New Roof," Judge Francis Hopkinson. The painter Charles Willson Peale, having returned from Maryland, acted as idea factory, artistic consultant, and set designer all in one. He procured decorations for the city and harbor, supervised the construction of floats, and fashioned costumes out of cloth and cardboard with his own hands. He even devised mottoes and guild insignias that were specific to America as a whole instead of individual states. Printer Benjamin Franklin Bache distributed a leaflet containing a public code of conduct, maestro Alexander Reinagle composed a "Fœderal March," actors from the Southwark Theater added a "Procession of the Thirteen States to the Temple of Liberty" to their repertoire, and Hopkinson himself penned "An Ode" honoring independence and the Constitution in the same breath.[44]

In its basic concept, the procession was similar to previous events, yet with 5,000 participants organized in eighty-eight divisions and stretching a mile and a half, it surpassed its predecessors in size, diversity, colorfulness, and splendor. Three contributions stood out in particular from the long train of farmers and their animals along with bands, militia, banner-waving artisans riding in portable workshops, representatives of the various professions, students and professors, politicians, judges, and assorted notables. The first of these was a representation of the Grand Federal Edifice, named "Temple of the Immigrants" by its creator Peale. Thirteen Corinthian pillars, three of which were unfinished, supported a domed roof. At the very top stood the goddess of prosperity lavishing the contents of her cornucopia on the citizens of America. Seated inside the building were representatives of the ten states that had by then adopted the Constitution, and printed along the base of the columns were the words: IN UNION THE FABRIC STANDS FIRM. Escorting this structure, which measured 11 meters from top to bottom, were 450 carpenters and architects.

An object of considerable attention was yet again a 10-meter-long, well-proportioned ship bearing the name *Union.* It majestically navigated its way through the streets in full sail with its twenty cannon and bustling crew. The hull of a British dinghy captured by the naval hero John Paul Jones had been given a new, elegant superstructure and draped with blue cloth. The wheels of the wagon pulling the display were covered to create the illusion of a ship sailing on ocean waves. Marching behind the *Union* were several hundred tradesmen engaged in the shipbuilding industry, exhibiting a scale-model shipyard and a ropery.

The third great attraction was a float conveying the Constitution. The document was held by the chief justice of the Pennsylvania Supreme Court, Thomas McKean, who stood high in the air together with two of his fellow Supreme Court justices inside a huge eagle, the symbol of the Union. Painted on the bird's breast were thirteen silver stars against a sky-blue background, alongside thirteen red and white stripes. In its right talon the eagle clutched an olive branch, the symbol of peace; in its left were thirteen arrows, representing the power of war. The spellbound spectators looked on with mingled delight and dismay when, at several points along the route, the monstrous construction threatened to topple over and spill the esteemed judges into the street.

Also popular was the blacksmiths' display featuring a hearth in which swords were melted down and remodeled into plowshares. The printers churned out English and German copies of Hopkinson's ode on their portable press and distributed them among the crowd:

Oh for a muse of fire! to mount the skies
And to a list'ning world proclaim—
Behold! behold! an empire rise!
An Æra new, Time, as he flies,
Hath enter'd in the book of fame.
On Alleghany's tow'ring head
Echo shall stand—the tidings spread,
And o'er the lakes, and misty floods around,
An Æra NEW resound.

. . . .

Hail to this festival! all hail the day!
Columbia's standard on HER ROOF display:
And let the PEOPLE's Motto ever be,
"UNITED THUS, and THUS UNITED—FREE."[45]

Small packets containing the ode and the wording of the official toasts were addressed to the governors of the ten ratifying states and sent off at regular intervals via carrier pigeon. Bringing up the rear of the parade was the unusual spectacle of seventeen Christian ministers of various denominations walking arm in arm with the Jewish rabbi. Taken as a whole, the parade was designed to illustrate the continuity of colonization, Revolution, Independence, and Constitution. Ratification was portrayed as the logical conclusion of the prolonged struggle for political and religious freedom, and represented the consummation of national unity.

James Wilson delivered the official address on Bush Hill around 1 p.m. He was forced to shout above the sound of artillery fire from ships on the Delaware River, as the signal to begin the cannon salutes had been given a little prematurely. The central theme of Wilson's speech was the benefits of the Constitution—peace, prosperity, and the continual progress of the arts and sciences. These rewards were contingent upon the citizens' persistent striving for such "internal Virtues and Accomplishments" as piety, frugality and moderation, industriousness, regard for the common weal, and a "warm and uniform Attachment to Liberty, and to the Constitution." A good constitution, Wilson continued, was "the greatest Blessing, which a Society can enjoy. Need I infer that it is the Duty of every one who enjoys its Benefits to use his best and most unremitted Endeavours for preserving it pure, healthful and vigorous? For the Accomplishment of this great Purpose, the Exertions of no one Citizen are unimportant." Wilson concluded with the magnificent image of fields of grain and plantations of fruit trees spreading ever farther westward, rivers and lakes dotted with merchant ships, and cities filled with citizens enjoying a rich and varied cultural life: "With heartfelt Contentment Industry beholds her honest Labours flourishing and secure. Peace walks serene Hand in Hand protecting, enlivening and exalting all. Happy Country! May thy Happiness be perpetual!"[46]

At the banquet that afternoon, no fewer than 17,000 people—nearly half the population of Philadelphia—gathered around long tables shielded from the sun by canvas canopies. The first of the ten toasts was dedicated to "the People of the United States," the last to "the entire Family of Mankind." Served were 4,000 pounds of roast beef, 2,500 pounds of smoked ham, 500 pounds of cheese, 13,300 liters of beer, and 3,600 liters of cider. Federalists had managed to collect £400 prior to the banquet to cover expenses, falling far short of their expectations.[47]

In the *Pennsylvania Mercury,* Benjamin Rush related an anecdote about a "worthy German" who had been allowed to carry one of the large guild banners. Upon returning home that evening, deeply moved by the day's events, he enjoined his wife "to take care of the flag 'till next time he should be called upon to carry it, and if I die, (said he) before I can have the honor again, I desire that you would place it in my coffin, and bury it with me."[48] It was said that foreigners who had watched the parade praised it "in the highest terms, and many of them who have seen the splendid processions of coronations in Europe, declare, that they all yield, in the effect of pleasure, to our hasty exhibition instituted in honor of our Fœderal Government."[49] The *New Jersey Journal* was certain the Philadelphia procession had outshone "any thing of the kind ever exhibited on this Continent before."[50] Across the ocean, John Brown Cutting found Hopkinson's colorful description of the "singularly splendid" event reprinted in London newspapers and transmitted it to Jefferson in Paris.[51]

Not to be outdone, the organizers of the New York procession were determined to raise the bar higher still, but were faced with less than favorable political conditions. Originally scheduled for the 4th of July, the parade was postponed several times as the ratifying convention lingered on. When July 23 arrived, the final date set for the parade, there was still no official word from Poughkeepsie. Distressed Federalists were forced to go on with the celebration in the vague hope that the mass demonstration by the residents of the state's largest city would finally open the eyes of dissenters at the convention.[52] The long preparation also had its advantages, giving planners ample time to design particularly elaborate costumes, insignias, and allegorical presentations. The arrangements committee, led by Richard Platt, kept in constant contact with the heads of guilds and other occupational groups. Its members laid out the parade route, instructed the residents of pertinent neighborhoods to sweep the streets and sidewalks, and assigned each group of participants a meeting point near the start of the procession.

The marchers, up to 5,000 strong, were arranged in ten divisions, six of which comprised delegations of tradesmen and laborers. Farmers led off the procession as usual, this time joined by the discoverer of the New World, "Columbus in his Ancient Dress—on Horseback." The artisans' most spectacular float had been produced with the help of upholsterers, cabinet makers, chair makers, and fringe makers. It came in the shape of a "Federal Chair of State," seven feet high and four feet wide, covered with light-blue satin, and borne on an elaborate platform. Seated in the chair was the genius of wisdom, accompanied by the genii of morality under the motto "The reward of virtue." On the right-hand side rode a costumed boy representing Liberty and holding a scroll entitled "Federal Constitution"; on the left was Justice, symbolically gripping a scale in one hand and a sword in the other. Ten golden stars gleamed on the canopy, while thirteen rays of gold culminating in stars radiated from the float's dome-shaped roof. Crowning it all was a globe on which a bald eagle was perched, "with expanded wings ready to fly away the moment her liberty is invaded."

Booksellers, bookbinders, and printers led by Hugh Gaine and Samuel Loudon displayed a functional "Federal Printing-Press" from which they handed out fresh copies of two odes composed for the occasion by William Pitt Smith and Samuel Low.[53] The printers' banner pictured Benjamin Franklin circumscribed by his slogan "Where Liberty dwells, there is my Country." Two mottoes extolled the art of printing as "Ars Artium omnium conservatrix" and "the Palladium of the Constitution, and the Centinel of Freedom."

The seventh position was reserved for the Federal Ship *Hamilton* drawn by ten horses. Federalists had collected pledges to finance the construction of this seaworthy frigate armed with thirty-two real cannon and measuring twenty-seven feet at the keel by ten feet at the beam, with "galleries and everything complete and in proportion both in hull and rigging." A number of trees had to be removed along the parade route to ensure the safe passage of the *Hamilton*, its captain, Commodore Nicholson, and its crew of over thirty through the city. Along the way, the *Hamilton* took on a pilot, saluted the members of Congress watching the activities from the Fort, and answered the thirteen cannon volleys fired from a Spanish warship anchored in the harbor.

The ninth section of the parade consisted of merchants, traders, lawyers, and students accompanied by professors from Columbia College in "academical habits." Joining them were members of the New York Philological Society, dressed in black and promoting "the principles of a Federal language," that is, American English. The tenth and final division contained the clergy—once again including rabbis—along with doctors, foreign diplomats, and officers. An unexpected silence filled the air as the marchers and floats passed by the estimated 20,000 spectators, "which gave a solemnity to the whole transaction suited to the singular importance of its cause. No noise was heard but the deep rumbling of the carriage wheels, with the necessary salutes and signals. A glad serenity enlivened every countenance, while the joyous expectation of national prosperity triumphed in every bosom."[54]

The organizers had contrived a particularly lavish setting for the banquet held afterward at the farm of city councilman Nicholas Bayard. Pierre L'Enfant, the future planner of the national capital, had designed an architectural wonderwork in the shape of a fan covering 880 × 600 feet, with seating for 6,000 people. At the fan's vortex were three pavilions connected by a huge table in the shape of a half-circle. Fanning out from this were ten 440-foot-long colonnades, each of which was capped by a garden house decorated with flags. The congressmen and other dignitaries dined in the prominent central pavilion, on which the allegorical figure of glory trumpeted in a "New Era." The embellishments and flags depicted the defining events of the Revolution: the Declaration of Independence, the alliance with France, and the peace treaty with England. Seating was surely in short supply, as the crowd was estimated at 10,000–15,000.

The foreign guests of honor were most awed by the ease with which this large gathering was dispersed at the conclusion of the festivities. Platt attributed the small number of drunkards to the natural self-discipline of freemen, and to the fact that only "federal beverages," meaning beer and cider, had been served. He thanked the farmers and tradesmen, on behalf of the organizing committee, "for their punctual attendance on the parade, their regularity in the march, and their strict decorum on the dismission from the Procession." In order "to diffuse the joy to all classes of citizens," some of the leftover food was donated to the prisoners in Percy Castle.[55]

"Yesterday we had the Grandest Procession I believe that has been in America," Evert Bancker informed his nephew, "and Europeans say they have not seen any to come up to it in the Old Countries." From Samuel Blachley Webb's perspective, it had been "the most brilliant [display] ever seen in America, and probably few of the oldest City's in Europe ever excelled in a procession of the kind." Noah Webster summed up the operation, reported to have cost over £5,000, in his diary as, "Very brilliant, but fatiguing."[56] Of all the newspapers in the city, only Thomas Greenleaf's *New York Journal* dared to belittle and satirize the Federal Procession.[57] When news of the ratification in Poughkeepsie reached the City on July 26, emotions began to boil over. The first reaction was joy and jubilation, but at night an angry mob marched through the streets, breaking windows and hissing in front of Governor Clinton's house before demolishing Greenleaf's print shop. This incident could not detract from the procession itself, however, described by one New York resident as "the most natural, tasty, august, and sublime Scene ever before exhibited in America."[58] In fact, some New Yorkers attributed the ultimate adoption of the Constitution by the deadlocked parties at Poughkeepsie to the effects of the city's sensational procession. This was mere speculation, but it seems safe to say that the wave of public celebrations culminating in the Fourth of July festivities of 1788 strengthened the momentum of the ratification process. During the summer months, the newspapers seemed to have concluded that nothing else even bore reporting on. "The northern papers present nothing to our view but accounts of processions in almost every town," the *Wilmington Centinel* apologized to its Antifederal readers on August 6. The parades in Exeter, Concord, Hartford, New Haven, Newport, Trenton, and Newark were nearly on a par with the original event in Boston. Procession fever even gripped parts of the South, for example along the Virginia coast: "We hear of nothing at present but processions, federal ships, and balloons. The Towns vie with each other in shewing their demonstrations of joy."[59] Though state capitals and commercial centers were unquestionably the site of the most spectacular events, many other localities organized festivals as well. Even small towns in the country now jumped on the celebration bandwagon, which eventually reached such frontier and backcountry communities as Pittsfield, Massachusetts; Kinderhook, New York; Pittsburgh, Pennsylvania; Lexington, Virginia; and Chatham, South Carolina.

The landscape was occasionally more than just a scenic backdrop and could itself be used to illustrate the promise of future grandeur embodied in the Constitution. Congregating in a shady grove, the residents of Head of Elk, Maryland, couched their lofty aspirations in a toast—"May the seat of the Federal Government be fixed at the junction of the three states, viz., Maryland, Delaware, and Pennsylvania"—a description which corresponded to the exact location of Head of Elk itself.[60] Almost at the same time and only a short distance away, participants in the procession at Havre du Grace were gathering for refreshments: "Mutual good will, and the rising glory of America, appeared to pervade every heart . . . whilst the majestic Chesapeake in one view, and the boundless and luxuriant Susquehanna on the other, anticipated to every generous breast the future growing celebrity of this elegant and unrivalled spot."[61]

Expectations of an entirely different nature were at the heart of a Fourth of July celebration by a group of black residents in Providence. According to the *United States Chronicle*, they hoped the new government would soon put an end to the slave trade. Toasts were proposed to "the nine states," the merchants of Providence (some of whom profited handsomely from the import of human beings), George Washington (himself a slave owner), the Humane Society of Philadelphia, and, above all, the fate of their kinsmen and kinswomen still in bondage: "May the Natives of Africa enjoy their natural Privileges unmolested"; "May the Freedom of our unfortunate countrymen . . . be restored to them"; "May Unity prevail throughout all Nations."[62]

The Significance of the Ratification Celebrations

Propaganda, Violence, and Accommodation

In order to gain a deeper understanding of their meaning, the ratification celebrations must be analyzed and interpreted at least on four different levels: as instruments of political propaganda, they helped Federalists to widen their base of support in the population; in a material and psychological sense, the processions demonstrated renewed confidence in the American economy and faith in progress; in the larger historical context, they were manifestations of the search for national identity and a desire to measure up to the metropolitan culture of Europe; finally, their characteristic mixture of secular and religious rituals and symbols laid the foundation for an original republican festive culture in the United States.

As an integral part of the ratification debate, the celebrations contributed—partly by design and partly by accident—to the weakening of the opposition and the triumph of the Constitution. The grand processions were invariably organized by Federalist committees dominated by merchants (Boston excepted) whose productions became more and more professional. The prominent position granted to representatives of the farming community in all parades was not simply designed to illustrate—as a concession to the Harringtonian ideal of an "agrarian republic"—the fundamental importance of crop production and stockbreeding. It also clearly showed where Federalists had pinpointed the source of Antifederalist opposition and on whom they wished to make the strongest impression. In the estimation of Hannah T. Emery, experiencing the well-organized procession of Boston citizens would "tend to convince the country people more, than the most elegant reasoning."[63]

Prior to the parade in Biddeford, Maine, Jeremiah Hill assured George Thatcher that local Federalists would endeavor "to give no offence to greek nor Jew, federal nor Antifederal, but become all things to all Men if by any means we can gain Some." He became even more explicit a short time later: "The federal party has taken and are taking every measure to promote and encourage Peace Union and Harmony by paying particular Attention to the Anti's especially those of any influence." William Widgery (who had voted against ratification in the Massachusetts convention, but who promised to support the Constitution once it was ratified) apparently enjoyed the extraordinary attention lavished on him at the Boston procession. "I must Tel you," he wrote George Thatcher, "I was never Treated with So much politeness in my Life as I was afterwards by the Tradesmen of Boston, Merchants & every other Gentleman." After the ninth state had ratified, Jeremy Belknap was even so gracious "as to endeavor to abolish the distinction of fed and antifed."[64]

Not everywhere did such a spirit of harmony and conciliation reign. In places where Antifederalists held a clear majority, they remained among themselves and celebrated the Fourth of July in a simple, "*true* REPUBLICAN stile."[65] There were also scattered reports from the backcountry of counter-celebrations, featuring the burning of the Constitution or its symbolic burial. On some occasions, the opposition reacted angrily or even violently to Federalist celebrations. Serious incidents took place in Carlisle in western Pennsylvania, in Providence, Rhode Island, and in Albany, New York. They provided a glimpse of the potential for violence and showed that the peaceful transition to a new system of government was not to be taken for granted.

The confrontation in Carlisle began on December 26, 1787, in connection with an unauthorized town meeting called to proclaim the adoption of the Constitution by the State of Pennsylvania. The plan was thwarted, however, by a mob of dissenters armed with staves, clubs, and stones, who drove the outnumbered Federalists from the square, then celebrated their victory by burning a copy of the Constitution. The next day the two armed groups faced off, though both sides were reluctant to start a fight. Federalists subsequently restaged their celebration while the Antifederalists, under the leadership of a militia captain supposedly guided by divine inspiration, burned effigies of James Wilson and Thomas McKean. This induced state authorities to start legal proceedings, which in February 1788 led to the arrest of twenty-one rioters. Seven of them refused the offer of a parole in order to draw attention to their plight as victims of political persecution. Their followers promptly mobilized militia companies from three counties and descended on Carlisle on March 1 with a band of 1,000 men determined to free the jailed men.

Federalists were prepared to defend the public buildings by force of arms, but in the face of this invasion of country militiamen, assented to a discussion. Arbiters from both sides drew up an agreement calling for the release of the seven prisoners, a joint petition to the state government, and the withdrawal of the militia. On March 20, the Supreme Executive Council in Philadelphia was more than willing to grant a petition signed by ten Federalists and eight Antifederalists to have the case dismissed. Still, the situation remained tense in and around Carlisle throughout the entire year. Federalists accused the opposition of playing up the affair to demonstrate their strength and arouse anti-Constitution sentiments in the backcountry. The advance of the "banditti" on Carlisle, editorialized the *Federal Gazette* on March 22, proved the absolute necessity of a strong federal government, for there was no worse form of despotism than the "licentious proceedings of an uncontrolled rabble." For their part, Antifederalists intensified their petition campaign against the Constitution and compelled the publishers of the *Carlisle Gazette* to show more "balanced reporting."[66]

Bloodshed was barely avoided in Providence, Rhode Island, where Federalists somewhat provocatively invited their opponents to a combined celebration of New Hampshire's ratification and Independence Day. Instead of participating in the festivities, several hundred armed Antifederalists gathered under the leadership of two justices of the State Supreme Court on the eve of the Fourth of July and took up threatening positions near Federalists, who were busy preparing the obligatory roast ox for the planned banquet. Emissaries from Providence were sent out around 11 p.m. to inquire into the purpose of the siege. Antifederalists replied that they could not permit the Constitution to be mentioned in one breath with Independence, let alone coupled with the celebration of it. Leaders from both sides met on the morning of the 4th of July to work out an agreement. After some hesitation, Federalists consented to commemorate Independence only and refrain from firing salutes or proposing toasts to the Constitution or the nine states that had ratified it. In return, the leaders of the mob ordered their men to disperse and not to disturb the festivities. The 4th of July was then celebrated without further incident.[67]

In Albany, where party spirit ran extremely high and the opposing groups were equally well organized and highly motivated, a serious clash could not be avoided. The altercation was preceded by the news of ratification in Virginia, which exacerbated an already tense situation. Even though Antifederalists had provoked their foes on the morning of July 4 by publicly burning a copy of the Constitution along with a broadside announcing the Virginia decision, a common parade from the courthouse to the old fort was still held around noon. Following the commemoration of Independence, adherents of both parties retired to their favorite taverns. That evening, around 800 to 1,000 Federalists held a procession to the fort to restore the honor of the "desecrated" Constitution. They erected a 4-meter-high liberty pole, affixed the Constitution to it, and fired off a 10-gun salute. Holding up a second copy attached to a pole, they marched back to town, choosing a route that happened to pass by their adversaries' assembly hall.

Though far outnumbered, Antifederalists—among them Jeremiah Van Rensselaer and Abraham G. Lansing—took up the gauntlet and fought a half-hour-long pitched street battle with the intruders. Before being forced to retreat, they inflicted severe injuries on several marchers with stones, clubs, and bayonets. Their plan to call up militia reinforcements from the countryside for a counterattack was happily dropped on the insistence of moderate voices, who ascribed the affair to both sides' overconsumption of alcohol. An escalation of the conflict, which might have resulted in fatalities, was thus avoided. The New York *Daily Advertiser*'s detailed account of the "bloody affray" in Albany was carried by over thirty newspapers, often garnished with urgent pleas to preserve peace and good order.[68] The mood in Albany remained tense and subdued. When Federalists celebrated New York's ratification with a Grand Procession at the beginning of August, they invited their opponents to join in the merriment, but were soundly rebuffed. The partisan rivalry had poisoned personal relationships and split the town into two camps.[69] A similar situation prevailed in New York City, where the Antifederalist minority was shocked by the brutality of the "Greenleaf riot."

The troubles in Carlisle, Providence, Albany, and New York City clearly demonstrate the potential explosiveness of the ratification struggle.[70] Especially the efforts to use public celebrations for propaganda purposes could produce unintended consequences. Nevertheless, open acts of violence were by far the exception to the rule and, thanks to the intervention of moderate forces on both sides, they remained isolated incidents. Of particular importance was the circumstance that alternatives were still available to Antifederalists, despite an overwhelming Federalist triumph, in the form of an amended Constitution or a second General Convention. In fact, in many states, Federalists were victorious at least partly because they promised amendments. Consequently, staunch opponents of ratification were disappointed and frustrated, but not desperate. Neither side could predict the outcome of the amendment movement with any certainty. Political acumen thus mandated that both parties avoid any actions that would appear to confirm charges of fostering anarchy or despotism.

When the Richmond convention ended, people in Virginia consciously tried to avoid any provocation. "There is no rejoicing on Acc. of the Vote of ratification," wrote Patrick Henry's son-in-law Spencer Roane. "It wd. not be prudent to do so; & Federalists behave with moderation and do not exult in their Success."[71] Another Virginian praised both state parties for having "conducted themselves with great moderation and candour; and no rejoicings were permitted to aggravate the feelings of so respectable a minority."[72]

It was more common that opponents of the Constitution tried to stem the tide of ratification celebrations by attacking their excessive costs or by satirizing and ridiculing them in the newspapers.[73] On most festive occasions, however, the organizers were pleased to note that citizens who had been skeptical, or had even actively opposed the Constitution, caught the spirit of the occasion and partook in the celebrations. "Many, who have been unfriendly to the Federal cause, joined in the hilarity of the day," noted the *New Hampshire Spy* on July 1 in connection with the parade in Dover. The same phenomenon was observed on June 26 by the *United States Chronicle* in Providence: "The wavering, and several of those who have heretofore appeared against the Constitution, now heartily joined in the general Joy." Opposition delegates sat alongside their Federalist peers at the banquet in Charleston before departing from the city "in good humor."[74] Despite the intensity of the debate in Poughkeepsie, Philip Schuyler sought to cultivate a "spirit of forbearance and conciliation." He advised a relative to trust in the critics' good intentions and respect their honest opinions.[75] In an extra edition of the *Independent Journal* reprinted thirty-four times, it was reported in regard to New York City's celebration that a number of those who had previously opposed ratification "drank freely of the Federal Bowl, and declared that they were now perfectly reconciled to the New Constitution."[76]

Federalists frequently spent considerable sums on these politically expedient acts of accommodation and rapprochement. Henry G. Livingston, for example, invited five hundred guests to his "Federal Village," while John Langdon treated the "patriotic citizens" of Portsmouth to a well-publicized feast in honor of Maryland's ratification.[77] Other friends of the Constitution donated funds for the procession banquets. There can be no doubt that these conciliatory gestures generally fulfilled their purpose, even if accounts by pro-Constitution newspapers were surely not free of exaggeration or wishful thinking. At all events, the rising tide of Federalist support was also indirectly confirmed by the *Wilmington Centinel,* an opposition paper. After gleefully reporting in mid-July that only three houses in the whole city had been decorated after the adoption of the Constitution in Virginia, the printer was forced to acknowledge just one month later that the entire community enthusiastically welcomed the outcome of the Poughkeepsie convention.[78] Switching to the winning side was easier than holding one's ground against the stiff wind of majority opinion. In a suggestive way, the celebrations showed unrelenting critics that they were running the risk of political isolation and social quarantine. At once an appeal and a warning, they coaxed the opposition into line with Federalist attitudes. On the other hand, critics of the Constitution could keep up the pressure for amendments more efficiently by joining the festivities than by cultivating a defiant mood.

The Rising Empire of Commerce and Trade

The majority of participants in the processions and a good number of organizers were members of the urban middle class, who were pleased to have an opportunity to demonstrate their enterprising spirit and dynamism. These were the people who had suffered the most during the postwar depression, alternately buffeted by money shortages and inflation, and were now the first to discern signs of relief. From the tradesmen's perspective, the parades essentially represented the symbolic banishment of economic hardship and optimism for the future. The feeling that the storm had been weathered and brighter days were in store was manifested in the rising-sun metaphor. Echoing the *Pennsylvania Gazette,* the Trenton *Federal Post* proclaimed the current situation was "indeed, like that of the glorious sun, when his powerful beams first dispel the darkness and terror of a tempestuous, awful night. . . . The œconomy, the industry, the virtue, and the steady perseverance of The People in the principles which have led to this great reformation in our government, can alone raise Our Sun to its meridian height." Similar emotions were aroused by the procession in Baltimore: "In this elegant place . . . the American character, emerging from Depression, was exhibited in all its glories."[79]

The spectacular parades not only signaled the end of a difficult period, they also bore witness to the incredible diversification and strengthening of the American economy since the end of the Seven Years War. As the final decade of the eighteenth century approached, the processions provided Americans with a welcome stage to display the skills they had acquired and which were essential to the survival and prosperity of an independent nation. There was a general conviction that the people of the United States could now stand comparison with the rest of the world when it came to their diligence and resourcefulness, degree of specialization, and the craftsmanship and quality of their products. The people desired self-affirmation, observed the reaction of foreigners, and sought words of praise like those offered by George Washington upon receipt of the ship *Federalist:* this "specimen of American ingenuity" proved "that Americans are not inferior to any people whatever in the use of mechanical instruments and the art of ship-building."[80]

The workers' pride in their achievements was accompanied by demands for the protection of domestic industries and the replacement of imported "luxury goods" by American-made products. The messages on signs carried by marchers in the processions were unambiguous. "While Industry prevails, we need no foreign nails," declared Baltimore nailsmiths. Such sentiments were echoed by their fellow craftsmen, the silversmiths: "No importation and we shall live." Furriers, breech makers, and glovers in New York walked behind a banner which read, "Americans, encourage your own manufacturers." Chair makers held up a picture of a Windsor chair circumscribed by the words "Free Trade" and "The federal states in union bound / O'er all the world our chairs are found." As explained by a Baltimore newspaper, the tradesmen were all relying on the new government to bring about "an increase of their different manufactures, from the operation of uniform duties on similar articles imported into the United States." Consequently, "foreign articles" were eschewed at the banquets in favor of "federal food" and "federal beverages."[81] The citizens of Philadelphia were reminded that "Home brewed is best," while New Yorkers were advised, "Ale, proper drink for Americans." Many a toast to the health and prosperity of the American economy contained elements of a similar nature.

There was a general conviction that the crisis could only be resolved by working together and avoiding clashes between classes and special interests: "May a just sense of their mutual interest and dependence on each other, forever unite the husbandman, the merchant and mechanick."[82] The processions were thus unquestionably tied to real social issues. The vehicle through which occupational groups expressed their pressing needs and concerns was economic nationalism. Those most affected did not content themselves with thinking up slogans. The clothing industry attempted to exploit the desire for increased national self-reliance by creating federal buttons and federal hats. A manufacturer in Baltimore proved that republican simplicity did not entail being deprived of the latest fashions, announcing in November 1788 the opening of a "Federal Manufactury" for the production of leather and fur garments "in the most modern and elegant style."[83]

By way of the Federal Processions the urban middle classes staked their claim to a position of economic and political equality with the elite. During the Revolution as well as during the struggle for ratification, they had shown themselves to be a national force, and were now demanding their just reward for supporting the Federalist cause. Boston merchants were quick to perceive that the expectations of the mechanics and laborers could not be satisfied by empty phrases. They therefore pooled their resources and commissioned three new ships from local shipyards, as the *Massachusetts Centinel* joyfully reported on March 26, 1788: "This unequivocal proof of federalism . . . will be a great relief to a number of our industrious mechanicks, whom the decline of commerce . . . had deprived of employment." A short time later, tradesmen's committees from various cities personally presented the new Congress with their demands for a stable currency, government promotion of economic development, and protectionist measures. Even if they had wanted to, Hamilton and Congress could not have ignored these demands.[84]

Constructing a National Identity

In their manner of organization as well as their key symbols and slogans, the processions provided a historical validation for the adoption of the Constitution. The figures, images, names, and mottoes were arranged to create the impression that the new system of government was an inevitable and universally accepted link in an unbroken chain of events from the discovery and settlement of America to the Revolution and the War of Independence. Just as the Revolution, the Constitution represented the final step toward the foundation of an American nation-state. The struggle for ratification was seen as the continuation and culmination of the struggle for independence. Federalists in Providence decorated a major bridge with the flags of the Rhode Island regiment, "which had been often displayed with Glory and Bravery in the Face of very powerful Enemies."[85]

This interpretation of the past necessitated the sacrifice of the Articles of Confederation, now often portrayed as a temporary aberration worthy only of ridicule and contempt. Such an attitude was conveyed by the incineration of a dilapidated ship named "Old Confederation," or by floats depicting craftsmen attempting to repair a worn-out object before finally casting it aside and making a new one. The Union's first constitution had no place in a national heritage in which all citizens could be proud. The sight of the Philadelphia parade aroused a sense of "political joy" in Benjamin Rush: "The connection of the great event of Independence—the French Alliance—the Peace—and name of General Washington, with the adoption of the Constitution, was happily calculated to unite the most remarkable transports of the mind which were felt during the war with the great event of the day, and to produce such a tide of joy as has seldom been felt in any age or country."[86]

In this connection, the word "federal" came to replace the word "national," which still had unpleasant connotations that seemed threatening to the states' existence. Some proponents of the Constitution, though, preferred the terms "national" and "nation." Jeremy Belknap congratulated Rush in July 1788 "on the erection of the ninth pillar of the *national* (for Mr Adams says we must not call it *federal*) Edifice." Rush himself summed up the Philadelphia procession with the words, "'Tis done! We have become a nation";

and Jonathan Jackson thought it was time "that we should assume a national character, and opinions of our own."[87] The use of "federal" was so popular and was understood by most Americans to be synonymous with "national." Rush was of the opinion that the processions with their images, songs, and banners had so impressed young people in Philadelphia "that 'fœderal' and 'union' have now become part of the 'household words' of every family in the city."[88] The term "federal" was soon attached to everything the people held dear. As explained by a writer in the *Massachusetts Gazette,* the word expressed "national honour, dignity, freedom, happiness, and every republican privilege," in marked contrast to "anti-federalism," which stood for "anarchy, confusion, rebellion, treason, sacrilege, and rapine."[89] People were soon making profuse—and occasionally rather odd—use of the word. No longer content to be merely carpenters, shoemakers, and butchers, tradesmen now referred to themselves as federal carpenters, federal cordwainers, and federal butchers; the people had federal ideas, federal principles, federal sentiments; they demanded federal measures, fired off federal salutes, washed federal meat down with federal beverages, wore federal hats, and were overcome with federal joy. Even discussions were held in a style of federal purity with the help of a federal dialect.[90] The word "federal," therefore, had become the favorite expression of the collective identity of the American people.

This sense of identity was augmented by the crafting of national symbols that appealed to the peoples' hearts and minds in equal measure and whose meaning escaped no one. Two of the most important were the Federal Ship and the Federal Edifice, or Federal Temple. Newspaper publishers had established a connection between the Constitution and a ship at an early stage of the debate with their ever popular, allegorical "Ship News." They contrasted the successes of the flagship *Union* or *Constitution,* to whose fleet a gleaming new frigate was added each time a state ratified, with the gradual decline and sinking of the Antifederalist *Old Confederation.* The widespread usage of the ship symbol was surely related to the fact that it was both simple and complex, thus capable of creating diverse associations. Ships were identified with the discovery of America and the voyages of the Pilgrims in search of the promised "New Jerusalem" in the West. On a more mundane level, ships were of course a central mode of transportation in the eighteenth century, something familiar to nearly every American. The great advances in shipbuilding were largely due to the enormous increase in overseas trade, as well as the expansion of coastal and inland navigation. Reflections on the future of the United States were nearly always combined with images of majestic naval fleets protecting trading vessels and warding off potential enemies. It was certainly no coincidence that most ships in the processions were heavily armed. The diverse associations flowed together in the "Ship of State," which was sure to steer clear of all perils with George Washington at the helm.

A wide variety of building metaphors appeared under different names: the Grand Republican Superstructure; the Great Federal Superstructure; the Grand Federal Edifice; the National Edifice; the Glorious Fabric; the New Roof; the Fœderal Temple; the Grand Federal Dome; the Temple of American Liberty; and, towering over the rest, the Great Dome of Federal Empire. These figurative expressions were soon given visual form as cartoons in the press, floats in the parades, and structures assembled at the sites of ratification celebrations. The central idea here was not the political symbolism attached to fallen pillars, etc. Rather, the buildings were designed to illustrate the innovative principle of federalism itself, the interconnections and interdependencies between the central government and the states. It was not by chance that temples were constructed and not, say, pyramids. The interplay of the individual architectural components lent temples the appearance of harmonious unity, their arches suggesting a dynamic tension. A degree of hierarchy remained, however, with the federal government representing the roof supported by the states as pillars. Yet pillars and roof together formed a single frame which allowed every component to retain its fundamental integrity.[91] The Articles of Confederation also fared poorly in architectural comparisons, "being placed . . . out of the perpendicular, like the hanging tower of Pisa."[92] The juxtaposition of temple and dome is indicative of efforts to combine classical form and aestheticism with Christian values. The Federal Temple could have been borrowed from ancient Greece or the Roman Republic just as well as from the Old Testament. It sheltered the eternal torch of liberty—a beacon of light for the politically oppressed and religiously persecuted peoples of the world. As Christian symbols were adapted for secular purposes, the patriotism evinced by the citizens assumed an unmistakably religious aspect and fervor.

The Constitution itself only gradually became the focal point of the celebrations. By the time of the Fourth of July parade in Philadelphia, however, it had been elevated to the status of Jefferson's Declaration of Independence. The scroll was laid in the hands of the Chief Justice of the Pennsylvania Supreme Court to remind the people that constitutional law and judicial authority would soon play a greater role in their lives than before. In the words of Benjamin Rush: "The triumphal car was truly sublime—It was raised above every other object. The Constitution was carried by a great Law-officer, to denote the elevation of the government, and of law and justice, above every thing else in the United States."[93] In the New York parade, a life-sized representation of Washington held a parchment entitled "The Federal Constitution." These were the initial stages of the worshiping of the Constitution as a sacred document, just as envisaged by Thomas Paine in *Common Sense* in 1776. His CONTINENTAL CHARTER would render an American king redundant: "Yet that we may not appear to be defective even in earthly honors, let a day be solemnly set apart for proclaiming the Charter; let it be brought forth placed on the divine law, the Word of God; let a Crown be placed thereon, by which the world may know, that so far as we approve of monarchy, that in America THE LAW IS KING."[94] To avoid abuses of power, it was advised that the crown be destroyed at the conclusion of the ceremony and its fragments spread among the people, for whose rights it stood.

Just as they employed artistic modes of expression, the Federal Processions were themselves public works of art. They rendered the Federalist ideology tangible by converting its message into movement, images, and sound. A profound understanding of mass choreography was required for organizers to arrange the various divisions of the parades into columns of marchers sometimes stretching for miles, then guide the stately exhibitions to their destination. Ideally, all floats, costumes, colors, and banners, even the music, were coordinated to form an audiovisual whole. Artistically inclined individuals like Charles Willson Peale, Francis Hopkinson, and Alexander Reinagle in Philadelphia, or Noah Webster, Samuel Low, and Pierre L'Enfant in New York, went to great lengths to turn these expectations into reality. At other locations as well, architects, painters, poets, actors, musicians, and composers contributed to the aesthetic design of the parades and the entertainment of the spectators. They built temples and colonnades, modeled figures, designed illuminations, set off fireworks, and painted allegorical pictures and portraits of Washington for public display; they wrote songs, recited poems, and put on plays; they composed marches, odes, and hymns, set Psalms to music, and held concerts. Never before in the history of the Union had so many renowned members of the cities' cultural elite joined together in a common cause.

Yet neither the range of activities nor their magnificence could conceal the fact that, measured by European standards, the development of the fine arts in America was still in its infancy. Though cultural productivity had increased since the Revolution, it was still underdeveloped in many respects, offering potentiality more than actual quality. Among the obstacles facing artists was a widespread popular belief that certain forms of expression, most notably the theater, were not compatible with Christian values and republican principles. Moreover, talented Americans were forced to walk a fine line in literature and the fine arts between neoclassical imitation and republican originality. Those seeking inspiration or improvement continued to travel to London, Paris, or Rome if they could afford it. Still, during the period of the debate over the Constitution there appeared a number of artistic innovations which heralded a new phase of development. These included the first anthology of American songs, published by Francis Hopkinson in September 1788; the first American landscapes, painted by Ralph Earl in 1788–89; and the first American novel, *The Power of Sympathy*, written by William Hill Brown in January 1789. Two months later, the Pennsylvania legislature ended the restrictive cultural policies of the Constitutionalist Party. By repealing the anti-theater laws, new avenues of expression were opened for authors and actors.[95]

Against this backdrop, the adoption of the Constitution seemed to signal the dawn of a new age. Local artists viewed the processions as an ideal platform for reaching out to a wide audience beyond their small circle of intellectuals. They felt the American republic was now maturing and in need of a homegrown national culture that went beyond simple imitation. To them, "liberty" spelled progress in practical matters like a national copyright law for literary productions and, above all, government support of the fine arts. This would enable them to break free from the cultural hegemony of the Old World and hold their own against Europe. George Washington shared their conviction that America should not be a mere extension of England but become a refuge for the fine arts, an equal partner in the Atlantic "Republic of letters."[96] This desire for artistic self-affirmation and recognition manifested itself in various ways during the ratification celebrations. In the process, the line became blurred between cosmopolitanism and cultural nationalism. Noah Webster, William Dunlap, and their friends in the New York Philological Society were probably correct in their assertion that any attempt by America to stand on its own feet must begin with language as the foundation of a true national culture. They went to extremes, however, in their rejection of everyday language and their efforts to return to the Saxon origins of English as the basis for a new "federal language."[97] Irrespective of the wisdom of such ideas, the public festivals of 1788 clearly showed that the passion aroused by the debate over the Constitution was not restricted to political and economic considerations.

The fine arts and education were almost always named in one breath during the deliberations. Both supporters and adversaries of the Constitution perceived an axiomatic connection between freedom, science, and the arts. If they could establish constitutional safeguards for liberty, culture and education would flourish. The fruits of good schooling and occupational training should be made available to nearly everyone they maintained, not just the elite. There were scattered calls for the introduction of general education and a system of national universities. A knowledgeable citizenry was believed to be a precondition for the survival of a republic. "Ignorance is the enemy of liberty, the nursery of despotism," pronounced David Ramsay. Once provided with the "means of education," the "yeomanry" would have nothing to fear "from any man or any association of men, however distinguished by birth, office, fortune, or abilities."[98] Federalists paid homage to the republican ideal of universal education by including students, teachers, and professors in the processions. Also important in this context was the participation of the printers, the disseminators of knowledge. In James Wilson's opinion, the republican parades served an educational purpose, both then and in the future: "They may *instruct* and *improve,* while they *entertain* and *please.* They may point out the elegance or usefulness of the sciences and the arts. They may preserve the memory, and engrave the importance of great *political events.* They may represent, with peculiar felicity and force, the operation and effects of great *political truths.*"[99]

Festive Culture and Civil Religion

In the final analysis, the celebrations were intended to represent dramatically the new republican society and sanctify its institutions, values, doctrines, and ideals. While the order of marchers within each division may have been decided by lot, the overall arrangement of the processions was anything but arbitrary. The underlying idea was to convey the image of a progressive society founded on liberty and equality yet still structured, orderly, and disciplined. This order was created by the citizens themselves, who voluntarily obeyed their Constitution and their elected government. It was precisely this penchant for order and self-discipline that gave a republic the strength to resist the threat of anarchy on the one hand and despotism on the other. The egalitarian spirit was best expressed in ceremonies of shared food and drink. At the banquet tables, the deference normally shown to the elite by the "ordinary" citizens gave way to mutual respect, even to occasional gestures of submission on the part of the educated, wealthy, and influential. Such comments as "the inhabitants dined together in the most perfect harmony," or "party differences subsided at the social table," often appeared in newspaper reports. Here again the religious undertones were unmistakable: "Harmony and friendship displayed themselves in their divinest form, soothing every turbulent passion."[100] Donations were collected for prison inmates and the needy to show that even the lowest elements of society were not forgotten or excluded.

As opposed to Thomas Greenleaf's biting satire, Federalist newspapers in New York praised the "triumphant dignity" of the procession, "sanctioned by the majesty of a Free People." From an ideological standpoint, the parades were intended as counter-examples of Old World pageantry, known to many Americans through hearsay at least. In his assessment of the Philadelphia procession, Benjamin Rush dedicated a long passage to the observation that Europeans celebrated their rulers, while the American people were celebrating themselves: "Every tradesman's boy in the procession seemed to consider himself as a principal in the business. Rank for awhile forgot all its claims, and Agriculture, Commerce, and Manufactures, together with the learned and mechanical Professions, seemed to acknowledge by their harmony and respect for each other, that they were all necessary to each other, and all useful in cultivated society. These circumstances distinguished this Procession from the processions in Europe, which are commonly instituted in honor of single persons. The military alone partake of the splendor of such exhibitions. Farmers and Tradesmen are either deemed unworthy of such connections, or are introduced like horses or buildings, only to add to the strength or length of the procession. Such is the difference between the effects of a republican and a monarchical government upon the minds of men!"[101] The Philadelphia masons expressed the same conviction in their proud motto: "Both buildings and rulers are the works of our hands." There was also doubt as to whether such large masses of people could even be assembled in Europe's cities without the risk of turmoil. An awareness of America's position as a constitutional and social role model for the rest of the world was revealed in toasts such as the following from Fredericksburg, Maryland: "May the Example of the New World enlighten the Nations of the Old!"[102]

Federalists not only presented an alternative to European feudalism and absolutism, they also carefully distanced themselves from the conditions that had prevailed during the Revolution and under the Articles of Confederation. The quest for conformity and direct participation characterizing the Revolution era was now contrasted with the calculated rationality which marked the framing of the Constitution. "The rejoicings were the dictates, not of wild enthusiasm, but of sober reason," observed the Boston *Independent Chronicle* in respect to the festivities in Salem. It was also said to have been a "cool and deliberate examination" of the Constitution that made Federalists out of Marlboro residents.[103] An editorial on the jubilation in Cambridge, Maryland, contained an obvious reference to the risks of direct democracy and the shortcomings of state legislatures in preceding years. It was reported that the activities had been held in the spirit of harmony and accord, free "from the riotous and disorderly disposition that is in some measure characteristic of popular assemblies."[104] The discipline exhibited during the celebrations was meant to provide a taste of the calmness, orderliness, predictability, and security that would reign under the new system of government. Citizens were expected to prove themselves worthy of the Constitution by displaying proper behavior at the parades and banquets. Indeed, this had apparently been the case in Newmarket, New Hampshire: "The propriety of their conduct marked them as Federalists and friends to good order and good government."[105]

It was occasionally maintained that the celebrations had a direct bearing on the existence and well-being of republican society extending far beyond the actual events themselves. This was meant by some observers in the conventional sense of a taming of the party spirit and the suppression of state particularism. They consequently welcomed the "laudable impulse to national festivity, at the prospect before us, of exterminating the noxious seeds of separation and disunion, which we find so fatal to human nature." Others hoped the celebrations might help teach the heterogeneous, diffuse population the "principles of social life," thus strengthening social cohesion.[106] There were still others who saw the underlying purpose of the events as the legitimation and strengthening of republican institutions. Precisely because the United States was born of a Revolution that made the right to resist authority one of the cornerstones of its political system, the right to rule required a foundation that was beyond all doubt. The stability of monarchies was upheld by an administration backed by military force, coupled with the loyalty of the people and a nobility to a ruler or dynasty ordained "by the grace of God." In a republic, by contrast, the government's power stemmed from the citizens' voluntary decision to delegate authority. As a consequence, the American republic had to be more than merely the sum of its individual citizens, states, and interest groups. Its continued existence was contingent upon whether the people, who were in charge of their own destiny, would develop a feeling of responsibility for the common good. To achieve this, the people needed a vision that combined the past with the future, transcended all special interests, and bound the nation from within. The public celebrations were one way of fostering this collective identity and eulogizing the nation's true calling, its highest values and creeds in symbols and ceremonies.

These ideas were not new, having been conceived long before in Europe. In his *Contrat social* of 1762, and even more so in the *Considérations sur le gouvernement de Pologne* of 1772, Jean-Jacques Rousseau expounded on the combined religious and secular elements of a cult designed to place the constitution and institutions of a republic on sound footing. Complemented by the system of education, this "civil religion" was to cultivate social sentiments conducive to political and social stability. The American version of this theory evolved largely independently of the European debate and—like Rousseau's arguments—had its origins in antiquity. Educated in the classics, John Adams was one of the first who, in 1776, began to consider the need for and suitable manner of regular Independence Day celebrations.[107] Though the ratification festivities were pervaded by allusions to religion, these were rarely as explicit as the remarks in a letter published in the *United States Chronicle* on the eve of the 4th of July, 1788. In response to doubts regarding the appropriateness of publicly celebrating major events, the author began with a reference to the annual Jewish Passover festival before pointing out that the Greeks, in particular, had enjoyed a large number of "public Celebrations" throughout the year: "They indeed constituted the greatest Part of their Religion.—Those of *Panthea,* of *Bacchus,* and *Eleusis* were very remarkable, especially the latter, instituted in Honour of Husbandry (the farmer's profession) and in Commemoration of *Ceres,* who taught the Art of Husbandry, particularly the *Cultivation of Corn, and making Bread.*—This Festival was celebrated annually, at Athens, with great Religion and Purity, but with vast Magnificence and Show, attended by a Procession very numerous, and which generally consisted of Thirty Thousand Persons. The Romans had also a great Number of stated Festivals, as the Saturnalia, Cerealia, Luparcalia, Neptunalia, &c. and we had among Christians and Mahometans of all sects, a great Number of Festivals, making Part of the outward or ceremonial Religion of every Country."

This was followed by an enumeration of the advantages Americans could derive from festivals of this nature. People from various parts of the country would congregate, "with a Disposition to be pleased with each other; and their Eating and Drinking together from the same Table, and from the same animal Food, where Friendship and good Humour prevail, is not easily forgotten—and the Recollection, that all met together in Friendship, and that all were pleased and disposed to love and serve each other, on such a particular Occasion, has a Tendency to endear that Occasion to all who were thus present.—The establishment of any particular Form of Government, is a Matter of Sentiment among a free People, and the Strength of that Government depends upon the good Opinion People in general have of it;—it is therefore good Policy, and a sure Mark of Patriotism and public Virtue, to endeavour as much as possible that all Ranks and Orders of People should be pleased with, and should wish to support it, and nothing has a greater Tendency to this than for the People of all Conditions to assemble together, at certain Times, to join in the Celebration of the Government under which they live."

A rather derisive remark by the Frenchman Victor Du Pont, who had witnessed the New York procession, indicates that beyond intellectual circles even average Americans were showing a decided interest in ancient traditions. "The toys of these peoples," he wrote to his father, "who are very young still who always have at their lips the word Roman and who compare these parades to the public games of that great people are sometimes very amusing for an unimpressed observer."[108]

The religious dimension of the celebrations did not go unnoticed by most commentators; in fact, most welcomed it. The Constitution itself was of a purely secular nature, as perturbed Antifederalists often noted. The formal segregation of religious institutions from the civil government was also proceeding rapidly in the states. In light of the strong support for this trend, there was hardly anyone who still clung to the illusion that Americans could be induced to accept a state religion. At the same time, many citizens perceived a correlation between religion and civic virtue. They remained convinced that if republican institutions were deprived of the spiritual and ethical underpinnings of the Christian faith, corruption and decline would be the result. The Reverend Joseph Haven commended the "temporal blessings" of the Constitution, but added: "If wisdom, virtue, and integrity, and a public spirit prevail: in short, if we observe the Christian religion, we shall be a happy, a flourishing, wealthy, and renowned people."[109]

Federalists placed great emphasis on the participation of the clergy in the processions in order to demonstrate, as Benjamin Rush explained, the "connection between religion and good government. . . . Pains were taken to connect Ministers of the most dissimilar religious principles together, thereby to shew the influence of a free government in promoting christian charity. The Rabbi of the Jews, locked in the arms of two ministers of the gospel, was a most delightful sight. There could not have been a more happy emblem contrived, of that section of the constitution, which opens all its power and offices alike, not only to every sect of christians, but to worthy men of *every* religion."[110]

An article published by "An American" in the *Fayetteville Gazette* on September 14, 1789, asserted that the founding of nations had always been accompanied by "public worship of the Deity." Solon, Romulus, and Jerobeam, for example, had purportedly sought the help of religion to ensure their newly established polity would be stable and enduring. Americans would therefore also be well advised to maintain and share in the costs of a "public religion": "There never has been a nation great or happy, where the subject's obedience to human laws did not receive a sanction from the obligation of religion." Yet this public religion would have to be encompassing and tolerant enough to transcend the barriers of the disparate confessions and avoid offending the sensibilities of any group, including the Jewish community. An ideal solution had already been suggested by the ratification celebrations, where Jewish-Christian symbols had been employed to create a common cult enabling citizens to honor the *"novus ordo seclorum,"* regardless of their religious persuasion. At the center of this new order was the Constitution, providing not only a national frame of government but also the basis for a collective identity of the American people. In this sense, the adoption of the Constitution marked the beginning of a new republican festive culture. At the Federal Processions and in the newspapers, a development could already be observed which would "sanctify" the Constitution and put it on an equal footing with the Declaration of Independence. It was the aim of the *Massachusetts Centinel* not only to report on the New York procession for the benefit of its readers but to preserve these events for posterity. Future generations ought to know "that their fathers had wisdom to accept a constitution framed for their happiness, and in honor of which these noble and federal festivals were first instituted—originating in the metropolis of Massachusetts, and extending universally through the Union."[111] The Grand Federal Processions with their blending of secular and religious elements, their communal spirit, and their aesthetic realism set a new standard for public celebrations. In the center of festive activity stood the American city, featuring all its local and regional specialties. However, the acting together of the (respectable) inhabitants of a diverse and at the same time well-ordered municipality was meant to reflect the envisaged community of an independent, sovereign, and self-governing nation. The lack of a national center was compensated for by a competitive spirit among the various cities and states, and by a common devotion to republican principles and constitutional government. Another distinguishing characteristic of the processions was the fact that the mass of participants did not play roles at a stage set for others, but represented themselves, their daily work, and their products in a realistic way. In celebrating the new Constitution, therefore, Americans laid the foundation for a distinct festive culture, whose forms, style, and spirit can still be observed in public life in the United States today.[112]

George Washington as Integrator

No one was better suited to reconcile the opposition with the Constitution than George Washington. Although he was known to support ratification, his name had more of a pacifying than polarizing effect. In public statements, Washington always made a deliberate effort to reach out to moderate critics and avoid any personal affronts. Harsh remarks were reserved for confidential discussions and private correspondence intended for a small circle of leading Federalists. He thus created the impression of a man calmly following developments and who would reunite the parties when all was settled.[113] Washington treated the prospect of himself becoming the first president in the same manner. He knew he was needed, and was surely attracted to the idea. Yet he hesitated, seemingly leaning more toward rejecting than accepting such a possibility.

This corresponded to the image people had of him and that he himself worked hard to maintain: the image of a New World Fabius bravely, deliberately, sensibly, and modestly dedicated to obeying the will of the people; or a Cincinnatus, the plain yet noble servant of the state in ancient Rome, who returned to the plow after fulfilling his duty to his country. In the portraits of Washington painted by Charles Willson Peale, kindness and vigor merge to form an expression of benevolent, fatherly sternness.[114] There was a general belief that his actions were motivated not by ambition but by a sense of justice and selfless duty. Although skeptics were quick to point out that Washington had yet to prove himself as a politician or lawmaker, even Antifederalists admitted they were not concerned about the fate of the Union under the new Constitution as long as Washington was at the helm. The problems were expected to begin when he relinquished the position.[115] Even at Antifederalist 4th of July celebrations, mentioning Washington's name with respectful and courteous regard was not considered a violation of the "true Republican style." Willie Jones forcefully denied ever having referred to Washington as a "scoundrel": "I have long thought and still think him the first and best character in the world."[116]

By the end of the War of Independence, songs and poems were already appearing honoring Washington as the *Pater Patriae* and paying effusive reverence to his name.[117] Federalists benefited considerably from the positive reactions to Washington's name during the ratification debate. He was regarded as a man who "stood above parties" like no other, a man who would unify all well-disposed Americans, heal the wounds, and pave the way for harmony and progress. The "good Angel" that had accompanied him in the past would surely not desert him in the future, wrote David Humphreys in late September 1787: "What will tend, perhaps, more than any thing to the adoption of the new System, will be an universal opinion of you being elected President of the United States, and an expectation that you will accept it for a while."[118] A month later, Gouverneur Morris beseeched Washington to make another personal sacrifice for the common good:

> I have observed that your Name to the new Constitution has been of infinite Service. Indeed I am convinced that if you had not attended the Convention, and the same Paper had been handed out to the World, it would have met with a colder Reception, with fewer and weaker Advocates, and with more and more strenuous Opponents. As it is, should the Idea prevail that you would not accept of the Presidency it would prove fatal in many Parts. Truth is, that your great and decided Superiority leads men willingly to put you in a Place which will not add to your personal Dignity, nor raise you higher than you already stand. . . . They will listen to your Voice, and submit to your Control; you therefore must I say *must* mount the Seat.[119]

No one but Washington, the *State Gazette of North Carolina* wrote on September 22, 1788, was in a position to balance the "jarring interests of so many different provinces." "There is no other man in whom the Mass of the people have sufficient confidence," pronounced William Tilghman in late January 1789. "I have great hope that his popularity, moderation & Patriotism, assisted by wise & liberal measures on the part of Congress, will calm that spirit of opposition which seems to threaten the happiness of the Continent."[120] This view was confirmed by former critics of the Constitution. The General Committee of the United Baptist Churches of Virginia wrote to Washington in May 1789 that only one thought had comforted them in the face of all their doubts and concerns: "The plan must be good, for it has the signature of a tried, trusted friend, and if religious liberty is insecure in the Constitution, 'the Administration will certainly prevent all oppression, for a WASHINGTON will preside.' . . . The very name of Washington is music in our ears."[121]

The Federal Processions of 1788, in which the name and images of Washington figured so prominently, can be seen as spontaneous public acclamations to the presidency long before the ballots were cast in the first presidential election. The veneration of Washington reached new heights during his inauguration in April 1789. Charles Thomson, the secretary of the Confederation Congress, conveyed the news to Washington on April 14, 1789, that he had been unanimously elected president. On April 16, the president-elect departed for New York accompanied by Thomson and David Humphreys. In marked contrast to Washington's request for "a quiet entry devoid of ceremony," the trip became a triumphal procession of unparalleled proportions.[122] At every stop along the way he was exalted in ceremonious welcoming addresses, church bells rang, salutes were fired off, and there were guards of honor, parades, banquets, and illuminations. In Philadelphia, 20,000 spectators looked on as Washington, in the saddle of a white horse, crossed the

Schuylkill River on a bridge transformed by Charles Willson Peale into an allegorical *via triumphalis* with twenty-foot-high Roman arches. Flags proclaimed the NEW ERA and the RISING EMPIRE, while Peale's daughter Angelica, dressed as the goddess of victory, lowered a laurel wreath onto Washington's head with the help of a special mechanical contrivance. There was more pageantry at the bridge leading to Trenton, where a chorus of white-robed girls scattered flowers and sang a "Gratulatory Ode."

On the morning of April 23, the three travelers were met in Elizabethtown by a congressional delegation that accompanied them for fifteen miles to Manhattan. A small boat flotilla escorted their ship, which had been constructed from materials taken from the *Hamilton* and equipped with a canopy and red curtains. Decorated sailboats pulled alongside the vessel en route to hail Washington and sing songs based on the melody to "God Save the King." A huge crowd awaited the arrival of the party in New York Harbor amid a virtual sea of flags. Washington disembarked to the sound of cannon fire, church bells, and the cheering of the masses, then, followed by Governor George Clinton, slowly pushed his way through the rows of people who had lined up to see—or perhaps even touch—the president-elect.

For a week, the entire city celebrated and paid homage to Washington. Houses were embellished with his portrait above inscriptions such as "The Father of His Country," and at night his countenance gleamed from transparent paintings. There were also attempts to cash in on the event. Vendors peddled boxes of tobacco, for example, made of colorful papier-mâché and featuring the words "God Save the President Washington." The general himself had seen the "finger of Providence" in the ratification process,[123] and the inauguration ceremony on April 30 added to the aura of sacredness surrounding the new Constitution. Standing on a small portico of Federal Hall, overlooking the crowd at Wall and Broad Streets, Washington put his right hand on the Bible and solemnly took the oath of office. In his inaugural address to the members of Congress, given in the Senate Chamber of Federal Hall, the president professed deep gratitude for the recurrent intervention of divine providence in American affairs: "No people can be bound to acknowledge and adore the Invisible Hand which conducts the affairs of men more than those of the United States. Every step by which they have advanced to the character of an independent nation seems to have been distinguished by some token of providential agency." And he reminded his audience one more time that "the preservation of the sacred fire of liberty and the destiny of the republican model of government are justly considered, perhaps, as *deeply*, as *finally*, staked on the experiment intrusted to the hands of the American people." In the evening, the festivities culminated in a two-hour display of fireworks, larger and more spectacular than anything of its kind ever before seen in America. This in turn rekindled the spirit of celebration in many towns and cities across the country, triggering new scenes of jubilation.

For Federalists, Washington's inauguration constituted both a conclusion and a beginning. It was the conclusion of the Revolution and the "Birthday of the Federal Government"[124]—and in a larger sense, the birth of America's existence as a nation. Like the Federal Processions, it was intended to honor past achievements while providing a vision of the country's seemingly unlimited prospects for the future. Once again, the sovereign people were to play the leading role:

> We praise ourselves; exalt our name,
> And in the scroll of time, we claim
> An int'rest in thy bays.[125]

Some observers wondered whether the idolization of Washington and the pompous celebrations were not a little excessive. The painter John Trumbull thought he detected the "odour of incense" at the inaugural celebrations, and quipped that the people had "gone through all the Popish grades of worship at least up to the *Hyperdoulia*." The *Boston Gazette* warned in reference to Vice President John Adams: "FLATTERY is the bane of freedom, the thief of liberty."[126] Virginia congressman Thomas Tudor Tucker complained in a letter to his brother St. George Tucker "that [the government] has infused into the Minds of People here the most intolerable rage for Monarchy that can be imagined. Verily I believe that a very great proportion are ripe for a King & would salute the President as such with all the Folly of Enthusiasm."[127]

For a time, the voice of distrust was lost in the tide of jubilation and optimism, and in the desire for authority, harmony, and security. The celebrations must be credited with reconciling a growing number of citizens with the Constitution and integrating them into the new order. Washington's inauguration, with its strong emphasis on personal leadership and presidential dignity, added another, more European-like element to American festive culture and civil religion. During the 1790s, this "federal style" sometimes threatened to overshadow the reverence for republican principles and values. Yet Washington's aversion to opulence, exaggerated etiquette, and effusive praise, as well as the opposition's predilection for "republican simplicity," forced Federalists to show self-restraint and helped to prevent excesses.[128]

7

The Creation of the Bill Of Rights

I wish the Constitution which is offered had been made more perfect, but I sincerely believe it is the best that could be obtained at this time—and, as a constitutional door is opened for amendment hereafter, the adoption of it under the present circumstances of the Union is in my opinion desirable.

GEORGE WASHINGTON TO FORMER VIRGINIA GOVERNORS, SEPTEMBER 24, 1787

A constitutional mode of altering the constitution itself is, perhaps, what has never been known among mankind before.

JAMES IREDELL, ADDRESS BEFORE THE HILLSBOROUGH CONVENTION, AUGUST 1788

We might as well have attempted to move mount Atlas upon our shoulders. In fact, the idea of subsequent amendments, was little better than putting ourselves to death first, in expectation that the doctor, who wished our destruction, would afterwards restore us to life. . . . The great points of free election, jury trial in criminal cases, and the unlimited right of taxation, and standing armies remain as they were.

RICHARD HENRY LEE TO PATRICK HENRY, SEPTEMBER 14, 1789

Amendment Recommendations and the Movement for a Second Convention

Fundamental Rights and Structural Amendments

On September 13, 1788, the Confederation Congress in New York City officially recognized that the Constitution had been ratified in the prescribed manner by the necessary number of states and had therefore gone into effect. At the same time, the delegates adopted an election ordinance, which had already been drafted by a committee in early July, stipulating the dates for the first federal elections. The delay had been caused by a bitter dispute over the meeting place of the new government, which was finally settled in favor of "the present Seat of Congress."[1] The unresolved problem of amending the

Constitution also caused anxiety and apprehension among the population. Circulating in the thirteen states were several documents with, all in all, over two hundred suggestions for improvements to the Constitution. The force and legitimacy of these amendment proposals varied depending on their source and manner of origin. The objections published in September and October 1787 by Richard Henry Lee, George Mason, and Elbridge Gerry were merely the expression of their private opinions. Other than their wide dissemination, the prominence of the authors, and the comprehensiveness of their vision, they differed little from the numerous other points of criticism printed in newspaper essays, pamphlets, and broadsheets. Also unofficial, yet vested with considerable authority, was the *Dissent of the Minority of the Pennsylvania Convention,* published on December 18, 1787. Although Federalists had prevented the list of fifteen amendments from being recorded in the minutes of the convention, the newspaper and pamphlet versions were soon regarded as the official position of the dissenting faction.[2]

Proponents of the Constitution in Massachusetts had been forced to accept a major compromise. The nine amendments they acceded to may have only been recommendations for Congress, yet they were endorsed by the convention and included in the Form of Ratification. Moreover, the Boston convention instructed the congressional representatives from Massachusetts to push for the implementation of their proposals. This procedure was emulated in the course of the year by conventions in South Carolina, New Hampshire, Virginia, and New York. In the process, the amendments grew in number, became more precise, and were more systematically arranged. The circular letter sent by the New York convention to the other states even went so far as to stipulate details for the convening of a second general convention to revise the Constitution on the basis of the proposed amendments. In August 1788, North Carolina's refusal to adopt the Constitution without previous changes again underscored how urgent the problem had become.

Increasingly, the debate began to focus on the distinction between amendments designed to protect basic civil rights and "substantial" amendments focusing on the structure and principles of the new system of government. An explicit division of this kind was first introduced by Virginia delegates and was subsequently adopted by the New York and North Carolina conventions. The first group was subsumed under the title of "Bill of Rights"; the second was often described as "alterations." No one really knew how many people actually wanted either type of change. If the conventions could be considered representative of the population, a majority of citizens backed the demand for amendments.[3] William Shippen estimated, somewhat more conservatively, that at least half of the constituents still wanted to see the Constitution revised, regardless of the fact that it had already gone into effect.[4] In Jefferson's view, some concessions should be made even if only a minority in a few key states supported the movement for amendments: "The minorities are too respectable not to be entitled to some sacrifice of opinion in the majority. Especially when a great proportion of them would be contented with a bill of rights."[5] This was easier said than done, however, in the prevailing political climate after the adoption of the Constitution. Some critics abandoned their opposition after being convinced that amendments would be implemented, thus creating the impression that the calls for proposals were neither as serious nor as widely supported as originally assumed. This in turn encouraged those who wanted to leave the Constitution as it was and had only made concessions for tactical reasons.

The 210 amendments that had been set out by eight ratifying conventions or their minorities by the fall of 1788 comprised about 100 different ideas.[6] The desire for a Bill of Rights was nearly universal. The individual articles were normally taken from the enumerations of rights existing in the states since the Revolution. The Bill of Rights proposed by the Virginia convention, for example, closely resembled the Virginia Declaration of Rights enacted in 1776. This is not surprising considering both documents were penned by George Mason. For the first time, the Virginia Declaration of Rights had systematically organized the diverse ideas and condensed them into sixteen articles. Not content to list such fundamental rights as life, liberty, and property ownership, it went on to lay down the basic principles of existence in society. All people were deemed by nature free and independent; all power was vested in and emanated from the people; the authority to govern was a trust and based on the consent of the people; the role of government was solely to provide for the well-being, security, and protection of the citizens; if it proved unfit for this purpose, the majority had the right to revoke the authority to govern and alter, reform, or abolish the existing system. Other principles derived from these rights, such as the right to vote, to have a trial by jury, and to maintain a well-regulated militia, as well as the freedom of the press and religion. Also included were provisions on criminal procedure drawn from the Habeas Corpus Act. It is astounding that in 1787 a knowledgeable lawyer like James Wilson was evidently unaware of the existence of this document.[7]

The amendments proposed by several ratifying conventions echoed the principles of the Virginia Declaration, which were often referred to as simply the "principles of 1776." Leading the list of specific demands was the right to a jury trial in civil cases, propounded by seven conventions or their minorities. The freedom of religion was mentioned six times, though there were some discrepancies as to what this concept entailed. Receiving five mentions each were the freedom of speech and the press, the right to bear arms, provisions outlawing the quartering of soldiers in private homes without the consent of the owner or proper legal authorization, and protection against arbitrary searches and arrests. Contained in four lists were the right to assemble and to petition the government, as well as the right to a speedy and public trial. These articles were thus designed not only to shield the citizens' private sphere from unjustified government intrusion but to secure those rights that enabled them to actively participate in the political process. In actuality, there was no serious resistance to any of these proposals. The only question was whether it was really necessary to include them in the Constitution or whether they were not already adequately safeguarded by the individual state constitutions or declarations of rights.

The bridge between the "alterations" and the "substantial" changes were suggestions that combined individual and group rights with structural revisions. The most important examples of this included the demand for a stricter separation of powers, set forth by the Pennsylvania minority and supported by the conventions in Virginia and North Carolina; the right of the constituents to instruct their delegates, affirmed by three conventions; the prohibition of trade monopolies, contained in four lists; and the ban on standing armies in times of peace, mentioned six times.

The largest share of amendments fell into the "alterations" category, demands which were considerably more controversial than the enumeration of basic rights. These proposals were a bone of contention both within the Antifederalist camp and between them and their adversaries. This is where such issues as slavery and qualified legislative majorities for commercial laws and trade agreements came into play, subjects that elicited equally emotional—albeit diametrically opposed—reactions in the North and South. This group also contained numerous provisions that were of special importance to the opposition but were adamantly rejected by Federalists. As disparate as the individual demands may have seemed, they all pointed in the same direction and served a common goal: shifting the balance of power in the new system away from the federal government and enabling the states to resist a central administration thought prone to corruption and abuse. The New York convention openly expressed this objective. The delegates wanted to require all federal officeholders to swear an oath "not to infringe or violate the constitution or rights of the respective states." The "alterations" are also important for another reason. Since detailed alternatives to the Constitution were rare, the reform proposals offer an extraordinary insight into the type of federal system envisioned by leading oppositionists.

The changes related to all three branches of government, and in some cases would have significantly reduced the scope of their authority. Antifederalists considered Article III of the Constitution particularly ambiguous and in need of reform. They wanted to see the jurisdiction of the federal courts more clearly defined, the Supreme Court's say in political decisions narrowly restricted, and the establishment of federal courts in the states kept to a minimum. Three conventions thought there should be no inferior federal courts at all except for admiralty cases. The original jurisdiction of the federal judiciary was to be limited to cases where the United States was a party (suggested by 3 states); disputes between two or more states (3); cases pertaining to international treaties (3), foreign emissaries (3), or admiralty and maritime law (3); conflicting titles issued by two states for the same piece of land (3); or disputes between a state (or its citizens) and a foreign nation (1). Areas where jurisdiction was explicitly denied included criminal proceedings within a single state and litigation between an individual citizen and a state. Finally, the federal courts were to be prohibited from unilaterally expanding their jurisdiction (2), as well as interpreting contracts in a manner which was incompatible with a state's constitution (3). Two conventions suggested that decisions of the Supreme Court could be appealed to a special commission appointed by the president and approved by Congress.

The push for amendments did not spare the office of the president. Antifederalists wanted to prevent the executive from joining forces with the Senate to create a hereditary monarchy or a dictatorship. They proposed limiting the president's tenure to two four-year terms (3), adding an executive council (2), and restricting the power to grant pardons (1). In time of war, the president was only to be given command over the army with the express consent of Congress (2), and impeachment proceedings would be decided by a simple majority vote in the Senate (1). Official documents and declarations were to be published in the name of the people of the United States and not in the name of the president (1).

Antifederalists' preference for a strong legislative branch applied to the individual state governments but not to a central legislature that was, in their view, removed from the people and too small in relation to the population. Amendments therefore also aimed at modifying the composition, authority, and operating methods of Congress. One of the most common demands involved the creation of small voting districts to increase the number of delegates and make Congress more representative (6). Antifederalists particularly resented the right of Congress to intervene in state election procedures. This was to be eliminated (8), along with Congress's exclusive jurisdiction over the federal capital (3). Other amendments forbade Congress from creating monopolies (4), granting titles of nobility (3), regulating the militia (4), or ratifying treaties that conflicted with state constitutions (3). Several conventions called for requiring a two-thirds or three-fourths majority in Congress to keep a standing army in peacetime (5), pass commercial legislation (3), or ratify trade agreements (2) or agreements involving U.S. land claims (3). Clauses such as these were often indicative of special regional interests. The desire for more openness was manifested in proposals requiring public admission to the deliberations in both houses (1) as well as the publication of their minutes (3) and budgets (2). The existence of the Senate was no longer questioned, out of deference to the small states. But there were isolated propositions stipulating that impeachment proceedings against senators should not be instituted in the Senate itself (2), that each state should have the right to recall its senators (1), and that their interim appointments should be made by the state legislature and not the governor (1).

Some of these ideas were not uniformly supported by Antifederalists, and others were mutually exclusive. Of crucial importance to the future relationship between the states and the federal government were two other recommendations that appeared in a prominent position in nearly all convention resolutions and minority opinions. One of these was the "tax amendment" permitting Congress to collect direct taxes under exceptional circumstances only. Congress would first have to prove that its other sources of income were insufficient to its needs and that the states could not or would not provide the additional funds. This condition was sure to meet with the approval of the rural population, which carefully distinguished between direct taxes on property and indirect taxes on imported goods and whose fear of oppressive duties and tyrannical "tax-gatherers" had fueled the struggle against England.[8]

The main purpose of this type of stipulation was to secure the states' sovereignty and check the financial aspirations of the federal administration. Import duties would still have provided the Union with an "independent income," something nationalists had been demanding since 1781, and the revenues from these sources may have sufficed under normal conditions. To Patrick Henry's mind, this one argument outweighed all others.[9] In times of crisis, however, Congress would have been placed at the mercy of the state legislatures. In Federalists' estimation, the implementation of this change would have been a throwback to the situation under the Articles of Confederation, thus robbing the new system of its central purpose. Subjecting the federal government's right to tax to such severe restrictions, complained Tench Coxe, "will re-establish the Supremacy of the state legislatures, the real object of all their Zeal in opposing the system."[10]

The effects of the other popular amendment, based on Article II of the Articles of Confederation, would have been no less profound. It would have established that all authority not *expressly* delegated to Congress remain with the states. This was an attempt to go beyond the Federalists' argument that the Constitution created a "government of enumerated powers," and would have negated the implied powers suggested in the "necessary and proper" clause. The states would have gained useful legal ammunition in the disputes likely to ensue with the Union over the distribution of power by shifting the burden of proof to the federal government.

Had the opposition been successful in achieving its most important aims, the central government would have been deprived of a considerable share of its economic, military, and political power. This Antifederalist version of the Constitution would have been considerably different from the Federalist version of a truly national government. To be sure, the new system would have formally transformed Congress into a "real" government with separated powers and improved its financial position, yet in other respects it would have resembled the loosely knit confederation of old.

The Push for a Second Constitutional Convention

Calls for a second general convention to discuss the states' amendment proposals had already begun during the deliberations in Philadelphia and had never ceased. The circular letter sent out by the Poughkeepsie convention was especially alarming to Federalists because it energized the discussion and revived Antifederalists' fading hopes in this regard. Until nine states had ratified, it was assumed the Confederation Congress had the right to call a second convention. Once the Constitution had gone into effect, however, a two-thirds majority of states would have to petition Congress in accordance with Article V. Any amendments subsequently proposed by the convention would also require the approval of three-fourths of the states. The same was true of amendments submitted to the states by Congress of its own accord. Federalists preferred this route if amendments were necessary at all. With the exception of Edmund Randolph, there was not a single prominent proponent of the Constitution who believed any good could come out of holding a second convention. Federalists feared this method because they were apprehensive about the opposition's true intentions.

The anxiety over the "measure of all others to be dreaded," as Benjamin Lincoln put it, began to take on a hysterical aspect toward the end of the summer and into the fall of 1788.[11] The New York circular letter seemed to fit into a pattern of events foreshadowing a new crisis. The letter was closely followed by the shocking news of the rejection of the Constitution in North

Carolina at the beginning of August, again coupled with the demand for a second general convention.[12] Federalists ascribed this move to the Union-wide Antifederalist correspondence, on which they now had more information. By June, Benjamin Lincoln had become convinced that Antifederalists were determined to do everything in their power to disrupt the new order.[13] Madison warned a short time later of an apparent plot "of regularly undermining the government" before it had even been given a chance: "I suspect the plan will be to engage 2/3 of the Legislatures in the task of undoing the work; or to get a Congress appointed in the first instance that will commit suicide on their own Authority."[14] Maryland was especially shaken by persistent rumors of a "settled system of opposition" and a "premeditated plan . . . to destroy, by particular amendments, our federal government."[15] These fears were driven by the assumption that Samuel Chase and Luther Martin would not rest until they had exacted revenge for their defeat at the ratifying convention.

Federalists were also becoming more aware of the dangers presented by the "interregnum" between the adoption of the Constitution and the opening session of the new Congress. The election ordinance of September 13 had specified that the members of the electoral college were to be appointed by the states on January 7, 1789, that they were to cast their votes on February 4, and that the new government was to convene two months later in New York City. The states were allowed to establish their own deadlines and procedures for electing members of the House of Representatives and the Senate. Because of the dispute over the national capital, Federalists feared that disgruntled southern voters would flock to their opponents. There was a span of six months to be bridged, time enough for the opposition to benefit from a swing in public opinion, thus creating new complications for the Constitution. At that point, a weak Union government was still in place which commanded little respect and whose legitimacy was already being questioned. Virginian Theoderick Bland asked friend Henry Lee, for instance, how an institution could still demand personnel and money when it had expired the preceding June, "without leaving a last Will and Testament . . . thus will doubts and difficulties arise at the threshold of this Business—and while an actual Interregnum prevails, a kind of sham government is carrying on the most Important functions of a real one."[16]

Federalists believed a second convention would only extend this period of uncertainty and perhaps even derail the reform entirely. Considering the condition of the present Congress, a return to the Articles of Confederation seemed out of the question and the dissolution of the Union inevitable. Just when their goal appeared within reach, Federalists suddenly found themselves on the brink of disaster, threatened on all sides by anarchy and chaos. In late July, an extremely disquieted Washington was convinced the opposition aimed "to undo all that has been done." In August, he expressed concerns that the New York circular letter would wreak havoc and conjured up visions of "a political shipwreck, without the aid of one friendly star to guide us into Port." Seeing the reform movement upended in clear view of the harbor would represent "the severest of all possible aggravations to our misery." As late as October he was still plagued by an "unusual degree of anxiety" and exhorted his friends not to relent in their fight against "premature amendments."[17]

In the meantime, the amendment issue had become fully entangled in a mesh of partisan politics, triggering a new wave of agitation. In Maryland, it dominated a rancorous, at times even ruthless, election campaign waged until the beginning of October for seats in the assembly. Federalists did everything possible to keep Samuel Chase and all other proponents of amendments out of the legislature, convinced that this was the only way to create favorable conditions for the upcoming federal elections and to ward off resolutions for a second convention. Since there was some backing for revisions in their own camp, they did not dismiss the idea of amendments altogether. They were careful to differentiate, however, between benign "federal amendments" and "antifederal amendments" designed to curb the power of Congress to levy taxes, restrict the jurisdiction of federal courts, and check the government's right to keep a standing army, moves which in their opinion amounted to the destruction the Constitution. They accused Antifederalists of pretending to support the new system while keeping the public in a permanent state of turmoil with their talk of a second convention. The authors and advocates of the Constitution were best qualified to institute changes in an orderly manner through Congress, they maintained, not the declared opponents of the plan.[18] Federalists defeated Samuel Chase and David McMechen by a slim margin in the Baltimore city elections held from October 6 to 9, 1788, and carried the rest of the state except for Harford, Anne Arundel, and Baltimore Counties.[19]

The party convention staged on September 3–6, 1788, in Harrisburg at the invitation of Pennsylvania Antifederalists, promised to generate still more political unrest. Delegates from thirteen counties and the city of Philadelphia took part in the event, regarded by Federalists as an "irregular" convention of the sort that had challenged government authority in the 1780s. Future Treasury Secretary Albert Gallatin had devised a radical program to use committees of correspondence and to intensify interstate collaboration in the drive for a second convention. The gathering seemed portentous enough for Federalists to smuggle in one of their members to take notes.[20]

The feared call for resistance did not materialize, however, for Gallatin and his acolytes were subdued by the moderate faction behind Charles Pettit, who favored peaceful negotiation within the framework of the new system. In the end, the convention agreed to present twelve amendments and urge the Pennsylvania Assembly to throw its weight behind their campaign for amendments. They also compiled an initial list of Antifederalist candidates for the federal elections, but kept it under wraps for the time being. Harrisburg may have been a disappointment for the "patrons of the scheme," as a relieved Madison observed, yet the friends of the Constitution could by no means relax in the face of this "run upon amendments."[21] After reading the secret notes taken at the convention, Thomas Hartley was certain the opposition remained determined "to distract this Country and embarrass the new Constitution. . . . They like no part of the System because it operates against their Power—but for the Moment they wish to appear under the plausible Pretentions of Amendments." "Cassius" could also discern nothing more than a change of tactics, a ploy he denounced in the *Federal Gazette:* "The insidious efforts of Antifederalists, to prevent the adoption of the new Constitution, having failed of success, they have now altered their plan, and are applying their strength to secretly undermine what they could not openly and fairly destroy."[22]

The amendments movement was still alive in New York as well. Melancton Smith presented a plan in late September supposedly outlining the simplest and quickest way to effect changes to the Constitution. A short time later, John Lamb's Federal Republican Committee informed all correspondents across the Union that a "society for the purpose of procuring the general convention" had been founded in New York City. Lamb's collaborators in New York and other states were encouraged to form similar organizations and advocate the election of "republican" delegates to the state legislatures and Congress. In November, another circular letter advanced the opinion that a worthy candidate for the office of vice president would be Governor Clinton, "who will be zealously engaged in promoting such amendments to the new Constitution as will render the liberties of the country secure under it."[23] A contributor to the New York *Daily Advertiser* calling himself a "Federalist who is for Amendments" expressed the hope that all those who had promised revisions at the Poughkeepsie convention would keep their word.[24] Hamilton wondered how the "rage for amendments" should best be handled and came to the conclusion it was "rather to be parried by address than encountered with open force."[25] The critics of the Constitution were also unrelenting in the New York legislature. A confrontation between the Antifederalist assembly and the Federalist senate blocked the appointment of the state's two senators for several months and prevented New York from passing legislation providing for the election of the first presidential electors.

Federalists were able to deduce the extent of the Lamb Committee's influence from remarks made by Thomas Person in North Carolina and Joshua Atherton in New Hampshire. Both initially suggested that the state legislatures should delay the congressional elections until a second convention had been approved. Atherton later modified his position somewhat, placing his faith in a Congress, "which shall contain a majority for stopping the operation of the new system until the amendments are incorporated."[26] Both positions were essentially the same as far as Federalists were concerned. Even in Massachusetts, where Antifederalism was thought defunct, there was a fierce clash between proponents and adversaries of amendments in advance of the federal elections. More and more articles had appeared in the newspapers since the end of August demanding that Federalists stick to the commitments they made in February and accusing them of dealing with the issue in a half-hearted, if not cynical, manner.[27] But Federalists denounced their opponents as "amendmenites" and "amendment mongers."

The greatest stronghold of amendment supporters was Virginia, whose legislature was more submissive to Patrick Henry's guidance than the ratifying convention had been. In the legislative session from October 20 to December 30, Henry attempted to set the stage for a second convention single-handedly. He first pressured both houses to elect two Antifederalists, Richard Henry Lee and William Grayson, to the U.S. Senate, and to exclude the Federalist candidate, James Madison, because of uncertainties regarding his stance on the amendments issue. He then had district lines drawn so that Madison's home county of Orange was merged with a district dominated by Antifederalists, which seemed to rule out any chance of Madison's getting elected to the U.S. House of Representatives. Finally, he proposed a resolution in accordance with the Poughkeepsie convention's circular letter applying to Congress to call a second general convention at the earliest possible date. The resolution, largely composed by Henry himself, stressed that the amendment proposals put forward by the Richmond convention were not founded in "speculative theory but deduced from principles which have been established by the melancholy example of other nations in different ages—So they will never be removed, untill the cause itself shall cease to exist." The desire for lasting protection of the "great and unalienable rights of Human Nature" was widely shared: "The anxiety with which our Countrymen press for the accomplishment of this important end, will ill admit of delay. The slow forms of congressional discussion and recommendation, if indeed they should ever agree to any change, would we fear be less certain of success.

Happily for their wishes, the Constitution hath presented an alternative, by admitting the submission to a Convention of the states." Federalists wanted to give Congress a free hand in dealing with the question of amendments. Yet as the outcome of the voting clearly showed, Antifederalists had an almost two-thirds majority in the assembly. The resolution was passed on November 14, then stylistically revised by the Senate before being forwarded in the form of a letter to Congress and the state executives by the end of the month.[28] The first official petition for a second convention had thus been submitted. There was no one on the receiving end, however, as the Confederation Congress had no jurisdiction over Article V of the Constitution and the new government was not to convene until the following March.

Federalists were defenseless in the Virginia legislature without Madison's leadership: "Intrigue, antifederalism and artifice go hand in hand," complained George Lee Turberville at the outset of the session. It appeared to Charles Lee that Federalists were afraid of their adversaries. They were even forced to swallow a resolution prohibiting members of the federal government from holding offices under the state constitution. By mid-November, Turberville's only hope was that the rest of the Union would regard the resolutions as a "Child of temporaryly triumphant faction."[29] The legislature's Antifederalist agenda apparently met with the approval of the general public. "The universal Cry is for Amendments, & the federals are obliged to join in it," crowed Patrick Henry.[30] Commentaries in the press indicated that the opposition had recovered from its defeat at the ratifying convention. "The anti's are in high spirits from their late successes," reported the Winchester *Virginia Centinel* on December 17, quoting a letter from Richmond. The only point of debate among newspaper writers was the most suitable method of instituting the changes. "A Republican" felt that a second convention was the best way to restore harmony and generate widespread support for the Constitution. Others criticized the pompous tone of the resolutions, which they saw as an attempt "to frustrate the design of putting in execution [the] plan of government," perhaps even aiming "to destroy the glorious fabric."[31]

From Congress, Madison kept a watchful eye on the proceedings in the Virginia legislature and was of two minds concerning the likelihood of a second convention. He expressed confidence that the plan was no longer seriously threatened. "I trust the Constitution is too firmly established to be now materially vulnerable," he assured Washington on November 5. Of the states that had ratified, Virginia was the only one "in which the Politics of the Legislature are at variance with the sense of the people, expressed by their Representatives in Convention."[32] But at the same time, he urged arguments against a second convention, suggesting that he still thought it a danger. He told Turberville "with great frankness" all that stood in the way of and spoke against a second convention. First of all, several states were so opposed to such a method that they would sooner forgo amendments entirely than lend their support to such an undertaking. Second, at least two-thirds of the states would have to petition Congress. This action seemed much more difficult than leaving the revisions up to Congress. Third, there was a danger that a specially elected convention would "consider itself as having a greater latitude than the Congress" to change the Constitution, and would attract "the most violent partizans on both sides" and reopen old wounds. This would provide the enemies of the new system with a "dangerous opportunity of sapping the very foundations of the fabric." Under the guise of trying to improve the Constitution, they might make demands that were popular in a certain part of the Union but were unacceptable in another. Anyone who had experienced the difficulties and dangers of the first convention "should tremble for the result of a Second, meeting in the present temper of America and under all the disadvantages I have mentioned." Fourth, Madison pointed out that one should not disregard the reaction that the mere thought of a second convention would elicit in Europe. This prospect would hang over the Constitution and the entire Union like a dark cloud. Dutch creditors had only averted the bankruptcy of the United States in the expectation of the swift, smooth, and definitive adoption of the Constitution. The success of the reform was important to Europe as well as America: "It is a well known fact that this event has filled that quarter of the Globe with equal wonder and veneration, that its influence is already secretly but powerfully working in favor of liberty in France, and it is fairly to be inferred that the final event there may be materially affected by the prospect of things here."[33]

Madison tirelessly bombarded his friends and acquaintances with arguments like these. He convinced Edmund Randolph and Henry Lee that the quest for a second convention was a "hopeless pursuit," and also managed to reassure Jefferson.[34] At the same time, Federalists stepped up their public relations campaign against the second convention movement. Tench Coxe published a new series of essays in the *Federal Gazette* under his pseudonym "An American Citizen." In Connecticut, Roger Sherman spoke out against a second convention as "A Citizen of New Haven." James Wilson attacked Antifederalists' "pretence of amendments" in a speech that was reprinted as far away as Massachusetts.[35] These prominent leaders were backed by a host of newspaper writers who pointed out again and again that the irreconcilable differences between the two parties, as well as conflicts within the opposition camp, rendered the idea of a second general convention hopeless from the start. The new Congress, by contrast, would be competent—and surely willing—to address any need for changes.

Since Rhode Island and North Carolina had not yet ratified, eight states were needed to force a second convention. Federalists swept the fall elections in Pennsylvania, Maryland, and New Jersey. The new Pennsylvania Assembly was consequently no more inclined than its predecessor to put the New York circular letter on the agenda. The delegates apparently never even saw the petition submitted by the Harrisburg convention in September.[36] In March 1789, they rejected Virginia's proposal for a second convention, on the grounds that the Constitution guaranteed the "fundamental principles which are calculated to ensure the liberties of their country. The happiness of America and the harmony of the Union depend upon suffering it to proceed undisturbed in its operations by premature amendments."[37] Federalist majorities in Maryland and New Jersey also blocked all measures aimed at bringing about a second convention. The New York circular letter was read before the Connecticut General Assembly, like all "public letters," but none of the critics of the Constitution ventured to put forward a motion for debate.[38] Antifederalists in New Hampshire and Massachusetts did not fare much better, despite having majorities in the lower houses. According to Joshua Atherton, New Hampshire Antifederalists had by now assumed the position: "It is adopted, let us try it."[39]

In Boston the New York circular letter was assigned to a legislative committee, yet no report ever materialized. Although Governor Hancock described the expectation of amendments as well founded in an address to the General Court on January 8, 1789, he warned that a second convention might result in the "dissolution of the Government." After arduous negotiations between the House of Representatives and the Senate regarding a proper response to Hancock, the legislature agreed to seek improvements "through the Congressional means of proposing amendments." Hence, Hancock informed the governors of New York and Virginia in February of the Massachusetts legislature's agreement with his position "that the calling of a general Convention at this period would be attended with great expense, if not dangerous to the Union."[40] This effectively extinguished all lingering hopes of securing a second convention. New York remained the only state other than Virginia even to submit a formal petition to Congress. A special session of the legislature put the final touches on the carefully worded letter on March 3 and officially delivered it to Congress on May 6, one day after the submission of the Virginia petition.[41] Two days earlier, on May 4, James

Madison announced on the floor of the House of Representatives his intention to introduce amendments on May 25.

The unspectacular end of the movement for a second convention again revealed the organizational and tactical weaknesses that had plagued the opposition throughout the ratification debate. A typical example of this was the lack of coordinated actions in Rhode Island and North Carolina, two states that dissenters could normally count on for assistance. The North Carolina legislature appointed delegates to the second convention upon receipt of the New York circular letter in November, and even authorized their remuneration, yet neglected to petition Congress for a convention. The Rhode Island legislature ordered Governor Clinton's letter printed and forwarded to the towns to decide whether the state should take part in a second convention. By the established deadline, only eight towns had answered in the affirmative. Most considered it pointless to discuss changing a constitution they had already rejected.[42] In any case, Congress would probably not have recognized a petition from a state that had not yet ratified the Constitution.

A major reason for the failure of the effort to call a second convention was the scarcity of reliable information, a problem even for an active organization like the New York Federal Republican Committee. At the time the Poughkeepsie convention proposed the circular, Antifederalists believed that the requisite number of states would join the crusade for a second convention. They were unaware of the change in public mood that had occurred since nine states adopted the Constitution. The respect for majority decisions, something they had preached themselves on numerous occasions, prevented many dissenters from pursuing a second convention. Federalists accommodated the public desire for restored order and a general willingness to accept the new system by proposing amendments themselves, and especially by offering prospects of a bill of rights—the precise tactic recommended by Hamilton in response to the "rage for amendments." In this way, Federalists effectively repelled the final drive for "structural" amendments and put an end to the campaign for a second convention. A number of Antifederalist politicians remained confident to the spring of 1789 that they could gain a majority in the new Congress. This induced them to waste a lot of effort on the selection and promotion of candidates that could have been applied to the pursuit of a second convention. One can only speculate on what would have happened if New York and Virginia had made their participation in the federal elections contingent upon the guarantee of a second convention. The Antifederalist factions under the guidance of Patrick Henry and George Clinton never even considered this possibility. Instead, they immediately focused their attention on the senatorial elections, the drawing of election districts for the House of Representatives, and the nomination of candidates. In the end, even the Harrisburg delegates seemed to have been more concerned about the congressional elections than amendments. The situation was similar in New Hampshire, Massachusetts, and South Carolina.

Some opponents of the Constitution later regretted having unconditionally consented to federal elections, thus acknowledging a system they had so long resisted. By delaying the elections they probably could have lent more weight to their calls for "structural" amendments than by placing their faith in the handful of Antifederalists who managed to win seats in Congress. These considerations notwithstanding, Antifederalists' participation was of the utmost importance for the successful conclusion of the ratification debate. A renewed polarization of political forces was thus avoided, the transition to a federal government was eased, and the Constitution acquired incontestable legitimacy. Subsequent developments would show that although Antifederalists' actions made the adoption of structural amendments almost impossible, they were not detrimental to the adoption of a bill of rights, and may have even accelerated the process. The deciding factor in Antifederalists' willingness to take part in the elections was not the expectation of victory. Rather, all signs indicate that the critics of the Constitution were now more than ever caught up in the flow of the ratification process in which they had been immersed since September 1787. Almost unnoticed even by themselves, they were swept along by the tide of events now surging toward their conclusion.

James Madison, the First Federal Congress, and the Bill of Rights

The First Federal Elections and the Revision of State Constitutions

The first federal elections began in November 1788 and were not concluded until July of the following year. Whereas the appointment of Senators was carried out by the state legislatures, the members of the House of Representatives were chosen by direct election. The legislatures had a hand in this as well, however, as they enacted the election laws. There was little controversy surrounding the selection of presidential electors on January 7, 1789, since the voice of the people had long spoken in favor of General Washington. Accordingly, all sixty-nine electors voted for Washington as President on February 4, 1789. The office of vice president fell to John Adams, who, as favorite of the "eastern states," received the second highest number of electoral votes.[43]

Since Federalists controlled most state legislatures, they had little trouble securing berths in the United States Senate for their candidates. In the unicameral legislatures in Pennsylvania and Georgia, Federalists competed against each other for the available seats. Other states, like South Carolina, chose their senators without notable friction between the upper and lower houses. In Massachusetts, the senate approved the assembly's appointment of Federalist Caleb Strong but repeatedly rejected the second candidate, Charles Jarvis, who was believed to support amendments. In the end, the House relented and endorsed the senate's preference, Tristram Dalton. The elections in New Hampshire followed the same pattern: the Federalist-dominated senate persistently refused to accept Nathaniel Peabody, an opponent of the Constitution, until the lower house finally dropped him in favor of a second Federalist candidate. The appointments in New York were delayed by a similar, though considerably more heated, conflict.[44] Virginia became the only state to send Antifederalists to the U.S. Senate. Hence, the Senate consisted of twenty Federalists (twenty-two after the two New York seats were filled) and only two Antifederalists.

The election of the fifty-nine representatives (North Carolina and Rhode Island were not yet included) naturally attracted the greatest public interest. In many states the election campaign, which began immediately after the promulgation of the election ordinance in September 13, 1788, was a continuation of the ratification struggle. The amendment debate dominated the statewide elections in Pennsylvania and Maryland. The issue of amending the Constitution was the deciding factor in several congressional districts in Virginia, New York, and Massachusetts as well, and it affected the results in parts of New Hampshire and South Carolina. Antifederalists refrained from nominating candidates in Connecticut, Delaware, and Georgia, where experience during the preceding two years had shown they had no chance of winning. In eight other states they ran in the hope of strengthening their position in the amendment negotiations in Congress. They had to overcome great obstacles, however, and appeared headed for a fiasco similar to the outcome of their movement for a second convention.

The source of their misfortune lay in Federalists' control of state legislatures and the growing indifference of opposition voters. In most states, Federalists were not averse to using the same tactics employed by the Antifederalist majority in the Virginia legislature. They devised election laws favoring their own candidates, much to the disadvantage of the proponents of amendments. The most obvious case was Maryland, where Federalists stipulated that voting would not be conducted on a district basis, so as to ward off defeats in such opposition strongholds as Baltimore, Harford, and Anne Arundel Counties. They were also opposed to statewide elections, which would have enabled other known Antifederalists to finish among the top six contenders. Instead, they came up with the idea of an at-large election that allowed each voter to choose a total of six candidates, one from each of six districts. The six candidates receiving the most votes would be declared the winners. This complex scheme to neutralize the heavily populated Antifederalist counties was hugely successful. All of the top six finishers were Federalists. Opposition leaders Samuel Chase and Luther Martin did not even bother to run.[45]

Statewide elections also allowed Federalists in Pennsylvania to keep the renitent backcountry at bay. The rural west had no chance against the eastern part of the state with a metropolis like Philadelphia, especially considering that the resistance had been waning since the Harrisburg convention. Antifederalists' "Harrisburg ticket" included two candidates of German descent, Peter Muhlenberg and Daniel Hiester, for tactical reasons. These two candidates, who had long abandoned their opposition to the Constitution, were the only members of the Antifederalist ticket to win.[46] The other six seats went to Federalists on the "Lancaster ticket," which also included a German, Frederick A. Muhlenberg. For all practical purposes, Antifederalists came up empty-handed. The fact that three of eight Pennsylvania congressmen had German names illustrates the growing political potency of the German American segment of the population.

Federalists also swept statewide elections in New Hampshire and New Jersey. In New Hampshire, each voter was allowed to mark three names on the ballot, in accordance with the number of representatives allocated to the state. To win a seat, a candidate was required to receive at least one-sixth of the total votes. No one achieved that feat during the first round of elections on December 15, 1788. Antifederalists Nathaniel Peabody and Joshua Atherton barely missed finishing among the top six candidates, who qualified for the runoff elections on February 2, 1789. The result: three Federalist representatives were chosen to follow the two Federalist senators, John Langdon and Paine Wingate, to Congress.[47]

In New Jersey, the Constitution became a contentious issue for the first time during the congressional elections. The conflict began when Abraham Clark linked his candidacy to the need for amendments. He had a fairly good chance of winning, thanks to his enormous popularity in East Jersey. As a preventive measure, the Federalist majority in the legislature mandated statewide elections and resorted to a rather curious interpretation of their own election law. The statute established that the polling stations were to open on February 11 and remain open until "legally closed."[48] After the results from seven of the eight East Jersey counties had been delivered to the State Council on February 23, Federalists simply kept the polling stations in West Jersey open to pile up votes in their favor. When Clark's supporters in the last East Jersey county of Essex decided to follow their example, the State Council declared the elections concluded and the four Federalists from West Jersey the winners. This maneuver by Clark's foes resulted in a record voter turnout of 16,000 citizens, or 44 percent of adult white males. East Jersey politicians challenged the legality of the election procedures, but to no avail. Clark himself was probably not incorrect in his assumption that Alexander Hamilton had had a hand in the affair.[49]

In view of the intense opposition in the inland areas of South Carolina and Massachusetts, Federalists in those states figured their chances were better if voting were conducted on a district basis. South Carolina's election law appeased the agitated backcountry while ensuring that at least a portion of the five-man delegation would come from the Lowcountry. Federalists battled it out among themselves in Charleston and the Georgetown-Cheraws district. David Ramsay became embroiled in a fierce feud with William Loughton Smith, whom he chided for living in England during the Revolution. Ramsay also insisted that his rival had not been a citizen of South Carolina for seven years, as required by law. Smith countered with a reference to Ramsay's Pennsylvania origins and his opposition to slavery. In the end, Ramsay was beaten not only by Smith but by another Federalist as well. Federalist Daniel Huger won unchallenged in the Georgetown-Cheraws district, while Antifederalists Aedanus Burke, Thomas Sumter, and Thomas Tudor Tucker won landslide victories in the other three districts.[50]

Massachusetts's election law also favored Federalists in the east over the critics of the Constitution in the interior parts of the state. Suffolk and Middlesex Counties, for example, home to 9.5 and 9 percent of the population, respectively, constituted separate districts, whereas the western counties of Berkshire and Hampshire (19 percent combined) were consolidated for voting purposes. The eastern section of the state was apportioned half of the eight seats despite comprising only one-third of the population; the other four seats were divided between the western counties and Maine (65 percent of the population). Federalists obtained majorities in three of the four eastern districts in the first round of voting. To win the election, a candidate had to receive at least a majority of the vote cast. If no one received a majority, another election was held. The most interesting battle was in Suffolk, where tempestuous young Fisher Ames defeated one of the major leaders of the independence movement, Samuel Adams. Ames, an opponent of amendments, easily carried every district except Boston, where he just edged out his esteemed opponent, who reportedly wanted to help Antifederalists in the South "tear down the pillars of the federal government."[51] The fourth district went to Federalist Benjamin Goodhue on the second ballot. Goodhue's bid was threatened more by internal party strife than by his rival, suspected Antifederalist sympathizer Congressman Nathan Dane.[52]

Maine's seat went to Dane's colleague George Thatcher, a candidate acceptable to Federalists but trusted by leading amendment proponents like Samuel Nasson and William Widgery. Runoff elections were required in the three backcountry districts; in fact, it took five ballots to decide the issue in Hampshire-Berkshire. There was a strange turn of events in Middlesex: both of the leading candidates, Nathaniel Gorham and Elbridge Gerry, withdrew from the race after the first round of balloting. The voters continued to favor Gerry, however, choosing him over Joseph B. Varnum, who had voted for ratification of the Constitution in violation of his instructions. Gerry hesitated but at length accepted the seat so he could push for amendments in Congress. Anyone aspiring to win an election in the Antifederalist stronghold of Worcester had to be a sworn supporter of amendments. This point was not lost on the three Federalists competing against the sole Antifederalist candidate, Jonathan Grout. Grout prevailed on the third ballot after he finally succeeded in galvanizing his party's grassroots support. Only on his fifth try did Theodore Sedgwick come out on top in Hampshire-Berkshire, on May 11, 1789. He, too, had no choice but to declare for amendments. Just as had been the case during the convention elections in the winter of 1787–88, Sedgwick was accused of using underhanded tactics to manipulate voters, though nothing was ever proven. Federalists must have been more than satisfied with the outcome of the federal elections in Massachusetts: they had the support of every member of the electoral college, both senators, and eight of ten representatives.

Antifederalists were sorely disappointed in New York and Virginia after entering the races with high expectations. And this time they could not use the election laws as an excuse, since they had either had a major say in their wording or had written them entirely themselves. The Clinton party apparatus in New York was unable to prevent three of six seats from going to Federalists. This was a major setback compared with the combined convention and general elections held in the spring of 1788. Antifederalists knew their chances were slim in and around New York City. It came as a severe shock, however, when they also lost in districts three (Dutchess and upper Westchester) and five (Columbia, Washington, Clinton, and eastern Albany). In the second district (Kings, Queens, Suffolk, and Richmond), they had agreed on a common candidate with Federalists, and their victory in district four (Ulster and Orange) was a matter of course. Their greatest success was the election of Jeremiah Van Rensselaer, the chairman of the Federal Republican Committee of Albany, in district six (western Albany and Montgomery).[53]

The critics of the Constitution in Virginia fared even worse, winning only three seats in ten congressional districts in the elections on February 2, 1789.[54] Of particular interest was the battle between future presidents, Madison and Monroe, in the fifth district. Patrick Henry had forced Madison to take this route to Congress by denying him a seat in the Senate and had even created additional obstacles through gerrymandering. Both candidates waged a systematic campaign. They sought the public support of prominent citizens in the district and wrote letters detailing their stance on various issues. The recipients of these letters shared them among acquaintances together with other political literature. Madison and Monroe occasionally traveled around the district together, debating at election gatherings. They devoted an inordinate amount of time to Culpeper County, which was likely to provide the swing vote. Madison suffered from frostbite on one particular occasion when the candidates spoke outside in the bitter cold after a church service.[55]

The key issue was amendments. Monroe backed all the amendments proposed by the Virginia convention and advocated a second convention. His opponent was said to be "dogmatically attached to the Constitution in every clause, syllable and letter," and his convictions would not let him support amendments, even if they fostered reconciliation. Madison used his public appearances to deny these rumors, which had not been spread by Monroe himself. He was especially determined to allay the Baptists' fears of encroachments on freedom of religion. He reminded their leaders of his instrumental role in bringing about the liberal reform of the relationship between religious denominations and the State of Virginia. He attempted to reassure churchgoers that the federal Constitution would have no detrimental effect on the status of the church or the freedom of worship. When doubts remained, he printed a letter in the *Virginia Independent Chronicle*, on January 28, 1789, formally pledging to push for the incorporation of all "essential rights" into the Constitution without delay, especially the freedom of conscience.[56] His victory over Monroe by a vote of 1,308 to 972 was probably attributable to this vow more than anything else.[57] The rivalry had no bearing on the respect both men had for each other, since "the distinction was duly kept in mind between political and personal views," as Madison informed Jefferson.[58]

Long before the meeting of the new government in New York City it had become clear that Federalists would control the first Congress. The opposition accounted for only two of twenty-two senators (Virginians Richard Henry Lee and William Grayson) and eleven of fifty-nine representatives—three each from South Carolina, New York, and Virginia, and two from Massachusetts. It was thus entirely in Federalists' hands which amendments—if any—would be added to the Constitution.

As New York and Virginia proved, Antifederalists' poor showing could not be put down to the election laws alone. Another important factor was the decrease in voter turnout registered in every state except New Jersey, usually to the disadvantage of the opposition. The drop in participation was particularly striking in New York, where only half of the 24,500 citizens who had voted in the convention elections returned to the polls. This was only partially due to the reactivation of property qualifications and the scheduling of the elections at a less favorable time of the year. It was also attributable to declining interest on the part of the voters, a problem which hurt Antifederalists more than their adversaries, as the results clearly showed. Around 6,000 fewer ballots were cast in Pennsylvania than had been the case during the general elections in October 1788. The low numbers in the western counties suggest the "real friends of liberty and republicanism" had accepted their fate.[59] In neighboring Maryland, 8,000 voters turned out (18.3 percent of adult white males) for the House elections, 2,000 more than for the ratifying convention but far below the 14,000 (33 percent) who voted in October 1788 in elections for the state legislature. In Massachusetts, 13.1 percent of adult white males (11,500) participated in the selection of representatives, as opposed to 27 percent in the convention elections conducted in the winter of 1787–88. The runoff balloting, on the other hand, drew up to 30 percent in some areas. The situation was reversed in New Hampshire, where 21.4 percent (5,126) voted in the first round but only 11–13 percent in the final balloting after the elimination of all Antifederalist candidates. The turnout in Virginia fell, from approximately 26.5 percent in the convention elections to about 22 percent in the congressional elections, and in South Carolina only 12.2 percent (3,500) cast votes for representatives. The selection of presidential electors aroused even less interest.[60]

One major reason for the triumph of Federalists and the apparent complacency of Antifederalists was that a number of moderate critics were comforted by the Federalists' assurances of amendments. As in Madison's campaign in Virginia, other Federalist candidates voiced support for a bill of rights. In New Hampshire, Atherton was forced to experience firsthand how guarantees of this kind could take the wind out of the critics' sails: "To carry on the farce the Federalists have taken the liberty to step onto the ground of their opponents, and, clothing themselves with their armor, talk high of amendments—and by a kind of duplicity, often successful if not discovered, are taking possession of the political citadel under the style of friends."[61]

The results of the first federal elections indicate that Antifederalists had by now inured themselves to the idea of living under a different form of government. Thomas B. Wait grumbled that most Antifederalists were just waiting for the guarantee of a bill of rights so they too could drop down and worship the Constitution. Like Wait's fellow resident of Maine, William Widgery, most citizens were confident that their desire for amendments would be fulfilled: "I think there can be no danger but that amendments would take place as soon as the New Congress is organized."[62]

The growing acceptance of the Constitution is also illustrated by the fact that its basic principles were soon being assimilated into state constitutions. A letter printed in the New York *Weekly Museum* on January 31, 1789, described public opinion in Georgia: "Our old State Constitution, which is much like that of Pennsylvania, consisting of a single house of Assembly, is found so defective, that a convention is ordered to frame a new one; our present ideas are, that the new one shall be nearly similar to the new federal constitution." Abraham Baldwin confirmed that the new constitution of Georgia, completed in May 1789 after three successive conventions, was in many respects a copy of the federal Constitution.[63] On August 15, 1789, the *New-York Daily Gazette* reported that South Carolina had called a constitutional convention "for the purpose of revising their state constitution, in order to render the same conformable to the federal constitution, and to improve a political system formed . . . at a time when the American mind . . . was only in its infancy. The adoption of the federal constitution was but half a revolution from anarchy to government . . . it does not repeal any of those errors, however manifest, but what actually interfere with it." The convention lasted from May to June 1790, after which the new state constitution went into force without ratifying proceedings.

The swing in mood was most conspicuous in Pennsylvania, where the state constitution was admired by some as the best manifestations of the "spirit of 1776," while others dismissed it as excessively democratic. George Bryan, one of its authors, called on his followers in July 1789 to counter a Federalist-sponsored petition campaign for a constitutional convention by gathering signatures against the proposal. Albert Gallatin predicted an "appeal to arms" should the citizens be forced to accept a new state constitution such a short time after the federal Constitution had gone into effect.[64] In the end, prominent Antifederalists like William Findley and John Smilie dutifully participated in the convention, which began in November 1789, presented a draft for public discussion in February 1790, and ratified the new state constitution on September 2, 1790.

"The federal cause has received a fresh confirmation by our convention," Coxe wrote to Alexander Hamilton at the outset of the convention. "For I think it may be justly said, that every recognition of the principles of the general constitution, and every step toward an efficient and well balanced government by any member of the Union, is a furtherance of the object." He then outlined the most important points:

> It has been determined:
>
> 1. That the legislative power ought not to be in a single house.
> 2. That the judges . . . should be appointed during good behaviour. . . .
> 3. That the executive power should be in a single person.
> 4. That the chief executive officer should have a qualified negative upon the proceedings of the legislature."[65]

The key objectives were to curb the power of the legislative branch, strengthen the executive, and create an independent judiciary.

These principles were also implemented a short time later by Kentucky, Vermont, Delaware, and New Hampshire, all of which adopted new constitutions or revised their old ones in 1792–93. Similar changes were discussed in New York, North Carolina, and Virginia. In Virginia the idea had the support of both Federalist Archibald Stuart and Antifederalist John Dawson. Stuart asked Madison if the dispute over the Constitution hadn't created "the most favorable crisis for this important business." According to a letter from Dawson to Tench Coxe in December 1789, the impression that the people were tired of "changes in government" persuaded revision proponents in the Virginia legislature "to say nothing about it at this session although we see and lament the defects in the present constitution." Unlike Coxe and Stuart, Dawson wanted to change the state constitutions in a way that would strengthen the individual states to better protect them from "encroachments of the general government."[66]

The Correspondence between Jefferson and Madison on a Bill of Rights

James Madison's support of amendments was not a mere ploy to get elected, nor was it based on a fear of Patrick Henry, as critics in his own party maintained. Though he doubtlessly felt bound by the promises extracted from him during the ratifying convention and repeated during his campaign for a seat in the House of Representatives, he was not necessarily obliged to take the initiative in the Federalist-led Congress. Madison's chief motivating factors were rather the overall political situation in the Union after the adoption of the Constitution and his change of heart on the issue of a bill of rights, the latter development having been significantly influenced by his correspondence with Thomas Jefferson. Like other Federalists, Madison was unwilling to accept ratification by only eleven states. The news he received from North Carolina in 1789 left little doubt that it would take a bill of rights, at the very least, to induce the people of that state to endorse the Constitution.[67] Although Rhode Island politics were unpredictable, Madison assumed more could be accomplished through amendments than threats. Moreover, he suspected that a refusal to enact amendments would cause a backlash in states like Virginia and Massachusetts that could have negative consequences for the work of the federal government. Amendments that did not compromise the Constitution's basic premises seemed to be an effective tool for separating the moderate from the radical critics and undermining organized opposition. By demonstrating a determination to follow through with their promises, Federalists could create a reservoir of trust that would help the new government rapidly implement the Constitution.

Beside these political considerations lay a changed outlook on the value of guaranteeing basic rights, a gradual development derived from Madison's written discussions with Jefferson. The latter welcomed the Constitution as an important step forward that must not be jeopardized. This did not prevent him, however, from expressing criticism and suggesting changes. He believed the lack of a declaration of rights was one of the Constitution's "principle defects" and "most glaring faults."[68] On July 31, 1788, he wrote to Madison that the Constitution was "a good canvas, on which some strokes only want retouching." The absence of a bill of rights regulating such matters as "Juries, Habeas corpus, Standing armies, Printing, Religion and Monopolies" was particularly conspicuous. "The few cases wherein these things may do evil, cannot be weighed against the multitude wherein the want of them will do evil. . . . I hope therefore a bill of rights will be formed to guard the people against the federal government, as they are already guarded against their state governments in most instances."[69]

Madison did not consider the issue to be urgent at this time, and he accused the opposition of using the dispute over fundamental rights to distract attention from their true objectives. He penned his first detailed, albeit clearly reserved, response to Jefferson's objections on October 17. Madison thought it "probable" that Congress would integrate into the Constitution additional safeguards for "public liberty and individual rights." He insisted that he was open to the idea of a bill of rights, but he did not consider the lack of one to be "a material defect." In any case, he would support the measure for no other reason "than that it is anxiously desired by others." What spoke against the idea was that the states retained all rights not expressly delegated; that it was difficult if not impossible to formulate an encompassing declaration of the "most essential rights"; and that sufficient protection was already provided by the limited power of the central government in conjunction with the vigilance of the states. He went on to point out that actual practice in America had proven the ineffectiveness of "parchment barriers" in preventing the arrogation of power by legislative majorities. The chief threat to "private rights" stemmed "from acts in which the Government is the mere instrument of the major number of the constituents. . . . Wherever there is an interest and power to do wrong, wrong will generally be done, and not less readily by a powerful and interested party than by a powerful and interested prince." In the case of a popular government, the political and physical power were in the same hand, "that is in a majority of the people, and consequently the tyrannical will of the sovereign is not to be controuled by the dread of an appeal to any other force within the community." Hence, a bill of rights was primarily of didactic value, since the political truths it contained would assume the character of "fundamental maxims of free Government" with time, "and as they become incorporated with the national sentiment, counteract the impulses of interest and passion." Attempts by the central government to usurp power could never be fully ruled out. Conversely, if governmental authority declined below a certain level, it must be feared that its influence would continue to weaken, "until the abuses of liberty beget a sudden transition to an undue degree of power."[70]

In the following months, Madison kept Jefferson up to date on developments surrounding the federal elections. For his part, Jefferson explained how important America's debate over the Constitution was to France, which was anxiously anticipating an assembly of the States General. Jefferson predicted on November 18 that if the estates' demands were not unreasonable it might be possible to devise a good national constitution. Clearly moved by the progression of events, he reported two months later that all of Paris had joined the effort to draw up a constitution and an enumeration of basic rights. Lafayette's draft of a "declaration of rights," to which Jefferson had contributed, contained "the essential principles of ours accomodated as much as could be to the actual state of things here."[71] On March 15, 1789, Jefferson answered Madison's letter of the preceding October, refuting his friend's arguments against a bill of rights. It was essential, Jefferson maintained, that such a document be appended to the American Constitution, "which leaves some precious articles unnoticed, and raises implications against others." Should a precise definition of all rights prove impracticable, then at least those rights that were easily established should be protected. The states' jealous protection of their authority could only be relied on if they were given entitlements that underpinned their opposition to the central administration. Jefferson felt the disadvantages of a declaration of rights were generally "shortlived, moderate, and reparable," whereas the consequences of their absence would be "permanent, afflicting and irreparable." He cleverly derived an additional justification for a bill of rights from Madison's obsession with the horrors of unbridled majority rule: the purpose of the amendments was not merely to limit the power of the executive branch; they were also designed to prevent the "tyranny of the legislatures," which would long remain the main problem in republican America. One particular benefit of a bill of rights was "the legal check which it puts into the hands of the judiciary. This is a body, which if rendered independent, and kept strictly to their own department, merits great confidence for their learning and integrity."[72]

The revolutionary events in France began to take up more and more space in Jefferson's letters. On May 11, 1789, he noted that the Revolution had so far been carried off "with the most unexampled success hitherto." After the storming of the Bastille, Jefferson delayed his return to the United States in order to witness events, "as will be for ever memorable in history." He was pleased to report toward the end of August that the French declaration of rights was completed and the constitution was in the planning stage. In both cases, the United States had served as an example: "In short ours has been professedly their model. . . . Our proceedings have been viewed as a model for them on every occasion . . . [our authority] has been treated like the bible, open to explanation but not to question."[73]

Jefferson at this point was still misinterpreting the events in France as a movement whose chief aim was to revolutionize the constitutional order. He experienced the social upheaval only from a distance, having returned to the United States at the beginning of December 1789. He carried with him a letter to Madison that was not mailed until January 9, 1790. Starting from the premise that no generation would assume more debt than it could pay back during its lifetime, Jefferson questioned the value of permanent constitutions in general: "On similar grounds it may be proved that no society can make a perpetual constitution, or even a perpetual law. The earth belongs always to the living generation. . . . Every constitution then, & every law, naturally expires at the end of 19 years." It is not hard to understand why he hesitated before sharing such unconventional thoughts with a friend who had just invested considerable time and energy in the conception of a constitution "for generations yet unborn."[74]

Madison did not directly respond to Jefferson's letter of March 15, 1789, which he received at the end of May. He no longer spoke of "conciliatory sacrifices," however, propounding instead "sundry amendments" that would largely satisfy the opposition. In late June he even apologized for ignoring several otherwise useful amendments that had no chance of obtaining a two-thirds majority in both houses of Congress as well as the approval of three-fourths of the states.[75] Above all, Jefferson's influence can be seen in the speech Madison gave on June 8, 1789, when he introduced his proposal for a bill of rights in the House of Representatives.[76] The arguments he used to dispel Federalists' reservations about a bill of rights are nearly indistinguishable from Jefferson's. He pointed out that the restrictions in Great Britain only applied to the power of the Crown and did not mention fundamental rights like freedom of the press and freedom of conscience. In the United States, by contrast, the people deemed it necessary "to raise barriers against power in all forms and departments of government." The greatest task was "to limit and qualify the powers of government, by excepting out of the grant of powers those cases in which the government ought not to act, or act only in a particular mode." Special attention, he said, must be paid to the legislature as the branch of government which was the most powerful, the most susceptible to abuse, and the most difficult to control. The real threat, in any case, was not so much the actions of Congress as transgressions committed by society in general. For this reason, the provisions must be primarily directed at the source of governmental power, the "body of the people, operating by the majority against the minority." It was questionable whether written declarations could protect basic rights against society itself, but since such "paper barriers" had a tendency "to impress some degree of respect for such rights, to establish the public opinion in their favor, and rouse the attention of the whole community, it may be one mean to controul the majority from those acts to which they might be otherwise inclined."[77]

The existence of bills of rights in the individual states sufficed to refute the common argument that an enumeration of rights was pointless or even harmful in a republican system. At the same time, these declarations were insufficient, Madison explained, because they were flawed in some cases and were not included in all state constitutions. It had often been said that there was no need for a bill of rights in the Constitution, for the simple reason that the general government possessed enumerated and precisely circumscribed powers only and thus could not possibly infringe on the citizens' basic rights and liberties. In fact, when the Constitution granted specific powers it also granted "certain discretionary powers with respect to the means, which may admit of abuse to a certain extent." Congress could freely decide, for example, how taxes should be collected. Depending on the circumstances, it might deem general searches of homes to be a "necessary and proper" method to enforce the collection. Here Madison was clearly distancing himself from James Wilson's "enumerated powers" theory, just as he had previously done in his letters to Jefferson, and admitting Antifederalists' concerns were justified.

The most plausible argument against a bill of rights—a point eloquently made by Hamilton in the 84th "Publius" essay—was the danger that specifying certain rights could be construed to mean all other rights had been surrendered and were now open to encroachment by the government. Madison proposed to avoid this problem by providing that the bill of rights "shall not be construed as to diminish the just importance of other rights retained by the people." He brushed aside the objection that in-state declarations had proved ineffective in the past, and he adopted Jefferson's view of the potential role of the judiciary. Under the new system of government, "independent tribunals of justice will consider themselves in a peculiar manner the guardians of those rights; they will be an impenetrable bulwark against every assumption of power in the legislative or executive; they will be naturally led to resist every encroachment upon rights expressly stipulated for in the constitution by the declaration of rights." An explicit affirmation of the "great rights of mankind" was possible, could be effective, and could be done without damaging the Constitution. "I do conceive that the constitution may be amended; that is to say, if all power is subject to abuse, that then it is possible the abuse of the powers of the general government may be guarded against in a more secure manner than is now done, while no one advantage, arising from the exercise of that power, shall be damaged or endangered by it." By acknowledging the material benefits of a bill of rights, Madison was extending his hand to the critics of the Constitution.

The Amendments before Congress

After the federal elections it was generally assumed that the new Congress would treat the amendment issue as a matter of priority. "I consider the first Congress as a second Convention," stated Samuel Osgood in February 1789.[78] This opinion was undoubtedly shared by most Antifederalists and even many proponents of the Constitution. Madison personally saw to it that the amendments were mentioned in President Washington's inaugural address of April 30, 1789, and in Congress's reply.[79] In this way, he hoped to reassure the public, while instilling a sense of urgency in the legislature. It appears, however, that he had overestimated both the ability of the opposition to put pressure on the majority and the willingness of his own party to compromise. For as soon as Federalists became fully aware of their dominant position in Congress, their interest in implementing immediate changes waned noticeably. In Massachusetts, Connecticut, and Maryland, in particular, the election results were interpreted as a clear vote against amendments. Some politicians openly admitted to having endorsed amendment recommendations at the ratifying conventions for tactical reasons only.

Most Federalist congressmen preferred to hide behind the argument that one should not be too hasty and that it would be better to wait a few years. Once the plan was put into practice, they said, it would become evident what changes were necessary and appropriate. Their real intention in many cases was to put off action on the problem indefinitely. Few Federalists agreed with Tench Coxe that immutable guarantees of "religious and civil liberty" were more likely to enhance rather than harm the reputation of the federal government in America and abroad.[80] At first Congress showed no inclination whatsoever to address the issue. The opposition saw no point in trying to force a debate on amendments, and the majority gave more priority to key legislative measures like the finance laws and provisions for the establishment of a federal judiciary. As a result, Madison had to wait five full weeks between his announcement on May 4 that he would propose amendments to the House on June 8. Had he not repeatedly stressed the urgency of the matter, it probably could not have been concluded during the first term of legislature.[81]

The delay tactics of his fellow party members caught Madison by surprise, as he was under the impression that the amendments he was going to propose would be acceptable to Federalists.[82] He had broken down the recommendations of the ratifying conventions into nineteen separate proposals, which he then condensed into nine articles.[83] Of the twenty-two amendments proposed by four or more states, fourteen were assimilated into his plan. He was understandably somewhat partial to the ideas submitted by the Richmond convention. All in all, he succeeded in incorporating nearly every right and liberty proposed by the ratifying conventions. The few exceptions included the right to free and frequent elections as well as the hunting and fishing rights so dear to the Pennsylvania minority. At the same time, he added two provisions which none of the states had demanded, but seemed important to him. The first of these established that no one could be forced to relinquish possession of private property for public use without fair compensation; the second prohibited the states from infringing on freedom of conscience or the press or the right of the accused to a trial by jury in criminal cases.

It was Madison's desire that the amendments be inserted directly into the text of the Constitution and not listed separately, in order to avoid misunderstandings. As he explained to the governor of North Carolina, his proposal served the dual purpose "of removing the fears of the discontented and of avoiding all such alterations as would either displease the adverse side, or endanger the success of the measure."[84]

In Congress Madison reaped more criticism than praise for his efforts, while public opinion was divided. Antifederalists suspected the plan was intended to split the opposition. Elbridge Gerry moved to postpone the debate until all amendment recommendations submitted by the states had been examined. Federalists, on the other hand, felt that Madison was acting in haste and running the risk of handing the opposition an undeserved triumph. Fisher Ames commented derisively that the proposal might placate people "who attend to sounds only, and may get the mover some popularity—which he wishes."[85] Pejorative epithets like "innocent," "nugatory," "premature," and "unnecessary" were used to describe Madison's amendments in the letters of other congressmen as well. The only generally positive response was from Madison's correspondents in Virginia, yet even they found fault with certain articles and suggested alternatives. Madison also detected a note of reproach in Edward Carrington's remark that the "patron of amendments" was starting to become popular with Virginia Antifederalists.[86] Typical of the mood in and around Philadelphia was the humorous yet, in effect, harsh criticism delivered by Richard Peters, the speaker of the Pennsylvania Assembly. Although Madison politely thanked Peters for sending a copy of his satirical poems, and justified his actions at great length, Peters remained convinced "that a Firmness in adhering to our Constitution 'till at least it had a longer Trial would have silenced Antifederalists sooner."[87]

Madison was also subjected to attacks in the newspapers after the plan was published in the New York *Daily Advertiser* on June 12. "If we must have amendments, I pray for merely amusing amendments, a little frothy garnish," concluded an anonymous writer in New York at the end of a twenty-eight-part series of articles in which he analyzed every suggested alteration. Under the pseudonym "Pacificus," Noah Webster addressed Madison directly in the *Daily Advertiser* and predicted his initiative would "revive the spirit of party, spread the causes of contention through all the states, call up jealousies which have no real foundation, and weaken the operations of the government." He also insisted that most people agreed "that paper declarations of rights are trifling things and no real security to liberty." For a sovereign people solemnly to declare itself unwilling to be robbed of its own rights was "a farce in government as novel as it is ludicrous."[88] It is not surprising under these circumstances that Madison, who had been backed only by his colleagues from Virginia during the initial discussion in the House of Representatives, found the whole affair "extremely difficult and fatiguing" and "exceedingly wearisome."[89]

After repeated delays, the House appointed a Select Committee on July 21 comprising one delegate from each state to address the amendment issue. During the week-long, closed-door deliberations, Madison was harried by his own party members much more than by the lone Antifederalist participant, Aedanus Burke of South Carolina. The committee tautened Madison's concept and rearranged his suggestions.[90]

Madison's original plan was nonetheless still relatively intact when the report of the select committee was finally put on the House agenda on August 13. It was discussed for a week in the Committee of the Whole and then for four more days in the House. In order to ensure he could muster the two-thirds majority needed to pass the measure, Madison had been wise enough to secure Washington's support in advance. He exhibited a letter in which the president stated, somewhat tepidly, that he expected no "evil consequences" from the amendments and therefore wished them a "favorable reception in both houses."[91] This hint reduced Federalist resistance to the proposal. The debate then reverted to a partisan dispute between them and Antifederalists, whose speakers—Gerry, Tucker, Burke, and Sumter—tried in vain to widen the discussion to include structural amendments recommended by the conventions. They had to content themselves with submitting their most urgently desired changes as supplementary proposals and defending them against sarcastic and condescending comments of the majority. Their suggestions included giving civil authorities control over the military, eliminating the power to create inferior federal courts with the exception of admiralty courts, curbing the right of the federal government to regulate elections, and incorporating the "tax amendment." They tried to strengthen the position of the states by inserting the word "expressly" in Madison's eighth amendment. By limiting the central government to only those powers expressly granted to it by the Constitution, they hoped to prevent the expansion of its power through the doctrine of "implied powers."[92]

All Antifederalist motions were defeated in emotional and heated debates. Thirty-nine of the forty-eight representatives rejected a restriction on the power to tax. Madison was also forced to make additional concessions to Federalists if his plan was to have good prospects of obtaining the requisite two-thirds majority. The rest of the preamble featuring the sentence "Government being intended for the benefit of the people, and the rightful establishment thereof being derived from their authority alone" fell victim to Federalists' aversion to overly democratic-sounding phrases. At the same time, the House increased the protection against searches and seizures and raised the maximum size of the House from 175 to 200. More important still, the majority was leaning toward Roger Sherman's suggestion of appending the amendments to the Constitution instead of integrating them into the text. Of all the concessions Madison had been forced to make until then, this was the one that bothered him the most.[93] On August 22, the House of Representatives approved seventeen amendments, and sent them to the Senate on August 24.[94]

The Senate in its closed-door sessions from September 2 to 9 made twenty-six changes, some of which were of such fundamental significance that an exasperated Madison complained they were "striking" at the "most salutary articles."[95] The protection of basic rights against infringement by the states was removed, along with the principle of separation of powers; the rest was edited, abridged, and compressed into twelve articles. Other important cuts involved the freedom of conscience, release from military duty for religious reasons, the minimum value of cases that could be appealed to the Supreme Court, and the right of the accused in criminal proceedings to a jury of the vicinage. The Senate altered the guarantee of freedom of religion and extended the last amendment to include the words "or to the people," to emphasize that not all "reserved powers" belonged to the states.[96] Richard Henry Lee and William Grayson of Virginia felt the Senate had "mutilated" and watered down the House's draft to such an extent that the remaining amendments were hardly worth the effort. Yet what angered them the most was the derogatory manner in which some of their colleagues spoke of the "great principles of Civil liberty," "the constitutional guarantees of basic freedoms," and the "democratic prerogatives." Lee reported that several senators even wanted to eliminate the reference to freedom of speech and the press, saying it only encouraged excesses and abuse. As Lee informed Patrick Henry, Federalists had been "wonderfully scrupulous" in formulating rights: "The English language has been carefully culled to find words feeble in their nature or doubtful in their meaning."[97] It was this bitterness that induced Lee and Grayson to write a letter to the Virginia House of Delegates containing warnings so ominous that even the critics of the Constitution dismissed them as "seditious and highly reprehensible."[98]

The House of Representatives reviewed the Senate draft from September 19 to 21 and expressed disagreement with some of the changes. The differences would have to be ironed out in a conference committee attended by three members from each chamber. James Madison, Roger Sherman, and John Vining eventually agreed to accept the Senate's version in toto on condition that three modifications were made. The first of these involved rewording the article pertaining to the size of the House, the second guaranteed a trial by jury in the district in which the crime was committed, and the last generally reinstated the original wording of the amendment on religious freedom.[99] The fact that the senators consented to these changes—particularly the third one—encouraged a fatigued Madison. The House of Representatives approved the compromise on September 24. The Senate followed on September 25, the date considered the birth of the Bill of Rights. President Washington forwarded the twelve amendments to the states for ratification at the beginning of October.[100]

Public Reactions and Ratification by the States

If staunch Federalists showed relief over the completion of the bill, it was mainly because they were glad to be rid of the bothersome issue of amendments so they could now turn their attention to more "serious" matters. Like Pennsylvanian George Clymer, most regarded Antifederalists as political hypochondriacs who should best be treated with "bread pills" and "neutral mixtures."[101] The amendments adopted by Congress did not pose a threat in their view. The revisions did not significantly restrict the ability of the federal government to act or give Antifederalists a political victory to be exploited in public. In Abraham Baldwin's estimation, the articles approved "will do no hurt and may give ground to antifeds to wheel around with a salve to their pride."[102] Fisher Ames, Theodore Sedgwick, and Robert Morris were also ultimately convinced that the amendments were more likely to put an end to Antifederalism than revive it.

Many moderate Federalists shared Jefferson's opinion of Madison's original amendments: "I like it as far as it goes; but I should have been for going further."[103] They would have preferred additional changes, such as replacing the vice president with an executive council, prohibiting trade monopolies and standing armies in times of peace, and improving protection for the militia and jury systems. Still, most were just glad they had at least partly managed to keep their promise of amendments, and were relieved to have concluded the monumental task of constitution making. The fact that Congress had reached an agreement on a bill of rights, wrote Edmund Pendleton, "will have a good effect in quieting the minds of many well meaning Citizens."[104]

In any case, Article V of the Constitution left the door open for further revisions, the necessity, nature, and scope of which could better be determined by time than by speculation. Madison's hope that the amendments would have a favorable effect on the political climate was soon confirmed. "As far as I can gather," he wrote to Washington on November 20, 1789, "the great bulk of the late opponents are entirely at rest, and more likely to censure a further opposition to the Govt. as now Administered than the Government itself." He proudly quoted a letter from a Baptist preacher in Virginia stating "that the amendments had entirely satisfied the disaffected of this Sect, and that would appear in their subsequent conduct."[105] Nevertheless, his disappointment over the vehement resistance to amendments in his own camp had alienated him from the nucleus of the Federalist Party, paving the way for his later gravitation to the opposition. Radical Federalists also noted that Madison was beginning to go his own way, and could become a dangerous political rival in the future.[106]

While most members of the opposition were disappointed over the outcome of the amendment debate, their constituents seemed satisfied. Men like Elbridge Gerry, Samuel Bryan, Thomas Tudor Tucker, Patrick Henry, and Richard Henry Lee regarded the amendments as not only of little use, but actually dangerous, in that they gave the people a false sense of security. Henry and Lee agreed that declarations of fundamental rights were pointless as long as the states and their citizens were deprived of the means to defend those rights if necessary. "We must not forget, that the liberties of the people are not so well received by the *gracious manner*, as by the *limitations* of power," warned the senator from Virginia. Henry concurred: "Right, without her Power & Might is but a shadow."[107] The amendments approved by Congress lacked "some essentials"—those "great points" which, to the minds of Grayson and Lee, included "free elections, jury trial in criminal cases, . . . the unlimited right of taxation, and standing armies." A few important rights had been established, Lee commented after the debate in the Senate, "but the power to violate them to all intents and purposes remains unchanged."[108]

At the core of the federal government's power was the right to tax. Only if this right were restricted could the proper relationship between the states and the Union be restored as far as Antifederalists were concerned. They consequently returned again and again to their demand for the elimination of the central government's right to collect direct taxes unless the states failed to provide revenue. Edmund Randolph informed Madison in August that Patrick Henry was satisfied with some of the proposed amendments, "but still asks for the great desideratum, the destruction of direct taxation." By the end of November 1789, according to another observer, the opposition to the new system of government had been "reduced to a single point, the power of direct taxation." Antifederalists were unhappy with the amendments because they stood in the way of their true objective, the revision of the tax article. "Never adventure direct taxation for years," Madison was advised by Lee's Federalist brother, Henry Lee, who was concerned about the stability of the political climate in Virginia.[109] There were also warnings from other states that the farmers feared nothing more than poll taxes and land taxes. The right of taxation was sacred to Federalists, however, and they were only prepared to accept certain restrictions regarding its practical application. Hamilton had predicted in July 1788 that direct taxes would remain an "impolitic measure" for years to come. Coxe described the danger of separatism in western Pennsylvania as "a strong Argument for preferring Revenue by impost to direct taxation."[110]

Elbridge Gerry, on the other hand, tried to prove that the central government could not subsist on import taxes and tonnage duties alone, and warned that both excise and direct taxes would be levied sooner or later. Moreover, he believed the people could no longer trust the judicial system to protect their rights. He viewed the Supreme Court together with the inferior courts created by the Judiciary Act of 1789 as an "awful tribunal" with nearly unlimited power to dispose of the life, liberty, and property of every citizen.[111] Ironically, it was precisely the strong, independent judiciary intended by Madison and Jefferson as a bulwark of civil rights that detracted from the merits of the Bill of Rights in the estimation of some Antifederalists.

Not all prominent adversaries of the Constitution took such a dim view of the situation as Elbridge Gerry and Richard Henry Lee, who were convinced the days of a free system of government in America were numbered. Most generally agreed with George Mason that, although a few "Material Amendments" were still needed, the Bill of Rights was certainly better than nothing at all.[112] Confident of the prospect of further improvement, they did not reject the idea of national unity out of hand. Above all, they had faith in the people's good judgment and their healthy distrust of authority. For the majority of former Antifederalists, the amendments ceased to be an issue after they had been approved by Congress. Madison's plan to separate the "well-meaning" Antifederalists from the headstrong ideologues and reconcile them with the new order had proven successful, at least on the surface. Elbridge Gerry indirectly confirmed the division between Antifederalist leaders and the rank-and-file when he wrote that Madison's proposals served no other purpose "than to reconcile those who had no adequate idea of the essential defects of the Constitution."[113]

It had become apparent during the creation of the Bill of Rights that the party lines established during the debate over the Constitution were beginning to dissolve and new political constellations were being formed in Congress. Madison was supported, for example, by Federalists from Virginia but not by those from Pennsylvania and New England. New Hampshire representative Samuel Livermore and one other Federalist in the House consistently voted with the opposition. There were also indications that not all

Antifederalists were as set on "structural" amendments as Gerry, Tucker, Lee, and Grayson. "Those who call themselves Antis," Grayson grumbled, "are so extremely lukewarm as scarcely to deserve the appellation."[114] One faction was focusing on obtainable goals while the other thought it better to accept defeat in the hope that the states would then insist on a second convention. Above all, the solidarity of southerners in opposition to the perceived threat of northern dominance was reasserting itself. Grayson observed that the conflicting interests of "carrying states" and "productive states" were by no means imagined. Congressmen from the South saw themselves forced into the role of a "defenceless naked minority." They believed the majority looked on the South as "the milk cow out of whom the substance would be extracted."[115] Federalists like Pierce Butler and William Loughton Smith from South Carolina thought no differently. Smith referred to the Massachusetts delegates as "great favorers of monarchy" and was deeply concerned about the fate of the South if John Adams should follow George Washington as president. Backed by a "phalanx of officers," Adams would allegedly create a "system of influence" in Congress that would prove ruinous to southern interests, especially where the system of slavery was concerned. However, Smith qualified this remark with the admission that, from an economical standpoint, Virginia, and not New England, was South Carolina's "greatest enemy."[116]

Anger over the northerners' egotistic behavior was already widespread in the South. Antifederalist John Dawson was not alone in his conviction that a northern "combination" was out to water down the amendments and push through their plans concerning the location of the national capital. Derogatory remarks about the states north of the Susquehanna were also made by the physician Walter Jones, who had been educated at the University of Edinburgh and William and Mary College. A former colleague of Madison's in the Virginia legislature and the ratifying convention, Jones believed the North was rapidly turning into a "Mixture of oligarchy & anarchy," as opposed to the structure of society in Virginia, that "great repository of republican principles." A separate southern confederation, an idea Jones had previously abhorred, "may one day, *possibly,* be a means of preserving our Liberty by a union of parts more homogeneous in their Nature, than the present may eventually be."[117] In Congress, Madison ordinarily played down the significance of sectional conflicts. During a heated debate on September 3, however, he allowed himself to be provoked into commenting that Virginia surely would not have joined the Union if the actions and arguments he had witnessed that day had been prophesied at the Richmond convention.[118] Surprising coalitions and constellations thus rang in the new era of American politics. The tensions eased somewhat after the "compromise of 1790," which met southern wishes for the national capital while giving way to the northern states on the question of funding the national debt and the assumption of the state debts.

Against this emotional backdrop, the ratification of the amendments was surprisingly uncontroversial and attracted little public interest. Nine state legislatures dispensed with the matter in the first ten months after Congress had approved the amendments. It took more than two years, however, for the decisive eleventh state to adopt the measure.[119] The first two amendments, dealing with representation and the remuneration of members of Congress, were not passed by the requisite three-fourths majority of states, which reduced the list to ten articles, much to Madison's chagrin.[120] New Jersey and Delaware dealt with the amendments just as quickly as they had previously adopted the Constitution. Yet two other states dominated by Federalists, Georgia rejected the amendments as premature, while the Connecticut legislature split—one house adopting ten and the other eleven of the twelve amendments. Maryland, South Carolina, and New Hampshire ratified around the turn of the year in 1789–90 without a word of protest from the once disputatious Antifederalist factions. Pennsylvania followed in March 1790 despite the return of Samuel Bryan's polemical "Centinel" series. A few problems were caused by the states with the strongest Antifederal parties. The opposition in the Massachusetts legislature put forward eight supplementary proposals, all of which were rejected. The lower house retaliated by blocking the ratification of the amendments at the last minute.[121] The New York legislature endorsed the amendments in February 1790 over the objections of the Clintonians, who dismissed what was left of Madison's plan as trivial, ambiguous, and useless. North Carolina and Rhode Island also accepted the plan, but still made a futile attempt to get Congress to discuss their own suggestions for amendments. In February 1791, Vermont ratified the Constitution and became the fourteenth state. Its legislature immediately adopted the proposed amendments.

In December 1789, the legislature in Virginia took up the amendments, along with the accompanying scathing letter from Senators Richard Henry Lee and William Grayson: "It is with grief that we now send forward propositions inadequate to the purpose of real and substantial Amendments, and so far short of the wishes of our Country."[122] Patrick Henry wanted the debate adjourned and turned his back on the legislature in disgust when his motion was rebuffed. Only a slim, one-vote majority, however, prevented the passing of a resolution calling on Congress to incorporate the remaining Virginia amendments into the Constitution. In the end, Edmund Randolph and a few other senators questioned whether the states' "reserved powers" were really secure, and the legislative term drew to a close leaving the issue unresolved. Madison was convinced that this delay would not harm the federal government and in fact would have the opposite effect on many Virginians, namely, that "of turning their distrust toward their own Legislature."[123] A year later, on December 15, 1791, Virginia became the eleventh state to ratify the amendments, thus permitting the Bill of Rights to come into force. Secretary of State Thomas Jefferson had the honor of informing the state governors of this development on March 1, 1792, and he sent them a copy of the ratification documents and the Bill of Rights commissioned from Thomas Greenleaf's print shop.[124]

It is one of the ironies of the debate over the Constitution that the Bill of Rights probably would not have been proposed without constant pressure from Antifederalists, yet it was subsequently adopted without much support or even against the resistance of their leaders. In fact, many viewed the Bill of Rights as a further link in the chain of defeats suffered by the opposition since the publication of the Constitution in September 1787. To do justice to the historical facts, it must nevertheless be emphasized that the Bill of Rights is not only a tribute to James Madison's immense skill as a politician, it is also the ideological legacy of the Antifederalists. It was their persistence that compelled Massachusetts Federalists to propose recommendatory amendments to the Constitution, thus hitting upon the key to resolving the standoff between the two parties. With the exception of the compensation amendment, every provision contained in the final version of the Bill of Rights had appeared in at least one—and in most cases several—of the lists of recommendations submitted by the state conventions or proposed by the dissenting Antifederalist minorities. Critical voters in the 5th congressional district and the Virginia legislature kept watchful eyes on Madison to ensure that he did not renege on his promises. A lot of the credit also goes to Thomas Jefferson as someone Madison listened to despite the fact that Jefferson's fondness for declarations of basic rights and his distrust of "energetic government" were, in many ways, more compatible with Antifederalist views than with Madison's. Fully in line with George Mason's conviction, the Bill of Rights upheld the general principle that governmental power is never absolute and, over time, etched this conviction in the public consciousness.

CONCLUSION

Constitution-Making as a Political and Cultural Process: America's Debate over the Constitution and the French Revolution

Or at least we may, with a kind of grateful and pious exultation, trace the finger of Providence through those dark and mysterious events, which first induced the States to appoint a general Convention and then led them one after another (by steps as were best calculated to effect the object) into an adoption of the system recommended by that General Convention—thereby, in all human probability, laying a lasting foundation for tranquility and happiness; when we had but too much reason to fear that confusion and misery were coming rapidly upon us.

GEORGE WASHINGTON TO JONATHAN TRUMBULL, JULY 20, 1788

The love of Liberty has fled from hence to France.

RICHARD HENRY LEE TO ARTHUR LEE, SEPTEMBER 18, 1789

These people seem to have catched the Flame of American Freedom; and in protecting the Rights & Liberty of others, have learned to assert their own.

GEORGE MASON TO SAMUEL GRIFFIN, SEPTEMBER 8, 1789

At the end of the debate over the Constitution, most Antifederalists signaled a willingness to accept and acknowledge the new system of government. For their part, Federalists now looked back with pride, knowing they had contributed to the success of one of the greatest revolutions in the history of mankind. "It exhibits an instance unparalleled in ancient and modern times, of a people rising from a state of anarchy, to liberty and order, without the horrors of a civil war, and forming a government not by public faction nor private ambition, but by a liberal and intelligent investigation," intoned the *Federal Gazette* in June 1790.[1] Two years earlier, Virginia physician William Brown had informed his Scottish mentor, Dr. William Cullen, that a "novelty in Politics" was taking place in America, namely "the effecting a considerable and important revolution in our Government, without bloodshed or violence of any kind, but with the deliberate consent of the People of a large number of independent Sovereignties covering a Country of 1500 miles Extent, and differing in climate, pursuits and interests."[2] "So thorough a revolution was never before effected by Voluntary Convention," wrote Edward Carrington around that same time, "and it will stand as a lasting monument of a wisdom and congeniality peculiar to America."[3] The making of the Constitution was equated with such historic events as the Reformation and the English revolutions of the seventeenth century, and it was exalted in an endless array of phrases as "a political revolution," "the glorious revolution," "one of the greatest of human revolutions," "a new phenomenon in the political and moral world," "the second great epoch of our history," the "second American Revolution," and "the most glorious and unparalleled occurence in the course of human events." Ancient Benjamin Franklin envisioned a European federation modeled on the American system.[4] In principle, mused Jonathan Jackson ("A Native of Boston"), the Constitution's modern federal structure could some day even serve as a prototype for a "World Government."[5]

There was growing conviction that this was the beginning of a new chapter in the "science of politics," and that Americans were at the forefront of a progressive movement toward more freedom, justice, and enlightened thinking. "It appears then that we live in an æra of the world," Tench Coxe observed in one of his "American Citizen" essays, "when the progressive wisdom of man has accomplished the abolition of ecclesiastical power, and discovered the materials to lay the foundation of free government . . . the progress of political knowledge had given us the more certain bases of the acknowledged rights of man, and the established principles of freedom."[6] Reacting to a letter in which the Reverend John Lathrop had spoken of "an age of astonishing improvement," George Washington predicted an "æra of still farther improvements." The Reverend John Blair Smith thanked Madison for his efforts "to establish freedom and happiness on fixed and rational principles."[7] An anonymous letter writer from Talbot County in Maryland was convinced "that the revolution of 1788 will be attended with much more important consequences to the interests of mankind in general, than that of 1688 was to Great Britain in particular."[8] In John Stevens's sixth "Americanus" essay, the spirit of enlightenment merged with a belief in historical progress and the Americans' sense of mission:

> It was not till the Revolution in England that any tolerable ideas of good Government were formed. Plato, Sir Thomas More and Harrington, before this period, had amused themselves with forming visionary schemes of perfect Governments, but, for the want of experimental knowledge, their plans are no better than romances. . . . But it is principally from

> our experience that we can derive just notions of the true foundations on which the liberties of the people rest. . . . Let us be thankful to an all-ruling Providence, which has enabled us to discover the clue by which we may finally extricate ourselves from the labyrinth of profound darkness and perplexity in which mankind have hitherto wandered, with only now and then a glimmering of light.[9]

Federalists had arrived at a new, dynamic understanding of history that was just beginning to take Europe by storm by way of the French Revolution.

It was considered a given fact that this "progress to greater perfection," which had culminated in the "best form of government in the world,"[10] would bring tangible material benefits for Americans and improve their position in relation to Europe. Writing in the *North Carolina Gazette* on December 19, 1787, an "Old Spy" could "clearly foresee that [America] will rise to a summit that will shake old Europe to its very centre . . . the will of fate is in our favour, and her decrees are irrevocable." In their response to an address by the Chief Justice of New Jersey, the members of the Essex County grand jury extolled the virtues of the new Constitution, "which will render the period of its establishment the most brilliant era in the annals of our history. . . . America . . . will raise into an empire of strength, beauty, and wide-extended renown."[11] A few observers believed the United States was already "the most glorious empire on which the sun ever shone," and the "happy land of universal liberty."[12] In the *Albany Register* of November 1, 1788, an "Adopted American" advised his countrymen to steer clear of "European broils":

> An extensive empire, such as Heaven designed this continent to form . . . will always guard against every external source of calamity. . . . We are as yet young as a nation; but no nation on earth ever made such rapid advances to maturity. . . . The operation of the new government . . . and the adoption of the amended constitution . . . will bind us indissolubly in mutual gratulation, and shortly raise us far above the scoffs of any contemptible British paragraphist.

The American Constitution could be taken by Europeans either as an example for emulation or as a challenge. The *Albany Journal* of August 4, 1788, conveyed this ambiguous message in the form of a "Federal Song," ironically sung to the tune of "Rule Britannia."

> Proud Europe hence may learn, and see,
> A Constitution self-controul'd;
> By wisdom, balanc'd, firm and free,

The dread and model of the world.
Raise, Columbia, raise thy voice,
Union is thy noble choice.

Those politically active circles in Europe that were receptive to republican values more or less shared this view. In September 1788, the artist John Trumbull wrote to his family in Connecticut:

> All of us who love you, (unfortunately our number is very small in comparison of those who fear, envy and detest you) rejoice without bounds in the triumph of Reason and Good Sense over the Spirit of Disunion and the prejudices of little interests:—you have given the World a new Lesson: and if the Example be as great in the future conduct of our Empire as it is in its formation, it will be glorious indeed.[13]

In a letter sent to America that same month, the Englishman John Penn, a former governor of Pennsylvania and delegate to the Albany Congress of 1754, commented: "As your New Government must now take place, undoubtedly your Country will far surpass this, as the arts and sciences and every thing that is polite and elegant will find place among you, and this poor little spot will have nothing but to envy your growing greatness."[14] Thomas Brand Hollis, a self-described "republican," informed John Adams of his high regard for the Constitution after examining it at his country estate. "The more I consider the new constitution of America the more I rejoice and congratulate myself & you. It is the wisdom of ages reduced to practice." The few critical remarks made by Hollis included an appeal for a more liberal immigration policy, "worthy of a people the preceptors of mankind."[15]

On the European mainland, activists like the Marquis de Lafayette and Philip Mazzei, who were themselves pushing for constitutional and political reforms, were heartened by the thought that the "mirage in the west" might have a bearing on other parts of the world. In August 1788, John Jay and Thomas Jefferson were congratulated as representing all Americans by C. W. F. Dumas in The Hague on their "plus illustre et depuis la création l'unique Example de Sagesse et de perfection progressive à tous les Gouvernements et de félicité vraie à tous les peuples du monde."[16] Madame d'Houdetot perceived the spirit of wisdom, reason, humanity, and enlightenment in the Constitution. If she could be born again, she imparted to Jefferson, there were only two countries she would want to live in: Switzerland and the United States.[17] She wrote to Franklin that the adoption of the Constitution had filled her with the "sweetest sentiments of which the human heart is susceptible, namely that of seeing the happiness of one part of the globe assured by the progress of reason and the success of the Enlightenment."[18]

The delegates to the French National Assembly not only referred to the American model in connection with the concept of fundamental rights, William Short proudly informed Madison from Paris in November 1789 that the United States was "constantly quoted & are authority in the national assembly." He quoted one member who, in the course of the debate over a suitable title for the King, had declared: "Voyez ces Americains qui dans un monde nouveau, ont crée vraiment un autre monde; ils ne dedaignent pas seulement les titres, ils les ont abolis par les decrets dont la gloire ne le sera jamais. Chez eux le Congrès, s'appelle le Congrès, Washington, Washington, Franklin, Benjamin Franklin, & tous les titres ne paroissant que les ridicules ou des puerilités auprès de ces glorieux noms."[19] The United States was a key source of inspiration for many adherents of the French Revolution up until 1791, especially as far as constitutional questions were concerned. Remarks critical of the Constitution's conservatism, such as those uttered by the Marquis de Condorcet at an early stage of the debate, were thus rarely heard at this juncture. As the revolution progressed and took a more radical turn, however, the American model lost its appeal until, in the end, it was only preserved in the underground in the hope of better times to come.[20]

Just as the French had turned their eyes to the United States in 1788–89, Americans now closely followed events in France and began to ponder the correlations and disparities between the two revolutions. It was beyond dispute that the "spirit of American liberty" was taking root in Europe; the only question was whether it had spread to the Old World or fled there. In July 1789, Mercy Otis Warren expressed doubts to her English friend Catharine Macaulay Graham as to whether the American pursuit of liberty had lived up to expectations, then added:

> I leave America to wait the success of the bold experiment and wonder a moment with you at the astonishing revolution in France. Would it not be surprising if that nation should reap greater advantages from the spirit of liberty lately diffused through this continent than Americans themselves may be able to boast, after all their successes and their struggles to become a free people? But I dare not pronounce, I only retrospect the past, and contemplate the probabilities of futurity. So various are the parties, the interests, and the principles, that no human calculation can decide on the fate of America or France.[21]

Federalists were both sympathetic to the cause of the French revolutionaries and concerned that their quest for liberty might degenerate into chaos and destruction.[22] As early as the summer of 1788, Washington exhorted the French to show "great moderation" and cautioned that the country and the common man would benefit most from "a gradual and tacit Revolution."[23] Upon learning of the "dreadful tumults" in Paris in September 1789, Madison drew comfort only from Jefferson's accompanying remark that the French continued to focus their attention on the "main object," the crafting of a constitution.[24] A lack of purpose in this regard, however, was the very point criticized two months later by the Pennsylvania Quaker Miers Fisher in a letter to Brissot de Warville:

> The Subversion of all Orderly Discipline & the total Inactivity of the States General with respect to maintaining the Peace of Society & the Safety of Individuals is to me astonishing—in so enlightened a Nation I expected that immediately after the first Burst of Joy, which the Victory of the People occasioned, the States General would have given their principal Attention to the Establishment of a new Government.

For the sake of humanity and the honor of the French nation, he hoped there was no truth to the reports of atrocities coming from Paris.[25] The artist John Trumbull concluded in June 1790 that even civilized nations were intellectually several hundred years behind the stage of development described by John Adams in his *Defence of the American Constitutions:*

> A spirit of liberty has indeed gone forth—a disposition to pull down Kings, nobilities, & hierarchies—but where is the disposition to establish just governments on their ruins? The opposers of arbitrary power are apt to consider all power as arbitrary—To say no more of America, what is now doing in France? Great things I must own—& France may perhaps be as near the period when a regular, well balanced constitution may be formed, as England was in the days of our wise Namesake, King John."[26]

In his correspondence with Samuel Adams, John Adams expanded this idea into general reflections on the course of history:

> Is the millennium commencing? Are the kingdoms of [this world] about to be governed by reason? Your Boston town-Meeting, and our Harvard College, have set the universe in motion. Every thing will be pulled down. . . . But what will be built up? Are there any principles of political architecture? Were Voltaire and Rousseau masters of them? Locke taught them the principles of liberty: but I doubt whether they have not yet to

> learn the principles of government. Will the struggle in Europe, be any thing more than a change of impostors and impositions?

He was not satisfied with Samuel Adams's reply, in which the latter asserted there had been no "golden age" and the future would have to rely on the beneficial effects of education: "I am for seeking institutions which may supply, in some degree, the defect." Conversely, John Adams's system of checks and balances, which juxtaposed the masses and the natural aristocracy, was not to his cousin's liking: "Is not the whole sovereignty . . . essentially in the people?" Samuel shot back, pointing to the principle of frequent elections and the orderly political proceedings in the American legislatures.[27]

James Madison remained optimistic, succumbing in 1791 for a while to the illusion that the French Revolution had—in much the same manner as the American Revolution—reached its happy conclusion: "The French revolution seems to have succeeded beyond the most sanguine hopes. The King by freely accepting the Constitution, has baffled the external machinations against it. And the peaceable election of a Legislative Assembly of the same complexion with their predecessors, and the regular commencement of their functions, have equally suppressed the danger of internal confusion."[28] In addition to misreading the external situation of France, Madison failed to note that the French revolutionaries had violated two principles which played a key role in the success of the American experiment: they did not seek the people's approval of the constitution by way of a valid process of ratification, nor did they dissolve the National Assembly and hold elections for a new parliament—despite their familiarity with the distinction between lawmaking and constituent powers.[29] All the errors and mistakes notwithstanding, the French Revolution ensured that the discussion of the key elements, nature, and consequences of a republican order was also kept alive in the United States, and was even expanded to include a new, comparative dimension.

The Dialectics of Progress and Tradition

The debate over the American Constitution is too complex to be explained with the help of standard sociological frames of reference or political-ideological clichés. Only in a very loose sense was this a social or class struggle. In reality, it was more a clash between two distinct attitudes, mentalities, and political cultures shaped by the divergent way the opposing groups experienced life. A large portion of the rural population and a small percentage of the elite were still strongly influenced by the radical republicanism of the early phase of the Revolution; the largest share of the Revolutionary elite was the product of a more liberal ideology and culture whose domain was extending more and more into the urban middle classes and the segments of the population living in the vicinity of cities. At the same time, there was a common foundation of shared convictions and values that was firm enough to preserve the people's faith in the soundness of republican institutions and prevent the two sides from breaking apart entirely. The Constitution polarized the population in the thirteen states, but the political and ideological differences were not as clear-cut and the party lines not as rigidly drawn as has often been assumed. The situation was rather characterized by a fusion or an amalgam of republican, liberal, and religious ideas in the minds of individuals "whose thinking changed as they attempted to assimilate and manage new phenomena and new events."[30] If the terms "conservative" and "radical" must be regarded as antitheses, both parties were—as paradoxical as this may sound—at once conservative and radical. Like many movements that see sociopolitical change as a threat and cling to the status quo, the opposition to the Constitution comprised nostalgic as well as radical elements. The Country ideology, with its preference for small republics, its emphasis on a virtuous and well-armed citizenry, and its insistence on the greatest possible representation of all social groups and interests, was no longer suited to the stage of development the United States had reached at the end of the eighteenth century. The staunch defense of state sovereignty coupled with a readiness to sacrifice the good of the Union to the prosperity of individual states was detrimental to the economic recovery of the country and to the formation of a national identity. Practice had shown that other components of the opposition ideology—such as annual elections and rotation of office; the fear of a standing army; the concept of a virtuous citizenry in a small, homogeneous republic; and the aversion to a securely funded public debt—were also outdated and impeded progress. The tendency to attribute all problems to a lack of moral rectitude—a shared element of traditional republican and Puritan thought—made it difficult to address structural flaws in the system of government. Moreover, the "communal" spirit, with its focus on harmony and conformity, a phenomenon that was more predominant in the backcountry than along the coast, hindered liberalization more than it promoted it, especially in religious and cultural matters.

For all that, it must be stressed that some meaningful ideals would have been lost if the new order had banned from American consciousness and political practice all values and principles revered by Antifederalists, including their emphasis on personal responsibility, self-determination, and strict control over public officeholders, their fondness for republican simplicity, and their eschewal of splendor and wastefulness. Of particular importance was their healthy distrust of centralism and bureaucratization, their aversion to an unrestrained lust for national glory, and, finally, their uncompromising defense of fundamental rights. All of these traits were more prominent among Antifederalists than among the proponents of the Constitution. This gave their politics an egalitarian dynamism which, despite the ballast of numerous antiquated ideas, looked ahead to the democratic future rather than pining for a return to the "good old days." It is telling that they found it easier than Federalists to overcome their reservations about party spirit and organization. They also refused to allow virtue and community spirit to be completely displaced by self-interest and institutional safeguards for maintaining a balance of economic interests. Their moral rigorism led them to condemn slavery, which they universally rejected in the North—and opposed in at least certain parts of the South—as incompatible with republican principles. Their weak following in the cities, however, suggests that their relatively narrow concept of republican citizenship had a limited appeal to the rising urban middle and lower classes. Antifederalists were still too attached to the agrarian conception of a free society to attract these groups. There was no place for the urban masses in this utopia, which may explain the opposition's frequent derogatory remarks about the "rabble" in the cities. Yet here, as in England, a movement was already underway that would modernize the outmoded republican ideas and give them a radical-democratic slant. The American adherents of this political philosophy would come into their own during the era of Jeffersonian Republicanism, and even more so in the Jacksonian period.

In the course of the ratification debate, Federalists increasingly freed themselves from the manacles of the traditional conception of history and politics. Their realization that the uniqueness of the situation in America both demanded new solutions and made them possible gave them an advantage over their adversaries. This awareness allowed them to approach the task of framing a new constitution in a more open, flexible, and pragmatic manner. In the scientific spirit of the day, they believed they were unearthing the fundamental laws of society and perceived constitution-making as an experiment—one that could still be revised yet pointed the way to a better future in a more perfect system. They saw themselves as agents of change and renewal and were perceived by others in the same vein. "An attempt to change the dogmas of a great people, is a task which the greatest writers upon law, government, or revolution, acknowledge to be big with consequences," cautioned a contributor to the *New York Journal.* Writing in the *Massachusetts Gazette,* "Agrippa" judged Federalists much more harshly: "Propositions, novel, erroneous and dangerous, are boldly advanced to support a system, which does not appear to be founded in, but in every instance to contradict, the experience of mankind."[31]

Federalists perceived that there were national issues of economic, political, and military importance that could only be resolved by a central government. They translated this realization into politics and constitutional law, undeterred by opposing opinions, even those of recognized authorities like Montesquieu. Their economic theories were influenced by such pioneers of the Industrial Revolution as Adam Smith, James Steuart, David Hume, and Adam Ferguson. Unconstrained by self-doubt or false modesty, they modeled their economic policies on Europe's most developed country, their former sovereign and military adversary, England. They were thus at the forefront of a secular modernization movement which would gradually encompass all Western countries and lead them into the new era of capitalism. They were still far removed, however, from the liberal notion that economic activity should be free from government intervention as much as possible, an idea which became popular in the nineteenth century. Unlike Antifederalists, with their fondness for small government, they preferred a strong central administration that took the initiative on economic issues and dictated the law of trade. In cultural matters they also tended to be more worldly and receptive to modern trends than the proponents of the Country ideology, whose strict moral code could easily take on an illiberal aspect. Federalists often combined their progressive stance with an elitist attitude that overtly questioned the ability of the people to rule themselves. Antidemocratic sentiments and their yearning for a static social order thus stood in contrast to their openness to rational economic reform and their energetic commitment to the process of modernization. This ambiguity occasionally made Federalists appear hypocritical, as if they were trying to hide their aversion to the egalitarian principles of popular sovereignty behind verbose professions of their dedication to a representative democracy.

There was nonetheless one group of Federalists for whom liberty, equality, and economic-cultural progress were not inherently contradictory: the urban artisans and laborers whose support of the new Constitution was based on their belief that it would serve both their own material needs and the democratization of society. In this respect, their ideas harmonized with those of their idol and advocate, Thomas Paine, who from his vantage point in England did not view the American Constitution as counter-revolutionary or as a betrayal of the ideals of 1776. He did have reservations about the prominent role of the president and the long terms of office for members of the Senate, but—like Thomas Jefferson—was convinced of the "absolute necessity of establishing some Federal authority." In a letter dated March 1788, he distinguished between natural rights of the first and second order: "I consider the individual sovereignty of the states retained under the Act of Confederation to be of the second class of rights. It becomes dangerous because it is defective in the power necessary to support it. It answers the pride and purpose of a few Men in each State, but the State collectively is injured by it."[32] For Paine, just as for artisans and mechanics in Boston, Philadelphia, New York City, Baltimore, and Charleston, the struggle for a new constitution was the direct continuation of the fight for political and economic independence and social equality.

In any case, Federalists as a group needed the ideological-political counterweight provided by the Antifederalist Party. This prevented them from yielding entirely to their elitist inclinations, on the one hand, or succumbing to an uncritical, rapturous affirmation of progress on the other. Antifederalists' firm resolve, often dismissed as backwards particularism, helped to ensure that the "revolution in favor of government" was not too extreme, and that political concepts which were too far removed from the people or were too authoritarian had no chance of success. Yet as much as the dissenters insisted on the right of the citizens to rule themselves, they also felt that strict democratic checks were indispensable, precisely because of what they considered man's natural susceptibility to the temptations of wealth and power. They disagreed among themselves over whether only the ruling classes and social elite were deserving of their distrust, or the entire populace. The concept of linear progress, on the other hand, was equally foreign to all Antifederalists. This is surely one of the points where they seem more "modern" to us than their "progressive" counterparts. Each party thus sought its own answer to the "paradox of human progress and human depravity."[33]

Federalists believed the Constitution represented a solution to this dilemma, even if they had to acknowledge the truth of their critics' warnings that no constitution, no matter how perfect, could by itself prevent corruption and moral decline. The nature of the debate dictated that Federalists stress the advantages of the new system, Antifederalists the drawbacks and the dangers of decline and degeneration. There is no question that the proponents of the Constitution clearly recognized America's enormous potential for development and more accurately foresaw the country's rise to world power.[34] Yet if all the adverse effects of this phenomenal ascent are added to the equation, it is evident that the skeptics in 1787–88 were not merely putting on a "parade of imaginary horribles."[35] As has nearly always been the case with predictions throughout history, the optimists were painting an overly rosy picture of the future, while the pessimists were conjuring up apocalyptic visions. In America as elsewhere, the reality was and is somewhere in between.

The Legitimation of the Constitution and the Union

The economic interests and ideologies that clashed during the framing of the Constitution were certainly important and will remain an object of critical research. Yet their significance can only be measured within the overall context of the debate. Without disputing the importance of economic factors or downplaying the valuable contributions made by such worthy individuals as Hamilton and Madison, it must be said that the greatest achievement of the years 1787–89 was the conception and successful conclusion of the process of ratification. The complexity of this operation resulted from its duration and the large number of people and institutions involved, including the thirteen state legislatures and conventions, the parties and politicians, the town meetings, the diverse interest groups and religious denominations. The interplay between the various levels of the debate, the interaction of its myriad components, and the permanent pressure of public opinion created a dynamic force that transformed America. In the course of the dispute, the newspaper business experienced an enormous boom, party formation entered into a new phase of development, long-established ideological maxims and doctrines were called into question, and a new festive culture and civil religion emerged from the ratification celebrations. Economic interests were now seen from a changed perspective, and the people generally took a different view of the past and future than they had before it all began. Although the terms "democracy" and "democratic" only gradually lost their negative connotations, and although not every American by far was allowed to participate, the events were driven by a democratic opinion-forming and decision-making process. In this regard, the ratification proceedings themselves represented an important stage in the transition to a modern civil society.

The success of this movement can be attributed to the attitudes and institutions created during the colonial period and transformed by the Revolution in such a way as to guarantee the openness of the political discussion. The legislatures and conventions, the town and county meetings, the grand juries and jury trials provided training grounds for democratic thought and behavior, a precondition for political participation. This applied in particular to the principle of respecting majority decisions, without which the Constitution would have been doomed to failure. Freedom of the press and freedom of speech created a climate and provided a forum for a productive political debate and a vibrant public sphere. At the conclusion of the long discussion, it was therefore fitting that these principles were embodied in the First Amendment. While their interpretation is difficult, and has been a frequent source of contention, no one questions their main purpose: ensuring the free examination of all matters affecting the public, thus preserving the general openness of the political discourse. For this reason, the First Amendment has been described as a "declaration of national policy in favor of the public discussion of all public questions."[36] Relevant Supreme Court opinions have included such fundamental observations as: "Authority here is to be controlled by public opinion, not public opinion by authority. . . . It is the function of the citizen to keep the Government from falling in error."[37] Seen from this perspective, the adoption of the Constitution represented a further step in the process of social self-organization and self-governance, set in motion by the Revolution or, in a more profound sense, by the settlement of North America. The final act of the Revolution, the making of the Constitution, was a "rational, legal, and deliberate process employed to correct defects in government."[38] Hence, the relationship between the form and content of the debate was defined by its purpose. If the government created by the Constitution can be characterized as a graduated system of mutually controlled powers, the ratification debate, as the element of public control, served as a final—perhaps even crucial—safeguard. Just as the checks and balances implemented by the framers of the Constitution were intended to energize the system, not encumber it, this new monitoring force did not weaken the government but rendered it more vigorous, effective, and stable.

In the Revolutionary state constitutions and the Articles of Confederation, the century's key doctrines of popular sovereignty, separation of powers, representation, and basic rights had been put into practice for the first time. In the 1780s, however, experience showed that the mechanisms designed to ensure the smooth functioning of these political orders were inadequate. A concentrated effort was required to revise them and bring them in line with the Union's needs. The old doctrines and principles were constructively modified, reinterpreted, and expanded to make room for the strict dictums of the rule of law and the dynamic concept of federalism. The new system of government acquired an incontestable legitimation through the process of public debate and ratification. It survived its first severe test, the partisan strife of the 1790s, and to date has only had to overcome one serious challenge, the Civil War of 1861–65. The ability to evolve and adapt, without which the Constitution could neither have been created nor ratified, was, is, and will always be of the utmost importance. When outdated ideas and worldviews are forced to make way for more realistic attitudes, spontaneity, reflexivity, and creative intelligence are in demand. Yet these qualities can only prosper in an environment where freedom of thought and expression liberate the spirit and break up fossilized systems of beliefs. Seen in this light, the debate over the Constitution was one of those unique moments of historical awakening in which prominent figures play a less important role than each and every individual. Society was no longer—as in times past—formed by the government, the government was formed by society. Far from being an obstacle to change, contrast, contradiction, and conflict proved a catalyst for intellectual achievement and were indispensable to the success of the movement. Political rivals locked in a common struggle, Federalists and Antifederalists made a lasting contribution to the construction of a common American identity and to the future of the United States and humankind.

NOTES

Abbreviations and Short Titles

AHR *American Historical Review*

AN Archives Nationales, Paris

Boyd Julian P. Boyd et al., eds., *The Papers of Thomas Jefferson,* 35 vols. to date (Princeton, N.J.: Princeton University Press, 1950–)

CtHi Connecticut Historical Society, Hartford

CtY Yale University Library, New Haven, Conn.

DAB *Dictionary of American Biography* (20 vols. New York, 1927–1936)

DHRC *The Documentary History of the Ratification of the Constitution,* ed. Merrill Jensen, John P. Kaminski, Gaspare J. Saladino, Richard Leffler, Charles H. Schoenleber (Madison, Wis., 1976–)

Diplomatic Correspondence *The Revolutionary Diplomatic Correspondence of the United States,* ed. Francis Wharton, 6 vols. (Washington, D.C., 1889)

DLC Library of Congress, Washington, D.C.

EHR *English Historical Review*

Elliot Jonathan Elliot, ed., *The Debates in the Several State Conventions, on the Adoption of the Federal Constitution . . . ,* 5 vols. (Philadelphia and Washington, D.C., 1866)

Evans Charles Evans, *American Bibliography,* 12 vols. (Chicago, 1903–34)

Farrand Max Farrand, ed., *The Records of the Federal Convention,* 3 vols. (New Haven, Conn., 1911)

FFC *Documentary History of the First Federal Congress,* ed. Linda Grant De Pauw, Charlene Bangs Bickford, Kenneth R. Bowling, and Helen E. Veit (Baltimore, 1972–)

FFE *The Documentary History of the First Federal Elections,* ed. Merrill Jensen et al., 4 vols. (Madison, Wis., 1976–89)

Ford, *Correspondence* Worthington Chauncey Ford, ed., *Correspondence and Journals of Samuel Blachley Webb,* 3 vols. (Lancaster. Pa., 1893)

JAH *Journal of American History*

Johnston, *Correspondence* Henry P. Johnston, ed., *The Correspondence and Public Papers of John Jay,* 4 vols. (New York, 1890–93)

McRee Griffith J. McRee, ed., *Life and Correspondence of James Iredell . . . ,* 2 vols. (New York, 1857–58)

Madison, *Debates* *Notes of Debates in the Federal Convention of 1787 Reported by James Madison,* ed. Adrienne Koch (Athens, Ohio, 1966)

MdHi Maryland Historical Society, Baltimore

MeHi Maine Historical Society, Portland

Mfm Microfiche Supplements in the *DHRC*

MHi Massachusetts Historical Society, Boston

MWA American Antiquarian Society, Worcester, Mass.

NC-Ar North Carolina Department of Archives and History, Raleigh
NCDAH North Carolina Division of Archives and History, Raleigh
NHi New-York Historical Society, New York City
NhHi New Hampshire Historical Society, Concord
NN New York Public Library, New York City
P-Ar Pennsylvania Museum and Historical Commission, Harrisburg
PHi Historical Society of Pennsylvania, Philadelphia
PPAmP American Philosophical Society, Philadelphia
PSQ *Political Science Quarterly*
RiHi Rhode Island Historical Society, Providence
Rutland Robert A. Rutland et al., eds., *The Papers of James Madison* (Chicago and Charlottesville, Va., 1973–)
SC-Ar South Carolina Department of Archives and History, Columbia
Smith, *Letters* Paul H. Smith, ed., *Letters of Delegates to Congress, 1774–1789,* 26 vols. (Washington, D.C., 1976–2000)
Storing Herbert J. Storing, ed., *The Complete Anti-Federalist,* 7 vols. (Chicago, 1981)
Syrett Harold C. Syrett, ed., *The Papers of Alexander Hamilton,* 27 vols. (New York, 1966–87)
WMQ *William and Mary Quarterly* [all cites are to the 3rd series unless otherwise indicated]

Editors' Introduction

1. *WMQ* 62 (2005): 553.

2. "Teaching the Nation's History," *Humanities: The Magazine of the National Endowment for the Humanities,* July/August 2004, www.neh.gov/news/humanitiesarchive.html.

3. The reference here is to the more traditional applications of historical methodology rather than to the methodologies of the "new new political history." For a historiographical analysis of the latter, see William G. Shade, "Déjà Vu All Over Again: Is There a New New Political History?" in *Beyond the Founders: New Approaches to the Political History of the Early American Republic,* ed. Jeffrey L. Pasley, Andrew W. Robertson, and David Waldstreicher (Chapel Hill, N.C., 2004), 387–412.

4. Jürgen is not the first historian to see the American experience as a potential template for Europe. See the bibliographical essay in David C. Hendrickson, *Peace Pact: The Lost World of the American Founding* (Lawrence, Kans., 2003), 285–89. Hendrickson's work itself might have been of use to Jürgen, although his construction of the Constitutional Convention as "an international conference conducted in secrecy among diplomatic plenipotentiaries of the states" (258–59), his doubts that the "struggle over the constitution turned on the issue of democracy versus aristocracy" (255), and his view that the Constitution "did not deny the democratic impulse so much as it directed and balanced it" (255) are not congenial to Jürgen's ideas, as will be discussed below.

5. For much of the first half of the twentieth century, a seminal force in early American history was Charles Beard's *An Economic Interpretation of the Constitution of the United States* (New York, 1913). It gave rise to a massive literature, for and against. For more recent, very well researched and persuasive studies on this subject, see Woody Holton, "'From the Labours of Others': The War Bonds Controversy and the Origins

of the Constitution in New England," *WMQ* 61 (2004): 271–307; Holton, "'Divide et Impera': Federalist 10 in a Wider Sphere," *WMQ* 61 (2004): 175–212; Holton, *Unruly Americans and the Origins of the Constitution* (New York, 2007); Terry Bouton, "A Road Closed: Rural Insurgency in Post-Independence Pennsylvania," *JAH* 87 (2000): 855–87; Bouton, "Whose Original Intent? Expanding the Concept of the Founders," *Law and History Review* 19 (2001): 661–71; Bouton, *Taming Democracy: 'The People,' The Founders, and the Troubled Ending of the American Revolution* (New York, 2007); Michael A. McDonnell, "Class War? Class Struggles during the American Revolution in Virginia," *WMQ* 63 (2006): 305–45; and Saul A. Cornell, *The Other Founders: Anti-Federalism and the Dissenting Tradition in America, 1788–1828* (Chapel Hill, N.C., 1999). For a rigorous statistical analysis of the economic factors that may have influenced the political debate over the Constitution, see Robert A. McGuire, *To Form a More Perfect Union: A New Economic Interpretation of the United States Constitution* (Oxford, 2003). Unlike Beard's work, which was founded on a rudimentary factual basis, these more recent studies are solidly grounded in hard data and immense research in manuscript sources (published and unpublished). For the importance of tax policy as a crucial issue leading to the calling of the Constitutional Convention and in the debate over ratification, see Roger H. Brown, *Redeeming the Republic: Federalists, Taxation, and the Origins of the Constitution* (Baltimore, 1993); and Calvin H. Johnson, *Righteous Anger at the Wicked States: The Meaning of the Founders' Constitution* (New York, 2005).

6. Jürgen is quoting from Federalist No. 33 and No. 34.

7. See Max Edling, *A Revolution in Favor of Government: Origins of the U.S. Constitution and the Making of the American State* (New York, 2003); Max Edling, "'So Immense a Power in the Affairs of War': Alexander Hamilton and the Restoration of Public Credit," *WMQ* 64 (2007): 287–326; and Max Edling and Mark D. Kaplanoff, "Alexander Hamilton's Fiscal Reform: Transforming the Structure of Taxation in the Early Republic," *WMQ* 61 (2004): 713–44.

8. Quoted in Hendrickson, *Peace Pact,* 201. Hendrickson gives primacy to the "Unionist Paradigm," which emphasized the importance of the Union in maintaining an American presence in the world.

9. There is now a vast body of Atlantic history and postcolonial history. See Bernard Bailyn, *Atlantic History: Concept and Contours* (Cambridge, Mass., 2005); Nicholas Canny, "The British Atlantic World: Working Towards a Definition," *The Historical Journal* 33 (1990): 479–97; Nicholas Canny, "Writing Atlantic History; or, Reconfiguring the History of Colonial British America," *JAH* 86 (1999): 1093–1114; Peter A. Coclanis, "Atlantic World or Atlantic/World," *WMQ* 68 (2006): 725–42; Jack P. Greene, "Colonial History and National History: Reflections on a Continuing Problem," *WMQ* 64 (2007): 235–50; and Hendrickson, *Peace Pact.* For all this, it is still a question whether there was an "Atlantic world," as opposed to a "British-American world." J. H. Elliott compares the British and Spanish empires, and although there are some similarities, there are also important differences—and there is little evidence that one affected the other. On the other hand, the ideas of Newton and Locke, once they became absorbed in Britain, "automatically came to form part of British American culture," and "the nature of eighteenth-century British Atlantic culture was such as to reinforce rather than undermine" the structures of American political freedom "to choose, reject, and hold account-

able those in position of authority" (J. H. Elliott, *Empires of the Atlantic World: Britain and Spain in America, 1492–1830* [New Haven, 2006], 332). For a daunting bibliography of Atlantic literature and history, see *WMQ* 65 (2008): 135–86.

10. See Jürgen Habermas, *Strukturwandel der Öffentlichkeit: Untersuchungen zu einer Kategorie der Bürgerlichen Gesellschaft* (Neuwied and Berlin, 1962), published in English as *The Structural Transformation of the Public Sphere: An Inquiry into a Category of Bourgeois Society,* trans. Thomas Burger and Frederick Lawrence (Cambridge, Mass., 1989). As Craig Calhoun has noted, "Efforts to understand the history, foundations, and internal processes of public discourse are gaining importance in several disciplines. . . . Surprisingly absent from the discussion, at least in English, has been one of Habermas's most important and directly relevant works, *The Structural Transformation. . . .*" The work was influential in German and translated into several languages, but not English (see Calhoun, *Habermas and the Public Sphere* [Cambridge, Mass., 1992], vii). Once it was translated, it became influential. For applications of the theory to the ratification of the Constitution, see David Waldstreicher, *In the Midst of Perpetual Fetes: The Making of American Nationalism, 1776–1820* (Chapel Hill, N.C., 1997); Simon P. Newman, *Parades and the Politics of the Street: Festive Culture in the Early American Republic* (Philadelphia, 1997); Simon P. Newman, William Pencak, and Matthew Dennis, *Riot and Revelry in Early America* (University Park, Pa., 2002); Len Travers, *Celebrating the Fourth: Independence Day and the Rites of Nationalism in the Early Republic* (Amherst, Mass., 1997); and Michael Warner, *The Letters of the Republic: Publication and the Public Sphere in Eighteenth-Century America* (Cambridge, Mass., 1990). For a slightly later period, see Jeffrey L. Pasley, *"The Tyranny of Printers": Newspaper Politics in the Early American Republic* (Charlottesville, Va., 2001). For a thorough and complex discussion of the application of the theory to the recent writing of early American history, see John L. Brooke, "Consent, Civil Society, and the Public Sphere in the Age of Revolution and the Early American Republic," in Pasley, Robertson, and Waldstreicher, *Beyond the Founders,* 207–50.

11. Jürgen Heideking, "Festive Culture and National Identity in America and Germany, 1760–1860," in *Republicanism and Liberalism in America and the German States, 1750–1860,* ed. Jürgen Heideking and James A. Henretta (Washington, D.C., 2002), 210.

12. Perhaps the first to use these celebrations as a method of deriving the ideology of the participants was Sean Wilentz, in his essay "Artisan Republican Festivals and the Rise of Class Conflict in New York City, 1788–1837," published in *Working Class America: Essays on Labor, Community, and American Society,* ed. Michael H. Frisch and Daniel J. Walkowitz (Urbana, Ill., 1983), 37–77. Wilentz is more interested in later processions than in the 1788 New York procession. He describes the processions as "public trade rituals" and "political festivals," and he properly notes that they "might once have appeared [and did] as anecdotal marginalia of labor history" (ibid., 38). But what Jürgen does that is quite different from Wilentz, is he derives the ideology not only of the workers who participated but of the Federalist organizers of the processions, and the political messages they intended to convey.

13. Morgan, "Honor Thy Founding Fathers," *Wall Street Journal,* April 23, 1997.

14. Edling, *Revolution in Favor of Government,* 7. See also *The Documentary History of the Ratification of the Constitution.*

15. Since this was written, we have had the opportunity to read the recently published

work by Pauline Maier, *Ratification: The People Debate the Constitution, 1787–1788* (New York, 2010). She, like Jürgen, has written a great history of the ratification of the Constitution, and, like Jürgen, she has utilized modern documentary editions, especially the *Documentary History of the Ratification of the Constitution.* Professor Maier's book also captures the many elements that shaped this seminal event in American history.

Introduction

1. The Constitution of the United States is the oldest written national constitution still in force today, followed by the constitutions of Belgium (1831) and Switzerland (1874).

2. The full quotation reads: "As the British Constitution is the most subtle organism which has proceeded from progressive history, so the American Constitution is the most wonderful work ever struck off at a given time by the brains and purpose of man" ("Kin Beyond the Sea," *North American Review* 126 [1887]: 185).

3. This can even be said for the otherwise groundbreaking study of Gordon S. Wood, *The Creation of the American Republic, 1776–1787* (Chapel Hill, N.C., 1969). See also James H. Hutson, "The Creation of the Constitution: Scholarship at a Standstill," *Reviews in American History* 12 (1984): 463–77.

4. Charles A. Beard, *An Economic Interpretation of the Constitution of the United States* (New York, 1913). See also Cecelia M. Kenyon, "'An Economic Interpretation of the Constitution' after Fifty Years," *Centennial Review* 7 (1963); John P. Diggins, "Power and Authority in American History: The Case of Charles A. Beard and His Critics," *AHR* 86 (1981): 701–30; and "Moving beyond Beard: A Symposium," *Radical History Review* 42 (1988): 7–47. An earlier attempt to link the party division between Federalists and Antifederalists with the conflicting interests of debtors and creditors had been made by Orin G. Libby, *The Geographical Distribution of the Vote of the Thirteen States on the Federal Constitution, 1787–1788* (Madison, Wis., 1894).

5. Jackson T. Main, *The Antifederalists: Critics of the Constitution, 1781–1788* (Chapel Hill, N.C., 1961); Cecelia M. Kenyon, ed., *Antifederalists* (Indianapolis, Ind., 1966); Cecilia M. Kenyon, "Men of Little Faith: The Anti-Federalists on the Nature of Representative Government," *WMQ* 12 (1955): 3–43; Robert A. Rutland, *The Ordeal of the Constitution: Antifederalists and the Ratification Struggle of 1787–88* (Norman, Okla., 1966); Steven R. Boyd, *The Politics of Opposition: Antifederalists and the Acceptance of the Constitution* (Millwood, N.Y., 1979).

6. This was also true for most investigations on the state level. See Staughton Lynd, *Anti-Federalism in Dutchess County, New York: A Study of Democracy and Class Conflict in the Revolutionary Era* (Chicago, 1962); and Linda Grant De Pauw, *The Eleventh Pillar: New York State and the Federal Constitution* (Ithaca, N.Y., 1966). See also James H. Hutson, "Country, Court, and Constitution: Antifederalism and the Historians," *WMQ* 38 (1981): 337–68.

7. *Documentary History of the First Federal Congress,* ed. Linda Grant De Pauw, Charlene Bangs Bickford, Kenneth R. Bowling, and Helen E. Veit (Baltimore, 1972–) (hereafter, *FFC*); *Documentary History of the First Federal Elections,* ed. Merrill Jensen et al., 4 vols. (Madison, Wis., 1976–89) (hereafter, *FFE*); *Documentary History of the Ratification of the Constitution,* ed. Merrill Jensen, John P. Kaminski, Gaspare J. Saladino, Richard Leffler, and Charles H. Schoenleber (Madison, Wis., 1976–) (hereafter, *DHRC*). These documentary histories and the editions of the papers of the Founding Fathers, such as

those of George Washington, Thomas Jefferson, James Madison, George Mason, and Alexander Hamilton, complement each other in an ideal way. Largely superseded by the *Documentary History of the Ratification of the Constitution* is, meanwhile, *The Complete Anti-Federalist,* ed. Herbert J. Storing, with the assistance of Murray Dry, 7 vols. (Chicago, 1981).

8. See, e.g., Forrest McDonald, *Novus Ordo Seclorum: The Intellectual Origins of the Constitution* (Lawrence, Kans., 1985); Michael Lienesch, *New Order of the Ages: Time, the Constitution, and the Making of Modern American Political Thought* (Princeton, N.J., 1988); Steven R. Boyd, *The Constitution in State Politics: From the Calling of the Constitutional Convention to the First Federal Elections* (New York, 1990); Saul A. Cornell, "The Political Thought and Culture of the Anti-Federalists" (Ph.D. diss., University of Pennsylvania, 1989); Saul A. Cornell, "Aristocracy Assailed: The Ideology of Backcountry Anti-Federalism," *JAH* 76 (1990): 1148–72; Richard Beeman et al., eds., *Beyond Confederation: Origins of the Constitution and American National Identity* (Chapel Hill, N.C., 1987); Leonard W. Levy and Dennis J. Mahoney, eds., *The Framing and Ratification of the Constitution* (New York, 1987); Peter S. Onuf, "Reflections on the Founding: Constitutional Historiography in Bicentennial Perspective," *WMQ* 46 (1989): 341–75; Patrick T. Conley and John P. Kaminski, eds., *The Constitution and the States: The Role of the Original Thirteen in the Framing and Adoption of the Federal Constitution* (Madison, Wis., 1988); Michael Allen Gillespie and Michael Lienesch, eds., *Ratifying the Constitution* (Lawrence, Kans., 1989); Herman Belz, Ronald Hoffman, and Peter J. Albert, eds., *To Form a More Perfect Union: The Critical Ideas of the Constitution* (Charlottesville, Va., 1992); Wilson C. McWilliams and Michael T. Gibbons, eds., *The Federalists, the Antifederalists, and the American Political Tradition* (New York, 1992); John P. Kaminski, *George Clinton: Yeoman Politician of the New Republic* (Madison, Wis., 1993); and Lance Banning, *The Sacred Fire of Liberty: James Madison and the Founding of the Federal Republic* (Ithaca, N.Y., 1995).

9. The discussion began with Bernard Bailyn, *The Ideological Origins of the American Revolution* (Cambridge, Mass., 1967; 13th ed., 1976); and J. G. A. Pocock, *The Machiavellian Moment: Florentine Political Thought and the Atlantic Republican Tradition* (Cambridge, 1975). The scholarly debate is summarized in Lance Banning, "The Republican Interpretation: Retrospect and Prospect," in *The Republican Synthesis Revisited: Essays in Honor of George Athan Billias,* ed. Milton M. Klein et al. (Worcester, Mass., 1992), 91–117; and Banning, *Sacred Fire of Liberty,* 214–19, 472–74. See also Paul Rahe, *Republics Ancient and Modern: Classical Republicanism and the American Revolution* (Chapel Hill, N.C., 1992). The most recent contributions are Christopher M. Duncan, *The Anti-Federalists and Early American Political Thought* (DeKalb, Ill., 1995); and Saul A. Cornell, *The Other Founders: Anti-Federalism and the Dissenting Tradition in America, 1788–1828* (Chapel Hill, N.C., 1999). See also chapter 1 of this book, under "The Philadelphia Convention and the Sovereignty of the People."

10. See especially Isaac Kramnick, "The 'Great National Discussion': The Discourse of Politics in 1787," *WMQ* 45 (1988): 3–32.

11. The debate over "American modernity" has been revived by Gordon S. Wood, *The Radicalism of the American Revolution* (New York, 1991). At the turn of the nineteenth century, Americans had become, according to Wood, "almost overnight, the most liberal, the most democratic, the most commercially minded, and the most modern people

in the world. . . . It was the Revolution, more than any other single event, that made America into the most liberal, democratic, and modern nation in the world" (6–7). See also "How Revolutionary Was the Revolution? A Discussion of Gordon S. Wood's *The Radicalism of the American Revolution*," *WMQ* 51 (1994): 677–716.

12. Washington's words echo in Abraham Lincoln's Second Inaugural Address, when the Civil War president professed his conviction that "truth and justice will surely prevail, by the judgment of this great tribunal, the American people."

1. Historical Background

1. "Ordinance for the Government of the Territory of the United States North-West of the Ohio River," July 13, 1787, in *DHRC*, 1:168–74.

2. Peter S. Onuf, *The Origins of the Federal Republic: Jurisdictional Controversies in the United States, 1775–1787* (Philadelphia, 1983).

3. See Brooke Hindle, *The Pursuit of Science in Revolutionary America, 1735–1789* (Chapel Hill, N.C., 1956); Kenneth Silverman, *A Cultural History of the American Revolution, 1783–1789* (New York, 1976); Alexandra Oleson and Sanborn C. Brown, eds., *The Pursuit of Knowledge in the Early American Republic: American Scientific and Learned Societies from Colonial Times to the Civil War* (Baltimore, Md., 1979).

4. "Articles of Confederation of the United States of America," November 15, 1777, in *DHRC*, 1:86–94.

5. Ibid.

6. Syrett, 2:649–74, 3:75–82, 99–106; Eric Foner, ed., *Paine: Collected Writings* (New York, 1995), 5–59, 91–176.

7. Grant of Power to Collect Import Duties, February 3, 1781, in *DHRC*, 1:140–41.

8. E. James Ferguson, *The Power of the Purse: A History of American Public Finance, 1776–1790* (Chapel Hill, N.C., 1961); Ferguson, "The Nationalists of 1781–1783 and the Economic Interpretation of the Constitution," *JAH* 56 (1969): 241–61.

9. For different views of the so-called "Newburgh Conspiracy," which was defused by Washington, see Richard H. Kohn, "The Inside History of the Newburgh Conspiracy: America and the Coup d'Etat," *WMQ* 27 (1970): 187–220; C. Edward Skeen, "The Newburgh Conspiracy Reconsidered," *WMQ* 31 (1974): 273–98; and Kenneth R. Bowling, "New Light on the Philadelphia Mutiny of 1783: Federal-State Confrontation at the Close of the War for Independence," *Pennsylvania Magazine of History and Biography* 101 (1977): 419–50.

10. *DHRC*, 13:60–70. For the use made of this letter during the ratification debate, see below at pp. <o>.

11. Standard works on the Confederation period are Edmund Cody Burnett, *The Continental Congress: A Definitive History of the Continental Congress from Its Inception in 1774 to March, 1789* (New York, 1941); Merrill Jensen, *The New Nation: A History of the United States during the Confederation, 1781–1789* (New York, 1950); Jensen, *The Articles of Confederation: An Interpretation of the Social-Constitutional History of the American Revolution, 1774–1781*, 7th ed. (Madison, Wis., 1970); Richard B. Morris, *The Forging of the Union, 1781–1789* (New York, 1987); and Jack N. Rakove, *The Beginnings of National Politics: An Interpretative History of the Continental Congress* (New York, 1979). The most important collection of sources is Paul H. Smith, ed., *Letters of Delegates to Congress, 1774–1789* (26 vols., Washington, D.C., 1976–2000).

12. *DHRC,* 1:146–50.

13. *DHRC,* 1:181–85.

14. *DHRC,* 1:187.

15. A prominent example is Patrick Henry, a member of the Virginia House of Delegates, who in May 1784 "saw Ruin inevitable unless something was done to give Congress a compulsory Process on delinquent States &c." (quoted in *DHRC,* 13:25).

16. Patrick T. Conley, "Rhode Island's Paper Money Issue and Trevett v. Weeden (1786)," *Rhode Island History* 30 (1971): 95–108; John P. Kaminski, *Paper Politics: The Northern State Loan-Offices during the Confederation* (New York, 1989).

17. The term "Shays's Rebellion" soon became common, although Daniel Shays was only one among several leaders of the uprising (see David P. Szatmary, *Shays's Rebellion: The Making of an Agrarian Insurrection* [Amherst, Mass., 1980]).

18. Washington to Henry Lee, October 31, 1786; and Washington to Madison, November 5, 1786, in *The Papers of George Washington: Confederation Series,* ed. W. W. Abbot, 6 vols. (Charlottesville, Va., 1992–97), 4:318–20, 331–32.

19. Stephen Higginson to Henry Knox, November 12, 1786, in Rutland, 9:155n4.

20. Rutland, 7:10. See also Lance Banning, "James Madison and the Nationalists, 1780–1783," *WMQ* 40 (1983): 227–55; and Banning, "The Hamiltonian Madison: A Reconsideration," *Virginia Magazine of History and Biography* 92 (1984), 3–28.

21. Rutland, 8:502.

22. Rutland, 9:345–58. See also Banning, *Sacred Fire of Liberty,* 115–21.

23. Rufus King to Theodore Sedgwick, quoted in John T. Agresto, "Liberty, Virtue and Republicanism, 1776–1787," *Reviews of Politics* 39 (1977): 488.

24. Charles F. Hobson, "The Negative on State Laws: James Madison and the Crisis of Republican Government," *WMQ* 36 (1972): 215–35.

25. Madison to Jefferson, New York, October 24, 1787, in Boyd, 12:276.

26. Madison to Jefferson, August 12, 1786, in Rutland, 111:95.

27. "Publius" 15, December 1, 1787, in *DHRC,* 14:325–26.

28. "Agrippa" II and III, *Massachusetts Gazette,* November 27 and 30, 1787, in *DHRC,* 4:322–24, 342–44.

29. "Hanno," *Massachusetts Gazette,* November 13, 1787, in *DHRC,* 4:225–27.

30. "Candidus" I, Boston *Independent Chronicle,* December 6, 1787, in *DHRC,* 4:398.

31. "A Federalist," *Boston Gazette,* November 26, 1787, in *DHRC,* 4:321.

32. "Federal Farmer": Letters to the *Republican* I, October 8, 1787, in *DHRC,* 14:20.

33. Conventions were traditionally seen as "defective parliaments" or "legally deficient bodies existing outside of the regularly constituted authority." In late eighteenth-century England, the very use of the word "convention" was sufficient "to provoke ministerialists and loyalists" (Clive Emsley, "Repression, 'Terror,' and the Rule of Law in England during the Decade of the French Revolution," *EHR* 100 [1985]: 808). See also Wood, *The Creation of the American Republic,* 311–12.

34. Thad W. Tate, "The Social Contract in America, 1774–1787: Revolutionary Theory as a Conservative Instrument," *WMQ* 22 (1965): 380.

35. Quoted in Robert J. Taylor, ed., *Massachusetts, Colony to Commonwealth: Documents on the Formation of the Constitution, 1775–1780* (Chapel Hill, N.C., 1961), 11.

36. Resolution of Concord Town Meeting, October 22, 1776, in Taylor, *Massachusetts, Colony to Commonwealth,* 45–46.

37. Ibid., 116–17.

38. Ronald M. Peters Jr., *The Massachusetts Constitution of 1780: A Social Compact* (Amherst, Mass., 1978); Edmund S. Morgan, *Inventing the People: The Rise of Popular Sovereignty in England and America* (New York, 1988); Willi Paul Adams, *The First American Constitutions: Republican Ideology and the Making of the State Constitutions in the Revolutionary Era* (Chapel Hill, N.C., 1980; expanded ed., Lanham, Md., 2001); Marc W. Kruman, *Between Authority and Liberty: State Constitution Making in Revolutionary America* (Chapel Hill., N.C., 1997); Peter Charles Hoffer, *Law and People in Colonial America,* rev. ed. (Baltimore, Md., 1998).

39. John Phillip Reid, *Constitutional History of the American Revolution* (Madison, Wis., 1995), 3–25. For colonial precedents, see Donald S. Lutz, *The Origins of American Constitutionalism* (Baton Rouge, La., 1988).

40. Foner, *Paine,* 33–35, 43, 52, 286.

41. Hamilton to James Duane, September 3, 1780, in Syrett, 2:400–402.

42. George Bancroft, ed., "Original Documents: A Hartford Convention in 1780," *Magazine of History* 8 (1882): 688–98.

43. Massachusetts Delegates (Elbridge Gerry, Samuel Holten, and Rufus King) to Governor James Bowdoin, New York, August 18, September 3, 1785, in Smith, *Letters,* 22:571, 610–14.

44. *DHRC,* 1:178.

45. *DHRC,* 1:187.

46. Rhode Island General Assembly to the President of Congress, September 15, 1787, in *DHRC,* 1:225–26. See also *DHRC,* 13:37–39.

47. Washington wanted the convention delegates to be unfettered by instructions so that they could "probe the defects of the [Articles of Confederation] to the bottom, and provide radical cures, whether they are agreed to or not. A conduct like this, will stamp wisdom and dignity on the proceedings, and be looked to as a luminary, which sooner or later will shed its influence" (Washington to Madison, March 31, 1787, in Rutland, 9:342–45; see also Madison's answer of April 16, 1787, ibid., 382–87).

48. *DHRC,* 1:232–43, 304–5.

49. For the various plans and drafts, see ibid., 1:243–96. The debate is documented in Farrand, 1:29–315. The best works on the Philadelphia Convention are Charles Warren, *The Making of the Constitution* (Boston, 1928); Carl Van Doren, *The Great Rehearsal: The Story of the Making and Ratifying of the Constitution of the United States* (New York, 1948); Max Farrand, *The Framing of the Constitution of the United States,* 20th ed. (New Haven, 1964); David G. Smith, *The Convention and the Constitution: The Political Ideas of the Founding Fathers* (New York, 1965); Clinton Rossiter, *1787: The Grand Convention* (New York, 1966); Catherine Drinker Bowen, *Miracle at Philadelphia: The Story of the Constitutional Convention, May to September 1787* (Boston, 1966); Christopher Collier and James Lincoln Collier, *Decision in Philadelphia: The Constitutional Convention of 1787* (New York, 1986); Forrest McDonald, *Novus Ordo Seclorum: The Intellectual Origins of the Constitution* (Lawrence, Kans., 1985); Calvin C. Jillson, *Constitution Making: Conflict and Consensus in the Federal Convention of 1787* (New York, 1988); and Herman Belz, Ronald Hoffman, and Peter J. Albert, eds., *To Form a More Perfect Union: The Critical Ideas of the Constitution* (Charlottesville, Va., 1992).

50. In his speech of June 30, 1787, Madison contended that the "great division of

interest" in the United States "did not lie between the large & small States: it lay between the Northern & Southern. And if any defensive power were necessary, it ought to be mutually given to these two interests" (Farrand, 1:486). In a letter to Jefferson, written in New York on October 24, 1787, Madison stated that the "great objects which presented themselves [at the Philadelphia Convention] were: 1. to unite a proper energy in the Executive and a proper stability in the Legislative departments, with the essential characters of Republican Government. 2. to draw a line of demarcation which would give the General Government every power requisite for general purposes, and leave to the States every power which might be most beneficially administered by them. 3. to provide for the different interests of different parts of the Union. 4. to adjust the clashing pretensions of the large and small states" (*DHRC*, 13:443).

51. *DHRC*, 1:255–60.

52. Banning, *Sacred Fire of Liberty* (Ithaca, N.Y., 1995), 141–42, Charles F. Hobson, "The Negative on State Laws: James Madison, the Constitution, and the Crisis of Republican Government," *WMQ* 36 (1979): 215–35.

53. Howard A. Ohline, "Republicanism and Slavery: Origins of the Three-Fifth Clause in the United States Constitution," *WMQ* 28 (1971): 563–84.

54. *DHRC*, 13:120. See also John P. Kaminski, *Secrecy and the Constitutional Convention* (Madison, Wis., 2005).

55. See Farrand, 1:153, 250, 274, 288–89, 291, 338–39, 512–14, 528, 530, 2:204–5, 211–12, 414.

56. Farrand, 1:215.

57. *DHRC*, 1:253–55; Syrett, 4:207–9.

58. Gerry maintained that Shays's Rebellion had taught him "the danger of the levelling spirit" (Farrand, 1:48).

59. Farrand, 2:623.

60. During the 1780s, Madison and Jefferson based their demand for a new Virginia state constitution on this argument (see Boyd, 6:294–96, 7:258–59, 359–61).

61. For the ratification of the Articles of Confederation by the states, see *DHRC*, 1:86–137.

62. Rutland, 9:352–53.

63. Farrand, 1:122–24; *DHRC*, 1:245. The method of state ratifying conventions had first been suggested by Stephen Higginson, a delegate to Congress from Massachusetts, in a letter to Secretary at War Henry Knox, dated February 2, 1787: "The most probable way in my mind, of meeting with Success, would be to have special State Conventions appointed, to whom the report of the general Convention should be referred, and they be directed to report to Congress their dissent or approbation thereof. And if nine of those State Conventions shall report in favour of the System, Congress shall be authorised thereupon, to declare it to be the federal Constitution of Government; and the States shall be compelled to conform themselves by it" (Knox Papers, Gilder-Lehrman Collection, New-York Historical Society). Neither Higginson nor Knox attended the Philadelphia Convention.

64. Farrand, 1:335, 2:88, 90.

65. Farrand, 2:88, 477.

66. In this sense, "Civis" in Maryland wrote at the beginning of 1788: "Although men of property, character and abilities, have too much retired from public employment since

the conclusion of the war, yet it is to be hoped, that, in this all-important crisis, they will again step forth, with a true patriotic ardour" (*Maryland Journal*, February 1, 1788).

67. Farrand 2:92, 468–69, 475–77, 561–62.

68. The question of sovereignty is still controversial; see, e.g., McDonald, *Novus Ordo Seclorum*, 279–81.

69. Farrand, 2:475–77.

70. In the end, George Washington was asked to take care of the papers and keep them secret. The quotations from Randolph, Gouverneur Morris, and King are in *The Debates in the Federal Convention of 1787 Which Framed the Constitution of the United States of America, Reported by James Madison*, ed. by Gaillard Hunt and James B. Scott (New York, 1920), 305, 499, 582–83.

71. Speech of August 31, 1787, in Farrand, 1:479. The powerful metaphor of "sooner chopping off one's right hand" than to vote for the adoption of the Constitution soon became part of the rhetoric of the ratification debate.

72. Madison, *Debates*, 306, 498–501, 580–82; Farrand, 2:645–47.

73. Madison, *Debates*, 577–79; Farrand, 2:641–43. Because of his weak health, Franklin asked James Wilson to read his speech to the delegates. In December 1787, the text appeared in two versions in Massachusetts and Virginia newspapers, both of which were thereafter reprinted many times all over the United States (*DHRC*, 13:212–15).

74. Farrand, 2:645.

75. George Read signed for the absent John Dickinson, bringing the number of signers to 39 (*DHRC*, 1:304).

76. *DHRC*, 1:317–18, 13:210–11.

77. Farrand, 2:622.

78. Debate in Congress, September 27, 1787, in *DHRC*, 1:331.

79. The debate is documented in *DHRC*, 1:322–42 and 13:229–42.

80. Richard Henry Lee to Samuel Adams, New York, October 27, 1787, in *DHRC*, 1:348. See also Richard Leffler, "Richard Henry Lee and the Early Opposition to the Constitution," *Documentary Editing* 9 (1987): 1–6.

81. William Bingham to Thomas FitzSimons, New York, September 21, 1787, in *DHRC*, 1:325.

82. Manuscript copies of Mason's *Objections to the Constitution*, dated 7 October 1787, would soon circulate in several states (*DHRC*, 13:346–51, 358–59).

83. *DHRC*, 1:345, 13:484–86.

84. Madison to Jefferson, New York, October 24, 1787, in *DHRC*, 13:452. See also *DHRC*, 1:322–42, 13:229–42.

85. *DHRC*, 1:332.

86. *DHRC*, 1:333.

87. *DHRC*, 1:337–39.

88. *DHRC*, 13:234. Several months later, Clark explained in a letter of July 23, 1788, to Thomas Sinnickson, that he had not been without reservations concerning the Philadelphia plan: "With all these imperfections about it, I nevertheless wished it to go to the States from Congress just as it did, without any Censure or Commendation, hoping that in Case of a general Adoption, the Wisdom of the States would soon amend it in its exceptionable parts" (Smith, *Letters*, 25:244).

89. Nathan Dane remained dissatisfied. In a letter written to Caleb Strong on October

10, 1787, he argued that the Constitution had been considered as "an entire New System, on its passage from the Convention to the people, and altogether extraneous to the powers of Congress—the warmest friends of it appeared to be extremely impatient to get it thro Congress, even the first day that it was taken up—they wanted Congress to approve of it, but objected to any examination of it by paragraphs in the usual mode of doing business." But Dane admitted that "very few members wanted any alterations. . . . Had Congress been of opinion that it was a subject within their cognizance, and taken time to examine it as so respectable a body ought always to do [in] such important cases, I think it is highly probable that Congress would have very strongly approved of the plan proposed" (*DHRC,* 13:357).

90. *DHRC,* 1:340.

91. Madison to Washington, New York, September 30, 1787; and Washington to Madison, October 10, 1787, in *DHRC,* 13:275–76, 358–59.

92. Carrington to Jefferson, New York, October 23, 1787, in *DHRC,* 13:438–41; Bond to the Marquis of Carmarthen, Philadelphia, September 29, 1787, in *DHRC,* 1:350. French chargé d'affaires Louis Guillaume Otto, who knew what had happened in Congress, found it surprising "that Congress itself is not in agreement over the great powers which the new Constitution allots it" (Otto to Comte de Montmorin, New York, October 23, 1787, in *DHRC,* 1:352–53).

93. "Centinel" II, Philadelphia *Freeman's Journal,* October 24, 1787, in *DHRC,* 13: 457–68.

94. Lee to Shippen, New York, October 2, 1787, in *DHRC,* 13:289. See also *DHRC,* 1:342, 13:281–83, 323–25.

95. Lee to Samuel Adams, New York, October 5, 1787, in *DHRC,* 13:324–25.

96. Lee may also have left a copy with George Washington when he visited Mount Vernon on November 11–12, 1787 (*DHRC,* 13:289, 14:365–66).

97. *DHRC,* 13:289, 14:365–66.

98. *DHRC,* 13:289, 14:365–66.

99. "Observations on the Plan of Government, proposed by the Convention, by R.H. L**, Esquire," in *DHRC,* 14:364–72.

100. New York *Daily Advertiser,* October 15, 1787, in *DHRC,* 13:383.

101. "Bill to Enforce Attendance . . . ," November 29, 1787, NCDAH, Legislative Papers.

102. This criticism was reflected in John Adams's three-volume *A Defence of the Constitutions of Government of the United States,* which had been published in London in 1787–88. The first volume arrived in America in April 1787 (*DHRC,* 13:81–90).

103. The deliberations of the Pennsylvania Assembly are documented in *DHRC,* 2:54–126. See also George J. Graham Jr., "Pennsylvania: Representation and the Meaning of Republicanism," in Gillespie and Lienesch, *Ratifying the Constitution,* 52–70.

104. The 250 petitioners from Germantown were hopeful that their city would become the seat of the new federal government (*DHRC,* 2:62, 134–38).

105. Robert Whitehill and other Antifederalist leaders had met with George Mason and discussed his objections to the Constitution (*DHRC,* 2:156, 13:347).

106. *DHRC,* 2:71, 76–78, 89, 93.

107. Tench Coxe to Madison, Philadelphia, September 28–29, 1787, in *DHRC,* 2: 121–22.

108. For a successful precedent in 1783, see *DHRC*, 2:110n4.

109. *DHRC*, 2:109–10.

110. *The Address of the Seceding Assemblymen* and *The Reply of Six Assemblymen* (October 8, 1787) are published in *DHRC*, 2:112–20; see also *DHRC*, 13:293–306.

111. *DHRC*, 2:224–37.

112. Otto to Montmorin, New York, October 10, 1787, in *DHRC*, 2:124–26.

113. Elbridge Gerry to James Warren, New York, October 18, 1787; Gerry to the Massachusetts General Court, October 18, 1787; and George Mason to Gerry, Gunston Hall, October 20, 1787, in *DHRC*, 13:407–8, 421–22, 546–55. See also *DHRC*, 4:94–100; and Boyd, *Politics of Opposition*, 19–20.

114. *DHRC*, 3:345–62.

115. *DHRC*, 363–71.

116. *DHRC*, 369.

117. *DHRC*, 370.

118. *DHRC*, 4:124–27. The speech was widely printed in newspapers from New Hampshire to Maryland.

119. *DHRC*, 4:34, 61–62.

120. The proceedings of the Massachusetts General Court, October 18–25, 1787, as well as newspaper reports and commentaries, are published in *DHRC*, 4:124–47.

121. *DHRC*, 4:148.

122. The relevant documents are printed in *DHRC*, 3:50–104 (Delaware), 133–95 (New Jersey), and 219–307 (Georgia).

123. *DHRC*, 8:127–29, 13:505.

124. For town and county meetings, see *DHRC*, 8:85–86 (Fredericksburg, October 20, 1787); 91–93 (Frederick County and Henrico County, October 22, 1787); and 96–97 (Petersburg, October 24, 1787).

125. Quoted in Washington's letter to Madison, October 22, 1787, in Rutland, 10:204.

126. *DHRC*, 8:110–18.

127. *DHRC*, 9:561.

128. On December 2, 1787, Archibald Stuart informed Madison that "there appears to be a Majority vs the Govt. as it now Stands & I fear since they have discovered their Strength they will adopt other Measures tending to its prejudice from this circumstance I am happy to find Most of the States will have decided on the Question before Virginia for I now have my doubts whether She would afford them as usual a good Example" (*DHRC*, 8:195–96).

129. See General Assembly proceedings, November 30–December 27, 1787, in *DHRC*, 8:183–93.

130. The text of the pamphlet, dated December 27, 1787, is printed in *DHRC*, 8:260–75.

131. Both Baltimore newspapers, the *Maryland Journal* and the *Maryland Gazette*, reported regularly on the state of the ratification question.

132. More tensions arose in connection with the House decision, by a vote of 28–22, to invite Maryland's delegates to the Philadelphia Convention to give a report. Maryland's *Act Electing and Empowering Delegates* to the Philadelphia Convention of May 26, 1787, had directed the deputies "to report the proceedings of the said convention, and any act agreed to therein, to the next session of the general assembly of this state." However, many Federalists loathed the idea of opening up the legislature to Luther Martin

as a platform for his critique of the Constitution. On November 29, the House of Delegates called on their three signatories to the Constitution, Daniel Carroll, Daniel of St. Thomas Jenifer, and James McHenry, who joined forces to respond against Martin's allegations regarding the "mischievous tendency" of the Constitution and the aristocratic and monarchical dispositions of its framers (see *DHRC,* 1:222, 14:278–96). Between December 28, 1787, and February 8, 1788, Luther Martin's detailed critique appeared in the Baltimore *Maryland Gazette.* In April 1788 an enlarged version was published by printer Eleazer Oswald of the Philadelphia *Independent Gazetteer* as a pamphlet entitled *The Genuine Information, Delivered to the Legislature of the State of Maryland* (see *DHRC,* 15:146–56, 204–10, 249–56, 296–302, 17:83–94).

133. The debates and resolutions appeared in print as *Votes and Proceedings of the House of Delegates; Votes and Proceedings of the Senate* (Annapolis, 1788).

134. William R. Davie to James Iredell, Halifax, January 22, 1788, in McRee, 2:217–18.

135. Williamson to Iredell, Philadelphia, July 22, 1787; and Maclaine to Iredell, Wilmington, August 29, 1787, in McRee, 2:167–68, 178–79.

136. North Carolina Senate-House Resolutions Calling Convention, December 6, 1787, in NCDAH, Legislative Papers.

137. Petry to Montmorin, Charleston, December 26, 1787, in Correspondence Consulaire B I 372, Charleston, vol. 1, 1784–1792, pp. 258–60, AN.

138. John Sullivan to Jeremy Belknap, October 4, 1787, in *Letters and Papers of Major-General John Sullivan,* ed. Otis G. Hammond, 3 vols. (Concord, N.H., 1930–39), 3:545–46.

139. New Hampshire General Court: Senate/House of Representatives, Journals of the Proceedings . . . Portsmouth, 11–14 December 1787, New Hampshire State Archives.

140. Hamilton's first anonymous attack against Clinton had already appeared on July 21, 1787, in the New York *Daily Advertiser* (*DHRC,* 13:136–38). See also Kaminski, *George Clinton,* 122–31.

141. Speech of January 11, 1788, in *DHRC,* 15:340–42. Clinton told the legislature that "from the nature of my office you will easily perceive it would be improper for me to have any other agency in this business, than that of laying the papers . . . before you for your information." See also Kaminski, *George Clinton,* 137–38.

142. See especially the first four "Countryman" essays by Hugh Hughes, published on November 21 and 23, and December 3 and 15, 1787, in *DHRC,* 19:271–74, 291–93, 347–52, 424–28.

143. The Yates-Lansing letter, dated December 21, 1787, formed part of Governor Clinton's report to the legislature. On January 14, 1788, the text was published in the New York *Daily Advertiser* and the *New York Journal* (*DHRC,* 15:366–70).

144. Richard Sill to Jeremiah Wadsworth, Albany, January 12, 1788, in *DHRC,* 20:602–3. At the beginning of its session, the legislature elected a Federalist-dominated delegation, headed by Hamilton, to represent New York in Congress.

145. The New York *Daily Advertiser* reported the debates in the assembly and in the senate on February 8 and 12, 1788. See also Kaminski, "New York: The Reluctant Pillar," in *The Reluctant Pillar: New York and the Adoption of the Federal Constitution,* ed. Stephen L. Schechter (Troy, N.Y., 1985), 73–77.

146. "You seem to be of opinion that there is a majority in both houses of the Legislature against the new Constitution. We have great doubts here, whether this is the case in the assembly. If it is, how can it be accounted for that they have chosen for the Delegates

[to Congress] the warmest advocates for the measure? You may say they out general you, but it amounts to the same thing, whether you are defeated by the superior skill of your enemy or by their superior strength, it is a defeat still" (Melancton Smith to Abraham Yates Jr., New York, January 28, 1788, in *DHRC*, 20:671).

147. Philip Schuyler to Stephen Van Rensselaer, Poughkeepsie, January 27, 1788, in *DHRC*, 20:700.

148. The *New York Journal* reported on the assembly debates on the oath, February 16–21, 1788.

149. On January 16, Lowndes argued that the slave trade "could be justified on the principles of religion, humanity and justice; for certainly to translate a set of human beings from a bad country to a better, was fulfilling every part of those principles" (see Debates in the S.C. House of Representatives, January 16–18, 1788, in Elliot, 4:253–342; and Storing, 5:148–59).

150. Journals of the Senate and the House of Representatives of the State of South Carolina, January 8–February 29, 1788, South Carolina State Archives.

151. *United States Chronicle*, November 1, 1787.

152. William R. Staples, *Rhode Island in the Continental Congress, 1765–1790* (Providence, R.I., 1870), 584–85.

153. "Providence Town Meeting: Report of a Committee Appointed on 24 March 1788," March 26, 1788, Providence Town Records, Rhode Island Historical Society.

154. "Newport Town Meeting: Report of the Committee Appointed to Draw Up Instructions to Delegates," March 28, 1788, Newport Town Records, Newport Historical Society.

155. John P. Kaminski, "Rhode Island: Protecting State Interests," in Gillespie and Lienesch, *Ratifying the Constitution*, 368–90; Patrick T. Conley, "First in War, Last in Peace: Rhode Island and the Constitution, 1786–1790," in Conley and Kaminski, *The Constitution and the States*, 269–94.

156. J. Q. Adams, Diary, October 29, 1787, in *DHRC*, 4:142n.

157. *Pennsylvania Gazette*, February 13, 1788.

158. Noah Webster, writing as "Giles Hickory" in the *American Magazine* (January/February 1788), counted this principle among the "received opinions of the present age," which he himself dared to question.

2. Public Discourses and Private Correspondence

1. Belknap to Ebenezer Hazard, March 3, 1784, quoted in Jackson T. Main, "The Antifederal Party," in *History of U.S. Political Parties*, ed. Arthur M. Schlesinger, Jr., 5 vols. (New York, 1973), 1:145.

2. Ibid.

3. "Americanus" (John Stevens Jr.), New York *Daily Advertiser*, November 23, 1787; Thomas Johnson to Washington, Annapolis, December 11, 1786, in *DHRC*, 14:404.

4. Jay to Washington, New York, January 7, 1787, in *Washington Papers: Confederation Series*, 4:503.

5. Coxe to Andrew Allen, Philadelphia, October 10, 1787, in *DHRC*, 13:360.

6. Webster, *Connecticut Courant*, November 20, 1786; Pintard to Elisha Boudinot, New York, September 22, 1787, in *DHRC*, 19:47.

7. J. Q. Adams, Diary, December 20, 1787, in Adams Papers, 2:331; Ellery to Benjamin

Huntington, Newport, May 10, 1787, Huntington Autograph Book, Jervis Library, Rome, N.Y.

8. Higginson to Henry Knox, Boston, November 15, 1786, in *Letters of Stephen Higginson, 1783–1804,* Annual Report of the American Historical Association for 1896, 1: 742–43; Sedgwick to Henry Van Schaack, Boston, May 29, 1788, Sedgwick Papers, MHi.

9. Alexander Donald to Jefferson, Richmond, November 12, 1787, in *DHRC,* 8:154–55.

10. Van Schaack to Sedgwick, Pittsfield, Mass., January 8, 1788, Sedgwick Papers, MHi.

11. Washington to Lafayette, May 28, 1788, in *DHRC,* 18:82–83.

12. "Alfred," Philadelphia *Independent Gazetteer,* December 13, 1787, in *DHRC,* 14: 432–35; "Impartial Examiner" I, *Virginia Independent Chronicle,* March 5, 1788, in *DHRC,* 8:461, 465; Baltimore *Maryland Gazette,* September 4, 1787; "An Old Whig" III, Philadelphia *Independent Gazetteer,* October 20, 1787, in *DHRC,* 13:428–29.

13. R. H. Lee to George Mason, May 15, 1787, in Rutland, 3:1096; Lee to William Shippen, New York, October 2, 1787, in *DHRC,* 13:289; Lee to John Lamb, June 27, 1788, in *DHRC,* 18:57–58.

14. Humphreys to Washington, New Haven, September 28, 1787, in *DHRC,* 13:261–62; Washington to Humphreys, Mount Vernon, October 10, 1787, in *DHRC,* 8:48.

15. Madison to Jefferson, June 6, 1787; New York, October 24/November 1, 1787, in Rutland, 10:29–30; *DHRC,* 13:448.

16. Stuart to John Breckinridge, Richmond, October 21, 1787, in *DHRC,* 8:89.

17. Gouverneur Morris to Washington, Philadelphia, October 30, 1787, in *DHRC,* 13:513–14.

18. Hamilton to Madison, New York, May 19, 1788, in Rutland, 11:53–54; Convention Speech, June 21, 1788, in Syrett, 5:37. In this respect, there was agreement between Hamilton, Madison, and Richard Henry Lee (see Lee to Patrick Henry, New York, September 14, 1789, in Richard Henry Lee, *Memoir of the Life of Richard Henry Lee,* 2 vols. [Philadelphia, 1825], 2:98–99). See also Erich Vollrath, "That All Governments Rest on Opinion," *Social Research* 43 (1976): 46–61.

19. *Georgia State Gazette,* June 21, 1788.

20. Petition of Providence Town Meeting, March 26, 1788, Providence Town Records, City Clerk's Office, Providence City Hall.

21. *Newport Herald,* July 3, 1788.

22. "Cato Uticensis," *Virginia Independent Chronicle,* October 17, 1787, in *DHRC,* 8:70; "Observator" V, *New Haven Gazette,* September 20, 1787, in *DHRC,* 3:349.

23. Federalist No. 1, October 27, 1787, in *DHRC,* 13:494.

24. John Preston to John Brown, February 10, 1788, in *DHRC,* 8:362.

25. Lee to Edmund Randolph, New York, October 16, 1787, in *DHRC,* 14:366–67; Melancton Smith to Gilbert Livingston, New York, January 1, 1789, Melancton Smith Papers, New York State Library.

26. "A Planter," *Virginia Independent Chronicle,* February 13, 1788, in *DHRC,* 9:565.

27. Washington's circular letter of June 8, 1783, was reprinted on March 15, 1787, in the Providence *United States Chronicle,* and was often quoted during the ratification debate (*DHRC,* 13:60–70, especially 63).

28. "Cato" I, *New York Journal,* September 27, 1787, in *DHRC,* 13:255–57.

29. "Caesar" II, New York *Daily Advertiser,* October 17, 1787, in *DHRC,* 13:396.

30. "Denatus," *Virginia Independent Chronicle,* June 11, 1788, in *DHRC,* 10:1599.

31. *DHRC,* 13:329, 475.

32. *DHRC,* 13:305–6, 562.

33. Madison to David Stuart, New York, October 30, 1787, in *DHRC,* 13:512.

34. "Agrippa" X, *Massachusetts Gazette,* January 1, 1788, in *DHRC,* 5:576.

35. "Lycurgus," October 29, 1787, in *DHRC,* 4:161–62; Ellery to Benjamin Huntington, Newport, July 21, 1789, Thomas C. Bright Autograph Collection, Jervis Library, Rome, N.Y.

36. Jefferson to Edward Carrington, May 27, 1788, in Boyd, 13:208–9.

37. Quotation from 1825 in Cecelia M. Kenyon, "The Declaration of Independence," *Fundamental Testaments of the American Revolution,* Library of Congress Symposia on the American Revolution (Washington, D.C., 1973), 45.

38. Francis Hopkinson to Jefferson, Philadelphia, July 17, 1788, in *DHRC,* 18:270–71.

39. New York *Daily Advertiser,* July 28, 1788.

40. "A Citizen of America" (John O'Connor), Pamphlet 1789, Evans 22072. See also the title of Robert A. Rutland's book, *The Ordeal of the Constitution* (Norman, Okla., 1966).

41. *Pennsylvania Gazette,* January 20, 1790; Letter from Charleston, New York *Daily Advertiser,* July 7, 1788; "Another True Federalist," *Fayetteville Gazette,* September 21, 1789.

42. Ridley to John Jay, December 12, 1787, M. Ridley Papers, MdHi; Carrington to Jefferson, October 23, 1787, and Carrington to William Short, October 25, 1787, in *DHRC,* 13:439, 469; Washington to Lafayette, June 18, 1788, in *DHRC,* 18:183–84; Madison to Jefferson, December 9, 1787, in *DHRC,* 14:395–98.

43. See "Appendix I: Speculation about the Prospects for the Ratification of the Constitution in Virginia, 23 October 1787–July 7, 1788," in *DHRC,* 10:1778–93.

44. Washington to Benjamin Lincoln, October 26, 1788, and Washington to Henry Knox, January 1, 1789, in *Papers of George Washington: Presidential Series,* ed. Dorothy Twohig et al. (Charlottesville, Va., 1987–), 1:70, 225.

45. Stuart to Madison, July 31, 1789, in Rutland, 12:319–20.

46. Hamilton to Theodore Sedgwick, November 9, 1788, in Syrett, 5:230–31; Platt to Winthrop Sargent, July 9, 1789, Sargent Papers, MHi. See also John P. Kaminski, *George Clinton: Yeoman Politician of the New Republic* (Madison, Wis., 1993), 178–89.

47. See, e.g., *DHRC,* 13:356–66, 505; and Rutland, 10:233–34.

48. W. Cranch to J. Q. Adams, January 22 and 27, 1788, Adams Papers, MHi.

49. James Breckinridge to John Breckinridge, December 14, 1787, in *DHRC,* 15:561–62. See also John Breckinridge to James Breckinridge, Grove Hill, January 25, 1788, in *DHRC,* 8:320–21.

50. Henrietta Maria Colden to Fanny Tucker, New York, December 28, 1787, in *DHRC,* 19:479.

51. When John Quincy Adams and his friends visited Gerry in July 1788, "we found Mrs. Warren there, and were in the midst of antifederalism: but quite in good humour" (entry for July 3, 1788, in *Diary of John Quincy Adams,* ed. David Grayson Allen et al. [Cambridge, 1981–]; see also *Adams Papers,* 2:424). And see James T. Austin, *The Life*

of Elbridge Gerry, 2 vols. (Boston, 1828–29), 2:84–85; and C. Harvey Gardner, ed., *Mercy Otis Warren and Elbridge Gerry: A Study in Dissent. The Warren-Gerry Correspondence, 1776–1792* (Carbondale, Ill., 1968).

52. Abigail Adams to Cotton Tufts, February 20, 1788, in *DHRC,* 14:474n3. The reference is to John Adams's *Defence of the Constitutions.*

53. *DHRC,* 17:104.

54. Ford, *Correspondence,* 3:110–11.

55. Mary Morris to Robert Morris, Philadelphia, December 13, 1787, in *DHRC,* 2:602.

56. Abigail Adams Smith to Abigail Adams, New York, June 15, 1788, in *DHRC,* 20: 1173. Historical background and analysis are provided by Linda K. Kerber, *Women of the Republic: Intellect and Ideology in Revolutionary America,* 2nd ed. (New York, 1986); Mary Beth Norton, *The Revolutionary Experience of American Women, 1750–1800* (Boston, 1980); and Norton, *Founding Mothers and Fathers: Gendered Power and the Forming of American Society* (New York, 1996).

57. Writing in the February issue of the *Worcester Magazine,* the Antifederalist "Maria" compared the Grand Procession to a "Royal Homage" in Europe: "Was I a gentleman, I would bear testimony against such proceedings, on such occasions, as I think it tends to the subversion of true republican principles, in as much as it controuls the bias of a citizen's mind, which ought to be free and uncountroulable by party measures."

58. William Fleming to Thomas Madison, Belmont, February 19, 1788, in *DHRC,* 8: 383–84.

59. Lee to George Thatcher, May 9, 1788, *Historical Magazine* 6 (1869): 348–49.

60. H. Van Schaack to Theodore Sedgwick, Pittsfield, Mass., December 14, 1787, in *DHRC,* 5:1005. At the time of the Massachusetts ratifying convention, Van Schaack's nerves were even more strained: "The perturbations of mind we are in can be better conceived than described. I can bring myself to think of nothing but this important matter; it is the last of my thoughts when I go to bed and the first in the morning when I awake. . . . Our friends in the State of New York are anxious beyond discription" (Van Schaack to Sedgwick, February 2, 1788, Sedgwick Papers, MHi).

61. J. Q. Adams to Dr. Oliver Fiske, January 31, 1788, American Antiquarian Society, Misc. Mss., box A, Adams Folder. See also *DHRC,* 4:67–68, 72–75; and *DHRC,* 14:220–29.

62. Letter of February 16, 1788, in *DHRC,* 7:1702.

63. J. Q. Adams to Nathaniel Freeman, February 25, 1788, quoted in *The Genesis of American Freedom, 1765–1795,* ed. Lawrence H. Leder (Waltham, Mass., 1961), doc. 35.

64. *Diary of John Quincy Adams,* March 4, April 3 and 25, July 3 and 5, 1788, 2:371, 384–85, 395–96, 424–26. See also Robert A. East, *John Quincy Adams: The Critical Years, 1785–1794* (New York, 1962).

65. *DHRC,* 8:475–78.

66. P. Thatcher to Jonathan Jackson, October 30, 1788, James Jackson Papers, MHi.

67. "Thoughts Upon the Political Situation of the United States," Worcester, August 14, 1788 (Evans 21173). See also *DHRC,* 18:326–31.

68. *Providence Gazette,* August 9, 1788.

69. Washington to Rochambeau, New York, August 10, 1790, in *Washington Papers, Presidential Series,* 6:232.

70. "Notes for the *National Gazette* essays: Influence of public opinion on Govern-

ment, December 19, 1791–March 3, 1792," in Rutland, 14:161–63; Banning, *Sacred Fire of Liberty*, 354–55.

71. Quoted in Philip G. Davidson, *Propaganda and the American Revolution, 1763–1783* (Chapel Hill, N.C., 1941), 345.

72. FDR was working on a manuscript of a speech which included this statement when he died on April 12, 1945 (Lloyd C. Gardner, *Spheres of Influence: The Great Powers Partition Europe, from Munich to Yalta* [Chicago, 1993], 258).

73. Hamilton to Washington, October 30, 1787, in Syrett, 4:306; Madison to Randolph, New York, October 21, 1787, in *DHRC*, 13:429–30. Thomas Hartley asked Tench Coxe to send him propaganda material for the Federalists' "Winter Campaign" in Maryland (Hartley to Coxe, York, January 11, 1788, Coxe Papers, PHi).

74. Introduction to *DHRC*, 13:xvii.

75. General press studies touch only briefly on the ratification debate. See Frank L. Mott, *American Journalism*, 2nd ed. (New York, 1959); Sidney Kobre, *Foundations of American Journalism* (Westport, Conn., 1958); Donald H. Stewart, *The Opposition Press of the Federalist Period* (Albany, N.Y., 1969); Culver H. Smith, *The Press, Politics, and Patronage: The American Government's Use of Newspapers 1789–1875* (Athens, Ga., 1977); and Bernard Bailyn and John B. Hench, eds., *The Press and the American Revolution* (Worcester, Mass., 1980). Important new information is provided by John K. Alexander, *The Selling of the Constitutional Convention: A History of News Coverage* (Madison, Wis., 1990).

76. Peters to John Adams, Belmont, Pa., June 15, 1789, Hull Collection of Letters Relating to the Adams Family, Smithsonian Institution.

77. In a letter to Richard Price, written in 1778, Turgot had argued that the bicameral system of most American states violated the theory of republicanism. Price published an extract of this letter in 1784 in London together with his own *Observations on the Importance of the American Revolution* (*DHRC*, 13:81–90).

78. *The Federalist: A Collection of Essays, Written in Favour of the New Constitution, by a Citizen of New-York* (New York, 1788). Because the thirty-first newspaper essay was divided, there were eighty-five numbered entries. For reactions to the series, as well as to the M'Lean volumes, see *DHRC*, 13:486–94, 15:223–25, 16:466–71.

79. Jefferson to Madison, November 18, 1788, in Boyd, 14:188.

80. Massachusetts Federalist Rufus King assumed that in New England Oliver Ellsworth's "Landholder" essays "would do more service our way, than the elaborate works of Publius" (*DHRC*, 15:71).

81. The *Debates* sold 266 copies (*DHRC*, 2:40–42, 16:75–80).

82. Evans 21242, in *DHRC*, 6:1132–37.

83. The Virginia *Debates*, based on the shorthand notes of David Robertson, a prominent Petersburg lawyer, appeared in three volumes between October 1788 and the summer of 1789. Totaling more than 600 pages, they were printed by Miles Hunter and William Prentis of the Petersburg *Virginia Gazette*. In 1805, Robertson published a second edition in one volume (*DHRC*, 9:902–6). The North Carolina *Debates* were used by Federalists during the campaign for the second convention, although they themselves considered the text "in many places defective" (William R. Davie to James Iredell, Newbern, July 1, 1789, Iredell Papers, Duke University; Archibald Maclaine to Iredell, Wilmington,

August 11, 1789, in *The Papers of James Iredell,* ed. Don Higginbotham et al. [Raleigh, N.C., 1976–], 3:499, 513).

84. *DHRC,* 5:569–71. Another example is *Fleet's Pocket Almanack for 1790,* which contained an unflattering portrait of the "backwards" citizens of North Carolina: "From a depreciated paper medium (like Rhode Island) and a deficiency of political knowledge, they in general are anti-federal. . . . Temperance and industry are not reckoned among their virtues. The general topics among the men, when cards and the bottle do not intervene, are negroes, the price of indigo, rice, tobacco etc. The time they waste in drinking, idling, and gambling, leaves the most of them very little opportunity to improve their plantations or their minds" (Almanac, Maine Historical Society, Portland, Maine).

85. Bernard Bailyn, ed., *Pamphlets of the American Revolution* (Cambridge, Mass., 1965).

86. This was Alexander Contee Hanson's definition of the ideal pamphlet. In Hanson's view, his "Aristides" came closer to this ideal than *The Federalist,* which was more of a treatise of government, displaying "learning and deep penetration," but "from its prolixity, tiresome" (*DHRC,* 15:521).

87. Only a few months after its publication, *Common Sense* had reached a circulation of 150,000 (G. Thomas Tanselle, "Some Statistics on American Printing," in Bailyn and Hench, *Press and Revolution,* 353).

88. Pennsylvania Antifederalists raised £15 sterling in order to get 1,400 copies of William Petrikin's pamphlet, *The Government of Nature Delienated,* printed. Petrikin hoped that more than 4,000 copies would be published (*DHRC,* 2:695).

89. *DHRC,* 14:18–54. The full title is *Observations Leading to a Fair Examination of the System of Government Proposed by the Late Convention; and to Several Essential and Necessary Alterations in It. In a Number of Letters from the Federal Farmer to the Republican.* The authorship question is discussed in *DHRC,* 14:14–18.

90. *DHRC,* 2:210–16, 13:405, 14:255–78, 16:272–91, 17:30–32, 83–94, 146–67, 229–31, 265–376, Mfm:Pa. 142, Mfm:Pa. 661. Most of these pamphlets are also printed in Storing and Dry, eds., *The Complete Anti-Federalist.*

91. *DHRC,* 13:297–306, 14:63–74.

92. *DHRC,* 13:381n2, 405–6, Mfm:Pa. 142.

93. *DHRC,* 2:339–50, 14:206–7.

94. Samuel Blachley Webb to Joseph Barrell, New York, April 27, 1788, in *DHRC,* 21:1509.

95. Washington to John Jay, May 15, 1788, in *Washington Papers: Confederation Series,* 6:275 (in the *Massachusetts Centinel*).

96. *DHRC,* 13:558–61, 15:517–554, 16:161–69, 17:74–83, 101–20.

97. Examples are David Ramsay's Oration in Charleston on the Occasion of South Carolina's Ratification, as well as Fourth of July orations by Simeon Baldwin (New Haven), James Wilson (Philadelphia), William Pierce (Savannah), Jonathan M. Sewall (Portsmouth), Harrison Gray Otis (Boston), and Enos Hitchcock (Providence) (*DHRC,* 18:158–65, 221–54).

98. *DHRC,* 14:447–48.

99. *DHRC,* 13:247–51, 430–31.

100. *DHRC,* 2:617–40, 13:293–97. On October 29, 1787, Eleazer Oswald, printer of the *Independent Gazetteer,* "respectfully" informed the public that "he has printed in a *hand-*

bill the fourth number of the OLD WHIG, as many of his customers were disappointed in receiving that piece owing to the rapid sale of his paper of Saturday [27 October]—The hand-bill is now for sale at the printing office" (*DHRC,* 13:497).

101. *DHRC,* 13:326–37, 534–38.

102. Boyd, *Politics of Opposition,* 56–58, 74–76. See also chapter 5, under "Ideology and Politics in the Conventions," below.

103. Boston *American Herald,* November 19, 1787.

104. Rush to John Adams, January 22, 1789, Adams Papers, MHi; Coxe to James Madison, September 9, 1789, in Rutland, 2:394–96.

105. *DHRC,* 13:49; Farrand 1:274.

106. New York *Daily Advertiser,* November 16, 1787. The newspapers themselves, their publishers, and their "correspondents" were the subject of a popular ditty called the "News-Mongers' Song" (*Albany Gazette,* November 15, 1787, in *DHRC,* 14:117–19).

107. Leonard W. Levy, *The Emergence of a Free Press* (New York, 1984).

108. "A Man of No Party," New York *Daily Advertiser,* October 19, 1787.

109. Ibid.

110. Jay to John Vaughan, Poughkeepsie, June 27, 1788, in *DHRC,* 20:923.

111. *Virginia Independent Chronicle,* January 23, 1788, in *DHRC,* 8:313–19.

112. Winchester *Virginia Gazette,* February 22, 1788, in *DHRC,* 8:401–8.

113. See "The Press and the Constitution," in *DHRC,* 13:312–23.

114. Belknap to Benjamin Rush, April 7, 1788, Rush Papers, Library Company of Philadelphia; *DHRC,* 13:573–74. See also Rutland, *Ordeal of the Constitution,* 148–49.

115. Clarence S. Brigham, *History and Bibliography of American Newspapers, 1690–1820,* 2 vols. (Worcester, Mass., 1947); Roger P. Bristol, *Index of Printers, Publishers, and Booksellers Indicated by Charles Evans in his American Bibliography* (Charlottesville, Va., 1961); G. Thomas Tanselle, ed., *Guide to the Study of United States Imprints,* 2 vols. (Cambridge, Mass., 1971); Edward C. Lathem, comp., *Chronological Tables of American Newspapers, 1690–1820* (Barre, Mass., 1972).

116. Seventy-six newspapers and two magazines covered the entire period, while the others either began to circulate in the course of the debate or ceased to exist. Among the eighty-nine newspapers, five were German-language: the *Maryland Chronicle* in Fredericktown, the *Germantowner Zeitung,* the *Neue Unpartheyische Lancaster Zeitung,* the *Gemeinnützige Philadelphische Correspondenz,* and the *Virginia Zeitung* in Winchester.

117. "A Man of No Party," New York *Daily Advertiser,* October 19, 1787.

118. Rollo G. Silver, *The American Printer, 1787–1825* (Charlottesville, Va., 1967), 115–17.

119. *DHRC,* 13:xxxiii–xxxiv (Introduction).

120. Fenno to John Barrett, Barrett Letters, Massachusetts Historical Society *Proceedings* 47 (1914): 16–17.

121. "Oriental Junius," *Cumberland Gazette,* December 13, 1787.

122. Judith M. Katz, "Connecticut Newspapers and the Constitution, 1786–1788," Connecticut Historical Society *Bulletin* 30 (1965): 33–44.

123. Stewart, *Opposition Press,* 16–18, 652–53n73. The ratio was better balanced if only white people were counted.

124. "Many" (Arthur Campbell), June 18, 1788, in *DHRC,* 10:1638–40.

125. Lee to Edmund Pendleton, May 26, 1788, in *DHRC* 9:879. Samuel Adams is

quoted in Jeremy Belknap to Ebenezer Hazard, June 14, 1789, in the Belknap Papers, Collections of the Massachusetts Historical Society, 5th Series, vols. 2–3 (Boston, 1877), 3:140–41. See also Rush to Henry Muhlenberg, February 15, 1788, in *DHRC,* Mfm:Pa. 432.

126. Quoted in Joel Munsell, *The Typographical Miscellany* (Albany, N.Y., 1850), 226.

127. Dieter Cunz, *The Maryland Germans* (Princeton, N.J., 1948), 170–71. See also Christopher L. Dolmetsch, *The German Press in the Shenandoah Valley* (Columbia, S.C., 1984), 110–11n23.

128. See *DHRC,* 13:337–39, 546–48, appendix 2: 593, 595.

129. See "The Controversy over the Post Office and the Circulation of Newspapers," in *DHRC,* vol. 16, appendix 2: 540–96. Hazard was one of the few Confederation officers whom Washington did not reappoint after taking the presidency. Congress reestablished the free exchange of newspapers among printers in 1792. A general survey is Richard R. John, *Spreading the News: The American Postal System from Franklin to Morse* (Cambridge, Mass., 1995).

130. The report of the Constitutional Convention, which consisted of the Constitution, two resolutions, and the letter of convention president George Washington to the President of Congress, was first published as a six-page broadside on September 18, 1787, by John Dunlap and David C. Claypoole, editors of the *Pennsylvania Packet* (*DHRC,* 13:199–200).

131. *New York Journal,* December 27, 1787.

132. Baltimore *Maryland Gazette,* February 15, 1788.

133. *Providence Gazette,* January 12, 1788.

134. *New Hampshire Gazette,* June 5, 1788.

135. *New Hampshire Recorder,* January 1, 1788, in *DHRC,* 13:480.

136. *DHRC,* 13:xxxv–xxxvi (Introduction).

137. Hazard to Belknap, New York, July 27 and October 14, 1788, Belknap Papers, MHi; Thomas McKean to William A. Atlee, Philadelphia, September 17, 1788, Atlee Papers, DLC; Henry Chapman to Stephen Collins, New York, June 20, 1788, Papers of Stephen Collins and Son, DLC; *Massachusetts Centinel,* August 16, 1788.

138. Dwight L. Teeter Jr., "The Printer and the Chief Justice: Seditious Libel in 1782–83," *Journalism Quarterly* 45 (1963): 235–42.

139. Philadelphia *Independent Gazetteer,* January 11, 1788.

140. Spotswood to Belknap, June 19, 1788, Belknap Papers, MHi.

141. Benjamin Rush to Henry Muhlenberg, February 15, 1788, in *DHRC,* Mfm:Pa. 432.

142. Philadelphia *Independent Gazetteer,* January 10, 1788.

143. *DHRC,* 13:xxxv–xxxvi (Introduction); Boyd, 13:642–44.

144. Franklin to Elizabeth Oswald, post August 3, 1788, Franklin Papers, American Philosophical Society Library.

145. *DHRC,* 13:xxxvii–xxxviii (Introduction).

146. *New York Journal,* December 6 and 11, 1787.

147. *DHRC,* 18:311–12.

148. Former state printer Samuel Loudon was convinced that the Clintonians wanted to punish him for publishing the "Publius" essays in his *New York Packet* (Syrett, 5: 341–42).

149. Eugene P. Link, *Democratic-Republican Societies, 1790–1800* (New York, 1942), 38.

150. Philadelphia *Freeman's Journal,* October 25, 1787. In the face of mounting criticism, Russell discarded this policy in November 1787 (*DHRC,* 13:xxxvi–xxxvii [Introduction], 312–23, 573–81).

151. *DHRC,* 10:1746–48, 18:381–83.

152. *Massachusetts Centinel,* August 2, 1788.

153. It did not take long, however, until he felt the wrath of a local Federalist: "Howard is a rank anti-federalist. . . . I have with a few others, withdrawn my subscription, and intend to procure another printer" (Archibald Maclaine to James Iredell, September 13, 1788, *Papers of James Iredell,* 3:436).

154. Evans 20597.

155. *Federal Gazette,* October 1, 1788. Brown was one of the first printers who published the debates of Congress under the new Constitution.

156. Nicholas Brown et al. to Bennett Wheeler, Providence, February 4, 1788, Brown Papers, John Carter Brown Library, Brown University; *Providence Gazette,* February 9, 1788.

157. Nicholas Brown et al. to Bennett Wheeler, Providence, February 4, 1788, Brown Papers, John Carter Brown Library, Brown University; *Providence Gazette,* February 9, 1788.

158. *American Herald,* August 21, 1788.

159. *Newport Herald,* June 19, 1788. Edes later professed he had been as impartial "as the times would admit" (ibid., October 22, 1789).

160. John Montgomery to James Wilson, Carlisle, March 2, 1788, in *DHRC,* 2:701–6.

161. *American Herald,* May 5, 1788.

162. *New York Journal,* March 3, 1788.

163. Philadelphia *Independent Gazetteer,* February 26, 1788. See also *DHRC,* vol. 16, appendix 2: 540–96 ("The Controversy over the Post Office and the Circulation of Newspapers").

164. Ledlie to Lamb, Hartford, January 15, 1788, in *DHRC,* 3:575–83; Atherton to Lamb, June 11 and 14, 1788, in *DHRC,* 18:45–47; Burke to Lamb, Charleston, June 23, 1788, in *DHRC,* 18:55–57; Bryan to Aedanus Burke, Philadelphia, post December 12, 1788, in *DHRC,* Mfm:Pa. 700.

165. Madison to Randolph, New York, October 21, 1787, in *DHRC,* 13:429–30.

166. *Massachusetts Spy,* October 16, 1788. In Maryland, John Vaughan had the impression that "much was written against [the Constitution] but it was the emanations of a very confined circle" (Vaughan to John Langdon, May 2, 1788, Langdon-Elwyn Papers, NhHi).

167. *Maryland Journal,* May 9, 1788.

168. Smith to David Gelston, ca. April 18–25, 1788, in *DHRC,* 21:1539.

169. In the 1790s newspapers were becoming more and more linked to national political agendas. Madison and Jefferson mainly published first in Philip Freneau's *National Gazette* (1791–93), then in Benjamin Bache's *Aurora.* Hamilton, by contrast, voiced his opinion in John Fenno's *Gazette of the United States.*

170. On January 7, 1788, the Boston *American Herald* published a parody which had a certain prophetic quality: "JULY the 9th, 1798. A Cabinet Council was holden yesterday, when it was resolved *nem. con.* that as the freedom of the press was relinquished, by the cession of 1787 and 1788, there shall be but one Gazette published in America. . . . The

Printer of the *Herald* was imprisoned for life.—The *Centinel,* having done much in 1787 for the establishment of the Empire of DESPOTISM, was allowed to EXIST two years longer, under the inspection of an opposite Insurance-Office" (*DHRC,* 5:639–42).

171. To Peter Gansevoort, New York, March 18, 1788, in *DHRC,* Mfm:N.Y.

172. Kinderhook, June 29, 1788, in *DHRC,* 21:1237–38.

173. Nasson to Thatcher, Sanford, February 26, 1788, in *DHRC,* 7:1708; Widgery to Thatcher, New Gloucester, September 14, 1788, in *Historical Magazine* 6 (1869): 352.

174. In early 1788 George Washington was embarrassed by the publication of a letter he wrote to Charles Carter, in which he had given his opinion "that there is no Alternative between the Adoption of [the Constitution] and Anarchy" (*DHRC,* 8:276–83).

175. Edmund Pendleton to Nathaniel Pendleton, November 25, 1788, Pendleton Family Papers, CtY.

176. *DHRC,* 8:97–109, 249–53; Boyd, 12:416–17, 475–77. Cf. Banning, *Sacred Fire of Liberty,* 281–86. Like all transatlantic correspondence in the eighteenth century, this dialogue suffered from delays caused by shipping conditions (see *DHRC,* vol. 14, appendix 2: 460–502).

177. Pickering's letter is perhaps the finest response to the "Federal Farmer" in the course of the ratification debate (*DHRC,* 14:193–206).

178. William Symmes Jr. to Peter Osgood Jr., November 15, 1787; and Samuel Osgood to Samuel Adams, January 5, 1788, in *DHRC,* 14:107–16, 15:263–67.

179. *DHRC,* 18:153–58.

180. Washington was hopeful that the example of Francis L. Lee, "on whose Judgment the family place much reliance," would dampen Richard Henry Lee's spirit of opposition (Washington to Madison, Mount Vernon, January 10, 1788, in *DHRC,* 8:291–93).

181. The Shippens's correspondence on the Constitution is published in *DHRC,* 2: 235–36, 288–89, 424, 549–50, 601–2, 14:462–63, 467–71; and in William Shippen Jr. to Washington, April 6, 1789, Washington Papers, DLC.

182. Abraham Bancker to Evert Bancker, Poughkeepsie, June 28, 1788; and Evert Bancker to Abraham Bancker, New York, July 2, 1788, in *DHRC,* 21:1229–31, 1246–47.

183. Boston, December 20, 1787, in *DHRC,* 15:49–51.

184. *Correspondence between Jeremy Belknap and Ebenezer Hazard,* Massachusetts Historical Society *Collections,* 1877–91. Both men corresponded with Mathew Carey, and Belknap also kept contact with Benjamin Rush in Philadelphia and David Ramsay in Charleston.

185. William Ellery Letterbook, 1786–94, Newport Historical Society; Thomas C. Bright Autograph Collection, Jervis Library, Rome, N.Y.

186. Henshaw to Sedgwick, Northampton, April 15, 1789, Sedgwick Papers, MHi.

187. *DHRC,* 18:32–68. For more detail, see chapter 5, under "Ideology and Politics at in the Conventions," and chapter 6, under "The Significance of the Ratification Celebrations."

188. According to Washington, the citizens of Maryland and Virginia were closely connected, "not only by the nature of their produce, but by the ties of blood and the habits of life" (Washington to William Smith et al., Mount Vernon, June 8, 1788, in *Washington Papers: Confederation Series,* 6:322).

189. *DHRC,* 13:223–24. See also George Washington on the Constitution, December 27, 1787–February 14, 1788, in *DHRC,* 15:135–43.

190. Following a meeting with the "Immortal General," a British visitor noted in his diary on February 12, 1788, that the conversation had "turned on the adoption of the New federal plan of government which he appears to be very much attached to. He said he had read with attention every publication both for and against it, in order to see wither there could be any new objections . . . he said he had sought in vain" (*DHRC*, 8:362–63). Between November 1787 and March 1788, Washington hosted, among others, Richard Henry Lee, Robert Morris, Gouverneur Morris, and James Madison.

191. This count is based on the files of the *DHRC*.

192. See excerpts from letters written by Rufus King to Madison, in Rutland, 10:419–20, 437–38, 455, 464–65, 481–82, 498–99. See also Stuart Leibiger, *Founding Friendship: George Washington, James Madison, and the Creation of the American Republic* (Charlottesville, Va., 1999).

193. Robert A. Rutland, "The Power of Prestige: George Washington and the Federal Constitution," in *Americana-Austriaca: Festschrift des Amerika-Instituts der Universität Innsbruck*, ed. K. Lanzinger (Wien, 1966), 116–28.

194. North Callahan, *Henry Knox: General Washington's General* (Philadelphia, 1958).

195. Jacob E. Cooke, *Tench Coxe and the Early Republic* (Chapel Hill, N.C., 1978).

3. The Debate over Basic Principles

1. New York *Daily Advertiser*, November 2, 1787.

2. Banning, The *Sacred Fire of Liberty*, 216.

3. John Adams to James Sullivan, New York, July 14, 1789, Adams Papers, MHi. When, in late September 1787, Cotton Tufts had asked for his opinion on the Constitution, Adams answered on January 23, 1788, that he was "much Mortified at the Mixture of Legislative and Executive Powers in the Senate, and wish for Some other Amendments—But I am clear for accepting the present Plan as it is and trying to Experiment. At a future Time Amendments may be made" (*DHRC*, 14:499–500).

4. *DHRC*, 14:14–18, 49, 15:386.

5. George Turner to Winthrop Sargent, Philadelphia, November 6, 1787, in *DHRC*, 13:565–66.

6. Wallace to William Fleming, June 29, 1788, in *DHRC*, 10:1694–95. Wallace's initial response to the Philadelphia plan had been much more critical (*DHRC*, 9:781–87).

7. John Breckinridge to James Breckinridge, Botetourt County, January 25, 1788; and William Nelson to William Short, York, July 12, 1788, in *DHRC*, 8:320–21, 10:1700–1704.

8. *Providence Gazette*, August 2, 1788.

9. Edmund Pendleton to Nathaniel Pendleton, Edmundsburg, November 15, 1788, Pendleton Family Papers, CtY.

10. Wilson was not as tolerant toward Antifederalists as this would suggest. He went on to say: "The sum of what I have wrote is just this. I think the whole amount of all the objections against the Constitution is ignorance, prejudice and absurdity; the production of narrow, warped minds, and leather headed politicians" (John Wilson to Rev. Samuel Wilson, Crowder Creek, July 10, 1788, L. C. Glenn Papers, Southern History Collection, University of North Carolina.

11. See John P. Kaminski, "Antifederalism and the Perils of Homogenized History: A Review Essay," *Rhode Island History* 42 (1983): 30–37.

12. See Paul A. Rahe, *Republics* (Chapel Hill, N.C., 1992); Christopher M. Duncan, *The Anti-Federalists and Early American Political Thought* (DeKalb, Ill., 1995); and Saul A. Cornell, *The Other Founders: Anti-Federalism and the Dissenting Tradition in America, 1788–1828* (Chapel Hill, N.C., 1999).

13. Since political thinking was in a state of flux during the ratification debate, it would be misleading to make clear distinctions and identify Antifederalists with a "neoclassical" republican ideology, and Federalists with a "modern" liberal ideology. The still ongoing scholarly controversy about the relationship between republicanism and liberalism in eighteenth-century America has shown that things are much more complicated. However, this study supports the thesis that Antifederalists were closer to the concepts, doctrines, and maxims of the British oppositionist (Old Whig, Country) tradition than Federalists who struggled to break free from its intellectual shackles. The fascinating historiographical debate was started by Bernard Bailyn (*The Ideological Origins of the American Revolution* [Cambridge, Mass., 1967]), Gordon S. Wood (*The Creation of the American Republic, 1776–1787* [Chapel Hill, N.C., 1969]), and J. G. A. Pocock (*The Machiavellian Moment: Florentine Political Thought and the Atlantic Republican Tradition* [Princeton, N.J., 1975]). Early summaries of the discussion are Robert E. Shalhope, "Toward a Republican Synthesis: The Emergence of an Understanding of Republicanism in American Historiography," *WMQ* 29 (1972): 49–80; Shalhope, "Republicanism and Early American Historiography," *WMQ* 39 (1982): 334–56; and Isaac Kramnick, "Republican Revisionism Revisited," *AHR* 87 (1982): 629–724. More recent contributions include Kramnick, "The 'Great National Discussion': The Discourse of Politics in 1787," *WMQ* 45 (1988): 3–32; Kramnick, *Republicanism and Bourgeois Radicalism: Political Ideology in Late Eighteenth-Century England and America* (Ithaca, N.Y., 1990); Saul A. Cornell, "Aristocracy Assailed: The Ideology of Backcountry Anti-Federalism," *JAH* 76 (1990): 1148–72; Joyce Appleby, *Liberalism and Republicanism in the Historical Imagination* (Cambridge, Mass., 1992); Rahe, *Republics;* Daniel T. Rogers, "Republicanism: The Career of a Concept," *JAH* 79 (1992): 11–38; and Lance Banning, "The Republican Interpretation: Retrospect and Prospect," in *The Republican Synthesis Revisited: Essays in Honor of George Athen Billias,* ed. Milton Klein et al. (Worcester, Mass., 1992), 91–117. See also Banning, *Sacred Fire of Liberty,* 195–233, 472–74.

14. *Genuine Information* III, January 4, 1788, in *DHRC,* 15:253.

15. "Centinel" I, October 5, 1787, in *DHRC,* 13:330; "Samuel," January 10, 1788, in *DHRC,* 5:683; "A Farmer" I, Baltimore *Maryland Gazette,* February 15, 1788, in Storing, 5:10; "Impartial Examiner" I, *Virginia Independent Chronicle,* February 20, 1788, in *DHRC,* 8:388. "Where are all these changes and revolutions to end?" asked a correspondent in the New York *Daily Advertiser* of June 14, 1788: "Your fathers, eternally restless, broke off from the House of Stuart; and ye, a restless progeny, first rebel against your *Mother Country* then break your Union, and rebel against *the Sister States;* and now, lastly, you divide the very members of your own political body."

16. Philadelphia *Independent Gazetteer,* December 13, 1787, in *DHRC,* 14:433.

17. Boston *Independent Chronicle,* December 6, 1787, in *DHRC,* 4:398.

18. Letter to George Mason, May 15, 1787, quoted in Storing, 1:26.

19. A Newport Man, *Newport Mercury,* March 17, 1788.

20. "Republican Federalist" III, *Massachusetts Centinel,* January 9, 1788, in *DHRC,* 5:664; "Cornelius," *Hampshire Chronicle,* December 11, 1787, in *DHRC,* 4:411.

21. "An Old Whig" I, Philadelphia *Independent Gazetteer,* October 12, 1787, in *DHRC,* 13:377.

22. The first author contrasting "fœderal" and "antifœderal" in this way was Noah Webster in an essay in the *Connecticut Courant* in November 1786 (*DHRC,* 13:193). During the winter of 1786–87, the *New Haven Gazette* attacked some representatives in Connecticut as "anti-federal men" because they had been granted the right to mint coins by the state legislature (*DHRC,* 3:371n6).

23. "A Columbian Patriot," in *DHRC,* 16:278. Mercy Otis Warren was referring to Wilson's speech in the Pennsylvania ratifying convention on November 24, 1787 (*DHRC,* 2:339–63).

24. "Sidney," *New York Journal,* December 4, 1788; "Veracitas," *Maryland Journal,* September 9, 1788.

25. *DHRC,* 4:405.

26. Antifederal Committee, Albany, Broadside, April 20, 1788, Evans 45221.

27. "A Countryman" II, December 13, 1787, in *DHRC,* 19:406.

28. David Thomas to Griffith Evans, March 3, 1789, Massachusetts Historical Society *Proceedings* 46 (1913): 370–71.

29. Speech of June 4, 1788, in *DHRC,* 9:930.

30. Montesquieu, *De l'esprit des lois,* bk. 9, chap. 1. Published in 1748, Montesquieu's work had been translated into English in 1750; by 1773, five editions of this English version had appeared in Europe. The first American edition came out in 1802 (Paul M. Spurlin, *Montesquieu in America, 1760–1801* [Baton Rouge, La., 1940]).

31. Montesquieu, *De l'esprit des lois,* bk. 8, chap. 19.

32. *DHRC,* 14:434–35.

33. "Agrippa" IV, *Massachusetts Gazette,* December 4, 1787, in *DHRC,* 4:382.

34. *DHRC,* 13:417–19.

35. "Z," *United States Chronicle,* March 27, 1788; "Denatus" I, *Virginia Independent Chronicle,* June 11, 1788; "Impartial Examiner" I, February 20, 1788; "A [Maryland] Farmer," April 15, 1788; and "Brutus" IV, November 29, 1787, in *DHRC,* 8:387–94, 10:1599–1607, 14:297–303; Storing, 5:65, 178–79.

36. "Brutus" I, in *DHRC,* 13:415. A detailed analysis of the taxing power followed in essays V through VIII.

37. "Brutus" II, *Dissent of the Minority,* in *DHRC,* 13:528–29, 15:22.

38. *DHRC,* 13:245, 334–35, 346, 464, 14:31–32, 174, 262–63, 301–3, 363–64, 15:19, 24, 240–43, 299.

39. "Brutus" XII, February 14, 1788; and "Brutus" XV, March 20, 1788, in *DHRC,* 16: 120–22, 431–35.

40. Louis G. Schwoerer, *"No Standing Armys!" The Anti-army Ideology in 17th-Century England* (Baltimore, 1974); John Phillip Reid, *In Defiance of the Law: The Standing-Army Controversy, the Two Constitutions, and the Coming of the American Revolution* (Chapel Hill, N.C., 1981).

41. "Federal Farmer" III, "Cato" V, "Philadelphiensis" II, *Dissent of the Minority,* "Centinel" VIII, and *Genuine Information* VII, in *DHRC,* 14:38–39, 182–85, 252–54, 15:19, 32, 232, 410–12.

42. "Agrippa" VII, December 18, 1787, in *DHRC,* 5:484.

43. "A [Maryland] Farmer," April 22, 1788, in Storing, 5:66.

44. *Virginia Independent Chronicle,* October 31, 1787, in *DHRC,* 8:138.

45. Donald S. Lutz, *Popular Consent and Popular Control: Whig Political Theory in the Early State Constitutions* (Baton Rouge, La., 1980). See also Marc W. Kruman, *Between Authority and Liberty: State Constitution Making in Revolutionary America* (Chapel Hill, N.C., 1997).

46. "A [Maryland] Farmer," in Storing, 5:68.

47. *Dissent of the Minority,* in *DHRC,* 15:26.

48. "Amicus," Charleston *Columbian Herald,* August 28, 1788.

49. "Centinel" II, Philadelphia *Freeman's Journal,* October 24, 1787, in *DHRC,* 13:458.

50. "Sidney," *New York Gazetteer,* January 29, 1787.

51. *DHRC,* 2:439.

52. "Federal Farmer" V, in *DHRC,* 14:48.

53. "Brutus" gave the number of 558 members of the House of Commons, each of whom represented on average 14,000 inhabitants (*DHRC,* 14:124).

54. *DHRC,* 17:366–70 ("Federal Farmer" XVIII); *DHRC,* 5:497 ("Candidus" II); *DHRC,* 5:858–60 ("Helvidius Priscus" IV); *DHRC,* 16:274, 285, 287 ("Columbian Patriot"). "Thomas Tinsel" predicted in a satirical way that Carolinians would soon "hear of the grandeur of our government at Vortex-Ville; how 1000 cannon were fired on the president's birth; how there was a grand procession, and a levee, a ball and an illumination; how the ambassador arrived, and was conveyed to his residence with proper pomp, between two ranks of federal soldiers . . . how he was entertained by the minister of finance at a dinner of 100 crowns" (*New York Journal,* April 24, 1788; reprinted from the *Wilmington Centinel*).

55. Storing, 5:20.

56. "A Countryman" I (De Witt Clinton), *New York Journal,* December 6, 1787, in *DHRC,* 19:374.

57. *DHRC,* 2:161.

58. *Worcester Magazine,* February 7, 1788, in *DHRC,* 5:879–81.

59. Storing, 5:89–90.

60. "Republican Federalist" III, *Massachusetts Centinel,* January 9, 1788, in *DHRC,* 5:661.

61. Speech in the State House Yard, Philadelphia, October 6, 1787, in *DHRC,* 2:167–68, 13:339.

62. "Landholder" IV (Oliver Ellsworth), December 10, 1787, in *DHRC,* 14:400.

63. "Giles Hickory," *American Magazine,* December 1787, in *DHRC,* 20:553.

64. Hamilton, Federalist No. 84, May 28, 1788, in *DHRC,* 18:127–32.

65. "Brutus" II, November 1, 1787, in *DHRC,* 13:526–27.

66. "An Old Whig" II, October 17, 1787, in *DHRC,* 13:402.

67. *DHRC,* 13:350 (George Mason), 386–90 ("A Democratic Federalist"); Storing, 1:64, 2:209n20, 3:58–61, 63n6, 4:123n5.

68. "There is a door opened for the Jews, Turks, and Heathen to enter into publick office. . . ." (*DHRC,* 5:880–81 ["A Watchman"]); *DHRC,* 14:252–53 ("Philadelphiensis" II); Storing, 4:242 ("Anti-Fœderalist" I); Storing, 4:246–48 ("David"); Storing, 5:125–27 ("A Proposal for Reviving Christian Conviction"). "Honestus" predicted "a toleration act, by which every Jew or Infidel could come into an office" (*Wilmington Centinel,* June 18, 1788).

69. "Federal Farmer," in *DHRC,* 17:343.

70. Samuel Chase to John Lamb, Baltimore, June 13, 1788, in *DHRC,* 18:47.

71. *DHRC,* 16:159 ("Philadelphiensis" X); Storing, 4:270. See also Robert W. Shoemaker, "'Democracy' and 'Republic' as Understood in Late 18th-Century America," *American Speech* 41 (1966): 83–95.

72. Storing, 3:171.

73. "Centinel" I, October 5, 1787, in *DHRC,* 13:331.

74. Du Ponceau to Edward Jones, Philadelphia, November 17, 1788, in Rev. W. Hooper, "Biographical Sketch of Edward Jones," *North Carolina University Magazine* 5 (1856): 349.

75. Storing, 5:23.

76. Ibid., 5:43; *DHRC,* 9:1061–63.

77. *DHRC,* 14:9–10 ("Cato" IV); *DHRC,* 15:206 (Luther Martin: "Genuine Information" II); *DHRC,* 16:365–66 ("Philadelphiensis" XI).

78. *Dissent of the Minority,* in *DHRC,* 15:30. Antifederalists found their fears confirmed by a thorough critique of the "New Government of America," which appeared in the London *Times* on April 1, 1788. Pointing toward the combined powers of the president and the senate, the author maintained: "From such a union in government, it requires no great depth of political knowledge to prophecy, that monarchy or aristocracy, must be generated" (reprinted in Baltimore *Maryland Gazette,* August 1, 1788).

79. This position was taken by Luther Martin from Maryland in *Genuine Information* I, in *DHRC,* 15:150–55. Large-state Antifederalists, however, tended to complain that a state like Delaware was allowed to elect as many senators as Virginia or Massachusetts. See also *DHRC,* 14:121; and Storing, 2:447n26.

80. *DHRC,* 13:415–16 ("Brutus" I); *DHRC,* 13:482 ("A Son of Liberty"); *DHRC,* 14:369 (R. H. Lee); *DHRC,* 15:24–25 (*Dissent of the Minority*); *DHRC,* 16:434–35 ("Brutus" XV); Storing, 6:184 (George Clinton).

81. *Independent Gazetteer,* October 6, 1787, in *DHRC,* 13:346. See also Mason's *Objections:* "The Judiciary of the United States is so constructed & extended, as to absorb & destroy the Judiciarys of the several States; thereby rendering Law as tedious intricate & expensive, and Justice as unattainable, by a great Part of the Community, as in England, and enabling the Rich to oppress & ruin the Poor" (ibid., 349).

82. Massachusetts *Debates,* January 26, 1788.

83. See Philadelphia *Independent Gazetteer,* May 8, 1788; speech by Benjamin Gale in the Killingworth town meeting, November 12, 1787, in *DHRC,* 3:421; "A Columbian Patriot," in *DHRC,* 16:277–78; and the *Carlisle Gazette,* March 5, 1788.

84. *DHRC,* 13:350. When the first printed version of Mason's *Objections* appeared in the North (*Massachusetts Centinel,* November 21, 1787), this argument was conspicuously missing. Federalists attacked the omission as "tricks [that] are not uncommon with the Enemies of the new Constitution" (*DHRC,* 14:147–49).

85. *DHRC,* 14:108–9 (William Symmes Jr.); *DHRC,* 4:417 ("Cornelius").

86. According to "Cato," the mildness of the climate, the fertility of the soil, slavery, and the value of the agricultural production of the southern states "naturally lead to luxury, dissipation, and a passion for aristocratic distinctions" (*DHRC,* 13:476).

87. "An American" (Tench Coxe), May 21, 1788, in *DHRC,* 9:833–41. See also "Publius" II (John Jay) and "Publius" XI and XII (Hamilton), in *DHRC,* 13:517–20, 14:209–15, 236–40; and "A Landholder" I, in *DHRC,* 13:561–64.

88. *Massachusetts Centinel,* December 12, 1787, in *DHRC,* 4:419.

89. *DHRC,* 14:166n8, 503–4, 523n3–4, 529n1. See also John P. Kaminski, ed., *A Necessary Evil? Slavery and the Debate Over the Constitution* (Madison, Wis., 1995).

90. See "Quaker Opposition to the Protection of Slavery in the Constitution," in *DHRC,* vol. 14, appendix 3: 503–30. In October 1787, the Warren Association in Massachusetts, representing forty-five Baptist churches, castigated "the horrid practice of sending our shipping to Africa" and the "heaven-daring wickedness of slavery" (*DHRC,* 14:509n9). Virginia Baptists discussed in March 1788 a petition to the legislature, "praying that the yoke of slavery may be made more tolerable" (Robert B. Semple, *A History of the Rise and Progress of the Baptists in Virginia* [Richmond, 1804], 102). See also James D. Essig, *The Bonds of Wickedness: American Evangelicals Against Slavery, 1770–1808* (Philadelphia, 1982).

91. "Brutus" III, in *DHRC,* 14:120–21. See also *DHRC,* 13:346, 405, 476, 14:60–61, 184, 253–54, 266; Storing, 3:206 ("Aristocratis"); and Storing, 4:255–66 (Consider Arms, Malachi Maynard, and Samuel Fields, "Reason for Dissent," *Hampshire Gazette,* April 9 and 16, 1788).

92. *Hampshire Gazette,* February 6, 1788.

93. Quoted in John Farmer, "Historical Sketch of Amherst, N.H.," New Hampshire Historical Society *Collections* 5 (1837): 79–81.

94. "A Countryman from Dutchess County" I, in Storing, 6:51.

95. *Maryland Journal,* November 30, 1787, May 10 and 23, 1788.

96. Rawlins Lowndes speech in the South Carolina House of Representatives, January 16, 1788, in *Debates which Arose in the House of Representatives of South Carolina . . .* (Charleston, 1788), 15, 16.

97. George Mason speech in the Va. Convention, June 17, 1788, in *DHRC,* 10:1342; and Patrick Henry speech in the Va. Convention, June 11, 1788, in *DHRC,* 9:1161.

98. *Massachusetts Centinel,* August 30, 1788.

99. William Dickson to Rev. Robert Dickson, Goshen, N.C., December 28, 1790, in James O. Carr, ed., *The Dickson Letters* (Raleigh, N.C., 1901), 37–39.

100. "Republican Federalist" III, *Massachusetts Centinel,* January 9, 1788, in *DHRC,* 5: 664; "Cornelius," *Hampshire Chronicle,* December 11, 1787, in *DHRC,* 4:411.

101. "An American Citizen" IV (Tench Coxe), in *DHRC,* 13:432.

102. Rutland, 11:150–51. See also Madison, Federalist No. 54, in *DHRC,* 16:107–11.

103. *DHRC,* 14:530n4.

104. Rush to John C. Lettson, September 28, 1787, in *DHRC,* 13:262–63. Pinckney is quoted in Elliot, *Debates,* 4:285–87.

105. Madison to Tench Coxe, New York, January 20, 1788, in Rutland 12:480–81. David Stuart believed that pointing out "the difference between the Objectors" had "the most weight with the common class" (Stuart to Washington, Fairfax, February 17, 1788, in *DHRC,* 9:583–84).

106. *DHRC,* 17:156.

107. One of the most elaborate alternatives was published by "Candidus" in the Boston *Independent Chronicle* of December 20, 1787 (*DHRC,* 5:493–500).

108. Benjamin Rush, "Address to the People of the United States," *American Museum,* February 1787, in *DHRC,* 13:45–46.

109. "Federalicus," *Maryland Journal,* August 12, 1788.

110. Stiles Diary, New Haven, December 24, 1787, in *DHRC,* 15:74; "Civis," *Maryland Journal,* July 11, 1788; "Landholder" VI, in *DHRC,* 14:402.

111. "Republican Federalist" III, *Massachusetts Centinel,* January 9, 1788, in *DHRC,* 5:664; "Cornelius," *Hampshire Chronicle,* December 11, 1787, in *DHRC,* 4:411.

112. Otto to Montmorin, New York, November 26, 1787, in *DHRC,* 14:229–30.

113. "Z," Philadelphia *Freeman's Journal,* May 16, 1787, in *DHRC,* 13:98.

114. Connecticut *Middlesex Gazette,* October 22, 1787, in *DHRC,* 13:394.

115. *DHRC,* 14:415.

116. *Pennsylvania Gazette,* May 30, 1787, in *DHRC,* 13:118.

117. *Virginia Independent Chronicle,* November 14, 1787, in *DHRC,* 8:159. Federalists often quoted from a letter written in January 1787 by the English clergyman and radical publicist Richard Price to Benjamin Rush, according to which Europeans had come to the conclusion "that you are falling to pieces, and will soon repent of your independence." Price's letter appeared in the Philadelphia *Independent Gazetteer* of May 16, 1787, and was reprinted in forty American newspapers (*DHRC,* 13:100–101). Price began his *Observations on the Importance of the American Revolution* in 1784 by remarking that the American Revolution would prove to be "the most important step in the progressive course of human improvements" since Christianization. While still working on the text, however, he began to question his "visionary expectations," and near the end he perceived the telltale signs of an impending political, moral, and cultural collapse. Should Americans lose sight of their republican virtues, and should the states' conflicts of interest get out of control, the "fairest experiment ever tried in human affairs" would end in failure. Near the climax of the ratification struggle, Henry Knox could assure Washington "that Doctor Price and all the friends of liberty in great Britain highly approve the Constitution and ardently wish its adoption" (Knox to Washington, May 25, 1788, in *Washington Papers: Confederation Series,* 6:291). Knox referred to a letter written by Price on March 24, 1788, to Arthur Lee in New York City. In September 1788, the *Pennsylvania Packet* printed an extract of another letter, dated June 16, 1788, in which Price admonished Americans that "no society can prosper, if, after a fair discussion, the minority will not submit to the decisions of the majority" (*DHRC,* 18:373, 406; see also Colin Bonwick, *English Radicals and the American Revolution* [Chapel Hill, N.C., 1977]). In the view of ordinary Englishmen, however, the American enthusiasm for the Constitution seemed to be "the bubble of the day that will soon vanish to nothing as all the rest of their new fangled constitutions . . . the people here think your late constitution was good enough if the laws was obeyed and without obedience they think the new one will be of no use" (Elias Ball to E. Ball, Frenchey [near Bristol, England], October 20, 1788, Ball Family Papers, Caroliana Library, University of South Carolina, Columbia).

118. See, e.g., a piece in the *Pennsylvania Herald,* June 9, 1787, in *DHRC,* 13:130–31.

119. Samuel Langdon, "The Republic of the Israelites an Example to the American States," Election Sermon, June 5, 1788, Exeter, N.H. (1788 pamphlet). Similar arguments were used by Benjamin Franklin in an article written under the pseudonym "K" in the Philadelphia *Federal Gazette,* April 8, 1788 (*DHRC,* 17:36–40). For references to the Bible in Connecticut, see *DHRC,* 3:347, 349, 361–62, 403–4, 585–86.

120. "A Landholder" II, *Connecticut Courant,* November 12, 1787, in *DHRC,* 3:401.

121. Hamilton, Federalist No. 1, in *DHRC,* 13:496.

122. Federalist nos. 6–8, in *DHRC,* 14:98–101, 132–35, 142–46.

123. Federalist No. 11 (Hamilton), in *DHRC,* 14:209–15. While representing the United States in London, John Adams was often told by the authorities "that there is not yet any national Government [in America], but as soon as there shall be one, the British Court will vouchsafe to treat with it" (Adams to John Jay, London, February 14, 1788, *Diplomatic Correspondence,* 2:826–27).

124. Federalist No. 5 (Jay), in *DHRC,* 14:87–91. See also Frederick W. Marks, "Foreign Affairs: A Winning Issue in the Campaign for Ratification of the United States Constitution," *PSQ* 86 (1971): 444–69.

125. *DHRC,* 9:1058–61; Storing, 1:86n4.

126. Speech in the Virginia House of Delegates, October 25, 1787, Petersburg *Virginia Gazette,* November 1, 1787, in *DHRC,* 14:403–4n10.

127. *DHRC,* 13:270, 14:280, 15:358–59.

128. Antifederalists did not dispute the necessity of economic progress and material prosperity, but for them it could only result from local and regional initiatives, not from the activities of a distant national government (see Drew R. McCoy, *The Elusive Republic: Political Economy in Jeffersonian America* [Chapel Hill, N.C., 1980]).

129. Stearns to Gorham, Billerica, January 22, 1788, in *DHRC,* 5:769.

130. *Virginia Independent Chronicle,* October 31, 1787, in *DHRC,* 8:139–40.

131. Federalist No. 1 (Hamilton), in *DHRC,* 13:494.

132. From Knox, [August 31?] 1787, Knox Papers, Gilder-Lehrman Collection, New-York Historical Society.

133. In his confidential "Conjectures About the Constitution" of September 1787, Hamilton gloomily predicted that in the course of a few years "the contest about boundaries of power between the particular governments and the general government and the momentum of the larger states in such contests will produce a dissolution of the Union" (*DHRC,* 13:278).

134. *Thoughts upon the Political Situation of the United States of America* . . . (Evans 21173). See also *DHRC,* 18:326–31.

135. "A Citizen of Philadelphia," *The Weaknesses of Brutus Exposed,* November 8, 1788, in *DHRC,* 14:72.

136. Farrand, 1:317. For Madison's historical studies, see Rutland, 9:3–22, 10:273–83. With the assistance of Alexander Hamilton, Madison expounded his ideas about "ancient and modern confederacies" in Federalist nos. 18–20 (in *DHRC,* 14:381–86, 390–95, 410–13).

137. James Madison Speech, Virginia ratifying convention, June 7, 1788, in *DHRC,* 9:1029, 1031.

138. Federalist No. 15 (Hamilton), in *DHRC,* 14:327, 329.

139. Federalist No. 16 (Hamilton), in *DHRC,* 14:341–42.

140. Federalist No. 9, in *DHRC,* 14:158–63. In Philadelphia, Hamilton characterized the Virginia Plan as deviating from "the *federal* idea, as understood by some, since it is to operate eventually on individuals" (Madison, *Debates,* 112).

141. *DHRC,* 2:342.

142. New York *Daily Advertiser,* November 2 and December 12, 1787, January 12, 1788.

143. *DHRC,* 15:380–86. Even some critics, such as Luther Martin and Richard Henry

Lee, spoke of a "partly national and partly federal government," or a "strange hotch-potch of both" (Storing, 1:9–11, 2:80n12, 350n9).

144. This was the message of Francis Hopkinson's allegory "The New Roof," published in the *Pennsylvania Packet* on December 29, 1787, which became very popular with Federalists all over the Union (*DHRC,* 15:179–88). As a poetic extension of his essay, Hopkinson published on February 6, 1788, "The RAISING: A NEW SONG for FEDERAL MECHANICS" (*DHRC,* 16:47–48). Other architectural metaphors used during the ratification debate were "the Grand Republican Superstructure" or the "Great Federal Superstructure," the "Grand Federal Edifice," the "Glorious Fabrick," and the "Great National Dome." These images of "state pillars" supporting the federal roof (i.e., the Constitution) were invented, or at least popularized, by printer Benjamin Russell of the *Massachusetts Centinel.*

145. Madison to Jefferson, New York, October 24/November 1, 1787, in *DHRC,* 13:443.

146. Pickering to Charles Tillinghast, Philadelphia, December 24, 1787, in *DHRC,* 14:201, 203. At the Philadelphia Convention, Hamilton had still subscribed to the theory that "two Sovereignties can not co-exist within the same limits" (Madison, *Debates,* 115). This maxim was again and again emphasized by Antifederalists during the ratification debate.

147. *DHRC,* 2:166, 344.

148. Federalist nos. 17 and 27, in *DHRC,* 14:352–56, 15:95–98.

149. Madison, *Debates,* 142 (June 27, 1787).

150. *DHRC,* 16:45.

151. "Government of the United States," *National Gazette,* February 4, 1792, in Rutland, 14:218.

152. Edmund Pendleton in the Virginia ratifying convention, June 5, 1788, in *DHRC,* 9:945; Hamilton in the New York ratifying convention, in Elliot, *Debates,* 3:37.

153. Memorandum by Franklin on the reverse side of a letter written by Francis Childs, January 31, 1788, Franklin Papers, PPAmP.

154. Madison to Mazzei, October 8, 1788, in Rutland, 11:278.

155. Dane to Moses Brown, June 7, 1788, Moses Brown Papers, Beverley Historical Society.

156. "A.B." to Elbridge Gerry, *Massachusetts Centinel,* November 14, 1787, in *DHRC,* 4:230.

157. Speech of October 6, 1787, in *DHRC,* 2:171.

158. "A Citizen of Philadelphia" and "A Landholder" III, in *DHRC,* 14:65, 68, 71, 141.

159. Federalist No. 30, in *DHRC,* 15:161.

160. *DHRC,* 13:342–43 (Wilson); *DHRC,* 15:274–75 (Ellsworth).

161. Federalist nos. 33 and 34, in *DHRC,* 15:4, 307. See also Gerhard Stourzh, *Alexander Hamilton and the Idea of a Republican Government* (Stanford, Calif., 1970).

162. Federalist nos. 35 and 36 (Hamilton), in *DHRC,* 15:59–64, 65–69; "Of a Standing Army," *Massachusetts Centinel,* January 1, 1788; "Tully," Baltimore *Maryland Gazette,* April 4, 1788.

163. Sullivan to Rufus King, Boston, September 23, 1787, in *DHRC,* 4:16–17; Pinckney is in Elliot, *Debates,* 4:258.

164. "A Citizen of Philadelphia," in *DHRC,* 13:301, 305.

165. *DHRC,* 2:418, 420.

166. *DHRC,* 14:84 (Ramsay); Syrett, 5:150–51 (Hamilton); *DHRC,* 2:349 (Wilson); *DHRC,* 13:432 (Coxe); *DHRC,* 8:164 ("A True Friend"); "An Annapolitan," Baltimore *Maryland Gazette,* January 31, 1788.

167. "A Country Federalist," Poughkeepsie *Country Journal,* Supplement, December 19, 1787.

168. James Wilson, speech in Pennsylvania ratifying convention, November 24, 1787, in *DHRC,* 2:343–44.

169. See, especially, Federalist No. 10 (Madison) and No. 35 (Hamilton), in *DHRC,* 14:175–81, 15:268–72; and Stevens in New York *Daily Advertiser,* December 12, 1787. See also Robert J. Morgan, "Madison's Theory of Representation in the Tenth Federalist," *JP* 36 (1974): 852–85; William B. Allen, "Federal Representation: The Design of the Thirty-Fifth Federalist Paper," *Publius* 6 (1976): 61–71; and David P. Epstein, *The Political Theory of 'The Federalist'* (Chicago, 1984). A typical Antifederalist critique of this argument, wrote "O" for the *American Herald,* February 4, 1788: "If the representatives must be chosen . . . from the natural or artificial aristocratic body in every state, the influence of the aristocratical parties will be more dangerous in proportion to the encrease of powers delegated to this Congress, and the abatement of the checks" (*DHRC,* 5:854).

170. John Adams to Henry Marchant, March 20, 1790, Adams Papers, MHi.

171. "The State Soldier" IV, *Virginia Independent Chronicle,* March 19, 1788, in *DHRC,* 8:510.

172. "Letter from New York," December 24 and 31, 1787. In 1787, there were between 1,600 and 1,700 state legislators (*DHRC,* 3:384, 392n8).

173. Madison, *Debates,* 115–16.

174. *DHRC,* 13:351 (Butler); *DHRC,* 2:138–39 (Coxe). A critical reader of the *Defence of the American Constitutions* could not help noticing that John Adams's enthusiasm for the British system of government far surpassed that of Montesquieu, Voltaire, and Hume: "He seems to wish that we should universally adopt the balance, and relinquish our present established systems, founded on the institutions of Woden and Thor and therefore altogether improper for this illuminated age of the world" (Baltimore *Maryland Gazette,* September 4, 1787; see also Storing, 5:68 ["A Farmer" from Maryland]).

175. *Virginia Independent Chronicle,* November 28, 1787, in *DHRC,* 14:242.

176. "Fabius" IX, in *DHRC,* 17:261–65; "Civis Rusticus," January 30, 1788, in *DHRC,* 8:331–40; Benjamin Rush to John Coakley Lettsom, Philadelphia, September 28, 1787, in *DHRC,* 13:262–63.

177. Federalist No. 39, in *DHRC,* 15:381.

178. "An American Citizen" I, II, in *DHRC,* 2:140–44. See also "A Citizen of America" (Noah Webster), in *DHRC,* Mfm:Pa. 142.

179. For instance, Gouverneur Morris spoke of a "well poised Machine" (in *DHRC,* 13:514), and Jedidiah Morse of a "grand machine constructed by wise men" (letter to his father, July 22, 1788, Morse Family Collection, Yale University Library). The metaphor of a complicated clockwork was used by John Adams in a letter to William Smith, May 20, 1790 (see Adams Papers, MHi).

180. *DHRC,* 14:177.

181. *DHRC,* 14:181.

182. *DHRC,* 16:46–47.

183. Madison's originality in this important aspect of constitutional interpretation has

recently been underlined by Banning (*Sacred Fire of Liberty,* 202–14, 467–70). See also John Zvesper, "The Madisonian System," *Western Political Quarterly* 37 (1984): 236–56.

184. In the 1790s, Madison began to distance himself from Hamilton. While composing *The Federalist,* he maintained, he and Hamilton had seen to it "not to give a positive sanction to all the doctrines and sentiments of the other; there being a known difference in the general complexion of their political theories" (Elizabeth Fleet, ed., "Madison's 'Detached Memoranda,'" *WMQ* 3 [1946]: 565). According to Morton White (*Philosophy, The Federalist, and the Constitution* [New York, 1987], 55), Madison had particularly stressed the protection of rights, while Hamilton put more emphasis on "energetic government."

185. "A Citizen of America," in *DHRC,* Mfm:Pa. 142.

186. Federalist No. 28 (Hamilton), in *DHRC,* 15:104.

187. "Cato" I, II, Charleston *City Gazette,* November 26, 1787, and December 10, 1787, in Storing, 5:137–44; Findley's speeches in the Pennsylvania ratifying convention, in *DHRC,* 2:367–587; "Agrippa" I–XVI, in Storing, 4:68–116.

188. Ezra Stiles to John Adams, Yale College, August 1, 1788, Adams Papers, MHi. See also David W. Robson, *Educating Republicans: The College in the Era of the American Revolution, 1750–1800* (Westport, Conn., 1985).

189. *Newport Herald,* November 6, 1788; Federalist No. 6 (Hamilton), in *DHRC,* 14:97.

190. "An Address to the Public Containing Some Remarks on the Present Political State of the American Republics," Exeter, N.H., January 1787 (Evans 19470).

191. Yates, "Essay Concerning the Defense of Political Liberty," December 31, 1789–February 1, 1790, Yates Papers, New York Public Library; Virginia General Assembly, House of Delegates, November 14, 1788, Extract from Journal, 105–7; Federalist No. 20, in *DHRC,* 14:413.

192. "All the people of the ancient republics lost their liberty, by being too liberal in bestowing too much power to their chosen leaders" ("Honestus," *Wilmington Centinel,* June 18, 1788). Mercy Warren tried to demonstrate that "the pride of a few families, the ambition of individuals, and the supineness of the people" had been responsible for the downfall of the Republic of Geneva (Lester H. Cohen, *The Revolutionary Histories: Contemporary Narratives of the American Revolution* [Ithaca, N.Y., 1980], 194–95).

193. "Barneveldt," *Newport Herald,* March 1, 1787.

194. *Newport Mercury,* March 3, 1788, in Storing, 4:251.

195. Speech of June 5, 1788, in *DHRC,* 9:966.

196. *Pennsylvania Herald,* October 17, 1787, in *DHRC,* 13:391. See also *DHRC,* 13:499, 14:127, 186, 15:209.

197. Speech of June 7, 1788, in *DHRC,* 9:1030. See also Madison's critical remarks on the Swiss canton's past and present in Federalist No. 19 (December 8, 1787), in *DHRC,* 14:394–95.

198. See Gordon D. Ross, "The *Federalist* and the 'Experience' of Small Republics," *Eighteenth-Century Studios* 5 (1972): 559–68; and Caroline Robbins, "European Republicanism in the Century and a Half Before 1776," *Library of Congress Symposia on the American Revolution: The Development of a Revolutionary Mentality* (Washington, D.C., 1972), 31–55.

199. "A Private Citizen," *Maryland Journal,* July 25, 1788; James Wilson, Speech of November 24, 1787, in *DHRC,* 2:342.

200. "A Freeholder," April 9, 1788, in *DHRC,* 9:720.

201. Adams to Arthur Lee, Braintree, Mass., July 18, 1788, in *DHRC,* 18:271–72.

202. *Massachusetts Gazette,* October 7, 1788.

203. *DHRC,* 18:250.

204. Speech of November 24, 1787, in *DHRC,* 2:362.

205. "A Countryman" I (Sherman); Federalist No. 17 (Hamilton), in *DHRC,* 14:107, 355.

206. *Massachusetts Gazette,* February 19, 1788; *Massachusetts Centinel,* February 23, 1788.

207. *DHRC,* 14:215.

208. *Massachusetts Centinel,* October 6, 1787, in *DHRC,* 13:344–45. Francis Hopkinson's Ode of July 4, 1788, began with the lines: "Oh for a muse of fire! to mount the skies / and to a list'ning world proclaim— / Behold! behold! an empire rise!" A "FEDERAL SONG to the tune of 'Rule Britannia,'" published in the *Albany Journal* of August 4, 1788, contained the following verses: "Behold Columbia's empire rise, / On freedom's solid base to stand; / Supported by propitious skies, / And seal'd by her deliverer's hand. . . . / Proud Europe hence may learn, and see, / A Constitution self-controul'd; / By wisdom balanc'd, firm and free, / The dread and model of the world" (*DHRC,* 18:246–47, 320–21).

209. *DHRC,* 14:418–22 ("Philadelphiensis" IV); *DHRC,* 15:234–40 ("Brutus" VII).

210. See *DHRC,* 4:194–99, 265–71 ("John De Witt" III, IV); *DHRC,* 13:399 ("Caesar" II); *DHRC,* 14:124–28 ("Cincinnatus" III); *DHRC,* 14:432–35 ("Alfred"); and *DHRC,* 17:60–62 ("Philadelphiensis" XII).

211. *American Herald,* November 19, 1787, in *DHRC,* 4:272.

212. *DHRC,* 4:381–83, 426–28.

213. "One of the People," *Massachusetts Centinel,* October 17, 1787, in *DHRC,* 13:395. See also Richard Koebner, "Two Concepts of Empire," in *The Reinterpretation of the American Revolution, 1763–1789,* ed. Jack P. Greene (New York, 1968), 111–21; and Norbert Kilian, "New Wine in Old Skins? American Definitions of Empire and the Emergence of a New Concept," in *New Wine in Old Skins: A Comparative View of Socio-Political Structures and Values Affecting the American Revolution,* ed. Erich Angermann et al. (Stuttgart, 1976), 135–52.

214. Baltimore *Maryland Gazette,* September 4, 1787.

4. Party Formation and Convention Elections

1. Jackson Turner Main, *Political Parties before the Constitution* (Chapel Hill, N.C., 1973). Main gathered information on more than 1,500 representatives serving between 1783 and 1788 in the legislatures of seven states. He groups them into "commercial-cosmopolitans" (552), "agrarian-localists" (539), and "neutrals" (412) (ibid., 24). See also Patricia U. Bonomi, ed., *Party and Political Opposition in Revolutionary America* (Tarrytown, N.Y., 1980).

2. *DHRC,* 15:506, 2:695–96.

3. *DHRC,* 8:506.

4. Pickering to Tillinghast, Philadelphia, December 24, 1787, in *DHRC,* 14:198.

5. *DHRC,* 2:198–99.

6. Van Vechten to Henry Oothoudt and Jeremiah Van Rensellaer, January 11, 1788, in *DHRC,* 20:600–601.

7. *Brunswick Gazette,* September 2, 1788.

8. Petry to Montmorin, Charleston, December 26, 1787, Correspondence Consulaire, B I 372, Charleston, 1784–1792, AN.

9. *DHRC,* 3:515–16, 15:79.

10. Gouverneur Morris to Washington, Philadelphia, October 30, 1787, in *DHRC,* 13:513–14.

11. Knox to Washington, Boston, October 3, 1787, in *DHRC,* 13:306–7.

12. Gibbs to Simeon Baldwin, Salem, October 31, 1787, in *DHRC,* 4:174.

13. McKean, speech of December 10, 1787, in *DHRC,* 2:543; *Pennsylvania Gazette,* September 26, 1787, in *DHRC,* 13:253 (this passage was reprinted in twenty-four newspapers).

14. *Massachusetts Centinel,* March 15, 1788.

15. *New York Packet,* June 6, 1788.

16. Buchanan to Tench Coxe, Baltimore, August 3, 1788, Coxe Papers, PHi.

17. Charles Tillinghast to Hugh Hughes, New York, January 27–28, 1788, in *DHRC,* 15:480; William Symmes Jr. speech in the Massachusetts ratifying convention, January 22, 1788, in *DHRC,* 6:1309.

18. Rutland, 11:358. In letters to Rufus King and Mazzei, Madison himself referred to a "federalist party" (ibid., 11:76, 389).

19. *Pennsylvania Gazette,* September 12, 1787, in *DHRC,* 13:193.

20. Arthur Bryan to [?], Annapolis, March 28, 1788, Lloyd Papers, Maryland Historical Society.

21. Carrington to William Short, New York, July 26, 1788, in *DHRC,* 18:293–94.

22. Francis to Nicholas Brown, November 11, 1787, Brown Papers, John Carter Brown Library, Providence, R.I.

23. *Pennsylvania Gazette,* October 10, 1787, in *DHRC,* 13:584 (this "squib" was reprinted in fifteen newspapers).

24. Smith to Abraham Yates Jr., Manor of St. George, June 12, 1788, in *DHRC,* 20:1151.

25. Tucker to Frances Bland Tucker, Richmond, October 27, 1787, in *DHRC,* 8:124–25.

26. Henry to Thomas Madison, Richmond, October 21, 1787, in *DHRC,* 8:88; Henry to Lee, November 15, 1787, in *FFE,* 2:374–75.

27. Sullivan to Richard Henry Lee, Boston, April 11, 1789, in Lee, *Memoir of R. H. Lee,* 2:152–53.

28. See, e.g., "Fair Play," Philadelphia *Independent Gazetteer,* October 4, 1787, in *DHRC,* 2:154.

29. John Adams to Henry Marchant, New York, March 20, 1790, Adams Papers, MHi.

30. Andrew Ellicot to John Nicolson, Baltimore, January 7, 1788, Nicholson Papers, P-Ar.

31. Lee to George Thatcher, Biddeford, Maine, January 23, 1788, in *DHRC,* 5:780–84.

32. Adams to Lee, Boston, December 3, 1787, in *DHRC,* 14:333–34.

33. Otto to Comte de Montmorin, New York, November 26, 1787, in *DHRC,* 14:229.

34. Sterling to Nicol, December 12, 1788, Sterling Collection, Nc-Ar.

35. Adams Diary, Adams Family Papers, MHi; Smith to J. Q. Adams, New York, June 8, 1788, MHi.

36. John Adams to Jabez Bowen, New York, June 26, 1789, Letterbook, MHi.

37. Adams to Roger Sherman, New York, July 20, 1789, in Charles Francis Adams,

ed., *The Works of John Adams, Second President of the United States,* 10 vols. (Boston, 1850–56), 6:432–34.

38. Storing, 5:191.

39. *DHRC,* 14:323.

40. New York *Independent Journal,* July 12, 1788.

41. *DHRC,* 14:50–51; Storing, 2:258–59.

42. Jackson to Henry Knox, Boston, March 15, 1788, Knox Papers, Gilder-Lehrman Collection on deposit at the New-York Historical Society.

43. Gardner to Nicholas Gilman, Portsmouth, June 14, 1788, Gardner Papers, NHi.

44. Hartley to Coxe, York, September 9, 1788, Coxe Papers, PHi.

45. George Brown to Theodore Sedgwick, Providence, June 18, 1790, Sedgwick Papers, MHi.

46. Washington to John Armstrong Sr., April 25, 1788, in *DHRC,* 17:214–17.

47. Hamilton to Madison, Poughkeepsie, July 19, 1788, in Rutland, 11:188.

48. See Madison's Federalist nos. 10, 50, and 51. Only in this sense can one say that he intended to use the Constitution "against" parties (see Richard Hofstadter, *The Idea of a Party System: The Rise of Legitimate Opposition in the United States, 1780–1840 [Berkeley, Calif., 1969],* 60–73). Madison's theory of the "extended Republic" contradicted previously held ideas. One tiny example of the contrary argument was made by the Pennsylvania Antifederalist "Alfred," who asserted it was proven fact that in "vast empires . . . *strong factions* are aptest to engender" (Philadelphia *Independent Gazetteer,* December 13, 1787, in *DHRC,* 14:434).

49. *Maryland Journal,* May 16, 1788.

50. Harrison to Washington, April 3, 1789, in *Washington Papers: Presidential Series,* 2:14.

51. Consider Arms, Malichi Maynard, and Samuel Field, "Reason for Dissent," *Hampshire Gazette,* April 9/16, 1788, in *DHRC,* 7:1743.

52. The history of Rome and Venice, thirty citizens wrote to the *Carlisle Gazette,* demonstrated the danger of an imperceptible decline toward "an odious and permanent aristocracy. This . . . will be the final consequence of the proposed Federal Constitution; and because we prize the felicity and freedom of our posterity equally with our own, we esteem it our indispensible duty to oppose it with that determined resolution and spirit that becomes freemen" (*Carlisle Gazette,* January 2, 1788, in *DHRC,* 15:228–29).

53. Quoted in Verner W. Crane, "Franklin's 'The Internal State of America 1786,'" *WMQ* 15 (1958): 226.

54. Elliot, *Debates,* 2:167.

55. Jefferson to John Rutledge Jr., Paris, February 2, 1788, in Boyd, 12:556–57. Ten years later, the future president underscored in a letter to John Taylor of Caroline the necessity of conflicts and party rivalry in a liberal republic: "In every free and deliberating society, there must, from the nature of man, be opposite parties, and violent dissensions and discords. . . . Perhaps this party division is necessary to induce each to watch and relate to the people the proceedings of the other" (quoted in Hofstadter, *Idea of a Party System,* 115).

56. "Atticus" II, Boston *Independent Chronicle,* October 18, 1787, in *DHRC,* Mfm:Mass.

57. Quoted in Morton Borden, ed., *The Antifederalist Papers* (East Lansing, Mich., 1965), 21.

58. *Report of a Committee of Correspondence*, New York, March 17, 1789, Evans 45535. A Federalist committee, chaired by Hamilton, countered with the question: "Have you not evidence, that the spirit of party, under [Governor Clinton's] fostering influence, has risen to a height prejudicial to the character and welfare of the state?" (April 28, 1789, in Syrett, 5:333–34). This exchange took place during the state gubernatorial elections.

59. In this category belong, among others, Theodore Sedgwick, a lawyer from Stockbridge, Massachusetts, who represented his state from 1785 to 1788; John Sullivan, a lawyer and Revolutionary general, the president of New Hampshire in 1788–89, and a U.S. senator from 1789 to 1801; Jeremiah Wadsworth, a merchant from Connecticut, delegate to Congress in 1787–88, and member of the U.S. House of Representatives (1789–95); Alexander Hamilton; the Pennsylvania merchant and financier Robert Morris; his partner Gouverneur Morris; the Pennsylvania lawyer-politician James Wilson; James McHenry, a Maryland merchant who served for a long time in the state senate; the North Carolina lawyer James Iredell, whom Washington in 1790 appointed as associate justice of the Supreme Court; and in South Carolina cousins Charles Pinckney and Charles Cotesworth Pinckney, both wealthy planters allied with other leading families, such as the Laurens and the Randolphs.

60. Among these moderate Federalists we find Pennsylvania's president Benjamin Franklin, the most famous American of his time; the Virginians Washington and Madison, although they held strong nationalist convictions; their countryman Edmund Pendleton, president of the High Court of Chancery, who warned that in constitutional matters one could not attain perfection; and (with some reservations) intellectuals, such as Tench Coxe, Benjamin Rush, Jeremy Belknap, Noah Webster, and Jedidiah Morse, whose nationalism was tempered by a desire for social, economic, and cultural reforms.

61. This radical orientation is well represented by William Widgery, Samuel Nasson, and General Samuel Thompson, energetic "self-made men" from the Maine district who in the Massachusetts convention fought against ratification; the leader of New Hampshire's opposition, Joshua Atherton, a lawyer and former Tory; the head of the Country Party in Rhode Island, Jonathan J. Hazard, a tailor by occupation; New York's popular governor George Clinton; Pennsylvanians George Bryan and Robert Whitehill, the one a Philadelphia merchant and state judge, the other—together with William Findley and John Smilie—a spokesman in the legislature and state convention for the western farmers; Maryland politicians Samuel Chase and Luther Martin, dynamic and enterprising but sometimes also reckless personalities; Virginian Patrick Henry, a lawyer, Revolutionary governor from 1776 to 1779, and wealthy planter and slave owner; Willie Jones from North Carolina, one of the most wealthy and well-educated planters in his state, but nevertheless fully committed to radical republicanism and to protecting the interests of small backcountry farmers; and Irish-born Aedanus Burke of South Carolina, a lawyer, Revolutionary officer, and state judge, who later served in the U.S. House of Representatives.

62. The dividing line between radical and moderate Antifederalists is not easy to be drawn, as the cases of Elbridge Gerry, Samuel Adams, George Mason, and Richard Henry Lee demonstrate. Their ideological convictions moved them toward determined resistance against the Constitution, but their feeling of responsibility for the common good had a restraining effect.

63. Prime examples are the governors of Massachusetts and Virginia, John Hancock

and Edmund Randolph. A similar indecision was shown by the Kentuckian Caleb Wallace, who in May 1788 confessed that he had first liked the Constitution, "but being much distressed for our National Faith and security I did not then so fully realize, as I have since done, the danger of introducing greater evils than those from which we have been delivered at the expense of much blood and treasure." Less than two months later, he was still "not better pleased with the New Federal Constitution . . . but I am much better reconciled to its adoption on account of the dangers the Union is exposed to from the greater imperfections of the old one. Of two evils I would choose the least If neither can be avoided" (*DHRC,* 9:781–84, 10:1694–95).

64. "Your people . . . must be able soon to discover that it is their intent to depend upon Gentlemen of character, Estate and information instead of being duped by upstart unprincipled characters" (Henry Van Schaack to Stephen Van Rensselaer, Pittsfield, June 5, 1788, in *DHRC,* 20:1132).

65. *DHRC,* 2:62, 64–65, 130–38. "Centinel" criticized "that frenzy of enthusiasm, that has actuated the citizens of Philadelphia, in their approbation of the proposed plan, before it was possible that it could be the result of rational investigation into its principles" (*DHRC,* 13:329).

66. For these Antifederalist petitions, see *DHRC,* 2:309–11, 589, 596, 642, 692–93, 709–25, 15:8, 44.

67. *DHRC,* 3:135–40. From the seat of Congress in New York City, Madison reported to Edmund Randolph on October 21, 1787: "N. Jersey appears to be zealous. Meetings of the people in different counties are declaring their approbation & instructing their representatives" (*DHRC,* 13:430).

68. *DHRC,* 3:359, 13:6–7, 354.

69. *DHRC,* 8:23–25; see also *DHRC,* 13:353, 358, 450, 455, 585. Other meetings took place in Berkeley County, Alexandria, Williamsburg, Fredericksburg, Frederick County, Henrico County, and Petersburg (*DHRC,* 8:22–23, 39–40, 85–86, 91–93, 96–97). On November 5, the legislature in Richmond received a "Petition of sundry freeholders of the County of Louisa" favoring a swift ratifying convention and the approval of the Constitution (Virginia Assembly, House of Delegates Journal, vi).

70. See this chapter, under "Party Spirit and Party Leaders," above.

71. Adelaide L. Fries, ed., *Records of the Moravians in North Carolina, 1752–1879,* 11 vols. (Raleigh, N.C., 1922–69), 5:2190.

72. Grand Jury to the Edenton District Court, November 12, 1787, in McRee, 2:181. In Columbia County, New York, the grand jury considered the Constitution at its winter session and resolved that "in our opinion every safeguard, which human foresight can suggest, for perpetuating to our posterity the blessings of Freedom" had been taken (John P. Kaminski, "New York: The Reluctant Pillar," in *The Reluctant Pillar,* ed. Stephen L. Schechter [Troy, N.Y., 1985], 82–83). Similar grand jury proceedings are recorded for Pennsylvania and South Carolina.

73. *DHRC,* 3:351, 13:374–75. The Philadelphia Baptist Association was comprised of the churches of the middle states.

74. *DHRC,* vol. 13, appendix 3: 597–98.

75. Burke to John Lamb, Charleston, June 23, 1788, Lamb Papers, NHi.

76. Peter Shaw, *American Patriots and the Rituals of Revolution* (Cambridge, Mass.,

1981); Dirk Hoerder, *Crowd Action in Revolutionary Massachusetts, 1765–1780* (New York, 1977).

77. Nisbet to Earl of Buchan, December 25, 1787, in *DHRC*, 15:88–89.

78. Coxe to Tilghman, October 23, 1787, Tilghman Collection, PHi; Tilghman to Coxe, Chester Town, November 25, 1787, Coxe Papers, PHi; Coxe to Madison, October 21, 1787, and January 16, 1788, in Rutland, 10:201–202, 375.

79. *DHRC*, 15:7–13.

80. Thomas Hartley to Tench Coxe, January 11, 1788, Coxe Papers, PHi.

81. Jean-Baptiste Petry to Comte de Montmorin, Correspondence Consulaire, B I 372, Charleston, 1:266, AN; Boyd, *Politics of Opposition*, 114–15.

82. *DHRC*, 15:147–48.

83. *DHRC*, 18:32–68.

84. *DHRC*, 3:470–71.

85. Nathaniel Gorham to Henry Knox, January 16, 1788, in *DHRC*, 5:730.

86. "KNOW YE," May 29, 1788.

87. *DAB*, 10:555–56.

88. William H. Riker, *The Strategy of Rhetoric: Campaigning for the American Constitution* (New Haven, Conn., 1996). See also Karl Tilman Winkler, *Politische Debattenkultur in England 1689–1750* (Stuttgart, 1998); and Günther Lottes, *Politische Aufklärung und plebejisches Publikum: Zur Theorie und Praxis des englischen Radikalismus im späten 18. Jahrhundert* (München-Wien, 1979).

89. At the Philadelphia Convention, John Francis Mercer and James McHenry had compiled a list of twenty delegates who, in their opinion, favored a "Kingly or national government." Martin got to see this list and used it during the ratification debate. See also Farrand, 2:192, 3:306, 319–24; and *DHRC*, 14:286, 295n14, 15:146–56.

90. "Centinel" XIV, in *DHRC*, 15:149.

91. Staughton Lynd, "Abraham Yates's History of the Movement for the United States Constitution," *WMQ* 20 (1963): 223–45. See also Stephan Wolf and Abraham Yates Jr., *Vergessener Gründervater der amerikanischen Republik* (Münster, 1997).

92. *DHRC*, 13:238–39.

93. Speech in Pennsylvania ratifying convention, December 12, 1787, in *DHRC*, 2:592.

94. Boston *Independent Chronicle*, October 4, 1787, in *DHRC*, 4:36–38.

95. *American Herald*, November 5, 1787, in *DHRC*, 4:195. "Centinel" XII proclaimed on January 23, 1788: "The authors and abettors of the new constitution shudder at the term conspirators being applied to them, as it designates their true character." (*DHRC*, 15:446). In her *History of the Rise, Progress, and Termination of the American Revolution*, published in 1805, Mercy Warren even saw international ramifications: "There has been a conspiracy formed against the dissemination of republican opinions, by interested and aspiring characters, eager for the establishment of hereditary distinctions and noble orders. This is a conspiracy formidable for on wealth and talents of its supporters in Europe, and not less so from the same description of men in America" (Storing, 6:244).

96. *Address of the Albany Antifederal Committee*, April 10, 1788, in *DHRC*, 21:1382.

97. *Maryland Journal*, April 1, 1788, in Storing, 5:74–78. According to "Monitor" (Boston *American Herald*, December 3, 1787), governments originally had been instituted for the "mutual benefit" of the people: "But at length different orders were created . . . the

original mild and ingenious manners of civil society were held in bondage, and obliged to submit to the dictates of those, whose pretended acts of benevolence were founded on the principles of avarice and superstition. Thus we find ambition will prevail, where authority is vested with wealth and power" (*DHRC*, 4:358–59).

98. Hamilton was convinced that an inequality of property would exist "as long as liberty existed, and that it would unavoidably result from that very liberty itself. This inequality of property constituted the great & fundamental distinction in Society" (Farrand, 1:398, 410, 422). Madison voiced similar views in Federalist No. 10 and No. 51. The Delaware politician Thomas Rodney saw a mixed government as the only escape from this dilemma: "Otherwise the common people for fear of oppression will ever be aiming at pulling down the rich to a level with themselves and the rich will ever be oppressing the poor for fear they should get this in their power; Between the two the laws would always be fluctuating" (Thomas Rodney to Caesar Rodney, Poplar Grove, June 14, 1788, Rodney Family Papers, DLC).

99. Baltimore *Maryland Gazette*, September 18, 1787.

100. *Hudson Weekly Gazette*, June 17, 1788; "Remarker," Boston *Independent Chronicle*, January 17, 1788. In Charles Pinckney's view, American society was characterized by its "mediocrity of fortune" (Charleston *State Gazette of South Carolina*, June 9, 1788).

101. The importance of rhetorical strategies for the outcome of the ratification debate has been stressed by William H. Riker in *The Strategy of Rhetoric: Campaigning for the American Constitution* (New Haven, Conn., 1996).

102. Jonathan Williams Sr. to Benjamin Franklin, Boston, October 10, 1787; and Henry Gibbs to Simeon Baldwin, Salem, October 31, 1787, in *DHRC*, 4:65, 174.

103. Henry Knox to Edward Carrington, New York, February 14, 1788, Knox Papers, Gilder-Lehrman Collection, on deposit at the New-York Historical Society.

104. *DHRC*, 4:293–94. St. John de Crèvecoeur, too, considered all Antifederalists as people "who want to Sacrifice the Glory, the Prosperity of this Country, to their Selfish, or rather hellish views; Such is I believe Messrs. Lee, Henry & Co" (Crèvecoeur to William Short, February 20, 1788, in *DHRC*, 16:151–52).

105. "Veracitas," Baltimore *Maryland Gazette*, September 9, 1788.

106. Washington believed "that whilst many ostensible reasons are assigned to prevent the adoption [of the Constitution], the real ones are concealed behind the Curtains, because they are not of a nature to appear in open day" (George Washington to Bushrod Washington, Mount Vernon, November 10, 1787, in *DHRC*, 14:86). In Madison's view, Patrick Henry used the demand for amendments to conceal his "real designs" of establishing a southern Confederacy (Henry to Edmund Randolph, New York, January 10, 1788, in *DHRC*, 15:326–27).

107. "An Old Spy," *North Carolina Gazette*, December 19, 1787.

108. Baltimore *Maryland Gazette*, December 18, 1787.

109. Broadside, Albany Institute of History and Art, reprinted in the *New York Journal*, April 29, 1788. The secret ballot was used for the first time in New York in the legislative election in 1786 and then in the convention election.

110. Lansing to Abraham Yates, July 20, 1788, in *DHRC*, 21:1330.

111. *Massachusetts Gazette*, November 20, 1787, in *DHRC*, 5:913.

112. *Massachusetts Centinel*, December 5, 1787, in *DHRC*, 5:925.

113. *Boston Gazette,* December 3, 1787; and *American Herald,* December 3, 1787, in *DHRC,* 4:367–69, 5:919.

114. In January 1788, the Boston tradesmen and mechanics put political pressure on Samuel Adams to vote for ratification (*DHRC,* 5:629–35). The New York *Daily Advertiser* reported a Federalist meeting of the "Master Carpenters of the city of New-York" and another one "of a large number of respectable Mechanics and Tradesmen at Vandewater's Tavern" (April 24 and 29, 1788). Newport mechanics resolved, according to the *Newport Mercury* of March 27, 1788, "that this Constitution was the only method of rescuing them and their country from impending ruin." In Providence, mechanics and manufacturers demanded a "Charter of Incorporation" and formed a committee of correspondence which later sent letters to similar organizations in other cities as well as to Congress and President Washington (*Providence Gazette,* June 17, 1790).

115. *Maryland Journal,* February 29, 1788.

116. Baltimore *Maryland Gazette,* August 22, 1788.

117. Baltimore *Maryland Gazette,* September 16, 1788.

118. Baltimore *Maryland Gazette,* April 15, 1788.

119. John Abert to Horatio Gates, April 14, 1788, Gates Papers, NN. See also Norman K. Risjord, *Chesapeake Politics,* 1781–1800 (New York, 1978), 288. In 1790, Germans accounted for 11.7 percent of the Maryland population. In Kentucky and Tennessee, their share was 14 percent; in Virginia, still 6.3 percent.

120. New York *Daily Advertiser,* April 28, 1788.

121. Syrett, 4:645–46; Broadside, April 20, 1788 (Evans 45222).

122. "You were addressed a few days since, in Dutch, by a person under the signature of *A King's County Farmer,* intended as a reply, to a publication of mine." (A Flat-Bush Farmer, "To the Inhabitants of King's County," April 21, 1788 [Evans 21502]). In 1790, 17.5 percent of the New York population was of Dutch origin, 8.2 percent were German, 8.1 percent Irish, and 7 percent Scottish.

123. In Pennsylvania, people of English origin were in the minority (35.3 percent) against the combined numbers of Germans (33.3 percent), Irish (14.5 percent), Scots (8.6 percent), and Others (8.3 percent).

124. "Centinel" admitted that the Revolutionary Test Laws had shifted the "weighty interest of the Quakers and tories" to the "Morris-Junto" ("Centinel" XX, Philadelphia *Independent Gazetteer,* October 23, 1788).

125. James H. Smylie, *American Clergymen and the Constitution of the United States of America, 1781–1796* (Ph.D. diss., Princeton University, 1958), 11.

126. Ruth Bloch, *Visionary Republic: Millennial Themes in American Thought, 1756–1800* (Cambridge, 1982).

127. Quoted in Smylie, *American Clergymen,* 126.

128. Benjamin Rush and Tench Coxe advocated "an ecclesiastical fœderal government for the advancement of morals" (see Rush to Belknap, June 24, 1788, Belknap Papers, MHi; and "A Friend of Society and Liberty" [Tench Coxe], *Pennsylvania Gazette,* July 23, 1788). See also William P. Trent, "The Period of Constitution-Making in the American Churches," in *Essays in the Constitutional History of the United States in the Formative Period, 1775–1789,* ed. J. Franklin Jameson (Boston, 1889), 186–262.

129. Henry Jackson to Henry Knox, Boston, November 11, 1787, in *DHRC,* 4:215; Lin-

coln to Washington, February 9, 1788, in *Washington Papers: Confederation Series,* 6: 104–5. A similar situation prevailed in Connecticut (see *DHRC,* 3:331, 354, 394–95).

130. *DHRC,* 13:374–75. The circular letter was criticized by a writer in the *New York Journal,* who maintained that churches "do not concern themselves, as churches, with worldly policy, or meddle with the government of states, or the politics of them" ("A Baptist," *New York Journal,* November 30, 1787). For a similar view, see *DHRC,* 13:573.

131. *A Concert for Prayer,* Exeter, N.H. (Evans 20284).

132. *DHRC,* 3:351.

133. Smylie, *American Clergymen,* 164–65, 351; *New York Packet,* June 10, 1788, in *DHRC,* 20:1138.

134. *New Haven Gazette,* October 18 and 25, 1787.

135. Smylie, *American Clergymen,* 231–33.

136. Ibid., 160–62; *DHRC,* 14:503–30.

137. Robert B. Semple, *A History of the Rise and Progress of the Baptists in Virginia* (Richmond, 1804), 102.

138. "A Planter," *Virginia Independent Chronicle,* February 13, 1788; letter from Fairfax County, March 24, 1788, Providence *United States Chronicle,* April 24, 1788.

139. *Providence Gazette,* March 20, 1788.

140. Smylie, *American Clergymen,* 173–75.

141. Quoted in John P. Kaminski, *Paper Politics: The Northern State Loan-Offices during the Confederation* (New York, 1989), 65, 104.

142. Robert J. Dinkin, *Voting in Revolutionary America: A Study of Elections in the Original Thirteen States* (Westport, Conn., 1982), 107–9.

143. Ibid., 129.

144. J. R. Pole, *Political Representation in England and the Origins of the American Revolution* (London, 1966).

145. Charles Roll Jr., "'We, Some of the People': Apportionment in the Thirteen State Conventions Ratifying the Constitution," *JAH* 56 (1969): 21–40; Kenneth S. Greenberg, "Representation and the Isolation of South Carolina, 1776–1860," *JAH* 64 (1977): 723–43.

146. Pole, *Political Representation,* 39.

147. Michael Zuckerman, *Peaceable Kingdoms: New England Towns in the Eighteenth Century* (New York, 1970).

148. Boyd, *Politics of Opposition,* 62, 71n69.

149. The Massachusetts convention elections are documented in *DHRC,* 5:888–1076; for the proceedings in Boston, see 5:909–38.

150. See the documents on the elections in Stockbridge and Great Barrington, Berkshire County, in *DHRC,* 5:957–61, 1034–43. On November 7, 1787, Federalist Samuel Henshaw of Northampton wrote to Henry Van Schaack: "For Heaven's sake, my dear Sir, I beseech you to be a Delegate if in your power—And if you have any influence with people in Stockbridge, exert it in favour of our Friend Sedgwick-[John] Bacon . . . must not be in Convention. He would poison a Host of Insurgents—and his Metaphysicks would give the Colic to all the friends of Government and Common Sense!" (*DHRC,* 5:1034–35).

151. Nathaniel Gorham to Franklin, Charlestown, December 15, 1787, in *DHRC,* 4: 377–78. See also *DHRC,* 4:369–380; and Bridge to Adams, Pownalborough (Wiscasset), May 4, 1788, Adams Papers, MHi.

152. "Several towns have instructed their delegates to oppose the Federal Constitution. I am informed almost Every town on this river [Connecticut] *disapproves* the new mode of Government" (Joseph Savage to Samuel P. Savage, Springfield, November 21, 1787, in *DHRC*, 4:291).

153. Federalist Jeremiah Hill complained in a letter to George Thatcher: "Shaysism appears to me to opperate the same in the Body politic, as epidemic's do in the human body" (Hill to Biddeford, January 1–2, 1788, in *DHRC*, 5:572–74).

154. "Queries," November 26, 1787, in *DHRC*, 5:992. King was elected in Newburyport, but also supported the Federalist candidate in Ipswich.

155. *DHRC*, 5:1005, 1035.

156. Theodore Sedgwick to Henry Van Schaack, Stockbridge, December 5, 1787, in *DHRC*, 5:1036.

157. The Worcester Town Meeting needed three ballots until Antifederalists Samuel Curtis and David Bigelow were "declared chosen" (*DHRC*, 5:1071).

158. *DHRC*, 5:967–69.

159. The Town Meeting of Gardner in Worcester County laconically "Voted Not to Send a Man to Convention—Five Voted that they Did not Like the proposed Constitution" (Town Meeting, December 27, 1787, in *DHRC*, 5:955).

160. Town Meetings of December 17 and 24, 1787, in *DHRC*, 5:1032–33.

161. Town Meeting and Instructions, November 27, 1787, in *DHRC*, 5:904–5.

162. *Worcester Magazine*, December 13, 1787, in *DHRC*, 5:1074. Two days earlier, the town meeting of Danvers, in Essex County, had decided "not to give their Delegates any Instructions—and left it with them to assent to, and Ratify the same or otherways, as they think most Advisable." Stoughton, in Suffolk County, voted on New Year's Day 1788, "after a mature and deliberate consideration on the subject," that the decision in convention "be left discretionary with the delegates." In Boston, one of the Stoughton delegates voted for, the other against ratification (*DHRC*, 5:950–51, 1043–44).

163. *Massachusetts Centinel*, January 9, 1788, in *DHRC*, 5:1018–19.

164. *DHRC*, 5:1017–23. Noah Webster ("Giles Hickory") praised Bourn's "noble conduct" in the *American Magazine:* his name "ought to be held in veneration by every true friend to his country, and his address to the electors on that occasion, ought to be written in letters of gold." However, "A Lover of Truth" maintained that the address was a Federalist forgery and that Bourn had resigned strictly for private reasons (*DHRC*, 5:1021–22).

165. *DHRC*, 5:995–98.

166. "Address of Samuel Chase to his constituents, the voters of Anne Arundel County, on the right of constituents to instruct their representatives," February 9, 1787, *American Museum*, October 1788; see also Chase, in the Baltimore *Maryland Gazette*, September 21, 1788. Similar arguments in favor of binding instructions could be heard in South Carolina, where Antifederalist Thomas Tudor Tucker considered "the explicit participation of the represented as the essential ingredient of any system of representation" (Greenberg, "Representation and the Isolation of South Carolina" [1977]). "A Voter" in North Carolina proposed to follow "the Irish method" of holding county meetings to discuss and issue instructions shortly after elections. This would oblige representatives "to stick closely to the intentions of their electors" (*Martin's North Carolina Gazette*, July 11, 1787). The right to instruct had been debated for the first time in America in the Virginia House of Burgesses in 1754 (Pole, *Political Representation*, 541–42).

167. Speech of McHenry, February 20, 1787, *American Museum,* October 1788; Hanson is quoted in James A. Haw, "Politics in Revolutionary Maryland, 1753–1788" (Ph.D. diss., University of Maryland, 1972), 448–49.

168. *American Museum,* March 1788. George Washington feared that the "insiduous arts" of the Constitution's opponents could produce instructions "that would shut the door against argument, and be a bar to the exercise of the judgment" (Washington to Madison, June 8, 1788, in *DHRC,* 10:1586).

169. A good example is Newbury in Essex County, Massachusetts, where opponents called a town meeting "for the purpose of *Instructing* their delegates." When the inhabitants arrived, however, Federalists had procured a majority, who voted "that they would *not* choose a Moderator to govern the meeting—and that the meeting be dissolved" (Newburyport *Essex Journal,* January 2, 1788). This event inspired one of the supporters of the Constitution to write a lengthy poem under the title "FEDERALISM *Triumphant:* Or, *The* JUNTO *Defeated*" (Newburyport *Essex Journal,* January 9, 1788, in *DHRC,* 5:985–90).

170. "Remonstrance of the inhabitants of Great Barrington to the Massachusetts Convention, 1788." The convention rejected the remonstrance and seated Elijah Dwight, who voted in favor of ratification. The affair is documented in *DHRC,* 5:957–65.

171. All twelve delegates finally voted "yes" in the convention. For the election campaign and voting procedures in Boston, see *DHRC,* 5:909–38.

172. *DHRC,* 5:944–46.

173. *DHRC,* 9:984–85.

174. Theophilus Parsons to Michael Hodge, Boston, January 14, 1788, in *DHRC,* 5: 708–9.

175. Nicholas Varga, "Election Procedures and Practices in Colonial New York," *New York History* 41 (1960): 249–77.

176. Webb to Joseph Barrell, New York, May 11, 1788, in *DHRC,* 21:1525.

177. Oothoudt to John McKesson, Albany, April 3, 1788, in *DHRC,* 21:1376.

178. Van Schaack to Henry Walton, Kinderhook, June 3, 1788, in *DHRC,* 21:1437.

179. Leonard Gansevoort to Peter Gansevoort, New York, March 18, 1788, in *DHRC,* 21:1576.

180. Abraham Bancker to Evert Bancker, May 4, 1788, in *DHRC,* 21:1534.

181. Quoted in Boyd, *Opposition Politics,* 75.

182. Livingston to James Duane, Manor Livingston, April 30, 1788, in *DHRC,* 21:1435; Van Gaasbeek to Major Severyn Bryn, Kingston, March 12, 1788, in *DHRC,* 21:1545–46.

183. Quoted in Kaminski, "Reluctant Pillar," 97.

184. Broadside, March 26, 1788, in *DHRC,* 21:1374–75.

185. *DHRC,* 21:1379–85. In 1937, a member of the Federal Writers' Project found a copy of this broadside in the Chamber of Commerce in Rome, New York, and sent it with the following commentary to President Roosevelt: "As you will observe, the main contention, strangely enough, was that the proposed constitution would deprive the people of their rights and liberties" (Roland P. Gray to Franklin D. Roosevelt, June 14, 1937).

186. See the *Hudson Weekly Gazette,* March 13 and 20, 1788, in *DHRC,* 21:1422–23, 1424; the Poughkeepsie *Country Journal,* March 4 and 18, 1788, in *DHRC,* 21:1440–41, 1446; and the *New York Journal,* February 29, 1788, in *DHRC,* 21:1543–44.

187. Tillotson to Livingston, Poughkeepsie, March 22, 1788, in *DHRC,* 21:1451.

188. "One of Yourselves" sounded the alarm: "Beware of Counterfeits! Yesterday a

very curious artifice was detected—Tickets were dealt out as Federal Tickets with the Governor at the head, but so folded down as not to be perceived" (see Broadside, April 30, 1788, *DHRC,* 21:1516–18; and "A Citizen," New York *Daily Advertiser,* May 1, 1788, in *DHRC,* 21:1519–20).

189. Kaminski, "Reluctant Pillar," 86–90; Kaminski, *George Clinton,* 139–48.

190. Van Schaack to Philip Schuyler, April 3, 1788, in *DHRC,* 21:1431.

191. From Peter Schuyler and Josiah Crane, Palatine, April 8, 1788, in *DHRC,* 21:1479; John C. Wynkoop to Peter Van Gaasbeek, May 3, 1788, in *DHRC,* 21:1568.

192. Boyd, *Politics of Opposition,* 76; Kaminski, "Reluctant Pillar," 86–87.

193. Yates to Abraham G. Lansing, Poughkeepsie, March 14, 1788, in *DHRC,* 20:861.

194. Cornelius C. Schoonmaker to Peter Van Gaasbeek, April 4, 1788, in *DHRC,* 21: 1553–54.

195. Albany Anti-Federal Committee to Benjamin Egbertsen et al., April 28, 1788, in *DHRC,* 21:1408.

196. Alexander Coventry Diary, April 30, 1788, in *DHRC,* 21:1435.

197. New York *Daily Advertiser,* April 28, 1788, in *DHRC,* 21:1511.

198. Webb to Hogeboom, May 4, 1788, in *DHRC,* 21:1523; Hazard to Sedgwick, June 5, 1788, in *DHRC,* 21:1528.

199. Wynkoop to Peter Van Gaasbeek, May 5, 1788, in *DHRC,* 21:1436.

200. Thirty-five of the sixty-three Antifederalist candidates had been running at the same time for a seat in the state legislature and the ratifying convention.

201. *DHRC,* 20:1102–5.

202. Bingham to Tench Coxe, New York, May 25, 1788, in *DHRC,* 20:1109–10.

203. Lansing to Abraham Yates, May 27, 1788, Yates Papers, NN.

204. Hamilton to Madison, May 19, 1788, in Syrett, 4:649–50.

205. Van Schaack to Henry Walton, Kinderhook, June 3, 1788, in *DHRC,* 21:1437. A correspondent of the Poughkeepsie *Country Journal,* June 3, 1788, felt the election results were more favorable to Federalists than they could have expected at the beginning of the year (see *DHRC,* 21:1466–67). In New York City, Abraham Yates had the impression that Federalists hoped "the Anties will not dare Refuse adopting the Constitution. They may Indeed adjourn, and adjourn again but they will at Last adopt it" (Yates to Abraham G. Lansing, Albany, June 1, 1788, in *DHRC,* 20:1123).

206. Lansing to Abraham Yates, Albany, June 1, 1788, in *DHRC,* 20:1122–23. On May 18 the committee had already started an attempt at cooperation with Antifederalists in several other states (*DHRC,* 9:811–29, 18:32–68).

207. Amariah Jocelin to J. Wadsworth, Wilmington, N.C., October 1789, J. Wadsworth Correspondence, CtHi.

208. James Mercer to John Francis Mercer, Richmond, December 12, 1787, in *DHRC,* 9:582.

209. Rhys Isaac, *The Transformation of Virginia, 1740–1790* (Chapel Hill, N.C., 1982); Risjord, *Chesapeake Politics.*

210. Wait to Thatcher, Portland, Maine, August 9, 1789, Wait Papers, MHi. In economic terms, Virginia was still overwhelmingly rural and agrarian. In 1790, only 18,500 of Virginia's 750,000 inhabitants (without Kentucky) were living in the nine principal towns.

211. In all, 170 delegates were to be elected, two from each of the state's eighty-four

counties and one each from Williamsburg and Norfolk Borough (see "The Election of Convention Delegates, 3–27 March 1788," in *DHRC,* 9:561–631).

212. Lear to John Langdon, Mount Vernon, April 3, 1788, in *DHRC,* 9:698–99.

213. Stuart to Washington, Abington, Fairfax County, February 17, 1788, in *DHRC,* 9:583–84.

214. Duncanson to James Maury, Fredericksburg, March 11, 1788, in *DHRC,* 8:478–80.

215. Carrington to Henry Knox, Fredericksburg, January 12, 1788, in *DHRC,* 9:583. On March 13, Carrington wrote to Knox that because of Patrick Henry's influence he felt "more anxiety upon the present occasion than ever I felt during the War. It has led me to commit myself in an election for a County [Powhatan] where the majority are opposed to me in sentiment, and it is highly probable I shall be rejected, yet I could not tamely submit the measure to its fate without such an effort" (*DHRC,* 9:607n6).

216. Jones to Madison, Richmond, February 17, 1788; and John Blair Smith to Madison, Hampden Sydney, June 12, 1788, in *DHRC,* 8:381, 9:607–8.

217. Madison to Washington, Orange, April 10, 1788, in Rutland, 11:20–21; John Brown to Madison, New York, May 12, 1788, in *DHRC,* 9:793–95. See also Boyd, *Politics of Opposition,* 108–9. In a letter to Brown, Innes complained about "the little regard Congress paid to our repeated applications for protection" against the Indians (Danville, April 4, 1788, Innes Papers, DLC).

218. "Letter from Rosegill, Va.," *Pennsylvania Packet,* May 10, 1788.

219. For Leland, see Rutland, 10:516n2, 540–42.

220. Crèvecoeur to William Short, New York, February 20, 1788, in *DHRC,* 16:151–52; Dawson to Madison, Fredericksburg, February 18, 1788, in *DHRC,* 9:601.

221. *DHRC,* 14:395–98.

222. "To the Freeholders of Albemarle County," *Virginia Independent Chronicle,* February 13, 1788, in *DHRC,* 9:565–69.

223. "I have no chance either in Stafford or Prince William [counties], & have therefore given up the pursuit" (Arthur Lee to Richard Henry Lee, Alexandria, February 19, 1788, in *DHRC,* 9:619–20; see also Boyd, *Politics of Opposition,* 106).

224. Mark to Gates, Shepherdstown, December 25, 1787, in *DHRC,* 9:571. Among the eighty-nine Federalists elected to the convention, forty-six had served as officers in the Continental Army and twenty-three as militia officers (McDonald, *We the People,* 262–63).

225. Mercer to John Francis Mercer, Richmond, December 12, 1787, in *DHRC,* 9:582.

226. Lee had been invited to run for a convention seat either in Westmoreland County or in Fauquier County. He declined out of fear for his health in Richmond. Federalists believed, however, that Lee felt uneasy in the company of radicals such as Patrick Henry and Meriwether Smith (*DHRC,* 9:617–21, 825–26).

227. Quoted in Risjord, *Chesapeake Politics,* 301.

228. Littleton Waller Tazewell, *Sketches of His Own Family,* 1823, in *DHRC,* 9:622–26.

229. For Westmoreland County, see *DHRC,* 9:617–21.

230. Madison to Washington, December 2, 1788, in Rutland, 11:376–78.

231. This incident was reported in 1823 by former U.S. senator Littleton Waller Tazewell (*DHRC,* 9:622–26).

232. The Orange County elections are reconstructed in *DHRC,* 9:595–647.

233. *DHRC,* 9:602–4. See also Banning, *Sacred Fire of Liberty,* 234–35.

234. *DHRC,* 9:611–13, 735–36. The second successful candidate was James Monroe, who did not clearly commit himself for or against ratification. In May 1788, he addressed a twenty-four-page turgid pamphlet under the title "Some Observations on the Constitution" to his constituents, in which he outlined his objections to the Philadelphia plan and demanded amendments (*DHRC,* 9:844–77).

235. Thomas to Griffith Evans, March 3, 1789, Massachusetts Historical Society *Proceedings* 46 (1913): 370–71.

236. *DHRC,* 9:569–70.

237. See, however, the "Instructions to Delegates to the State Ratifying Convention, Spotsylvania County, 1788," located in the James Monroe Papers and printed in *DHRC,* 9:611–12. The voters professed to confide in the integrity of their delegates "to do the best you can for the common good." Should nine states adopt the Constitution before the decision was to be made in Richmond, the delegates were authorized "to accept and ratify the same protesting agt. or declaring our dissent to such parts as shall be thought objectionable by a majority of the Body and pressing on the Congress when convened an early consideration and adoption of them into the System."

238. Carrington to Madison, April 8, 1788, in *DHRC,* 9:706–7.

239. *DHRC,* 8:385–87; *DHRC,* 8:433–36 ("Circular Letter to the Fayette County Court," Danville, Ky., 29 February 1788); *DHRC,* 9:884–85. Years later, one of the delegates from Fayette County, Humphrey Marshall, was attacked for having accepted the Constitution contrary to the instructions of his constituents. Marshall defended his vote in Richmond by arguing that he had given "no *pledge* to the people to vote against the ratification and had no *instructions* from them so to vote. . . . I stood in their place, and it was necessary only to understand the public interest, and pursue it according to my best judgment" (quote from A. C. Quisenberry, *The Life and Times of Honorable Humphrey Marshall* [Winchester, Ky., 1892], 24–26; see also *DHRC,* 10:1651–52n2).

240. *DHRC,* 9:606–7. See also Risjord, *Chesapeake Politics,* 302.

241. Charles Lee to Richard Henry Lee, April 6, 1788, in *DHRC,* 9:705–6.

242. *DHRC,* 9:626–31.

243. Carrington to Henry Knox, Richmond, March 13, 1788; and Carrington to William Short, New York, April 25, 1788, in *DHRC,* 8:491–92, 9:757–58. Cyrus Griffin considered Federalists "in point of virtues and real abilities" as much superior: "Henry is weighty and powerful but too interested—Mason too passionate—the Governor [Randolph] by nature timid and undecided—and Grayson too blustering" (Griffin to Madison, New York, April 14, 1788, in *DHRC,* 9:737–38).

244. Madison to Washington, Orange, April 10, 1788; and Madison to Jefferson, Orange, April 22, 1788, in *DHRC,* 9:732–33, 744–46.

245. Nicholas to Madison, Charlottesville, April 5, 1788, in *DHRC,* 9:702–5.

246. Assembly Proceedings, November 10, 1787, in *DHRC,* 2:238–41; William Shippen Jr. to Thomas Lee Shippen, Philadelphia, November 7–18, 1787, in *DHRC,* 2:235–36.

247. William Tilghman to Tench Coxe, Chester Town, April 20, 1788, Coxe Papers, PHi.

248. Baltimore *Maryland Gazette,* April 15, 1788.

249. *DHRC,* 3:92–104.

250. Thomas C. Parramore, "A Year in Hertford County With Elkanah Watson," *North Carolina Historical Review* 41 (1964): 448–63.

251. Benjamin Caswell, Affidavit on Dobbs County Riot, April 23, 1788, NCDAH; New York *Daily Advertiser,* June 30, 1788.

252. Maclaine to James Iredell, Wilmington, April 29, 1788, *Iredell Papers,* 3:396.

253. *DHRC,* 3:37–41.

254. *DHRC,* 3:94.

255. Harold Hancock, "Delaware becomes the First State," in Conley and Kaminski, *The Constitution and the States,* 21–36; Gaspare J. Saladino, "Delaware: Independence and the Concept of a Commercial Republic," in Gillespie and Lienesch, *Ratifying the Constitution,* 29–51.

256. *DHRC,* 3:119–25; Mary R. Murrin, "New Jersey and the Two Constitutions," in Conley and Kaminski, *The Constitution and the States,* 55–75; Sara M. Shumer, "New Jersey: Property and the Price of Republican Politics," in Gillespie and Lienesch, *Ratifying the Constitution,* 71–89.

257. *DHRC,* 3:173–76.

258. *DHRC,* 3:177–91.

259. Dinkin, *Voting in Revolutionary America,* 122–24.

260. "A Georgia Backwoodsman," *Gazette of the State of Georgia,* June 12, 1788. See also John P. Kaminski, "Controversy Amid Consensus: The Adoption of the Constitution in Georgia," *Georgia Historical Quarterly* 58 (1974): 244–61; Albert B. Saye, "Georgia: Security through Union," in Conley and Kaminski, *The Constitution and the States,* 77–92; and Edward J. Cashin, "Georgia: Searching for Security," in Gillespie and Lienesch, *Ratifying the Convention,* 93–116.

261. Washington to Samuel Powel, January 18, 1788, in *DHRC,* 3:263.

262. *DHRC,* 3:201–11, 219–64.

263. *DHRC,* 3:265–84.

264. "Marius," *Augusta Chronicle,* December 24, 1791, in *DHRC,* 3:211.

265. *DHRC,* 2:234.

266. *DHRC,* 2:226, 234, 259–60, 332.

267. Owen S. Ireland, "Partisanship and the Constitution: Pennsylvania 1787," *Pennsylvania History* 45 (1978): 315–32; Ireland, *Religion, Ethnicity, and Politics: Ratifying the Constitution in Pennsylvania* (University Park, Penn., 1995); Paul Doutrich, "From Revolution to Constitution: Pennsylvania's Path to Federalism," in Conley and Kaminski, *The Constitution and the States,* 37–53; George J. Graham Jr., "Pennsylvania: Representation and the Meaning of Republicanism," in Gillespie and Lienesch, *Ratifying the Constitution,* 52–70. See also John B. McMaster and Frederick D. Stone, *Pennsylvania and the Federal Constitution, 1787–1788* (Lancaster, Penn., 1888; repr., New York, 1970).

268. *DHRC,* 2:224–25.

269. "Dissent of the Minority," in *DHRC,* 2:622.

270. Christopher Collier, "Sovereignty Finessed: Roger Sherman, Oliver Ellsworth, and the Ratification of the Constitution in Connecticut," in Conley and Kaminski, *The Constitution and the States,* 93–112; *DHRC,* 3:315–32; Donald S. Lutz, "Connecticut: Achieving Consent and Assuring Control," in Gillespie and Lienesch, *Ratifying the Constitution,* 117–37.

271. In his *American Geography,* Jedidiah Morse emphasized the importance of the religious factor for Connecticut politics: "The clergy, who are numerous, and as a body

very respectable, have hitherto preserved a kind of *aristocratical balance in the democratical government* of the State, which has happily operated as a check to the *overbearing spirit of republicanism*" (quoted in Main, *Antifederalists,* 198n28).

272. See, e.g., *DHRC,* 3:393, 470–71, 514, 516, 544, 549.

273. See Farrand, 1:468–69; and *DHRC,* 3:328–29, 351–53.

274. *DHRC,* 3:405–55.

275. Hugh Ledlie to John Lamb, Hartford, January 15, 1788, in *DHRC,* 3:575–83.

276. Risjord, *Chesapeake Politics,* 276–93; Gregory Stiverson, "Necessity, the Mother of Union: Maryland and the Constitution, 1785–1789," in Conley and Kaminski, *The Constitution and the States,* 131–52; Peter S. Onuf, "Maryland: The Small Republic in the New Nation," in Gillespie and Lienesch, *Ratifying the Constitution,* 171–200; Eric Robert Papenfuse, "Unleashing the 'Wildness': The Mobilization of Grassroots Antifederalism in Maryland," *Journal of the Early Republic* 16 (1996): 73–106.

277. "The Convention are not to think for the people, but merely to declare the will of the people": "A Watchman," Baltimore *Maryland Gazette,* October 30, 1787. On November 6, 1787, a correspondent rhetorically asked in the same newspaper: "What freeman who has a sense of the value of liberty . . . would delegate to any body of men a right to reject what he approved of?" Similar arguments were used by "Freeman" in the *Maryland Journal* on February 19, 1788. Federalist Alexander Contee Hanson saw each convention delegate "under a sacred obligation, to vote conformably to the sentiments of his constituents" (Hanson to Madison, Annapolis, June 2, 1788, in Rutland, 11:69–71).

278. In early April, Lux proclaimed to the voters of Baltimore County: "It is my real opinion the members of convention should neither be shackled by instructions or promises; I would never have consented to stand, had I expected to be called on to declare my sentiments, for a child of five years could lisp out yes or no, as well as the most sensible man in the state" (*Maryland Journal,* April 4, 1788).

279. Carroll to Madison, May 28, 1788, in Rutland, 11:62–64; Alexander Contee Hanson to Tench Coxe, Annapolis, April 11, 1788, Coxe Papers, PHi.

280. In 1790, the number of free adult white males in Baltimore County was 4,214; in Ann Arundel County, 2,336; and in Harford County, 2,325. Similar numbers existed only in Baltimore Town (3,072), Frederick County (5,610), Washington County (3,040), and Montgomery County (2,592) (Pole, *Politics of Representation,* appendix 2: 554).

281. "A Republican," Baltimore *Maryland Gazette,* May 16, 1788.

282. *Maryland Journal,* April 15, 1788.

283. *Maryland Journal,* April 4, 1788.

284. Risjord, *Chesapeake Politics,* 288.

285. Carroll had been defeated in Anne Arundel County. In late January, 1788, he had already drafted a speech for the ratifying convention (Edward C. Papenfuse, ed., "An Undelivered Defense of a Winning Cause: Charles Carroll of Carrollton's 'Remarks on the Proposed Constitution,'" *Maryland Historical Magazine* 71 [1976]: 220–51).

286. Storing, 5:149n3; McDonald, *We the People,* 215n137.

287. Jerome J. Nadelhaft, "South Carolina: A Conservative Revolution," in Conley and Kaminski, *The Constitution and the States,* 153–79; Robert M. Weir, "South Carolina: Slavery and the Structure of the Union," in Gillespie and Lienesch, *Ratifying the Constitution,* 201–34.

288. Dinkin, *Voting,* 127–28.

289. Libby, *Geographical Distribution,* 44; McDonald, *We the People,* 216n139; Main, *Antifederalists,* 218–20.

290. Roll, "We, Some of the People," 30–32.

291. *DHRC,* 5:888–92. See also John J. Fox, "Massachusetts and the Creation of the Federal Union, 1775–1791," in Conley and Kaminski, *The Constitution and the States,* 113–30; and Michael Allen Gillespie, "Massachusetts: Creating Consensus," in Gillespie and Lienesch, *Ratifying the Constitution,* 138–67.

292. Main, *Antifederalists,* 207n57.

293. Dinkin, *Voting,* 117–19; Roll, "We, Some of the People," 26; Pole, *Political Representation,* appendix 2: 544–46.

294. Jere Daniell, "Ideology and Hardball: Ratification of the Federal Constitution in New Hampshire," in Conley and Kaminski, *The Constitution and the States,* 181–200; Jean Yarbrough, "New Hampshire: Puritanism and the Moral Foundations of America," in Gillespie and Lienesch, *Ratifying the Constitution,* 235–58.

295. Town Records, January 15, 1788, New Hampshire State Library.

296. The citizens of Sanbornton in Strafford County wanted to commit their delegate William Harper to ratification, but Harper "liked his opinion best, and finally voted against it." He explained "that the powers conferred upon the general government were too great; that the abundant patronage conferred upon some, and the independent tenure of office upon other departments, would tend to consolidation, and lead to the exercise of tyranny and oppression" (J. Farmer and J. B. Moore, eds., *Collections, Historical and Miscellaneous: Historical Sketch of Sanbornton, N.H.* [1824], 3:355; M. T. Runnels, *History of Sanbornton, N.H.,* 2 vols. [Boston, 1881–82], 1:135, 2:326).

297. Boyd, *Politics of Opposition,* 62–63.

298. Risjord, *Chesapeake Politics,* 306–17. See also Alan V. Briceland, "Virginia: The Cement of the Union," in Conley and Kaminski, *The Constitution and the States,* 201–23; and Lance Banning, "Virginia: Sectionalism and the General Good," in Gillespie and Liensch, *Ratifying the Constitution,* 261–99.

299. Main, *Antifederalists,* 225, 228.

300. Ibid., 285–86.

301. Dinkin, *Voting,* 124–26; Roll, "We, Some of the People," 24–26.

302. Newport Town Records, R.I. State Archives, Papers Relating to the Adoption of the Constitution.

303. Dinkin, *Voting,* 111–13 (historians' tabulations of the votes vary slightly).

304. *DHRC,* 14:503–30.

305. Patrick T. Conley, "First in War, Last in Peace: Rhode Island and the Constitution, 1786–1790," in Conley and Kaminski, *The Constitution and the States,* 269–94; John P. Kaminski, "Rhode Island: Protecting State Interests," in Gillespie and Lienesch, *Ratifying the Constitution,* 368–90.

306. Foster Town Meeting, R.I. State Archives.

307. According to Rhode Island Federalist Jabez Bowen, leaders of the Country Party had secretly discussed "that the Duties on all Goods Imported should be put very low . . . and that our Ports should be opened to all the World" (Bowen to John Adams, Providence, December 28, 1789, Adams Papers, MHi; see also Kaminski, *Paper Politics,* 232).

308. Risjord, *Chesapeake Politics,* 318. For a general view, see Alan D. Watson, "North Carolina: States' Rights and Agrarianism Ascendant," in Conley and Kaminski, *The Constitution and the States,* 251–68; and Michael Lienesch, "North Carolina: Preserving Rights," in Gillespie and Lienesch, *Ratifying the Constitution,* 343–67.

309. Bloodworth to John Lamb, June 23, 1788, in *DHRC,* 18:54. From the point of view of John Brown Cutting in London, the disappointing election results in North Carolina cried loudly for "interference of national authority and control" (Cutting to Jefferson, July 11, 1788, in Boyd, 13:331–32).

310. Risjord, *Chesapeake Politics,* 337.

311. Ibid., 337–41.

312. Dinkin, *Voting,* 122.

313. See Schechter, ed., *Reluctant Pillar,* 161; Roll, "We, Some of the People," 21–23.

314. John P. Kaminski, "Adjusting to Circumstances: New York's Relationship with the Federal Government, 1776–1788," in Conley and Kaminski, *The Constitution and the States,* 225–49; Cecil L. Eubanks, "New York: Federalism and the Political Economy of Union," in Gillespie and Lienesch, *Ratifying the Constitution,* 300–340. See also the older works of Staughton Lynd, *Anti-Federalism in Dutchess County, New York: A Study of Democracy and Class Conflict in the Revolutionary Era* (Chicago, 1962); and Linda Grant De Pauw, *The Eleventh Pillar: New York State and the Federal Constitution* (Ithaca, N.Y., 1966).

315. *New York Packet,* June 6, 1788.

316. Estimates of the comparative voting strength of the two parties on a national scale vary between "about equal" (William H. Riker, Evelyn Fink) and 52-to-48 in favor of Antifederalists (Jackson Turner Main) (see Riker, *Strategy of Rhetoric,* 20–21, 255). As Riker rightly points out, however, "the real issue was whether or not Federalists could win over 9/13, or 70 percent, of the state conventions."

317. Robert A. McGuire and Robert L. Ohsfeldt, "Self-Interest, Voting Behavior, and the Ratification of the United States Constitution" (unpublished typescript, Ball State University, Muncie, Ind., 1985).

318. *Maryland Journal,* February 29, 1788. A writer from New York stressed the factors of communication and information: "The cities of *New-York* and *Hudson* . . . are very *unanimous* in favor of the New Federal Government—and the city of *Albany* has a respectable majority. These cities . . . having the best means of information, *have not,* like many of the counties in this State, formed premature judgments" (*New York Packet,* June 13, 1788).

319. Risjord, *Chesapeake Politics,* 306–17.

5. State Ratifying Conventions

1. In Poughkeepsie, New York Federalist David S. Bogard shared a house with several Antifederalists, "where I can hardly speak without opposition" (Bogard to Samuel Blachley Webb, July 8, 1788, in *DHRC,* 21:1296). When Charles Tillinghast visited the Poughkeepsie convention, Governor Clinton offered him "part of his Bed—but Judge Smith procured me Lodgings" (Tillighast to John Lamb, June 21, 1788, Lamb Papers, NHi).

2. Freeman to John Quincy Adams, Medford, January 5, 1788, in *DHRC,* 5:617.

3. Duncanson to James Maury, Fredericksburg, June 7, 13, 1788, in *DHRC,* 10:1583.

4. *DHRC,* 2:269, 276–77, 364–68, 378.

5. *DHRC,* 2:312–13.

6. Debates of Massachusetts Convention, February 2, 4, and 5, 1788.

7. "Address of a Minority of the Maryland Ratifying Convention," Baltimore *Maryland Gazette,* May 6, 1788, in Storing, 5:92–100; Alexander Contee Hanson to James Madison, Annapolis, June 2, 1788, in Rutland, 11:69–71.

8. *DHRC,* 2:379; Massachusetts Convention Payroll, Massachusetts Archives Division, Constitutional Convention, 1788, 162.

9. Va. Treasury Office to Va. House of Delegates, October 24, 1788, Executive Communication, Vi; Convention Expenses, 2 June 1788–6 February 1789, in *DHRC,* 10:1564–68; Pay and Travel Vouchers to the Members of the South Carolina Convention, May 23–24, 1788, Legislative Papers, Sc-Ar.

10. North Carolina Convention (Hillsborough), Estimates of Allowances made to the Members of the Convention, August 1788, Papers of the Convention of 1788; N.C. Civil List for 1789, Legislative Papers, Nc-Ar.

11. Baltimore *Maryland Gazette,* May 9, 1788.

12. "To the Honorable the Convention of the State of Pennsylvania," Philadelphia *Independent Gazetteer,* November 22, 1787, in *DHRC,* 2:289–92.

13. *Massachusetts Centinel,* January 9, 1788, in *DHRC,* 5:666.

14. "To the CONVENTION *of* MASSACHUSETTS," Boston *American Herald,* January 14, 1788, in *DHRC,* 5:710.

15. "Junius," *Massachusetts Gazette,* in *DHRC,* 5:801.

16. *DHRC,* 5:704.

17. See, e.g., "A Pennsylvanian": "To the Honorable the CONVENTION of the STATE of NEW-York," *Pennsylvania Gazette,* June 11, 1788, reprinted in New York *Daily Advertiser,* June 14 and 17, 1788. See also "Denatus": "*To the* MEMBERS *of the* VIRGINIA FEDERAL CONVENTION, *collectively, and individually*" (*Virginia Independent Chronicle,* June 11, 1788, in *DHRC,* 10:1599–1607). The author used the occasion to recommend the establishment of academies for educating the youth in the subjects of morality, religion, law, and the art of war. He also made the unusual proposal to leave the final decision concerning the amendments recommended by state conventions to General Washington.

18. *Virginia Gazette and Weekly Advertiser,* June 19, 1788, in *DHRC,* 10:1656.

19. To Stephen Hooper, Boston, January 31, 1788, in *DHRC,* 7:1568.

20. Charleston *City Gazette,* May 20, 1788.

21. To Evert Bancker, Bancker Family Papers, NHi.

22. Hazard to Carey, New York, July 15, 1788, in *DHRC,* 21:1317–18. The first such edition was published in August 1788 by the Virginia printer Augustine Davis (*The Ratification of the New Fœderal Constitution, together with the Amendments, proposed by the Several States,* Richmond [Evans 21529]).

23. The "rules and regulations" of the state conventions are printed in the *DHRC.*

24. *DHRC,* 2:328, 382, 423. The service at the Lutheran church was attended by the convention delegates, Pennsylvania's Supreme Executive Council, the trustees and faculty of the university, "and a great number of citizens. . . . The Rev. Mr. Smith, assistant Lutheran minister, introduced the business by prayer; Dr. Helmuth concluded with a solemn short address to the audience, in the English language, and a prayer in the German" (letter of a participant to the *New York Journal,* December 11, 1787).

25. Massachusetts Convention Debates, January 9, 1788, in *DHRC,* 6:1162.

26. *DHRC,* 5:813–14.

27. *DHRC,* 3:180. On December 15, 1787, the *Pennsylvania Packet* published an extract of a letter from Trenton stating that "you see we hold public prayers in greater estimation in New Jersey than they were held in Pennsylvania, notwithstanding the members of our Convention consist, like yours, of gentlemen of *different* religious sects" (*DHRC,* 3:182).

28. *DHRC,* 3:535.

29. Virginia Convention Proceedings, June 2, 1788, in *DHRC,* 9:909.

30. *DHRC,* 2:529–31, 547–48, 587–88.

31. Massachusetts Convention Debates, January 19, 1788, in *DHRC,* 6:1254–56.

32. *DHRC,* 3:325, 584.

33. Syrett, 5:135–37. In Virginia, a difference of opinion regarding the outcome of elections in Hanover County led to a duel between Colonel William Fontaine and Thomas Macon in Richmond, resulting in serious injury to Macon. In a letter to Arthur Lee, Theodorick Bland stressed the fact that neither of the two men was a convention delegate: "I mention this to shew you that heats have not yet entered that body, and that they are not yet Ignited altho. Thunders Roll and lightnings flash every day both in the Natural and Political Atmosphere" (*DHRC,* 10:1617–18).

34. John Jay to Sally Jay, June 21, 1788; Jay to Washington, June 30, 1788; and Jay to John Adams, July 4, 1788, in Johnston, *Correspondence,* 3:340, 345–47.

35. *DHRC,* 10:1680–81.

36. Pole, *Political Representation,* 68.

37. *DHRC,* 2:330–31.

38. *DHRC,* 3:523.

39. John Quincy Adams Diary, February 21 and 22, 1788, in Allen, 2:364–66.

40. *New York Journal,* July 10, 1788.

41. Alexander White to Mary Wood, Richmond, June 10–11, 1788, in *DHRC,* 10:1591–92.

42. Extract of a letter from Richmond, New York *Daily Advertiser,* July 3, 1788, in *DHRC,* 10:1698–99.

43. *DHRC,* 2:547–49; "An Auditor," *Massachusetts Gazette,* January 25, 1788.

44. "Agrippa" XI, January 8, 1788, in *DHRC,* 5:649–51.

45. Hugh Ledlie to John Lamb, Hartford, January 15, 1788, in *DHRC,* 3:575–76. According to the Litchfield *Weekly Monitor,* however, "a very numerous and respectable audience attended the debates with great decency, who, when the decisive vote was summarily declared from the chair, clapped their hands for joy" (*DHRC,* 3:574–75).

46. Massachusetts Convention Debates, January 24, 1788, in *DHRC,* 6:1336.

47. Charleston *City Gazette,* May 21, 1788.

48. Several of these speeches are published in *DHRC,* 18:221–55. See also the chapter in this volume on ratification celebrations.

49. John Jay to Sally Jay, July 5, 1788, in Johnston, *Correspondence,* 3:347–48.

50. Frances L. Williams, *A Founding Family: The Pinckneys of South Carolina* (New York, 1978), 283.

51. Thomas Iredell to James Iredell, Edenton, May 27, 1788, in McRee 2:225.

52. See *New York Journal,* April 4, 1788; New York *Daily Advertiser,* April 11, 1788.

53. *DHRC,* 3:523, 574–74, 585–87.

54. Ezra Stiles Literary Diary, January 25, 1788, Stiles Papers, CtY; *Boston Gazette,* January 14, 1788, in *DHRC,* 5:717.

55. Nancy B. Oliver, "Keystone of the Federal Arch: New Hampshire's Ratification of the United States Constitution" (Ph.D. diss., University of California at Santa Barbara, 1972), 113–15.

56. See "Biographical Gazetteer," in *DHRC,* 2:727–34.

57. Schechter, *Reluctant Pillar,* 157–206.

58. Poughkeepsie *Country Journal,* July 1, 1788.

59. See Verstandig, *Emergence of the Two-Party System,* 40; Philip A. Crowl, "Anti-Federalism in Maryland," *WMQ* 4 (1947): 452.

60. Forrest McDonald, *We the People: The Economic Origins of the Constitution* (Chicago, 1958), 255–57.

61. Gore to Rufus King, December 12, 1788, in *DHRC,* 5:506–7; Belknap, "Notes of Debates," in Massachusetts Historical Society *Proceedings* 3 (1855–58): 295–304; Gorham to Henry Knox, January 16, 1788, in *DHRC,* 5:730; Gorham to James Madison, January 27, 1788, in Rutland, 10:435–36; Henry Jackson to Knox, January 20, 1788, Knox Papers, Gilder-Lehrman Collection on deposit at the New-York Historical Society; King to Madison, January 27, 1788, in Rutland, 10:436–37.

62. Massachusetts Convention Debates, January 25, 1788, in *DHRC,* 6:1346–48; Jeremy Belknap to Nathaniel Hazard, January 25, 1788, in *Correspondence Between Jeremy Belknap and Ebenezer Hazard,* Massachusetts Historical Society *Collections,* 1877–91, 3:9–11.

63. See McDonald, *We the People,* 199–200; Main, *Antifederalists,* 208–9.

64. Jackson to Knox, February 3, 1788, in *DHRC,* 7:1571; Gibbs to Washington, February 9, 1788, in *DHRC,* 7:1687; Silas Lee to George Thatcher, Biddeford, Maine, February 22, 1788, in *Historical Magazine* 6 (1869): 340, in *DHRC,* Mfm:Mass.

65. *DHRC,* 3:576.

66. Sullivan to [Knox?], Portsmouth, February 11, 1788, J. S. H. Fogg Autograph Collection, MeHi; Sullivan to Nathaniel Gilman, Durham, February 28, 1788, Gratz Collection, PHi; Lear to Washington, Portsmouth, June 22, 1788, in *Washington Papers, Confederation Series,* 6:349.

67. See Main, *Antifederalists,* 290; Oliver, *Keystone,* 106–8; and Nathaniel J. Eiseman, "The Ratification of the Federal Constitution by the State of New Hampshire" (master's thesis, Columbia University, 1937), 89–91.

68. William Peck to Knox, February 15, 1790, Knox Papers, Gilder-Lehrman Collection on deposit at the New-York Historical Society; Jabez Bowen to John Adams, Providence, March 9, 1790, and Marchant to Adams, Newport, May 29, 1790, Adams Papers, MHi; Vernon to Wadsworth, Newport, June 5, 1790, Wadsworth Papers, CtHi.

69. McDonald, *We the People,* 340–42.

70. Vaughan to John Langdon, Philadelphia, June 6, 1788, Langdon-Elwyn Papers, NhHi; De Saussure to Jedidiah Morse, Charleston, April 2, 1788, James T. Mitchell Autograph Collection, PHi; Burke to John Lamb, Charleston, June 23, 1788, in *DHRC,* 18:55–57.

71. McDonald, *We the People,* 217–19.

72. Main, *Antifederalists,* 289.

73. Ibid., 241–42.

74. See, e.g., Melancton Smith to Abraham Yates Jr., New York, January 28, 1788, in *DHRC,* 20:672; and James M. Hughes to John Lamb, Poughkeepsie, June 18, 1788, in *DHRC,* 21:1202.

75. See Crowl, *Anti-Federalism in Maryland,* 446–50; and McDonald, *We the People,* 155–57.

76. Timothy Bloodworth to John Lamb, June 23, 1788, in *DHRC,* 18:53–55; Jesse Benton to Thomas Hart, June 29, 1788, Thomas J. Clay Papers, DLC.

77. See Main, *Antifederalists,* 244–45; William C. Pool, "An Economic Interpretation of the Ratification of the Federal Constitution in North Carolina, *North Carolina Historical Review* 27 (1950): 119–21.

78. See Robert E. Thomas, "The Virginia Convention of 1788: A Criticism of Beard's *An Economic Interpretation of the Constitution,*" *Journal of Southern History* 19 (February 1953): 63–65; McDonald, *We the People,* 269–71; Risjord, *Chesapeake Politics,* 306–17.

79. Thomas Willing to William Bingham, Philadelphia, June 24, 1788, in *DHRC,* 10:1670–71; Randolph's Letter of June 18, 1788, quoted in Samuel Smith to Tench Coxe, Baltimore, June 22, 1788, in *DHRC,* 10:1666; Morris to Horatio Gates, Richmond, June 12, 1788, in *DHRC,* 10:1613; Archibald Stuart to John Breckinridge, Charlottesville, June 30, 1788, in *DHRC,* 10:1696.

80. For an excellent case study, see Christopher Grasso, *A Speaking Aristocracy: Transforming Public Discourse in Eighteenth-Century Connecticut* (Chapel Hill, N.C., 1999).

81. At the time of the Boston convention, Dwight Foster drafted a letter to his wife Rebecca, "in a publick House, a publick Room, in the Midst of a large Circle of People zealous upon Politicks" (Boston, January 16, 1788, in *DHRC,* 7:1529). Speeches given at the Poughkeepsie convention became the focus of heated discussions in the coffee houses and taverns of New York City (Abraham Yates to Abraham G. Lansing, June 29, 1788, in *DHRC,* 21:1240).

82. Peter Sylvester to Francis Sylvester, Kinderhook, July 25–28, 1788, Sylvester Family Papers, NHi.

83. Butler to the Rev. Weeden Butler, Maryville, March 2, 1788, P. Butler Letters, Department of Manuscripts, British Museum.

84. Edward Rutledge Jr. to John Rutledge Jr., Charleston, April 8, 1788, John Rutledge Jr. Papers, University of North Carolina.

85. R. C. Johnson to W. S. Johnson, June 28, 1788, R. C. Johnson Collection, Connecticut State Library.

86. Peter Van Schaack to Henry Van Schaack, Kinderhook, June 29, 1788, in *DHRC,* 21:1239.

87. Farrand, 3:87–90.

88. Tilghman to Coxe, April 11, 1788, Coxe Papers, PHi.

89. *New Hampshire Spy,* February 22, 1788. The debates of the Virginia convention are published in the *DHRC,* vols. 9 and 10.

90. Massachusetts Convention Debates, January 22 and February 5, 1788, in *DHRC,* 6:1307, 1448. Federalist Winthrop Sargent characterized Samuel Nasson, one of the principal opponents in the following way: "A little fellow who was a Quarter Master in our

Army by name of *Nason* is a great Speaker on their Side of the Question, but I think a good deal ignorant and much illiterate" (Sargent to Henry Knox, February 3, 1788, in *DHRC,* 7:1574).

91. South Carolina Convention Debates, May 20, 1788.

92. Jeremy Belknap to Ebenezer Hazard, Boston, January 25, 1788, in *DHRC,* 7:1548.

93. *DHRC,* 2:334, 3:586.

94. D. S. Bogard to Samuel Blachley Webb, Poughkeepsie, July 14, 1788, in Ford, *Correspondence,* 3:104–5; *New York Packet,* June 24, 1788; Spencer Roane to Philip Aylett, Richmond, June 26, 1788, in *DHRC,* 10:1713.

95. "Judge Dana spoke with a pathos which drew tears into the eyes of admiring spectators" (Nathaniel Freeman to John Quincy Adams, Medford, January 27, 1788, in *DHRC,* 7:1551). The editor of the *Massachusetts Centinel* apologized for the "feeble sketch" of the January 18 debates, because "captivated by the fire—the pathos—and the superior eloquence of [Dana's] speech—we forgot we came to take minutes—and thought to hear alone was our duty."

96. Belknap to Hazard, January 25, 1788, in *DHRC,* 7:1548.

97. George Benson to Nicholas Brown, Boston, January 29–30, 1788, Brown Papers, John Carter Brown Library, Providence, R.I.

98. James Breckinridge to John Breckinridge, Richmond, June 13, 1788, in *DHRC,* 10:1620–21.

99. Webb to Hogeboom, Poughkeepsie, June 24–25, in *DHRC,* 21:1222; Clarence E. Miner, *The Ratification of the Federal Constitution by the State of New York* (New York, 1921), 104, 115.

100. *DHRC,* 2:418, 422.

101. *DHRC,* 2:384–92, 423–33, 528–50, 571n1, 592–602.

102. "Helvidius Priscus" IV, *Massachusetts Gazette,* February 5, 1788, in *DHRC,* 5: 858–60.

103. Adams to William Cranch, February 16, 1788, in *DHRC,* 7:1702.

104. Crocker to George Thatcher, Boston, January 26, 1788, in *DHRC,* 7:1550–51.

105. *DHRC,* 3:547.

106. John Quincy Adams Diary, February 21–22, 1788; and Jeremiah Libby to Jeremy Belknap, Portsmouth, February 22, 1788, in Belknap Papers, 3:389–99, MHi.

107. Quoted in Rutland, 11:75.

108. Madison's superb performance at the Richmond convention is analyzed in detail in Banning, *Sacred Fire of Liberty,* 234–64, and in John P. Kaminski, *James Madison: Champion of Liberty and Justice* (Madison, Wis., 2006).

109. Quoted in Rhys Isaac, "Preachers and Patriots: Popular Culture in Virginia," in *The American Revolution: Explorations in the History of American Radicalism,* ed. Alfred F. Young (DeKalb, Ill., 1976), 152–53. Henry's rhetorical style reminded Jefferson of Homer's epic works (Storing, 5:209n1).

110. Quoted in Storing, 5:207.

111. Patrick Henry, Speech of June 4, 1788, in *DHRC,* 9:929–31.

112. James Breckinridge to John Breckinridge, Richmond, June 13, 1788, in *DHRC,* 10:1620–21.

113. James Madison, Speech of June 6, 1788, in *DHRC,* 9:989–90.

114. Grayson to Nathan Dane, Richmond, June 18, 1788, in *DHRC,* 10:1636–37.

115. Stuart to James Breckinridge, Richmond, June 19, 1788, in *DHRC,* 10:1651–52.

116. Patrick Henry, Speech of June 24, 1788, in *DHRC,* 10:1504–7. Still in 1816, Archibald Stuart remembered this dramatic scene in a letter to William Wirt: "I was with Mr. H[enry] in the Convention, when a storm rose in the midst of his speech, I sat too far from him to hear distinctly, but it was said he seemed to mix in the fight of his aetherial auxilaries, and rising on the wings of the tempest, to seize upon the artillery of Heaven, and direct its fiercest thunders against the heads of his adversaries" (published in *WMQ,* 2nd ser., 6 (1926): 340–43, and in the *DHRC,* 10:1511). See also the reminiscences of William Wirt and Spencer Roane, in the *DHRC,* 10:1511–12.

117. See John E. Buckley, "The Role of Rhetoric in the Ratification of the Federal Constitution, 1787–1788," (Ph.D. diss., Northwestern University, 1972); John R. Breitlow, "Rhetorical Fantasy in the Virginia Convention of 1788" (Ph.D. diss., University of Minnesota, 1972); and J. Thomas Wren, "The Ideology of Court and Country in the Virginia Ratifying Convention of 1788," *Virginia Magazine of History and Biography* 93 (1985): 389–408.

118. Platt to Winthrop Sargent, New York, August 8, 1788, in *DHRC,* 21:1352.

119. David S. Bogart to Samuel Blachley Webb, July 14, 1788, and Webb to Catherine Hogeboom, June 26–27, 1788, in Ford, *Correspondence* 3:104–5, 108; Philip Schuyler to John B. Schuyler, Poughkeepsie, June 26, 1788, Bancroft Papers, MHi; *New York Packet,* June 24, 1788. Hamilton's speeches are published in Syrett, *Papers of Alexander Hamilton,* vol. 5, and in the *DHRC,* vol. 22.

120. Abraham Bancker to Evert Bancker, Poughkeepsie, June 28, 1788, in *DHRC,* 21:1230.

121. Cornelius C. Schoonmaker to William Smith, Poughkeepsie, July 7, 1788, Manor of St. George Museum.

122. Christopher P. Yates to Congressman Abraham Yates, Poughkeepsie, June 27, 1788, Yates Papers, NN.

123. Bancker to Evert Bancker, Poughkeepsie, June 28, 1788, in *DHRC,* 21:1230.

124. Jay to Washington, Poughkeepsie, June 30, 1788, in *Washington Papers, Confederation Series,* 6:367; Hamilton to Madison, Poughkeepsie, July 2, 1788, in Syrett, 5:140–41.

125. *New York Morning Post,* July 14, 1788.

126. Isaac Roosevelt to Richard Varick, Poughkeepsie, July 22, 1788, Franklin D. Roosevelt Library, Hyde Park, N.Y. For the subtle political maneuver orchestrated by Clinton and his closest allies to permit the convention to vote in favor of ratification, see John P. Kaminski, *George Clinton: Yeoman Politician of the New Republic* (Madison, Wis., 1993), 148–66.

127. Other indications of the minority's intent to sabotage the convention were their failed proposal to disallow the use of the Pennsylvania State House for counting the votes following the election, and their vain attempt to prevent the adjournment of the legislature for the duration of the convention (*DHRC,* 2:266–78).

128. The convention was called to meet on November 20, but only thirty-eight of the sixty-nine delegates elected were present that day (*DHRC,* 2:322; Rutland, *Ordeal,* 55–59). For further information on the Pennsylvania convention as well as the other state ratifying conventions, see Conley and Kaminski, *The Constitution and the States;* and Gillespie and Lienesch, *Ratifying the Constitution.*

129. *DHRC,* 2:364–82.

130. *DHRC,* 2:444.

131. William Findley on 12 December, in *DHRC,* 2:510.

132. *DHRC,* 2:525.

133. *DHRC,* 2:362, 434, 439–40, 555–56, 579–81.

134. *DHRC,* 2:444, 465, 553.

135. *DHRC,* 2:603, 605–6.

136. *DHRC,* 2:610–16.

137. *The Dissent of the Minority of the Convention,* in *DHRC,* 2:617–40.

138. *DHRC,* 3:105–13 (Delaware); *DHRC,* 3:177–95 (New Jersey); *DHRC,* 3:269–84 (Georgia). There had evidently been some doubts, concerns, and differences of opinion in Georgia and New Jersey. According to two newspaper reports, Judge David Brearley, who had represented New Jersey in the Federal Convention, was forced to summon all his "persuasive eloquence" to allay the misgivings and counter the objections of some delegates in Trenton. Still, no concrete changes were proposed in any of the three early states.

139. A total of 174 delegates had been elected, of whom 168 or 170 participated (see *DHRC,* 3:536–39).

140. *DHRC,* 3:535, 540.

141. Perkins to Simeon Baldwin, January 15, 1788, in *DHRC,* 3:583–85.

142. *Connecticut Courant,* January 9, 1788, in *DHRC,* 3:554.

143. *DHRC,* 3:559.

144. Huntington to Governor Samuel Johnston of North Carolina, September 23, 1788, in *DHRC,* 3:560n3.

145. *DHRC,* 3:560–62.

146. *DHRC,* 3:579, 594–601. See also Bernard C. Steiner, "Connecticut's Ratification of the Federal Constitution," American Antiquarian Society *Proceedings* 25 (1915): 70–127.

147. *DHRC,* 5:624–25.

148. For the Massachusetts convention debates, see the *DHRC,* vol. 6. Early interpretations include Samuel B. Harding, *The Contest over the Ratification of the Federal Constitution in the State of Massachusetts* (New York, 1896); Arthur N. Holcombe, "Massachusetts and the Federal Convention of 1787," in *Commonwealth History of Massachusetts,* ed. A. B. Hart (New York, 1929), 3:366–406; and Rutland, *Ordeal,* 93–114.

149. King to Madison, January 20, 1788, in Rutland, 10:440–41, and in *DHRC,* 7: 1539–40.

150. *DHRC,* 5:787–88. See also George A. Billias, *Elbridge Gerry: Founding Father and Republican Statesman* (New York, 1976), 213–14.

151. In a letter to Knox, Henry Jackson described Gerry's behavior as "extraordinary & unaccountable, his friends are at a loss what can be his motives" (Jackson to Knox, January 23, 1788, in *DHRC,* 7:1546).

152. *Cumberland Gazette,* January 24, 1788, in *DHRC,* 7:1547.

153. George R. Minot, Journal, January–February 1788, in *DHRC,* 7:1599.

154. "Every measure & contrivance possible is used by both sides to gain proselites—as the Antifederals are more mixed in the Lodging Houses with those Neutral characters they have the best chance by private Conversations—while Federalists have the best of it in public" (Nathaniel Gorham to Henry Knox, January 20, 1788, in *DHRC,* 5:752).

155. *DHRC,* 5:629–35.

156. Jackson to Knox, January 20, 1788, in *DHRC,* 7:1538, and in *DHRC,* 6:1335. The funeral of Adams's son had taken place on January 19 (*DHRC,* 7:1538).

157. King to Horatio Gates, January 20, 1788, in *DHRC,* 7:1538–39; King to Knox, February 3, 1788, in *DHRC,* 7:1571–72; King to Madison, February 3, 1788, in Rutland, 10:465–66, and in *DHRC,* 7:1572.

158. George H. Haynes, "The Conciliatory Proposition in the Massachusetts Convention of 1788," American Antiquarian Society *Proceedings* 29 (1919): 294–311.

159. *DHRC,* 14:83–84.

160. John Avery to Madison, in Rutland, 10:376, and in *DHRC,* 5:745–46.

161. *Massachusetts Centinel,* January 26, 1788, in *DHRC,* 5:806–10.

162. King to Knox, January 27, 1788, in *DHRC,* 7:1553.

163. Lincoln to Washington, January 27, 1788, in *DHRC,* 7:1555. At the end, Belknap wrote: "The Antis would have had the question called much sooner, but the Feds. protracted the debates on paragraphs till they were *sure* of a majority" (Belknap to Hazard, February 10, 1788, in *DHRC,* 7:1584).

164. King to George Thatcher, January 30, 1788, in *DHRC,* 7:1562; Tristram Dalton to Michael Hodge, January 30, 1788, in *DHRC,* 7:1560.

165. Jackson to Knox, February 3, 1788, in *DHRC,* 7:1570–71.

166. "Portius," in the *Massachusetts Gazette* of February 8, accused Antifederalist "Helvidius Priscus," probably James Warren, of participating in "nocturnal scenes of conspiracy" (*DHRC,* 5:882).

167. For the many different estimates of party strength circulating in Massachusetts and in other states, see "Speculation about the Prospects for the Ratification of the Constitution in Massachusetts," in *DHRC,* vol. 5, appendix 1: 1077–1105.

168. Tristram Dalton to Stephen Hooper, January 31, 1788, in *DHRC,* 7:1563.

169. Jackson to Knox, February 3, 1788, in *DHRC,* 7:1571.

170. King to Madison, February 3, 1788, in Rutland, 10:465–66, and in *DHRC,* 7:1572.

171. "*S. Adams* had almost overset the apple-cart by *intruding* an amendment of his own fabrication. . . . A. has made himself unpopular" (Belknap to Hazard, February 10, 1788, in *DHRC,* 7:1583).

172. "Resolutions ratifying Constitution and proposing amendments. Commonwealth of Massachusetts, Massachusetts Convention, February 6, 1788" (*DHRC,* 6:1468–71).

173. Massachusetts Convention Debates, February 7, 1788. In Paris, William Short was deeply impressed by this conduct: "No example was ever more worthy of imitation than that of the minority of the Massachusetts Convention" (Short to William Smith, May 27, 1788, Gilpin Papers, Phi).

174. Washington to Benjamin Lincoln, January 31, 1788, in *Washington Papers, Confederation Series,* 6:74. As late as February 3, Lincoln had little hope for true conciliatory behavior from Antifederalists in the convention. He wrote to Washington that Federalists in Massachusetts could hardly have expected "that those men who were so lately intoxicated with large draughts of liberty and were thirsting for more would in so short a time submit to a constitution, which would further take up the reins of government, which in their opinion were too strait before" (*DHRC,* 7:1573).

175. John Quincy Adams, February 11, 1788, in *DHRC,* 7:1691.

176. Abraham G. Lansing to Abraham Yates Jr., Albany, June 22, 1788, in *DHRC,* 21: 1208.

177. See "Alleged Bribery and Corruption of Delegates to the Massachusetts Convention, 21 January–6 February," in *DHRC,* 5:759–67.

178. Massachusetts Convention Debates, February 5, 1788, in *DHRC,* 6:1444–48.

179. Madison to Washington, New York, February 15, 1788, in Rutland, 10:510.

180. Edward Carrington to Knox, Richmond, March 13, 1788, in *DHRC,* 8:491–92; John Avery Jr. to George Thatcher, Boston, February 13, 1788, in *DHRC,* 7:1692–94; Hazard to Belknap, New York, February 13, 1788, Belknap Papers, 5:19, MHi.

181. Jefferson to Thomas Lee Shippen, Paris, June 19, 1788, in Boyd 13:276–77.

182. *Journal of the Proceedings of the Convention: Extract from Miscellaneous Documents and Records Relating to New Hampshire,* vol. 10, comp. and ed. Nathaniel Bouton (Concord, N.H., 1877), 12–13.

183. Samuel Lane to Paine Wingate, Stratham, March 17, 1788, Lane Family Papers, NhHi.

184. Adams Diary, February 21, 1788; Jeremiah Libby to Belknap, Portsmouth, February 19 and 22, 1788, Belknap Papers, 3:388–90, MHi. In late 1786, William Plumer had described Peabody as an "infidel" and "blasphemer" who was deeply in debt and made his house a meeting place for "the vilest of men" (Plumer to John Hale, Londonderry, October 14, 1786, Letters of William Plumer, 1786–1787, *Publications* of the Colonial Society of Massachusetts [Boston, 1910], 11:383–403).

185. John Vaughan to John Dickinson, Philadelphia, March 9, 1788, Dickinson Papers, PPL; Lane to Paine Wingate, March 17, 1788, Lane Family Papers, NhHi.

186. Adams Diary, February 22, 1788.

187. *New Hampshire Gazette,* February 27, 1788.

188. Sullivan to Belknap, Durham, February 26, 1788, Belknap Papers, 3:393–94, MHi; Langdon to Washington, Portsmouth, February 28, 1788, in *Washington Papers, Confederation Series,* 6:132–33. See also "The Adjournment of the New Hampshire Convention," in *DHRC,* 16:179–85.

189. At the seat of Congress in New York City, Madison predicted that "the influence of this check will be considerable in this State and in several others" (Madison to Edmund Pendleton, March 3, 1788, in Rutland, 10:554). Madison's fellow Virginia delegate John Brown feared that the adjournment "will be productive of bad consequences as it will give fresh spirits & Confidence to the Malcontents who were beginning to dispair & relax in their opposition" (Brown to James Breckinridge, New York, March 17, 1788, in *DHRC,* 16:404).

190. Lear to George Washington, June 2, 1788, in *Washington Papers, Confederation Series,* 6:307.

191. Writing on April 10 from Orange County, Madison warned Washington that "the difference between even a postponement and adoption in Maryland, may in the nice balance of parties here, possibly give a fatal advantage to that which opposes the Constitution" (*DHRC,* 9:732–33). Washington, on his part, advised former Maryland governor Thomas Johnson on April 20 that an adjournment of the Annapolis convention "to a later period than the decision of the question in this State, will be tantamount to the rejection of the Constitution." Washington was later accused of having put pressure on Johnson, who acted as president of the Maryland convention (see "George Washington and the Maryland Convention," *DHRC,* 17:187–91).

192. William Tilghman to Tench Coxe, Chester Town, April 20, 1788, Coxe Papers,

PHi. See also Bernard C. Steiner, "Maryland's Adoption of the Federal Constitution," *American Historical Review* 5 (1899–1900): 22–44, 207–24; Rutland, *Ordeal,* 135–59; and Risjord, *Chesapeake Politics,* 289–93.

193. William Smith to Otho Holland Williams, April 28, 1788, Williams Papers, MdHi; *Maryland Journal,* April 29, 1788. For Chase's convention speeches, see Storing, 5:79–91.

194. Printed in *DHRC,* 17:240–41.

195. *DHRC,* 17:242–46; Storing, 5:92–100.

196. Daniel Carroll to Madison, May 28, 1788; Alexander Contee Hanson to Madison, Annapolis, June 2, 1788, in Rutland, 11:62–67, 69–70.

197. Storing, 5:101–6.

198. The Philadelphia *Independent Gazetteer* criticized the behavior of the Federalist delegates as "a striking display of the nature of power, and a sample of what the freemen of America would experience from the great Congress if established" ("A Freeman," Philadelphia *Independent Gazetteer,* May 13, 1788).

199. Washington to Daniel of St. Thomas Jenifer, April 27, 1788, in *Washington Papers, Confederation Series,* 6:211nl.

200. Tilghman to Coxe, Elk, June 11, 1788, Coxe Papers, PHi; *Maryland Journal,* May 20, 1788; Annapolis *Maryland Gazette,* June 19, 1788.

201. Ramsay to Lincoln, Charleston, March 31, 1788, Lincoln Papers, MHi.

202. *Journal of the Convention of South Carolina which Ratified the Constitution* (Atlanta, Ga., 1928). See also George C. Rogers Jr., "South Carolina Ratifies the Federal Constitution," *Proceedings* of the South Carolina Historical Association 31 (1961): 41–62.

203. Burke to Lamb, Charleston, June 23, 1788, in *DHRC,* 18:55–57; "A Planter," Charleston *City Gazette,* July 21, 1788.

204. South Carolina Convention Debates, May 26, 1788.

205. Ibid., May 22, 1788.

206. In order to infuse religious meaning into the oath for federal and state officeholders, it was proposed to change the phrase "but no religious Test shall ever be required" to "but no other religious Test shall ever be required." The South Carolina Amendments are printed in *DHRC,* 18:71–72.

207. Charleston *City Gazette,* May 23, 1788.

208. Rutledge to John Jay, June 20, 1788, Jay Papers, DLC; Rutledge to John Langdon, June 20, 1788, in Elwyn, *Letters,* 107.

209. Nathan Dane to Moses Brown, New York, June 7, 1788, in *DHRC,* 18:169–71.

210. For Hamilton's effort to set up a Federalist express system between the conventions of New York, New Hampshire, and Virginia in June 1788, see below and *DHRC,* 10:1672–75.

211. Clinton to Randolph, May 8, 1788, in *DHRC,* 9:788–93; see also *DHRC,* 17:395–98. This was the answer to the Virginia legislature's circular letter of December 27, 1787, signed by Randolph, which Clinton had received, after much delay, on March 7, 1788. Randolph forwarded Clinton's letter to his executive council; the Virginia ratifying convention was informed of it only after the delegates had adopted the Constitution.

212. Lamb to Richard Henry Lee, May 18, 1788, in *DHRC,* 9:814–15. Further documents and commentaries pertaining to this important episode are published in "The Second Attempt at Cooperation between Virginia and New York Antifederalists, 18

May–27 June," (*DHRC*, 9:811–29); and "The New York Federal Republican Committee Seeks Interstate Cooperation in Obtaining Amendments to the Constitution, May 18–August 6" (*DHRC*, 18:32–68).

213. *DHRC*, 18:38–45.

214. Edward Pole to Lamb, Philadelphia, June 20, 1788, Lamb Papers, NHi.

215. Lowndes to Lamb, Charleston, June 21, 1788, in *DHRC*, 18:50–51.

216. Atherton to Lamb, Amherst, June 11 and 14, 1788, in *DHRC*, 18:45–47.

217. New York Federal Republican Committee to New Hampshire, June 6, 1788, in *DHRC*, 18:38, 62; Atherton to Lamb, Amherst, June 23, 1788, in *DHRC*, 18:51–53.

218. When President John Langdon addressed the New Hampshire General Court in Concord on June 6, he dwelled on the financial and economic difficulties of the state but looked forward "with pleasure to the time . . . when by the blessing of divine providence, we shall be relieved in a great measure from those and many other embarrassments by the adoption of the proposed federal constitution." The Senate responded favorably to Langdon's speech. The same Federalist message was contained in Dr. Samuel Langdon's election sermon "The Republic of the Israelites as an Example to the American States," delivered on June 5 (see Journal of the Proceedings of the New Hampshire General Court, June 6–11, 1788; and *Dr. Langdon's Election Sermon* [Exeter, 1788]). For Federalist activities in the interlude after the Exeter convention, see Oliver, *Keystone*, 81–88; and Eiseman, *Ratification*, 60–77. All these propaganda efforts notwithstanding, Federalist Joshua Wentworth had to admit on the eve of the Concord meeting that "we have many members of the Convention opposed to the adoption of the Constitution" (Wentworth to Judge Sumner, Concord, June 16, 1788, Wentworth Papers, NhHi).

219. The town of Hopkinton, which in January had instructed its delegate to vote against ratification, now granted him the right "to act as he thought best for the public good" (Hopkinton Town Records, January 14 and June 14, 1788, New Hampshire State Library).

220. Journal of the Convention, June 18, 1788 (see n. 56). Atherton defended the right of each community "to choose their members in what way and manner they saw fit." Judge Samuel Livermore rejected such ideas as "subversive of all order and tending in their operation to introduce anarchy and confusion" (*New Hampshire Spy*, June 21, 1788).

221. Pierse Long to Paine Wingate, Portsmouth, July 4, 1788, Wingate Papers, NhHi.

222. "New Hampshire Convention Amendments, 21 June," in *DHRC*, 18:186–89. The seventh amendment limited the jurisdiction of the federal judiciary even further than had been proposed in Massachusetts.

223. Long to Wingate, July 4, 1788, Wingate Papers, NhHi. See also Eiseman, *Ratification*, 78.

224. Atherton to Lamb, June 23, 1788, in *DHRC*, 18:51–53.

225. *DHRC*, 10:1672–75, 18:211–13; Syrett, 5:2, 148–49; Gaspare J. Saladino, "The Federalist Express," in *New York and the Union: Contributions to the American Constitutional Experience* ed. Stephen L. Schechter and Richard B. Bernstein (Albany, N.Y., 1990), 326–41. Apparently, Hamilton had conceived the idea of an express system between Congress and the conventions of New Hampshire, Virginia, and New York in reaction to the activities of the Federal Republican Committee in New York City. An eyewitness described the arrival of the courier from Springfield, Massachusetts, in Poughkeepsie on June 24: "It was about noon, on a very hot day . . . when I saw an express rider, on a powerful horse

flecked with foam, dismount at the Court House door. . . . The courier was Col. William Smith Livingston. . . . The reading of that despach gave great joy to Federalists in the Convention, and they cheered loudly. . . . [Some people] formed a little procession, and led by the music of a fife and drum, marched around the Court House several times. In the evening they lighted a small bonfire. Before sunset Power had printed an 'Extra' on a sheet of paper seven by ten inches in size" (*DHRC*, 21:1217–18).

226. Langdon to Washington, Concord, June 21, 1788, in *Washington Papers: Confederation Series*, 6:348.

227. The Virginia convention is documented in *DHRC*, vols. 9 and 10. See also Rutland, *Ordeal*, 218–34, 245–53; and Risjord, *Chesapeake Politics*, 300–306.

228. For Randolph's letter of October 10, 1787 to the Virginia legislature, which was not published until late December, and on his "fence-sitting" attitude, see *DHRC*, 15:117–35.

229. *DHRC*, 9:931–36.

230. Grayson to Dane, June 4, 1788, in *DHRC*, 10:1572–73. See also Grayson to Lamb, June 9, 1788, in *DHRC*, 9:816–17.

231. Singleton to Charles Pettigrew, Kempsville, June 10, 1788, in *DHRC*, 10:1593–94.

232. *DHRC*, 10:1658–60, 1687–88.

233. *DHRC*, 10:1587–88.

234. Madison to Coxe, June 11, 1788, in *DHRC*, 10:1595–96.

235. Madison to King, June 13, 1788, in *DHRC*, 10:1618–19.

236. Madison to Washington, June 13, 1788, in *DHRC*, 10:1619–20. Although still weakened by a "bilious attack," Madison not only delivered several long speeches in the convention but wrote numerous letters to his friends and allies. Hamilton alone received seven communications from Madison, keeping him informed about the progress of the Virginia convention.

237. Bland to Arthur Lee, June 13, 1788, in *DHRC*, 10:1617–18.

238. See nn. 212 and 213, above.

239. Henry to Lamb, June 9, 1788, in *DHRC*, 18:39–40.

240. Mason to Lamb, June 9, 1788, in *DHRC*, 18:40–45.

241. Boyd, *Politics of Opposition*, 127–30.

242. Yates to Mason, Poughkeepsie, June 21, 1788, in *DHRC*, 9:825.

243. The navigation on the Mississippi River was debated on June 12 and 13 (*DHRC*, 10:1179–1258). Grayson returned to this problem in his speech of June 19 (*DHRC*, 10:1387–88).

244. *DHRC*, 9:989–998 (June 6); *DHRC*, 9:1028–35 (June 7); *DHRC*, 9:1142–54 (June 11); *DHRC*, 10:1222–26 (June 12); *DHRC*, 10:1239–42 (June 13); *DHRC*, 10:1272–74, 1282–84, 1287–89, 1294–96 (June 14); *DHRC*, 10:1301–3, 1311–12, 1323 (June 16); *DHRC*, 10:1338–40, 1343–45 (June 17); *DHRC*, 10:1376–78 (June 18).

245. *DHRC*, 10:1398–1401.

246. *DHRC*, 10:1407–9. Antifederalist hopes to win over all eight delegates from the counties of Ohio, Monongalia, Harrison, and Randolph received a blow when Zachariah Johnston, who was held in high regard in that region, declared himself in favor of ratification (John Vaughan to John Langdon, Philadelphia, June 16, 1788, in *DHRC*, 10:1631–32).

247. *DHRC*, 10:1412–19.

248. Morris to Alexander Hamilton, June 13, 1788, in *DHRC,* 10:1622.

249. Madison to Hamilton, June 22, 1788, in *DHRC,* 10:1665–66.

250. Madison to Washington, June 23, 1788, in *DHRC,* 10:1668–69. Mason had stated in the convention that the adoption of the Constitution "could not but be productive of the most alarming consequences. He dreaded popular resistance to its operation."

251. *DHRC,* 10:1473–81, 1512–15.

252. *DHRC,* 10:1498–1504.

253. One delegate, David Patteson of Chesterfield, voted with Antifederalists on amendments but sided with Federalists on ratification (*DHRC,* 10:1515, 1538–41).

254. *DHRC,* 10:1537.

255. *DHRC,* 10:1545–47.

256. *DHRC,* 10:1514–15. See also n. 240, above.

257. *DHRC,* 10:1556–57. See also Risjord, *Chesapeake Politics,* 305–6.

258. Archibald Stuart to John Breckinridge, Charlottesville, June 30, 1788, in *DHRC,* 10:1696. The convention debates and resolutions of June 27 are printed in *DHRC,* 10: 1550–59.

259. *DHRC,* 10:1560–62. See also Madison to King, June 25, 1788; Madison to Washington, June 25 and 27; and Madison to Hamilton, June 27, in *DHRC,* 10:1676, 1688–89; and Rowland, *Life of Mason* 2:273–74.

260. Madison to Washington, June 27, 1788, in *DHRC,* 10:1688–89.

261. Corbin to Benjamin Rush, July 2, 1788, in *DHRC,* 10:1697.

262. *DHRC,* 10:1674; and see n. 225, above. The New York *Independent Journal* reported Virginia's ratification on July 2 in an "extraordinary" issue. In Poughkeepsie, the news was disseminated by way of a broadside.

263. For a balanced account of the Poughkeepsie convention on the basis of all available sources, see Kaminski, *George Clinton,* 148–66. See also Kaminski, "New York: The Reluctant Pillar," in Schechter, *Reluctant Pillar,* 48–117; Schechter and Bernstein, *New York and the Union,* 226–422; and Rutland, *Ordeal,* 235–45, 254–66.

264. *The Debates and Proceedings of the Constitutional Convention of the State of New York Assembled at Poughkeepsie on the 17th June* (Poughkeepsie, N.Y., 1905; originally published by Francis Childs, 1788); *Journal of the Proceedings of the Convention of the State of New York, 1788* (New York, 1788). See also Elliot, *Debates,* vol. 2; and Syrett, 5:11–196.

265. Hamilton to John Sullivan, New York, June 6, 1788, in *DHRC,* 20:1126.

266. Lansing to Yates, Poughkeepsie, June 19, 1788, Gansevoort-Lansing Papers, NN; Lansing to A. Yates, Albany, June 22, 1788, in *DHRC,* 21:1208; Gelston to John Smith, New York, June 21, 1788, J. Smith Misc. Mss., NHi; Robert Yates to George Mason, Poughkeepsie, June 21, 1788, Emmet Collection, NN.

267. Convention Debates, June 20 and 21, 1788.

268. Richard B. Morris, "John Jay and the Adoption of the Federal Constitution in New York: A New Reading of Persons and Events," *New York History* 63 (1982): 133–64.

269. Syrett, 5:140–41.

270. DeWitt Clinton to Charles Tillinghast, Poughkeepsie, July 12, 1788, DeWitt Clinton Papers, Columbia University.

271. Syrett, 5:149, 156; Kaminski, "Reluctant Pillar," 108.

272. Abraham Bancker to Evert Bancker, Poughkeepsie, July 18, 1788, Bancker Family Papers, NHi.

273. Yates to George Clinton, New York, June 27, 1788, Yates Papers, NN.

274. Abraham G. Lansing to Abraham Yates Jr., Albany, July 20, 1788, Yates Papers, NN.

275. Smith to Dane, June 28, 1788, Dane Papers, Beverly Historical Society; Dane to Smith, July 3, 1788, in *DHRC,* 21:1254–59.

276. Osgood to Smith and Jones, July 11, 1788, in *DHRC,* 21:1308–10; Smith to Dane [ca. July 15, 1788], J. Wingate Thornton Collection, New England Historic Genealogical Society.

277. Hamilton to Madison, July 19, 1788, in Syrett, 5:177–78, 184–85; Madison to Hamilton, July 20, 1788, in Rutland, 11:188–89.

278. Isaac Roosevelt to Richard Varick, Poughkeepsie, June 22 [or 23], 1788, Franklin D. Roosevelt Collection, Roosevelt Library, Hyde Park, N.Y.

279. Convention Debates, July 23, 1788. See also Syrett, 5:193–95, and the map of New York on the convention vote, in *DHRC,* endpapers.

280. According to the Poughkeepsie *Country Journal* of July 29, after the vote on ratification, Governor Clinton "addressed the Convention very politely: the purport of which was, that until a convention was called to consider the amendments now recommended by this convention, the probability was, that the body of the people who are opposed to the constitution, would not be satisfied—he would however, as far as his power and influence would extend, endeavour to keep up peace and good order among them: To which the members and spectators were very attentive—and more than a common pleasantness appeared in their countenance" (*DHRC,* 18:296).

281. *DHRC,* 18:297–305. New among the recommendatory amendments was, e.g., the right of state legislatures to recall senators during their term of office in Congress.

282. *DHRC,* 18:306–7. The circular letter appeared in the Poughkeepsie *Country Journal* on August 5, and was reprinted in at least forty-two newspapers by the end of September.

283. Convention Journal, July 26, 1788.

284. For the Albany riot, see *DHRC,* 21:1264–75.

285. As early as May 29, John Jay had informed Washington that the idea was taking root "that the Southern part of the State will at all Events adhere to the Union, and if necessary to that End seek a Separation from the northern. This Idea has Influence on the Fears of the [Antifederalist] Party" (Jay to Washington, New York, in *DHRC,* 20:1119). On June 8, Hamilton told Madison that New York Federalists planned to respond to a rejection of the Constitution with a "separation of the Southern district from the other part of the state" (*DHRC,* 20:1135). During the Poughkeepsie convention, this motive reappeared in several speeches, in newspaper articles, and also in private letters written by members of both parties.

286. William Shippen predicted in late July, that one of the consequences of New York's rejection of the Constitution would be "that Congress will come here—and the new Government will be fixed here also." In August, he still believed that Philadelphia "must finally be the place" (William Shippen to Thomas Lee Shippen, Philadelphia, June 29 and August 21, 1788, Shippen Family Papers, DLC; see also "A Pennsylvanian" [Tench

Coxe], *Pennsylvania Gazette,* June 11, 1788; and Webb to Catherine Hogeboom, New York, July 13, 1788, in *DHRC,* 21:1314).

287. Webb to Hogeboom, July 27, 1788, in Ford, *Correspondence,* 3:112–13; Schuyler to Van Schaack, Poughkeepsie, July 25, 1788, New York State Library; Carrington to William Short, New York, July 26, 1788, Short Papers, DLC.

288. Schoonmaker to Peter Van Gaasbeek, Poughkeepsie, July 25, 1788, in Marius Schoonmaker, *The History of Kingston* (New York, 1888), 394–96.

289. Platt to William Smith, Poughkeepsie, July 28, 1788, Manor of St. George, Museum.

290. Lansing to Yates, August 3, 1788, Yates Papers, NN.

291. Gerry to Ann Gerry, Newport, July 28, 1788, Gerry Papers, MHi; Mason to John Mason, Gunston Hall, September 2, 1788, Rutland, in *Mason,* 3:1128–29.

292. Seth Johnson to Andrew Craigie, July 27, 1788, Craigie Papers, MWA; Knox to Washington, New York, July 28, 1788, in *Washington Papers, Confederation Series,* 6:405.

293. Madison to Edmund Randolph, New York, August 22, 1788, in Rutland, 11:237–38; Madison to Washington, August 24, 1788, in *DHRC,* 18:343–45.

294. Richard Dobbs Spaight to Levi Hollingsworth, New Bern, July 3, 1788, Hollingsworth Papers, PHi.

295. *Virginia Independent Chronicle,* August 20, 1788.

296. Journal of the Convention, held at Hillsborough, July–August 1788, Nc-Ar. A good report is contained in a letter written by John Wilson to his brother, the Reverend Samuel Wilson, August 18, 1788, in the L. C. Glenn Papers, Southern Historical Collection, University of North Carolina. See also Charles L. Raper, "Why North Carolina at First Refused to Ratify the Federal Constitution," *American Historical Association* 1 (1895): 99–108.

297. See Davie to Iredell, Halifax, July 9, 1788, in *Iredell Papers,* 3:408–9; Madison to Jefferson, New York, August 23, 1788, in Rutland, 11:238–39.

298. Convention Journal, August 2, 1788; Samuel Johnson to N.C. Delegates in Congress, August 25, 1788, Governors' Letterbooks and Papers, Nc-Ar; James Gordon to Madison, Germanna, Va., August 31, 1788, in Rutland, 11:245–46.

299. North Carolina Declaration of Rights, August 1, 1788, Broadside, Executive Papers, Delaware Hall of Records, Dover. The newspaper version, which appeared first in the *Wilmington Centinel* on August 20, 1788, was reprinted by twenty-three newspapers in ten states.

300. John Langdon to Nathaniel Gilman, Portsmouth, N.H., August 25, 1788, Personal Papers Misc., DLC. Jeremiah Hill used biblical language to convey his sense of indignation over the renegade state: "She hath lost her first Love, She hath gone a whoring after strange Gods, She hath polluted herself by her abominations, She hath lapsed from her original, primitive purety, let her alone, let her wallow in her filth, let her eat her swine husks till her poverty and Starvation cause her to look back to her federal Fathers, and sing the prodigal Song" (Hill to George Thatcher, Biddeford, Maine, August 29, 1788, Thatcher Papers, MHi).

301. "A Republican" (Hugh Williamson), New York *Daily Advertiser,* September 17, 1788. Privately, Williamson remained convinced "that a Want of honesty is at the Bottom with many of our Oppositionists" (Williamson to Iredell, September 22, 1788, in *Iredell Papers,* 3:440). See also John Swann to Iredell, New York, September 21, 1788 (*Iredell*

Papers, 3:438–39); and George Thatcher to William Thatcher, New York, September 19, 1788 (Thatcher Papers, MHi).

302. "We are now independent of all nations and states, our own not excepted," commented "ANTIFED. Senior" sarcastically in the *State Gazette of North Carolina* on November 3, 1788.

303. Davie to Iredell, Halifax, September 8, 1788, in *Iredell Papers,* 3:432; [Member of Tipton Party] to "Dear Sir," August 20, 1788, Draper Papers, WiHi; Amariah Jocelin to Jeremiah Wadsworth, Wilmington, October 1788, Wadsworth Correspondence, CtHi.

304. Davie to Iredell, Halifax, September 8, 1788 and November 1788; and Maclaine to Iredell, Wilmington, September 13, 1788, in *Iredell Papers,* 3:432, 457–58, 239–40; County Petitions in North Carolina State Papers, Duke University Library. See also Risjord, *Chesapeake Politics,* 337–41.

305. North Carolina Resolve Calling New Convention, November 21, 1788, North Carolina State Papers, Ratification of the Constitution, Duke University Library.

306. Williamson to Madison, Edenton, May 24, 1789, in Rutland, 12:183–84; Williamson to Nicholas Gilman, Edenton, May 28, 1789, Chamberlain Collection, Boston Public Library; *Massachusetts Centinel,* September 3, 1789; "A Citizen and Soldier": To the People of the District of Edenton (Newbern, 1788), reprinted in *State Gazette of North Carolina,* September 22, 1789.

307. The *State Gazette of North Carolina* had already warned on June 4, 1789: "We are doubtless to be considered as foreigners with whom there is not any commercial treaty, and in this case our vessels must pay the duty of half a dollar the ton in every port of the United States." In Congress, however, Williamson succeeded in winning a temporary exception from the law for North Carolina.

308. Printed in *State Gazette of North Carolina,* July 9, 1788.

309. Davie to Madison, Halifax, June 10, 1789, in Rutland, 12:210–12.

310. In Tennessee, as well as in Kentucky and Maine, the conviction was growing that the Constitution, instead of being an obstacle, would actually improve the chances for separate statehood under the Union (Risjord, *Chesapeake Politics,* 341, 641n73).

311. Journal of the Convention held at Fayette-Ville, November 1789, Nc-Ar. See also Albert R. Newsome, "North Carolina's Ratification of the Federal Constitution," *North Carolina Historical Review,* 17 (1940): 287–301.

312. Risjord, *Chesapeake Politics,* 340, 642n72.

313. Coxe to Hamilton, December 16, 1789, in Syrett, 6:11–13.

314. Madison to Johnston, New York, June 21, 1789, in Rutland, 12:249–51.

315. Pierce Butler to Iredell, August 11, 1789, in *Iredell Papers,* 3:511–12.

316. John P. Kaminski, "Political Sacrifice and Demise: John Collins and Jonathan J. Hazard, 1786–1790," *Rhode Island History* 35 (1976): 91–98.

317. Adam Stephen to Madison, Berkeley County, Va., September 12, 1789, in Rutland, 12:398–99; *Massachusetts Centinel,* October 29, 1788. Derogatory terms for Rhode Island included "the wandering sister," "our stray sister," "our little perverse sister," and "little W-h-r." John Adams thought that Rhode Island was "too small a part of America to dictate to all the rest." He gave the advice, however, to win its citizens over through "mildness and condescention" (Adams to Jabez Bowen, New York, May 18, 1789; and Adams to Henry Marchant, September 17, 1789, Adams Papers, MHi).

318. Bowen to Adams, Providence, May 19, 1789; and Adams to Bowen, New York, September 18, 1789, Adams Papers, MHi.

319. Coxe to Madison, Philadelphia, March 21 and 31, and April 6, 1790, in Rutland, 13:111, 130–33, 141.

320. Bowen to Adams, Providence, July 22, 1789, and February 15, 1790, Adams Papers, MHi.

321. Bowen to Adams, December 28, 1789, Adams Papers, MHi.

322. Marchant to Adams, Newport, January 18, 1790, and to William Marchant, January 25, 1790, Marchant Papers, RiHi. See also Kaminski, "Political Sacrifice," 93.

323. Robert C. Cotner, ed., *Theodore Foster, Minutes of the Rhode Island Convention,* 1–6 March 1790 (Providence, R.I., 1929; repr., New York, 1970); Staples, *Rhode Island in the Continental Congress,* 640–54.

324. Bowen to John Adams, Providence, February 15, 1790, Adams Papers, MHi; Ellery to Benjamin Huntington, Newport, March 8, 1790, Ellery Letters, RiHi.

325. *Providence Gazette,* June 13, 1789; *Federal Gazette,* April 5 and 6, 1790.

326. Bassett to George Read, New York, March 1, 1790, Richard S. Rodney Collection of Read Papers, Delaware Historical Society.

327. *The Diary of William Maclay,* ed. Kenneth R. Bowling and Helen E. Veit (Baltimore, 1988), entries for May 11, 14, and 18, 1790 (pp. 264, 268, 270–71).

328. Oliver Ellsworth to his wife, New York, June 7, 1790, CtHi.

329. Benson to Sedgwick, Providence, May 21, 1790, Sedgwick Papers, MHi.

330. Channing to Foster, Newport, May 18, 1790, Foster Papers, RiHi; Foster to Channing, Providence, May 24, 1790, Channing-Ellery Papers, RiHi.

331. John Brown and John Francis to Washington, Providence, June 11, 1790, Washington Papers, DLC.

332. Daniel Updike's "Journal of the Proceedings in Rhode Island Convention, 25–29 May 1790, With Form of Ratification and Proposed Amendments," in Staples, *Rhode Island in the Continental Congress,* 659–80. The Form of Ratification was printed as a broadside on May 31 under the title: "Rhode Island and Providence Plantation united to the Great AMERICAN FAMILY" (Evans 22847).

333. Vernon to Jeremiah Wadsworth, Newport, June 5, 1790, Wadsworth Correspondence, CtHi.

334. Louis Guillaume Otto to Comte de Montmorin, New York, June 1, 1790, Henry Adams Transcripts, French State Papers, Otto, 1789–1791, DLC. See also Madison to Monroe, New York, June 1, 1790, in Rutland, 13:233–34.

335. Quoted in "The Adjustment of Rhode Island into the Union in 1790," Rhode Island Historical Society *Publications* 8 (1900): 110–11.

336. Washington to Fenner, New York, June 4, 1790, in *Washington Papers: Presidential Series,* 5:470; Adams to Marchant, New York, June 1, 1790, Misc. Mss., RiHi.

337. Otto to Montmorin, June 1, 1790, Henry Adams Transcripts, French State Papers, Otto, 1789–1791, DLC.

338. Wynkoop to Cornelius Ten Brock, Hurley, N.Y., July 1, 1788, Ten Brock Papers, Rutgers University Library.

339. Sullivan to Adams, Boston, July 2, 1789, Adams Papers, MHi.

6. Republican Festive Culture

1. Whitfield J. Bell, "The Federal Processions of 1788," New-York Historical Society *Quarterly* 46 (1962): 38. See also Kenneth Silverman, *A Cultural History of the American Revolution* (New York, 1976), 570–87. For a more systematic approach to this phenomenon, see Jürgen Heideking, "The Federal Processions of 1788 and the Origins of American Civil Religion," *Soundings* 77 (1994): 367–87.

2. Belknap to Ebenezer Hazard, Boston, May 15, 1788, in *Correspondence between Jeremy Belknap and Ebenezer Hazard,* 3:39–41. Antifederalist Abraham Yates resented the continuous bell-ringing in New York City as "uselessly irritating and Improper in the Situation we are in" (Yates to Abraham G. Lansing, June 29, 1788, in *DHRC,* 21:1240).

3. Henry Jackson to Henry Knox, Boston, February 6, 1788, in *DHRC,* 21:1580.

4. Adams Diary, February 7–8, 1788, in *DHRC,* 7:1633.

5. "Light horsemen, artillery, etc., etc., mustered and going out to meet his Excellency, President Langdon" (Jeremiah Libby to Jeremy Belknap, Portsmouth, June 23, 1788, Belknap Papers, 3:412, MHi).

6. Williams to Dr. Philip Thomas, Baltimore, May 14, 1788, Williams Papers, MdHi.

7. Letter from Talbot, Maryland, *Pennsylvania Packet,* July 22, 1788; *Newport Herald,* July 3 and 31, 1788; Philadelphia *Federal Gazette,* June 4, 1790.

8. Philadelphia merchant Levi Hollingsworth received mail from his customer Jacob Broom of Wilmington, N.C.: "I congratulate you on the adoption of the Fœderal Constitution by Virginia—an event of vast Importance to the United States, the present generation and their posterity; for tho' it will be but the 1/13 spoke in the Wheel of Government it is an important one" (Broom to Hollingsworth, July 2, 1788, Hollingsworth Papers, PHi). The Philadelphia firm of Coxe and Frazier expected that "the administration of Justice thro[u]out the Union will be as certain & perfect as the Courts of Great Britain, which alone can establish us in the Confidence of foreign Countries." They hoped that Philadelphia would "become the Seat of the new Government which will encrease the Demand for West India Articles, & will have a favorable effect . . . on business in general" (Coxe and Frazier to James O'Neal, July 10, 1788; and Coxe and Frazier to Stephen Blackett, July 11, 1788, in *DHRC,* 18:255–56).

9. Annapolis *Maryland Gazette,* May 8, 1788; Providence *United States Chronicle,* July 31, 1788.

10. *Pennsylvania Packet,* July 22, 1788; Charleston *City Gazette,* June 19, 1788.

11. Charleston *State Gazette of South Carolina,* January 25, 1790.

12. *Newport Herald,* July 10, 1788.

13. The first toast was to "the United States of America," the second to "the Western world, perpetual Union, on principles of equality, or amicable Separation." No love was lost for Indians, however: "May the Savage enemies of America, be chastised by arms" (*Kentucky Gazette,* July 5, 1788, in *DHRC,* 10:1730–31).

14. Celebration in Fredericksburg, *Maryland Journal,* July 11, 1788.

15. Washington to Tobias Lear, Mount Vernon, June 29, 1788, in *DHRC,* 10:1715–16. The festive echo of Virginia's ratification is fully documented in *DHRC,* 10:1709–59.

16. *Connecticut Journal,* July 9, 1788; and *Norfolk and Portsmouth Journal,* July 9, 1788, in *DHRC,* 10:1732–36.

17. *State Gazette of North Carolina,* December 3, 1789.

18. *Federal Gazette,* March 8, 1788; Webb to Joseph Barrell, New York, February 17, 1788, in *DHRC,* 7:1641–42; Hazard to Belknap, New York, July 17, 1788, in *DHRC,* 21:1323. A participant of celebrations in Pittsfield in western Massachusetts rhymed: "And 'twas not look'd upon as sinful / that every man should drink his skin ful" (Louie M. Miner, *Our Rude Forefathers: American Political Verse, 1783–1788* [Cedar Rapids, Iowa, 1937], 253).

19. Jeremy Belknap, *Notes of Debates, January 9 to February 6, 1788,* in *DHRC,* 7:1597–98; Knox to Robert R. Livingston, New York, February 13, 1788, Livingston Papers, NHi.

20. James Buchanan to Tench Coxe, Baltimore, April 29, 1788, Coxe Papers, PHi; Jeremiah Libby to Jeremy Belknap, Portsmouth, June 23, 1788, Belknap Papers, 3:412, MHi.

21. *Providence Gazette,* July 12, 1788.

22. Silverman, *Cultural History,* 420–21, 541.

23. Shippen to Thomas Lee Shippen, December 12, 1788, in *DHRC,* 2:601.

24. *DHRC,* 2:591, 600–602, 609, 646–51.

25. The delegates formally thanked the tradesmen's committee on February 11: "We are happy to find that our decisions have so fully corresponded with the sentiments and wishes of our constituents" (*Massachusetts Centinel,* February 13, 1788, in *DHRC,* 7:1626–27).

26. Detailed report in *Massachusetts Centinel,* February 13, 1788, in *DHRC,* 7:1623–24.

27. Jackson to Knox, February 13, 1788, in *DHRC,* 7:1626; *Massachusetts Centinel,* February 13, 1788, in *DHRC,* 7:1628.

28. Samuel Salisbury to Stephen Salisbury, Boston, February 10, 1788, Salisbury Papers, MWA; Isaac Winslow Jr., to Knox, Boston, February 10, 1788, Knox Papers, Gilder-Lehrman Collection on deposit at the New-York Historical Society; Rev. James Cogswell Diary, February 22, 1788, CtHi.

29. Jackson to Knox, Boston, February 10, 1788, in *DHRC,* 7:1614; Lincoln to Washington, February 9, 1788, in *DHRC,* 7:1624.

30. Charles Willson Peale, *Autobiography,* 125–27, PPAmP; Daniel Carroll to Madison, Georgetown, April 28, 1788, in Rutland, 11:30–31; *Maryland Journal,* May 2, 1788.

31. In a letter to Tench Coxe, James Buchanan announced "great doings allmode de Boston" (Buchanan to Coxe, Baltimore, April 28, 1788, Coxe Papers, PHi).

32. Thomas and Samuel Hollingsworth to Levi Hollingsworth, Baltimore, April 27–28, 1788, Hollingsworth Papers, PHi.

33. The colorful report in the *Maryland Journal* of May 6, 1788, was soon reprinted by twenty-two newspapers all over the Union.

34. Washington to William Smith et al., June 8, 1788, in *Washington Papers: Confederation Series,* 6:322–23; entries for June 9 and July 24, 1788, in *The Diaries of George Washington,* ed. by Donald Jackson and Dorothy Twohig, 6 vols. (Charlottesville, Va., 1976–79), 5:339, 366.

35. William Evans, Bill for Federal Expenses, Enoch Pratt Free Library, Baltimore; *Massachusetts Gazette,* May 23, 1788.

36. Hollingsworth to Levi Hollingsworth, Elkton, May 6, 1788, Hollingsworth Papers, PHi; Pringle to John Holker, Baltimore, May 4, 1788, Misc. Mss. Collection, CtY.

37. St. John de Crèvecoeur to William Short, New York, June 10, 1788, in *DHRC,* 18: 174–75.

38. Descriptions of the "Grand Procession" were given on May 29 in the Charleston *State Gazette* and the *Columbian Herald.* The latter report, featuring the "Order of March," was taken up by thirty-four newspapers in most of the states. A letter published in the Charleston *City Gazette,* also on May 29, foreshadowed important economic changes: "The people in the back parts of this state, are very anxious to get the machines for ginning, carding and spinning cotton. . . . Each state must play into each others hands as much as possible . . . which will cement us together, so that we shall be not nominally but really an united people."

39. "We have not observed this rank in either of the former Processions," the *Salem Mercury* in Massachusetts told its readers on June 10.

40. Ramsay to Benjamin Lincoln, June 20, 1788, Lincoln Papers, MHi. The text of the oration was published in the *Columbian Herald* on June 5, and somewhat later it also appeared as a twelve-page pamphlet (*DHRC,* 18:158–65).

41. Charleston *Columbian Herald,* May 29, 1788.

42. "New Hampshire Federal Procession," *New Hampshire Gazette,* June 26, 1788. "We have copied your State in having a procession, but a Boston gentleman who was present told me we really exceeded you" (Jeremiah Libby to Jeremy Belknap, June 30, 1788, Belknap Papers 3:414–15, MHi).

43. Thomas Willing to William Bingham, June 29, 1788, Gratz Collection, PHi. Three days after the event, the *Pennsylvania Packet* boasted that the parade "far exceeded the expectations of all who saw it, and that in the opinion of men of taste, both citizens and foreigners, it has seldom been surpassed in Europe, and never equalled in America." A recent interpretation is Laura Rigal, "'Raising the Roof': Authors, Spectators and Artisans in the Grand Federal Procession of 1788," *Theatre Journal* 48 (1996): 253–77.

44. *DHRC,* 18:246–49. Hopkinson was also the author of the official "Account of the Grand Federal Procession," which appeared simultaneously, on July 9, 1788, in the *Pennsylvania Gazette, Pennsylvania Journal,* and *Pennsylvania Packet* (later published as a pamphlet; see Evans 21149, 21150). A German translation under the title "Die grosse Bundesschaftliche Proceszion" was provided by the editors of the *Gemeinnützige Philadelphische Correspondenz* on July 15, 1788. Another detailed description was given by Benjamin Rush, in the form of a letter, "Observations on the Fourth of July Procession in Philadelphia" (*Pennsylvania Mercury,* July 15, 1788, in *DHRC,* 18:261–69).

45. The last verses referred to the "roof" metaphor which Hopkinson had popularized with his allegorical work "The New Roof" and his poem "The Raising: A New Song for Federal Mechanics." One of the floats at the parade was also called "THE NEW ROOF, OR GRAND FŒDERAL EDIFICE."

46. "James Wilson's Notes of Address On Occasion of Procession in Honor of Pennsylvania's Adoption of the Constitution," July 4, 1788, Wilson Papers, PHi; excerpts are printed in *DHRC,* 18:242–46.

47. William Shippen Jr. to Thomas Lee Shippen, Philadelphia, June 28, 1788, Shippen Family Papers, DLC.

48. *DHRC,* 18:268.

49. *Pennsylvania Mercury,* July 15, 1788.

50. *New Jersey Journal,* July 16, 1788. In response to such claims, Benjamin Russell took it upon himself to remind the public of the birthplace of the republican festivals:

"Boston does not stand in the lowest grade of Processional rank. It must be considered . . . that it was here the production of originality—performed in the winter season" (*Massachusetts Centinel,* July 23, 1788).

51. August 30, 1788, in Boyd, 13:551. See also Hopkinson to Jefferson, July 17, 1788 (ibid., 13:369–71).

52. "We had need to rejoice with trembling, as it is more than probable if this State should reject the constitution, it will occasion a civil war" (Jedidiah Morse to his father, New York, July 22, 1788, in *DHRC,* 21:1334).

53. *DHRC,* 18:290–92. Samuel Low's comedy *The Politician Out-Witted,* which played in New York City during 1788–89, was squarely set in the context of the ratification debate. The political controversy over the Constitution is alienating two families and almost prevents the marriage of their offspring. At the end, however, the loving couple concludes for themselves that of all constitutions the constitution of matrimony is most important (Silverman, *Cultural History,* 577–78).

54. Official report, written by Noah Webster and signed by Richard Platt, August 2, 1788, New York *Independent Journal* and New York *Daily Advertiser.* See also Sarah H. Simpson, "The Federal Procession in the City of New York," New-York Historical Society *Quarterly* 9 (1925): 39–57; Richard Leffler, "The Grandest Procession," *Seaport: New York's History Magazine* 21 (1987/88): 28–31; and Paul A. Gilje, "The Common People and the Constitution: Popular Culture in New York City in the Late Eighteenth-Century," in *New York in the Age of the Constitution, 1775–1800,* ed. Paul A. Gilje and William Pencak (Rutherford-Madison, N.J., 1992), 48–73.

55. This good deed was probably initiated by Platt himself, who served as secretary of the Society for Distressed Prisoners (Simpson, "Federal Procession," 53). In his capacity as treasurer of the New York chapter of the Society of the Cincinnati, Platt had participated in a 4th of July celebration in City Hall. The presiding officers at that occasion were Friedrich Wilhelm Baron von Steuben and Alexander Hamilton.

56. Bancker to Abraham Bancker, July 24, 1788, in *DHRC,* 21:1338; Webb to Catherine Hogeboom, July 25, 1788, in *DHRC,* 21:1619; Webster Diary, July 23, 1788, in *DHRC,* 21:1604.

57. *New York Journal,* July 24, 1788, in *DHRC,* 21:1614–17.

58. Letter from New York, August 2, 1788; and *Maryland Journal,* August 19, 1788, in *DHRC,* 21:1666.

59. William Nivison to Thomas Ruston, Suffolk, Va., July 9, 1788, Coxe Papers, PHi. As part of Norfolk's celebration, "a Balloon (constructed by Mr. Balfour) ascended, amidst the acclamation of a numerous group of spectators" (*Virginia Gazette and Winchester Advertiser,* July 2, 1788; *Norfolk and Portsmouth Journal,* July 2, 1788).

60. *Pennsylvania Mercury,* July 15, 1788.

61. Baltimore *Maryland Gazette,* July 8, 1788.

62. *United States Chronicle,* July 17, 1788, printed in Kaminski, *A Necessary Evil?,* 114.

63. H. T. Emery to Mary Carter, Boston, February 10, 1788, Cutts Family Papers, Essex Institute Library.

64. Hill to Thatcher, Boston, February 14 and 28, 1788, in *DHRC,* 7:1696, 1716; Widgery to Thatcher, February 9, 1788, in *DHRC,* 7:1690; Belknap to Benjamin Rush, June 22, 1788, Rush Papers, Library Company of Philadelphia.

65. Report from Kingston, Ulster Co., *New York Journal,* July 12, 1788, in *DHRC,* 21:1282.

66. The "Carlisle Riot" and its aftermath is documented in *DHRC,* 2:670–725.

67. The affair was followed by a bitter dispute in the newspapers. State Justice William West defended the Antifederalists' actions, arguing that to honor the Constitution was to insult the state of Rhode Island and the vast majority of its citizens, who had rejected the proposed system in a March referendum. He even went so far as to offer examples of more fitting toasts: "1. Confusion to all usurpers and tyrants throughout the thirteen States. 2. The old Confederation, with proper amendments. 3. May the sons of freedom in America never submit to despotic Government. 4. May each State retain their sovereignty in the full extent of republican Governments. . . . 8. May we have well-regulated militia in lieu of standing armies. . . . 13. May the Merchants and Landholders be convinced their interest depends on the support of each other." Outraged over West's article, Federalists denounced the illegal restriction of democratic liberties, the corruptness of civil servants who acted like gang leaders, and the general state of lawlessness in Rhode Island: "Unhappy indeed are the times in which we are fallen, when armed violence is preferred to the laws of the land, even by those whose duty it is to administer them" (see *United States Chronicle,* July 10, 1788; *Connecticut Gazette,* July 11, 1788; *Providence Gazette,* July 12, 1788; and *Newport Herald,* July 17 and 24, 1788).

68. New York *Daily Advertiser,* July 10, 1788, in *DHRC,* 21:1266–67. For the Antifederal point of view, see "Extract of a letter from Albany, July 6," *New York Journal,* July 14, 1788, in *DHRC,* 21:1267–69.

69. However, Abraham G. Lansing's colorful description of the Albany procession reveals his fascination with republican festive culture (Lansing to Abraham Yates Jr., Albany, August 3, 1788, Yates Papers, NN).

70. Some private letters contain speculations about the outbreak of open hostilities. Should New Hampshire reject the Constitution, wrote Nicholas Gilman to John Sullivan, he was "apprehensive the sword will be drawn and your Excellency's early predictions be verified" (New York, March 23, 1788, N.H. Misc. [Peter Force], DLC). "At present the City and lower part of the State seem resolved to defend the constitution by force," reported Richard Penn Hicks from New York City (Hicks to John Dickinson, July 15, 1788, Logan Papers, PHi). The possibility of a civil war was discussed in Victor Du Pont to Pierre Samuel Du Pont de Nemours, New York, July 1–26, 1788, Eleutherian Mills Hist. Library. Antifederalist "counter-celebrations" in the backcountry, featuring the burning or symbolic burying of the Constitution, reminded nervous Federalists of Shays's Rebellion and earlier agrarian uprisings.

71. Roane to Philip Aylett, Richmond, June 26, 1788, in *DHRC,* 10:1713.

72. Letter from an Alexandria gentleman, June 30, 1788, published in the *Connecticut Gazette,* July 11, 1788, in *DHRC,* 10:1713n. On July 4th, Richmond's citizens celebrated Independence Day but toasted also to "the civil revolution of the year 1788" (*DHRC,* 10:1743–44).

73. New York City's Federal Procession reminded Virginian John Randolph of Roanoke of the preparations "which were made in Don Quixote for the wedding of Camacho and the rich and the fair Quiteria" (Randolph to St. George Tucker, New York, July 30, 1788, in *DHRC,* 21:1625). Antifederalist newspapers associated the constant ringing of

bells with death and funerals: "On Saturday last a gentleman observed to his friend that the bells were ringing; his friend requested to know the reason; on which he replied,—that they rung 'for the funeral of the liberties of Maryland'" ("A Subscriber," *New York Journal*, May 5, 1788). Eleazer Oswald's Philadelphia *Independent Gazetteer* reduced Boston's parade to the mock verses of *The Contract*: "There they went up, up, up, / And there they went down, down, downy, / There they went backwards and forwards, / And poop for Boston towny!" (Philadelphia *Independent Gazetteer*, February 19, 1788; see also Silverman, *Cultural History*, 576). Greenleaf's satirical remark that during New York's procession the potters had been "accidentally separated from their clay" triggered the attack on his print shop (*New York Journal*, July 24 and 25, 1788, in *DHRC*, 21:1614–17).

74. Letters from Charleston, May 27 and June 20, 1788, New York *Daily Advertiser*, June 7 and July 7, 1788.

75. Schuyler to John B. Schuyler, Poughkeepsie, June 26, 1788, Bancroft Papers, MHi; see also Samuel A. Otis to George Thatcher, New York, July 17, 1788, in *DHRC*, 21:1323.

76. New York *Independent Journal*, Extraordinary, July 28, 1788.

77. Poughkeepsie *Country Journal*, August 19, 1788; *New Hampshire Spy*, May 10, 1788.

78. *Wilmington Centinel*, July 16 and August 20, 1788.

79. *Pennsylvania Gazette*, July 2, 1788; *Federal Post*, July 8, 1788; *Maryland Journal*, May 2, 1788.

80. Washington's address of June 8, 1788, published in the Baltimore *Maryland Gazette*, June 24, 1788.

81. *Maryland Journal*, May 6, 1788; Henry Hollingsworth to Levi Hollingsworth, Elkton, May 6, 1788, Hollingsworth Papers, PHi.

82. Toast of the artisans' committee in Boston, *Independent Chronicle*, February 14, 1788, in *DHRC*, 7:1630–31.

83. Baltimore *Maryland Gazette*, November 4, 1788.

84. In 1789, the "Providence Association of Mechanics and Manufacturers" tried to coordinate its lobbying activities with those of similar organizations in Connecticut and New York (letters of April 30, 1789 to New London and New York City, Annie Burr Jennings Memorial Collection, CtY; New York *Daily Advertiser*, May 13, 1789).

85. *United States Chronicle*, July 21, 1788.

86. *DHRC*, 18:262.

87. Belknap to Rush, June 22, 1788, Rush Papers, Library Company of Philadelphia; Rush's "Observation," July 15, 1788, in *DHRC*, 18:266; Jackson, "A Native of Boston" (pamphlet), Worcester, August 14, 1788 (Evans 21173). See also *DHRC*, 18:326–31. On July 18, 1788, John Adams wrote to Arthur Lee: "You and I should not materially differ, I fancy, if we Were to compare Notes of a perfect Commonwealth. But I consider the present Project, as a commencement of a national Government, to be a valuable Acquisition" (*DHRC*, 18:271–72).

88. *DHRC*, 18:268.

89. *Massachusetts Gazette*, January 18, 1788, in *DHRC*, 5:744.

90. *Newport Herald*, July 10, 1788.

91. Robert L. Alexander, "The Grand Federal Edifice," *Documentary Editing* 9 (1987): 13–17. Benjamin Russell's *Massachusetts Centinel* was especially ingenious in making use of the metaphors of dome, temple, and pillars. See also *DHRC*, 10:1746–48, 18:381–83.

92. William Pierce, "An Oration Delivered at Christ Church, Savannah, on the 4th of July, 1788," in *DHRC,* 18:253.

93. *DHRC,* 18:264.

94. Quoted in Foner, *Paine,* 34.

95. Silverman, *Cultural History,* 587–98.

96. Washington to Lafayette, May 28, 1788, in *Washington Papers, Confederation Series,* 6:297–98.

97. Silverman, *Cultural History,* 585.

98. Quoted in Arthur H. Shaffer, *The Politics of History: Writing the History of the American Revolution, 1783–1815* (Chicago, 1975), 31. In his work *On the Education of Youth in America,* Rush advocated in 1790 the construction of a national identity through historical and political education. Every American child should be made familiar with the history of the country and its founding fathers: "As soon as he opens his lips, he should rehearse the history of his country; he should lisp the praise of Liberty and of those illustrious heroes and statesmen who have wrought a revolution in his favor" (41).

99. Oration of July 4, 1788, in *DHRC,* 18:242–46.

100. *Brunswick Gazette,* July 8, 1788.

101. *Pennsylvania Mercury,* July 15, 1788, in *DHRC,* 18:263. Shortly after experiencing the ratification celebrations in America, the French artist Jacques-Louis David became one of the most prominent organizers of revolutionary festivals in France. His aim was to place "the people" in the center of public rituals: "National festivals are instituted for the people; it is fitting that they participate in them with a common accord and that they play the principal role there" (quoted in Silverman, *Cultural History,* 580; see also Mona Ozouf, *Festivals and the French Revolution* [Cambridge, Mass., 1988]).

102. *Maryland Journal,* July 11, 1788. Similar sentiments had already prevailed on the occasion of Pennsylvania's ratification in December 1787: "May America diffuse over Europe a greater portion of political light than she has borrowed from her" (*DHRC,* 2: 607).

103. *Independent Chronicle,* July 10 and 17, 1788.

104. *Maryland Journal,* May 16, 1788.

105. *New Hampshire Spy,* July 12, 1788.

106. *Norfolk and Portsmouth Journal,* July 16, 1789; Charleston *State Gazette of South Carolina,* December 11, 1788.

107. Adams to Abigail Adams, Philadelphia, July 3, 1776, in *Letters of Delegates to Congress, 1774–1789,* ed. Paul H. Smith, 26 vols. (Washington, D.C., 1976–2000), 4:376.

108. Victor Du Pont to Pierre Samuel Du Pont de Nemours, New York, July 26, 1788, in *DHRC,* 18:311n.

109. "A Sermon Preached in Rochester, New Hampshire," November 27, 1788, quoted in Franklin McDuffee, *History of the Town of Rochester, N.H., 1722–1890,* 2 vols. (Manchester, N.H., 1892), 1:147–48.

110. *DHRC,* 18:265.

111. *Massachusetts Centinel,* August 8, 1788.

112. Recently, several studies of American festive culture in the early national period have been published. See especially David Waldstreicher, *In the Midst of Perpetual Fetes: The Making of American Nationalism, 1776–1820* (Chapel Hill, N.C., 1997); Len Trav-

ers, *Celebrating the Fourth: Independence Day and the Rites of Nationalism in the Early Republic* (Amherst, Mass., 1997); and Simon P. Newman, *Parades and the Politics of the Street: Festive Culture in the Early American Republic* (Philadelphia, 1997). The "religious dimension" of American public life concerned Robert N. Bellah in his famous article "Civil Religion in America" (*Daedalus* 96 [1967]: 1–21), which opened a fascinating scholarly debate and inspired much additional historical research. Particularly for the early period, see Catherine L. Albanese, *Sons of the Fathers: The Civil Religion of the American Revolution* (Philadelphia, 1976).

113. When from time to time one of Washington's private letters appeared in a newspaper, it immediately caused a sensation throughout the country (see *DHRC,* 5:788–96).

114. Silverman, *Cultural History,* 428–29.

115. Samuel Adams to Richard Henry Lee, Boston, August 29, 1789, in Harry Alonzo Cushing, *The Writings of Samuel Adams,* 4 vols. (New York, 1904–1908), 4:335–37.

116. *State Gazette of North Carolina,* October 20, 1788.

117. John P. Kaminski and Jill Adair McCaughan, eds., *A Great and Good Man: George Washington in the Eyes of His Contemporaries* (Madison, Wis., 1989).

118. Humphreys to Washington, New Haven, September 28, 1787, in *DHRC,* 13:261–62.

119. Morris to Washington, Philadelphia, October 30, 1787, in *DHRC,* 13:513–14.

120. Tilghman to Tench Coxe, Chester Town, January 25, 1789, Coxe Papers, PHi.

121. Letter drafted by Rev. John Leland, Richmond, May 8–10, 1789, in *The Writings of Elder John Leland,* ed. L. F. Greene (New York, 1845; repr., 1969), 52–54.

122. The following account is based on Silverman, *Cultural History,* 598–608.

123. Washington to Jonathan Trumbull Jr., Mount Vernon, July 20, 1788, in *DHRC,* 18:273–75.

124. Fisher Ames to John Lowell, New York, March 4, 1789, Auction Catalog, Paul C. Richards-Autographs (ca. 1982–83).

125. Quoted in Silverman, *Cultural History,* 607. The *Massachusetts Centinel* published another installment of its popular "Ship News": "The Federal Ship. Just launched on the Ocean of Empire, the Ship Columbia, [GEORGE WASHINGTON, Commander] which, after being thirteen years in dock, is at length well manned, and in very good condition."

126. Quoted in Silverman, *Cultural History,* 599.

127. Thomas Tudor Tucker to St. George Tucker, May 15, 1789, in "Randolph and Tucker Letters," *Virginia Magazine of History and Biography* 42 (1934): 50–52. The Senate's search for a dignified form of address for the president and vice president was also disconcerting for devoted republicans. One of the ideas brought up but finally rejected—much to the disappointment of the Boston printer Benjamin Russell—was "His Majesty the President of the United States" (Joseph T. Buckingham, *Specimens of Newspaper Literature* [Boston, 1850], 57). When Jefferson in Paris heard that Congress had settled on the modest form "the President of the United States," he praised the American government's "genuine dignity . . . in exploding adulatory titles; they are the offerings of abject baseness, and nourish the degrading vice in the people." In the French National Assembly, the simplicity of American titles was considered exemplary (see Rutland, 12:338, 363, 421, 449).

128. Simon P. Newman, "'Principles or Men?' George Washington and the Politi-

cal Culture of National Leadership, 1776–1801," *Journal of the Early Republic* 12 (1992): 477–507.

7. The Creation of the Bill of Rights

1. *DHRC,* 18:364–67; *FFE,* 1:132–33.

2. Some months later, the minority of the Maryland convention in Baltimore followed this example, but their "Address of a Minority" caused much less excitement than the Pennsylvanian "Dissent of the Minority."

3. "If because a person is for amendments, he is to be called an antifederalist, the great majority of the United States are antifederalist" ("An Old German," Baltimore *Maryland Gazette,* September 23, 1788).

4. William Shippen Jr. to Thomas Lee Shippen, Philadelphia, November 18, 1788, Shippen Family Papers, DLC.

5. Jefferson to Madison, Paris, November 18, 1788, in Boyd, 14:188.

6. The proposals are printed in *FFC,* vol. 4. See also Helen E. Veit, Kenneth R. Bowling, and Charlene Bangs Bickford, eds., *Creating the Bill of Rights: The Documentary Record from the First Federal Congress* (Baltimore, 1991); and Jack N. Rakove, *Declaring Rights: A Brief History with Documents* (Boston, 1989).

7. See *DHRC,* 2:384–92, 423–33, 528–50, 571n1, 592–602.

8. Thomas P. Slaughter, "The Tax Man Cometh: Ideological Opposition to Internal Taxes, 1760–1790," *WMQ,* 41 (1984): 566–91.

9. See David Stuart to Washington, Abingdon, September 12, 1789. In the Virginia convention, Henry had criticized the federal government's power of direct taxation as emanating from "the visionary projects of modern politicians" (Henry speech of June 7, 1788, in *DHRC,* 9:1045).

10. Coxe to Robert Smith, Philadelphia, August 5, 1788, Coxe Papers, PHi.

11. Lincoln to Theodore Sedgwick, Boston, September 7, 1788, Sedgwick Papers, MHi.

12. After their defeat in Hillsborough, some North Carolina Federalists clutched at the straw of a second general convention: "It appears to me that the States should immidiately concur in calling another Convention, it would satisfy the Honest part of the opposition—and stop the mouths of the rest" (William R. Davie to James Iredell [November 1788], in *Iredell Papers,* 3:458).

13. Lincoln to Washington, Boston, June 3, 1788, in *Washington Papers: Confederation Series,* 6:309–11.

14. Madison to Washington and to Hamilton, Richmond, June 27, 1788, in *DHRC,* 10:1688–89.

15. Robert Smith to Tench Coxe, Baltimore, July 31, 1788, Coxe Papers, PHi; "Federalism," *Maryland Journal,* Extraordinary, September 26, 1788.

16. Bland to Lee, Richmond, October 28, 1788, published in *Southern Literary Messenger* 28 (1859): 43–44.

17. Washington to James McHenry, Mount Vernon, July 31, 1788; Washington to Charles Pettit, August 18, 1788; Washington to Benjamin Lincoln, August 28, 1788; and Washington to Madison, September 23, 1788, in *Washington Papers: Confederation Series,* 6:409, 447–48, 482–83, 534; Washington to Benjamin Lincoln, October 26, 1788, in *Washington Papers: Presidential Series,* 1:70–73.

18. "A Real German": Dialogue between "Anti" and "Federal"; "A Federalist"; and "Federalicus," Baltimore *Maryland Gazette,* August 1, September 30, and October 3, 1788.

19. *FFE,* 2:107–9.

20. *FFE,* 1:258–60.

21. Coxe to Madison, Philadelphia, September 10, 1788; Madison to Randolph, New York, September 14, 1788, in Rutland, 11:249, 253.

22. Hartley to Coxe, September 9, 1788; *Federal Gazette,* October 9, 1788, in *FFE,* 1:266, 311. Alexander Graydon, however, considered the Harrisburg amendments as "extremely moderate." In his opinion, the real motive of the opposition was "to let themselves down as easy as possible and to come in for a share of the good things the new Government may have to bestow" (Graydon to Lambert Cadwalader, Louisbourg, Pa., September 7, 1788, in *FFE,* 1:265).

23. John Lansing to Abraham Yates and Melancton Smith, October 3, 1788, Lamb Papers, NHi; *FFE,* 1:16.

24. New York *Daily Advertiser,* November 22, 1788.

25. Hamilton to Theodore Sedgwick, New York, November 9, 1788, in Syrett, 5:230–31.

26. Quoted in *FFE,* 1:16.

27. The bitterness of the opposition was heightened by Federalist statements which openly disavowed the amendment promises: "The proposed amendments . . . have effected the purpose for which they were intended—i.e. *conciliation* . . . alterations ought not to be further thought of—until found by *experience,* wanting" ("SENEX," *Massachusetts Centinel,* September 20, 1788). The controversy is documented in *FFE,* 1:450–76.

28. Second Convention Resolutions, November 14–20, 1788, in *FFE,* 2:273–79; *DHRC,* 10:1761–68.

29. Turberville to Madison, Richmond, October 27 and November 10, 13, and 16, 1788, in Rutland, 11:319, 339–41, 343–44, 346–47; Charles Lee to Washington, Richmond, October 29, 1788, and Mason to John Francis Mercer, Gunston Hall, November 26, 1788, in *FFE,* 2:268–69, 380.

30. Henry to Richard Henry Lee, Richmond, November 15, 1788, in *FFE,* 2:374–75.

31. "A Republican," *Virginia Independent Chronicle,* August 27, 1788; Winchester *Virginia Gazette,* November 19, 1788; Winchester *Virginia Centinel,* December 17, 1788.

32. Rutland, 11:334–35.

33. Madison to Turberville, New York, November 2, 1788, in Rutland, 11:330–32.

34. Rutland, 11:237–40, 257–59, 304–5, 371–73.

35. "An American Citizen," "Thoughts on the Subject of Amendments," *Federal Gazette,* December 4, 10, 24, and 31, 1788; "A Citizen of New Haven," *New Haven Gazette,* December 25, 1788; Extract of James Wilson's Speech at Philadelphia, *Massachusetts Centinel,* December 13, 1788.

36. *FFE,* 1:264n3.

37. Thomas Mifflin to Virginia Governor Beverley Randolph, Philadelphia, March 6, 1789, Letterbook, P-Ar. See also Boyd, *Politics of Opposition,* 138n55.

38. Jeremiah Wadsworth to Henry Knox, Hartford, November 2, 1788, Knox Papers, Gilder-Lehrman Collection, NHi.

39. Atherton to Lamb, February 23, 1789, Lamb Papers, NHi.

40. Hancock to Massachusetts General Court, January 8, 1789, Hancock Papers, Smithsonian Institution; "Massachusetts General Court: Answer to Governor Hancock's

Message," February 3, 1789, Secretary of the Commonwealth, Resolves, 1789, Archives Division, MHi; Gov. Hancock to Governors Clinton and Randolph, Boston, February 21, 1789, Misc. Collection, Huntington Library; Executive Communications, Virginia State Library.

41. Extracts from the *Journal of the Assembly of the State of New-York*; and extracts from the *Journal of the Senate of the State of New-York,* December 11, 1788–March 3, 1789 (Albany, 1789). See also DePauw, "Anticlimax of Antifederalism," 108.

42. DePauw, "Anticlimax of Antifederalism," 105–6.

43. The election of the president and vice president is documented in *FFE,* 4:1–300.

44. *FFE,* 3:513–56.

45. *FFE,* 2:123–43, 158–203.

46. *FFE,* 1:229–372. Tench Coxe was confident that Daniel Hiester (or Heister), who had voted against ratification, would respect the Federalist sentiments of his fellow Germans, "and he will also, I think, from being rather fond of public office, feel the federalism of the state" (Coxe to Madison, January 27, 1789, in Rutland, 11:429–33). See also "The German Vote and the 1788 Congressional Election," in Ireland, *Religion, Ethnicity, and Politics,* 283–84.

47. *FFE,* 1:767–852. One of the congressmen elected, Benjamin West, declined his election, and on June 22 Abiel Foster was elected.

48. *FFE,* 3:17, 62–179.

49. Clark to Jonathan Dayton, [March 1789], *FFE,* 3:144. See also Richard P. McCormick, "New Jersey's First Congressional Election, 1789: A Case Study in Political Skullduggery," *WMQ* 6 (1949): 237–50.

50. *FFE,* 1:173–74.

51. Boyd, *Politics of Opposition,* 146.

52. For the elections in Massachusetts, see *FFE,* 1:433–40, 543–742.

53. *FFE,* 3:436–512.

54. *FFE,* 2:247–97, 310–409.

55. Rutland, 11:438n1.

56. See Madison to George Eve, January 2, 1789; Madison to Thomas Mann Randolph, Louisa, January 13, 1789 (printed in the *Virginia Independent Chronicle,* January 28, 1789); and Madison to a Resident of Spotsylvania County, January 27, 1789 (printed in the Fredericksburg *Virginia Herald,* January 29, 1789), in Rutland, 11:404–6, 415–17, 428–29.

57. Election result published in Fredericksburg *Virginia Herald,* February 12, 1789, in *FFE,* 2:346.

58. Madison to Jefferson, March 29, 1789, in Rutland, 12:37–40; see also Monroe to Jefferson, February 15, 1789, in Boyd, 14:557–59.

59. *FFE,* 1:227–29, 233.

60. Robert J. Dinkin, *Voting in Revolutionary America: A Study of Elections in the Original Thirteen States, 1776–1789* (Westport, Conn, 1982), 107–9.

61. Atherton to Lamb, Amherst, February 23, 1789, in *FFE,* 1:839.

62. Wait to George Thatcher, Portland, August 15, 1788, Thatcher Papers, Boston Public Library; William Widgery to Thatcher, New Glocester, September 14, 1788, *Historical Magazine* 6 (1869): 352–53.

63. Baldwin to Joel Barlow, New York, January 10, 1789, Baldwin Collection, CtY.

64. Bryan to Robert Whitehill, Philadelphia, [July 1789], Whitehill Papers, Hamilton Library, Cumberland County Historical Society; Gallatin to Alexander Addison, Fayette County, Pa., October 7, 1789, Gallatin Papers, NHi.

65. Coxe to Hamilton, Philadelphia, December 16, 1789, in Syrett, 6:11–13.

66. See Stuart to Madison, Richmond, October 21, 1787, in Rutland, 10:202–3; Dawson to Coxe, Richmond, October 26 and December 12, 1789, Coxe Papers, PHi. See also Alexander White to Madison, Bath, August 16, 1788, in Rutland, 11:232–34. Also at stake was a fundamental revision of the common law, which had remained largely intact during the Revolution.

67. See Rutland, 12:210–12, 274–75, 284–85, 346–48.

68. Jefferson to John Rutledge Jr., February 2, 1788; and Jefferson to William Carmichael, August 12, 1788, in Boyd, 12:556–57, 13:502. See also "Americans Abroad Comment on the Constitution," in *DHRC,* vol. 14, appendix 2: 460–502.

69. Boyd, 13:442–43.

70. Rutland, 11:295–300.

71. Letters of November 18, 1788, and January 12, 1789, in Boyd, 14:187–90, 436–40. See also Joyce Appleby, "America as a Model for the Radical French Reformers of 1789," *WMQ* 28 (1971): 267–86.

72. Boyd, 14:659–63.

73. Letters of May 11, July 22, and August 28, 1789, in Boyd, 15:121–24, 299–301, 364–69.

74. Jefferson letter of September 6, 1789, answered by Madison on February 4, 1790, in Boyd, 15:384–98; Rutland, 13:18–26. In his response, Madison again emphasized the importance of political stability: "The evils suffered & feared from the weakness in Government, and licentiousness in the people, have turned the attention more toward the means of strengthening the former, than of narrowing its extent in the minds of the latter." See also Banning, *Sacred Fire of Liberty,* 265–90.

75. Letters of March 29, May 23 and 27, and June 30, 1789, in Rutland, 12:37–41, 182–83, 185–87, 267–72.

76. Rutland, 12:196–210.

77. Rutland, 12:204–5.

78. Osgood to Elbridge Gerry, New York, February 19, 1789, Gerry Papers, DLC.

79. Rutland, 12:120–24, 132–34, 141–42.

80. Coxe and Frazier to James Clark, Philadelphia, May 11, 1789, Coxe Papers, PHi.

81. For details of the legislative process, see *Creating the Bill of Rights.* The debates in Congress, as well as the public response, are covered in Kenneth R. Bowling, "'A Tub to the Whale': The Founding Fathers and the Adoption of the Federal Bill of Rights," *Journal of the Early Republic* 8 (1988): 223–51.

82. See Madison to Edmund Pendleton, April 8, 1789; and especially Madison to Edmund Randolph, April 12, 1789, in *Creating the Bill of Rights,* 229, 230.

83. Actually only in eight, since Madison's ninth point concerned only changes in the numbering of the Articles of the Constitution (*FFC,* 4:9–12).

84. Madison to Governor Samuel Johnson, New York, June 21, 1789, in Rutland, 12: 249–51.

85. Ames to Thomas Dwight, June 11, 1789, in *Creating the Bill of Rights,* 247.

86. Carrington to Madison, Richmond, September 9, 1789, in Rutland, 12:392–94.

87. See Madison's correspondence with Peters, in Rutland, 12:283–84, 301–3, 346–48, 353–56.

88. New York *Daily Advertiser,* August 14, 1789, in *Creating the Bill of Rights,* 275–77; Rutland, 12:334–35.

89. Madison to Pendleton and to Randolph, New York, August 21, 1789, in Rutland, 12:348–49.

90. *Creating the Bill of Rights,* 29–33.

91. Washington to Madison, May 31, 1789, in *Creating the Bill of Rights,* 242.

92. In this respect, Antifederalists received some support from southern Federalists who feared that Congress in the future could interfere with the system of slavery (see William L. Smith to Edward Rutledge, August 10, 1789, in *Creating the Bill of Rights,* 273). Maryland Representative William Smith described the tense atmosphere: "Very high words passed in the house on this occasion, & what nearly amounted to direct challenges, the weather was excessive hot, & the blood warm" (Smith to Otho Holland Williams, August 22, 1789, ibid., 285).

93. Madison foresaw ambiguities, "as the question will often arise and sometimes be not easily solved, how far the original text is or is not necessarily superceded, by the supplemental act" (Madison to Alexander White, August 24, 1789, in *Creating the Bill of Rights,* 287–88).

94. *Creating the Bill of Rights,* 37–41.

95. Madison to Pendleton, September 14, 1789, in *Creating the Bill of Rights,* 296.

96. *Creating the Bill of Rights,* 47–49.

97. See Lee to Francis Lightfoot Lee, September 13, 1789; Lee to Patrick Henry, September 14 and 27, 1789; and Grayson to Henry, September 29, 1789, in *Creating the Bill of Rights,* 294–96, 298–300.

98. Lee and Grayson to the Speaker of the Virginia House of Delegates, September 28, 1789, in *Creating the Bill of Rights,* 299–300. See also Carrington to Madison, December 20, 1789, in Rutland, 12:462–65.

99. Conference Committee Report, September 24, 1789, in *Creating the Bill of Rights,* 49–50.

100. *FFC,* 4:47–48.

101. Clymer to Tench Coxe, New York, June 28, 1789, Coxe Papers, PHi.

102. Baldwin to Joel Barlow, New York, September 29, 1789, Baldwin Collection, CtY.

103. Jefferson to Madison, Paris, August 28, 1789, in Boyd, 15:364–69; Rutland, 12:360–65.

104. Pendleton to Madison, September 2, 1789, in Rutland, 12:368–69.

105. Madison to Washington, Orange, November 20, 1789, in Rutland, 12:451–53.

106. On June 5, 1790, John Trumbull warned John Adams that Madison was becoming more and more "a Southern Partizan, & loses his assumed candor & moderation" (Hartford, Adams Papers, MHi).

107. Lee to Samuel Adams, May 10, 1789, Lee Family Papers, CtY; and Henry to Lee, August 28, 1789, in *Creating the Bill of Rights,* 289–90.

108. Grayson to Henry, June 12, 1789; Richard Henry Lee to Charles Lee, August 28, 1789; and Richard Henry Lee to Patrick Henry, September 14, 1789, in *Creating the Bill of Rights,* 248–49, 290, 295–96.

109. Randolph to Madison, Fredericksburg, August 18, 1789; Hardin Burnley to

Madison, Richmond, November 28 and December 5, 1789; and Henry Lee to Madison, Richmond, November 25, 1789, in Rutland, 12:345–46, 454–57, 460–61.

110. Hamilton to Nathaniel Chipman, Poughkeepsie, July 22, 1788, in Syrett, 5:1789; Coxe to Madison, Philadelphia, April 21, 1789, in Rutland, 12:93–97. In principle, however, Hamilton and Coxe agreed with Jonathan Trumbull, who was of the opinion that "direct Taxation to a moderate amount is the strongest link in the chain of Government, & the only measure, which will make every man feel that there is a Power above him in this world" (Trumbull to John Adams, Hartford, June 5, 1790, Adams Papers, MHi).

111. Gerry to John Wendell, New York, September 14, 1789, J. S. H. Fogg Autograph Collection, MeHi.

112. George Mason's judgments became more benevolent as time went by. See his letters to John Mason, July 31, 1789; to Samuel Griffin, September 8, 1789; and to Jefferson, March 16, 1790, in Rutland, *Mason,* 3:1162–64, 1170–72, 1189.

113. Gerry to John Wendell, New York, September 14, 1789, J. S. H. Fogg Autograph Collection, MeHi.

114. Grayson to Henry, June 12, 1789, in *Creating the Bill of Rights,* 248–49

115. Grayson to Henry, September 29, 1789, in *Creating the Bill of Rights,* 298–300.

116. William L. Smith to Edward Rutledge, August 10, 1789, in *Creating the Bill of Rights,* 273.

117. Jones to Madison, September 15, 1789; and Dawson to Madison, September 18, 1789, in Rutland, 12:403–4, 410–11.

118. Rutland, 12:371–72. On May 9, 1789, Madison had still assured Jefferson that the interests and ideas of the northern and southern states in general were "less averse than was predicted by the opponents or hoped [feared?] by the friends of the new Government. Members from the Same State, or the same part of the Union are as often separated on questions from each other, as they are united in opposition to other States or other quarters of the Continent" (ibid., 12:142).

119. Patrick T. Conley and John P. Kaminski, *The Bill of Rights and the States: The Colonial and Revolutionary Origins of American Liberties* (Madison, Wis., 1992).

120. The second amendment concerning the compensation for the services of senators and representatives was finally ratified on May 7, 1992, when it became the 27th Amendment to the Constitution.

121. Together with Connecticut and Georgia, Massachusetts ratified the first ten amendments on the occasion of the sesquicentennial of the Bill of Rights in 1939 (John M. Murrin, "From Liberties to Rights: The Struggle in Colonial Massachusetts," in Conley and Kaminski, *The Bill of Rights and the States,* 97).

122. Lee and Grayson to the Speaker of the Virginia House of Delegates, September 28, 1789, in *Creating the Bill of Rights,* 299–300.

123. Madison to Washington, January 4, 1790, in Rutland, 12:466–67. See also Brent Tarter, "Virginians and the Bill of Rights," *Virginia Cavalcade* 32 (1982): 62–75; and Warren M. Billings, "'That All Men Are Born Equally Free and Independent': Virginians and the Origins of the Bill of Rights," in Conley and Kaminski, *The Bill of Rights and the States,* 364–66.

124. See Rutland, 14:85–86, 123, 140–41, 151–52; and Edward Dumbauld, *The Bill of Rights and What It Means Today* (Norman, Okla., 1957), 159.

Conclusion

1. Letter from Newport, *Federal Gazette,* June 14, 1790.

2. William Brown to Dr. William Cullen, Alexandria, July 19, 1788, Misc. Mss. Coll., PPAmP.

3. Edward Carrington to William Short, New York, July 26, 1788, in *DHRC,* 18:293–94. Short was Jefferson's secretary in Paris.

4. "I do not see why you might not in Europe carry the Project of good Henry the 4th into Execution, by forming a Federal Union and One Grand Republick of all its different States & Kingdoms, by means of a like Convention, for we had many Interests to reconcile" (Benjamin Franklin to Pierre Samuel Du Pont de Nemours, Philadelphia, June 9, 1788, in Smyth, *Writings of Franklin,* 9:658–60). See also *DHRC,* 2:583; and Franklin to Ferdinand Grand, Philadelphia, October 22, 1787, in Farrand, 3:131. Tench Coxe wrote as "An American" that the United States under the Constitution had "all the Advantages in America, which Henry IV hoped to produce by universal monarchy in Europe" (*Pennsylvania Gazette,* May 28, 1788).

5. *DHRC,* 18:326–31.

6. *Pennsylvania Gazette,* December 3 and 10, 1788.

7. Lathrop to Washington, Boston, May 16, 1788; and Washington to Lathrop, June 22, 1788, in *Washington Papers: Confederation Series,* 6:280, 349; Smith to Madison, June 12, 1788, in Rutland, 11:121.

8. *Pennsylvania Packet,* July 22, 1788.

9. New York *Daily Advertiser,* January 12, 1788. See also William Pierce's Fourth of July oration in Savannah, Georgia, in *DHRC,* 18:249–54.

10. Mathew Carey to Christopher Carey, Philadelphia, May 23, 1789, Carey Letterbook, Lea and Febiger Collection, PHi.

11. *New Jersey Journal,* July 9, 1788.

12. "By an American," *Fayetteville Gazette,* September 14, 1789.

13. John Trumbull to Jonathan Trumbull, London, September 3, 1788, Jonathan Trumbull Papers, CtY.

14. From John Penn, Ramsgate, September 23, 1788, Printed Auction Sale Catalog, Henkels No. 842 (April 1900), Item no. 378.

15. Brand Hollis to John Adams, November 4, 1788, Adams Papers, MHi.

16. C. W. F. Dumas, August 9 and 14, 1788, in Boyd, 13:511–12.

17. Madame d'Houdetot to Jefferson, August 26, 1788, in Boyd, 13:546–47.

18. Madame d'Houdetot to Benjamin Franklin, quoted in Echeverria, *Mirage in the West,* 163.

19. Short to Madison, Paris, November 17, 1789, in Rutland, 12:449.

20. See Durand Echeverria, "Condorcet's 'The Influence of the American Revolution on Europe,'" *WMQ* 25 (1968): 85–108; Robert R. Palmer, "The Fading Dream: How European Revolutionaries Have Seen the American Revolution," in Lackner and Philip, *Essays on Modern European Revolutionary History,* 89–104; and Joyce Appleby, "America as a Model for the Radical French Reformers."

21. Mercy Otis Warren to Catharine Macaulay Graham, Boston, [July 1789], Warren Papers, MHi.

22. This motif of decline and degeneration balancing the hope for unlimited prog-

ress can be found in both Federalist and Antifederalist writings (see Lienesch, *New Order of the Ages,* 204–14; see also the contributions in Barlow, Levy, and Masugi, *The American Founding*).

23. Washington to Lafayette, Mount Vernon, June 18, 1788, in *Washington Papers: Confederation Series,* 6:336–37.

24. Madison to Pendleton, New York, September 23, 1789, in Rutland, 12:419–20.

25. Fisher to Brissot de Warville, Philadelphia, November 12, 1789, Scioto and Ohio Land Co., Letters to Warville, NHi. See also Beatrice F. Hyslop, "American Press Reports on the French Revolution, 1789–1794," New-York Historical Society *Quarterly* 53 (1969): 34–63.

26. Trumbull to John Adams, Hartford, June 5, 1790, Adams Papers, MHi.

27. See John Adams to Samuel Adams, New York, September 12 and October 18, 1790; and Samuel Adams to John Adams, Boston, October 4 and November 20, 1790, in William V. Wells, *The Life and Public Service of Samuel Adams,* 3 vols. (Boston, 1866), 3:299, 300–302, 302–8, 308–14; and Cushing, *Writings of Samuel Adams,* 5:340–44. Benjamin Franklin kept an ironical distance from the enthusiasm over the Constitution. In 1789 he wrote that "everybody appears to promise that it will last; but in this world nothing is certain but death and taxes."

28. Madison to Edmund Pendleton, Philadelphia, December 18, 1791, in Rutland, 14:157.

29. The first revolutionary constitution had been proclaimed by the National Assembly on September 3, 1791, and was subsequently affirmed by the king. The ratification procedures for the constitutions of 1793, 1795, and 1799 served merely as a propagandistic cover for political faits accomplis (Charles Borgeaud, *Établissement et revision de constitutions en Amérique et en Europe* [Paris, 1893]).

30. Banning, *Sacred Fire of Liberty,* 215. Michael Lienesch has argued that a mixture of republican and liberal concepts was institutionalized in the Constitution and has continued to characterize American politics ever since (Lienesch, *New Order of the Ages*).

31. *New York Journal,* May 29, 1788; "Agrippa" XV, January 29, 1788, in *DHRC,* 5:823.

32. Paine to Jefferson, [March 1788], in Boyd, 13:5.

33. William Gribbin, "Republican Religion and the American Churches in the Early National Period," *Historian* 34 (1972): 71.

34. According to Isaac Kramnick, Hamilton spoke "the state-centered language of power," and "his zeal to push aside any intermediary bodies between the state and individuals . . . were also heavily influenced by his perceptive reading of the patterns of state-building in Europe" (Kramnick, "The 'Great National Discussion': The Discourse of Politics in 1787," *WMQ* 45 (1988): 3–32, especially 24–26).

35. Quoted in Kenyon, *Antifederalists,* lxv.

36. Zechariah Chafee, quoted in Dumbauld, *Bill of Rights,* 150.

37. Quoted in ibid., 114, 115n43.

38. George M. Dennison, "The 'Revolutionary Principle': Ideology and Constitutionalism in the Thought of James Wilson," *Review of Politics* 39 (1977): 174.

BIBLIOGRAPHY

Editors' Note

Professor Heideking provided his German readers with a bibliography of almost a hundred pages. Many of the references were old and obscure. To shorten the English edition, we talked about deleting the bibliography altogether and letting the readers rely upon the extensive footnotes for bibliographic references. When finishing the preparation of this manuscript, it was decided to provide a short bibliographic essay describing the most important manuscript repositories and newspapers. A select listing of secondary sources is also provided.

Primary Sources

The single most important source used in writing this book was *The Documentary History of the Ratification of the Constitution* (*DHRC*). Twenty-one volumes of this magisterial work have been published by the State Historical Society of Wisconsin and are available from the University of Virginia Press's electronic imprint, Rotunda (www.rotunda.upress.virginia.edu). Thanks to a grant from the Alexander von Humboldt Foundation, Professor Heideking was able to reside in Madison, Wisconsin, for a year in 1983, as part of the vast research done for his book. In addition to using the published volumes of *DHRC*, Professor Heideking used the supplemental documents available on microfiche and the thousands of manuscripts and contemporary printed documents (newspapers, broadsides, and pamphlets) that had not yet been published in the *DHRC*. In his book Heideking cited the repositories that own these primary sources, but many of these documents can now be found in the published volumes of the *DHRC*.

The most voluminous and most important collections of manuscripts cited in this volume can be found in the Library of Congress. Other repositories, with collections that primarily accentuate their home state's history, include the Historical Society of Pennsylvania, the Massachusetts Historical Society, the New-York Historical Society, and the New York State Library. In addition, hundreds of manuscript collections from more than a hundred different repositories are cited in the footnotes throughout this volume. The town records for Massachusetts, Connecticut, New Hampshire, and Rhode Island are particularly important, especially for the election of delegates to state conventions.

Newspapers, broadside, and pamphlets are critical in any study of the debate over the ratification of the Constitution. Some of these printed primary sources had a national circulation, while others had either a regional or only a statewide circulation. Some newspapers were even more restricted, with only a local circulation. About ninety-five newspapers were printed at any one time during the ratification debate. Most were weeklies. About a half dozen were dailies (six days per week), and another half dozen were printed twice weekly. Only about six newspapers were Antifederalist. Another six were neutral, while the vast majority of newspaper printers were Federalists, as illustrated by the kinds of material they published. The most important Antifederalist newspapers included the *New York Journal,* the Philadelphia *Independent Gazetteer,* the *Boston Gazette,* and the Philadelphia *Freeman's Journal.* The first two had the broadest circulation. The most important Federalist newspapers, with the most extensive circulation, included the *Pennsylvania Gazette,* the *Massachusetts Centinel,* the New York *Daily Advertiser,* and the *New York Packet.* All of the newspapers for this study are now available online from Readex Corp.

In addition, three monthly magazines carried much of the debate over the Constitution. Most important, with a national (and even international) circulation, was the *American Museum* published in Philadelphia by Mathew Carey. Other magazines included the *Columbian Magazine,* also published in Philadelphia, and the *American Magazine,* published in New York.

Secondary Sources

Albion, Robert G. "New York Port in the New Republic, 1783–1793." *New York History* 21 (1940): 388–403.

Arnold, Douglas M. "Political Ideology and the Internal Revolution in Pennsylvania, 1776–1790." Ph.D. diss., Princeton University, 1976.

Bancroft, George. *History of the Formation of the Constitution of the United States of America.* 2 vols. New York, 1885.

Bates, Frank G. *Rhode Island and the Formation of the Union.* New York, 1898.

Beeman, Richard B. *The Old Dominion and the New Nation, 1788–1801.* Lexington, Ky., 1972.

Beeman, Richard B., Stephen Botein, and Edward C. Carter II, eds. *Beyond Confederation: Origins of the Constitution and American National Identity.* Chapel Hill, N.C., 1987.

Berlin, Ira, and Ronald Hoffman, eds. *Slavery and Freedom in the Age of the American Revolution.* Charlottesville, Va., 1983.

Bernstein, Richard B. *Are We to Be a Nation? The Making of the Constitution.* Cambridge, Mass., 1987.

Bielinski, Stefan. *Abraham Yates, Jr., and the New Political Order in Revolutionary New York.* Albany, N.Y., 1975.

Bishop, Hillman M. "Why Rhode Island Opposed the Federal Constitution." *Rhode Island History* 8 (1949).

Black, Frederick R. "The American Revolution as a 'Yardstick' in the Debates on the Constitution, 1787–1788." *Proceedings of the American Philosophical Society* 117 (1973): 162–85.

Bogin, Ruth. *Abraham Clark and the Quest for Equality in the Revolutionary Era, 1774–1794.* Rutherford, N.J., 1982.

Bordelon, Joseph M. "The Antifederalists and the Agrarian Republic: Securing the Blessings of Liberty through a Less Perfect Union." Ph.D. diss., University of Dallas, 1974.

Boyd, Steven R. *The Politics of Opposition: Antifederalists and the Acceptance of the Constitution.* Millwood, N.Y., 1979.

Bradford, M. E. *Founding Fathers: Brief Lives of the Framers of the United States Constitution.* 2nd ed., rev. Lawrence, Kans., 1994.

Brant, Irving. *James Madison.* 6 vols. Indianapolis, Ind., 1946–61.

Brooks, Robin. "Alexander Hamilton, Melancton Smith, and the Ratification of the Constitution in New York." *William and Mary Quarterly,* 3rd ser., 24 (1967): 339–58.

———. "Melancton Smith: New York Anti-Federalist, 1744–1798." Ph.D. diss., University of Rochester, 1964.

Bruchey, Stuart. "The Forces Behind the Constitution: A Critical View of the Framework of E. James Ferguson's *The Power of the Purse.*" *William and Mary Quarterly,* 3rd ser., 19 (1962): 429–38.

Brunhouse, Robert L. *The Counter-Revolution in Pennsylvania, 1776–1790.* Harrisburg, Penn., 1942.

Buckley, John E. "The Role of Rhetoric in the Ratification of the Federal Constitution, 1787–1788." Ph.D. diss., Northwestern University, 1972.

Burnett, Edmund Cody. *The Continental Congress: A Definitive History of the Continental Congress from Its Inception in 1774 to March, 1789.* New York, 1941.

Collier, Christopher. *Roger Sherman's Connecticut: Yankee Politics and the American Revolution.* Middletown, Conn., 1971.

Crowl, Philip A. *Maryland During and After the Revolution: A Political and Economic Study.* Baltimore, 1943.

Daniell, Jere R. *Experiment in Republicanism: New Hampshire Politics and the American Revolution, 1741–1794.* Cambridge, Mass., 1970.

Davis, Joseph L. *Sectionalism in American Politics, 1774–1787.* Madison, Wis., 1977.

DenBoer, Gordon. "The House of Delegates and the Evolution of Political Parties in Virginia, 1782–1792." Ph.D. diss., University of Wisconsin, Madison, 1972.

DePauw, Linda G. "The Anticlimax of Antifederalism: The Abortive Second Convention Movement, 1788–1789." *Prologue* 2 (1970): 98–114.

———. *The Eleventh Pillar: New York State and the Federal Constitution.* Ithaca, N.Y., 1966.

Eidelberg, Paul. *The Philosophy of the American Constitution: A Reinterpretation of the Intention of the Founding Fathers.* New York, 1968.

Eiseman, Nathaniel J. *The Ratification of the Federal Constitution by the State of New Hampshire.* Washington, D.C., 1938.

Elkins, Stanley M., and Eric L. McKittrick. "The Founding Fathers: Young Men of the Revolution." *Political Science Quarterly* 76 (1961): 181–216.

Feer, Robert A. "Shays's Rebellion and the Constitution: A Study in Causation." *New England Quarterly* 42 (1969): 388–410.

Ferguson, E. James. *The Power of the Purse: History of American Public Finance, 1776–1790.* Chapel Hill, N.C., 1961.

Freehling, William W. "The Founding Fathers and Slavery." *American Historical Review* 77 (1972): 81–93.

Gillen, Jerome J. "Political Thought in Revolutionary New York, 1763–1789." Ph.D. diss., Lehigh University, 1972.

Goddard, Henry P. *Luther Martin: The Federal Bull-Dog.* Baltimore, 1887.

Goldwin, Robert A., and William A. Schambra, eds. *A Decade of Study of the Constitution.* Washington, D.C., 1979.

Goodman, Paul. *The Democratic-Republicans of Massachusetts: Politics in a Young Republic.* Cambridge, Mass., 1964.

Greene, Evarts B., and Virginia D. Harrington. *American Population before the Federal Census of 1790.* New York, 1932.

Greene, Jack P. "Revolution, Confederation, and the Constitution, 1763–1787." In *The Reinterpretation of American History and Culture,* edited by W. H. Cartwright and R. L. Watson Jr., 259–95. Washington, D.C., 1973.

———. "The Role of the Lower Houses of Assembly in Eighteenth Century Politics." In *The Reinterpretation of the American Revolution, 1763–1789,* edited by Jack P. Greene, 86–109. New York, 1968.

Grigsby, Hugh B. *The History of the Virginia Federal Convention of 1788.* Edited by R. A. Brock. 2 vols. Richmond, Va., 1890–91.

Groce, George C., Jr. *William Samuel Johnson: A Maker of the Constitution.* New York, 1937.

Hall, Van Beck. *Politics without Parties: Massachusetts, 1780–1791.* Pittsburgh, Penn., 1972.

Harding, Samuel B. *The Contest over the Ratification of the Federal Constitution in the State of Massachusetts.* New York, 1896.

Harmon, George D. "The Proposed Amendments to the Articles of Confederation." *South Atlantic Quarterly* 24 (1925): 298–315, 411–36.

Haw, James A. "Politics in Revolutionary Maryland, 1753–1788." Ph.D. diss., University of Maryland, 1972.

Hawke, David F. *Benjamin Rush: Revolutionary Gadfly.* Indianapolis, Ind., 1971.

Haynes, George H. "The Conciliatory Proposition in the Massachusetts Convention of 1788." *Proceedings of the American Antiquarian Society* 29 (1919): 294–311.

Henderson, H. James. "The Structure of Politics in the Continental Congress." *Essays on the American Revolution,* edited by S. G. Kurtz and James H. Hutson. Chapel Hill, N.C., 1975.

Hoffer, Peter C. "The Constitutional Crisis and the Rise of a Nationalistic View of History in America, 1786–1788." *New York History* 52 (1971): 305–23.

Hoffman, Ronald. *A Spirit of Dissension: Economics, Politics, and the Revolution in Maryland.* Baltimore, 1973.

Hoffman, Ronald, and Peter J. Albert, eds. *Sovereign States in an Age of Uncertainty.* Charlottesville, Va., 1981.

Hunter, William C. *The Commercial Policy of New Jersey under the Confederation, 1783–1789.* Princeton, N.J., 1922.

Hutson, James H. "Country, Court, and the Constitution: Antifederalism and the Historians." *William and Mary Quarterly,* 3rd ser., 38 (1981): 337–68.

Ireland, Owen S. "The Ratification of the Federal Constitution in Pennsylvania." Ph.D. diss., University of Pittsburgh, 1966.

Isaac, Rhys. *The Transformation of Virginia, 1740–1790.* Chapel Hill, N.C., 1982.

Jameson, John Franklin, ed. *Essays in the Constitutional History of the United States in the Formative Period, 1775–1789.* Boston, 1889.

Jensen, Merrill. *The Articles of Confederation: An Interpretation of the Social-Constitutional History of the American Revolution, 1774–1781.* Madison, Wis., 1940.

———. *The New Nation: A History of the United States during the Confederation, 1781–1789.* New York, 1950.

Jordan, Philip H., Jr. "Connecticut Politics during the Revolution and Confederation, 1776–1789." Ph.D. diss., Yale University, 1962.

Kaminski, John P. "Controversy Amid Consensus: The Adoption of the Federal Constitution in Georgia." *Georgia Historical Quarterly* 58 (1974): 244–61.

———. "Paper Politics: The Northern State Loan-Offices during the Confederation." Ph.D. diss., University of Wisconsin, Madison, 1972.

———. "Political Sacrifice and Demise: John Collins and Jonathan J. Hazard, 1786–1790." *Rhode Island History* 35 (1976): 91–98.

———. "The Reluctant Pillar." In *The Reluctant Pillar,* edited by Stephen L. Schechter, 48–117. Troy, N.Y., 1985.

Ketcham, Ralph. *James Madison: A Biography.* New York, 1971.

Libby, Orin G. *The Geographical Distribution of the Vote of the Thirteen States on the Federal Constitution, 1787–8.* Madison, Wis., 1894.

Lynd, Staughton. *Class, Conflict, Slavery, and the United States Constitution: Ten Essays.* Indianapolis, Ind., 1967.

Main, Jackson Turner. *The Antifederalists: Critics of the Constitution, 1781–1788.* Chapel Hill, N.C., 1961.

———. *Political Parties before the Constitution.* Chapel Hill, N.C., 1973.

———. *The Social Structure of Revolutionary America.* Princeton, N.J., 1965.

Marks, Frederick W., III. *Independence on Trial: Foreign Affairs and the Making of the Constitution.* Baton Rouge, La., 1973.

McCormick, Richard P. *Experiment in Independence: New Jersey in the Critical Period, 1781–1789.* New Brunswick, N.J., 1950.

McDonald, Forrest. *E Pluribus Unum: The Formation of the American Republic, 1776–1790.* Boston, 1965.

———. *Novus Ordo Seclorum: The Intellectual Origins of the Constitution.* Lawrence, Kans., 1985.

———. *We the People: The Economic Origins of the Constitution.* Chicago, 1958.

Meyers, Marvin, ed. *The Mind of the Founder: Sources of the Political Thought of James Madison.* Indianapolis, Ind., 1973.

Middlekauff, Robert. *The Glorious Cause: The American Revolution.* New York, 1982.

Miner, Clarence E. *The Ratification of the Federal Constitution by the State of New York.* New York, 1921.

Mintz, Max M. *Gouverneur Morris and the American Revolution.* Norman, Okla., 1970.

Mitchell, Broadus, and Louise Pearson. *A Biography of the Constitution of the United States: Its Origin, Formation, Adoption, Interpretation.* New York, 1964.

Morrill, James R. *The Practice and Politics of Fiat Finance: North Carolina in the Confederation, 1783–1789.* Chapel Hill, N.C., 1969.

Morris, Richard B. *The Forging of the Union, 1781–1789.* New York, 1987.

———. "John Jay and the Adoption of the Federal Constitution in New York: A New Reading of Persons and Events." *New York History* 63 (1982): 133–64.

Munroe, John A. *Federalist Delaware, 1775–1815.* New Brunswick, N.J., 1954.

Murphy, William P. *The Triumph of Nationalism, State Sovereignty, the Founding Fathers, and the Making of the Constitution.* Chicago, 1967.

Nadelhaft, Jerome J. *The Disorders of War: The Revolution in South Carolina.* Orono, Me., 1981.

Newsome, Albert R. "North Carolina's Ratification of the Federal Constitution." *North Carolina Historical Review* 17 (1940): 287–301.

Norton, Joseph M. "The Rhode Island Federalist Party, 1785–1815." Ph.D. diss., St. John's University, 1975.

Obrecht, Everett D. "The Influence of Luther Martin in the Making of the Constitution of the United States." *Maryland Historical Magazine* 27 (1932): 173–90, 280–96.

Ohline, Howard A. "Republicanism and Slavery: The Origins of the Three-Fifths Clause in the United States Constitution." *William and Mary Quarterly,* 3rd ser., 28 (1971): 563–84.

Oliver, Nancy E. B. "Keystone of the Federal Arch: New Hampshire's Ratification of the United States Constitution." Ph.D. diss., University of California, Santa Barbara, 1972.

Polishook, Irwin H. "Peter Edes's Reports of the Proceedings of the Rhode Island General Assembly, 1787–1790." *Rhode Island History* 25 (1966): 33–42, 87–97, 117–29; (1967): 15–31.

———. *Rhode Island and the Union, 1774–1795.* Evanston, Ill., 1969.

Pool, William C. "An Economic Interpretation of the Ratification of the Federal Constitution in North Carolina." *North Carolina Historical Review* 27 (1950): 119–41, 289–313, 437–61.

Rakove, Jack N. *The Beginnings of National Politics: An Interpretative History of the Continental Congress.* New York, 1979.

Rapport, Leonard. "Printing the Constitution: The Convention and Newspaper Imprints, August–November 1787." *Prologue* 2 (1970): 69–89.

Roche, John P. "The Founding Fathers: A Reform Caucus in Action." In *The Reinterpretation of the American Revolution, 1763–1789,* edited by Jack P. Greene, 437–68. New York, 1968.

Roll, Charles W., Jr. "'We, Some of the People': Apportionment in the Thirteen State Conventions Ratifying the Constitution." *Journal of American History* 56 (1969): 21–40.

Rutland, Robert A. *The Birth of the Bill of Rights, 1776–1791.* Chapel Hill, N.C., 1958.

———. *The Ordeal of the Constitution: The Antifederalists and the Ratification Struggle of 1787–1788.* Norman, Okla., 1983.

Schechter, Stephen L. *The Reluctant Pillar: New York and the Adoption of the Federal Constitution.* Troy, N.Y., 1985.

Schick, James B. "The Antifederalist Ideology in Virginia, 1787–1788." Ph.D. diss., Indiana University, 1971.

Schwartz, Bernard. *A Commentary on the Constitution of the United States.* 5 vols. New York, 1963–68.

Shoemaker, Robert W. "'Democracy' and 'Republic' as Understood in Late Eighteenth Century America." *American Speech* 41 (1966): 83–95.

Smith, Edward P. "The Movement towards a Second Convention in 1788." In *Essays in the Constitutional History of the United States,* edited by John Franklin Jameson, 46–115. Boston, 1889.

Smylie, James H. "American Clergymen and the Constitution of the United States of America, 1781–1796." Ph.D. diss., Princeton Theological Seminary, 1958.

Staples, William R. *Rhode Island in the Continental Congress, 1765–1790.* Providence, R.I., 1870.

Steiner, Bernard C. Connecticut's Ratification of the Federal Constitution." *American Antiquarian Society Proceedings* 25 (1915): 70–127.

———. “Maryland’s Adoption of the Federal Constitution.” *American Historical Review* 5 (1899–1900): 22–44, 207–24.

Szatmary, David P. *Shays’s Rebellion: The Making of an Agrarian Insurrection.* Amherst, Mass., 1980.

Trenholme, Louise I. *The Ratification of the Federal Constitution in North Carolina.* New York, 1932.

Turner, Lynn W. *The Ninth State: New Hampshire’s Formative Years.* Chapel Hill, N.C., 1983.

Van Doren, Carl C. *The Great Rehearsal: The Story of the Making and Ratifying of the Constitution of the United States.* New York, 1948.

Watlington, Patricia. *The Partisan Spirit: Kentucky Politics, 1779–1792.* New York, 1972.

Webking, Robert H. “Melancton Smith and the Letters from the Federal Farmer.” *William and Mary Quarterly,* 3rd ser., 44 (1987): 510–28.

Wilentz, Sean. *Chants Democratic: New York City and the Rise of the American Working Class, 1788–1850.* New York, 1984.

Willis, Edmund P. “Social Origins of Political Leadership in New York City from the Revolution to 1815.” Ph.D. diss., University of California at Berkeley, 1967.

Wood, Gordon S. *The Creation of the American Republic, 1776–1787.* Chapel Hill, N.C., 1969.

Yazawa, Melvin, ed. *Representative Government and the Revolution: The Maryland Constitutional Crisis of 1787.* Baltimore, 1975.

Young, Alfred F. *The Democratic Republicans of New York: The Origins, 1763–1797.* Chapel Hill, N.C., 1967.

INDEX

Note: Individual entries falling within certain broader subject areas appear grouped under the following main entries: Great Britain, philosophical and political writers, and pseudonyms. Also, please look under individual state names for entries on those state conventions.